Power & Piety

Monastic Houses of Medieval Britain

Volume 1 - Northern England

Günter Endres & Graham Hobster

ISBN-13: 978-0-9958476-0-6

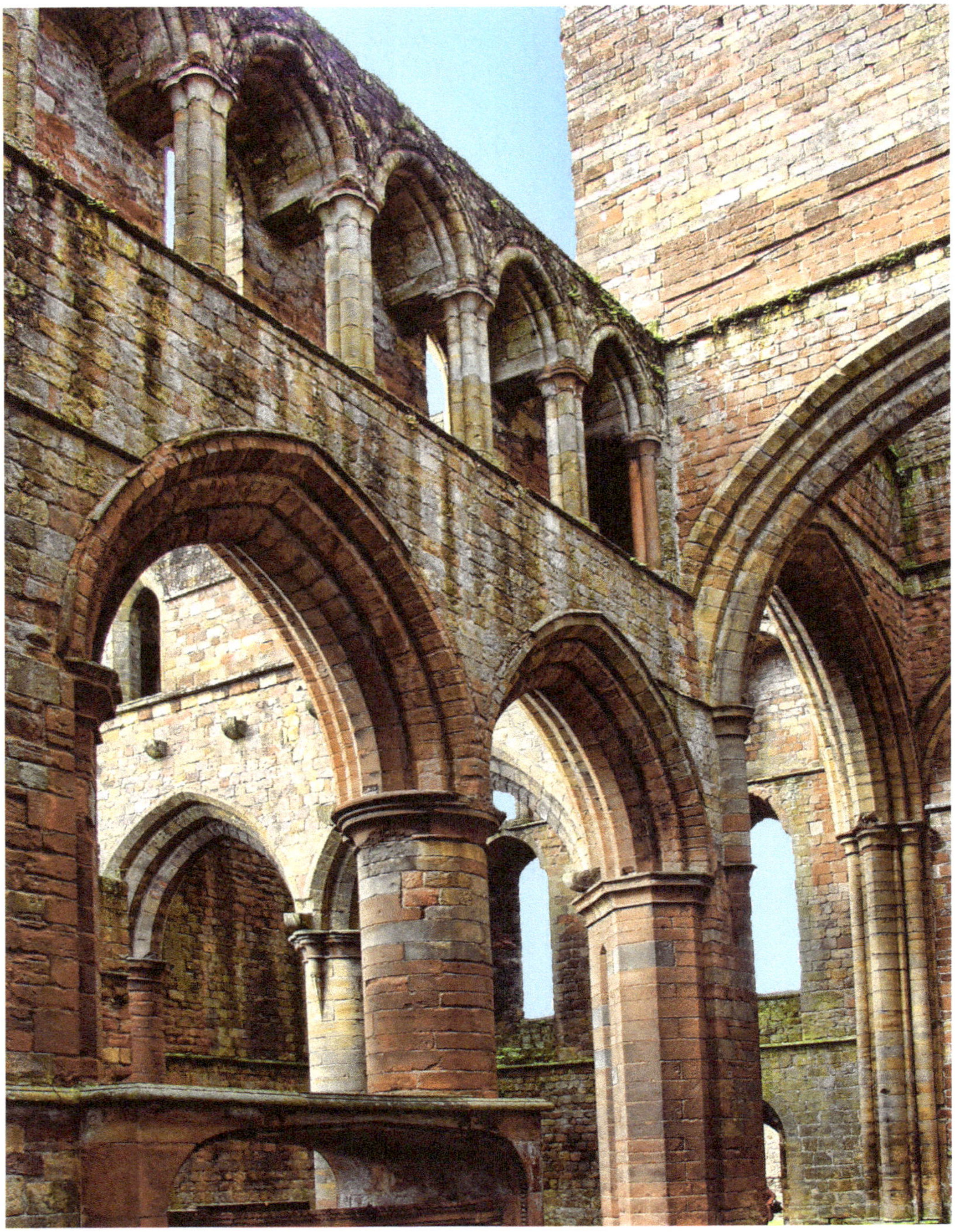

Lanercost Priory

Contents - Volume 1 - Northern England

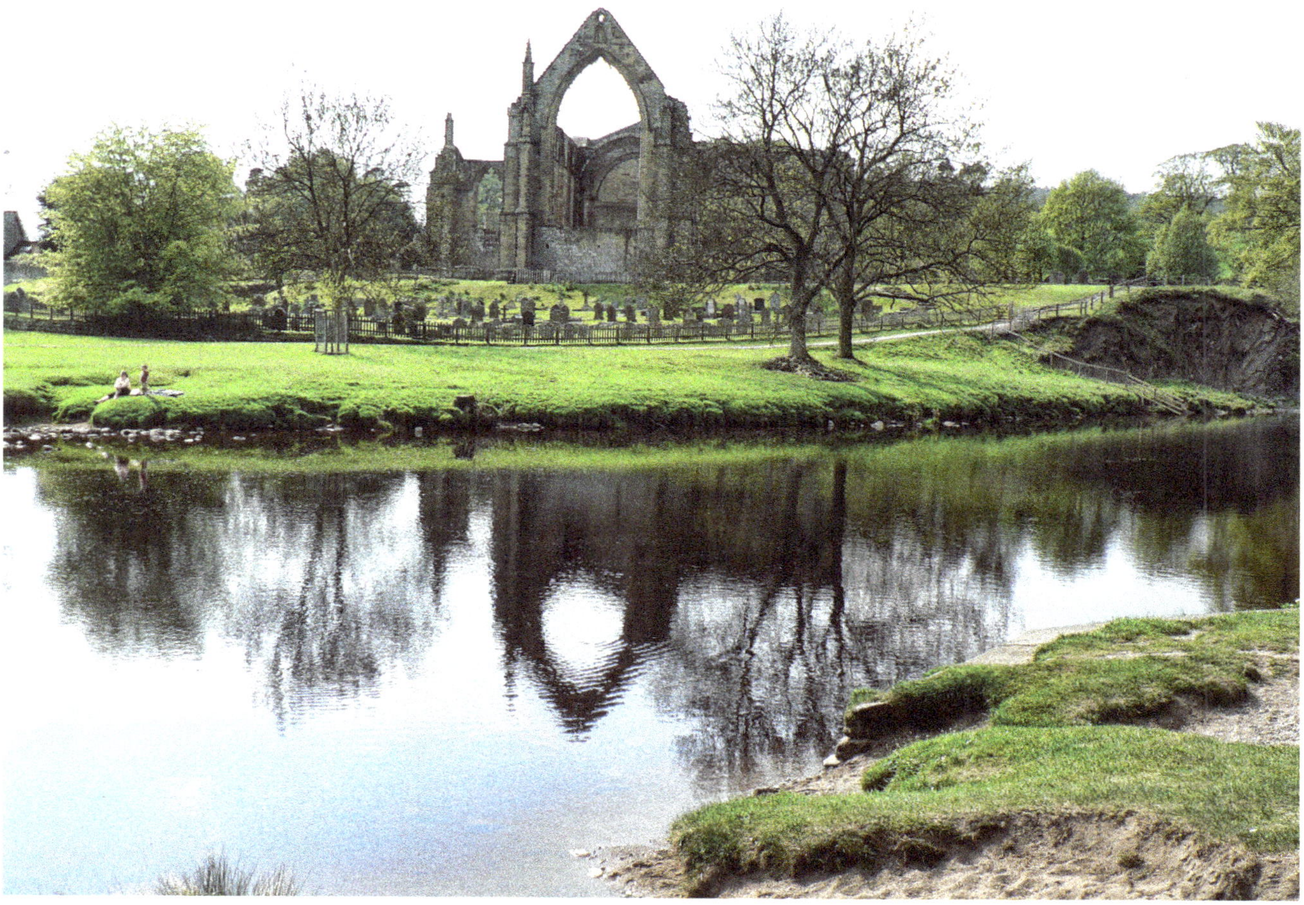

Bolton Priory

Foreword

Robert Houghton, Augustine Webster and Robert Lawrence are not names that leap easily to most people's minds, yet their lives and deaths mark the beginning of the end of one of the most influential social, religious and cultural phenomena in English history. These three men were Carthusian monks, and the first religious victims of the English Reformation. They were executed in 1534, close to their London monastery, for refusing Henry VIII's Act of Supremacy, by which he claimed authority over the English Church. They are recognised as the first martyrs of the English Reformation, and were canonised as saints by Pope Paul VI in 1970. Most remarkably, within six years of their execution, every one of the five hundred or so religious houses in England had been destroyed, and numerous other monks had shared the Carthusians' fate.

What the Carthusian martyrs represented was the end of a tradition in this country which had played a significant part in shaping English society. When Pope Gregory the Great, at the end of the sixth century, sent monk missionaries to England, Christianity was already present, but monks including St Augustine of Canterbury and St Cuthbert spread a form of monastic life, that was both stable and missionary.

The monks embedded Christianity in the culture and institutions of Anglo-Saxon, and later Norman society. They did so by establishing settled monastic communities. These became the focus of prayer and worship which not only shaped the lives of the monks but also drew thousands of pilgrims to pray and seek assistance in times of difficulty, or simply to experience the presence of God.

Particularly after the Norman occupation in the eleventh century, the monasteries played a key role in the political and economic life of the country, as they expanded into agricultural empires, creating wealth and employment, especially from the farming of sheep. The wool industry would become the dominant source of wealth in the medieval economy, so that the abbots who ran the monasteries became powerful economic and political figures. Fountains Abbey, founded in North Yorkshire in 1132 became one of the richest and most powerful. At its dissolution in 1539, although only thirty monks remained, it yielded a wealth of over £1100.

The real wealth of the monasteries, however, lay in their spiritual and cultural legacy to English society. The monasteries and their occupants were familiar to the whole population; it is said that no-one in England could walk more than five miles without meeting a member of a religious order. The monasteries provided education for rich and poor alike, and were the resource to which the poor looked for shelter, food, health care, advice and protection in times of difficulty. They provided the social institutions at the heart of English society that enabled it to function in relative peace and stability.

Nevertheless, by Henry VIII's time, there were many critics of the monasteries, who accused the monks of laziness, greed, corruption and failure to fulfil their charitable and spiritual duties. There were certainly some religious houses in which this was true, but recent historians have taken a more measured view, and recognised that, like any other human institutions, the monasteries had weaknesses but also many strengths.

Among the strengths were the remarkable artistic, literary and architectural enterprises, a few of which survived the sixteenth century dissolution, to give us a glimpse into a world of exquisite beauty. Rare examples of illuminated manuscripts such as the Lindisfarne Gospels, and medieval tombs such as that of Edward the Confessor in Westminster Abbey remind us of the true purpose and achievement of the monasteries. It is worth recalling that many of our most spectacular cathedrals, including Canterbury, Worcester, Salisbury and Durham, all began life as monastic churches, and in a few cases, such as Gloucester, the beautiful and evocative monastic cloisters survive.

The splendour that remains in those buildings gives us an insight into what stood until the 1530s on sites that, in many cases are now little more than shadowy outlines in stone, or romantic ruins. In many cases, the buildings in which thousands of people committed their lives to God, and in which God was glorified in word and action for a millennium, have entirely disappeared from the landscape. Gunter Endres' exhaustive account of the monasteries of England and Wales will prevent them from disappearing from our consciousness. In his text, maps and illustrations he records faithfully the presence of the monasteries all over England and Wales. He reminds us that what remains is not merely a network of fragmented buildings, however beautiful, but the legacy of the people and the prayers that created places of holiness, and the holiness of place, and served society so well.

Cardinal Vincent Nichols
Archbishop of Westminster

Introduction

A journey of discovery

What is it that makes grown men and women scour the countryside for what some would regard merely as 'a pile of broken stones'? Is it a sense of history and a desire to learn more of our religious past, or is it an appreciation of changing architectural styles. Could it be admiration for the achievements and fortitude of a group of monks or nuns determined to seek a solitary life, or may we ourselves be seeking spiritual renewal and reflection as we tread softly on once holy ground. Perhaps it is a little of all these things. As we stand among the remains of soaring churches and quiet cloisters, or worship in churches that have survived the Reformation in one form or other, we become part, for a moment at least, of a thousand years and more of history, which neither plunder, nor wilful destruction, neglect, nor the ravages of time, have been able to obliterate. It is a humbling experience.

Having unsuccessfully set forth towards the priesthood, which, as a young Catholic boy in Germany I had believed to be my calling, it took no great leap of faith to find myself fascinated by the medieval flowering and ultimate destruction of monasticism in the British Isles. While I consider Henry VIII's despoiling and dismantling of the monastic establishments, driven as it was by the King's break with Rome and the need to finance the strengthening of his defences against the French, vandalism on a breathtaking scale, it has to be acknowledged that the monastic Orders played a not inconsiderable part in their downfall. By the fifteenth and sixteenth century, scores of the faithful of both sexes had increasingly succumbed to secular temptations and pleasures, which, together with the trappings of power and wealth for many, provided a heady cocktail that led to an alarming spiritual decline. Yet, for some five hundred years, these monasteries were a key part of the social fabric of a then largely feudal society.

While I have focused intensively on the text, both in evaluating the remains and providing brief histories, my good friend and collaborator, Graham Hobster, has applied his considerable photographic and layout skills to create what we modestly consider a major work on this extensive subject and one that has been designed to encourage the reader to learn about these numerous ancient survivals. These range from the great abbeys of Battle, Bury St Edmunds, Furness, Fountains, Glastonbury, Rievaulx and Westminster, to minimal and sometimes uninteresting, yet historically significant, fragments of stone. Monastic hospitals, of which there were many, had to be left out because of limitations of space. I cannot take credit for the wealth of historic information accompanying the photographs. I merely summarised the often intriguing, but always interesting histories of the various houses many eminent persons have painstakingly assembled over centuries from ancient documents.

During our near twenty-year collaboration, we have visited virtually all the monastic remains described in this book and have taken numerous photographs. Others have generously permitted the use of their photographs in places we have been unable to reach. Our selection, while limited by restrictions of size, has been made to illustrate some of the more interesting features on each site, as well as the elaborate architectural detail that has survived in many monasteries. It is hoped that these might encourage a visit when in the vicinity, or persuade some intrepid adventurers that a long journey would be worthwhile. We believe that there are no major omissions and, for the first time, there is a comprehensive illustrated guide to lead the way.

Had it not been for the preservation efforts of the Ministry of Works in the early twentieth century and continued under English Heritage and the National Trust, helped by more sympathetic landowners and numerous volunteers, many of these wonderful ruins in England would have been lost forever. And with them a large part of a monastic heritage that dates back to the close of the sixth century. I fear, however, that many of the lesser remains still in private hands may in time disappear. Not through wilful destruction, as in the past, but through sheer neglect and disinterest. It must not be allowed to happen.

Günter Endres

Acknowledgements

Completing a work of this extent would not have been possible without the comprehensive records of the Victoria County History project, English Heritage Pastscape, the National Trust, CADW, the guidance of Medieval Religious Houses of England and Wales by David Knowles and R Neville Hadcock, and others listed below. The kind assistance of a great number of owners and occupants who allowed us access to the medieval remains, many of which are incorporated in their private homes, was also invaluable, as has been the help of friends and acquaintances who took the trouble to visit several sites in their locality to take photographs, particularly Maurice Wickstead in Devon, Richard Croft in Lincolnshire, Michael and Lucien Anderson in Yorkshire, Patrick Allen in Dorset, and Tony and Georgia Gill in Lancashire.

Our appreciation also extends to Adrian Fletcher in Australia who photographed a number of cathedral priories, and the following who gave permission to use their, mostly copyrighted photos: Andrew Abbott (Depedale), John Armagh (Bicknacre/Carisbrooke/Holmcultram/Marham/Peterstone/St Benet/St Helens/Seton/Wix), Howard Barber (Pentney), Dave Barlow (Ravenstonedale/Wetheral), Jonathan Billinger (Llangua), Eugene Birchall (Dunkeswell Church), Gary Bothwell (Cammeringham), Jenny Bradwell, Milton Keynes Discovery Centre (Bradwell), Colin Brammer (Haverholme), Janette Brasier (Tywardreath), Eva Bredsdorff, Powysland Museum (Strata Marcella), Jeff Buck (Beddgelert), Richard Burke (Otterton), David Burrows (Bradenstoke), Marian Byrne (Rosedale), Dr Brian Callingham (Cambridge White Friars), Dave Carter † (Scilly), Matthew Champion (Walsingham), Elli Constantatou (St Osyth), Edward Cross (Flitcham), Erskine Crum (Bridge End), Stefan Czapski (Anckerwycke), Ashley Dace (Bruisyard/Bungay/Dunwich/Langley), Steve Daniels (Steventon), Catherine Davies (Holystone), Manju Deva (Tetbury), Nicholas Dumbell (Bradbourne), Tony Ethrington (Montacute), Keith Evans (Minsmere), Ed Fordham (Kilburn), Patrick Friedman (Wroxton), Su Gough (Thetford), Andy Grieve (St Anthony in Roseland), Clive Hanley (Caldey Island/Monkton), Matthew Hatton (Basedale), David Hinde (Wolston), Dave Hitchborne (St Gilbert), Richard Hoare (Markby), Justin Hobson/Country Life (Stoneleigh), Richard Humphrey (Spalding) , Jerome Jackson (Poulton), Przemyslaw Jahr (Beaulieu), Malcolm Jones (Rosedale), Rebecca Jones (Barlynch), John Lawson (Handale), Malcolm Locking (Louth Park), Phil McGahan (Thetford), Alan Marsh (Pill), John Meadows (Stamford Grey Friars), David Medcalf (Bardsey), Peter Morrell (Ranton), Dr Iris Musa (Cardiff Black Friars), Martin Norgate (Holmcultram), Martin Pearman (Blackborough), David Pennant (Malpas),Tim Pickford-Jones (Newcastle Austin), Adam Poole (St Michael's Mount), Paul Pursgove (Morville), Adrian S Pye (Old Buckenham), Arthur Roe (Burton), Alan Rosevear (Exeter St Nicholas), Evelyn Simak (Broomholm), Dr Anna Skarżyńska/RCAHMW (St Tudwal/Strata Marcella), Amanda Slater (Coventry Charterhouse), Jack Smith (Wymondham, main), Stuart Spicer (Broomholm), David Striker (Aldeby), Jeff Thomas (Ellerton), Richard Torrens (Flaxley/St Anthony's Well), Peter I Vardy (Vale Royal), Sue Vermeer(Rosedale), Geoff Thomas (Ellerton), John Whitworth (Latton), Bill Wilcox (Hickling), Stephen Woodcock Photography (Lincoln Greyfriars), Rob Woodward (Southampton Greyfriars), Jonathan Wright (Sibton), Ian Yarham (Dartford), Mark Ynys-Mon (Thorney), and Zorba the Greek (Dodnash).
Apologies if we have missed anyone.

With very few exceptions, access to private sites was kindly granted by the owners or affiliated associations over many years and we also want to express our gratitude for their help. Again, apologies for any inadvertent omissions.

Bedfordshire Julie Benson (Chicksands); **Buckinghamshire** Jenny McLellan (Bradwell), Sisters Victoria and Jane (Burnham); Rev David Hiscock (Chetwode), David Brown (Missenden), Rev Laurence Meering (Newton Longville), Philippa Peters (Notley); **Cambridgeshire** Amanda Goode (Emmanuel College), Simon Hawkey (Jesus College), Lynn (Hinchingbrooke), Philip O'Donoghue/Merv Fox (Ramsey); **Cornwall** Ruth Parsons (Minster); **Essex** Christopher Foyle (Beeleigh), Rev Antoinette Smith (Blackmore), Rev Stephen Richmond Northfield (Hatfield Peverel), John Whitworth (Latton), Michael Leach, Essex Society for Archaeology and History (Leighs); **Hampshire** David Cullum (Pamber), Susan Tomkins (Beaulieu); **Kent** Sister Benedict (Minster in Thanet), Robin Levey (Minster in Sheppey); Reverend Ali Duguid (Davington), Faversham Joinery (Faversham), Stephen Jones, Headmaster, Dover College (Dover), Sue Moynan (St Radegund's), Leanda Smith (Bilsington), Annette Best-Shaw (Boxley); **Leicestershire** David (Launde), Rev Jane Curtis/Simon Hammond (Owston); **Lincolnshire** Jean Morris (South Kyme); Dave Hill (Sempringham); **Northamptonshire** Revd Elizabeth Cowley/Ruth Thomson (Catesby); **Norfolk** Anthony Robinson and Clare Carrol (Great Massingham), Richard Benton (Horsham St Faith), Shaun Canon (Norwich Blackfriars), Garlinda and Henry Birkbeck (West Acre), Mike Canham (Norwich Carrow), Brigid Everitt (Norwich St Leonard); **Nottinghamshire** Ann Whyte (Beauvale Priory); Robert Howard (Felley); Derek Adlam, FSA (Welbeck); **Oxfordshire** Alexandra Dury and Ruth Waddle (Deaf and Hard of Hearing Centre/Oxford

Black Friars), Maurice Kirtland (Thame); **Somerset** Sir Cameron Mackintosh/Michael Le Poer Trench (Stavordale), Roger Woodland (Hinton); **Shropshire** David and Julie Wilde (Alberbury); **Staffordshire** Paul and Tom Docksey (Dieulacres); **Suffolk** Robin and Elizabeth Sutton (Little Welnetham), Mrs Campbell (Eye), Amy-Rose Ford (Butley), Caroline Ball (Hoxne); **Surrey** Mrs M Rubin (Newark), Dave Saxby (Merton); **Sussex** The late Miss Morvyne Mary Martia Fenwick-Owen (Langney), Johnny Rowell and Lisa Davies (Hardham), the late Sir Arthur Watts (Tortington), Laura Ponsonby and Ian Russell (Shulbrede); **Warwickshire** Tony Dipple (Combe), Jenny Leadbetter (Merevale), Chris Lowe (Pinley), Mel Speirs (Studley); **Wiltshire** Heather Ault, Wiltshire Museum (Monkton Farleigh), D Stevens (Maiden Bradley); **Yorkshire** David Hepworth (Kirklees), Alan Maddocks (Esholt), Harriet Corner (Coverham), Jim Gleave (Marrick), Lee Lowther (Ellerton), Winifred Delf (Richmond St Martin's).

Sources

Victoria County History	Web: www.victoriacountyhistory.ac.uk
English Heritage	Web: www.english-heritage.org.uk; www.pastscape.org.uk
National Trust	Web: www.nationaltrust.org.uk
The Landmark Trust	Web: www.landmarktrust.org.uk
CADW	Web; www.cadw.wales.gov.uk
Royal Commission on the Ancient and Historical Monuments of Wales	Web: www.rcahmw.gov.uk
Monastic Wales	Web: www.monasticwales.org
David Knowles and R Neville Hadcock	Medieval Religious Houses England and Wales; Longmans, Green and Co. London, 1953
Roy Midmer	English Medieval Monasteries (1066-1540); Heinemann, London, 1979
Roland W Morant	The Medieval Abbeys and Priories of England and Wales A Resource Guide, Trafford Publishing, Victoria, British Columbia, Canada, 2004
Historic England	Web: www.historicengland.co.uk
Sir William Dugdale	*Monasticon Anglicanum*, Sam Keble, Hen. Rhodes, London, 1693
Thomas Tanner	*Notitia Monastica*, Oxford, 1695

Further Reading

M R James	Abbeys; The Great Western Railway, London, 1926
F H Crossley	The English Abbey; B T Batsford, London, 1935
Abbot Gasquet	The Greater Abbeys of England; Chatto & Windus, London, 1908
Derry Brabbs	Abbeys and Monasteries; Weidenfeld and Nicolson, London, 1999
John Mason	Haunted Heritage; Collins & Brown, London, for English Heritage, 1999
Brian Bailey	Ordnance Survey Guide to Great British Ruins; Cassell, London, 1991
William Beattie	The Castles and Abbeys of England; Virtue, Spalding and Company, London, 1862

Explanatory Note

The entries in this book are listed alphabetically within each medieval county and their location is shown by Ordnance Survey reference. The closest village or hamlet, main road, and an approximate straight-line distance from the nearest larger town are given in the gazetteer, to aid identification on a map, as many are situated in remote areas. Contact details are provided where public access is permitted, but many are in private hands and have no public right of access, although a request for a visit is welcomed by many of the more historically minded owners. Conditions of access will need to be checked before planning a visit.

Coverage is limited to abbeys and priories for men and women of the monastic orders, all of which, except for the indigenous Gilbertines, originated on the Continent, and the houses of the Mendicant Friars. Not included are the numerous hospitals and secular colleges. Photographic coverage is limited to those sites where some masonry, however minimal, remains visible.

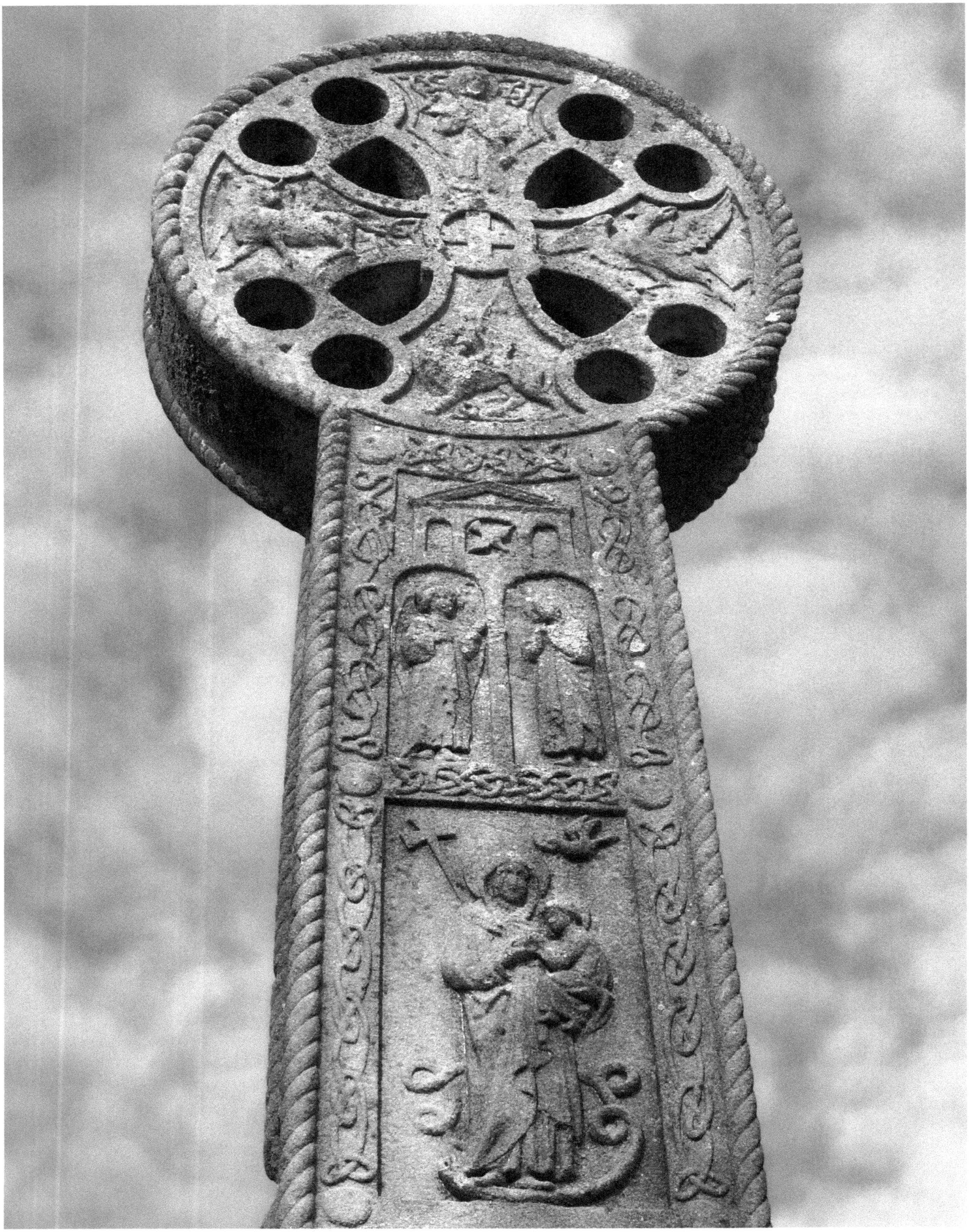

St Augustine's Cross, Isle of Thanet

The Spread of Medieval Monasticism

The monastic ideals of communal brotherhood can be traced all the way back to the rule of St Benedict (cAD 480-547) whose followers were bound by strict vows of personal poverty, chastity, obedience to the abbot, and a commitment to remain within the Order for life. The day in all later Benedictine monasteries was divided into three distinct areas of activities, the most important of which were eight periods of worship, known as the 'Opus Dei' or Work of God, starting with Matins at 2 am. A significant portion of the day was also set aside for meditation, while the remaining time was devoted to manual labour, which included maintenance of buildings and production of food and clothes. English monasticism began with the arrival of St Augustine and his missionaries in Canterbury in AD 597, and his monastery, established on land granted by King Ethelbert of Kent, became the first Benedictine house to be established on English soil.

A different, more reclusive way of life was preached by St Aidan and his Celtic disciples, mostly in the north, although their influence eventually extended as far south as Glastonbury. St Aidan founded the first religious community on Lindisfarne, also known as Holy Island, at the invitation of King Oswald of Northumbria in AD 635. Christianity spread through the land, with many establishments catering for both men and women, until cruelly halted by the arrival of the Danes, who burnt most of the monasteries and showed no mercy to their inhabitants. A few religious communities were rebuilt and struggled on in one form or another, entering a more peaceful period after King Alfred the Great (AD 849-899) had defeated the Danes. This led to a spiritual revival inspired by Dunstan, Abbot of Glastonbury and later Archbishop of Canterbury. Dunstan reintroduced the Benedictine doctrine, later changing the emphasis of formal worship in his *Regularis Concordia*, which sought to standardise the structure of daily life at all English monasteries. He died in AD 988 and was canonised in 1029.

The Norman Conquest in 1066 led to a fundamental change in monasticism, with many new houses founded by Norman lords on land given to them by William the Conqueror as reward for loyalty and support during the Conquest, in an earnest belief that in so doing, it would assure them a place in heaven. A great building boom ensued, led by Lanfranc, Archbishop of Canterbury from 1070, whereby the largely wooden late Saxon abbeys were replaced by grand churches, chapter houses, and refectories in stone. In those early days, the monasteries continued the rule of St Benedict, which had a particularly strong following in Normandy.

Crusade for stricter and simpler life

The first Crusade to retake the Holy Land from the Infidels generated further enthusiasm for monasticism, and soon many different Orders were established, with a constant stream of people from all classes of society seeking the religious life. Unlike the Benedictine houses, which were all independent establishments, the new Orders put their abbeys and priories under the control of a mother house, whose abbot was head of all and wielded great power. It was the desire for a more austere lifestyle in the service of God that gave rise to these other foundations, which considered the rule of St Benedict to be too lax. The most notable were the Cluniac and Cistercian Orders, both reformed Benedictines. The Cluniac Order was founded in Cluny in AD 910 by Berno, a monk, and Count William of Aquitaine, and became renowned for its almost obsessive form of worship, taking virtually no part in manual labour and putting aside little time for study. Its churches and cloisters were much more ornate, and its lavish hospitality legendary. There were some 45 Cluniac houses in England, Wales and Scotland, starting with the great priory of St Pancras in Lewes, Sussex, founded in 1078.

The Cistercian Order became the most powerful of all. It came into being in 1098 when a group of disenchanted monks from Molêsme, led by Abbot Robert, set up a new community in the forests around Cîteaux in Burgundy. Little progress was made until Stephen Harding, an Englishman from Sherborne in Dorset, became its second abbot and was joined in 1113 by St Bernard, when the new Order began to spread at extraordinary speed. Known as the White Monks because of their coarse, undyed wool habits, the Cistercians sought out remote and isolated locations, and their rules prohibited anything suggesting pride or superfluity. Consequently, the churches of the new Order, while magnificent in scale, were simple in execution and devoid of adornment. Through a system of granges, worked by lay-brothers, the Cistercians became great cultivators and sheep farmers. New abbeys were colonised by monks from existing monasteries, usually by an abbot and twelve monks (for the twelve apostles), and the first Cistercian house to be founded in England was that of Waverley in Surrey, established in 1128. Some 150 Cistercian houses followed in England, Wales and Scotland. All its churches were dedicated to the Blessed Virgin Mary. In 1147, the Savignac Order was incorporated into the Cistercians, involving the transfer of some English foundations, including the first Savignac house of Furness, which had been founded in 1127. The Order had been established by Vitalis of Savigny, near Mortain in Normandy in 1112, and was part of the same movement towards a stricter and simpler life that had given birth to the Cistercians.

The most austere of all monastic orders were the Carthusians, founded in 1084 by St Bruno at La Grand Chartreuse near Grenoble. The Order distinguished itself by its strict adherence to St Bruno's ideal, even when others were later tempted by worldly pleasures. But is was a life of total isolation, with each monk living in a separate cell and rarely meeting his brethren except during some church services, and never leaving his cloister. They completely shut themselves away from the world and made no contribution to society. A notable absentee from Carthusian monasteries was the infirmary, for when a monk was taken ill he was attended to in his cell and, upon death, was buried in his clothes in the, usually large, cloister garth. Such a harsh existence was quite forbidding and the Order remained small in number, with only nine monasteries established in England, where they were known as Charterhouses. The first Carthusian priory to be founded was at Witham in Somerset in 1182. There were none in Wales, and none in Scotland.

Bernard d'Abbeville (1046-1117), who set up a monastery in the forest of Tiron in Picardy in about1066 after a quarrel with Cluny, founded the Order of Tiron, which was based on the Benedictine creed, but added hard manual labour. Its adherents were known as Tironensians or Grey Monks. The Order spread rapidly through France, and also to England, Wales, Scotland and Ireland. There were seven houses in England. The Grandmontines, or Order of Grandmont, was founded by St Etienne of Thiers towards the end of the eleventh century. It appears to have modelled itself on the strict Carthusian rule, but has also been claimed by the Augustinians and Benedictines as branches of their Orders. Although the Order was acclaimed in France in the twelfth century, its popularity lasted less than a century and later disputes and scandal led to a slow decline. Outside France, the Order possessed only five houses, three of which, all small, were in England.

The Order of the Holy Trinity, or Trinitarians, was founded in 1193 in the area of Cerfroid to the north-east of Paris by St John de Matha and Felix de Valois. The Trinitarians followed the rule of St Augustine, with additional constitutions, and wore white robes, with a red and blue cross on their breasts. They came into England in 1224, where the lands, revenues, and privileges of the canons of the Holy Sepulchre were given to them upon the demise of that Order. The Trinitarian house at Mottenden in Kent was the first of ten established in England. The Canons Regular of the Holy Sepulchre was also based on the Augustinian rule, but without having to endure the long choral duties and stern discipline. This secular confraternity was probably founded in 1114 and grew up around the most Holy Places during the Crusades. This Order had only two houses in England. The ruined church of the one at Thetford can still be seen. The Bridgettines, or Order of the Most Holy Saviour, was founded by St Birgitta of Sweden around 1350, and approved by Pope Urban V in 1370. The Order was open to men and women, with each monastery having an enclosed community of nuns, with monks attached to act as chaplains, but under the government of the abbess. Syon Abbey, founded in 1431, was the only English house. Another little known Order was that of the Valliscaulians, founded in Burgundy and confirmed by Pope Innocent III in 1205. Its rules were partly drawn from the Cluniac and Cistercian Orders. There were only three houses outside France and Germany, all in Scotland

An interesting, and the only purely English Order, was the Gilbertines, founded in 1131 by Gilbert, then rector of Sempringham in Lincolnshire. Gilbert initially founded a house for nuns, but then revived the double monastery of Saxon times, with the canons regular following the rule of St Augustine and the nuns that of St Benedict. After the confirmation of the Rule by Pope Eugenius III in 1148, the Order of Sempringham was put under papal 'protection', and as the new Order was purely English, and the houses were all in England, the Gilbertines enjoyed great royal favour, especially from Henry II and the three Edwards. Gilbertine houses, of which there were 26, were notable for their complete segregation of the sexes, with the priory church divided throughout its length. The walls were of a height that prevented canons and nuns making eye contact, but still enabled the nuns to hear the mass being said on the other side. The nuns lived in a cloister to the north of the church and were guarded at all times. Not all Gilbertine priories were double houses. The Bonhommes, or Boni Homines, had only two houses in England. They followed the rule of St Augustine and were indistinguishable from the canons regular in their daily life. The origins of this Order are unknown, but it appears to have been English.

Popular move into the community

Somewhat more sociable were the Augustinian and Premonstratensian Orders of canons, introduced into England in 1106 and 1143 respectively. From their dress, the former were known as the Black Canons and the latter as the White Canons. Both followed the rule of St Augustine, Bishop of Hippo in North Africa, not the St Augustine who arrived in Canterbury in AD 597. Although living in cloister, they had much more freedom and contact with the outside world, venturing out to preach and tend to the spiritual needs of the local communities, while also inviting people to share church services at the priory. As a result, the Augustinian canons proved very popular in many regions. Yet, they never achieved the prosperity of other Orders, probably because they were a disparate group until united in a Grand Union in 1243. Nevertheless, a total of some 361 houses existed in the country. The Premonstratensian Order of canons was founded in 1121 by St Norbert in the small isolated hamlet of Premontré, near Laon in north-eastern France. While following the rule of St Augustine, its constitution was modelled on the Cistercians, with the mother house at Premontré retaining control over the 49 houses established in England. Like the Cistercians, the Premonstratensians chose secluded places and colonised new houses from existing abbeys, but rarely exceeded the minimum of an abbot and twelve canons. The first Premonstratensian settlement in England was at Newhouse in Lincolnshire, founded in 1143.

The established Orders, while having played a major role in the development of learning, agriculture and the arts, began accumulating land and wealth, but increasingly neglected to attend to the spiritual and physical needs of the masses. Especially the poor and uneducated in the medieval cities, particularly in the suburbs where disease and vice were rampant, were largely ignored by the established church. This neglect gave rise to a new religious phenomenon, that of the preaching friar. Also signed up to a life of personal poverty, chastity and obedience, the new friars were not confined to the precincts of a monastery, but travelled through the country, receiving their income in the form of alms. The friars owned no property and took heed of the preaching of Arnold of Brescia, who proclaimed that monks and clerics who possessed property could not be saved. In London, York, Warwick, Oxford, Bristol, Lynn and elsewhere, their convents stood in the suburbs abutting the city walls.

Among the more prominent mendicants were the Dominicans, or Black Friars, also known as the Order of Preachers, which was founded by St Dominic in 1215 at Calaroga in Old Castile and came to England in 1221, basing itself in Oxford. The Black Friars had been preceded in 1209 by the Franciscans, or Order of Friars Minor, also known as Grey Friars, founded by St Francis and St Clare of Assisi. The Franciscans arrived in Canterbury a year after the rule of the Order was approved by Pope Honorius in 1223. In 1517, Pope Leo X divided the order into two autonomous branches, Conventual Friars Minor and Friars Minor of the Regular Observance. There were six houses of Observant Friars in England, but all were dissolved by Henry VIII in 1534, after the Observants objected to his proposed divorce from Katherine of Aragon. A third branch, the Capuchin Friars Minor, was established in 1525, but had no houses in the British Isles. The Carmelites, or Brothers of the Blessed Virgin Mary of Carmel, also known as White Friars, which had their origins during the Crusades in 1156, first arrived at Hulne in the wilds of Northumbria in 1242, while the Austin Friars, or Hermits of St Augustine, essentially a union of various isolated movements, started out in Suffolk around 1230. These popular friars encouraged learning through the establishment of schools and valuable libraries, but this often brought them into conflict with the universities, with opposition also from the bishops and secular clergy, as the Church exempted these new Orders from episcopal jurisdiction.

The Dominicans, Franciscans, Carmelites and Austin friars were not the only mendicants in existence, but the Second Council of Lyons, in1274, with the enthusiastic backing of the Dominicans and Franciscans, legislated against any of the smaller groups, which could not prove their existence prior to the Fourth Lateran Council of1215, which had promulgated orthodox beliefs and had prohibited the creation of new Orders. These were suppressed and its members assimilated into the remaining Orders. Among the smaller Orders were the Friars of the Penance of Jesus Christ, or Friars of the Sack, so named after their shapeless dress, which was made of coarse sackcloth. The Order apparently originated in Italy and came to England in 1257, setting up a house in London, one of 16 in England. The Crutched Friars, or Crossed Friars, also came to England from Italy, making their first appearance at Rochester in 1244 and establishing the first of 10 houses at either Colchester or Reigate. The friars observed the rule of St Augustine and wore brown or black habits, later changed to blue. Each friar carried a wooden staff surmounted by a cross and also had a cross of red cloth sewn on their habit. The Order of the Blessed Mary, known as the Pied Friars or Friars de Pica, was founded in Marseille around the middle of the thirteenth century and were first established in London. There were three known houses of this most obscure Order in England.

Refuge for the gentle born

In addition to the double houses, there were in England and Wales some 138 pure nunneries. More than half belonged to the Benedictine Order, about a quarter to the Cistercian Order, the latter localised almost entirely in Lincolnshire and Yorkshire, and 17 following the Augustinian rule. There were also small numbers of monasteries of Premonstratensian and Cluniac nuns, a single house of the Order of St John of Jerusalem at Buckland, which followed the Augustinian rule, a single foundation of Dominican nuns at Dartford, and six houses of Franciscan nuns, known as The Minoresses, or The Poor Clares, the most prominent having been in the City of London. About twenty had the status of abbeys, with the rest having been priories. They were distributed all over the country, and only Surrey, Lancashire, Westmorland and Cornwall were without.

In contrast to most of the houses of monks and canons, many communities struggled on with inadequate endowments and generally endured a life of poverty. The imbalance between the male houses and the nunneries can best be illustrated by returns in the *Valor Ecclesiasticus* of 1535, which showed that on average, the nunneries' income was less than half that of the monks and canons, while the average number of religious was larger. The most numerous houses were in the Midlands, but they were also small and among the poorest. The nunneries in Yorkshire and the North suffered additionally from the frequent incursions of the Scots, who pillaged their lands, burnt their monasteries and often dispersed the nuns. The wealthiest and most famous were all located south of the River Thames.

The nunneries were essentially aristocratic institutions, referred to as 'refuge for the gentle born'. With few acceptable jobs available to those ladies born into noble families, the choice simply lay between marriage and taking the veil, and many found the latter a much preferable alternative. In the fourteenth century, with the emergence of the rich and powerful merchant class, daughters of the well to do citizens also entered the monasteries, as did women from ordinary backgrounds later. Many from all three classes, while initially leading a pious life, soon succumbed to worldly temptations, as did their male counterparts. As early as 1298, apparently because of the alleged licentiousness of the nuns, Pope Boniface issued a papal decretal, known as the *Periculoso*, under which the nuns of all Orders "ought henceforth to remain perpetually cloistered in their monasteries … wholly separated from the public and worldly gaze and, occasions of lasciviousness having been removed, may most diligently safeguard their hearts and bodies in complete chastity". Episcopal records show that the bishops attempted to enforce the decretal, but this was not always successful.

Alien houses

Following the Norman Conquest and the distribution of lands in England by William the Conqueror to his trusted followers, many of the newly enriched Norman lords granted some of their possessions to abbeys in their homeland, many of which they themselves had founded. The Norman abbots sent monks across the Channel whose sole duty was to manage the English estates and sent back to the mother house any income received from rents, tithes and spiritualities. Some of these alien estates were merely granges with perhaps a single monk or prior in residence, but others were fully established conventual priories, usually with a prior and three to four monks, and rich foundations in their own right. The fairly constant state of war between England and France engendered some unease among the later Kings, who were becoming increasingly suspicious that the money sent regularly overseas was being used to finance the war.

The first to seize these alien priories was King John, who compelled them to pay into the Royal Treasury the 'apport' they had been forwarding to the continent. When Edward I went to war against France in 1295 to recover Gascony, which had been retaken by Philip IV, he seized all alien priories, which then numbered about 120, and used their revenues to pay for the war. At the same time, the King relocated many of the monks in southern coastal areas, which he considered as possible spies, to other religious houses that were at least twenty miles from the sea, to prevent any help being given to their homeland. Edward II followed his example, but frequently allowed the priors to continue as custodians for a monetary consideration. When Edward III came to the throne in 1327, he restored many of the alien priories to their original owners and waived the arrears of payments due to the Crown. However, Philip VI's confiscation of the Duchy of Aquitaine and the county of Pothieu in 1337 marked the beginning of the Hundred Years' War with France, and resulted once again in their seizure. The alien houses remained in the hands of the Crown for twenty-three years, but with the peace of 1361 most of them were restored, only to be again sequestrated eight years later when the war was renewed. In the time of Richard II the alien priories continued mostly in the hands of the Crown and all foreign monks were expelled. Their end finally came in 1414 under Henry V, when the King was petitioned at the Parliament of Leicester, to dissolve all alien priories, even if peace was to return. More than 50 were suppressed and their revenues taken into the King's hands. Many were granted to Henry's supporters, friends and families, with others given to his new monasteries of Syon Abbey and Sheen Priory. His son, Henry VI, used the revenues of some towards the founding of Eton College, and King's College, Cambridge.

Dissolution of the Monasteries

In the fourteenth century, there were nearly 900 monastic establishments in England and Wales, not counting hospitals and the Templars and Hospitallers warrior monks, but by then, the enthusiasm for the religious life had begun to wane. The abbots in the larger houses had become landowners on a grand scale, many had grown rich and powerful and had taken on a secular lifestyle that differed little from that of the wealthy gentry. Many took an active part in the political life of the nation and often did the bidding of the King. Austerity began to give way to indulgence, vows of chastity were sometimes openly flouted, and many houses slid into debt, with a resultant dilapidation of the conventual churches and other buildings. In addition, the Black Death in 1348/49 robbed most communities of monks and lay-brothers and further accelerated the decline.

Episcopal visitations to the abbeys and priories

became more frequent and resultant reports, especially from the larger establishments, sometimes made grim reading. Some reforms were initiated towards the close of the fifteenth century by a number of church leaders through closing smaller, unsustainable monasteries, mostly poor Benedictine and Augustinian houses for men and nuns, although all were accommodated in other establishments. A more concerted effort was made in 1525 by Cardinal Thomas Wolsey, who used his powers as papal legate to dissolve some 30 decayed and dissolute monasteries, whose income was to fund a grammar school in Ipswich and Cardinal College, Oxford. Wolsey fell out of favour with Henry VIII and died, being spared the wholesale destruction of the monasteries that was to follow.

There was a marked change in 1535, when Thomas Cromwell, now Henry VIII's vicar-general, entrusted the visitation to his own men, who were tasked with reporting back on standards pertaining within these religious establishments. Combined with the introduction of the *Valor Ecclesiasticus* that same year, a full-scale undertaking to assess what property was owned by the church in England and Wales, this was the clearest indicator of what was to come. Having left these preliminary tasks to Cromwell, Henry VIII showed his hand with the Act of Suppression, under which all the lands and property of religious houses with an income of less than £200 a year, as assessed by the *Valor*, were to be transferred to the Crown. The King used the highly suspect reports of Cromwell's agents, especially those from Thomas Legh and Richard Layton, who alleged that "manifest sin, vicious, carnal and abominable living is daily used and committed amongst the little and small abbeys," as justification for the closure. Many of these were either false or greatly exaggerated. At the same time, praise was heaped upon the larger houses, many of whose abbots sat in Parliament and whose assent to the Act was required. As the Act was relatively moderate and fair compensation and pensions were offered to the monastic communities, it easily passed through Parliament in March 1536. Some 300 houses fell within this Act, but around 77 were allowed to continue upon payment of a fine, boosting the royal coffers by at least £15,000 a year. The 1536 Act did not apply to the houses of the mendicant friars.

Vandalism on a breathtaking scale

The decline in standards and need for reform was not in dispute, but proved merely a pretext and the real motive for Henry's suppression of the minor houses soon became clear. While some at the time thought it may have been influenced by the King's split with Rome and to remove a possible threat to his newly founded Church of England, it was the need to stave off royal bankruptcy and to finance his defensive measures against the perceived threat from the French that was behind the King's overzealous attack on the monasteries. Crown tenants were installed in the suppressed houses, but everything of value, such as precious metals, altar furnishings, bells and roofing lead was carted off to the Tower of London. The altar plate and vestments went to the King's jewel house, and bells were recast as cannon and the lead used as shot. Most despicably, many precious books and irreplaceable documents from some of the most important libraries in the land were used to stoke the fires that burned roof timbers from churches and monastic buildings. It was vandalism on a breathtaking scale.

But worse was to come after Henry VIII crushed a revolt in the north, the so-called Pilgrimage of Grace, which started in October 1536, when barrister Robert Aske led nine thousand insurgents into York where he drove out the King's tenants and arranged for the expelled monks and nuns to return to their houses to resume religious observance. In his Narrative to the King, Aske had declared: "In all parts of the realm, men's hearts much grudged with the suppression of the abbeys, and the first fruits, by reason the same, would be the destruction of the whole religion in England." Henry VIII, reneging on promises made during negotiations with the leaders, crushed the rebellion without mercy. Abbots were declared traitors in an act of attainder and executed, often under the flimsiest of pretexts, and those larger houses that had assisted the rebels were immediately forfeited to the Crown and the remaining religious forced out. Those against whom no substantial case could be made were cajoled into surrender. All pretence of reform had been swept aside, and the King was now clearly intent on eliminating the monasteries altogether. Henry cleverly bypassed Parliament by being able to show that the abbots surrendered their houses 'voluntarily'. But, as he set the terms of surrender, for which there were no longer any legal controls, abbots had no real choice but to accept, before the then reasonably generous financial terms were being withdrawn. A few tried to resist the royal will, but were summarily dealt with. After the surrender of the last house at the end of1540, there were no religious houses left anywhere in England and Wales. More than 10,000 monks, canons, friars and nuns were pensioned off and dispersed and their houses and lands granted to royal favourites or sold.

The abbeys, priories and nunneries suffered from deliberate destruction, especially of the churches, cloisters and chapter houses, pillaging of stone for local buildings and roads, or from simple neglect. Weather and time did the rest. Some monastic quarters were converted into mansions by their new owners, and a few of the great churches were repaired to be used by the parish, but not before the townspeople were able to compensate the Crown with cash. The attempted revival of monastic life under the Catholic Queen Mary in 1553 was minimal and was extinguished after the Queen's death in 1558.

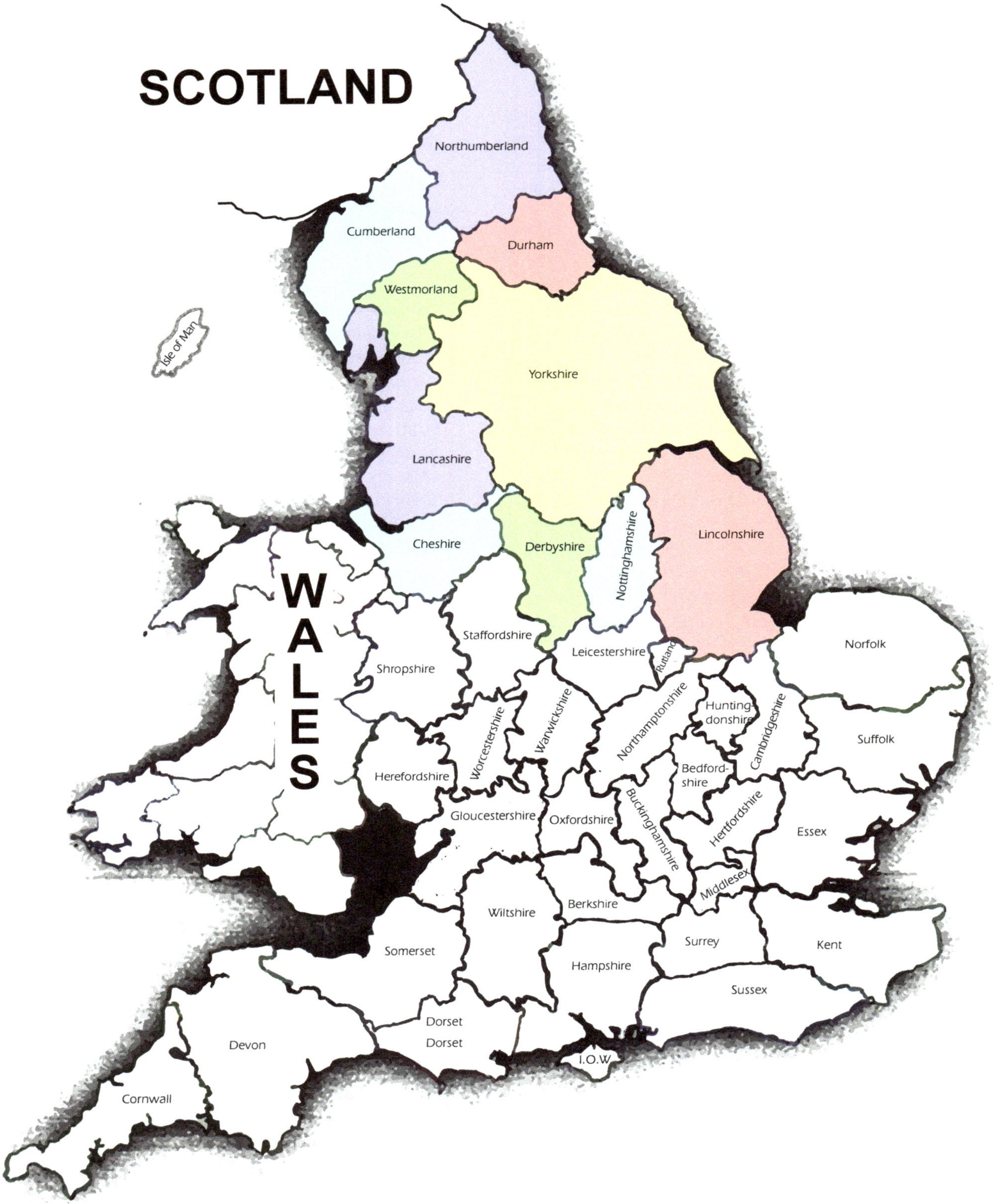
SCOTLAND
Northumberland
Cumberland
Durham
Westmorland
Isle of Man
Yorkshire
Lancashire
Cheshire
Derbyshire
Nottinghamshire
Lincolnshire
WALES
Staffordshire
Leicestershire
Rutland
Norfolk
Shropshire
Worcestershire
Warwickshire
Northamptonshire
Hunting-
donshire
Cambridgeshire
Suffolk
Herefordshire
Bedford-
shire
Gloucestershire
Oxfordshire
Buckinghamshire
Hertfordshire
Essex
Middlesex
Wiltshire
Berkshire
Somerset
Surrey
Kent
Hampshire
Sussex
Dorset
Dorset
I.O.W.
Devon
Cornwall

County-by-County Description of Abbeys and Priories with Map and Gazetteer

Volume 1 – Northern England

Volume 2 – Southern England

Volume 3 – East Central England

Volume 4 – West Central England and Wales

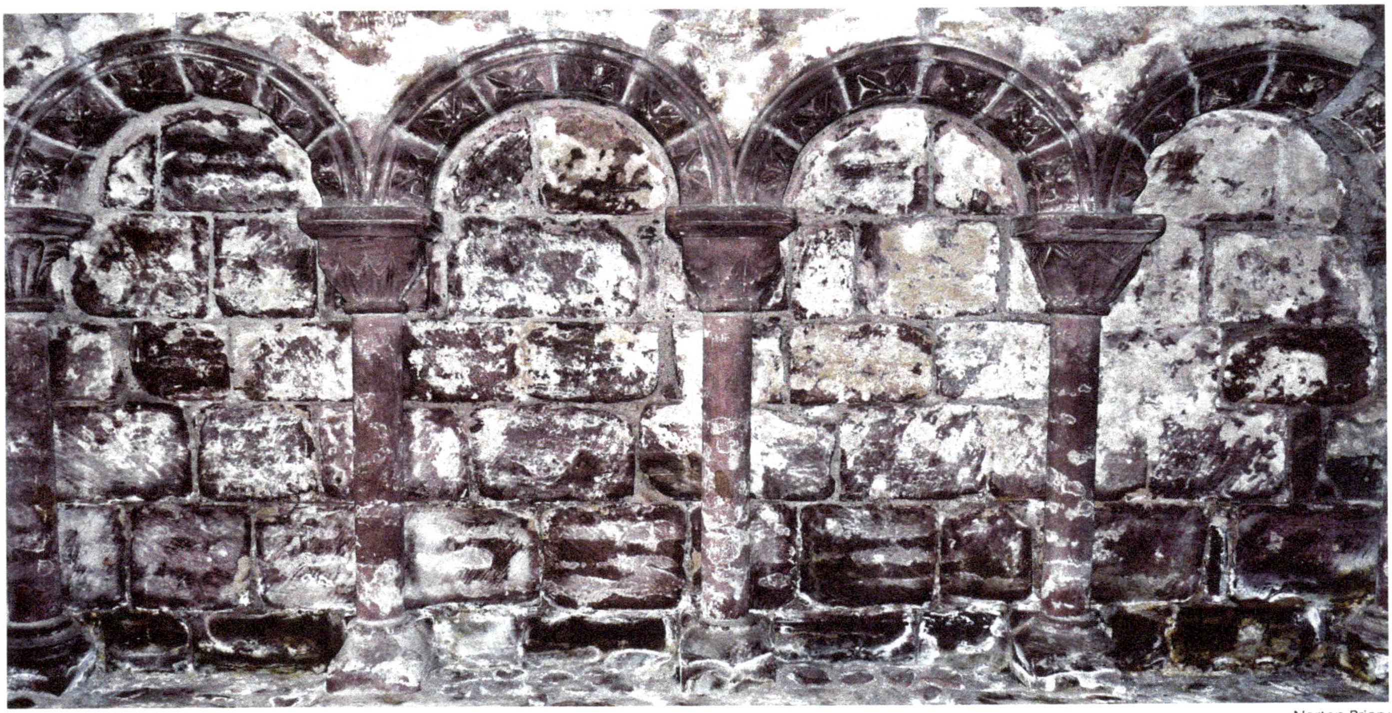

Norton Priory

Cheshire

Royal Palatine

A history of almost 2,000 years lies below and within the cathedral of Chester, but monasticism possibly came to the city in AD 660, with the building of a church. Nothing else is known until the relics of St Werburgh were brought to Chester in AD 875 and laid to rest in a new church, specially built in AD 907 by King Alfred the Great's daughter, Ethelfleda, known as the Lady of the Mercians, probably for secular canons. The abbey was restored in 1075 by Leofric, Earl of Mercia, and by Lady Godiva, but was razed to the ground in 1090 for reasons unknown. The present structure was begun in 1093, when Hugh d'Avranches (Lupus), first Earl of Chester, persuaded Anselm, Abbot of Bec-Herlouin and one of the greatest theologians of his day, to establish a Benedictine monastery. The abbey became prosperous, but religious life deteriorated in later centuries. The shrine of St Werburgh was desecrated on the Dissolution, but the church was saved and designated as the cathedral of the new See of Chester. No trace remains *in situ* of the priory of St Mary, founded in Chester for Benedictine nuns by another earl of Chester in c1140. What buildings survived its suppression in 1538, were largely destroyed in 1645 during the bloody siege of Chester in the Civil War. Reconstructed archways can be admired in a local park.

As the only populous conurbation in the county, three of the main Mendicant Orders of friars established themselves at Chester. Regrettably, nothing has survived from the Dominican (Black) Friars, who arrived in the town in 1236, or the Franciscan (Grey) Friars, who followed only a year after. The Carmelite (White) Friars first moved to Chester in 1279, but most of the buildings were destroyed following its suppression, to make room for a mansion. Almost nothing is known of the Friars of the Sack.

The massive cranes of the dockyard cast their shadows over the former spiritual place of Birkenhead Priory, founded in 1150 on the north-eastern shore of the Wirral. Host to English Kings and battleground for Royalists and Parliamentarians, the priory played its part in shaping life in the Wirral. Insubstantial endowments, expenses incurred from the Kings' visits and other demands on hospitality caused considerable financial distress. The surviving ruins include the guest hall and chapter house. Hidden away in the borderlands at the southern edge of the county stands a Gothic mansion, which incorporates parts of Combermere Abbey, a Savignac foundation, which later became Cistercian. It founded several daughter houses, but its reputation as an 'evil place' appears to have been well deserved. The Cistercian abbey of Vale Royal, founded by Prince Edward, later Edward I, was to be the grandest of all monastic houses in Britain, but the royal purse was not deep enough to quite fulfil the King's ambition. The King became disinterested when all his time was taken up with his war against the Welsh. In spite of mismanagement and misdeeds, which prompted the governing body of the Order to describe Vale Royal as 'damnable and sinister', the abbey was quite wealthy. It is rather unfortunate that nothing has survived within the country mansion that took its place after its dissolution in 1539. Another prominent Cistercian house was Stanlaw Abbey, built on a low-lying promontory, but flooding and fire devastated many of its buildings, forcing the monks to move to Whalley Abbey. Only an overgrown wall remains, but nothing has survived from the short-lived Cistercian abbey of Poulton on the River Dee. The monks were later relocated to Dieulacres in Staffordshire.

The most important monastic remains in Cheshire are those of Norton Priory, a house of Augustinian canons, founded in 1115 on the south bank of the River Mersey. The priors were of some importance, and one in particular, Richard Wyche, was instrumental in raising the priory's status to that of a mitred abbey in 1391. When the King's commissioners arrived in !536 to take the surrender, they were faced by a large, hostile crowd, soon dispersed by an army of soldiers. There are many surviving features, both *in situ* and in the excellent on-site museum. Of particular interest is the well-preserved cellarer's undercroft with a finely carved original doorway. Mobberley Abbey was a short-lived house for a small number of Augustinian canons, while Warburton Priory, a cell of the Premonstratensian abbey of Cockersand, also had a short history.

The only alien cell was the priory on Hilbre Island, given to the abbey of St Evroul-sur-Ouche in Normandy. The priory appears to have been a place of pilgrimage to the shrine of St Hildeburgh, after whom the island was named. Nothing has survived to remind of its existence.

Gazetteer

Birkenhead Priory Priory Street, Birkenhead, Wirral, Merseyside (SJ 328885). Tel: 0151 666 4010. Free access

Chester St Mary's Priory NW of castle walls, Chester, Cheshire (SJ 403659). Re-erected arches in local park

Chester St Werburgh Abbey In city centre, Chester, Cheshire (SJ 406665). Web: www.chestercathedral.org

Chester Black Friars To north of Black Friars in city centre, Chester, Cheshire (SJ 403866). No visible remains

Chester Grey Friars Near Watergate in city centre, Chester, Cheshire (SJ 402662). No visible remains

Chester Sack Friars S of New Crane Street, Chester, Cheshire. No visible remains

Chester White Friars Near Whitefriars in city centre, Chester, Cheshire (SJ 404661). No visible remains

Combermere Abbey On A350, 6.5km (4 miles) NE of Whitchurch, Cheshire (SJ 587441). Tel: 01948 662876. www.combermereabbey.co.uk

Hilbre Island Priory Hilbre Island, Wirral, Merseyside. No visible remains

Mobberley Priory Church Lane, Mobberley, 5km (3 miles) W of Wilmslow, Cheshire (TJ 789802). No visible remains

Norton Priory/Abbey Tudor Road, Manor Park, Runcorn, Cheshire. (SJ 548830). Tel: 01928 569895. www.nortonpriory.org

Poulton Abbey On Old Pulford Brook, Poulton, near Wallasey, Wirral, Merseyside (SJ 404584). No visible remains

Stanlaw Abbey Stanlow Point, Wirral Peninsula, 5km (3 miles) SW of Runcorn, Cheshire (SJ 427773). Minimal remains, not accessible

Vale Royal Abbey Whitegate, Northwich, Cheshire (SJ 638699). Minimal remains

Warburton Priory Off B5159, to the W of Warburton village, 10km (6 miles) E of Warrington, Greater Manchester (SJ 696896). Minimal remains

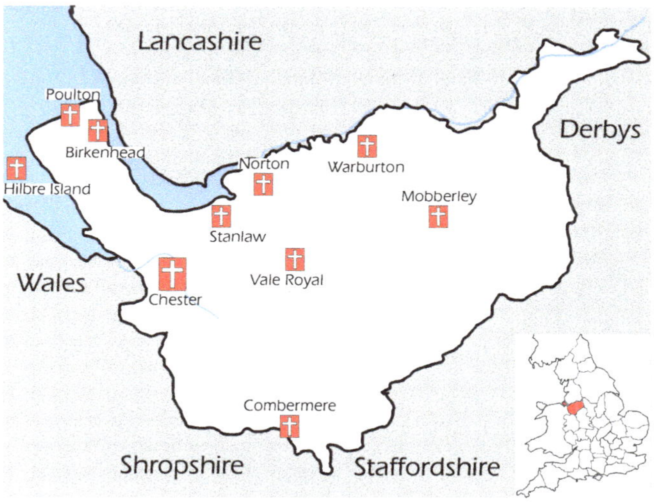

Birkenhead Priory

St James the Great • Benedictine 1150–536

This small and much disturbed monastic site has almost slipped below the radar of those seeking the spiritual heart of the city, yet its sparse remains were once a vital part of life around the Mersey. Host to English Kings and battleground for Royalists and Parliamentarians, its near four hundred years of history are punctuated by events that shaped life in the Wirral. However, a certain degree of neglect is now eating away at the crumbling buildings and the massive cranes of the dockyard cast an overwhelming presence over a once uplifting and spiritual place. Yet, amid the dark shadows, it is still possible to block out the noisy industrial surroundings and set aside precious moments of peaceful reflection. There is also much still of interest to the architectural historian, both within the ruined walls and in the on-site museum.

Today, the late twelfth century but heavily restored chapter house, the oldest standing building on the Wirral and still incorporating some Norman architecture, is the focal point of the erstwhile priory grounds on the headland. It is consecrated as an Anglican chapel and is still used for regular services on the upper floor, formerly believed to have been the scriptorium, dating from 1375. Inside, the chapter house has two bays of quadripartite vaulting carried on clustered shafts with trumpet corbels. Of the church, which was dedicated to St James the Great, only the truncated north wall is still visible where it joined the chapter house, with scars of walling and the base of a shaft also discernable against the ruinous west range. The priory church was about 36.5m (120ft) long by 15.8m (52ft) wide and comprised a four-bay nave, north and south transepts, choir and sanctuary.

The west range, dating from c1250 but remodelled in the fourteenth century, comprises the guest hall and monks' parlour and prior's solar and chapel over. Of interest are the fireplaces at both levels, a passage linking the guest hall and monks' parlour, several decorated doors and windows, and a cornice with stone carvings of flower heads interspersed with grinning and scowling faces. A springing for the vaulting of the cloister passage roof is also visible. The fourteenth century refectory has an undercroft with rib vaulting, carried on octagonal shafts and moulded corbels. A short distant away is the tower of the ruined church of St Mary, the first parish church of the town.

Birkenhead Priory was founded on a wooded headland on the north-eastern shore of the Wirral peninsula in 1150 by Hamo de Massey, third baron of Dunham Massey, who endowed his Benedictine foundation with lands and churches. The first community was said by Leland to have comprised the prior and fifteen monks. The small early church was rebuilt between c1200 and1250, at which time the other major elements of the house had been completed. King Edward I visited in 1275 and again in 1277, as the area was of strategic importance close to the borders of Wales and the Irish Sea. However, the insubstantial endowments, expenses incurred from the King's visits and the rebuilding of the church caused considerable financial distress. Another irksome problem was the increased use of the public road to the Mersey ferry, which crossed the priory court, although this was resolved with royal permission in 1284 to divert the road and enclose the priory with a wall.

The burdens of hospitality were also great, as there were no inns for weary travellers between Chester and the Mersey crossing. The monks, therefore, successfully petitioned the royal council for permission to build lodgings and sell food to travellers delayed from crossing the Mersey by inclement weather. The priory's financial situation improved following a grant by Edward III, which gave the monks the right to ferry men, horses and goods across the Mersey and charge a reasonable fee. The priory itself used the ferry to sell goods at Liverpool market. The additional income enabled the building of the great hall and scriptorium. There were no serious disorders in the house and life among the decreasing community proceeded without much upheaval. In 1381 there were only five monks, including the prior, in residence.

Not much is known of the next hundred and fifty years. With an annual net value estimated in 1535 at £90 13s, Birkenhead Priory was included in the list of the smaller monasteries destined for dissolution, which occurred in summer 1536 when the last prior, John Sharpe, signed the Deed of Surrender. The priory lands were leased immediately to Ralph Worsley, a member of the royal household, who purchased the site in 1545. A manor house was built c1600 where the old hostel stood, but was demolished in the nineteenth century. Birkenhead Priory was occupied by royalists and fortified in 1644, but quickly surrendered to the Parliamentarians.

Photos – clockwise from top left

Ruined west range with guest hall
Passage linking the guest hall and monks' parlour
Springing of roof vaulting of cloister walk
Internal view of guest hall
Cornice with stone carvings of flowers interspersed with grotesque faces
Intact chapter house now used as a chapel

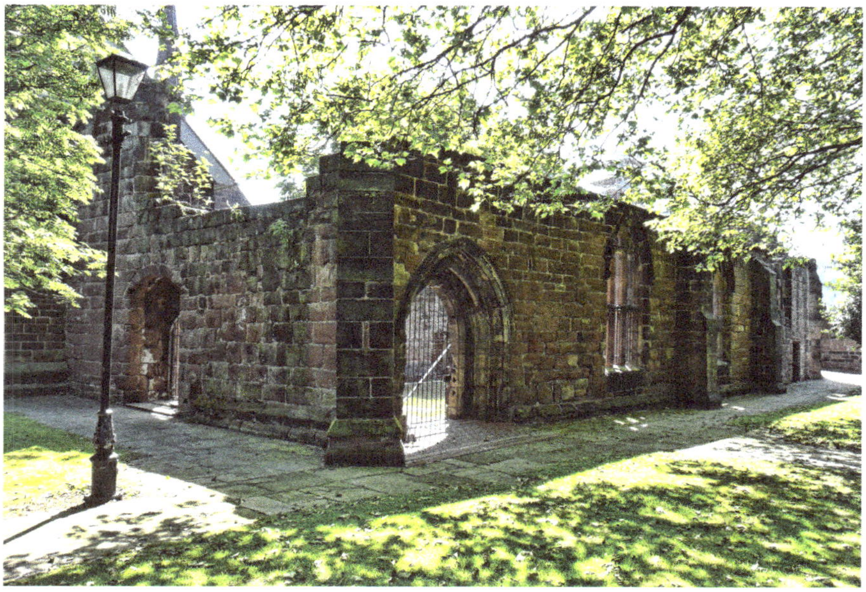

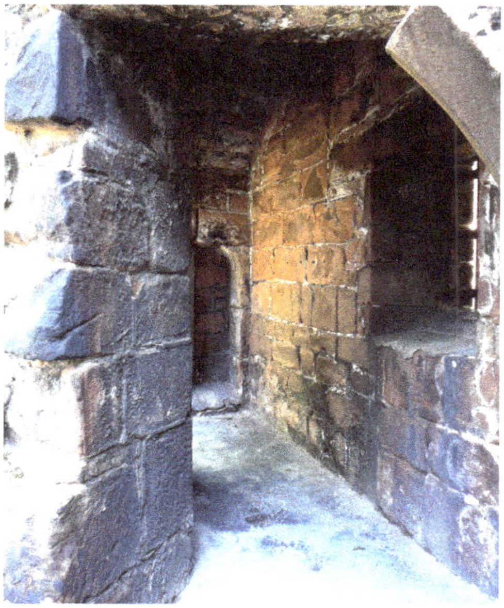

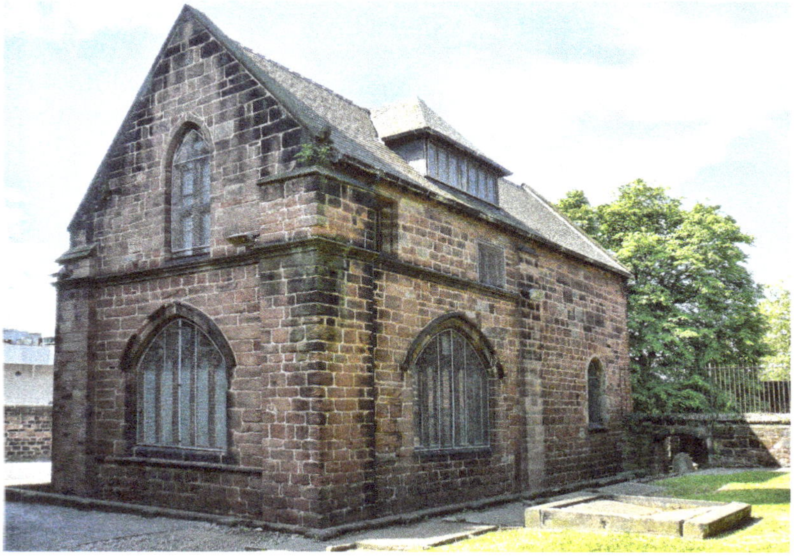

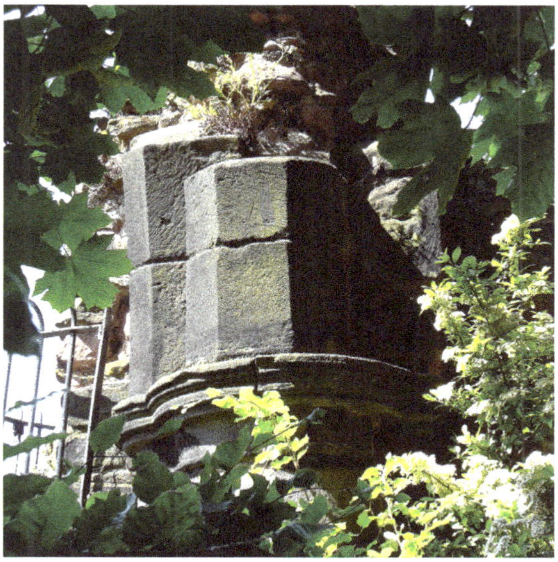

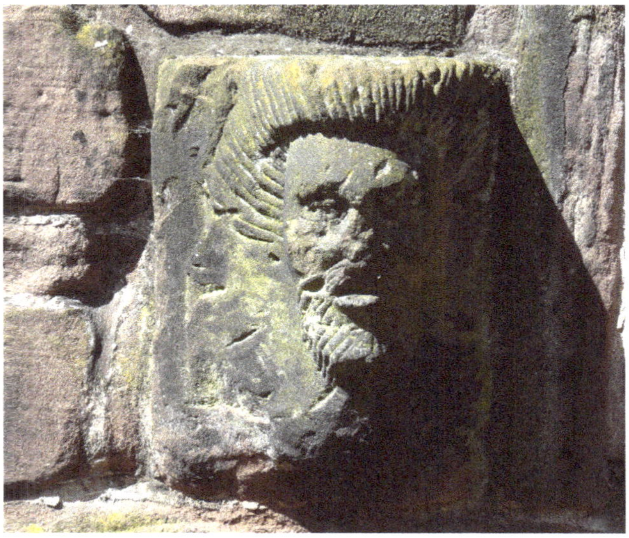

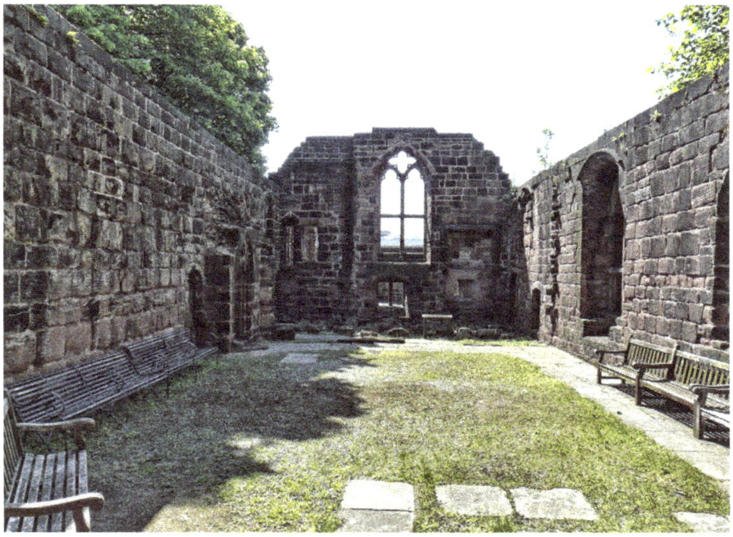

Chester Abbey

St. Werburgh • Benedictine 1093–1540

Chester's St Werburgh Abbey, now the Cathedral Church of Christ and the Blessed Virgin, has survived almost unscathed from medieval times, notwithstanding the nineteenth century restoration of Sir George Gilbert Scott. Apart from the church, most of the monastery buildings are still standing and include the cloisters, Norman undercroft, parlour and chapter house. The refectory and abbey gatehouse have also been restored and are well preserved. The church measures 108m (355ft) in length, with 56m (185ft) across the transepts, topped by a 39m (127ft) high tower. Built of sandstone with an attractive hue of red, the construction exhibits a progression of architectural styles, from the Romanesque to various forms of Gothic.

The cathedral is chiefly noted for its fine choir stalls, whose amazing woodwork dates from 1380 and comprises elaborately carved canopies and misericords, each a piece of art. Among the many fascinating carvings, which of course includes St Werburgh, is one of the Elephant and Castle, where the elephant has horse's hooves! It was carved either as a quirky piece of fun, or, more likely, the craftsman had never seen an elephant before. The sharp-eyed will also spot the Chester Imp, an unusual carving of the Devil in chains, high up at the clerestory level of the nave. With it goes a story of a monk, who was walking along the upper gallery and saw the devil looking through the window. Rather worried about this apparition, the monk confided in the abbot, who told him to put up a carving of the Devil in chains, so that he would know what would happen to him if he dared to return. There are also details of Arthurian legends, Aesop's fables, and fabulous mythical birds. A post-medieval image, some 200 years old, is also of great interest. It shows the Virgin and Child painted on the web of a caterpillar and is the only one of this Tyrolean art form in Britain. The carved shrine of St Werburgh in the Lady Chapel dates from about 1300. St Werburgh was the daughter of King Wulfhere of Mercia and St Ermenilda, daughter of King Ercombert of Kent. She became a nun at Ely and had no associations with Chester during her lifetime.

As the bustling city bombards the senses from all around, it is difficult to imagine that a history of almost 2,000 years lies below and within the cathedral and, according to legend goes even back to prehistoric times when a Druid temple was said to have existed on the site. This was succeeded by a Roman temple dedicated to Apollo, which may have been replaced by a church in the fourth century. Greater certainty is attached to the building of a church in AD 660. The relics of St Werburgh were brought to Chester in AD 875 and laid to rest in a new church, probably for secular canons, specially built in AD 907 by King Alfred the Great's daughter, Queen Ethelfleda, known as the Lady of the Mercians. The abbey, as it was then, was restored in 1057 by Leofric, Earl of Mercia, and by Lady Godiva. For reasons yet to be ascertained, the abbey was razed to the ground in 1090 and the canons evicted. No trace of it now remains.

The present structure has its origins in 1093, when the nephew of William the Conqueror, Hugh d'Avranches (Lupus), first Earl of Chester, persuaded Anselm, the abbot of the great abbey of Bec-Hellouin in Normandy and one of the most renowned theologians of his day, to establish a Benedictine monastery. Work on the church began immediately and completion of the monastic complex was achieved in about 1250 with the construction of the chapter house. All over Europe, the Gothic architectural style was beginning to replace the Romanesque form and reconstruction of Chester started in 1260 and was not completed until early in the sixteenth century with the west end. The plague had carried away much of the work force, which led to a 130-year break in construction.

The abbey became prosperous, with many benefactors enabling the monks to increase their income from many manors, churches, tithes, as well as a ship and ten nets at Anglesey. Its net income in 1535 was a considerable £1,003 5s. According to a monk called Lucian who c1195 wrote a description of Chester, *De Laude Cestrie*, the community was virtuous, learned, and provided liberal hospitality. Fourteenth century visitations discovered a deterioration of religious life, which caused concern then and appears to have worsened over the next two hundred years. The monks later also found themselves in frequent conflict with the city fathers over the abbey's extensive jurisdiction over Chester and its high privileges.

The abbey was dissolved in January 1540 and the shrine of St Werburgh was desecrated. The good news was that Henry VIII designated the church as the cathedral of the new See of Chester, preventing the destruction suffered by most other monastic establishments. The last abbot, Thomas Clarke, became dean of the newly established cathedral in July 1541.

Photos - clockwise from top left

The abbey church built in attractive red sandstone
Ornately carved west façade
Vaulted cloister walk
Reconstructed abbey gateway
Entrance to the chapter house
Nave with vaulting and gilded roof bosses

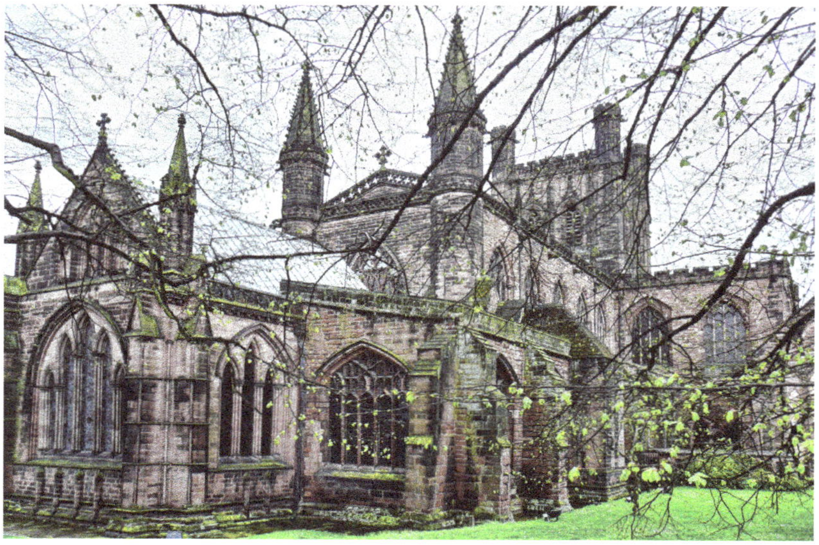

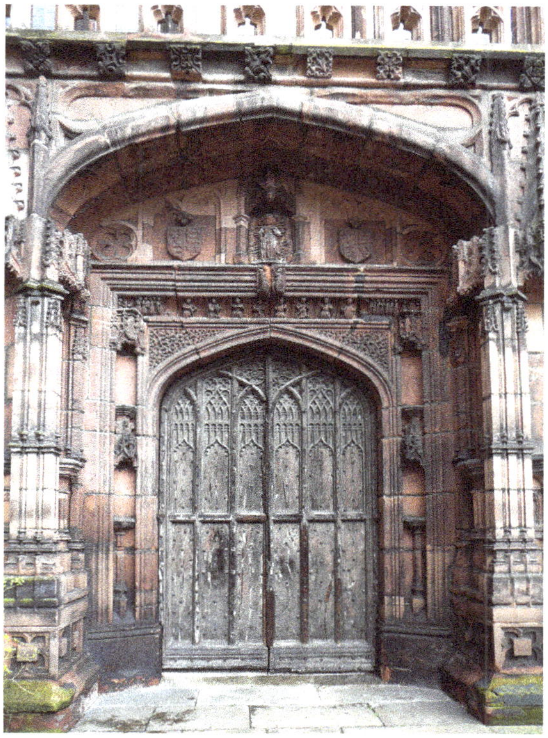

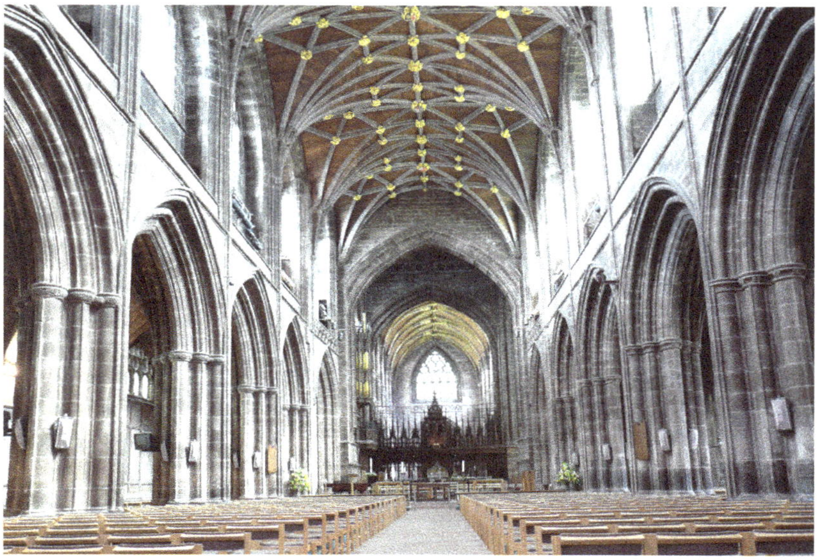

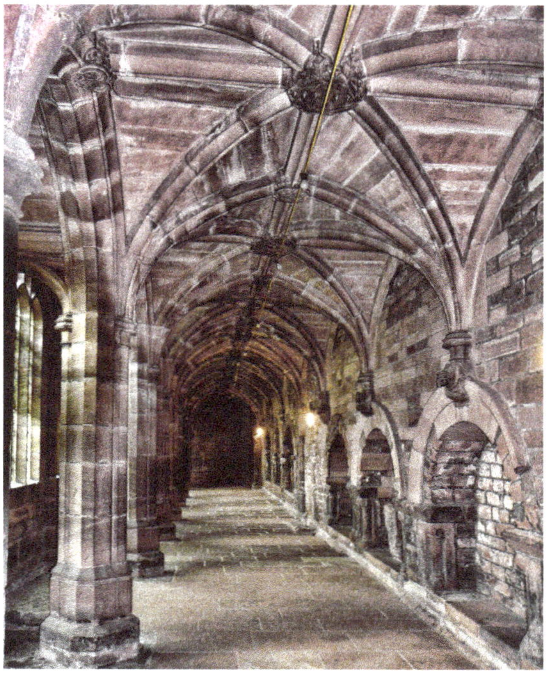

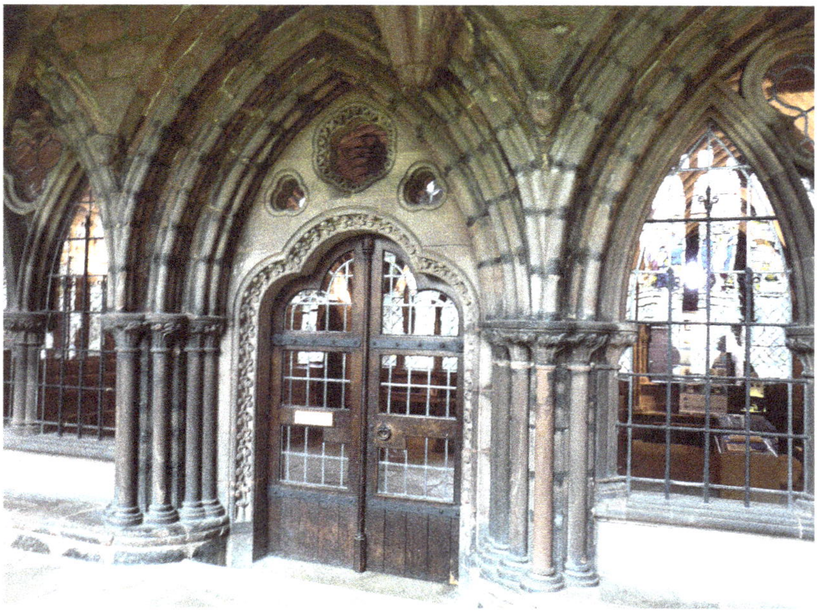

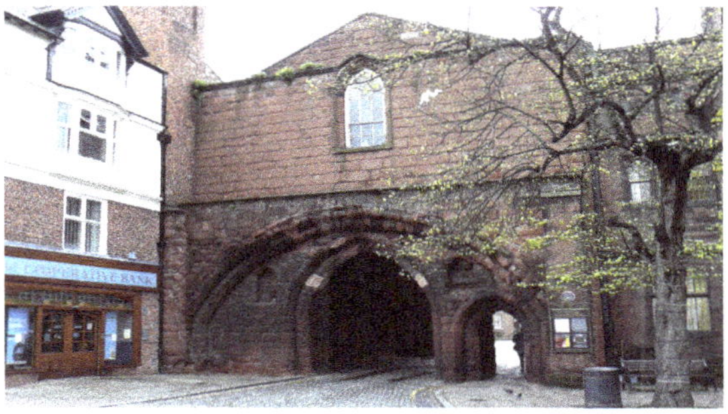

Chester Priory

St Mary • Benedictine nuns c1140–1536

Not a trace remains above ground of this Benedictine house for nuns dedicated to the Virgin Mary, which, like many other buildings, were destroyed in 1645 during the bloody siege of Chester in the Civil War and left to decay. Only Nun's Road, which runs through part of the priory's lands, reminds of this ancient foundation first mentioned in Saxon times, although a re-erected archway can still be seen in Grosvenor Park, and the porch of the church of St Mary-Within-the-Walls, next to the castle, incorporates stone from the old convent. A seventeenth century plan shows a rectangular church with nave and north aisle, in later excavations determined as having measured 18.9 x 16.8m (62 x 55ft), a cloister to the south, and enclosures, including an outer court to the north and west of the church.

While there is some early uncertainty, it is generally accepted that the founder was Ranulph II, Earl of Chester, who, in c1140, granted some land to a community of nuns. The founder's daughter Lucy became the second prioress. Ranulph's son, Hugh II, gave them the church of Over and, although the nuns subsequently received many benefactions, these were small and the house was never wealthy. The nuns were partially supported by regular alms from the earls of Chester up to the early thirteenth century, together with a quarter of the tithes of the expenses of the royal household when the King was in the town. Other help came in the form of oaks and fuel from the royal forests to enable the nuns to maintain the buildings. However, when Bishop Roger Northburgh visited the house in 1331, he found that revenues were barely able to support the community and forbade the prioress to admit any more nuns without his permission. Poverty was eased somewhat in 1362, when the Black Prince granted them the advowson of a church and chapel in Wales. Injunctions were issued in the fifteenth century for mismanagement, and laxity of rules, but the state of the house improved under Prioress Margery Pasmyche, who reported in 1519 that the priory was free of debt. With an annual net income of £66 18s, the priory came well within the 1536 Act of Suppression of the smaller monasteries, but was allowed to carry on upon payment of £160. Prioress Elizabeth Grosvenor and eleven nuns were pensioned off following the dissolution of the house in August 1538. In 1642, the estate and nunnery buildings were granted to Urian Brereton, whose most illustrious descendant, Sir William Brereton, became the leader of the Parliamentarian forces in Cheshire. A hundred years later, the ruins were removed to improve the approach to the new shire hall.

Chester Black Friars

St Nicholas • c1236–1538

The street of Black Friars is all that recalls the Dominican friars who, under the patronage of Alexander Stavensby, Bishop of Coventry and Lichfield, established themselves on the south side of Watergate around 1236, at first probably making use of the nearby chapel of St Nicholas. Work on a new church, also dedicated to St Nicholas, began soon after the foundation, and by 1276, the monks could draw on fresh water for their domestic quarters and kitchens through a pipeline they themselves had laid from a spring at Boughton, some two kilometres away. The Provincial Chapter of the Dominicans held at Chester in 1312 would suggest that the monastery had by then been completed. The church was subsequently rebuilt and enlarged at least three times, but the last, and grandest, was still incomplete when the priory, along with the other religious establishments in the city, was dissolved in August 1538. The only items of value listed by the King's commissioners were the stained glass and lead roofs. The estate was leased to Thomas Smythe and Richard Sneyde, whose successors presided over the asset stripping and thorough demolition of the buildings and levelling of the site.

Chester Grey Friars

St Francis • c1237–1538

Nothing remains today of this house of Franciscan friars, but the fact that the area bounded by Watergate Street, Bedward Row, St Martin's Way and the City Walls once formed its precinct, gives a fair indication of the size of this monastery. The priory was founded in 1237 or 1238, only a year or so after the Dominicans, who opposed its foundation on the grounds that there would not be enough alms forthcoming in the small town to support both institutions. It is not known if their fears were realised, as history has left few records. The Grey Friars appear to have lived an uneventful life, but were always the poorest of the religious foundations in Chester. By 1529, they had become so impoverished that they were compelled to let out the nave and three aisles of the church to merchants and sailors of Chester, as a place for storing and repairing sails and other things requisite for their ships, on the understanding that the merchants undertook all necessary repairs to the church. Together with the other two Chester religious houses on this side of the city, the unfortunate Franciscans finally surrendered their house to Richard Ingworth, Bishop of Dover, in August 1538. The Deed of Surrender was signed by Warden William Wall and seven friars. Although their estate passed through the hands of several owners over the next 250 years, the priory buildings survived remarkably well until falling into the hands of developers. Its destruction, and in particular of the tall steeple of the church, which had long served as a guide to mariners entering the Port of Chester, was lamented by antiquarian William Webb who wrote: "It was a great pitie that the steeple was put away, being a great ornament to the citie. This curious spire steeple might still have stood for grace to the citie had not private benefit, the devourer of antiquitie, pulled it down with the church..".

Chester Sack Friars

-1274–c1300

Almost nothing is known of this house of the Friars of the Penitence of Jesus Christ, more popularly known as Friars of the Sack, which was founded before 1274, when the Order was suppressed by the Council of Lyons. In 1277, Edward I sent the community 5s for food and made a further donation in 1284. The friars probably dispersed before 1300.

Chester White Friars

St Mary • 1290–1538

The Friars mansion standing in its extensive grounds in the heart of the city was the result of the tearing down in 1592 by Thomas Egerton, the Attorney-General, of the church and other buildings of the community of Carmelite Friars, more popularly known as the White Friars. The monastery and its lands in its final form were bounded by Commonhall Street, Bridge Street, White Friars (formerly White Friars Lane) and Weaver Street. The Carmelites first moved to Chester in 1279, but it was not until 1290 that Hugh Payn granted them land in what was then merely a suburb. The priory church was rebuilt and enlarged several times, culminating in 1495 with the reconstruction of the tower to include a tall and graceful steeple. The Dissolution came in 1538 when ten friars were dispossessed. Most of the buildings were destroyed to make room for a mansion, but the large monastic church remained in use until 1592.

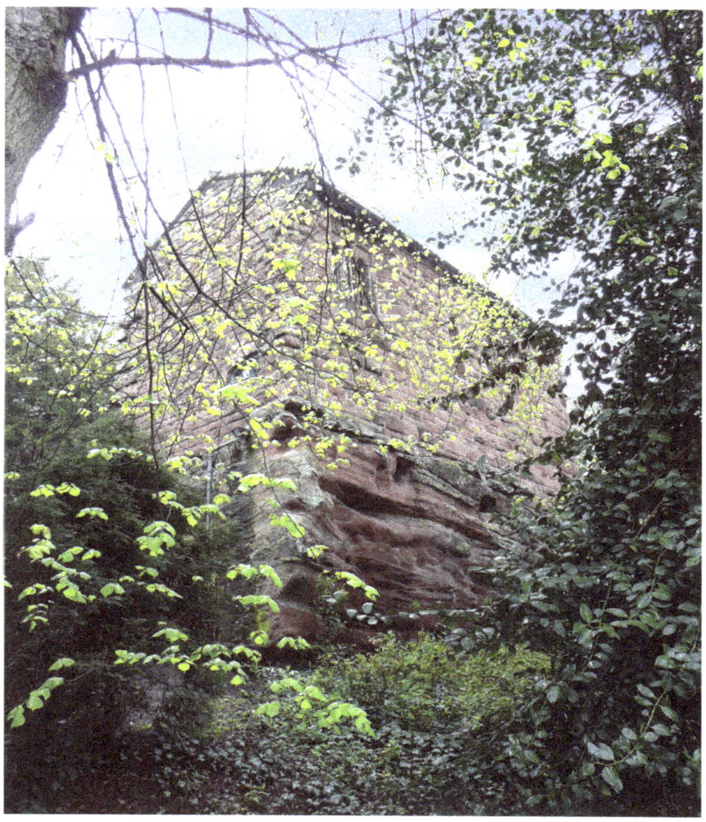

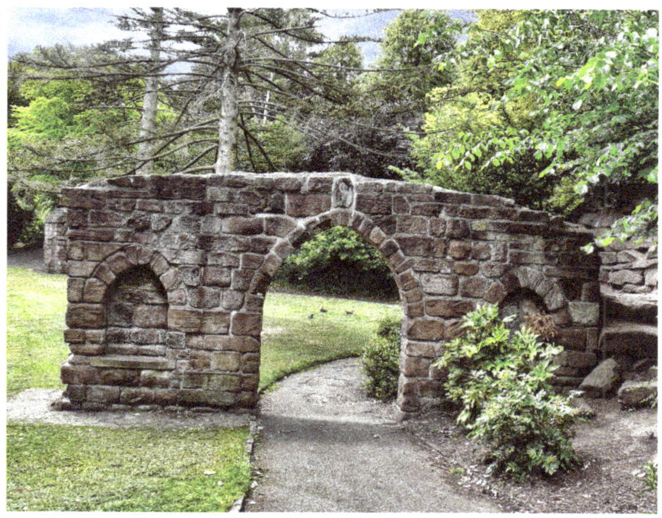

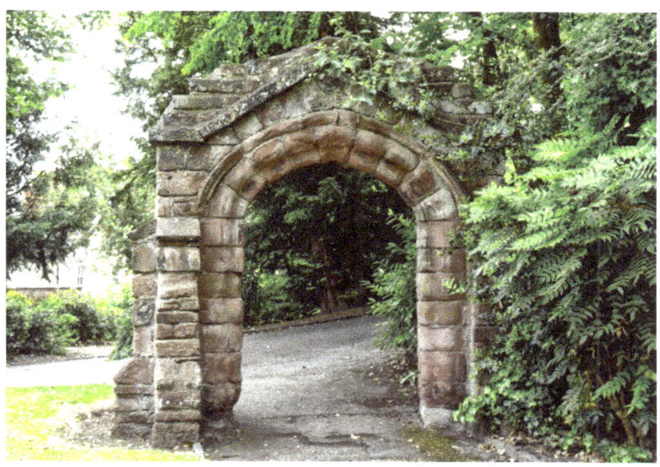

Photos – clockwise from above

Remodelled anchorite cell built in the fourteenth century as a retreat for monks

Reconstructed archways from Chester Priory of St Mary

Combermere Abbey

St Mary & St Michael • Savignac/Cistercian 1133–1538

Little may be left of this original Savignac foundation dedicated to St Mary and St Michael, but the site, hidden away in the borderlands at the extreme southern edge of Cheshire, where the county nudges Shropshire and Staffordshire, retains its rural character to this day. Much of the wooded tracts have been replaced by parkland, but the Mere, from which its name is derived, is still a focal point, as well as an important environment for birds. The splendid house with its Victorian Gothic embellishments was originally built in the mid-sixteenth century and incorporates portions of the south cloister and adjacent rooms, probably the kitchens, and a short length of the east range. The timber-framed upper storey of the south range includes the late medieval refectory, dating from c1500, with a hammer-beam roof displaying the abbey's arms on each spandrel. Abutting the east end of the south side of the refectory is a smaller room, which may have been the misericord. The abbey church and other buildings were demolished soon after the Dissolution. Combermere Abbey is now run as an organic dairy farm, but guided tours are available once a week between April and September. Intricately carved choir stalls at St Mary's Church at Nantwich are said to have come from the abbey. St Mary's belonged to the monks of Combermere who used the wall oven in the church to bake bread for the sacrament.

The abbey was founded in 1133 by Hugh de Malbank, who endowed the house with nearby lands, a mill and several churches, with the charter witnessed by Ranulph II, Earl of Chester. Under William, the first abbot, Combermere established a daughter house at Poulton, later moved to Dieulacres in Staffordshire, and from 1154, for a time, St Mary's Abbey in Dublin and Basingwerk Abbey in Flintshire also came under Combermere's jurisdiction. Attempts to settle monks at Church Preen in Shropshire were thwarted by the abbot of Wenlock. Other daughter houses were acquired in 1178 at Stanlaw, later translated to Whalley in Lancashire, followed in 1219 by another at Hulton in Staffordshire.

Although the abbey expanded moderately through sheep farming and wool production, by 1275 it was in debt, and its impoverished state continued more or less throughout its history. One of the abbots was accused of counterfeiting gold coins, in an effort to ease the abbey's precarious financial position. In 1412, Henry, Prince of Wales, took the abbey into his own hands and entrusted its management to the chamberlain of Chester. But mismanagement was not the only culprit responsible for disturbing the abbey's tranquility. Its history was punctuated by often violent local disputes, which sometimes resulted in attacks on the abbey, murder and horse rustling, with the consequent retribution by the abbot, who also took up arms. Feuds too soured the atmosphere between the abbots of Combermere and the daughter houses of Whalley and Hulton, and other nearby monasteries. Its reputation as an 'evil place' appears to have been well deserved.

In the *Valor* of 1535, its net income was valued at a respectable £225 9s, but when the King's commissioners visited the house the following year, they found that it carried debts of £160. Appeals by Abbot John Massey to Thomas Cromwell to spare the abbey fell on deaf ears, and in July 1538, he and twelve monks signed the Deed of Surrender and were pensioned off. In August 1539, the abbey and its lands were granted to Sir George Cotton, who proceeded to demolish the church and most of the claustral buildings, to make room for a mansion. The Cottons, later Lords Combermere, remained in possession until 1919.

Hilbre Island Priory

St Mary & St Hildeburgh • Benedictine c1138–1538/9

There is some evidence that Hilbre was a place of pilgrimage to the shrine of St Hildeburgh, an unknown saint after whom the island was named, but more certainty surrounds its establishment as a cell to the Abbey of St Evroul-sur-Ouche in Normandy by Norman lord Robert of Rhuddlan. A single monk was said to have lived there before the island was transferred c1138 to the Benedictine abbey of St Werburgh in Chester. It appears that there were probably no more than two monks on the island, who maintained a small chapel dedicated to St Mary, collected tithes in West Kirby and managed a depot for sheep and cattle in Meols. The island also remained a minor place of pilgrimage to 'Our Lady of Hilbre' throughout the thirteenth and fourteenth centuries. It would be more accurate to describe Hilbre as a monastic grange, rather than a priory cell, although the last monk on the island, Thomas Wengham, has been titled as prior. It was dissolved c1538/9. Nothing has survived to remind of its existence. Thomas Wengham left the island in about 1550.

Mobberley Priory

St Mary & St Wilfrid • Augustinian c1206–c1245

This was a short-lived house for a small number of Augustinian canons regular, founded c1206 by Patrick de Mobberley. A paucity of endowments appears to have made the priory economically unviable, in spite of the modest lifestyle of the canons, which led Gilbert de Barton to annex the lands and church to Rocester Abbey in Staffordshire sometime between 1228 and 1230. In name at least, the priory continued to exist for a while, at least until the building of the present church, which was begun in 1245. It has been suggested that the church replaced an earlier Saxon building, said to have been erected by St Wilfrid about AD 690, following his exile from Northumbria.

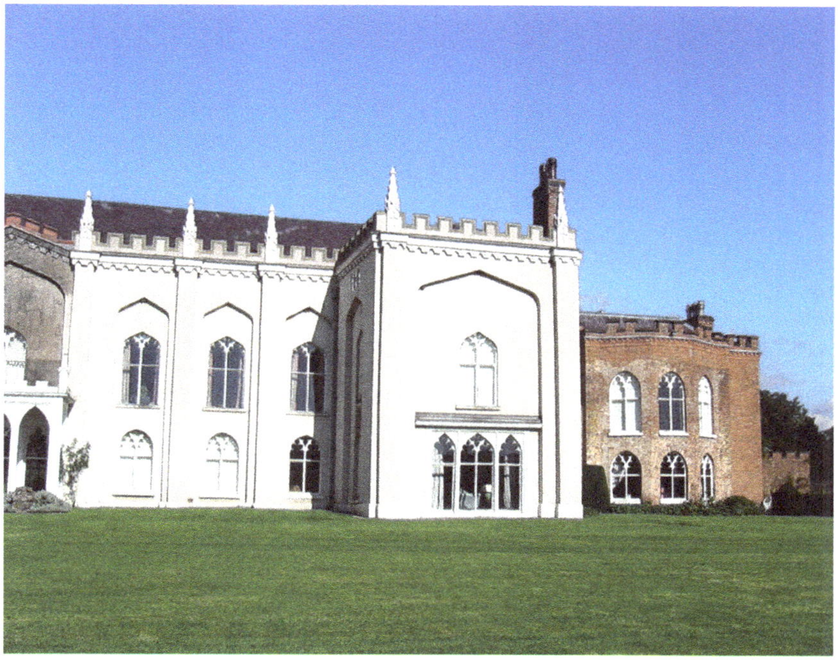

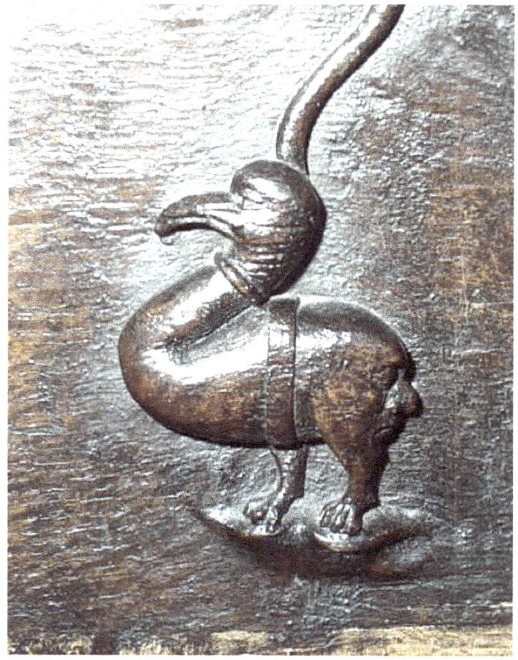

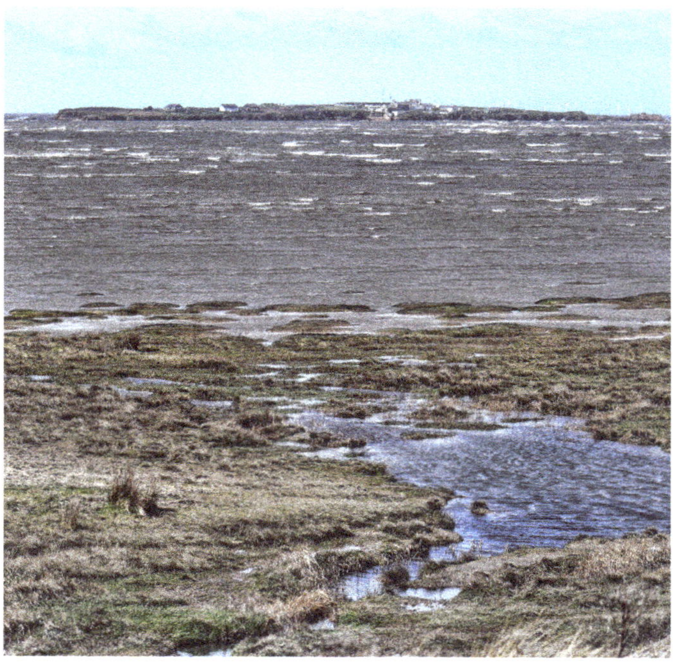

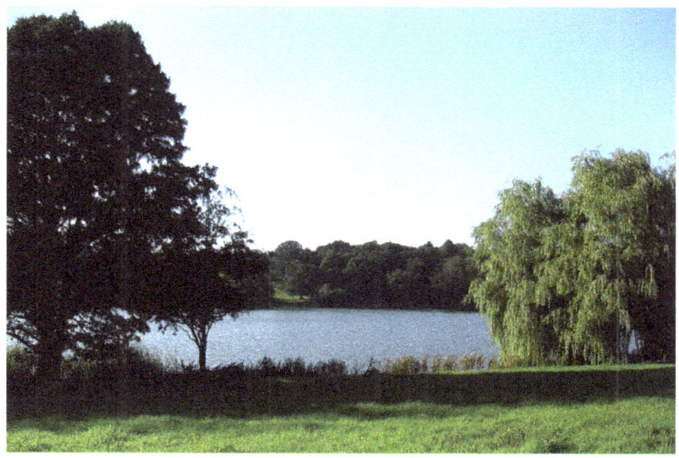

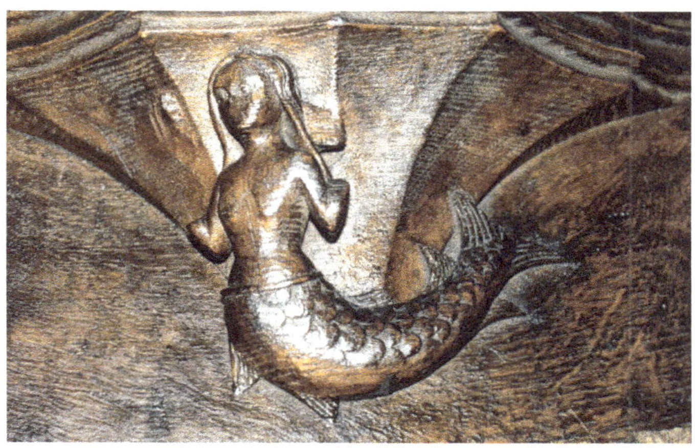

Photos - clockwise from top left

Combermere Abbey House
Carving of parson's nose at Nantwich
The Mere after which the abbey was named
Choir stall carving of mermaid
View of Hilbre Island from the Wirral

Norton Priory/Abbey

St Mary & St Christopher • Augustinian 1115–1536

Finding the remains of the Augustinian priory of St Mary and St Christopher in a swathe of leafy woodland, green fields and well-kept parks to the north of the Bridgewater Canal and in the midst of the encircling industrial landscape is not easy, but very rewarding and most unexpected. So are the surviving features of this early foundation, both *in situ* and in the excellent on-site museum, through which the visitor is guided and where the main artefacts are parts of a reconstructed cloister arcade, a large collection of medieval glazed floor tiles and remains of a kiln where the tiles were fired, several carved sepulchral slabs, and a bell pit for casting the church bells. Norton, which since its foundation has looked out upon a great and stormy river, chose St Christopher, the Christ-bearer symbolising the Christians' passage over the stormy waves of a troublesome world as its second saint. The saint's giant sandstone figure, once painted in bright colours and placed under a canopy looking towards the River Mersey, now stands in a separate gallery near the entrance to the priory. Some 3m (10ft) tall and dated to about 1350, it is the largest medieval stone sculpture in Britain and is one of the highlights of a visit.

There is still more to explore of what are considered the most important monastic remains in Cheshire. None more so than the undercroft of the cellarer's range, entrance to which is gained by two finely decorated doorways, one of which is an original, the other a Victorian replica, although at first glance it is difficult to distinguish between the two. The older doorway from the late twelfth century is in good condition. The three orders of semi-circular arches on colonettes are carved with typically Norman zigzag work. The medieval undercroft is seven bays long and two bays wide and contains a transverse wall and brick wine bins, which are later additions. The southern four bays have ribbed vaults, while the three northern bays have groined vaults. The fine vaulting springs from short octagonal columns with capitals. A passage at the northern end is notable for stone benches under blind arcading on both sides, each consisting of four round-headed arches, which are enriched with elaborate human heads, animals and stiff-leaf foliage.

A short climb to an observation point affords a birds-eye view of the monastic complex, where some walls of the church and other buildings have survived to a height of a few feet in places. The size of the church with a length of 91.5m (300ft) comes to immediate attention and is the result of several expansion programmes, the last probably the result of a consuming fire in 1326, which also led to the building of a new, larger chapter house, cloister arcades and reredorter. After the priory's elevation to abbey status in 1391, the abbot's quarters were extended by the addition of a tower house to the west range, a gatehouse built at the entry to the outer court, and a northern aisle added to the nave of the church.

In 1115, William fitzNigel, the second Baron of Halton, founded this house of Augustinian canons on the south bank of the River Mersey where it narrows to form Runcorn Gap. The community had barely settled at Runcorn when his son William fitzWilliam removed them in 1134 to the wild woods of Norton, beneath the shadow of Halton Castle. Prior Richard cultivated the area to support sheep and cattle and grow crops. The priory was endowed with several churches, the tithes of at least eight mills, the rights of common in four townships, and one-tenth of the profits from the Runcorn ferry. From the foundation of the priory until the palatine jurisdiction of the Norman earls of Chester ceased, the prior of Norton was a man of some importance. He sat in the local Parliament and appeared at many public functions, styled the Lord Prior. King Edward II visited the priory in 1323 while staying at nearby Halton Castle and, in1347, Edward III demanded two sacks of wool from the prior to boost funds for his wars with France.

Financial mismanagement for most of the fourteenth century and severe flooding in 1331 decimated the priory's income, but the situation improved from 1366 with the appointment as prior of Richard Wyche who, in 1391, was instrumental in raising the priory's status to that of a mitred abbey. After his death in 1400, the fortunes of the abbey declined and by 1429, the church and other buildings were described as being ruinous. In 1535, the worth of the abbey was assessed at £180 7s. When the King's commissioners arrived at Norton in October 1536, they faced a hostile bunch of 300 local people, but an army of soldiers led by Piers Dutton soon dispersed the crowd. The last abbot, John Birkenhead, and four of the canons were arrested and sent to prison, but were later discharged and pensioned off. The abbey was stripped of all valuables and was sold to Sir Richard Brooke, who demolished most of the monastic buildings and erected a mansion.

Photos - clockwise from top left

Well-preserved undercroft of the cellarer's range
Foundations of chapter house
column capitals of doorway with scallop and foliage decorations
Medieval floor tiles produced by the canons
Passage with blind arcading and stone seats
Finely carved late twelfth century doorway

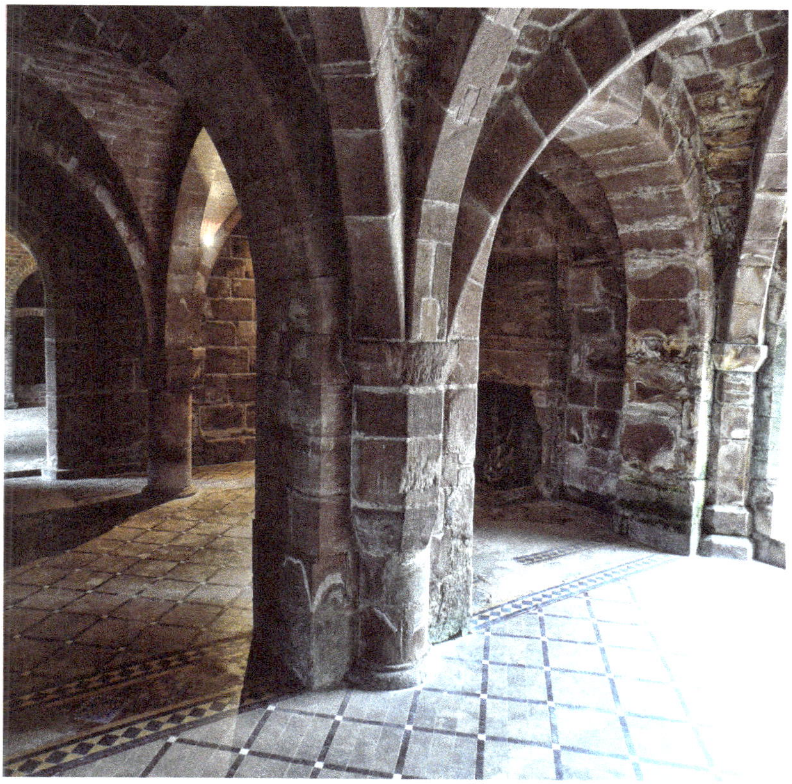

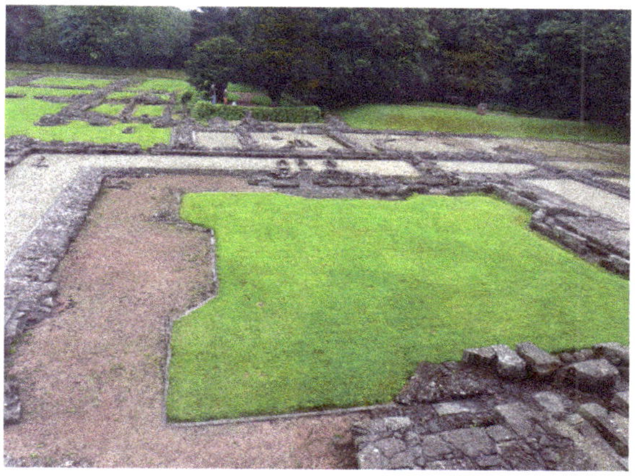

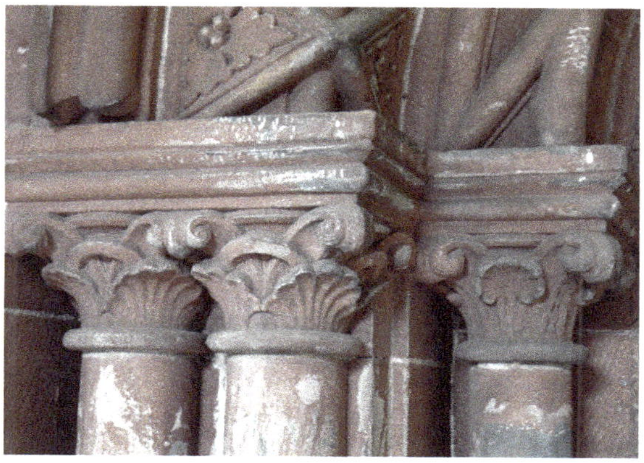

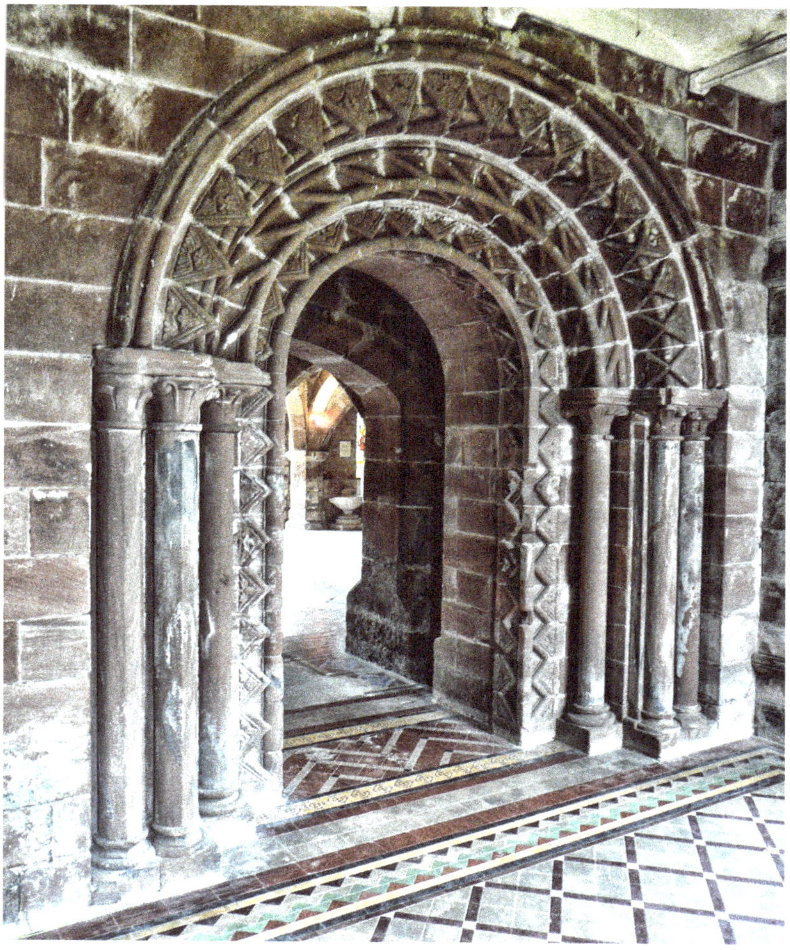

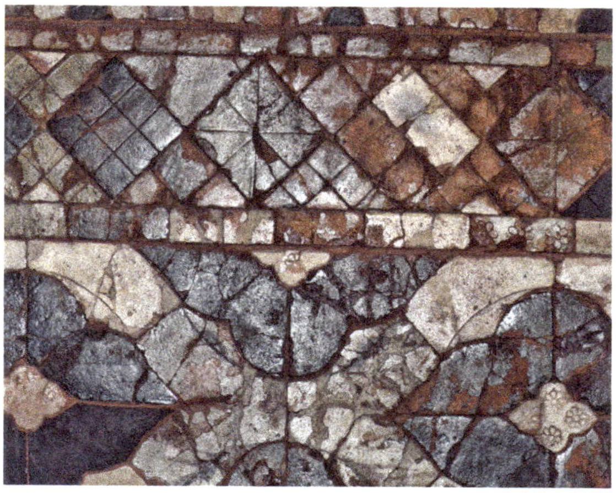

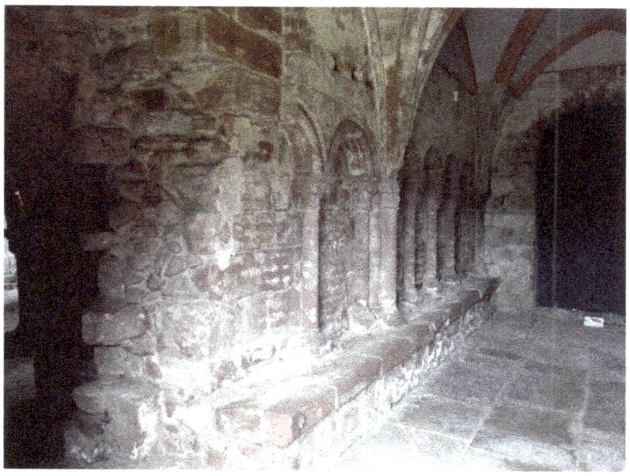

Poulton Abbey

St Mary • Cistercian c1146–1204

Nothing at all is visible from this short-lived Cistercian abbey on the River Dee, nor has its exact location been identified. It was founded between 1146 and 1153 by Robert Pincerna, butler to Ranulf de Gernon, second Earl of Chester, as a daughter-house of Combermere Abbey. Combermere supplied a small community of monks who arrived at Poulton in 1158. The original foundation charter, the earliest in Cheshire, has survived. The abbey obtained a mass of endowments of lands, with successive earls of Chester being particularly generous benefactors. However, Ranulph de Blundeville, the sixth earl, relocated the monks to Leek where he founded Dieulacres Abbey in 1204. Poulton was retained as a grange and prospered, becoming the most important Cistercian estate in the country, with huge swathes of land, which have conservatively been estimated at 3,000 acres. Although much was waste land and of poor quality, the highly skilled monks were able to drain bogs, establish complex field drainage systems, and a series of fishponds, some of which still exist.

Stanlaw Abbey

St Mary • Cistercian 1178–1296

At Stanlow Point, a low-lying promontory in the south-east of the Wirral peninsula where the small Gowy rivulet mingles with the River Mersey, stand the sparse overgrown remains of a once prominent Cistercian abbey. The site, always remote, is now separated from the hinterland by the Manchester Ship Canal, making access extremely difficult. In any case, even when overcoming such obstacles, the visitor will find little evidence above ground that would throw light on the extent and layout of this religious foundation and the grange that succeeded it. The only upstanding remains are two unidentified sandstone walls up to 3m (5ft) high, which were incorporated into a now demolished farmhouse. At the western end of one of the walls is a re-used medieval doorway. Prominent among the buried remains is part of a tunnel, which formed the main drain into the Gowy. Antiquarian sources record that a circular rock-cut crypt containing lead coffins was exposed by flooding, but its exact location is no longer known. The abbey was founded in 1178 by John fitzRichard, sixth Baron of Halton and Constable of Chester, and was colonised from Combermere. The abbey acquired considerable wealth, especially in Lancashire, but the choice of building in exposed marshland was not an inspired one. In 1279, the Mersey burst its banks and inundated the land, and in 1287, after a fierce storm, the church tower and chapel collapsed and damaged surrounding buildings. The abbey's misfortunes were further compounded two years later with more flooding and a raging fire that devastated many of its buildings. It was the last straw for the long-suffering community. The abbot successfully appealed to the Pope for permission to move to a more suitable site and with his consent and that of Edward I and Henry de Lacy, tenth Baron of Halton, twenty monks transferred to Whalley Abbey in Lancashire's Ribble Valley in 1296, six more moved elsewhere, and only the abbot and five monks remained to administer the site as a grange to Whalley.

Vale Royal Abbey

St Mary, St Nicholas & St Nicasus • Cistercian 1274–1539

Vale Royal Abbey was founded and endowed by Prince Edward, later Edward I, to become the grandest of all monastic houses in Britain. Even though the royal purse was not deep enough to quite fulfill the King's avowed ambition, it is regrettable that none of the buildings have survived. The country mansion that rose from the largely demolished buildings and is now part of a prestigious golf club, displays no obvious external signs of a religious past, but one survival is the former gate chapel provided by the monks to serve travellers, which is now St Mary's parish church. Fearful of his life while crossing the stormy Channel from France in 1263, Prince Edward vowed that if he were to reach England safely, he would build an abbey of unprecedented size and grandeur. Edward granted a charter in 1270 together with a generous gift of land and churches. The site given to the Cistercian Order was a secluded location in Darnhall and the first monks from Abbey Dore led by Abbot John Chaumpeneys arrived in 1274. However, the site proved unsuitable for the huge buildings planned, and strong resistance from the local population forced Edward, who had by then become King Edward I, to move the abbey to nearby Over in 1277, which henceforth became known as Vale Royal.

The abbey was to be an expression of the King's piety and symbol of royal power and wealth. The abbey church in particular was to represent the King's ambition. Royal masons under the leadership of Walter of Hereford, probably the greatest architect of his time, started work on an elaborate Gothic edifice that was to exceed in size and splendour any others in the land. The cruciform church was to be 116m (380ft) long, with a central tower and a semi-circular east end with a chevet of thirteen radiating chapels. Each of the transepts also incorporated three eastern chapels. The cloister to the south was to be 42m (138ft) square. The splendour of the church was to be matched by the chapter house, refectory, dormitory and surrounding domestic buildings. The King made large donations of cash and materials, but he soon became distracted by his war against the Welsh and in 1290 declared that he wanted nothing further to do with the abbey. Work stopped for many years but the situation improved somewhat in the 1350s when Edward, the Black Prince, donated substantial funds for the completion of the abbey. Disaster struck in 1360 when a hurricane brought the arcades of the unfinished nave crashing down, but under the patronage of Richard II, the abbey was finally completed, but not on the grand scale originally envisaged.

Problems with building works were compounded by a catalogue of misdeeds over the next 150 years that had the governing body of the Cistercian Order describe Vale Royal as "damnable and sinister". The abbots were harsh and oppressive landlords and monastic officials were often attacked and on occasions, large-scale violence ensued, which led to the murder of Abbot Peter in 1339. Another abbot, Henry Arrowsmith, was hacked to death in 1437 by a group of men including the vicar of Over, in retribution for a rape he allegedly committed, but was acquitted of. Lax discipline and gross mismanagement was the order of the day, but the abbey entered a quiet period after an investigation in 1455. The abbey was initially to house 100 monks, but barely more than twenty were in residence at any one time. In spite of mismanagement, the abbey's net worth was assessed in the *Valor* of 1535 at a substantial £518 19s. Although the last abbot, John Hargreaves tried bribery to avoid the impending closure of the abbey, leased out its lands to friends and associates, and realised other assets, the end came in March 1539. The King's commissioner, Thomas Holcroft, demolished the church and, after he was granted the abbey site and its estates in 1544, he used many of the abbey buildings to form the core of his huge mansion. In 1615, the abbey came into the hands of the Cholmondeleys who supported the King during the Civil War. As a result, it was extensively looted and the south wing of the house burned down by Parliamentarian forces.

Warburton Priory

St Mary & St Werburgh • Premonstratensian c1187-1271

Warburton Priory on the south bank of the River Mersey, close to the ancient church of St Werburgh, was a short-lived cell of the Premonstratensian abbey of Cockersand. It was probably established around 1187 by John the Constable, after whose death in 1190, Adam de Dutton gave the moiety of the vill of Warburton to the church of St Mary and St Werburgh and the Premonstratensian canons. Several grants of land on both sides of the Mersey enabled the canons to engage in sheep farming, but the priory ceased to exist when the abbot of Cockersand sold the advowson of the chapel and all lands and rights to Geoffrey de Dutton II in 1271. It has been suggested that the timber framed part of the north wall of the nave of the now abandoned church is all that is left of the priory chapel.

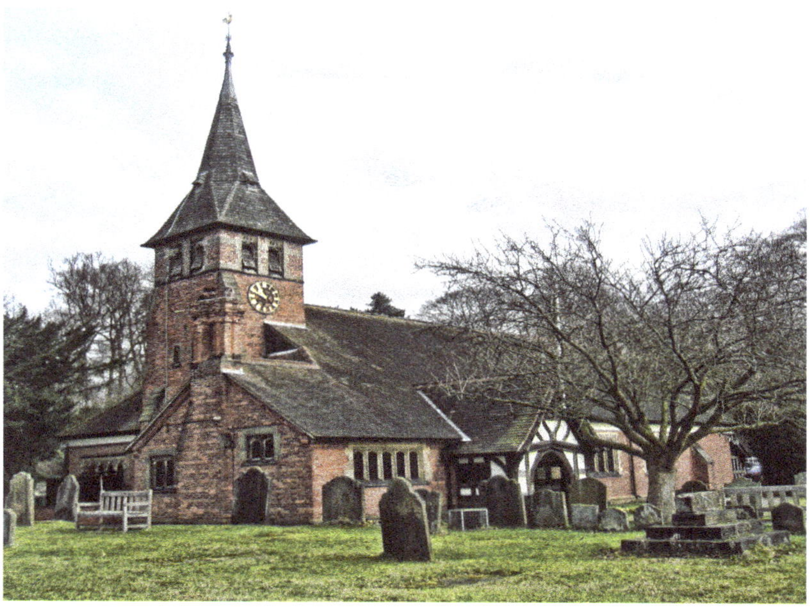

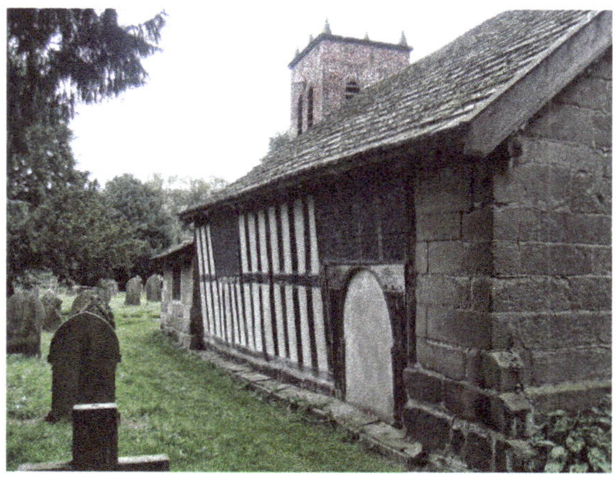

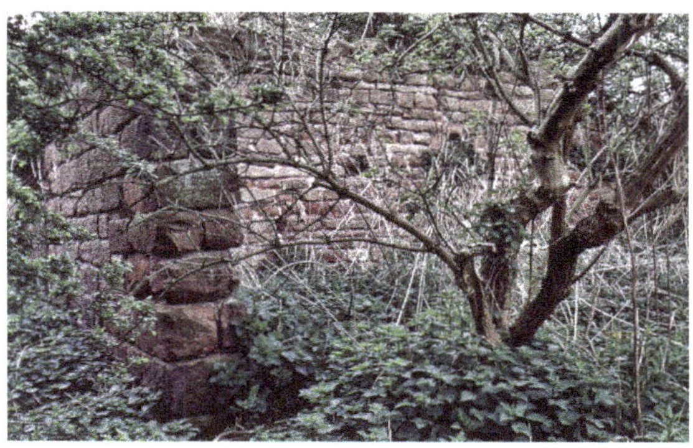

Photos – clockwise from above

Former gate chapel of Vale Royal Abbey
Timber framing from former Warburton Priory chapel
Sparse red sandstone survival from Stanlaw Abbey

Cumberland

War and Peace

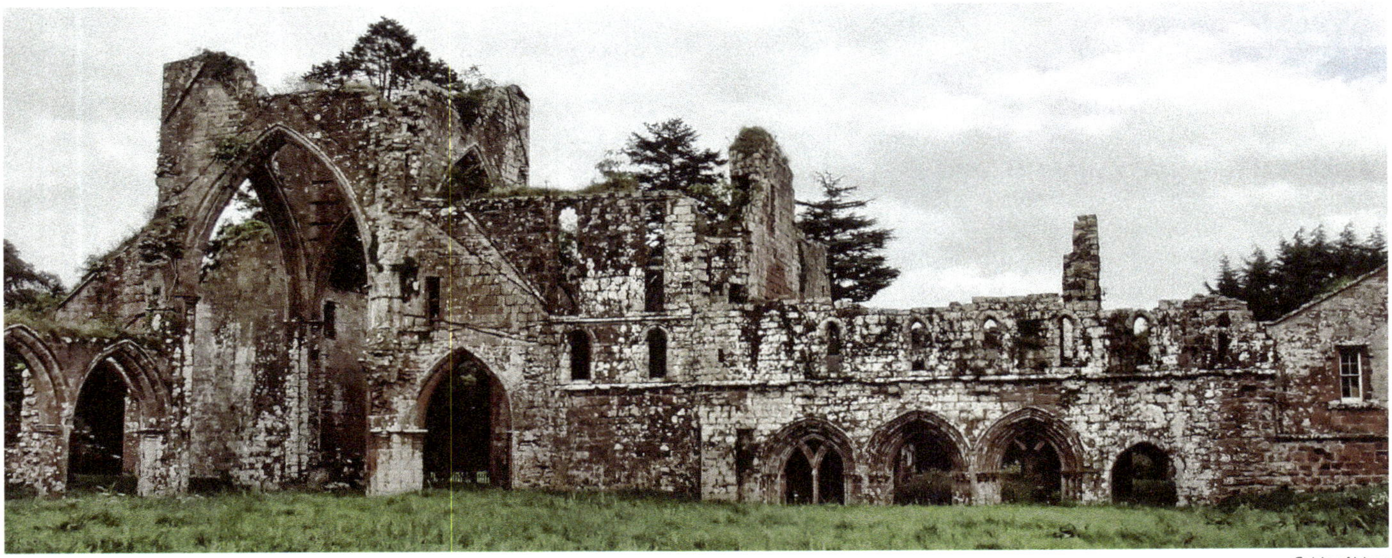

Calder Abbey

The term of Cumberland was first recorded in AD 945, when, according to the *Anglo-Saxon Chronicle,* the area was ceded by King Edmund to Malcolm I of Scotland. It reverted to England in 1092, following the invasion of Carlisle by William II (Rufus), who created the Earldom of Carlisle, only to be reclaimed by King David I of Scotland after the death of Henry I. In 1157, Henry II resumed possession and formed two counties: Westmorland and Carliol, the latter becoming known as Cumberland from 1177. The border between England and Scotland was firmly established by the Treaty of York in 1237.

Being a remote area of lakes, forests and mountains, the county proved attractive to the monastic Orders. The first monastic foundation was the richly-endowed Benedictine priory of Wetheral, founded in 1088 by Ranulph le Meschines, Lord of Copeland. Unfortunately, during the border wars the monks were frequently forced to flee, but wholesale destruction, with the exception of the gatehouse, was not wrought by the Scots but by the Dean and Chapter of Carlisle after the Dissolution. The Augustinian priory of St Mary at Carlisle was founded in 1122 by Henry I, and became the new cathedral upon the establishment of the diocese of Carlisle in 1133. It history too was marked by the Scottish conflicts and a series of fires, which caused much destruction. As the only major town in Cumberland, Carlisle also had two houses of the Dominican and Franciscan friars, while Austin friars settled at Penrith, all arriving in the thirteenth century.

The small Benedictine priory of St Bees replaced a pre-Norman church sometime after 1120. In 1138, Ranulph le Meschines founded the abbey of Calder, which was colonised by Savignac monks from Furness Abbey. Throughout the next 200 years, the abbey's close proximity to the border with Scotland made for a troubled history. The Scots themselves founded the Cistercian Holmcultram Abbey in 1150, when the land was under their control, but this did not protect the community from later Scottish raids. The Augustinian house of Lanercost Priory also had a peaceful beginning, founded in 1166 by Robert de Vaux, but as elsewhere, this did not last and as a result of frequent raids and the need to continuously rebuild, its wealth started to dwindle.

Religious associations of women did not flourish in Cumberland. The rough life and continual warfare in this border county did not encourage nuns to the area, nor were good endowments forthcoming. Although the Benedictine nunnery of Seton at Lekeley was far removed from the Scottish frontier, in a secluded position on the south-western seaboard, it always struggled in an environment of financial poverty. Only a single fragment of the church wall has survived, but nothing can now be seen of Armathwaite Priory, another Benedictine nunnery, probably founded in 1089. It suffered heavy losses during the border conflicts, but some compensation and additional endowments enabled the nuns to keep their heads above water.

Gazetteer

Armathwaite Priory Priory Farm, on minor road between Armathwaite and Staffield, Armathwaite, Cumbria (NY 537429). No visible remains

Calder Abbey Off minor road, 1km (0.5 miles) E of Calder Bridge, Cumbria (NY 050063). Tel: 01946 841147

Carlisle Black Friars Blackfriars Street, Carlisle, Cumbria (NY 400557). No visible remains

Carlisle Cathedral Priory The Abbey, Carlisle, Cumbria (NY 399560). Tel: 01228 548151. Web: www.carlislecathedral.org.uk

Carlisle Grey Friars Off A7 Lowther Street, Carlisle (NY 402558). No visible remains

Holmcultram Abbey Abbeytown, Cumbria (NY 177508). Church in use

Lanercost Priory On minor road off A69, Lanercost, 3km (2 miles) NE of Brampton, Cumbria (NY 556637). English Heritage; Tel: 01697 73030. Web: www.lanercostpriory.org.uk

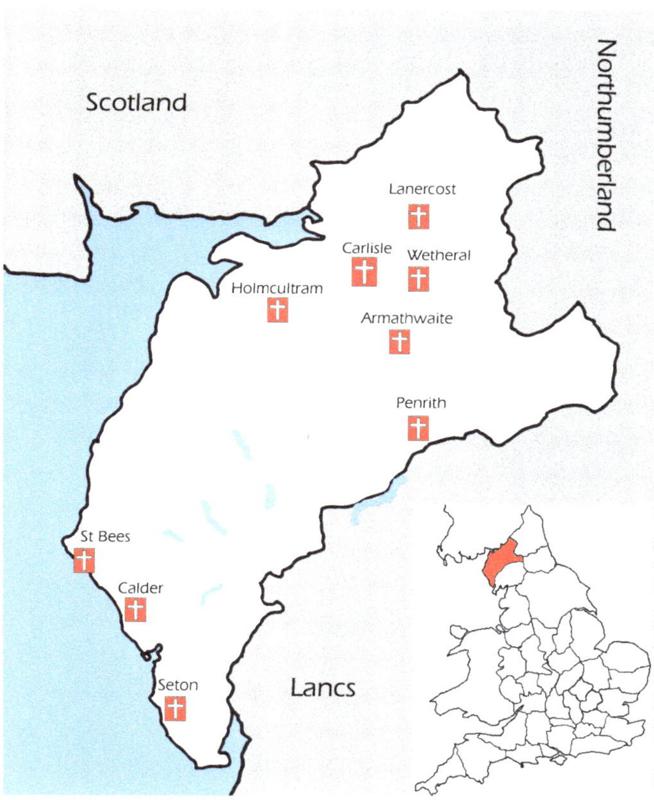

Penrith Austin Friars The Friarage, Friargate, Penrith, Cumbria (NY 518301). No visible remains

St Bees Priory The Priory, on B5345, off the A595, 4km (2.5 miles) W of Egremont, Cumbria (NX 968121). Tel: 01946 822279. Web: www.stbees.org.uk

Seton Priory On minor lane, off A 595, Bootle, Cumbria (SD 107899). Private

Wetheral Priory Off B6263, S of Wetheral village, 10km (6 miles) E of Carlisle, Cumbria (NY 469542). English Heritage; Tel: 01228 625600

Armathwaite Priory

St Mary • Benedictine nuns 1089–1537

There is nothing to be seen today of this Benedictine nunnery, which was located in a lovely glen near where the Rivers Croglin and Eden meet between Armathwaite and Ainstable. Just as all physical evidence has disappeared, so has much of its history, beginning with a spurious charter that attributes the foundation to King William II (Rufus) in the year 1089. Adding further to the mystery was a claim to the liberty of sanctuary, based on a sanctuary stone, about 3m high, inscribed with a cross and the words 'Sanctuarium 1088', which was placed on rising ground above the priory. What is certain is that the priory suffered heavy losses during the Scottish wars, for which the nuns were partly compensated by Edward II who granted pasture in Inglewood Forest, and by Edward III in 1331, when they were excused payment of £10 due to the Crown for victuals bought in the previous reign. The nuns also received several bequests in the fourteenth century, which enabled them to keep their heads above water.

The priory appears to have been dissolved soon after July 1537, when Prioress Anne Derwentwater and three nuns received pensions. Its value in 1535 amounted to just £19 2s. Its buildings and possessions, including the rectory of Ainstable, were leased to Leonard Barowe of Armathwaite in 1538, but the manor was later sold by Edward VI. Only names remind of the priory's existence. There is Nunclose in Inglewood Forest, and the field where the sanctuary pillar was standing is still called Cross Close. A stone from the old buildings inserted in the northwest end of the present house bears the following couplet: 'Though veiled Benedictines are remov'd hence. Think of their poverty, chastity, faith, obedience'.

Calder Abbey

St Mary • Savignac/Cistercian 1134–1536

Often referred to as one of the most enchanting abbeys in the British Isles, the appeal of Calder Abbey is heightened by a slightly unkempt and overgrown appearance, as nature has been allowed to intrude undisturbed on its weathered stones. The downside is that nature's encroachment and lack of maintenance have made Calder Abbey unsafe. It is not, therefore, presently open to the general public, but the visitor can wander carefully among the ruins by prior arrangement with the owner of the nearby eighteenth century mansion, which was built largely from parts of the south claustral ranges and domestic buildings. But, even if access cannot be achieved, the short walk along the attractive footpath from the small hamlet of Calder Bridge, along the river from which the abbey takes its name, will bring the traveller to the edge of the ruins. This is close enough to appreciate its tranquil setting surrounded by wooded hills and admire the attractive arches of the church. Halfway between the village and the abbey stands the Sanctuary stone. It is said that if any criminal or man on the run reached the stone, he or she could claim sanctuary and safety within the abbey precinct.

A fair part of the abbey church still stands to a good height, dominated by the four tall Gothic arches that supported the central crossing tower, now some 19.5m (64ft) high, also including some sections of the chancel and transepts. The east end of the choir has entirely gone. Particularly charming is the series of arches that have survived from the north arcade, which separated the nave and the aisle. In an arched recess in the south side of the choir is the sedilia, where officiating clergy sat during mass. The west doorway into the church has also survived, as has the dormitory undercroft, and there are remnants of the library, chapter house, refectory and lay brothers' range. An effigy of a knight in mail armour can be found in the north transept, which is believed to be that of the abbey's main benefactor, John Le Fleming. It is believed to date from around the beginning of the fourteenth century.

The abbey was founded in 1134 by Ranulph le Meschines, Lord of Copeland, for a colony of monks from the Savignac foundation at Furness and, as was usual, was dedicated in honour of the Blessed Virgin Mary. The twelve monks and their abbot, Gerald, settled on the site and begun to build their monastery, but its location close to the border left it wide open to attack from Scottish raiders. One of these forays, led by King David I in 1138, forced the monks to abandon the new abbey and return to Furness. However, the abbot of Furness refused to take them in because, so the story goes, Gerald refused to resign his office of abbot and agree to the demotion of Calder Abbey to a priory. It was argued that two abbots could not inhabit the same monastery together. Gerald and his monks then journeyed to Yorkshire to found the great abbey of Byland. Calder Abbey was recolonised in 1142 by another group of monks from Furness under Abbot Hardred, who rebuilt the abbey in stone in the years up to 1210. In 1147, along with all other Savignac foundations, Calder Abbey became a Cistercian house.

The new colony of monks was able to sustain the abbey with the help of gifts and endowments, which included several churches in the locality. It is also worth mentioning that in 1338, prior to the Scottish raid, an agreement had been reached between the lords of Egremont and the abbey, giving monks rights to take reasonable amounts of wood for their essential needs from within the Forest of Copeland. Among the principal benefactors were John Le Fleming, whose family continued its support throughout the generally uneventful history, the Countess of Albemarle, William de Esseby and the Huddleston family. Other income came from rich salmon and trout fishing in the Calder and the extensive grazing for flocks of sheep in the vicinity. The abbey, nevertheless, remained relatively poor, with the number of monks never increasing above the original thirteen. Calder Abbey just about survived another Scottish raid in 1322, this time by Robert the Bruce, but by 1381, there were only four monks and three lay-brothers in residence.

In February 1536, Henry VIII sent one of his knights, Sir Thomas Legh, to turf out the monks and take possession of the abbey and its estates. The clear annual value of Calder Abbey at the Suppression was just over £50. The community had shrunk to nine monks, including Abbot Richard Ponsonby. Sir Thomas adapted some parts for occupation, while stone robbers demolished large sections of the other abbey buildings, adding to the dereliction. The property changed hands several times thereafter. Much of what was left was incorporated into a mansion built on the site in the eighteenth century. A passage under the house is said to still lead to one of the monks' original accommodation blocks.

Photos - clockwise from top

Ruined crossing tower and nave arcade
Entrance to chapter house
South-East corner of cloister
Triple sedilia with trefoiled heads

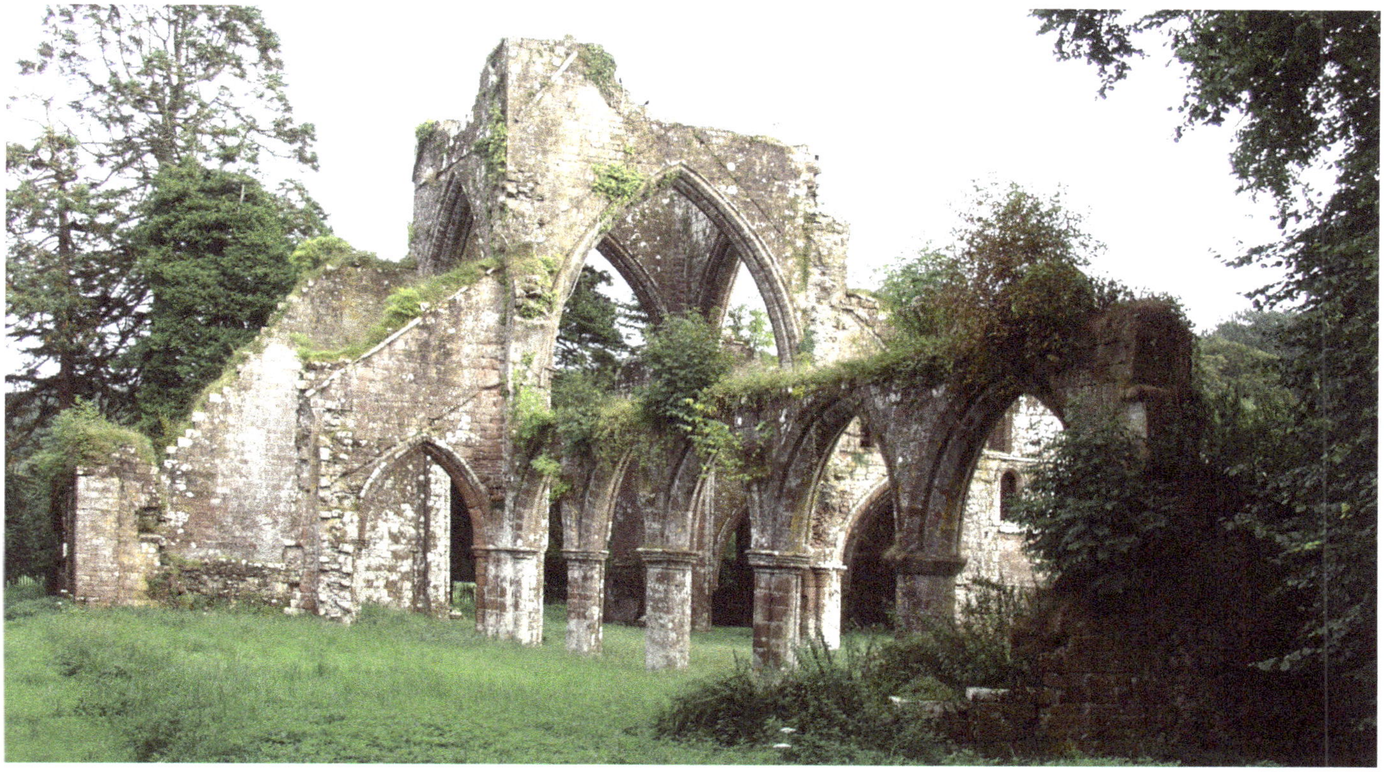

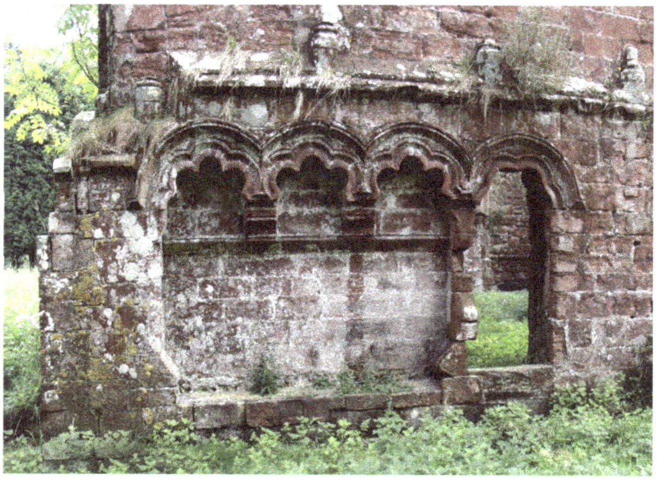

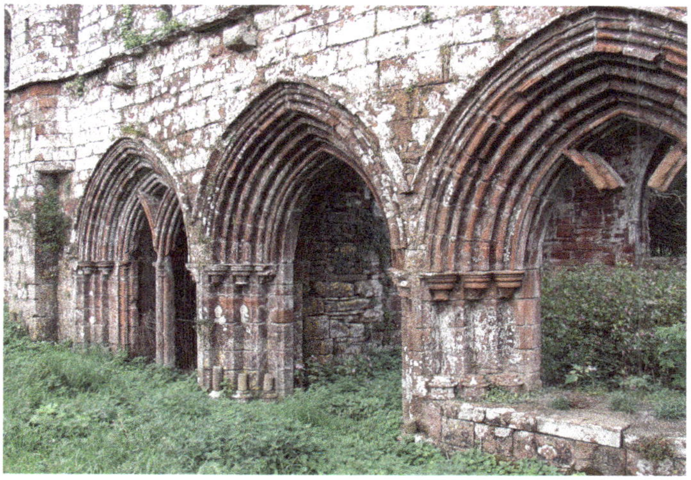

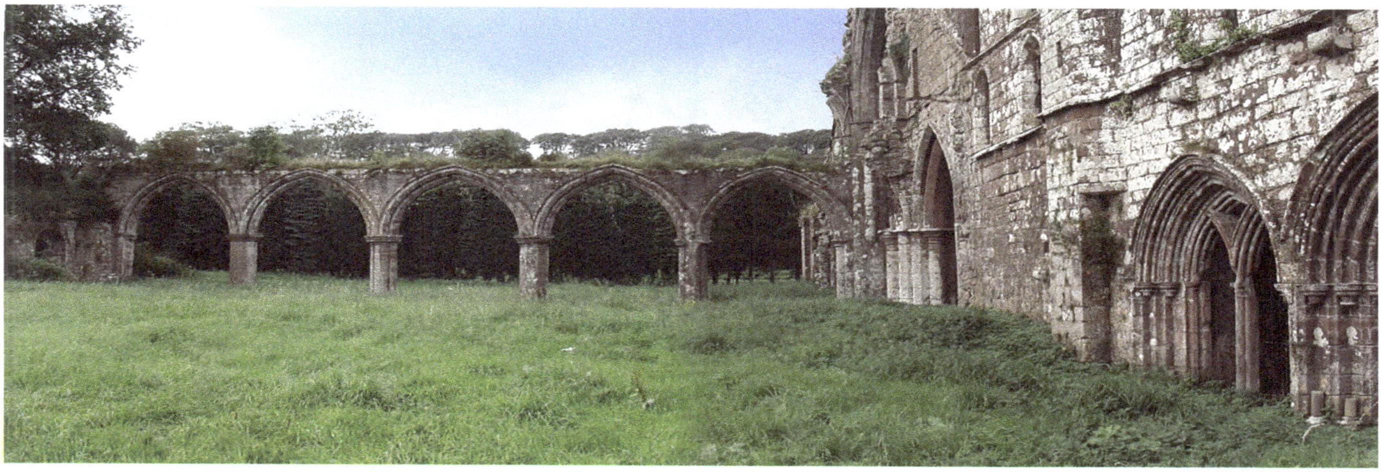

Carlisle Cathedral Priory

St Mary • Augustinian 1122–1540

Carlisle Cathedral started life as the Augustinian Priory of St Mary, founded in 1122 by Henry I, who visited the town that winter. Henry made his English confessor and chaplain, Athelwold, the first prior of his new community, and in 1133 established the Diocese of Carlisle and the priory church as its cathedral. In 1140, the bishop allowed the canons to join the Victorine Order, but this is unlikely to have taken place. The church was most probably built on the foundations of an earlier pre-Norman place of worship and underwent much rebuilding until the fifteenth century, with minor alterations and restorations completed subsequently. The building is constructed in a mix of red calciferous and ashlar sandstone, with its stepped buttresses carried up as lacework pinnacles. The battlemented tower fell in 1380, but was rebuilt in 1401. The twelfth century aisled nave, which had been used as the parish church since its construction, was originally of seven bays, but this was drastically shortened in 1645, leaving just two bays with a fragment of a third remaining as buttresses, giving the Cathedral a rather truncated appearance. The net effect is that the large new choir, which replaced the existing Norman structure in the mid-thirteenth century, appears disproportionate to the remainder of the church. The south transept with the chantry chapel of St Catherine and parts of the north transept are the only survivals from the early days of the monastery.

While the external appearance may not have the architectural elegance of other cathedrals, there is much to admire within. Features of special interest include the chancel in Decorated style and the east window, described as unsurpassed in size and beauty, with its tracery containing some very fine fourteenth century stained glass. In St. Wilfrid's Chapel is the Brougham Triptych, a magnificent sixteenth century carved Flemish altarpiece. There is also a very fine renovated barrel-vaulted painted ceiling in the choir dating from the fourteenth century and, in the north and south aisles, medieval paintings depicting the life of St. Cuthbert, St. Augustine and St. Anthony, and the figures of the twelve Apostles. The carved capitals of the main pillars in the choir represent activities associated with the months of the year and the early fifteenth century choir stalls and misericords are notable examples of medieval carving. The Gothic screen of 1542 on the north side of choir is also worth seeing. The Cathedral's stained glass dates from the fourteenth to the twentieth centuries. Only ruins remain of the canons' dormitory, which formed the east range of the cloisters, fragments of which are attached to the south face of the cathedral and extend northwards for the east end of the refectory. The arches are in Decorated style, with remnants of vaulting ribs on the corbels.

The cathedral priory shared the turbulent history of this border city, which in the past has been invaded by the Romans and Vikings, and fought over by the English and the Scots for many centuries. The priory suffered frequently from Scottish invasions and raids, and was devastated in 1292, when a great fire destroyed much of the city. The new choir and east end were left a mass of ruins, the north transept was badly damaged, and the conventual buildings perished almost entirely. Fire again caused much damage in 1316 and 1363. Although rebuilding after the first fire started almost immediately, a lack of funds slowed progress, and it was probably unfinished when an ailing Edward I came to Carlisle in 1307 to meet his Parliament and organise an expedition into Scotland. At that same time, the cathedral resounded with the voice of the Papal Legate excommunicating Robert the Bruce and pronouncing a terrible curse upon the usurper of the Crown of Scotland. In 1297, Carlisle Cathedral had been the venue when Robert Bruce swore his allegiance to the English Crown in front of his future nemesis Edward I, 'the Hammer of the Scots'. A few months after meeting his Parliament, a stricken Edward I mounted his horse and rode away through the gateway of the priory to lead his army into Scotland. He was destined never to reach it and died within sight of the Scottish coast.

The priory was dissolved in January 1540 and the last prior, Lancelot Salkeld, became the first dean, and two of the canons regular became prebendaries of the new chapter, which was founded by Henry VIII the following year. The King changed the dedication of the church, from the Blessed Virgin to the Holy and Undivided Trinity. Much of the stained glass was destroyed and statuary defaced in the times of Edward VI and Elizabeth I, but greater damage occurred in 1646, when Carlisle was besieged and taken by the Scottish Army. Scottish soldiers returned to the cathedral in 1746, but this time as prisoners. The final indignity was suffered in 1764, when, as part of general repairs, 'a great amount of ancient work was destroyed'.

Photos - clockwise from top

The drastically shortened Cathedral Church of St Mary
Choir with barrel-vaulted ceiling and great east window
Carved column capital in choir representing the month of January
Ruined arches of dormitory
Attractive roof boss in passage with Tudor roses

Photos courtesy of Adrian Fletcher

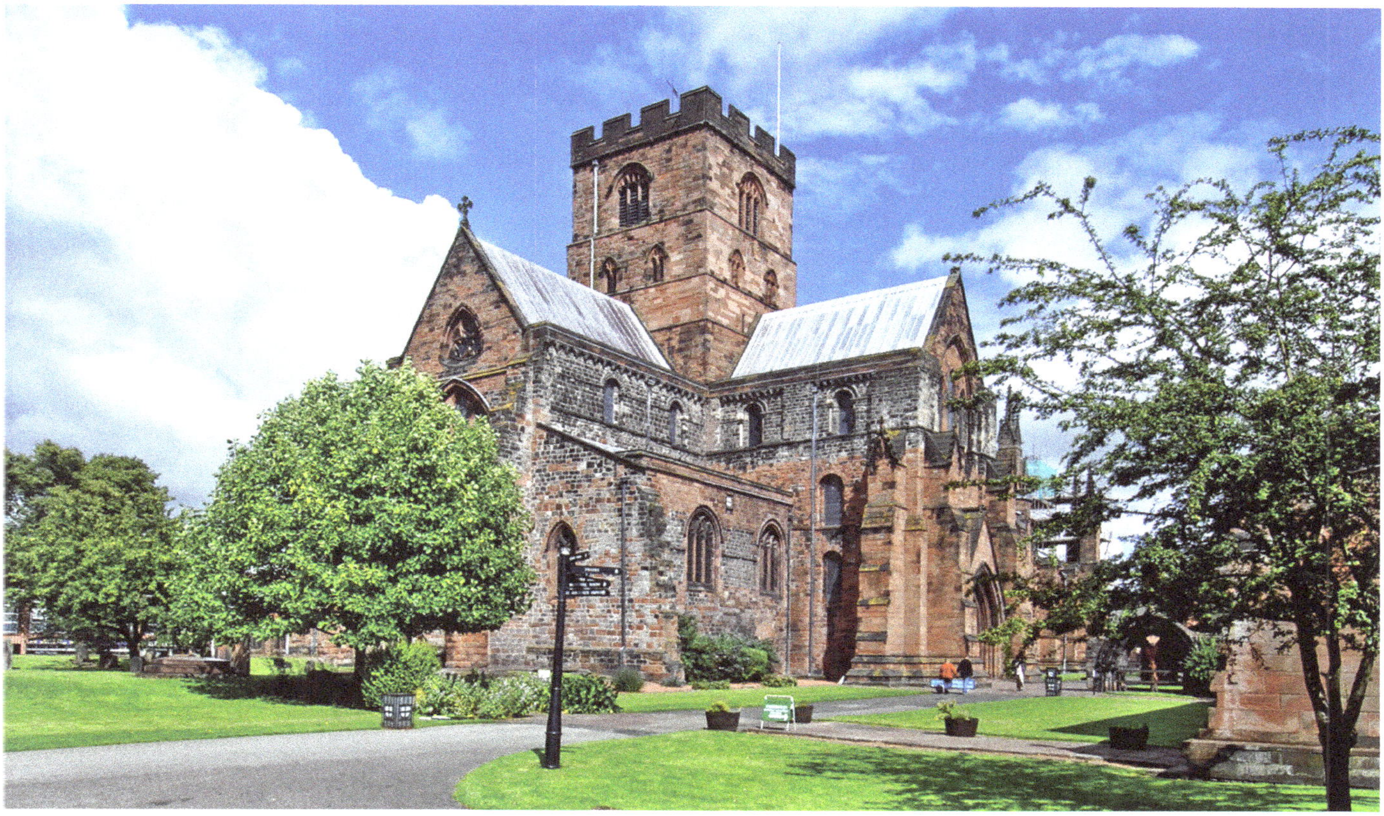

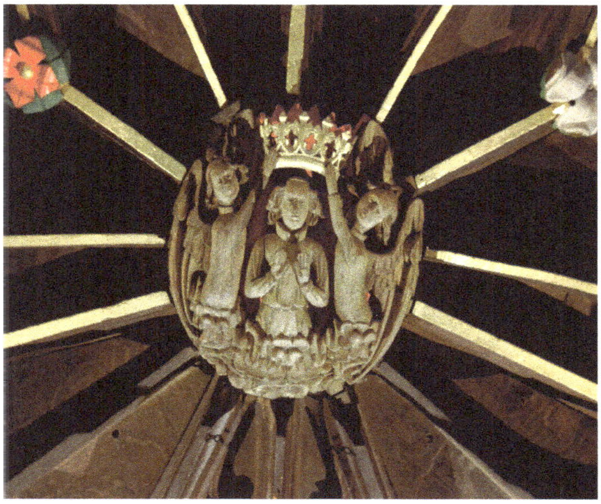

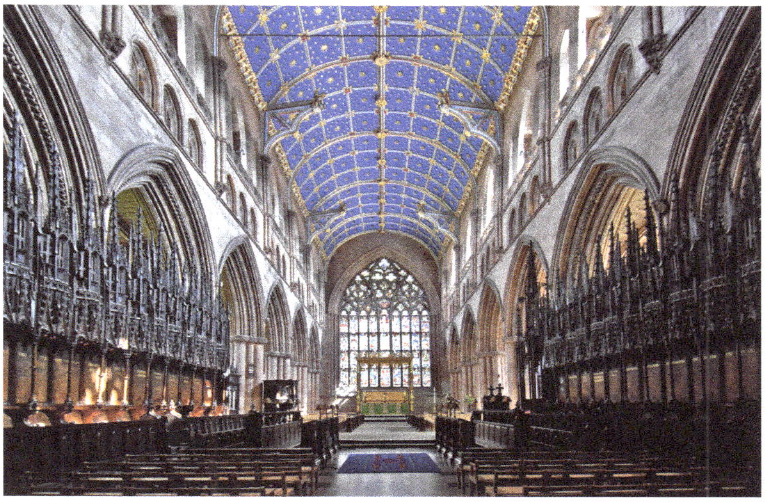

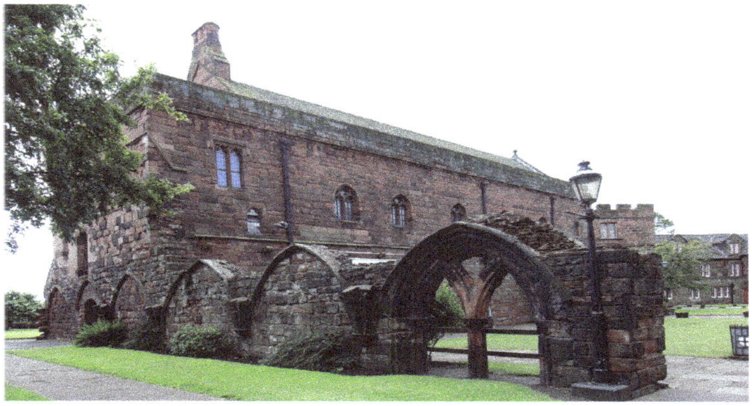

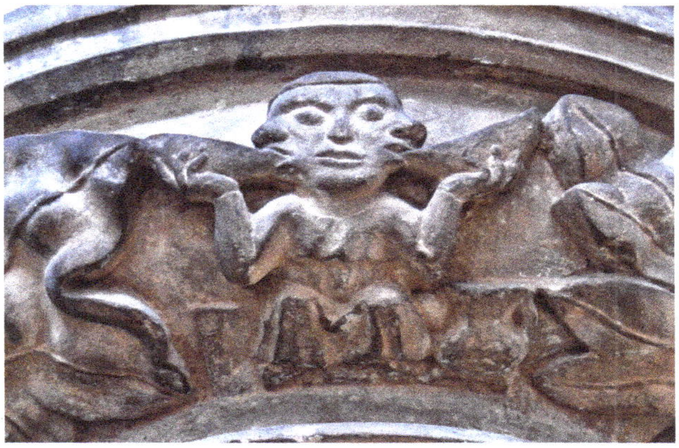

Carlisle Black Friars

1233–1539

The Dominican Friars, or Friars Preacher, came to Carlisle in 1233 and settled without the city walls. The friars obtained permission from the King to erect a house on the public highway, but this was pulled down in 1237 because it was causing an obstruction. Even before, they appear to have gained a foothold within the walls, where they re-established themselves and built their church and dwelling place with gifts of timber from Inglewood Forest in 1239 and 1244. Being situated close to the city walls made them vulnerable to assault, but the worst happened in 1292, when a great fire reduced the whole city to ashes. The friars set about rebuilding their house and in 1300, Edward I stayed on several occasions during his military expeditions against the Scots. The King compensated the friars for their hospitality and disruption caused by the royal train, but the house survived largely from alms and bequests in wills from local people who valued the work of the Friars Preacher. They were generally held in high regard, the priors being called upon to frequently assist in the settlement of disputes between monasteries and secular clergy. The priory was surrendered to Richard Ingworth, Bishop of Dover, in 1539 and leased out in 1541 to Sir Thomas Warton. The site was bounded on the north by Heads Lane, on the south by Bush Brow, (now Victoria Viaduct), on the west by West Walls, and on the east by Blackfriars Street. Excavations have located the cemetery, cloister garth, and part of the church, but the lack of stonework made it impossible to identify the individual parts, or any construction details.

Carlisle Grey Friars

St Francis • 1233–1539

According to the *Chronicle of Lanercost*, the Franciscans, or Friars Minor, settled within the city walls of Carlisle in an area to the east of English Street on the Feast of Assumption in August 1233. The friars received a gift of twenty oaks from the royal forest in 1235 to enable them to erect their church, with another twenty pieces of timber granted later that same year for the friars' dwellings. In 1280, King Edward I gave six oaks, presumably for the enlargement of their abode. Their location close to the walls left them vulnerable to attacks on the city, but disaster struck from an entirely different direction, when an all-consuming fire devastated the whole of Carlisle in 1292. The priory was rebuilt, apparently from the foundations up, and was once again in a habitable state when Edward I stayed there in 1300 on his expedition against the rebellious Scots. The friars received royal gifts as compensation for the expenses incurred by the royal household, but the alms received from the populace were generally insufficient. However, the Friars Minor were well regarded and were able to boost their income through legacies. Along with the others in the region, the priory was surrendered to Henry VIII's commissioner, Richard Ingworth, Bishop of Dover, in 1539. Friars Court behind Devonshire Street marks its approximate location, which was said to have been between the present Bank Street and Devonshire Street. Nothing at all is left.

Holmcultram Abbey

St Mary • Cistercian 1150–1538

The abbey was founded in 1150 by Prince Henry, son of King David I of Scotland, who then ruled Cumberland. Prince Henry gave the land to the Cistercian abbey of Melrose in the Scottish Borders. King Henry II of England extended his protection over the abbey after he re-established his authority over the area in 1157. The abbot of Melrose sent a colony of monks who cleared the forests and drained large tracts of the Solway marshes to make their new home habitable. Construction work on the monastic complex was virtually complete by 1200. The abbey attracted many benefactors on both side of the Solway, who lavished gifts and land, which enabled the community to become the largest supplier of wool in the northwest of England, with an estimated flock of more than 6,000 sheep. Salt and fish production also added considerably to its income. The resultant wealth and its isolated location not far from the border attracted Scottish raiding parties which, from 1216 onwards, plundered the abbey on many occasions. Edward I stayed in the abbey during his campaign against Scotland in 1299, and was also there the day he died in July 1307. His entrails are said to have been deposited at the abbey, while his body was carried to Westminster for entombment. The abbot was summoned to Parliament and to the great councils of state between 1294 and 1312, attesting to the importance of the house.

The threat from the Scots was ever-present, and the worst devastation was caused by Robert the Bruce in 1319, in spite of the fact that his father, the Earl of Carrick, was buried in the abbey church. For a time, the monks had to find shelter in neighbouring religious houses. By 1428, the house was reported to have been in a state of disrepair and, although the pope offered an indulgence for anyone willing to contribute to its rebuilding, progress was exceedingly slow. In spite of its turbulent history, it was valued at a significant £477 in the *Valor* of 1535, and there were still twenty-four monks resident at the time of the Dissolution in March 1538. The abbey church was saved for the parish and to serve as a refuge against the Scots, but when Bishop Nicholson visited Holmcultram in 1703 he was shocked that it had been left to fall into disrepair. The tower had fallen in 1600. Bishop Nicholson immediately set about organising the reduction of the nave, removal of the side aisles and general restoration. Further remodelling was undertaken subsequently, but arson by local youths in 2006 claimed much of the fabric of the church and it took a considerable sum of money to once again effect its restoration. The original records of the abbey, including the cartulary, were, alas, completely destroyed.

The parish church of today comprises six of the nine bays of the nave of the original abbey church, but in spite of its greatly reduced size, there is much to study and admire in the solid red sandstone building, beginning with the wonderful Norman west doorway, and a fine arcade of pillars. Fragments of tombstones, inscriptions, medieval tiles and stone carvings are displayed in the porch. Of the claustral buildings, nothing at all has survived.

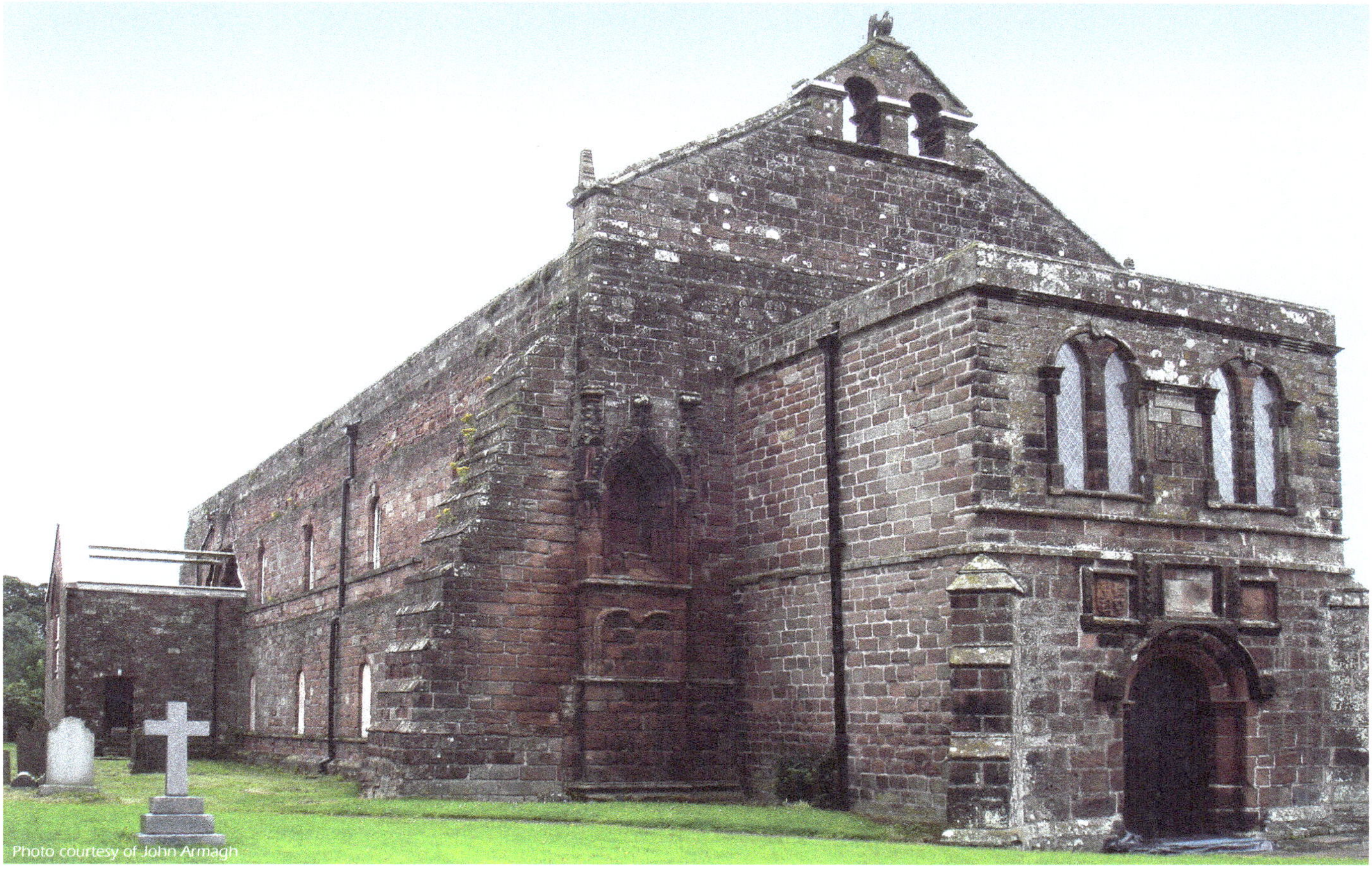

Photo courtesy of John Armagh

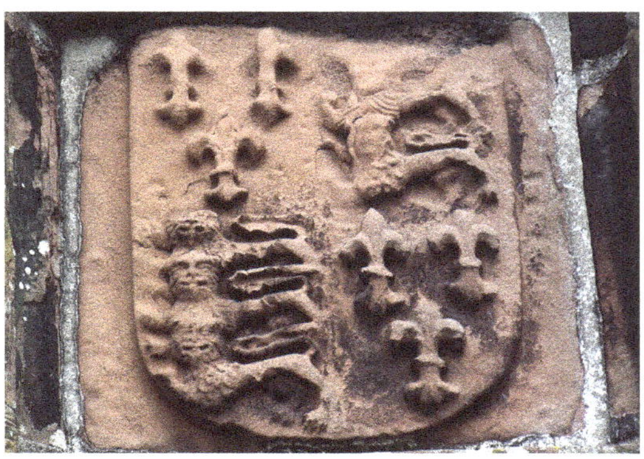

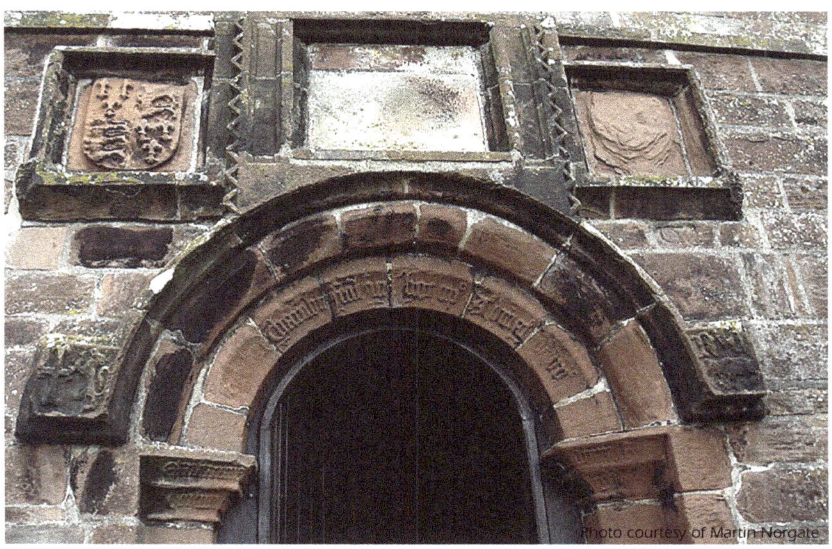

Photo courtesy of Martin Norgate

Photos of Holmcultram - clockwise from top

Former abbey church of St Mary
Norman west doorway and arms of
Abbot Robert Chambers

Lanercost Priory

St Mary Magdalene • Augustinian 1166–1536

Part parish church and part ruin, Lanercost Priory reposes in a quiet rural area of Cumbria amid isolated farms and cottages, and within a stone's throw of Hadrian's Wall. The rural ambience and tranquillity is heightened by the presence of grazing cattle that are allowed to roam freely in surrounding fields. Today, not a single marauding Scot can be seen approaching menacingly on the horizon, although many now come in peace. It was not always so, for the priory's history in the fourteenth century was marked by a great deal of turbulence and much wanton destruction. It started peacefully enough in 1166 when it was founded by Robert de Vaux and consecrated three years later. Augustinian canons are believed to have come from Pentney in Norfolk. With a generous endowment, building began on a grand scale, with much of the stone used from Hadrian's Wall, and was completed about 1220. The canons went about their daily lives in prayer and work, undisturbed by secular events for most of the next century. Its close proximity to the Scottish border later proved a perpetual temptation to the Scots, while also being useful to the English army defending the homeland.

Soon after a visit by King Edward I and Queen Eleanor in 1280, it suffered its first raid by the Scots, but worse was to come. In 1296, marauding Scots burned out the cloister, and the following year, with repairs barely completed, William Wallace destroyed more of the monastic buildings. Edward I then used it as a military base and visited again in 1300, and once more in 1306, when he fell ill and, with a retinue of 200 people, had to spend the winter at Lanercost, before retiring to his favourite castle at Brough to die. Robert the Bruce vented his anger on Lanercost for the hospitality given to the English King by throwing its occupants into prison and plundering its treasures. Always the canons continued to build and rebuild, only to suffer yet another devastating raid in 1346, when King David II of Scotland ransacked and desecrated the priory church, and wasted its lands. As a result of these frequent raids, the priory's wealth continued to dwindle, yet still had what was left of value seized by the Crown on its dissolution in 1536. The land was granted to Sir Thomas Dacre of nearby Naworth Castle, who turned the west range of the priory into a private residence.

The nave of the priory church was re-roofed in 1740 to become the parish church, which is still in use today and dominates the site. From the original crossing tower to the east, however, the church remains roofless, but the structure has survived with every detail remarkably complete in spite of the ravages of time and weather. The church features progressive architectural styles, reminiscent of a continuous building programme, ranging from the sturdy Norman piers and round-headed arches, to the more elegant pointed lancet windows in the Gothic style. Of note on the west front of the parish church is a figure of St Mary Magdalene, the patron saint of the priory, which was carved in about 1270, but it is the empty shell enclosing the transepts, crossing, choir and sanctuary that gives Lanercost's history an atmospheric shape. The ruined tombs of Roland de Vaux, nephew of the priory's founder, and of Sir Thomas Dacre, who died at the battle of Flodden, span the centuries of the priory's existence.

The Prior's Tower is a four storey medieval stone fortified tower, with an adjoining two storey range to the west. It was extensively remodelled in the sixteenth century by the Dacres as a dwelling, when a large fireplace was built on the first floor of the west range (now known as Dacre Hall) and new windows inserted in the tower. The Vicarage Tower is known as King Edward's Tower after Edward I lodged there on his three visits to Lanercost. It is a thirteenth century two-storey stone Pele Tower, with a line of dog-tooth ornament below the parapet. Nothing but foundations have survived from the claustral buildings in the east range, with minimal fragments of the cloister, chapter house and dormitory, but this is more than made up for by a splendid vaulted undercroft in the south range, believed to have been the cellarium under the refectory. Inside can be found examples of masons' marks scratched into the stone, several medieval carvings and some Roman altars found along Hadrian's Wall. Once through the ruined archway of the former gatehouse, Lanercost Priory beckons to be explored.

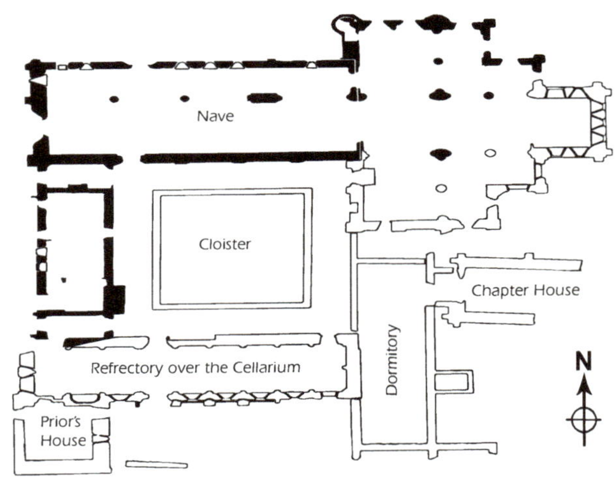

Photos – clockwise from top

The Priory Church, part complete and part ruined
Springing of stone arch with dogtooth decoration
Prior's Tower and Dacre Hall fronting the cloister
Ornate altar tomb in the transept
Vaulted cellarium under the refectory

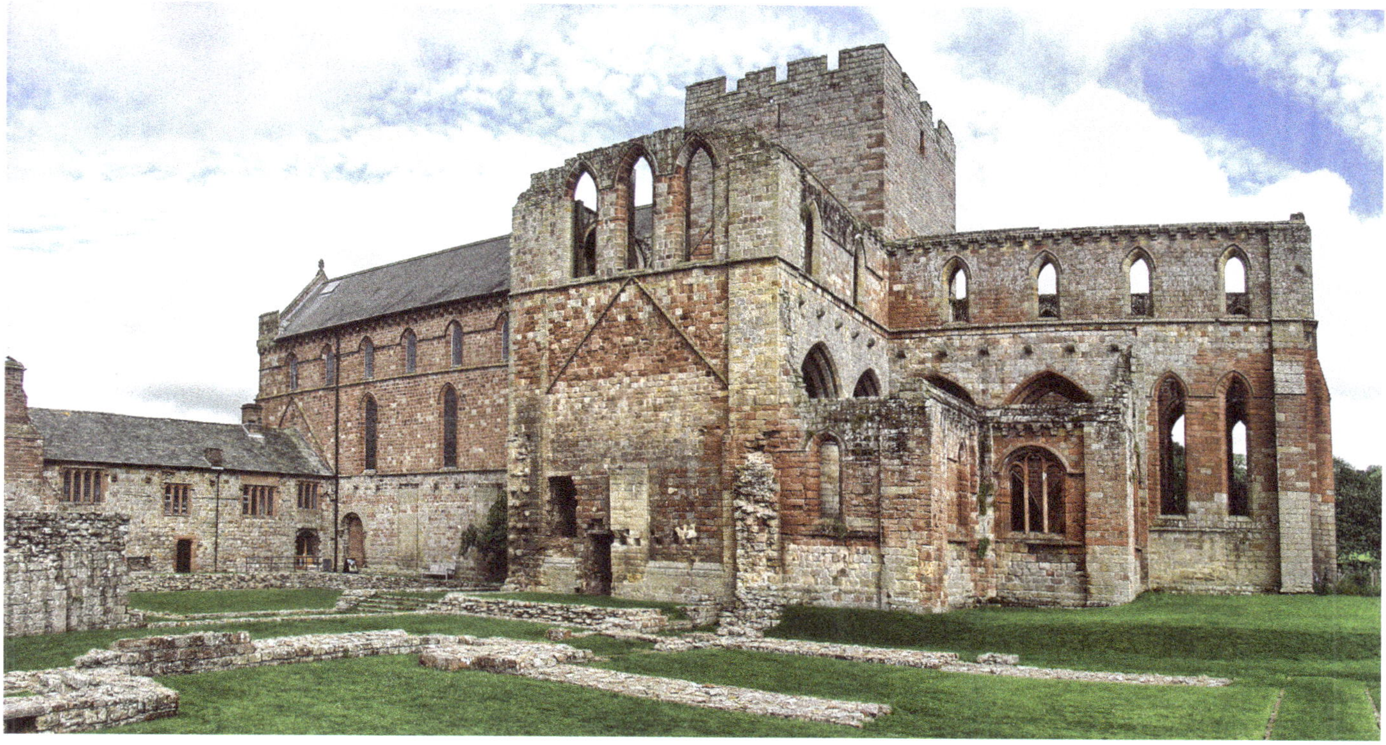

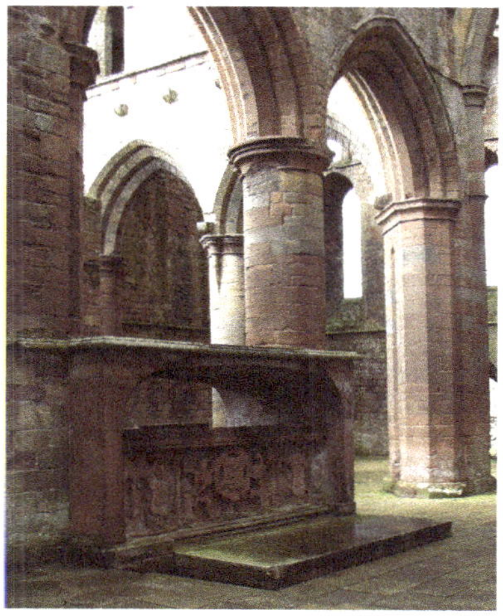

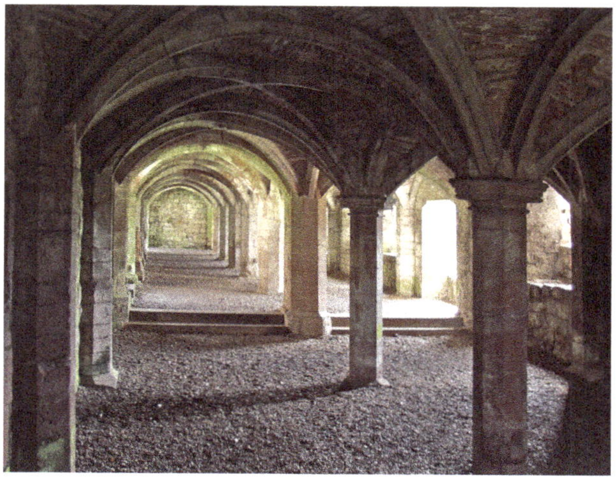

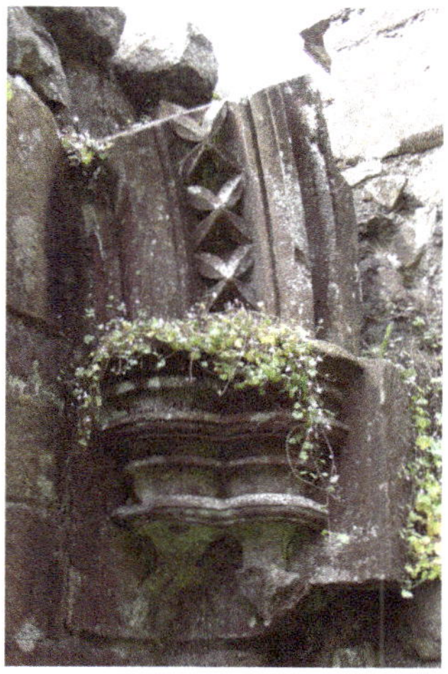

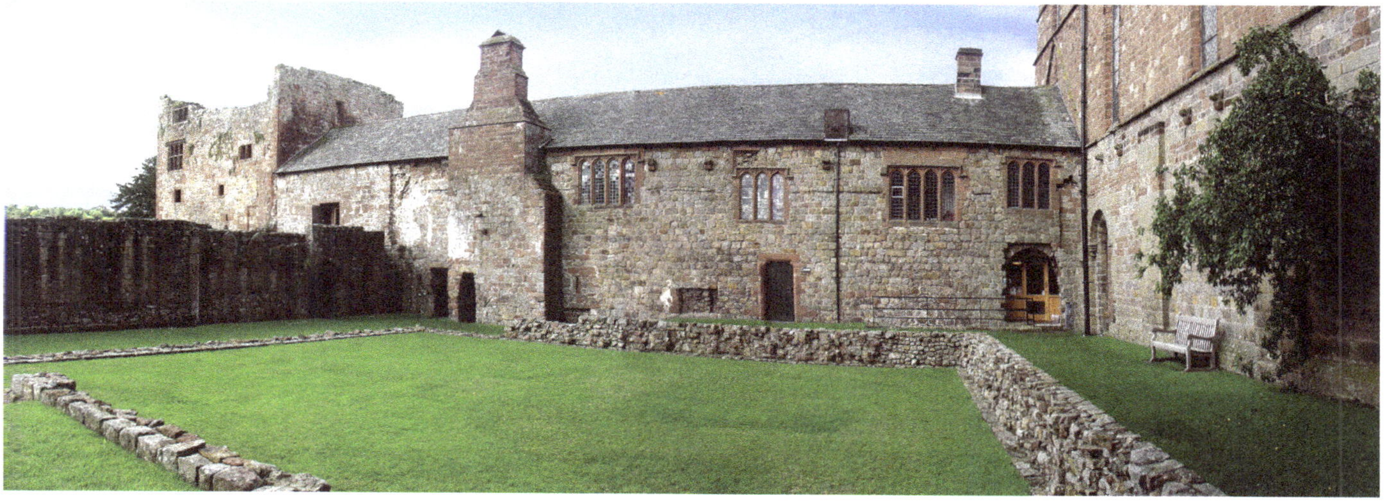

Penrith Austin Friars

St Mary & St Augustine • +1291–1539

The Friars Eremites of St Augustine established themselves in Penrith between 1291 and 1300 and John de Penrith granted them a piece of land to expand their property. Further grants for the same purpose were made in 1331 and 1333 by John de Crumbewell. However, with voluntary alms proving insufficient, the friars resorted to creative measures to boost their income, including persuading successive bishops to appoint first the prior and then the sacrist to the church of Newton Reigny, which had been vacant for some time. Richard Ingworth, Bishop of Dover, suppressed the priory in 1539. Nothing at all is left from the priory buildings, but the Augustinian friars are remembered in a house called the The Friarage, which was built on the site in 1717, and a street known as Friars Gate. Excavations have found part of the friars' cemetery.

St Bees Priory

St Mary & St Bega • Benedictine +1120–1539

The pretty church at St Bees is all that remains of a small Benedictine monastery, whose origin is shrouded in mystery, with many a fancy tale woven around the shadowy figure of St Bega. Supposedly the daughter of an Irish King, St Bega is said to have fled Ireland at the end of the ninth century to escape a marriage that had been arranged between her and a Viking Prince or Chieftain, and arrived in Cumbria the day before Midsummer Eve. She struck a deal with the local lord that she should be able to claim all the land that would be under snow the next day. Miraculously, three miles of the surrounding landscape were indeed covered in snow, so the legend goes. Physical evidence confirms that there was a church on the site before the Normans came, but this was replaced sometime after 1120 by a small Benedictine house, founded by William le Meschines, Lord of Egrement, for six monks and a prior. It was a subsidiary cell of the great abbey of St Mary and consecrated by York's Archbishop Thurstan. In recognition of the worship of St Bega by the local community, the new priory church incorporated a chapel dedicated to her. Another variation of the 'snow miracle' is said to have taken place when a dispute arose over the extent of the priory lands. On the day of examination of the boundaries, there was thick snowfall on all the surrounding land but not a flake upon the lands of the priory.

It is a long, narrow and twisting road that leads to St Bees from anywhere and was well chosen for its isolation. Set at the edge of the village overlooking flat marshy fields leading to the seashore, it is protected from the worst of storms by large mature trees all around the site, and lies almost hidden from view. The still atmospheric if badly weathered arches of the West Door and the base of the tower date from the time of the original Norman building, while the arches in the nave are in the Early English style, which came in slightly later. The impressive monastic chancel, also in the Early English style, was built at the east end before 1190, with an aisle added to the south in the same period. Also of interest within the church are many grave slabs from the Middle Ages, carved with ornate crosses, knights, men at arms, and an unusual archer. A twelfth century stoup and piscina are also worth taking a closer look at.

The impressive Norman west door makes a fine entrance to the treasures within. It comprises five decreasing semicircular arches, which spring from decorated capitals and are ornamented with typical carved beak head designs of men and serpents, although many of the details have been worn away by time and weather. The dripstone above the outer arch is embellished with a trefoil design, representing the Holy Trinity. Not to be missed is the pre-Conquest Beowulf Stone, forming a lintel between the church and the vicarage, which depicts St Michael killing the dragon. Nothing remains of the extensive range of other monastic buildings.

The priory's lands and ecclesiastical jurisdiction over many churches and chapels extended throughout the Western Lakes, stretching to Eskdale, Ennerdale, Loweswater and Wasdale, and even included property on the Isle of Man and in Ireland. These endowments, and the relic of a bracelet said to have belonged to St Bega, contributed to St Bees becoming the third-richest monastic house in the county. The monks were active in coal mining and sheep rearing. The priory was enlarged in about 1190 with the construction of a monastic chapel at the east end, with another chapel added between 1270 and 1300. Its isolation kept it away from mainstream politics and its peaceful history was interrupted only in 1315, when St Bees was raided and damaged by Scot James Douglas who came south after the Battle of Bannockburn. There is a record of an earlier raid, but no date is known. The end came with suppression in October 1539. Only the nave was retained as a parish church, with the chancel and chapter house both demolished. Some of the cloister range was retained as a residence for the parish priest, but this was demolished in 1816 to make way for the theological college.

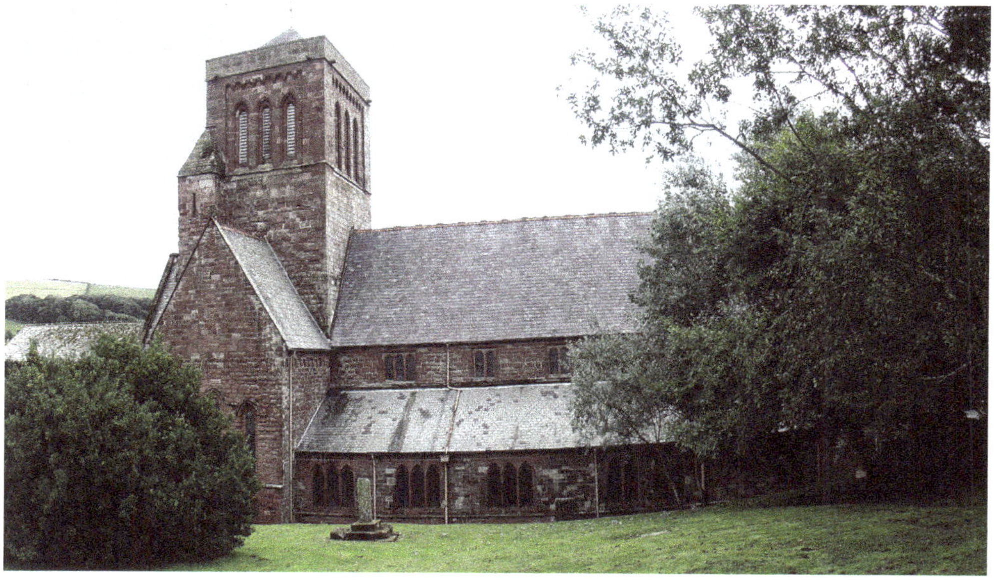

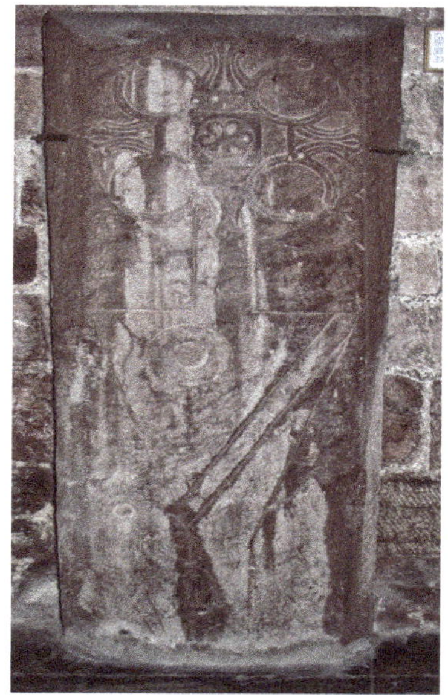

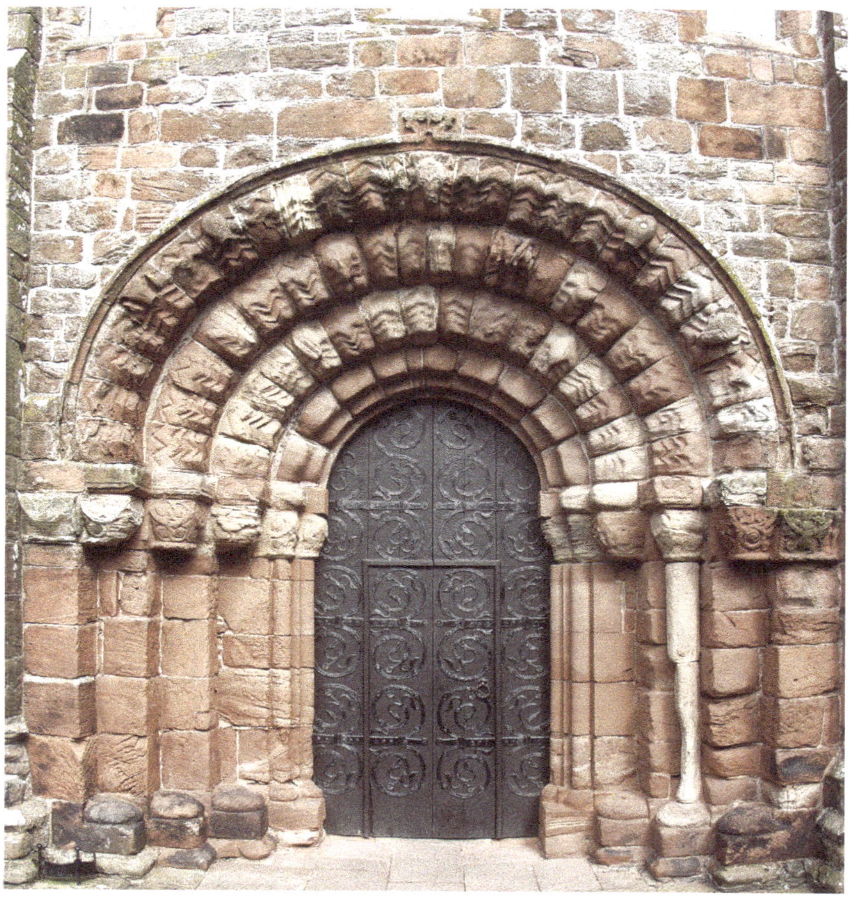

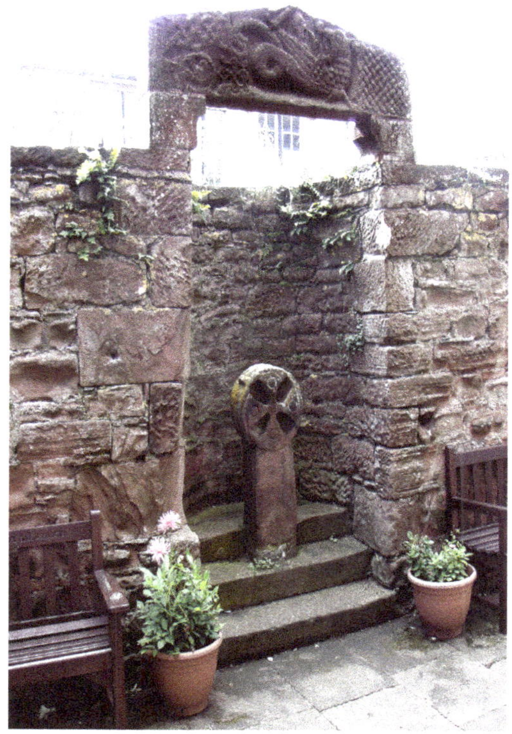

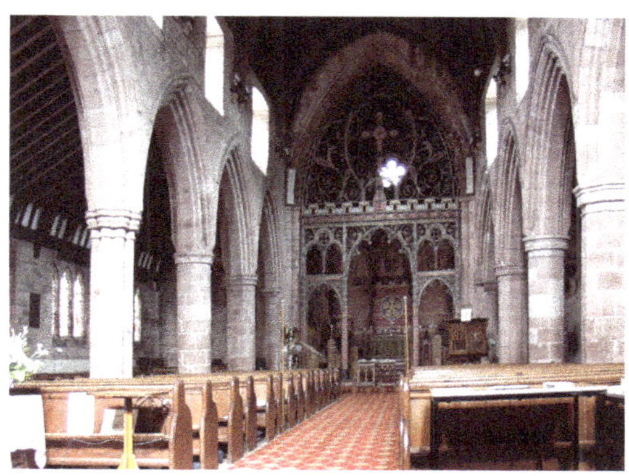

Photos of St Bees Priory – clockwise from top left

The pretty and still isolated priory church
One of many beautifully incised tomb slabs
Pre-conquest Beowulf stone depicting St Michael slaying the dragon
The monastic chancel built in the late twelfth century
Arches of the West Door dating from the original Norman church

Seton Priory

St Mary • Benedicitine nuns 1184–1537

A single fragment is all that has survived to remind of the one-time existence of this Benedictine nunnery founded at Lekeley towards the close of the twelfth century, probably in 1184, by Henry, son of Arthur, Lord of Millom. Located in a secluded picturesque position beneath rising ground of Corney on the south-western seaboard, the tough life in the border country and dearth of valuable endowments ensured that the community always struggled in an environment of financial poverty. From time to time, the situation became so dire that first Archbishop Gray in 1227, and then Henry, Duke of Lancaster in 1357, made several grants to sustain the house. Archbishop Gray gave the nuns the church of St Michael at Irton, while the duke appropriated to the convent the hospital of St Leonard at Lancaster, with all its lands and possessions. Abbot Thomas York of Holmcultram helped in 1459 through leasing all the lands of the abbey between Esk and Lekely to the prioress for twelve years. In the midst of their struggles, the nuns appear to have maintained their spiritual equilibrium, as nothing of blame attached to the community has been recorded. Only one discordant note recalls the forced entry into the nunnery of an eight-year old girl who, after several years at the priory, managed to escape and get married.

In the *Valor* of 1535, the net worth of the priory was returned at only £12 12s, and it was duly dissolved in the first wave of closures in the following year. Only the prioress, Joan Copeland or Seton, and one nun were then left. In 1537, the priory and its lands were leased to Hugh Askew of the King's household. The buildings were demolished and only the east wall of the chancel with its three tall lancet windows and fragments of associated walls have survived the destruction. What appears to have been a monumental slab of a prioress is built into the wall of a barn at High Hyton not far from the nunnery. Although one end of the slab has been broken off and lost, part of an inscription cut on either side of a pastoral crook can still be read. It says: *+HIC IACET ... DENTONA AN.*

Wetheral Priory

Holy Trinity, St Mary & St Constantine • Benedictine 1088–1539

At the end of a tiny single-track country lane stands a solitary red sandstone gatehouse, all that now remains of a once thriving Benedictine priory. Had it not been for the fact that the gatehouse was used as a vicarage after the Dissolution, even that little gem would not have survived the destruction wrought by the Dean and Chapter of Carlisle. The dean ruthlessly demolished the rest of the priory walls to build a prebendal house in Carlisle, ignoring a plea by a Mr Howard, who offered sufficient compensation to leave the ruins standing. The gatehouse is notable for a fine elliptical archway, through which visitors would have entered the priory. Stairs lead up to a large room above, with a spiral stair giving access to a chamber on the second level. The two floors could have served as guest rooms for visitors and travellers seeking shelter. Although nothing else is left of the priory, the gatehouse would have given access to grand monastic buildings, including a chapel, school, domestic quarters and monastic offices.

The priory was founded in 1088 by Ranulph le Meschines, who had granted the manor of Wetheral to the Benedictine abbey of St Mary in York two years earlier. Populated by eight monks, Wetheral Priory was dedicated to the Holy Trinity, St Mary and St Constantine, and was richly endowed by numerous benefactors, one of whom, Richard I, granted it many privileges, exemptions and immunities. One of the more interesting privileges was the right of sanctuary to criminals for offences committed outside its bounds, conferred by Henry I and also by later Kings. The bounds, which did not reflect the extent of the manor, were marked by six crosses, within which no such refuge was allowed. During the border wars, the monks and other inhabitants were frequently forced to flee from the plundering Scottish hordes and took refuge in St Constantine's cells a short distance from the priory. Said to have been dug into the face of perpendicular rock some 12m (40ft) above the River Eden by Constantine, the son of a Scottish monarch, the cells were hidden behind trees and were approached by a wooden ladder or plank, drawn up afterwards to prevent anyone following. Each cell was divided into three apartments, each with its own window and a communal chimney in the centre. Apart from the monks' own safety, this hidden place was also used to safeguard the plate, vestments and relics of the priory. Wetheral was surrendered in 1539 by the last prior, Ralph Hartley, to Henry VIII, who, in 1542 granted it to the Dean and Chapter of Carlisle. Its annual worth was £128. Oliver Cromwell sold the priory to Richard Banks after the Civil War, but it came back to the Dean and Chapter upon restoration of the monarchy.

Photos – clockwise from top left

Red sandstone gatehouse of Wetheral Priory
Interior views of gatehouse
St Constantine's cave
Fragment of church of Seton Priory

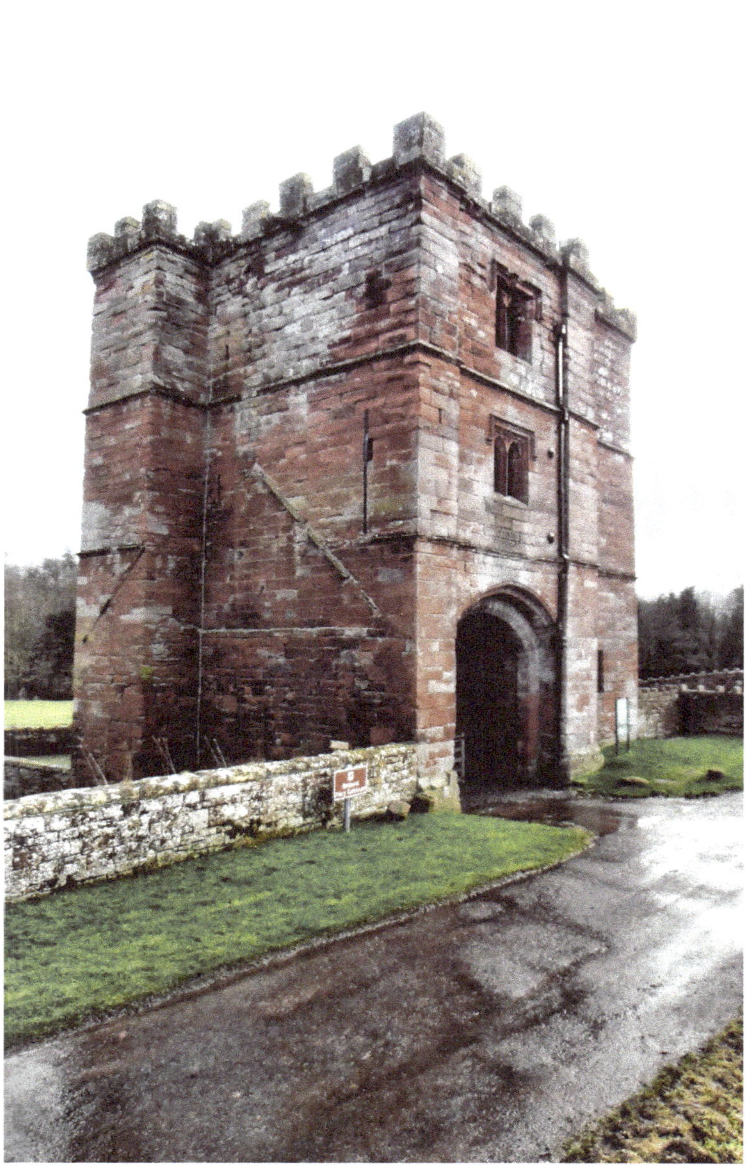

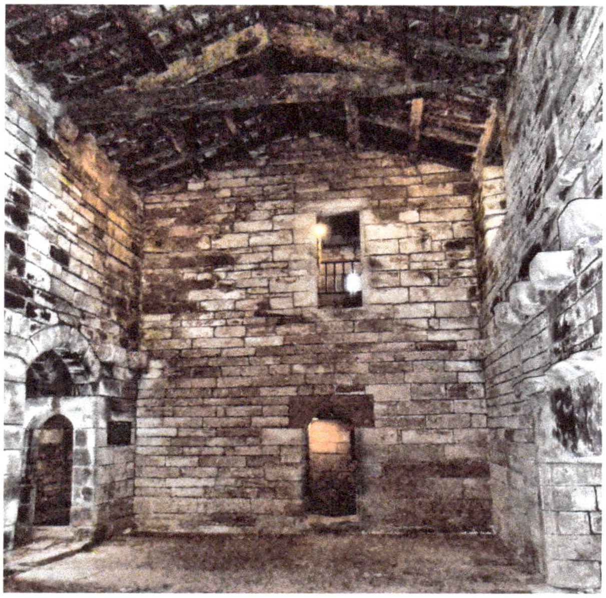

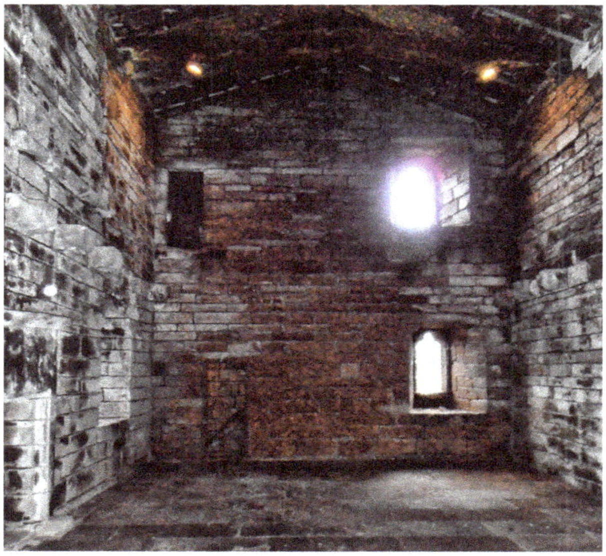

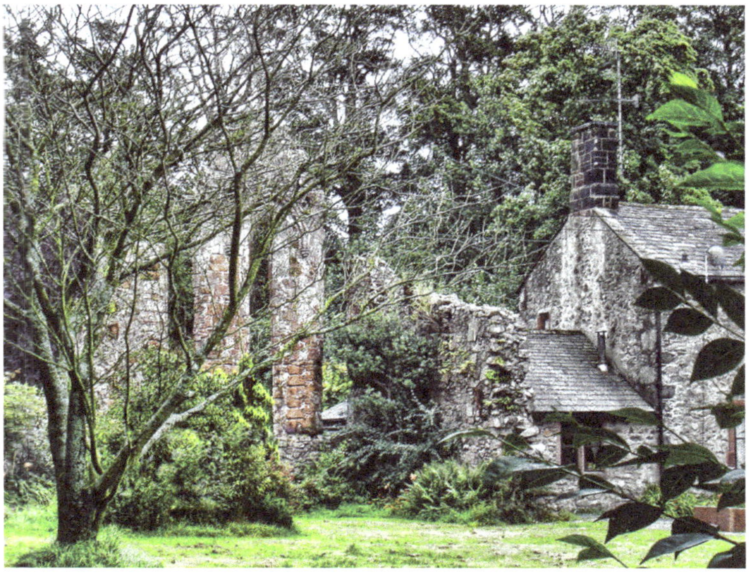

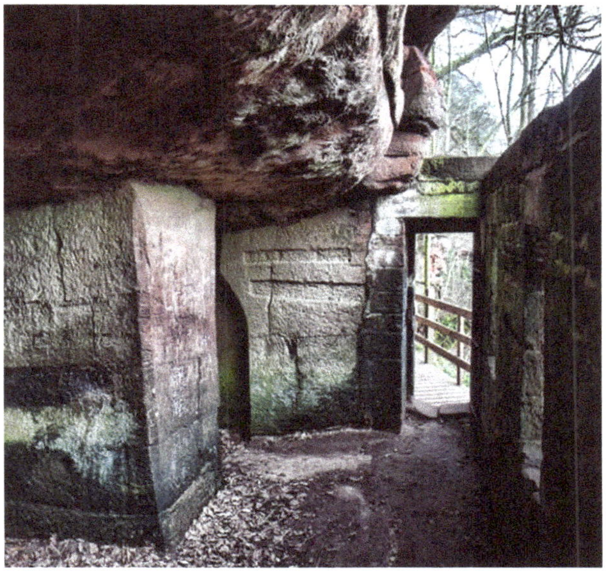

Derbyshire

Outside Influence

The name of the county was first recorded in 1049 in the Old English form of Deorbyscir, having previously been an administrative division of the Kingdom of Mercia and later part of Danelaw. It was the Danes who established the town of Derby. After the Norman Conquest, the county was divided into six hundreds. Large areas of land were granted to William Peverel and Henry de Ferrers, both of whom are thought to have fought at the Battle of Hastings. The de Ferrers became Earls of Derby and supported some monastic foundations.

However, Derbyshire was not rich in monasteries, with many of its churches and manors, and much of its lands, owned by monasteries outside the county, which wielded considerable influence. The Peak District was particularly devoid of monasteries, but boasted some forty monastic granges involved in sheep farming and some lead mining. Surprisingly, the Benedictines made little impression in the post-Conquest era, with only a small foundation for nuns at King's Mead in Derby, and the Cistercians had not a single house in the county.

The less strict Augustinian Order dominated religious life from the twelfth century, which was begun with the founding of a large-scale abbey at Darley in c1146, having moved there from the smaller house of St. Helen's, which was just outside the walls of the county town. Augustinian canons also established themselves at Repton in 1172, having moved from the much smaller foundation at Calke. Repton had once been a great missionary centre of Mercia, with an important abbey of nuns. Two smaller houses existed at Gresley and Breadsall, but both faced a continual struggle against poverty. Augustinian canons from Dunstable also served the church at Bradbourne. A small Cluniac cell of Bermondsey was founded in Derby in 1140, and the town was also served by the Dominicans, the only house of mendicant friars in the county. There were also two houses of Premonstratensian, or White Canons, at Beauchief, near Sheffield, and at Depedale (Dale).

Gazetteer

Beauchief Abbey Abbey Lane, Beauchief, 6.5km (4 miles) from city centre, Sheffield, South Yorkshire (SK 333819). Tel: 0114 235 3263. Web: www.beauchiefabbey.org.uk

Bradbourne Priory Mill Lane, off B5056, Bradbourne, 6.5km (4 miles) NE of Ashbourne, Derbyshire (SK 208527). Church in use

Breadsall Priory Moor Road, Off A61, Morley, 5km (3 miles) NE of Derby, Derbyshire (SK 381414). Private: Tel: 01332 832235

Calke Priory Calke Abbey, Ticknall, 14.5km (9 miles) S of Derby, Derbyshire (SK 368226). National Trust; Tel: 01332 863822. No visible remains

Darley Abbey Darley Street, Darley Abbey, Derby, Derbyshire (SK 353384). The Abbey; Tel: 01332 558297

Depedale (Dale) Abbey Off Dale Lane, Dale Abbey village, 6.5km (4 miles) NE of Derby, Derbyshire (SK 437387 and SK 439385). Remains visible, but limited access

Derby Abbey Garden Street, off A601 St Alkmund's Way, Derby, Derbyshire (SK 350367). No visible remains

Derby Black Friars Friar Gate, off A601 Stafford Street, Derby, Derbyshire (SK 348363). No visible remains

Derby Priory St James Street, Derby, Derbyshire (SK 352362). No visible remains

Derby (Kings Mead) Priory Nunnery Court, Nun's Street, Derby, Derbyshire (SK 344367). No visible remains

Gresley Priory Church Street, of A444, Church Gresley, Swadlincote, Derbyshire (SK 293181). Church in use; Tel: 01283 222966

Repton Priory The Lodge, Repton, 11km (7 miles) SW of Derby, Derbyshire (SK 304272). Remains incorporated in private school

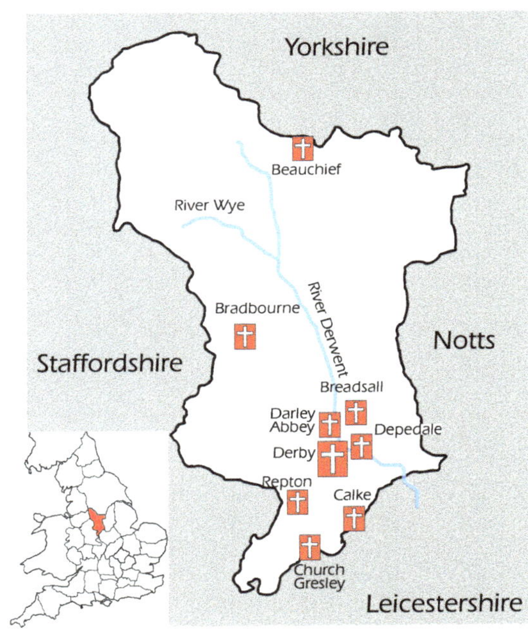

Beauchief Abbey

St Mary & St Thomas ▪ Premonstratensian c1175–1537

Not far from the sprawling conurbation of the famous steel town, Beauchief Abbey is said to be Sheffield's hidden secret. It is named after the fair headland that overlooks the dale and the area has retained its natural beauty, the ruins being still surrounded by fine ancient woodlands, and the much more modern trappings of golf courses. Only the twelfth century western bell tower of the abbey remains, now attached to the small chapel of St Thomas dating from 1662, which was built around the original nave. The tower is freely accessible via an Early English arched doorway under a fourteenth century window, but the active chapel, which is kept locked when no services are in progress, can be visited by appointment, The foundation of many of the other monastic buildings can be explored and provide a good picture of the extent of what was once a fairly wealthy abbey. Easily recognisable is the apsidal chapter house. The waters of the three medieval fishponds are a magnet for wildlife, and the stream that fed the ponds and supplied the abbey with water also still runs. Nearby Beauchief Hall was built in 1671 using stone from the abbey.

The abbey, now situated in South Yorkshire, was founded c1175 by Robert fitzRanulph, Lord of Alfreton and Noreton, and High Sheriff of Nottingham and Derbyshire. The Premonstratensian house was dedicated to the Blessed Virgin and the slain St Thomas Becket. No evidence has been advanced that proves the legend that Robert was implicated in the murder of Thomas and that the establishment of the abbey was his atonement for the wrong done to the Archbishop of Canterbury. However, Robert gifted all his lands and other possessions including several churches to the abbey, renounced the world and joined the Order.

The community of up to fifteen canons plus lay-brothers enjoyed a peaceful existence, generating good income from farming, iron smelting, mineral extraction, woodland industries and mills on the River Sheaf. Regular visitations found little wrong with the management and spiritual well-being of the abbey. Only disputes over property and minor misdemeanours of some canons have been recorded. The death of the last abbot, John Greenwood, alias Sheffield, in April 1536 delayed its dissolution until February the following year. It was valued at £126 3s and sold to Sir Nicholas Strelley for almost twice that sum.

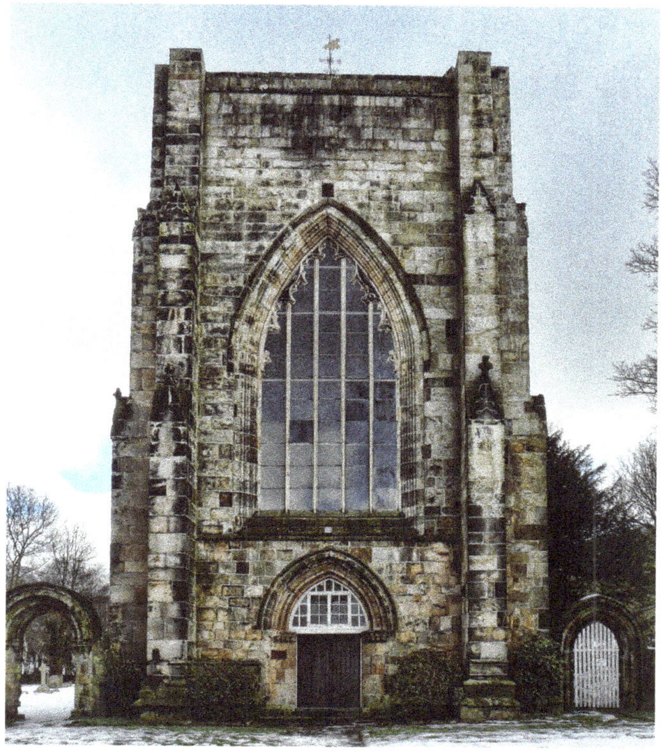

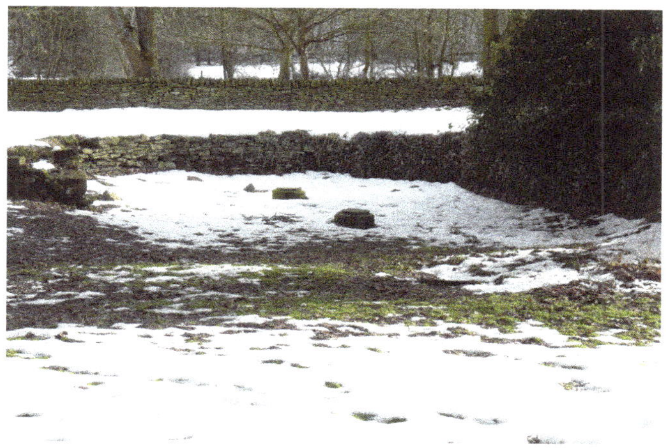

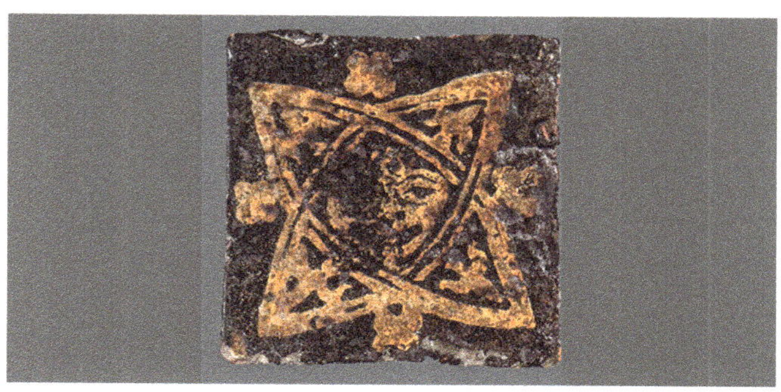

Photos from top

Western bell-tower
Foundations of the apsidal chapter house
Medieval floor tile from the Abbey

Bradbourne Priory

All Saints • Augustinian 1205–1540

Some uncertainty surrounds the status of this establishment and the only known facts are that the church was given by Geoffrey de Cauceis in 1205 to Dunstable Priory, which sent four Augustinian canons to serve the church at Bradbourne, its three chapelries at Tissington, Brassington and Ballidon, and associated lands. The gift was confirmed by William de Ferrers, Earl of Derby. It may have served under a warden as a small cell to this Bedfordshire house until its dissolution in 1540. The church of All Saints stands among the green hills and grey limestone outcrops of the White Peak, commanding an elevated position with fine views. Built in the Early English and Perpendicular styles, it has considerable remains of Norman and Saxon work. Particularly prominent is the massive Norman tower with a Saxon lower stage and a stair turret in the north-east angle. The south doorway has three orders of mouldings, one of which displays typical beak-head carvings, with the other two adorned with various indistinguishable animals. A Saxon cross shaft in the churchyard dates from around AD 800.

Breadsall Priory

Holy Trinity • Augustinian c1260–1536

The remains of a thirteenth century doorway with roll moulding inside the Breadsall Priory hotel, golf and country club, is all that has survived from this small priory for Augustinian canons, first founded c1260 by either Richard Curzon or his son Robert, who granted the community parcels of land in Horston and Horsley. The endowments of the house, however, were so slender, that it seems to have supported at most two canons beside the prior. Its history proceeded without upheaval, but it was clearly a struggle to keep the house functioning. In the *Valor* of 1535, its clear annual value was a mere £10 17s and only Prior William Pendylton was left. He duly surrendered the priory at the Dissolution of the lesser monasteries the following year, and received a small pension of only five marks. The buildings and lands were granted in 1552 to Henry, Duke of Suffolk, who sold it that same year to Thomas Babington. The priory church and other structures were razed to the ground to enable a later owner, Sir John Bentley, to build the Elizabethan E-plan house in the late sixteenth century. Some exceptionally thick walls in the house may be from the medieval priory.

Calke Priory

St Giles • Augustinian -1120–1538

A small monastic house for Augustinian canons, dedicated to St Giles, was founded in the woods south of the River Trent before 1120 by Richard d'Avranches, second Earl of Chester, to whom the King had given the manor of Ticknall. The earls and other benefactors endowed the new foundation with the church at Calke, as well as lands, woods and mills in the neighbourhood. The canons came into conflict with the powerful abbey of Chester, which appears to have confiscated its church and property. However, about 1125, the abbot promised to restore the church and all property taken away by him or his men to the canons of Calke. The priory had a short-lived independent existence. After the death of Ranulf de Gernon, fourth Earl of Chester in 1153, Calke, together with most of his estates, became part of the dowry of his widow, Maud of Gloucester, Countess of Chester. Maud initially granted the nearby church of St Wystan at Repton to the canons at Calke, but having built a new priory there, she transferred the Augustinian community from Calke to her new foundation in 1172. The Countess stipulated that Calke was to remain a cell to Repton.

Nothing is known of its history during the fourteenth and fifteenth centuries and with no more than two or three canons present, it has been suggested that monastic life as such lapsed and Calke became merely a grange. It ceased to exist when Repton Priory was dissolved in 1538. The site of the priory was granted in 1547 by Edward VI to John, Earl of Warwick, after which its ownership changed frequently. Nothing at all now exists from the priory and the present building, given the confusing name of Calke Abbey in 1808, is an amalgam of two structures that have stood on the same site, including an Elizabethan mansion and a huge remodelling project into a large country house, undertaken between 1701 and 1704.

Darley Abbey

St Mary • Augustinian c1146–1538

Darley Abbey was a re-foundation in c1146 of the Abbey of St Helen in Derby by Robert de Ferrers, second Earl of Derby, and sanctioned in 1154 by King Stephen and his successor Henry II. Robert gave to the new foundation several churches, arable and meadow lands and 'as much wood as one cart can bring from the woods of Duffield and Chaddesden'. There appears to have been a problem with the intended site, and it was not until 1160 after Hugh, rural dean of Derby, gave all his lands at Little Darley, that enabled Prior

Albinus and most of his Augustinian canons to remove to the new site on the River Derwent, some one mile to the north. With a steady flow of grants and gifts, the abbey of St Mary became the wealthiest monastic foundation in Derbyshire, with extensive holdings, not only in its home county, but also in neighbouring Nottinghamshire and Staffordshire. Henry III granted three charters in 1229, which confirmed the possessions of the abbey, including those given by Henry II, Earl Ferrers and Hugh, the dean. In 1216, Pope Honorius III commissioned the prior and two other religious to adjucate in a dispute between the chapter of York and the priory of St Oswald. From that time onwards, the prior was frequently called upon to take part in papal and diocesan commissions. Royal visitors included Henry III in 1251, when he granted the abbey a market at Ripley and a three-day fair on the feast of St Helen, and Edward I in 1293.

But its powerful position in the land did not prevent its brush with poverty early in the fourteenth century, as the failure of the harvest, heavy mortality of its cattle, a certain amount of mismanagement, and the fall-out from occasional disputes over tithes, caused great concern. However, this appears to have been only temporary, as by the time of the *Valor* of 1535, the clear annual worth of the abbey was given as £258 13s, which enabled it to avoid the 1536 closure of the smaller monasteries. Its stay of execution lasted only another two years. Abbot Thomas Page, Prior Richard Machyn, the sub-prior and ten canons signed the Deed of Surrender in October 1538. The abbey buildings and lands were immediately handed over to Robert Sacheverell, who held it for the Crown, before they were granted in 1540 to Sir William West, who used its stone for the construction of the first Darley Hall in Darley Park. Only two buildings, although much reconstructed, may have survived the destruction. One is the Abbey Inn, which is thought to have been the abbey's bakehouse and still retains a spiral stone staircase and a beehive bread oven. It has been used as cottages and shops in the past and has been known to have ghostly visitations. The other survival forms part of a private house in Abbey Lane, and some medieval stonework from the abbey is incorporated in houses at the bottom of Old Lane. Also traced to the abbey is a burial ground beneath Hill Square.

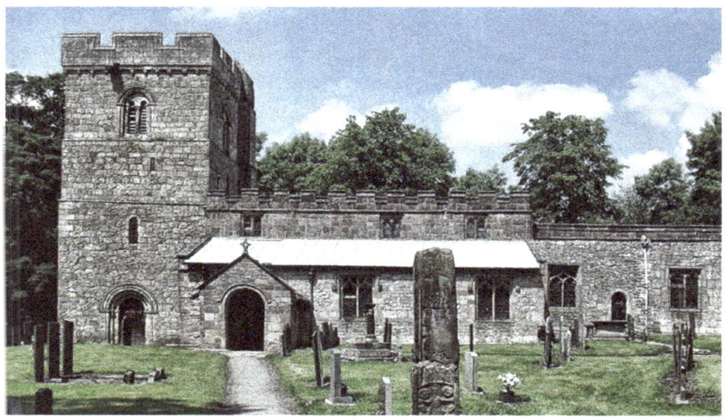

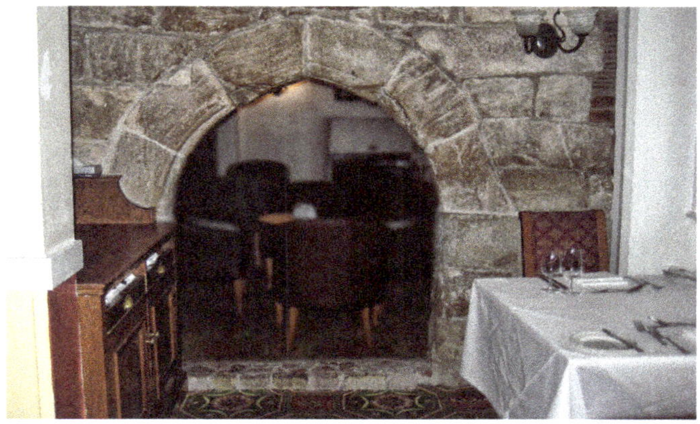

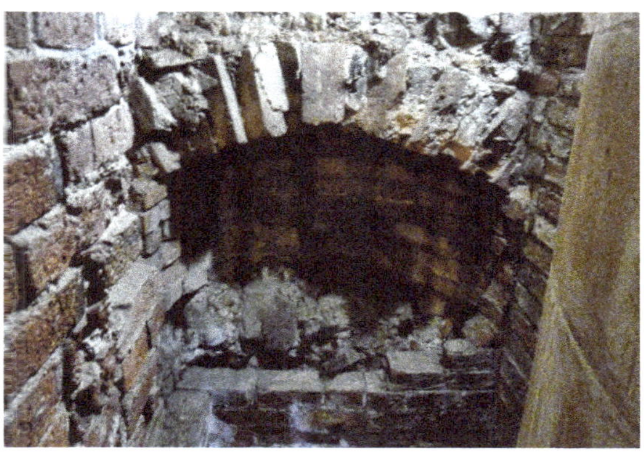

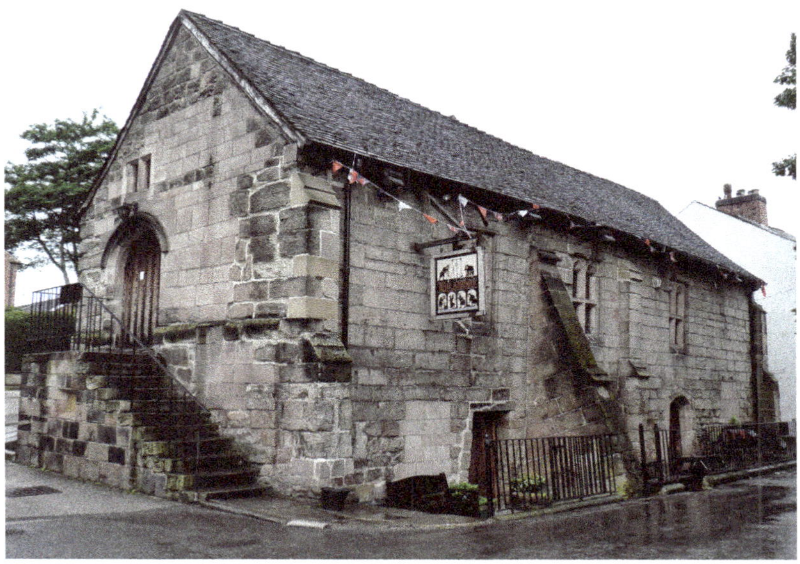

Photos - clockwise from top left

Bradbourne All Saints Church
Thirteenth century doorway from Breadsall
The Abbey Inn at Darley Abbey
Probable medieval bread oven

Depedale (Dale) Abbey

St Mary • Augustinian/Premonstratensian 1162–1538

The stark outline of the 12.2m (40ft) high great east window of the church, now alas without tracery, standing in isolation in the picturesque South Derbyshire countryside, is the most prominent of the remains of this abbey for Premonstratensian canons. Other stonework from the abbey, some decorated, was incorporated into houses in the small village, while other parts found their way into various local churches after the Dissolution. Stained and painted glass, floor tiles and an entire porch were taken to Morley, where the most notable features from Dale Abbey are the stained glass windows, mostly in the north chancel chapel, which used to glaze the cloister arcades. The windows display stories from Invention of Holy Cross and St Robert of Knaresborough. Chaddesden received a window frame, and benches and bench ends with poppy heads found their way to Radbourne.

The ornately carved font cover also went to Radbourne, but has since been returned to the All Saints chapel, as has the fifteenth century octagonal stone font, decorated with shields on the cardinal sides, which was recovered from a garden. The tiny chapel, measuring just 7.9 x 7.6m (26 x 25ft), is associated with the origins of the abbey, and, together with the attached Tudor house, is thought to have formed part of the infirmary. The oldest part of the chapel is the wall below the hymn board, which dates back to the 1150s. Also worth seeing is a late thirteenth century medieval painting on the north wall, depicting the Annunciation, Visitation and Nativity. In sharp contrast, the cruciform abbey church with crossing tower appears to have been of impressive proportions, with the transepts extending 30.5m (100ft) across. The cloister was 25.9m (85ft) square.

The abbey's beginnings are cloaked in mystery and folklore, peppered by a sprinkling of fact, and come from a chronicle written in the middle of the thirteenth century by Thomas de Musca, a canon of the house. One tale concerns a god-fearing Derby baker who, after the Virgin Mary appeared in his dreams, was guided to Depedale, then a desolate wooded and marshy valley far from habitation, in c1130. There he lived as a recluse in a cave hewn out of the sandstone cliffs on the slopes of the valley. This is still well-preserved and worth a visit. When Ralph fitzGeremund, Lord of Ockbrook and Alvaston, chanced upon the hermit, he took pity on him and granted an income, which he used to build a small chapel. A lady who became known as the 'Gome' or godmother of the Dale later settled there and built on to the hermit's chapel. Also told is the legend of the outlaw Uthlagus who, while resting in the Dale, had a vision in which he saw a golden cross reach high into the sky and men of all nations gathering to worship. Upon waking he told his companions what he had seen and proclaimed that the dale was holy ground and he would no longer pursue his wicked ways.

A little more certainty pertains to the arrival from Calke Abbey of five Augustinian canons under prior Humphrey in 1162. The inhospitality of the place caused them to withdraw a short while later, after which William de Grendon, Lord of Dale, invited six Premonstratensian canons from Tupholme Abbey in Lincolnshire to take their place. After toiling unsuccessfully on a scrap of infertile land, the canons were recalled by the abbot after only seven years. William then brought five canons from Welbeck Abbey, but they too succumbed to poverty and soon lost heart. Finally, with better endowments, a Premonstratensian abbey was established and colonised by nine canons from Newhouse Abbey.

Although the canons arrived in c1195, the date of the official foundation of the abbey by Geoffrey de Salicosa and his wife Matilda has been given as 1204, when it was dedicated to the Virgin Mary. Under the first abbot, Walter de Senteney, and his successors, the abbey's possession and influence increased, and it later owned around 24,000 acres of land, much of which would have been leased out for production or grazing. But it was never a large house, accommodating no more than twenty-four canons at the height of its powers. Apart from the odd dispute over possessions and occasional spiritual lapses, the abbey enjoyed a good reputation throughout its long existence.

Its worth, assessed in the *Valor Ecclesiasticus* of 1535 at £144 12s, brought the abbey well within the limit for the suppression of smaller houses in 1536, but a payment to the King delayed the inevitable by only two years. In October 1538, Dale Abbey and all its possessions in Derbyshire, Nottinghamshire, Leicestershire and Northamptonshire were surrendered to the Crown by Abbot John Bebe, the prior and fifteen canons, and granted to Sir Francis Pole of Radbourne.

Photos – clockwise from top left

The ruined great east window of the abbey church
Remains of abbey built into local house
Tiny All Saints Chapel attached to later house
Former gatehouse
Hermit cave hewn out of sandstone cliff

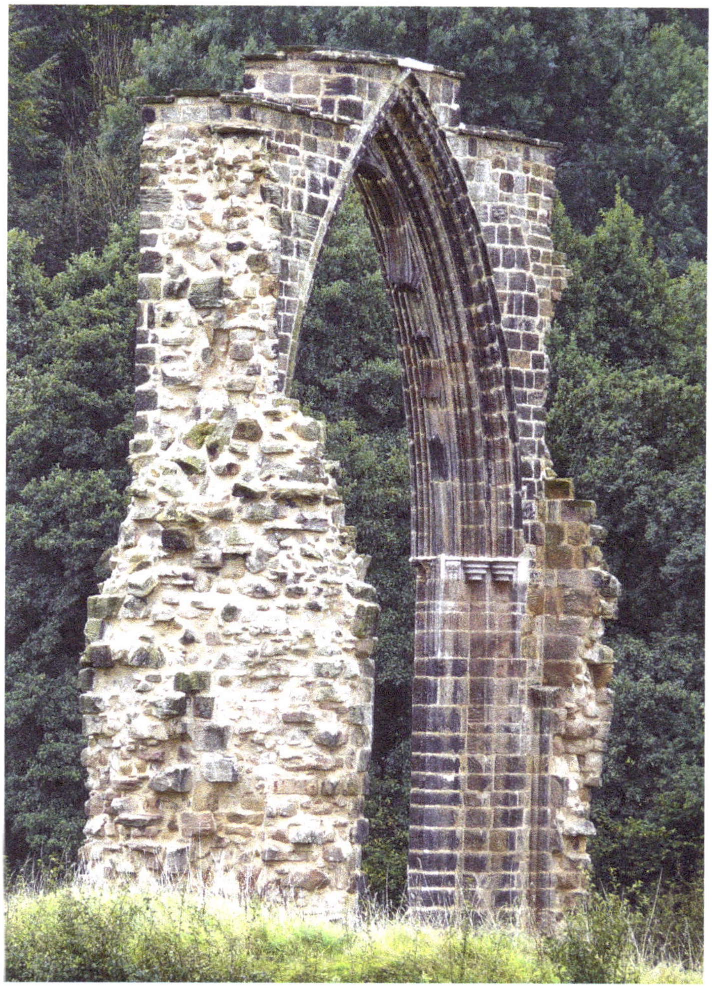

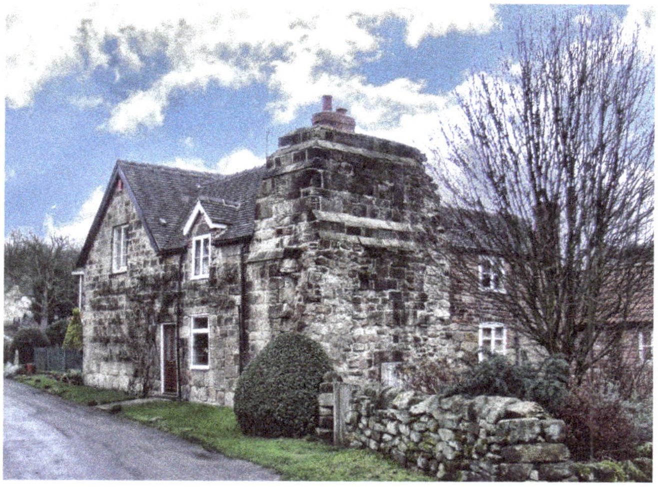

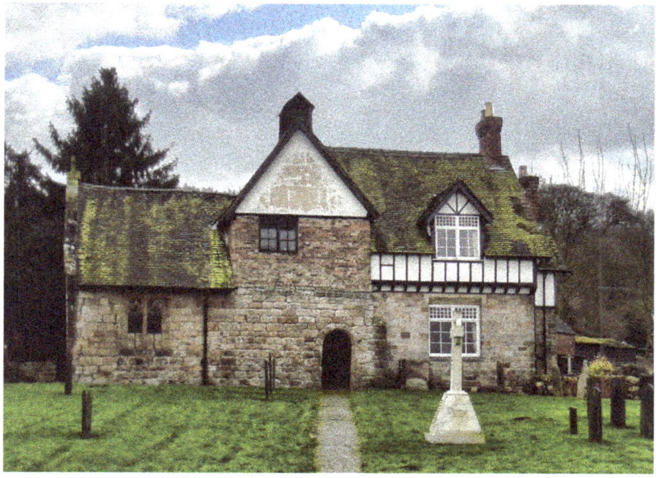

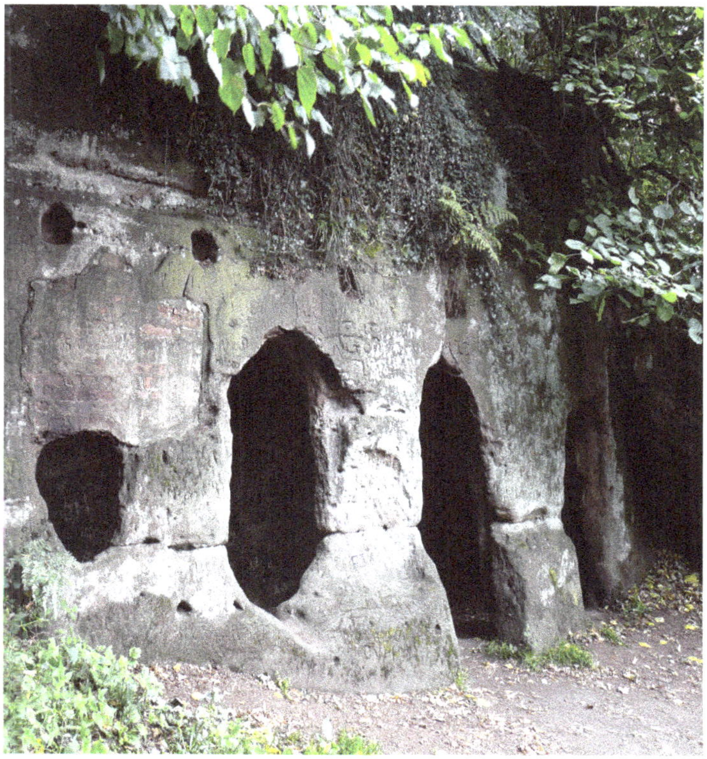

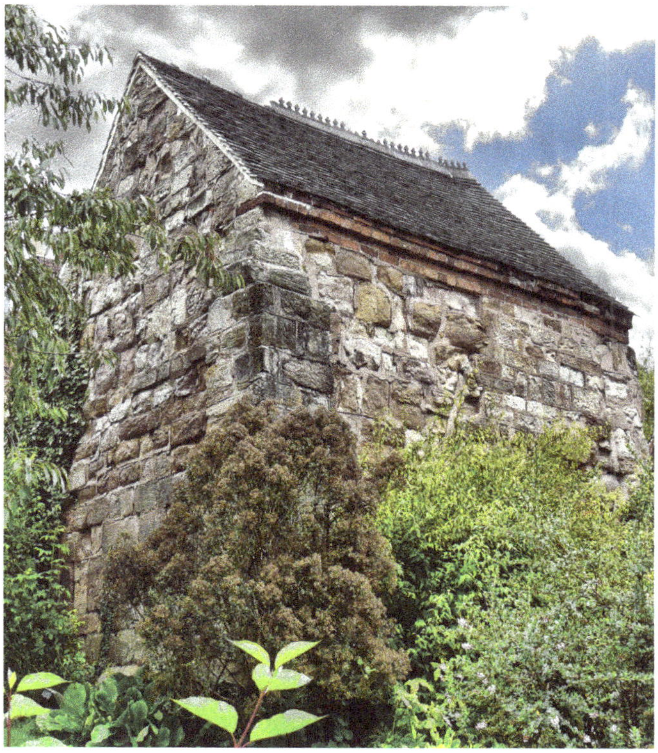

Derby Abbey

St Helen • Augustinian 1137–c1146

The abbey of St Helen was founded in 1137 in the reign of King Stephen by Robert de Ferrers, first Earl of Derby, who endowed his new foundation with several churches, meadows and arable lands. After his death in 1139, his son, another Robert, second Earl of Derby, confirmed all these grants and added, in perpetuity, 'as much wood as a cart can bring from the woods of Duffield and Chaddesden'. Abbot Albinus and his Augustinian canons obtained further lands from Hugh of Derby to build a church and monastery. However, in c1146, the earl translated the community to nearby Darley, where he refounded the abbey. Only an oratory remained at the former place just outside the walls of the town, near the church of St Alkmund.

Derby (Kings Mead) Priory

St Mary • Benedictine nuns c1160–1536

A house for Benedictine nuns, known as St Mary de Pratis, was founded by the abbot of Darley around the year 1160. It was situated to the west of the town in an area still called Nuns' Green, on the north bank of the Markeaton Brook. The nuns possessed a number of water mills, lands and several local manors, which enabled a comfortable lifestyle, but the community was impoverished during the march of the Black Death. Its quiet existence was interrupted in the reign of Henry VI, when Prioress Isabella de Stanley was sued by the abbot of Burton, who accused her of having failed to pay rent due to him for twenty-one years. As the priory was in debt, this situation was probably not a surprise. By 1535, its annual revenues had dwindled to just £18 6s. The nunnery was dissolved in 1536 and granted in 1541 to Francis, Earl of Shrewsbury, who, in the following year, sold it to Thomas Sutton. The later development of the area obliterated any remnants of this religious house.

Derby Priory

St James • Cluniac 1140–1536

A small chapel on the north side of Markeaton Brook was built in the Saxon era and was given in 1140 to the Cluniac Priory of Bermondsey by Waltheof, a Saxon nobleman who was said to have been the first person to have lost his head by order of William the Conqueror. The prior of Bermondsey consequently established a small cell in Derby, together with a hospital for the poor and infirm, which was being managed by a prior and perhaps two monks. The endowments were insufficient and the community always found it a struggle to make ends meet. At a general visitation of English Cluniac houses in 1279, the cell was in debt and the church roof in bad repair. The situation barely improved over the next hundred years, and the loss of two actions brought in 1396 by Prior Peter, who accused various chaplains of having stolen his hay and of having beaten him and stolen some of his property, did nothing to improve matters. When, in 1325, the Crown seized most alien monasteries, including Bermondsey, which was a dependency of the abbey of La Charité-sur-Loire, St James was allowed to remain under the prior, in exchange of an annual payment to the Crown, which it was later allowed to forgo. The priory church and attached hospital were accidentally burnt down in 1335 and rebuilt. The charter of denization granted to Bermondsey in 1395 also applied to the cell of St James, enabling it to escape the final suppression of alien houses. Prior Thomas Gainsborough surrendered the house to the King's commissioners, Dr Thomas Legh and Richard Layton, in 1536. Its annual value barely exceeded £11.

Derby Black Friars

Annunciation of Our Lady • -1239-1539

The Dominican friars obtained a site just outside the walls of the old town, within the parish of St Werburgh, sometime before 1239. The friars enjoyed the patronage of Henry III, who contributed to the building of the conventual church. Building works appear to have progressed slowly, as Edward I also made a monetary gift for the construction in 1275. Over the next hundred years, the community was able to enlarge its house through several grants of lands and meadows, which gradually expanded the precinct boundaries. The Provincial Chapter was held at Derby in 1310, 1346 and 1376, for which the friars received financial assistance for food and other expenses from Edward II and Edward III. When Edward II visited the house in 1323, he bestowed 8s 8d, which covered a day's food for twenty-six friars. In 1344, the priory suffered a severe attack when local men broke into the precinct, beat the friars and servants, and carried off goods and chattels. The reasons for this assault have never been fully explained. When the threat of dissolution became real, most of the friars withdrew, leaving only the prior, Lawrence Sponor, and five friars to sign the house over to the King's commissioners in January1539. Its annual value was estimated at only £18 16s. The house and land of the priory was rented out to John Sharpe. The priory was located in the area of the Friary Hotel, to the east of Stafford Street, but several excavations in connection with redevelopment have found no traces of its existence.

Gresley Priory

St Mary & St George • Augustinian c1135–1536

The Church of St Mary and St George at Church Gresley retains little of the original priory church, whose nave was used by the parishioners and the chancel by the Augustinian canons as the priory chapel. When the church was repaired soon after 1816, most of the priory ruins to the east were swept away and the outer walls almost entirely rebuilt and new windows inserted. All that was left from the priory was the fifteenth century embattled western tower and two decorated arches of the arcade, supported by an octagonal pier. The chapter house, cloister, refectory and other conventual buildings had long since disappeared.

This small priory for four or five canons was founded c1135-40 during the reign of King Stephen by William de Gresley, who provided nearby arable land and meadows for the new community, to which eventually was granted the advowson of the church of Lullington and a mill at Castle Gresley. Although his descendants continued their benefaction, the barrenness of the lands and inability of the prior to increase the number of canons kept the house small and poor. On the spiritual side, little untoward has been reported. Its clear annual value in the *Valor* was assessed at only £31 6s, which sealed its fate with the smaller houses in 1536. Prior John Okeley and two canons were pensioned off. The site of the priory was immediately assigned to 'Henry Churche of the Households' and repeatedly changed hands thereafter. The fabric of the priory fell into decay.

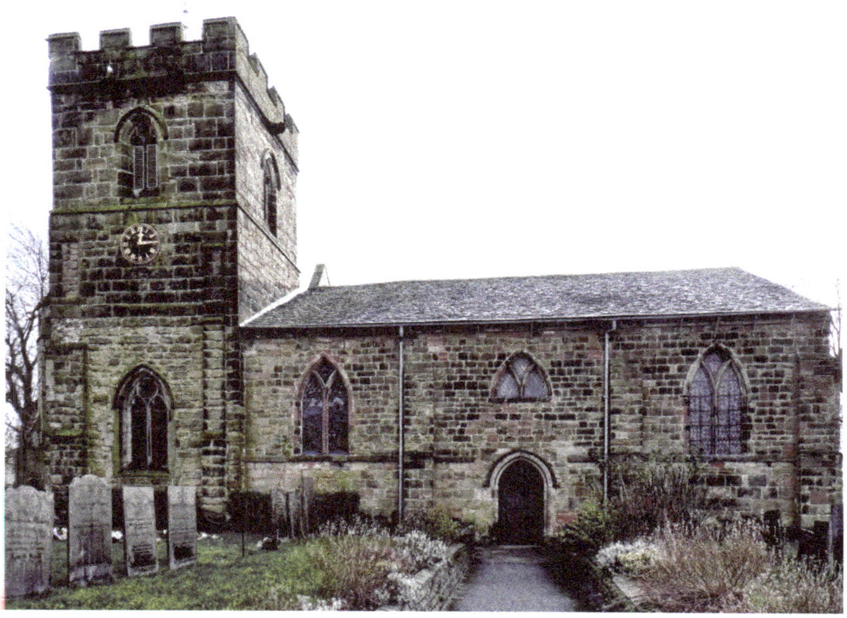

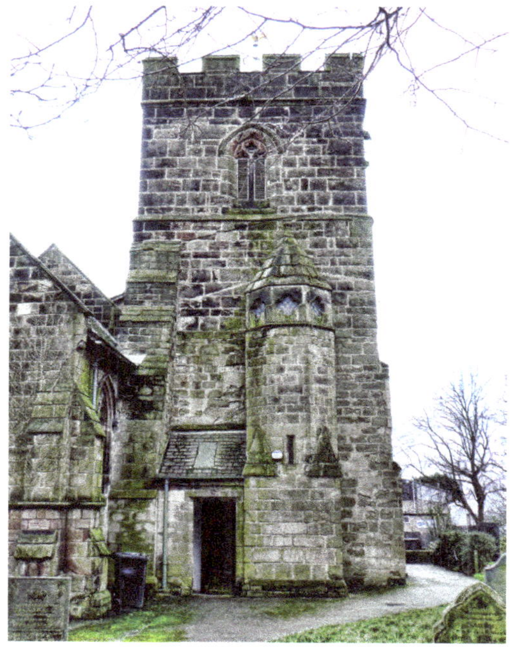

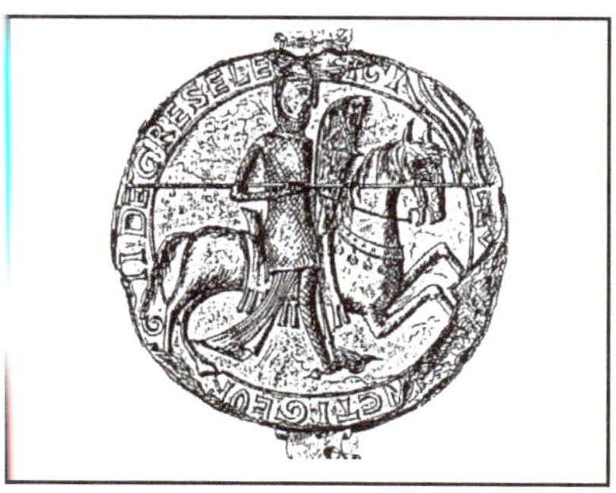

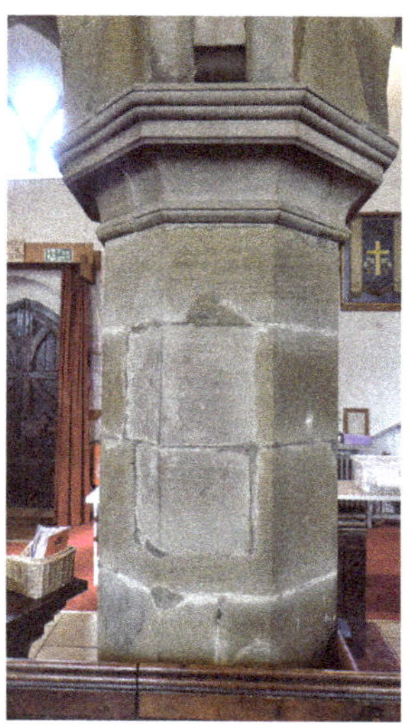

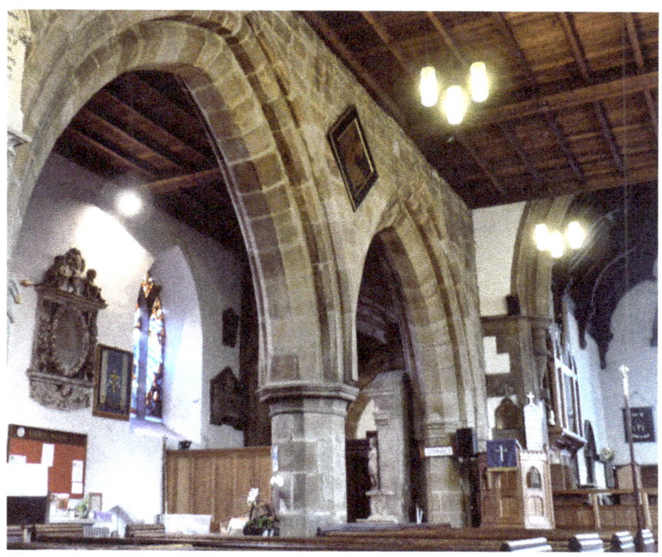

Photos - clockwise from top left

The former Gresley priory church
Fifteenth century church tower
Nave arcade from former priory
Octagonal pier
Seal of Gresley Priory at time of Prior Richard (d 1281)

Repton Priory

Holy Trinity • Benedictine 1172–1538

A Benedictine abbey was first established at Repton during Saxon times about the year AD 653, traditionally by St David. The foundation of the abbey followed the arrival of four priests sent from Northumbria to convert the Mercian royal family from its paganism, so that a royal wedding could take place between the son of a Mercian King and a Northumbrian princess. Repton was then a capital of the Kingdom of Mercia, which covered a vast area of the country, and also the chief residence of the royal family. Although throughout its existence it was described as famous and venerable, little is known of its daily life, other that it was a double monastery under the rule of an abbess. In AD 697, when Alfthritha held the post of abbess, St Guthlac came to Repton to do penance for his sins, but soon left to take up the life of a hermit. Cynehard, King Sigebert's brother, was buried at Repton after being killed in battle with Cynewulf, King of Wessex, in AD 786. King Wiglaf and his grandson St Wystan were also buried in the abbey church. The abbey largely perished at the hands of the Danes in AD 873-4, but the abbey church of St Wystan was used as a defended strongpoint by the Vikings. The church was remodelled and enlarged in later centuries but still retains substantial Anglo-Saxon work, especially the crypt, which is said to pre-date that at Lastingham by two centuries. Nikolaus Pevsner wrote: "the chancel and the crypt form one of the most precious survivals of Anglo-Saxon architecture in England".

Monastic life returned to Repton in 1172, when Maud, who, with the consent of her son Hugh de Kevelioc, fifth Earl of Chester, had begun building a priory dedicated to the Holy Trinity c1153, effected the transfer of the community of Augustinian canons from Calke Priory of St Giles. Maud stipulated that Calke was to remain as a cell to the new foundation at Repton.

The only building of Repton Priory still substantially complete is the priory guest house, now known as the Old Priory, which was built c1400 and was converted into a school for boys. It has a fine timber roof. Also extant is the entrance arch of the priory gatehouse, which has been dated to c1250, but was moved to its present position in 1905. There are foundations of the east end of the priory church, cloisters and adjacent buildings, most notably the west range, which includes the library and an undercroft. Also still extant is the old priory precinct wall of ashlar, which virtually encircles the original priory lands, sloping down to Repton Brook and to Milton, where the priory mill was located. It has been restored and altered in places. It is also thought that the Old Stone House in the High Street has been constructed from dressed stone taken from the priory.

A charter of Henry III, dated 1272, confirmed the priory's possessions of the church at Repton, its eight chapelries, and several more churches, including one in Essex. Regular endowments of arable land, meadows and woods in Derbyshire and Nottinghamshire helped to increase its annual income, although it was never rich. In 1327, at the beginning of the reign of Edward III, the prior was made surveyor of the tolls taken on goods passing over Swarkeston Bridge, a civic duty he performed for several years. Some events disturbed life at the priory in the fourteenth century. First, a lay-brother, William de Repton, was assaulted and taken away, together with the prior's goods in 1302, and in 1337 there was illegal interference in the priory's temporal affairs by one of the King's servants. Bishop Stretton indicted the community, town, and parish church of Repton for a grave disturbance during his visitation in 1364. The entire community of the town, bearing swords and staves, and bows and arrows, attacked the bishop's retinue, which almost resulted in the bishop's death, and laid siege to the priory, for which act the ringleaders were excommunicated.

In the *Valor Ecclesiasticus* of 1535, the net annual value of Repton Priory was returned as £118 8s, which brought it well within the limit of the smaller monasteries. As a consequence, Repton had to submit to a visitation in 1536 by the King's commissioners, Thomas Legh and Richard Layton. Although their report painted a dire, but entirely false picture of the inhabitants, Henry VIII permitted the priory to continue on payment of a heavy fine of £226 13s. It was to no avail, as the priory was surrendered in October 1538 to Dr Legh by the sub-prior, Ralph Clerke, and eight canons. Prior John Young had died three days before the surrender. Thomas Thacker, steward to Thomas Cromwell, took possession the day after, but it was his son Gilbert who, fearing that Queen Mary would resurrect the monastic Orders, had most of the buildings, including the beautiful church, demolished in one day, saying "he would destroy the nest, for fear the birds should build therein again".

Photos – clockwise from top left

Former cloister garth with prior's guest house
Ancient wooden door to prior's guest house
Relocated gatehouse arch of mid-thirteenth century
Foundations of priory church
Clustered columns in former nave of priory church
Stairs to dormitory and parlour alongside

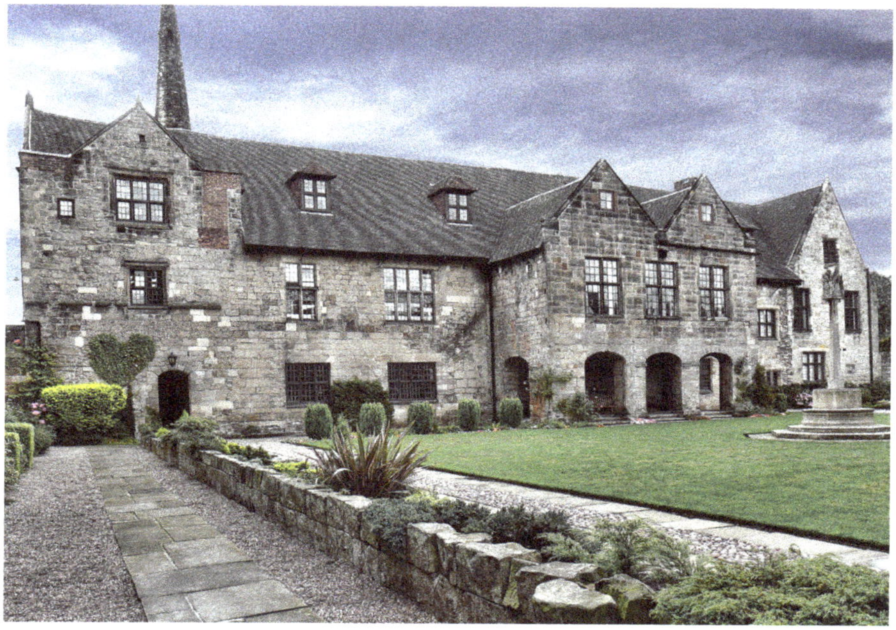

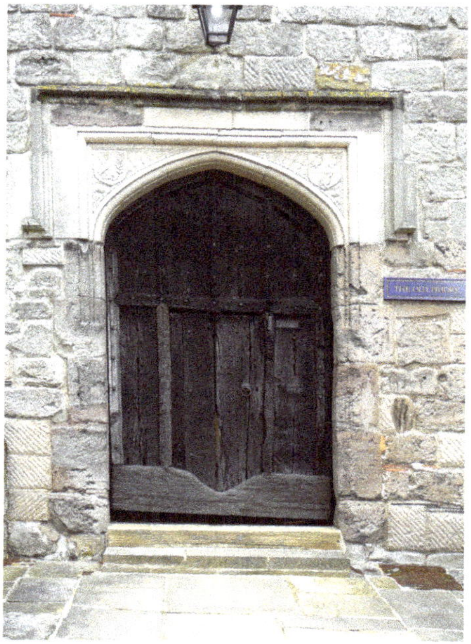

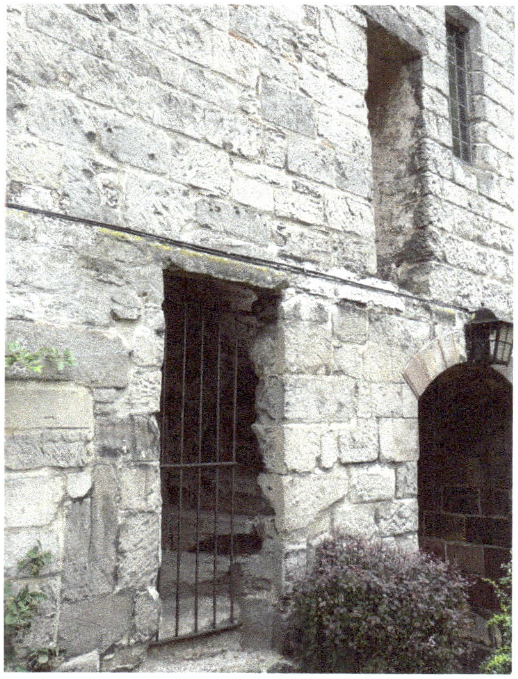

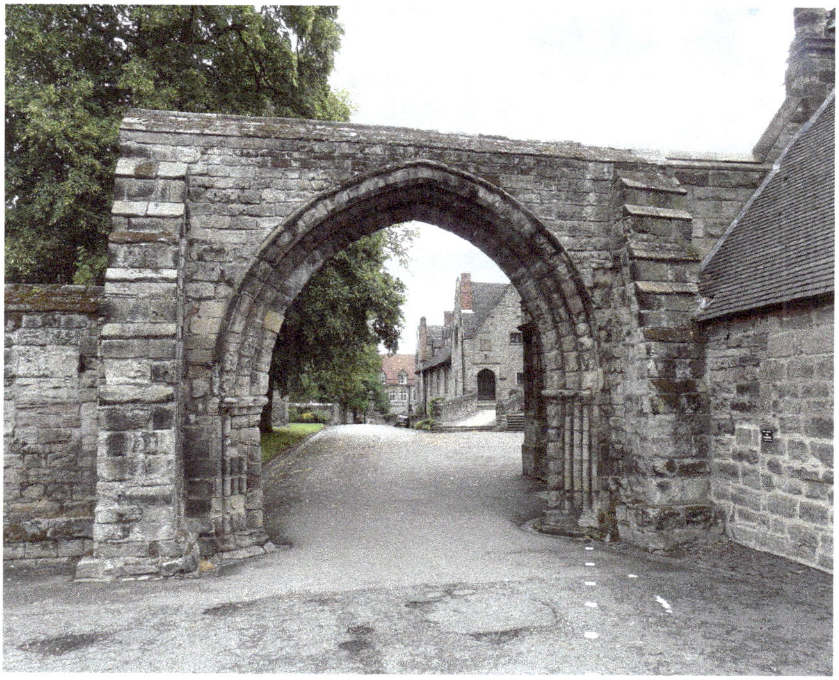

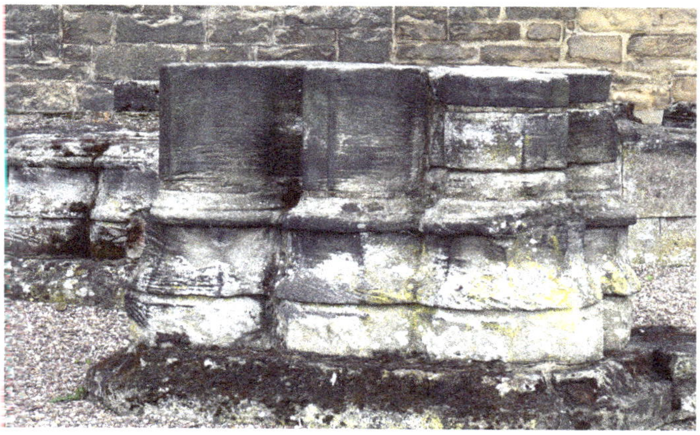

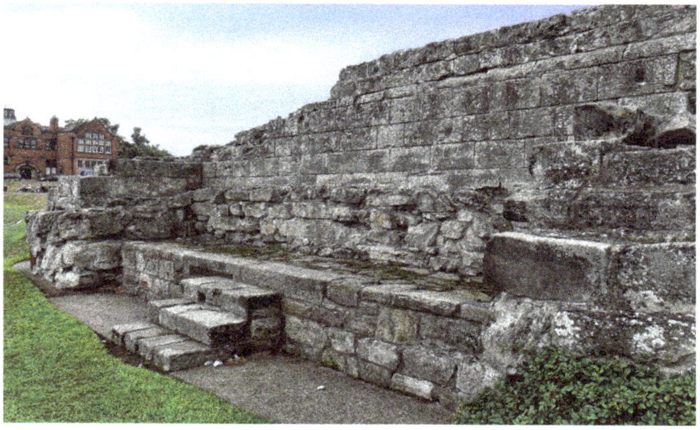

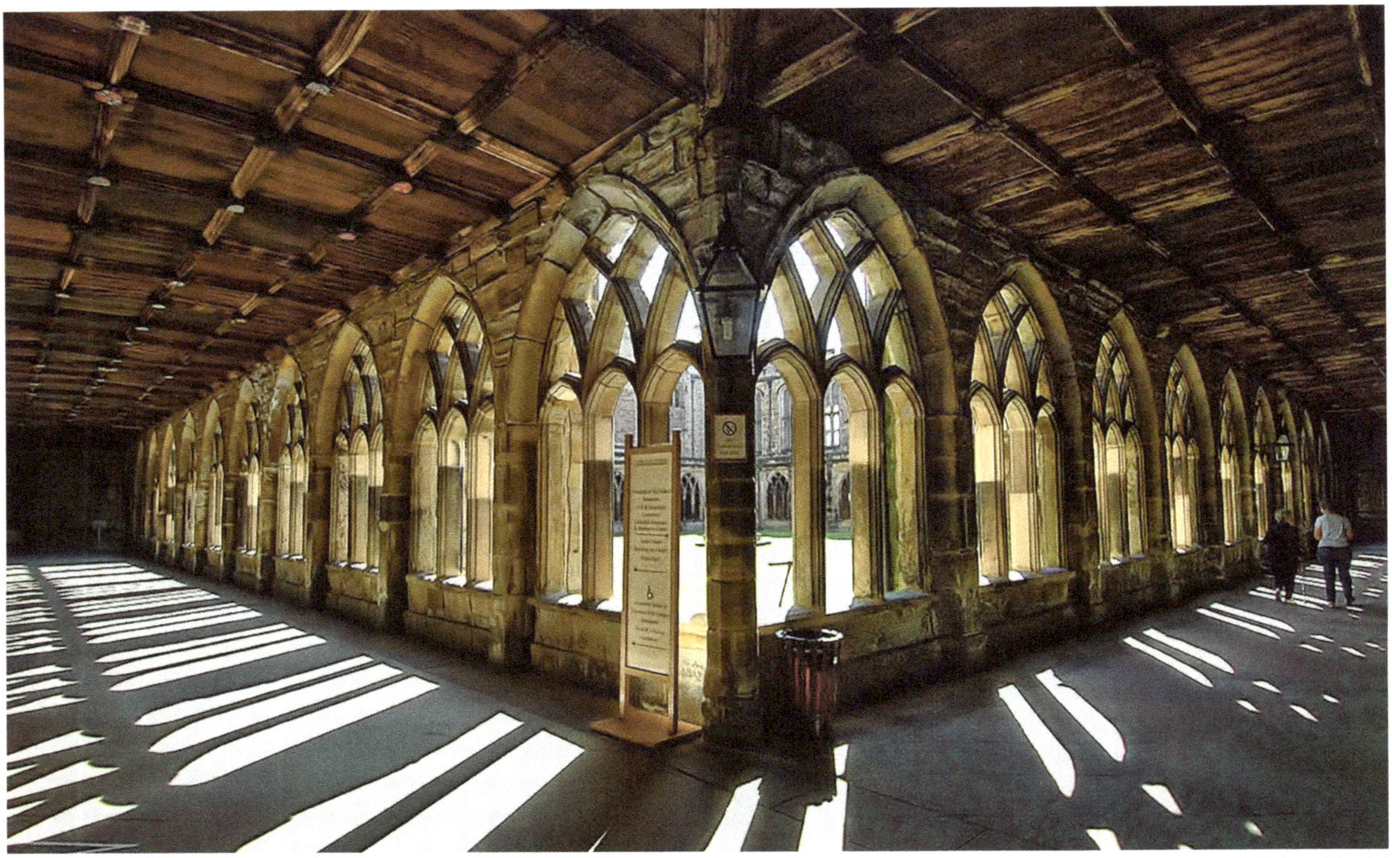

Durham Cathedral

Gazetteer

Barnard Castle Austin Friars On A67, Barnard Castle, County Durham. (NZ 050161) No visible remains

Baxterwood Priory (NZ 256424). Possible location, but no visible remains

Durham Cathedral Priory Palace Green, Durham City, County Durham (NZ 273412). Tel: 0191 386 4266. Web: www.durhamcathedral.co.uk

Finchale Priory On minor road between A167 and A690, 5km (3 miles) NE of Durham, County Durham (NZ 297471). English Heritage: Tel: 0191 386 3828

Hartlepool Black Friars Details or location unknown

Hartlepool Grey Friars The Friarage, The Headland, Hartlepool, Cleveland (NZ 530338). Private

Jarrow Priory In Jarrow, on minor road N of A185, 8km (5 miles) NE of Newcastle-on-Tyne, Tyne and Wear (NZ 339652). English Heritage: Tel: 0191 489 7052

Neasham Priory In Neasham village, 6.5km (4 miles) SE of Darlington, County Durham (NZ 323101). No visible remains

Owton Priory Nothing known and no visible remains

Wearmouth Priory St Peter's Way, Monkwearmouth, Sunderland, Tyne and Wear (NZ 402577). Church in use; Tel: 0191 567 3726

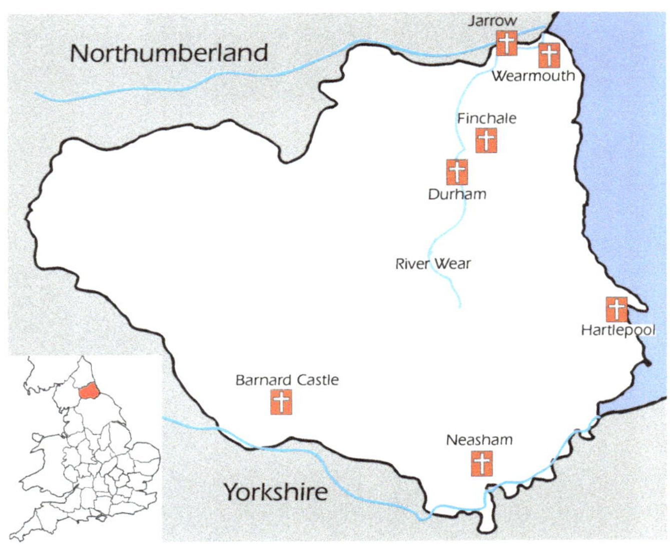

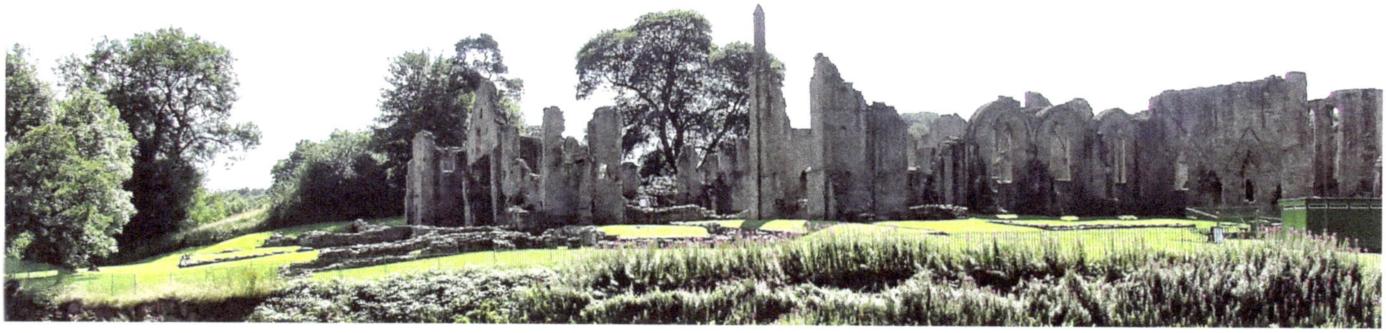

Finchale Priory

Durham

Private Shire

The territory that became known as County Durham was originally a liberty under the control of the Bishops of Durham. In AD 883, the See was moved from Lindisfarne to Chester-le-Street and, together with the remains of St Cuthbert, to Durham in AD 995, after repeated raids by Vikings. When the county of Northumberland was created, Durham was considered within its bounds. This was vehemently disputed by the bishops and, after a decision by Parliament in 1293, Durham became a County Palatine, a de facto private shire under the bishops. The bishops had the power to raise armies and call their own Parliament, until these powers were curtailed by Henry VIII.

At the heart of the county is the magnificent Durham Cathedral, which replaced several previous churches on the site and became the Benedictine cathedral priory of St Cuthbert and power base of the prince-bishops. It houses the tombs of St Cuthbert and the Venerable Bede. Finchale Priory is one of the most historic sites in Durham, having first been mentioned in AD 792, when an important synod of the Northumbrian church was held there. The Benedictine priory was established in 1196 and from the fourteenth century was used as a holiday retreat by the monks from Durham Cathedral. Even older are Jarrow and Wearmouth Priories, both of which had connections with the Venerable Bede, and both became Benedictine cells of Durham Cathedral. Benedictine nuns were present at Neasham, and Gilbertine canons or nuns may have had a house at Owton. Some uncertainty remains about the Augustinian house of Baxterwood. A short-lived house of Austin friars existed at Barnard Castle, while Dominicans and Franciscans settled in Hartlepool.

Barnard Castle Austin Friars

1381– ?

A house of Austin Friars was founded in 1381, but appears to have lapsed almost at once, because no mention of it was made in a list of houses in 1387. There has been conjecture that an old building to the east of Thorngate, on which the words 'Soli Deo honor et Gloria' were cut in stone, had the appearance of a religious building, but no confirmation has been possible.

Baxterwood Priory

St Mary • Augustinian c1180–1196

Towards the end of the twelfth century, c1180, Henry Pudsey, a son of Bishop Pudsey, conferred the vills of Wingate and Haswell, probably to the Augustinian canons of Gisburn, to found a monastery at Haswell. This was to be dedicated to the Virgin Mary, but it is doubtful if any construction work was actually begun at Haswell, as soon afterwards the possessions were transferred to a new priory at Baxterwood on the River Browney, close to the city of Durham. Known as 'The New Place upon the Browney', it was colonised by canons from Gisburn, under the superintendence of Stephen. However, the Benedictine monks from Durham made life difficult for the new foundation until, so wrote Geoffrey of Coldingham, Henry Pudsey agreed in 1196 to abandon the canons and transfer his lands to Finchale, where a new Benedictine priory was founded with monks from Durham. The fact that no trace of foundations have been discovered in Baxterwood, in spite of the exact location being known, would suggest that building work either never got started, or was abandoned before any substantial completion.

Durham Cathedral Priory

St Mary & St Cuthbert • Benedictine 1080–1540

The grandeur of the Cathedral Church of Durham is immeasurably enhanced by its strategic location on the summit of a rocky peninsula created by a loop in the River Wear. The west towers and central lantern tower rise high above a precipitous wooded cliff that falls to the river, dominating the surrounding city nestling in its shadow. The great length of the cathedral, measuring 143m (496ft) can best be appreciated from Palace Green. It has been described as "one of the greatest architectural experiences of Europe" and is renowned as a masterpiece of early Norman craftsmanship, much of which can still be admired. The cathedral was more than a place of worship, its splendour also reflects the role of the prince-bishops in reinforcing political and military control over England's northern lands. The nave, choir and transepts, completed in 1133, are all Norman, and include the Galilee Chapel at the east end, which was added in 1175. The Chapel of the Nine, facing St Cuthbert's tomb, was built in Gothic style between 1242 and 1280. The lowering of the floor below the level of the main body of the church, the slender ribs of the vaulting and the tall narrow lancet windows have created an enhanced sense of height. The two western towers were built between 1217 and 1226, while the taller central tower in Perpendicular Gothic is of fifteenth century construction. Although the cloister was begun in Norman times, it contains much work from the fifteenth century and later. Only the roof is original, as is the monks' door, decorated with ironwork, which leads into the cloisters. The Sanctuary Knocker on the north door reminds that criminals were able to claim sanctuary in the cathedral until their offences had been pardoned by the King.

The cathedral contains many treasures from its time as a Benedictine cathedral priory under the prince-bishops of the Palatine. Of most historical significance are the tombs of St Cuthbert behind the High Altar and of the Venerable Bede in the Galilee Chapel. St Cuthbert, the greatest saint of the north, died in AD 687 and, after many vicissitudes, was buried in a magnificent shrine in the Norman cathedral, which became a centre of pilgrimage in the Middle Ages. The Venerable Bede, the most famous scholar and historian, died in AD 735, and his bones were brought to Durham in 1022. Both shrines were destroyed during the Reformation. The magnificent screen between the High Altar and St Cuthbert's tomb was a gift from the Nevilles, one of the most influential local families, whose chantry is located in the nave. It was designed by Henry Yevele, the finest mason/architect of the fourteenth century and was carved from Caen stone between 1372 and 1380 by the King's masons in London. Also of medieval interest are the twelfth-century wall paintings behind the most northerly altar of the Galilee Chapel of a bishop and a King, thought to represent St Cuthbert and St Oswald, and depictions of the Crucifixion and the martyrdoms of some of the apostles on the south wall of the northernmost aisle. The bishop's throne above the Hatfield chantry was built by Thomas Hatfield, Bishop of Durham (1344-1381), and founder of Durham College (now Trinity College) Oxford. More treasures from the cathedral's history can be seen in the St Cuthbert Exhibition, including his wooden coffin and cross, and in the monks' dormitory, begun in 1398 and completed in 1404. It still retains its splendid original hammer-beam roof with twenty-eight oak beams.

The present cathedral replaced the 'White Church' built in AD 995 by a Saxon monastic community to house the relics of St Cuthbert, which the Benedictine monks had carried and protected since the first Viking raids in AD 875. Bishop William de St Carileph (1081-1096), who had been appointed the first prince-bishop by William the Conqueror in 1080, founded the new Benedictine Priory of St Cuthbert in 1083. Bishop William, together with Prior Turgot, laid the foundation stone for the cathedral church in 1093, having seen Europe's great Romanesque architectural style during a brief exile in France. The building was largely completed by 1140. The new foundation differed from most other monasteries in that it was under the care of a bishop, rather than an abbot, although the prior exercised a good deal of day-to-day authority. Several additions and repairs were made by succeeding bishops. St Cuthbert's tomb was destroyed on the orders of Henry VIII in 1538. The monastery was finally surrendered to the Crown in December 1540, but the cathedral was refounded in January 1541. The last prior, Hugh Whitehead, became the first dean of the new secular chapter, and twelve former monks became the first canons. Many historic furnishings and artefacts were destroyed subsequently, and the cathedral suffered further indignities when Oliver Cromwell used it as a makeshift gaol in 1650 to incarcerate 3,000 Scottish prisoners, of whom 1,700 died within its walls for lack of food, water and heating.

Photos – clockwise from top left

Durham Cathedral standing high above the river Wear
Prior's door leading to the cloister
East end of church with fine rose window
The magnificent Norman Galilee Chapel
Ornate floor of the choir
Sanctuary knocker on north door

Photos courtesy of Adrian Fletcher

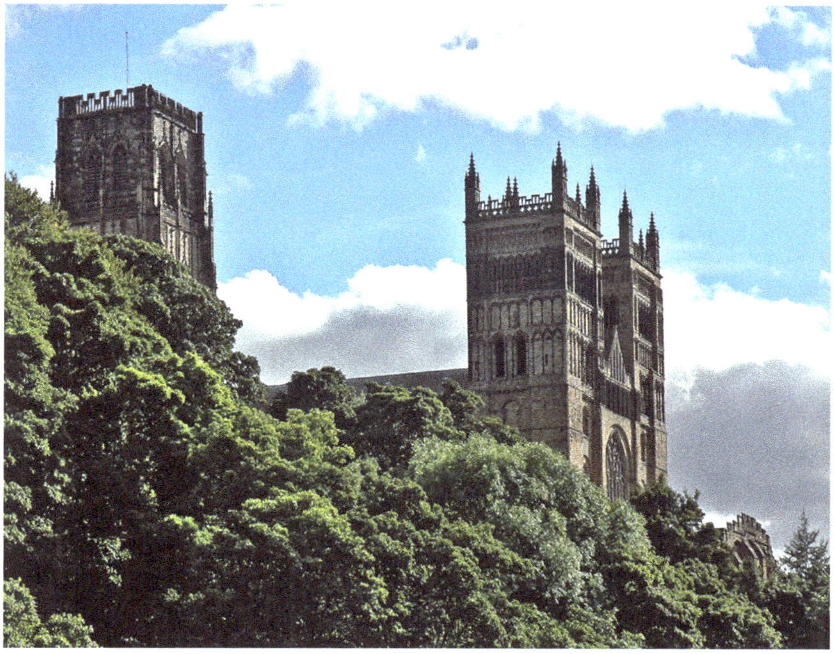

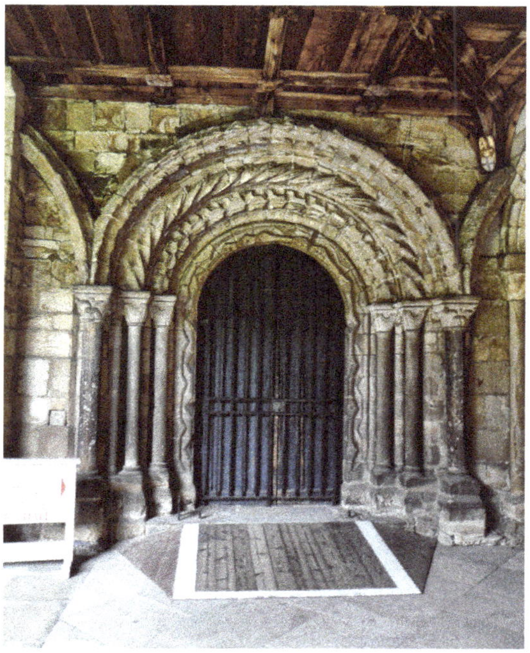

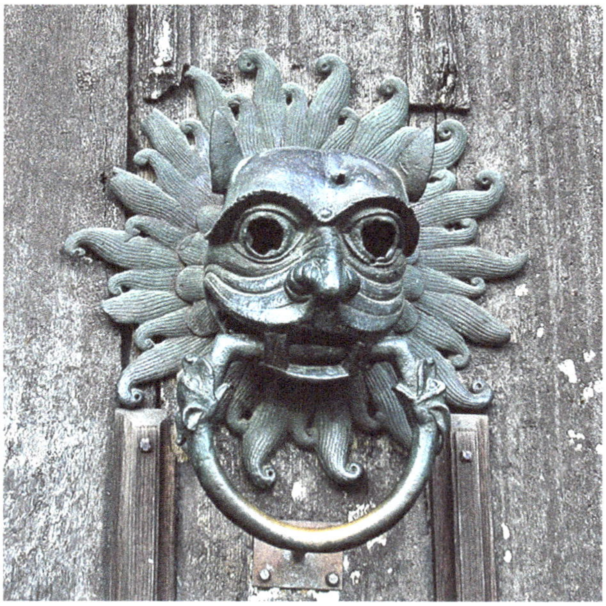

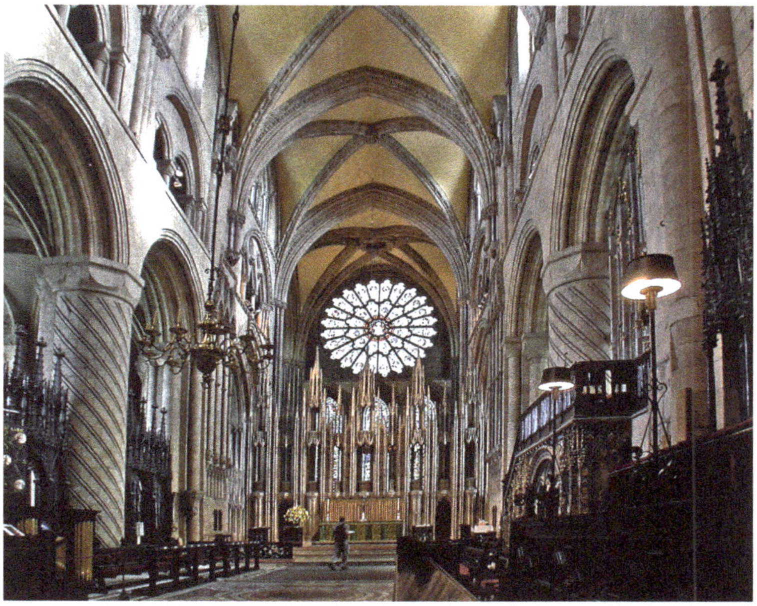

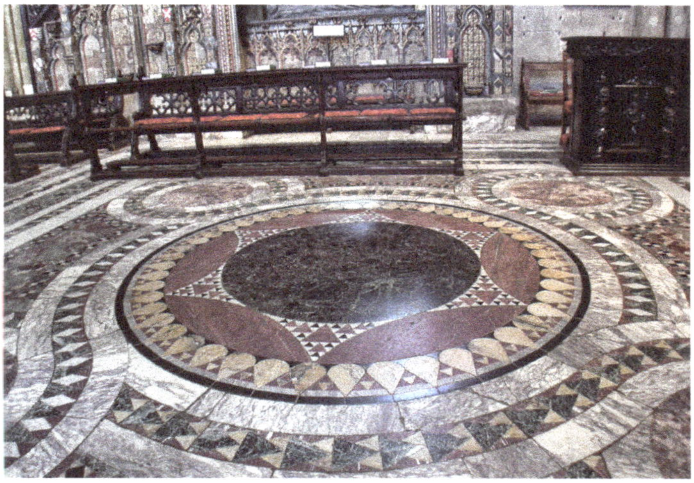

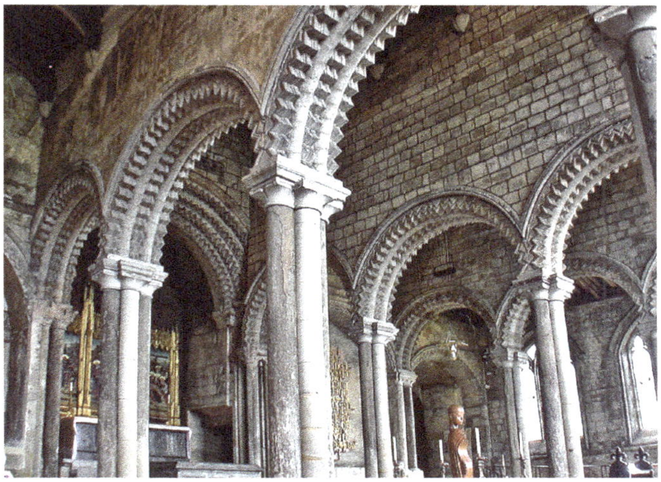

Finchale Priory

St Mary, St John the Baptist & St Godric • Benedictine 1196–1538

The priory is no longer the place of solitude of bygone days, now being surrounded by a working farm and scarred somewhat by the presence of a caravan park to the south, but it still occupies a scenic spot on the banks of the River Wear. The trappings of the present should also not distract from the fact that Finchale is one of the most historic sites in Durham. It was first mentioned in AD 792, when an important synod of the Northumbrian Church was held there to discuss church discipline, followed by two more meetings in AD 798 and AD 810. It reappears in history in 1104 as a hermitage of St Godric, who lived there in a simple hut for sixty years and was laid to rest in the stone chapel of St John the Baptist, fragments of which are still extant at Finchale. After his death at the grand old age of 105, Finchale passed to the priors of Durham Cathedral. In 1196, Henry Pudsey, son of the bishop of Durham, established a Benedictine priory on the site, and the new community of Prior Thomas, formerly sacrist at Durham, and eight monks, quickly erected temporary buildings, before embarking on constructing a permanent monastic complex.

Remodelled many times since, the walls of the priory church and those of several other buildings remain standing, making exploration an interesting experience. The church boasts some fine tracery in the choir and the filled-in arches in the nave, as well as heavily decorated capitals on the arcade columns. On the south wall is an outstanding double piscina, alongside two carved seats of the sedilia. Other notable features are a superb stone-vaulted cellar underneath the refectory, the three entrance arches to the Chapter House, and substantial parts of the Prior's Hall.

From the fourteenth century, the priory had four resident monks and a prior, but the monks of Durham Cathedral used it as a holiday retreat, visiting in groups of four and staying for three weeks at a time. The church was drastically reduced in size and the refectory system appears to have been abandoned in the fifteenth century, when parts were turned into chambers for the visiting monks. According to legend, the Durham monks may have travelled via a secret passage, which was discovered by a blind fiddler in the eighteenth century. The sounds of his fiddle could be heard above ground as he walked through the tunnel with his dog, but the music abruptly stopped when he reached Framwell Bridge over the River Wear. He was never heard or seen again, although his dog was said to have emerged later with a ghostly look on his face. Finchale Priory was suppressed in 1538.

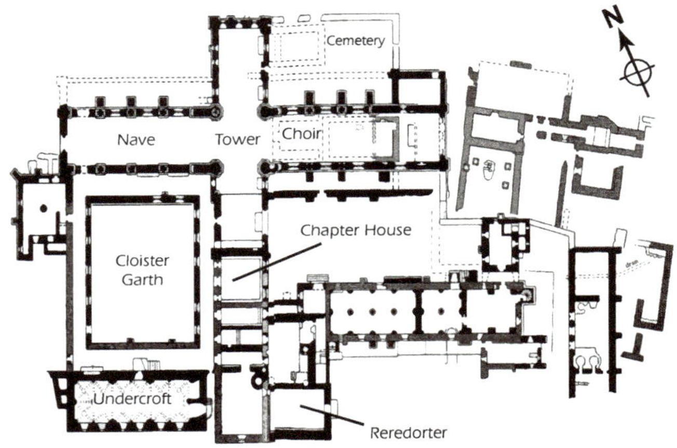

Hartlepool Black Friars

A house for Dominican friars is believed to have been established sometime before 1259, but with no later records, it is likely to have had a short existence.

Hartlepool Grey Friars

-1239-1538

The old walls surrounding the Friarage, a late sixteenth century mansion converted into a hospital in 1867, now known as St Hilda's Hospital, contain many fragments of ancient stonework, which, together with foundations visible between the present house and the Friary Barn, are believed to be from the Franciscan priory founded before 1239. The location of an early Saxon monastery, said to have been founded around AD 640 and destroyed by the Danes in the ninth century, is also thought to have been in the same vicinity at or near St Hilda's Church. Many Saxon and medieval architectural fragments are incorporated within the church. Excavations by the Cleveland County Archaeology Section have shown that the priory had an aisled church, possibly with a central tower, cemetery and well. The church was 57.3m (188ft) long and 15.2m (50ft) wide at its west end. It was founded, probably by Robert de Brus VI, sometime before the first mention of the priory in 1240, when Henry II granted a tunic to each of the friars, but nothing else of note has been recorded of its history. It was dissolved in 1538 and leased out. At the time, the house contained a warden, Richard Threlkeld, and eighteen friars.

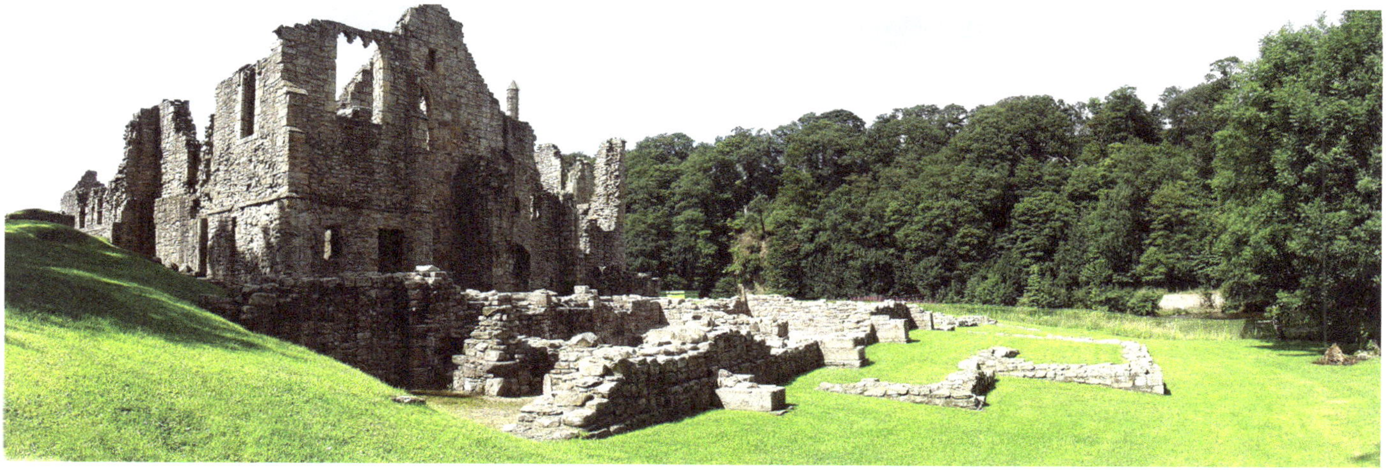

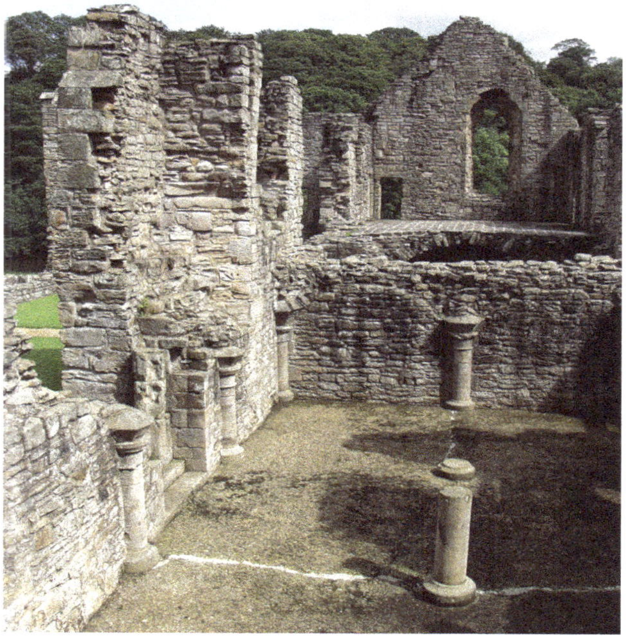

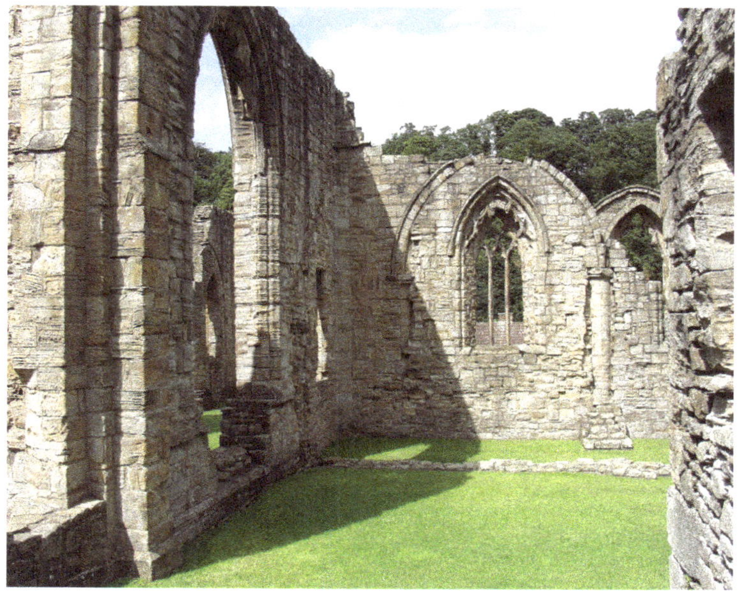

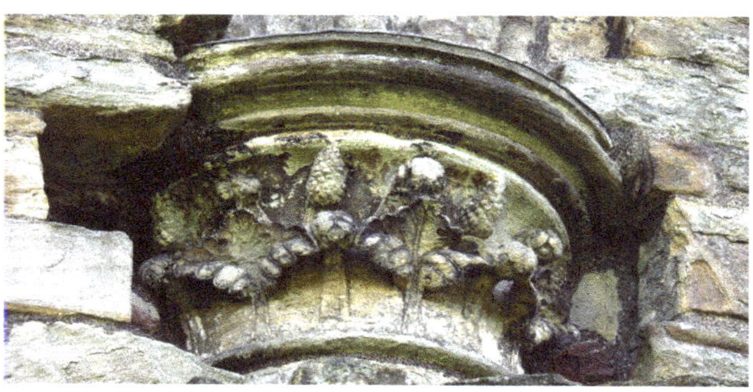

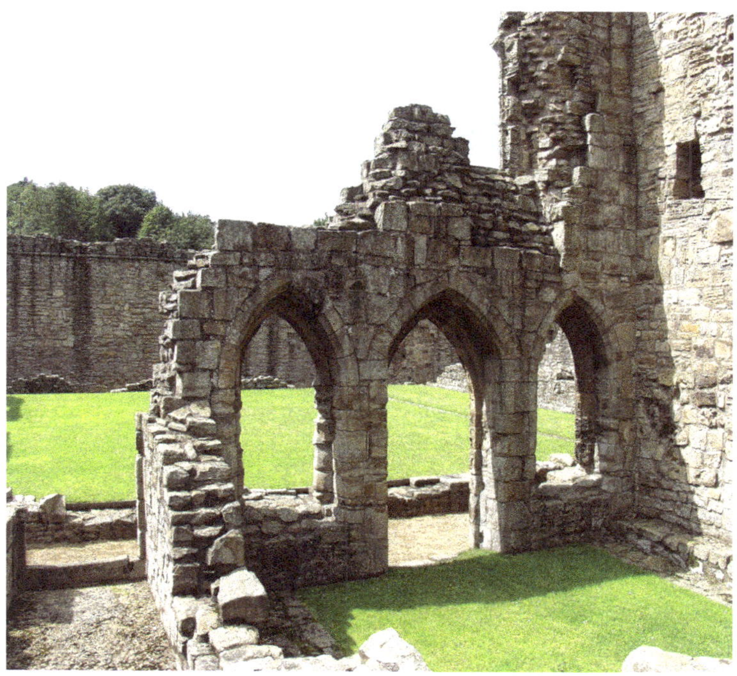

Photos of Finchale Priory – clockwise from top

Priory remains from across the River Wear
Fine traceried window in choir
Chapter house entrance arches
Vine-leaf decoration on column capital
Prior's Hall and camera beyond

Jarrow Priory

St Paul • Benedictine 1074–1536

A monastery dedicated to St Paul was first founded on this site in Jarrow in AD 681 on land between the rivers Tyne and Wear given by King Ecgfrith of Northumbria to Benedict Biscop, Abbot of the nearby St Peter's Monastery in Wearmouth, which he had founded in AD 674. Benedict, later to become known as St Benet, sent Ceolfrith together with ten monks and twelve novices to run the new Benedictine house, which, like Wearmouth, was also built by stonemasons and glaziers from Gaul. Rather than being a separate house from Wearmouth, it was effectively one monastery on two sites and managed as such. St Paul's Church was dedicated in AD 685 and quickly gained a reputation for ecclesiastical learning when the Venerable Bede lived and wrote here at the turn of the eighth century. The remains of this Anglo-Saxon monastery and later medieval buildings now form part of the Bede's World complex, established to celebrate the life of one of Europe's greatest monastic scholars. He is the only Englishman to have been named a Doctor of the Church.

The original church, once a free-standing chapel in the monastery and one of the earliest stone buildings in Northumbria, still survives as the chancel in St Paul's Church, the active parish church of Jarrow. In the wall of the tower, which links two separate Anglo-Saxon churches built with Roman stone, is the oldest surviving dedication stone of any church in England, dating from AD 685. High in the south wall of the church are three small, deeply recessed and tiny windows - round, oval and arched - retaining what is considered among the oldest coloured glass in Europe. The glass in the middle window was made in the monastery's own workshops.

No written accounts have been found detailing the centuries after Bede's death in AD 735, but archaeological evidence suggests that the Danes attacked the monastery, probably in AD 794, leading to a slow decline. It is also possible that sometime later, Scottish raiders attacked and badly burnt the monastery leading to eventual closure. However, a monastery for Benedictine monks was re-founded on the site in 1074 by Aldwin, Prior of Winchcombe, who had travelled north with two monks from Evesham to visit the sites of the Northumbrian saints described by Bede. Walcher, Bishop of Durham, donated both sites on which, according to Symeon of Durham, "the unroofed walls alone were standing, and they exhibited scarce any vestige of their ancient dignity". The monks proceeded to rebuild the monastery to the Benedictine layout and it remained a small cell dependent on Durham Cathedral Priory until it was dissolved by Henry VIII in 1536. The annual net value had been assessed in 1535 at a lowly £38. The monastic estates were sold, but St Paul's Church continued in use as the parish church of Jarrow.

Neasham Priory

St Mary • Benedictine nuns -1156–1540

This priory for Benedictine nuns was the only religious house within County Durham which remained outside the control of the powerful prince-bishops. Situated on the River Tees, the house was founded for eight nuns, probably by an early baron of Greystoke. The foundation date is unknown, but a bull from Pope Adrian IV of 1156-7, confirming the privileges of the monastery, also stated that it was by then already well established. Its grants included land, a mill and churches in County Durham and Yorkshire, and the pope exempted the nuns from paying tithes, but the house was never wealthy.

Its history appears to have been uneventful, but any difficulties encountered were overcome by the bishops of Durham, some of whom were also benefactors. In the fifteenth century there were periods of deterioration of morals, and a gradual ruination of the church, cloisters and other buildings. In 1504, Princess Margaret stopped at the gate of the priory while on her bridal journey to Scotland, but it is not known if she entered. Prioress Jane Lawson and seven nuns surrendered the priory into the King's hands in December 1540. In spite of a net annual income of only £20 17s, the priory had escaped the 1536 closure of the lesser monasteries. The site, church, bell tower and cemetery were granted to her brother, James Lawson. A nineteenth century house, known as Neasham Abbey, now stands on the approximate site of the nunnery, and there are no *in situ* remains. A wall containing a reconstructed Gothic window standing in Darlington town centre is purported to have come from the priory. A large stone carving in the treasury of Durham Cathedral is a more likely remnant from Neasham.

Owton Priory

St Mary

The only record of this house dates from 1204, when King John confirmed the foundation of the Gilbertine Priory of St Mary in Owton or Oveton in Hartness. It is most likely that it was never more than a grange.

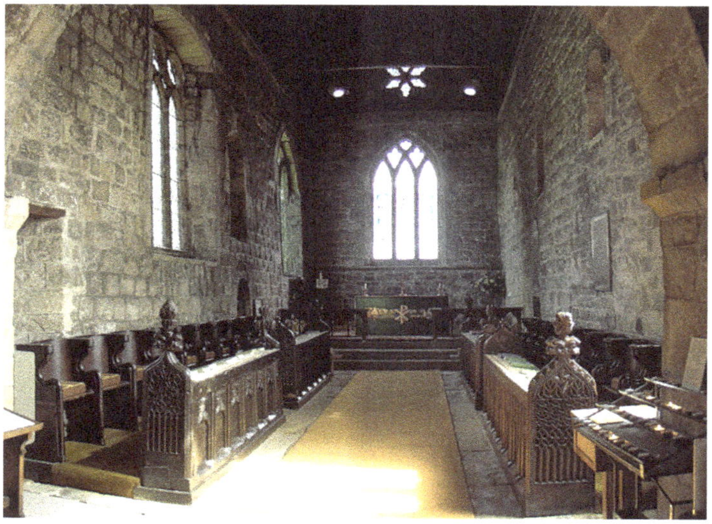

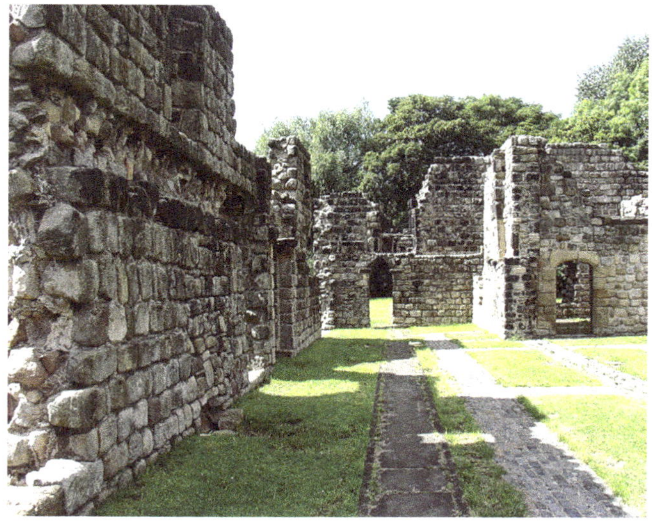

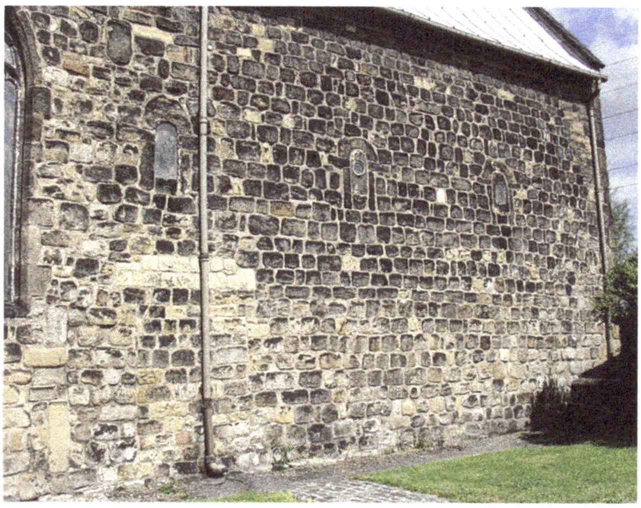

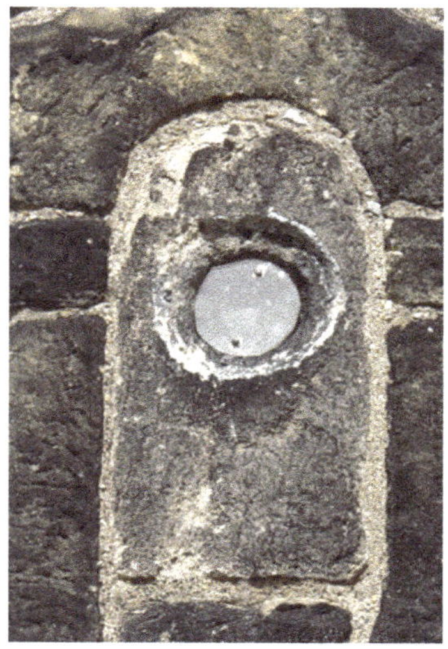

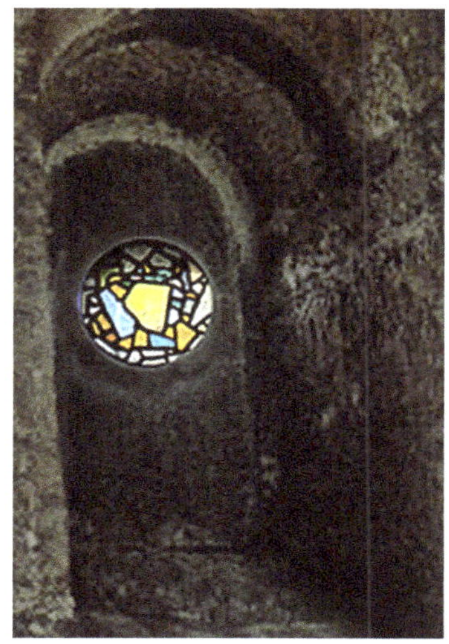

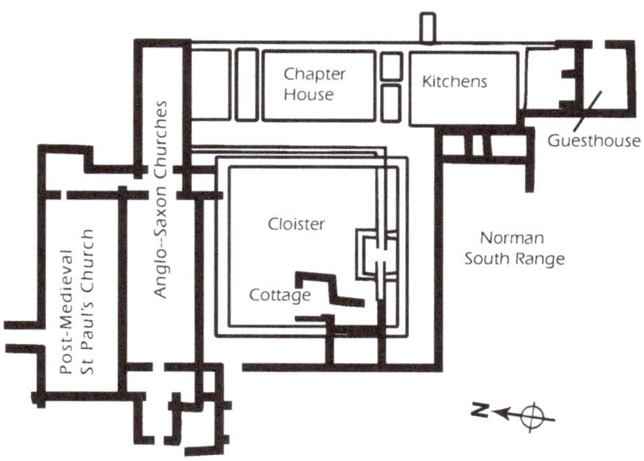

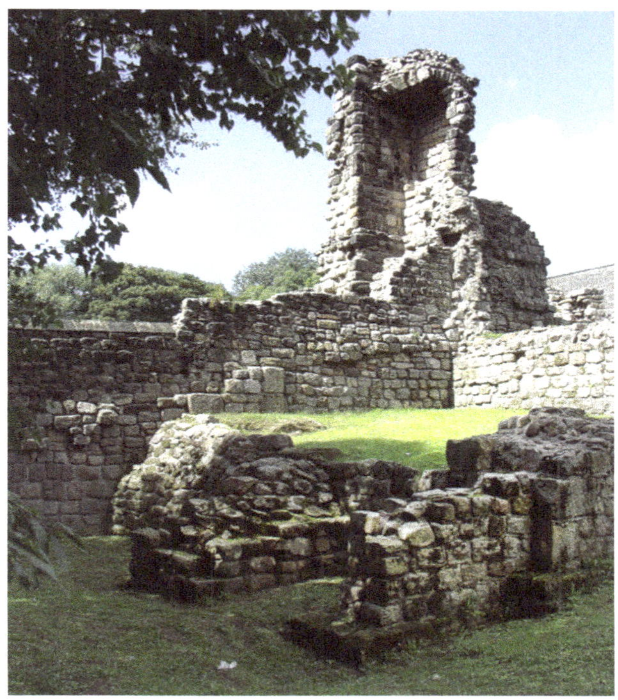

Photos of Jarrow Priory - clockwise from top left

Church of St Paul incorporating Anglo-Saxon structure
View of post-medieval cottage
Round window with Anglo-Saxon glass
Remains of guesthouse
South wall of church with tiny windows
Close-up external view of round window

Wearmouth (Monkwearmouth) Priory

St Peter • Benedictine 1074–1536

In a small green oasis at Monkwearmouth on the north bank of the mouth of the River Wear, in the midst of an industrial area that once was the shipbuilding and coalmining centre, stands the parish church of St Peter, whose largely Saxon tower points ramrod straight to heaven. Although heavily reconstructed in the late nineteenth century, much still remains from its golden age when it formed the heart of the joint Benedictine monastery of Wearmouth-Jarrow. When opening the ancient oak door from the west porch into the church, the realisation that Benedict Biscop, who founded the priory in AD 674, St Ceolfrith and the Venerable Bede, the great teacher, scholar and historian, all walked through this same doorway, is a quite spiritual experience. Unravelling the layers of history is challenging, but a local guide can be of immense value.

Little of the original building remains, but the high west wall and the porch beyond are part of the Saxon monastic church, which was about the width of the main nave, but shorter than the current church. The stonework of the wall has been exposed, but this would have been covered in plaster and paint. High on the wall are two small windows with lathe-turned stone balusters, and the small door above the main door leads into an upper chamber above the porch, whose function is uncertain. The floor is the only modern part of the porch, which otherwise dates from the seventh century and is one of the finest examples of that period. Close inspection of the base of each side of the entrance archway will reveal much weathered Saxon stone carvings of entwined serpents with birds' heads and fish tails. Above are more stone balusters, similar to those in the west wall.

The upper part of the tower was probably added in the eleventh century, when the church and monastery was restored by Aldwin of Winchcombe, but the lower section dates from Saxon times. The broad band of stones above the entrance to the porch was a carved frieze of animals, but time has obliterated any detail. A little higher up on the porch are the badly worn remains of a large statue, which probably represented Christ or St Peter, the patron saint of the church. Also visible are the faint outlines on the stonework of the original roofline of the porch. The effigy of a monk on the north wall is believed to be one of the 'Masters of Wearmouth', who were put in charge of the monastery when it became a cell of Durham in Norman times. Extensive excavations by Professor Rosemary Cramp in the 1960s revealed the remaining structures of the monastery, but these were covered up and only a stone outline indicates their position.

Much of the monastery's early history has been learned from the writings of the Venerable Bede, who entered Wearmouth in AD 680 at the age of only seven and received his education first from Benedict Biscop, and later from Ceolfrith. The three holy men ensured that its reputation as a centre of Christian culture and learning spread throughout Europe and beyond. Benedict Biscop, a Northumbrian nobleman, founded the monastery in AD 674 on land provided by Ecgfrith, King of Northumbria. He brought over stonemasons and glaziers from Gaul, who taught the English the art of making coloured glass, while also adorning the church with painted and turned stone carvings. Biscop also brought many works of art from Europe, adding to the beauty of the monastic church. Upon being gifted more land by Ecgfrith, Biscop founded another monastery at Jarrow, dedicated to St Paul, in AD 681. Rather than being a separate house, it was effectively one monastery on two sites and managed as such.

After his death in AD 689, Benedict Biscop was succeeded by Ceolfrith, under whose abbacy the Anglo-Saxon monasteries grew and flourished for two hundred years. But when Northumbria came under sustained attack from the Danes, both monasteries suffered violence and destruction, most probably in AD 974, leading to a long period of uncertainty, unrest and poverty. Scottish raids added further hardship.

In 1074, Aldwin, Prior of Winchcombe, and two monks from Evesham travelled north to visit the sites of the Northumbrian saints mentioned by Bede, which Symeon of Durham described as "the unroofed walls alone were standing, and they exhibited scarce any vestige of their ancient dignity". The monks began to rebuild the monastery and, although later instructed to abandon their work and return to Durham, St Peter's, like St Paul's at Jarrow, became a Benedictine cell of Durham Cathedral Priory in 1083 and was managed by a master and two or three other monks. The monastic church also served the local community until dissolved by Henry VIII in 1536. Its annual net value had been assessed in 1535 at just £25. The monastic estates were sold, but St Peter's Church continued in use as the parish church of Wearmouth.

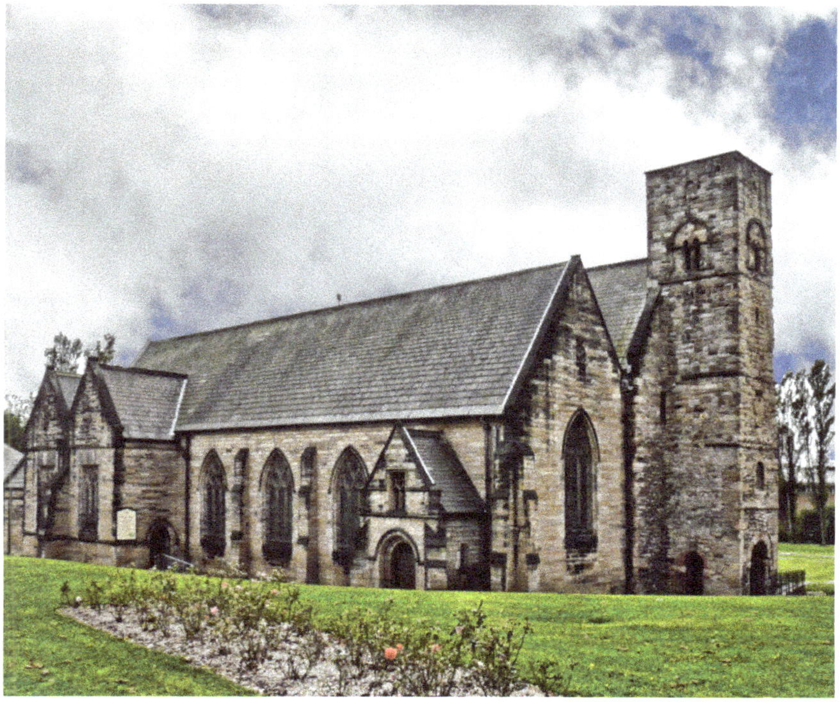

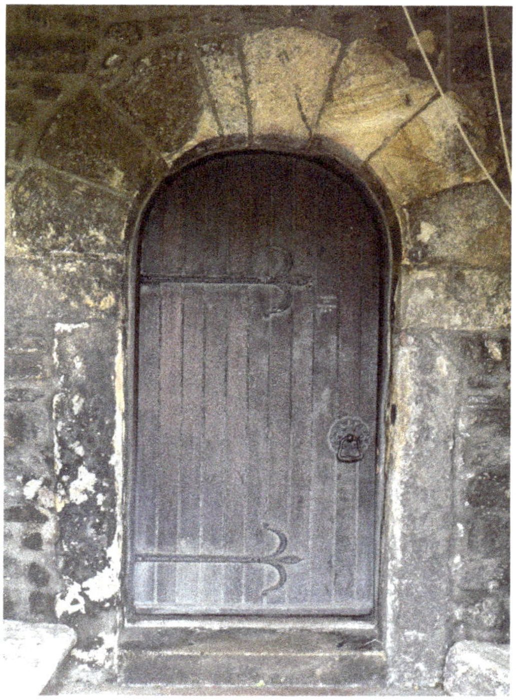

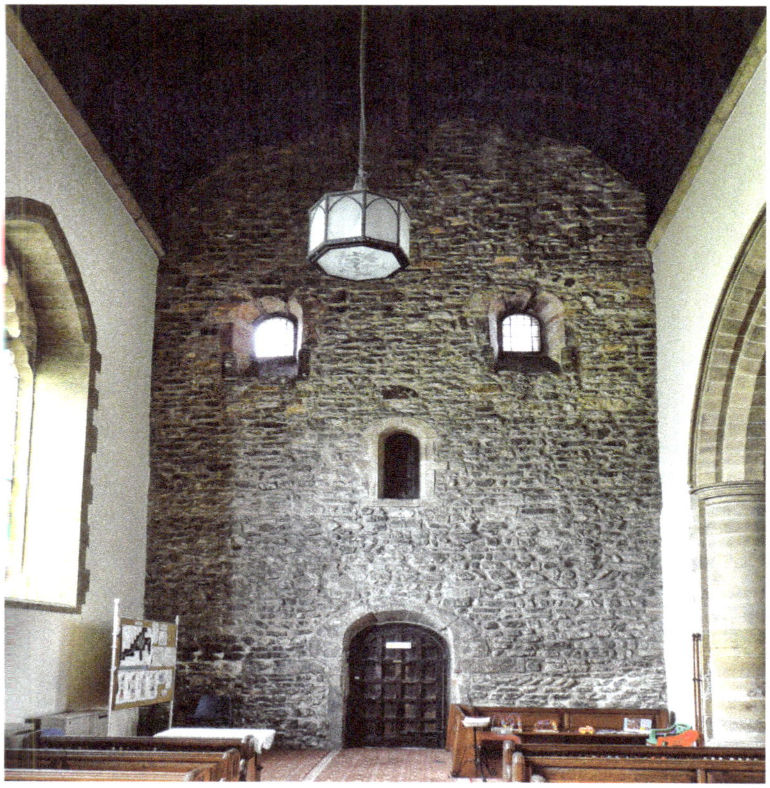

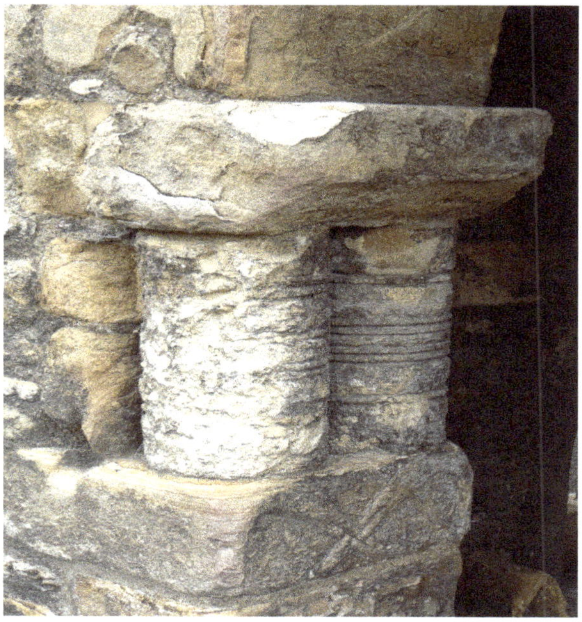

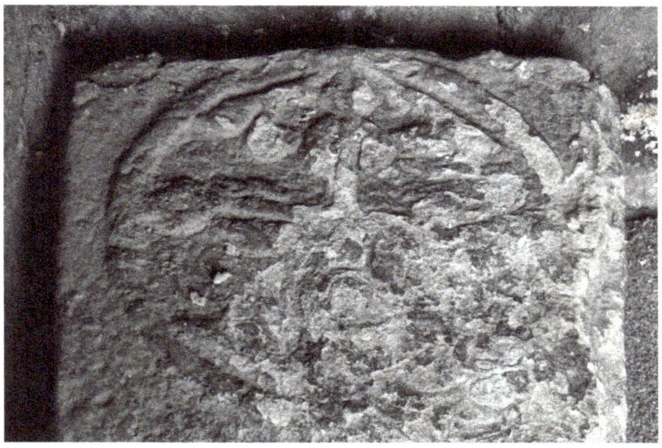

Photos - clockwise from top left

The church of St Peter with its largely Saxon tower
Ancient oak door in the west porch
Exposed Saxon stonework in west porch
Carved gravestone known as the Herebricht Stone
The high west wall was part of the original Saxon church

Lancashire

Entrenched Catholicism

Lancashire, which derives its name from the city of Lancaster, was established in 1182, later than many other counties. During the eighth century, the area was incorporated into the Anglo-Saxon Kingdom of Northumbria. After the Norman Conquest, the lands between the Ribble and the Mersey, together with Amounderness, were given by William I to Roger de Poitou, who also soon acquired Lonsdale, Cartmel and Furness. The county was divided into six hundreds. Its relative isolation and entrenched Catholicism resulted in a vigorous defence of its monastic heritage against the forces of the Reformation.

The most impressive monastic remains are those of Furness Abbey, which wielded much influence in medieval England. It was founded in 1127 as a Savignac house with monks from Tulketh Abbey on the Ribble, which was the first house of the Order in England. Furness became Cistercian when the Savignac Order was absorbed in 1147, and became the second wealthiest Cisterican abbey after Fountains in Yorkshire. Monks from Furness set up the short-lived Wyresdale Abbey towards the close of the twelfth century, but this ceased to exist, when the monks moved to Ireland in 1204. Another Cistercian foundation was that of Whalley Abbey, much of whose history was marked by friction with nearby Sawley Abbey. The principal Benedictine house was Lancaster Priory, established in 1094 by Roger de Poitou as a cell of the Abbey of Saint Martin of Séez in Normandy. It had a chequered history, but the church has survived, although this has undergone major reconstruction. Other Benedictine priories were established at Lytham, Penwortham and Upholland.

William Marshall, later Earl of Pembroke, founded Cartmel Priory for Augustinian canons c1189 and decreed that the parishioners should always have the right to worship in the priory church. This gesture saved the church from destruction. A large, early Victorian mansion stands on the site of Conishead Priory, another Augustinian house. Only part of the tower has survived of the Augustinian priory at Burscough, but not a vestige is left of Cockerham Priory, a cell of the Augustinian abbey of St Mary de Pratis at Leicester.

Premonstratensian canons settled on a bleak and windswept headland overlooking Cockerham Sands, where a small hospital and hermitage were standing in 1184. This later became Cockersand Priory, before being elevated to abbey status. An attractive octagonal chapter house and a few low walls of the church remain. A farm now occupies the site of Hornby Priory, another Premonstratensian foundation. Kersal Priory was a small cell of the Cluniac priory of Lenton in Nottinghamshire. Little is known of a house of Dominican friars in the county town of Lancaster and nothing visible has survived. Austin Friars settled in Warrington before1308 and Franciscans (Grey Friars) in Preston before 1260.

Gazetteer

Burscough Priory Abbey Lane, Burscough, 3km (2miles) NE of Ormskirk, Lancashire (SD 434099). Private; minimal remains

Cartmel Priory In town centre, Cartmel, Grange-over-Sands, Cumbria (SD 379788). Tel: 01539 536261. Web: www.cartmelpriory.org.uk

Cockerham Priory Minor lane, off B5272 Main Street, Cockerham, 10km (6 miles) S of Lancaster, Lancashire. Exact location unknown

Cockersand Abbey On headland, Thurnham, 10km (6 miles) SW of Lancaster, Lancashire (SD 427537). Private

Conishead Priory Off A5087 Priory Road, Ulverston, Cumbria (SD 301761). No visible remains

Furness Abbey Manor Road, off A590, 2.5km (1.5 miles) N of Barrow-in-Furness, Cumbria (SD 218717). English Heritage; Tel: 01229 823420

Hornby Priory Priory Lane, off A683 Melling Road, Hornby, 13km (8 miles) NE of Lancaster, Lancashire (SD 577690). No visible remains

Kersal Priory Off Littleton Road, Salford, Greater Manchester (SD 810015). No visible remains

Lancaster Priory Castle Hill, Lancaster, Lancashire (SD 474620). Church in use; Tel: 01524 63200. Web: www.lancasterpriory.org

Lancaster Black Friars Friar Street, Lancaster, Lancashire (SD 479616). No visible remains

Lytham Priory Lytham Hall, Balham Road, Lytham, Lancashire (SD 357280). No visible remains

Penwortham Priory Priory Crescent, Penwortham, Preston, Lancashire (SD 522288). No visible remains

Preston Grey Friars Near A59 Ring Way, Preston, Lancashire (SD 524295). No visible remains

Tulketh Abbey Tulketh Crescent, Ashton-on-Ribble, Preston, Lancashire (SD 522301). No visible remains

Upholland Priory Church Street,, off A577, Up Holland, 5km (3 miles) E of Sklemersdale, Lancashire (SD 523050). Church in use; Tel: 01695 622938. Web: www.stthomasthemartyr.org.uk

Warrington Austin Friars Friars Lane, Warrington, Lancashire (SJ 606879). No visible remains

Whalley Abbey The Sands, Whalley, off A59, 10km (6 miles) NE of Blackburn, Lancashire (SD 730360). Tel: 01254 828400. Web: www.whalleyabbey.org

Wyresdale Abbey Off Strait Lane, Abbeystead, 11km (7 miles) SE of Lancaster, Lancashire (SD 561542). No visible remains

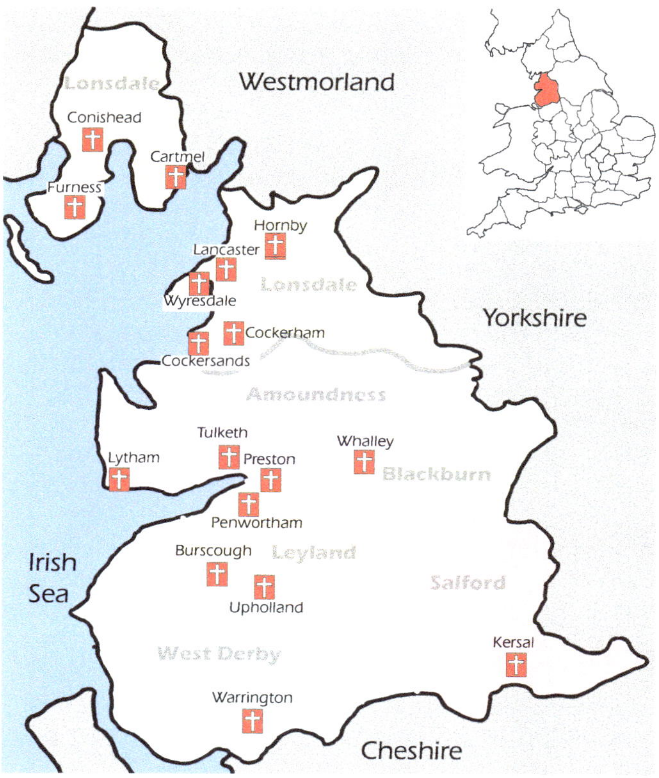

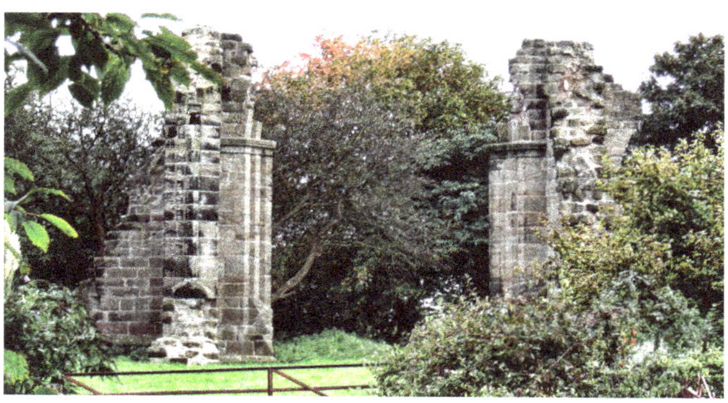

Two clustered pillars from the north arch of Burscough Priory

Burscough Priory

St Nicholas • Augustinian c1189–1536

Travellers on the East Lancashire section of the Lancashire and Yorkshire Railway will have the best view of the sparse ruins of Burscough Priory, a house of Augustinian canons, dedicated to St Nicholas. Situated in a beautiful and fertile valley not far from Martin Mere, which was the largest lake in Britain before being drained, it now stands on private land with no public access. Excavations in 1886 by local antiquarian, James Bromley, uncovered the layout of the priory church, which measured 53.6m (176ft) x 25.6m (84ft) across the transepts. Architectural remains recovered indicated that the church was substantially rebuilt in the Transitional Gothic style early in the thirteenth century and, according to Britton, had a beautiful crossing tower with tall lancets and slender shafts of columns carried in clusters to a great height. The cloister on the south side of the church measured approximately 20.7m (68ft) x 20.7m (68ft). All that is left standing are two clustered pillars of the north arch, which supported the central tower. A portion of the north wall of the chancel is attached to one of the pillars on the eastern side, while to the north of it is part of the east window of the north transept and, at the base, is a canopied recess, in which stood the piscina. The bells of the priory church now hang in Ormskirk Parish Church.

A stone-lined interment with a stone lid decorated with two foliated crosses found near the altar was almost certainly that of the founder of the priory, Robert fitzHenry, Lord of Lathom, who, in c1189, granted the house extensive lands and several churches. Over the next two hundred years, the priors were able to expand their territory and also boost their income from a market and five-day fair at nearby Ormskirk, granted by Edward I and Edmund, Earl of Lancaster, in 1286. The priory became the final resting place of the Lathoms and their successors, the Stanleys, earls of Derby, but no traces remain of any sepulchre. The priory is said to have flourished and generally maintained good order until the mid-fifteenth century, when charges were brought against a prior and one of the canons of divination, sortilege and black art and, somewhat later, another prior was living with a woman in a state of incontinency. In February1536, Prior Hugh Huxley and five canons surrendered the house and subscribed to the King's supremacy. At that time, the priory also maintained forty servants. Its annual value was estimated at £80 7s. The priory site and estate, which included a 'watermill, windmill, dovecote, 100 acres of land with meadow and other lands including 10,000 acres of moors, moss and turbary, with a free fishery in Martin Mere', was given by the Crown in 1547 to Sir William Paget, who sold it back to the Earl of Derby two years later.

Cartmel Priory

St Mary • Augustinian c1189–1537

The cruciform priory church of St Mary and St Michael and the gatehouse are all that has survived from the destruction wrought in the name of Henry VIII, but the church still forms the beating heart of this lovely Cumbrian village of ancient houses, nestling alongside the River Eea. Its stunning location in a wide and verdant valley surrounded by wooded hills probably has changed little since the Augustinian canons first took up residence here more than 800 years ago. The priory church is impressive, both in terms of size and with regard to its craftsmanship, embodying the changing times of monastic architecture from Norman, through Decorated to Perpendicular.

One external feature instantly noticeable is the central bell tower, which sits at a 45-degree angle on top of the original square tower, thought to be unique in England. This arrangement is believed to have been designed to prevent the nave arches from cracking and causing serious damage. In the south wall at the western end of the church is Cromwell's Door. It is pitted with bullet holes, said to have been made when local people shot at Parliamentarian soldiers who were stabling their horses in the nave during the Civil War. The south porch was built in 1626 to protect the main entrance, which dates from about 1200 and comprises several orders of decorated semi-circular arches that spring from three slender columns.

There is also much to admire within, much of which dates back to medieval times. Pride of place must go to the forty-five exquisitely carved misericords, which date from 1440 and are of exceptional quality. Each is different and demands closer inspection, but particularly noteworthy is the depiction of the green man, who is probably associated with the legend of the priory's foundation, the mermaid with twin tails, the elephant and castle, the Holy Trinity, and Alexander the Great flying with the help of eagles. In the south choir aisle stands the traceried chantry chapel with the tomb of Sir John Harrington and his wife, Joan. The building of the chapel between 1327 and 1347, however, has partially destroyed the ornate sedilia, which now comprises only two seats instead of three. Also in the sanctuary is the tomb of William de Walton, one of the earliest priors of Cartmel. The blocked arch in the north wall was the doorway to the night stairs, down which the canons entered the church from their dormitory. Norman dogtooth and chevron patterns can be seen in the archway of the piper choir, the oldest part of the priory church.

The fortified gatehouse on the edge of the market square was built, along with a precinct wall, between 1330 and 1340, primarily to protect the priory precinct following raids by Robert the Bruce. There would have been a guardroom on the east side and a porter's lodge on the west. The Great Room on the first floor was the manor court, which dealt with disputes over land owned by the priory. After the Dissolution, it became the village grammar school.

Cartmel Priory was founded c1189 by William Marshall, Baron of Cartmel and afterwards first Earl of Pembroke, who endowed the house with the whole district of Cartmel, granted to him out of the demesne of the Honour of Lancaster by Henry II. William later became an advisor to King John at the signing of Magna Carta and was Regent of England after the King's death in 1216. The first community at Cartmel comprised a prior and twelve Augustinian canons who came from Bradenstoke Priory in Wiltshire, where William's father was buried. From the outset, William decreed that the parishioners should always have the right to worship in part of the priory, and it was this gesture that saved the priory church from complete destruction 350 years later. The canons later acquired some of William's Irish estates, which brought them into conflict with the Augustinian canons of St Thomas' Abbey in Dublin. An interesting duty of the priory was to provide guides for those crossing the Cartmel Sands on the west of the peninsula and the Kent Sands on the east side. The 'Conductor of the King's people over Cartmel Sands' was paid £6 a year.

Some structural damage to the church in the fifteenth century resulted in extensive reconstruction work from 1440. This included the replacement of the lancets at the east end with one huge window, which still retains some medieval stained glass, the carving of the misericords and the extension of the bell tower. There are great gaps in the recorded history of the priory, but there appears to have been little untoward, although priors were accused from time to time of depravity, mismanagement and incontinence. The priory was surrendered by the last prior, Richard Preston, in autumn 1536. The canons were later re-instated during the Pilgrimage of Grace, but were unable to halt the final suppression in 1537. The prior, meanwhile, had fled to the King's forces. The priory's annual value assessed the previous year was £88.16s. There were strong objections to the Dissolution and when four canons, including the sub-prior, and ten husbandmen from Cartmel tried to stop the King's commissioners from removing the corn from the priory's barns, they were summarily executed. The lead was stripped from the roofs of the cloister walks and other buildings, but the church was saved for the parish. The priory was granted to Thomas Holcroft in 1540, and its Irish manor of Kilrush to Thomas, Earl of Ormond, in 1558. Cartmel Priory languished in poor repair for eighty years until George Preston began to restore the church. The Preston memorial with the family coat of arms is located in the nave of the church

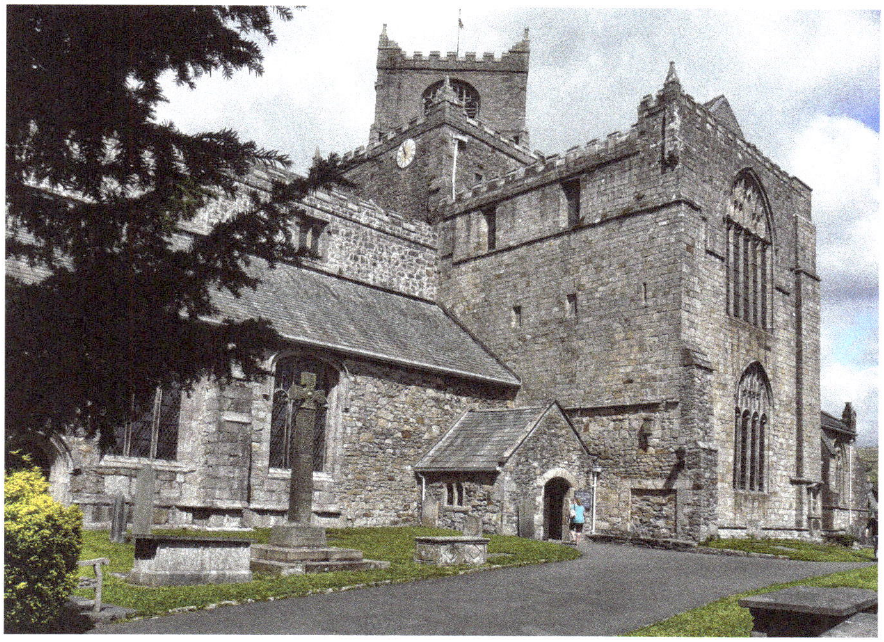

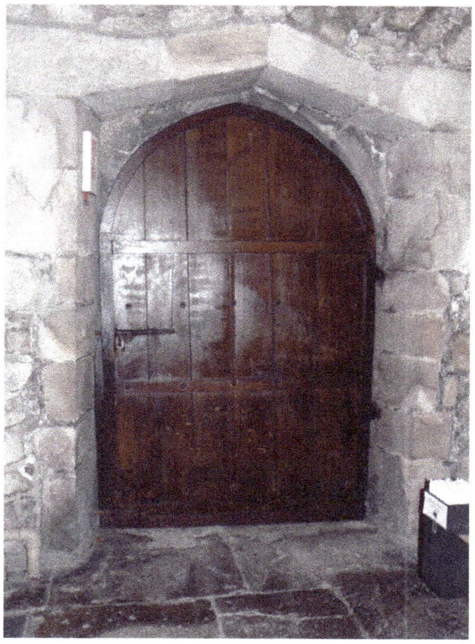

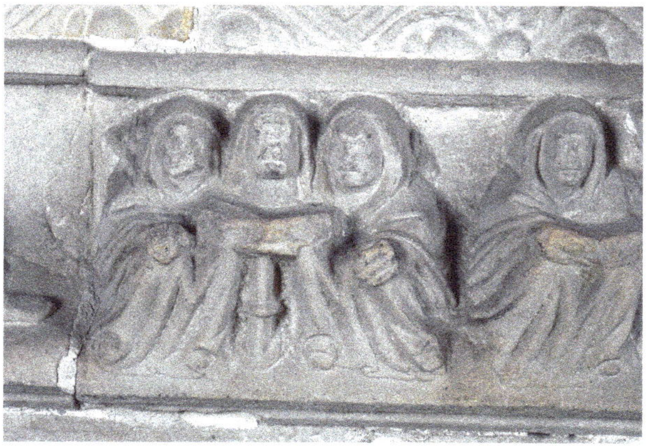

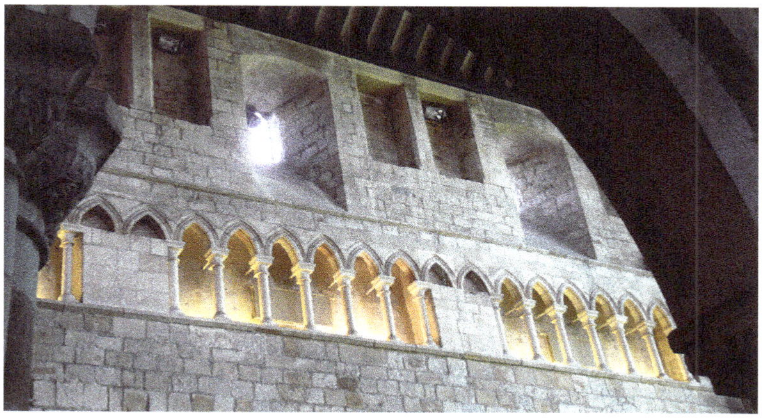

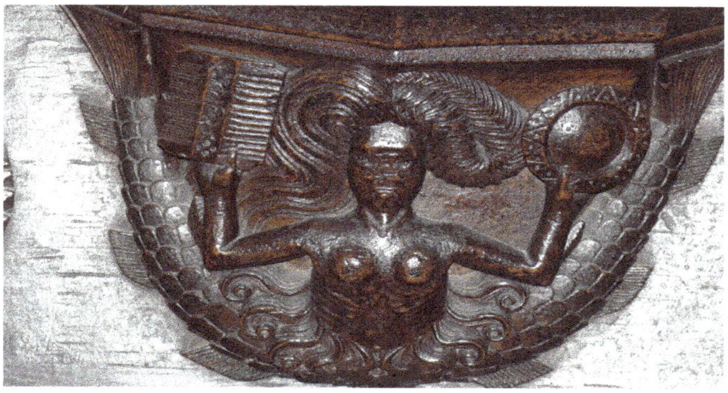

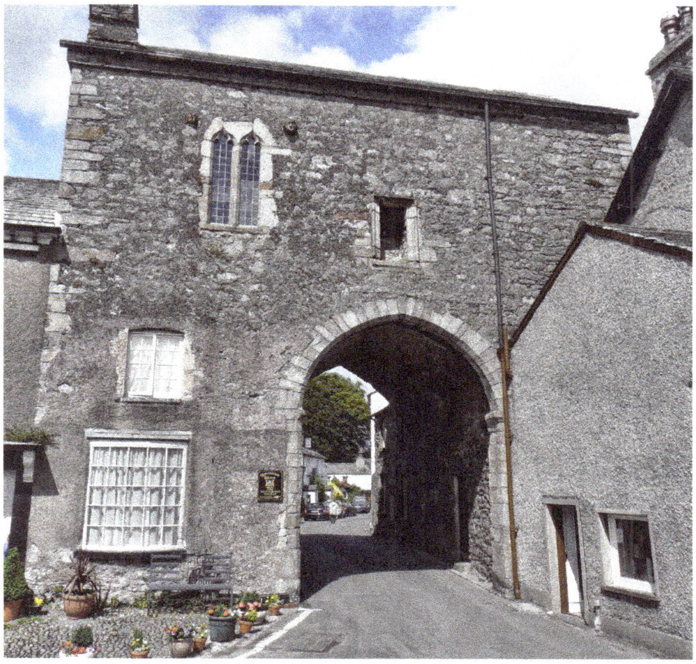

Photos – clockwise from top left

Cruciform priory church and angled central tower
Cromwell's Door
Arcaded triforium
Priory gatehouse in town square
Medieval misericord of lady with mirror and comb
Carving of figures on Harrington memorial

Cockerham Priory

St Mary de Pratis • Augustinian 1207–1477

Not a vestige is left of this priory cell of the Augustinian abbey of St Mary de Pratis (St Mary in the Meadows) at Leicester, which had been given the church and manor of Cockerham by William de Lancaster between 1153 and 1156. The cell appears to have come into being in 1207 or 1208, after a long-running dispute over the division of the manor between the Abbey of Leicester and the monastic hospital (later abbey) at Cockersand, which was founded on part of the manor lands. Only three or four canons were present at Cockerham, but after 1334, there appears to have been a canon warden only, who managed the Lancashire estates. The Black Death in 1349 is said to have halved the income, which probably never fully recovered. In 1477, the estate, then valued at £99 10s, was leased out to one John Calvert. It has been conjectured that the present heavily reconstructed parish church of St Michael, commonly known as the Church in the Fields, originated as the priory church, with the west tower dating from c1400.

Cockersand Abbey

St Mary • Premonstratensian -1184–1539

On an exposed and often bleak and windswept headland, overlooking Cockerham Sands between the estuaries of the Rivers Lune and Cocker, next to a farmstead, stands a rather attractive octagonal building with Gothic windows, a modern embattled parapet and three-stage buttresses on the east side. It looks rather forlorn and out of place, but is a welcome discovery in a surprising location. The only drawback is that it is on private land with no public access, although a fair view of it can be had from the distant lane. The much restored building of local red sandstone was the chapter house of the former abbey of Cockersand and, together with a few crumbling low walls of the church nave and the north and south transepts, is all that has survived from this house of Premonstratensian canons. The chapter house is a good example of thirteenth century work. It measures 8.4m (28ft) across internally, with a vaulted roof carried on a central shafted pillar. Blind arcading on the west side matches the windows opposite to provide a unified design all around. The pointed arches are of three moulded orders and hood mould, springing from angle shafts, with moulded capitals and bases. Of note is a trefoiled inner arch on the west side. The nineteenth century slated roof is surmounted by a cross. The building is rectangular on the external western face, and the wide round-headed doorway has been partially restored with modern stonework. From the mid-eighteenth century to about 1861, the chapter house was used as the family mausoleum of the Daltons of Thurnham Hall.

Cockersand Abbey started life before 1184 as the small hospital of St Mary de Marisco (St Mary of the Marsh), with local hermit Hugh (Garth) becoming its first master. It was established on land given by William de Lancaster, second Baron of Kendal. More fertile land in the adjoining township of Thurnham was added by William de Furness, Lord of Thurnham, from 1186. The canons came from Croxton Abbey in Leicestershire. In 1190, Pope Clement III took the hospital under his protection and conferred privileges that would suggest its acceptance as a fully established priory. In the midst of disputes over boundaries, tithes and pasture with Leicester Abbey on whose lands it was situated, the priory was elevated to abbey status sometime after 1192, but also continued as a hospital. King John bestowed favours on the abbey, which also benefited from a large number of grants, although most of these were small. The sea continuously threatened to wash away the walls that protected the abbey buildings and internal harmony was damaged with indiscipline, disobedience and violence, as well as several other minor disorders. On the positive side, ten poor men were provided with bed and board on a daily basis. In 1535, the net value of the abbey was assessed at £157 14s, but in 1536, the King's commissioners raised this to £282 7s, which ensured its survival for another few years. In January 1539, the house was surrendered by Abbot Robert Poulton and twenty-one canons, all of whom received pensions. John Kitchen, of Hatfield, Hertfordshire, who farmed the site after the Dissolution, bought it from the Crown in 1543. Upon the marriage of his eldest daughter Anne to Robert Dalton of Thurnham Hall, it passed to that family.

Conishead Priory

St Mary • Augustinian 1188–1536

A large early Victorian Gothic revival building now stands on the site of a twelfth century Augustinian priory, originally founded in 1167 by Gamelda Pennington as a hospital for the 'poor, decrepit, indigent and lepers' of the Ulverston area. The foundation was also claimed by William de Lancaster II, Baron of Kendal. In 1188, the hospital was raised to priory status, dedicated to the Virgin Mary. One of her girdles was kept at Conishead as a holy relic. The new status encouraged further endowments of land, cattle, tithes and fishing rights and the canons also became actively involved in the Furness iron industry, which boosted its income, but also brought the priory into conflict with the monks of nearby Furness Abbey. This 150-year rivalry between the two religious houses was finally settled in 1338, when Edward II confirmed all the grants by bestowing a royal charter on Conishead. In 1316, the priory had suffered greatly during the Scottish invasion. In 1525, it was threatened with suppression, as Cardinal Wolsey was encouraged to take it into the King's hands for his new college at Oxford. The priory survived following intervention by the Duke of Suffolk, but was finally dissolved in 1536, in spite of strong local opposition, having been valued at £97, well below the £200 threshold for the closure of the lesser monasteries. Present in the house at the Dissolution were Prior Thomas Lord, eight canons and an ex-prior. In 1540, the estate was granted to William Stanley, Lord Monteagle, but came into the hands of Sir William Paget.

Some of the stone was used to restore the tower of Ulverston's parish church of St Mary, and the remainder for the building of a large country house, since replaced by a Victorian Gothic-style house. Recent excavations of the site have discovered that the main church stood on the site of the present south lawn. It was a small cruciform structure with nominal transepts and a nave about 30m (100ft) long. The hospital, almshouses and domestic buildings occupied the same site as the present house. Carved sandstone blocks from the medieval chapter house can still be seen in the south wall of the present building.

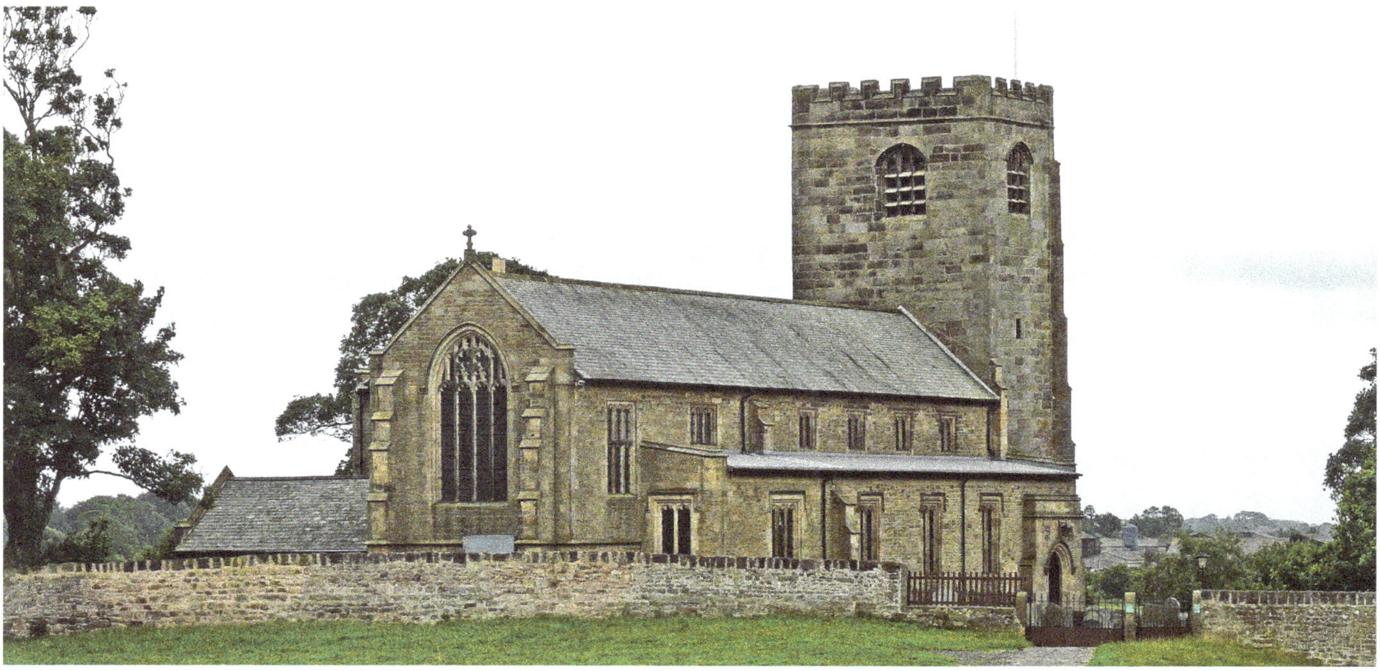

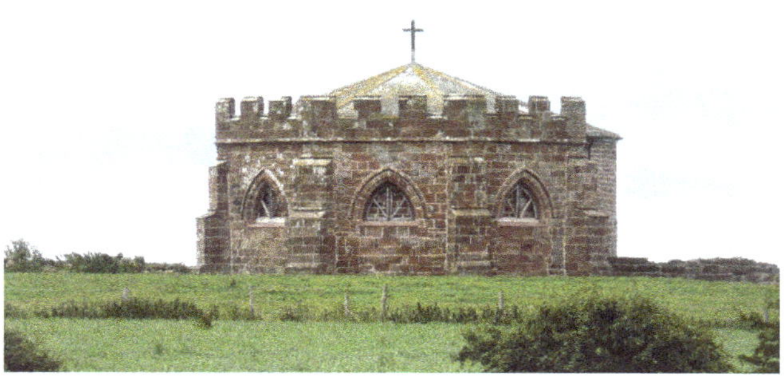

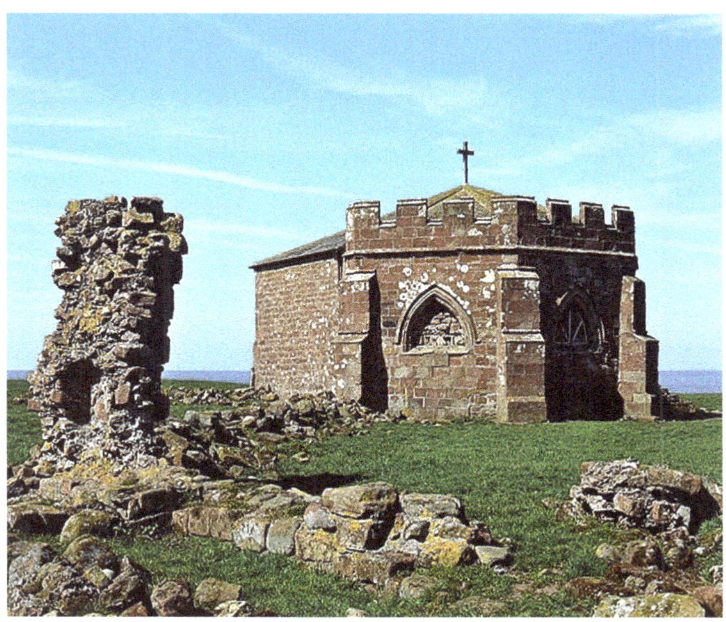

Photos - clockwise from top

The parish church of St Michael at Cockerham is said to have been reconstructed around the former priory church, with the tower dating from early in the fifteenth century

The Cockersand chapter house with ruined masonry of the abbey church

Chapter house from the north-east

Furness Abbey

St. Mary • Savignac/Cistercian 1127–1537

On the peninsula that stretches out into the sandy seas of Morecambe Bay stand the substantial warm red sandstone ruins of Furness Abbey. Nestling in the depths of a once remote valley, known a long time ago as Benkansgill, or Valley of the Deadly Nightshade, the extensive remains with their intricate design features still make a powerful statement about the wealth and influence the abbey wielded in medieval England. But, alongside the material expressions, the ruined buildings of Furness Abbey also retain a spiritual atmosphere, which transcends the centuries of destruction and strife. When the first colony of monks arrived in this secluded valley in 1127, they came from Tulketh on the Ribble, where Ewan d'Avranches from Savigny established a monastery on land given by Stephen, Count of Blois, who was later to become King of England. The new site included large areas of forests, pastures, fisheries and mills, with a share in the salt works and mines, which enabled Furness to grow rapidly, and to send forth monks to found other abbeys in England, as early as 1134. It also developed close relations with the Isle of Man and Irish abbeys.

In 1147, Furness Abbey was absorbed into the Cistercian order, but only after some considerable resistance from Peter of York, the fourth abbot of Furness. Further grants from King Stephen and later benefactors helped the abbey to achieve much power and influence, becoming the second richest Cistercian abbey after Fountains. Apart from owning almost the entire peninsula, it had accumulated lands and possessions in numerous counties of England. The abbey owned ships and developed a harbour on Walney Island, to promote its trade in wool and iron ore, or in smelted iron from its own furnaces. The monks were also actively engaged in smuggling and built a castle on Piel Island for protection, not only against pirates, but also to keep out the King's customs men. A fourteenth century Pele Tower at nearby Dalton was used as an administrative centre and court house.

Raids by the Scots in 1316 and 1322, famine and the Black Death, which robbed the abbey of many lay-brothers, led to a slow decline. Simmering disputes between Furness Abbey and surrounding landowners also began to surface and blighted its relatively peaceful existence. The abbey also had obligations, being required to furnish soldiers to the King at times of need. Such a contingent of 'Furness men' was engaged in the Battle of Flodden in 1513. Being implicated in the Pilgrimage of Grace rebellion, the abbey became the first of the larger houses to fall. In 1537, Abbot Roger Pyle was forced to choose between death and surrender and he duly signed Furness and all its possessions to the King, because of the "misorder and evil lives, both unto God and our prince, of the brethren of the said monastery". Shortly afterwards, the hammer and axe were taken to the buildings, which were further diminished by local plundering, especially of the sculpted stonework. Its annual income had been assessed at more than £805.

Given the scale of the destruction, it is quite surprising that so much has survived. The substantial remains of the church date from the thirteenth century, when the original Savignac church was enlarged. The perpendicular tower at the west end was built within the late Norman aisled nave, which was 57m (160ft) long and 20m (65ft) wide but has now largely disappeared. The 39m (129ft) wide transepts and the chancel, however, are more or less complete, having been rebuilt in the fifteenth century. The presbytery has some wonderful sedilia, crowned by intricately carved canopies. Five stunning Norman arches on the eastern edge of the cloister have been preserved, the largest in the centre leading into the chapter house. Unfortunately, this is now without its vaulted ceiling, twin lancet windows and polished dark marble offset by lime-washed walls. Little survives of the south and west ranges, except the small infirmary chapel, which is complete with vaulting, circular wall benches, window tracery and the remains of an elaborate piscina. There is a legend that when the monks arrived at the Valley of the Deadly Nightshade, the poison of the plants was rendered harmless.

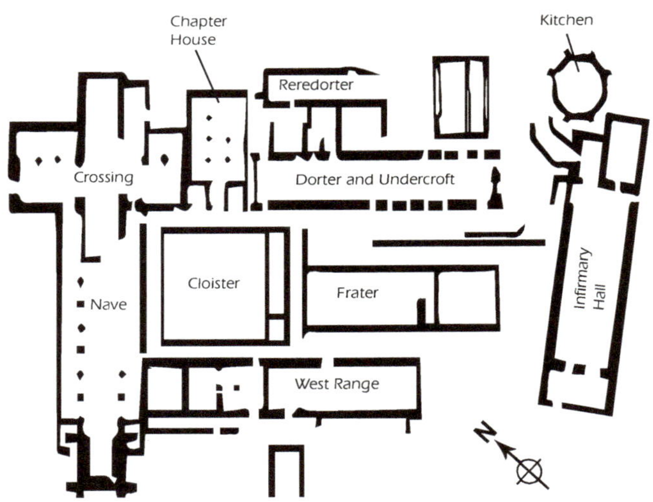

Photos – clockwise from top

The abbey reposing serenely in the Valley of the Deadly Nightshade
The tall crossing piers and walls continuing to defy gravity
Attractive ornamentation found at many locations in the abbey
Entrance arches to the chapter house
Buttery and chapel standing almost complete

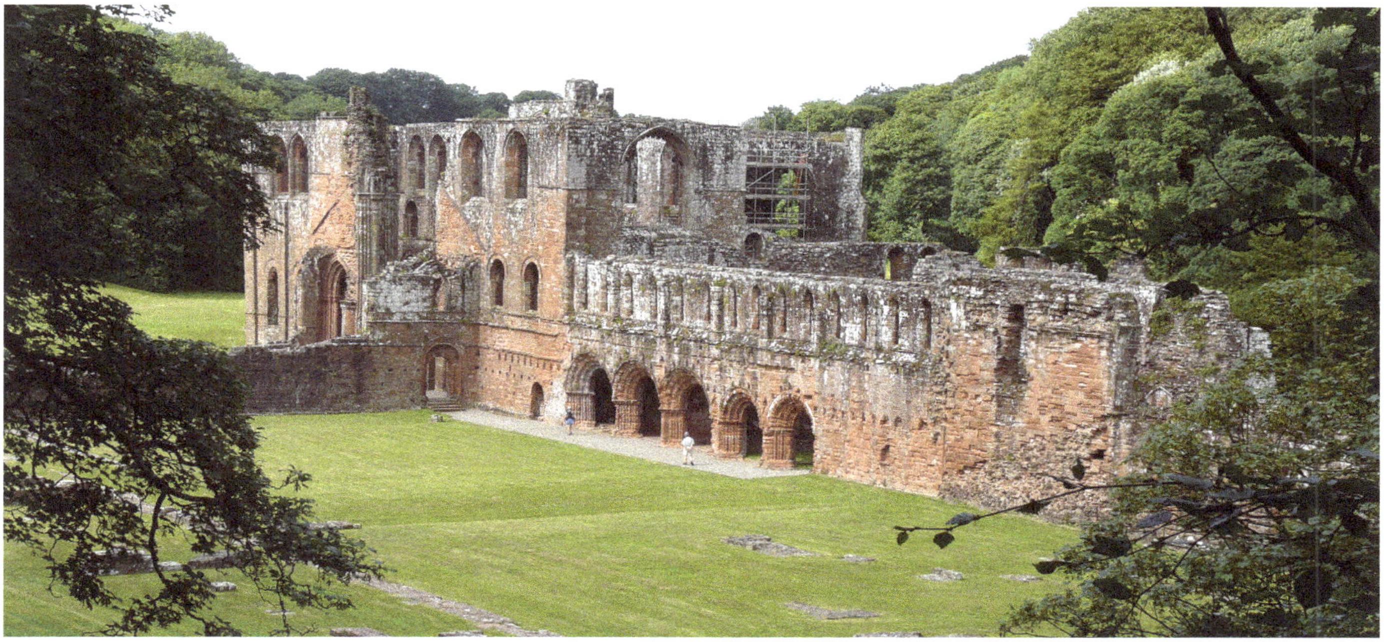

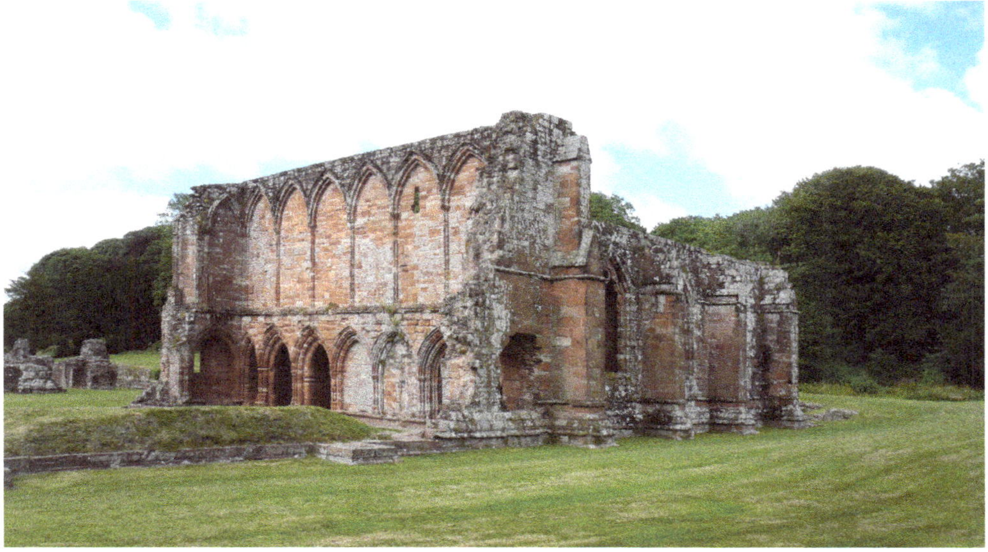

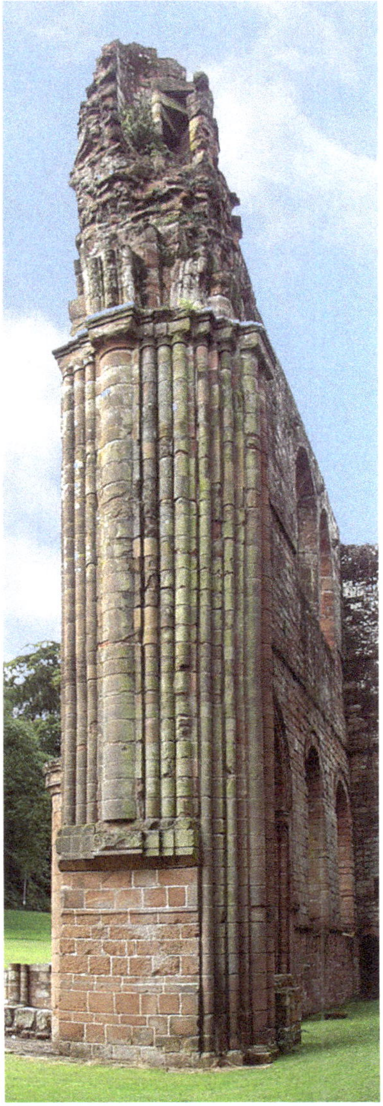

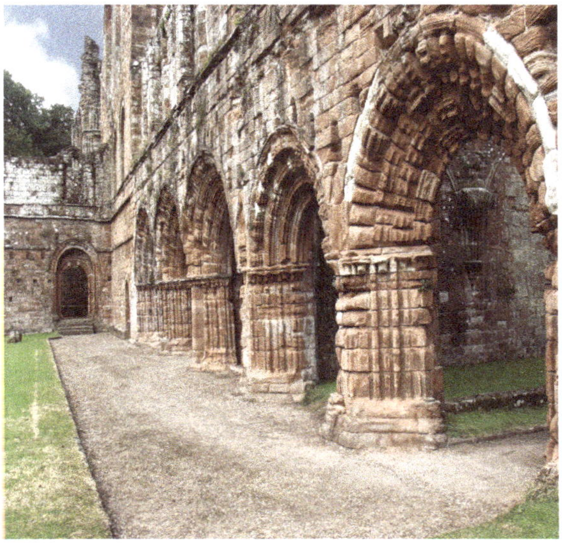

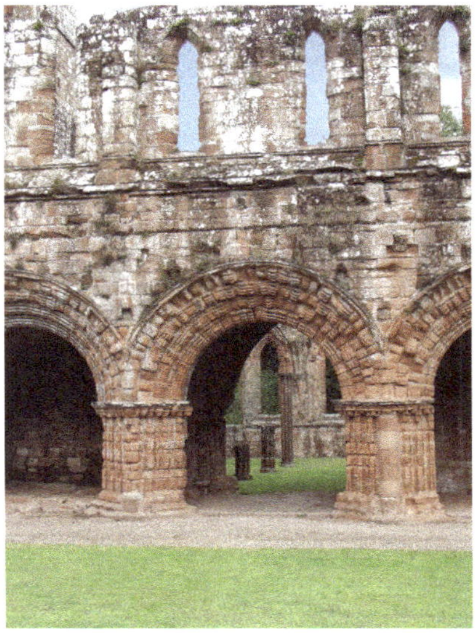

Hornby Priory

St Wilfrid • Premonstratensian -1200–1538

A farm now occupies the site of this small house of Premonstratensian canons, founded in the second half of the twelfth century. The founder was probably Roger de Montbegon III, who gave the canons in alms 100 acres of land, but his father Adam, or his grandfather Roger II, have also been suggested. The canons came from Croxton Abbey in Leicestershire, of which the priory was a dependent cell. It may originally have been a hospital. Very little of its history has been recorded, the only events that apparently disturbed life at the community were a dispute over the advowson of Melling between the prior and Countess Margaret de Burgh in 1246, and in 1292, when the prior sued for lands at Wrayton. The priory was separately surrendered in February 1536 by Prior William Halliday and two canons, but this was cancelled and the final dissolution was made with Croxton in September 1538, the surrender being signed by Prior John Consyll and two canons. The site was acquired in 1544 by Thomas Stanley, second Lord Monteagle.

Kersal Priory

St Leonard • Cluniac 1143/1153–1538

This small cell of the Cluniac priory of Lenton in Nottinghamshire was founded between 1143 and 1153 by Ranulf de Gernon, fourth Earl of Chester, who granted the hamlet of Kersal, together with rights of fishery in the Irwell and pasture. Between 1174 and 1176, Henry II regranted the priory to Lenton and was described in his charter as a hermitage. Apart from a mention of a dispute with the rector of Manchester over the burial of parishioners at Kersal, the history of the cell is blank. Only one prior, John of Ingleby, who held the post in 1332, is known, and there was probably only one monk in residence beside the prior. As all Cluniac houses in Britain were considered as alien, Kersal was temporarily seized by the Crown in c1371, but, together with Lenton, was made denizen by Richard II in 1392-3. The income of the priory in 1535 was a mere £9 6s, but it survived the closure of the smaller monasteries in 1536 and was dissolved with Lenton in April 1538. Nothing has survived.

Lancaster Priory

St Mary • Benedictine 1094–1414

The Priory Church of St Mary and the nearby castle, standing within the Roman fortifications high above the River Lune, are potent reminders of the historical significance and importance of the ancient county town. Although the church underwent a major reconstruction in Perpendicular style in the fifteenth century, much of medieval interest remains, not least the magnificent carved choir stalls of oak, the third–oldest in England dating from 1340. That the canopies are, as Pevsner describes them, "about the most luxuriant canopies in the country", is indisputable. The embroidered panels behind the stalls are modern. Also survived have fourteen finely carved medieval misericords, although many were mutilated during the Civil War. The carvings depict, among others, a winged figure with feathers and a bird's claw on the left bearing a shield, and on the right another with headdress and beast haunches. The faces are mutilated. Another, highly detailed tableau probably represents a baptism, with two kneeling figures, male and female, facing a font, and two praying nuns to the left and three other figures, two females with a man between them, to the right. On display near the south-west door is a replica of an Anglian Runic Cross, which was discovered in the churchyard in 1807. The original is now in the British Museum. Built of sandstone, the aisled church comprises a four-bay nave and four-bay chancel with a clerestory under a continuous roof, a south porch, and a four-stage west tower, the last-named dating from 1753. The original tower was considered unsafe and dangerous and was demolished.

A church stood on the site from about AD 630, of which a Saxon doorway has survived, but in 1094, Roger de Poitou established a Benedictine priory as a cell of the Abbey of Saint Martin of Séez in Normandy. Roger's liberal endowments included almost all of his demesne lands in the county, together with hunting, pannage and fishing, as well as many churches, although several of these were soon lost. The dependency on the abbot of Séez was at first close, but after the loss of Normandy, the Crown asserted control over the appointment and removal of the priors. The priory's history was often marred by disputes and litigation over land, tithes and other rights, especially with the houses at Furness and Cockersand, as well as with the town. Heavy taxes as a result of the wars with France greatly affected the life of the community, and in 1397, Richard II granted custody of the house to Cockersand Abbey. In 1414, however, when Henry V seized all alien monasteries, Lancaster was assigned to the King's new Bridgettine foundation of Syon. Although the nuns later leased out the priory and its estates, the abbess and convent retained a chamber and stable as a lodging. On the dissolution of Syon Abbey in 1540, 'the late priory of Lancaster' was valued at £216 13s. In 1557, the Crown sold the possessions to Robert Dalton of Bispham.

Lancaster Black Friars

c1260–1539

Little is known of this house of Dominican friars and nothing visible has survived. It was founded about 1260 by Sir Hugh Harrington and, in 1291, the archbishop of York instructed three friars to preach the Crusade on Holy Cross Day, one at Lancaster, another in Kendal, and the third in Lonsdale. Land was granted in 1311 for the enlargement of the site. The house was surrendered in 1539 and, together with the priories of Preston and Warrington, was sold by the Crown to royal servant Thomas Holcroft in June 1540.

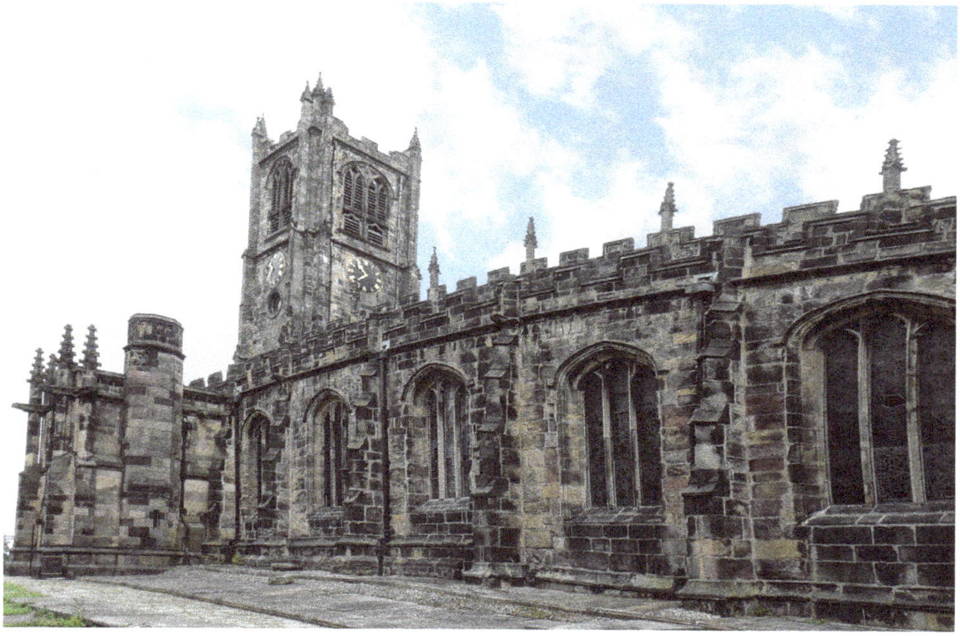

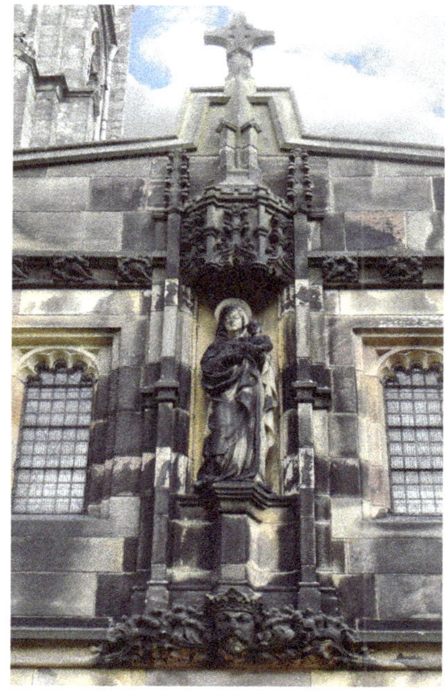

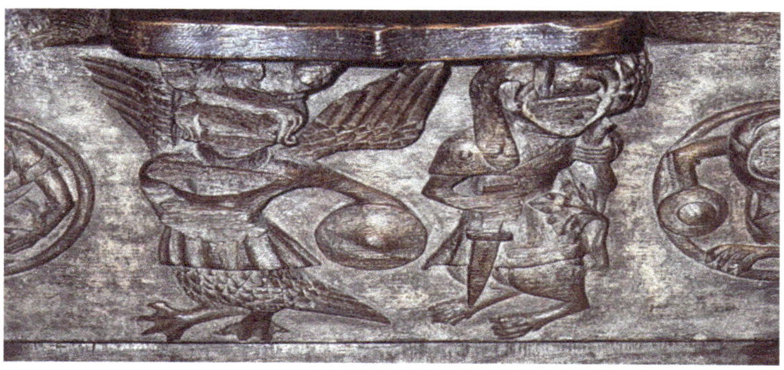

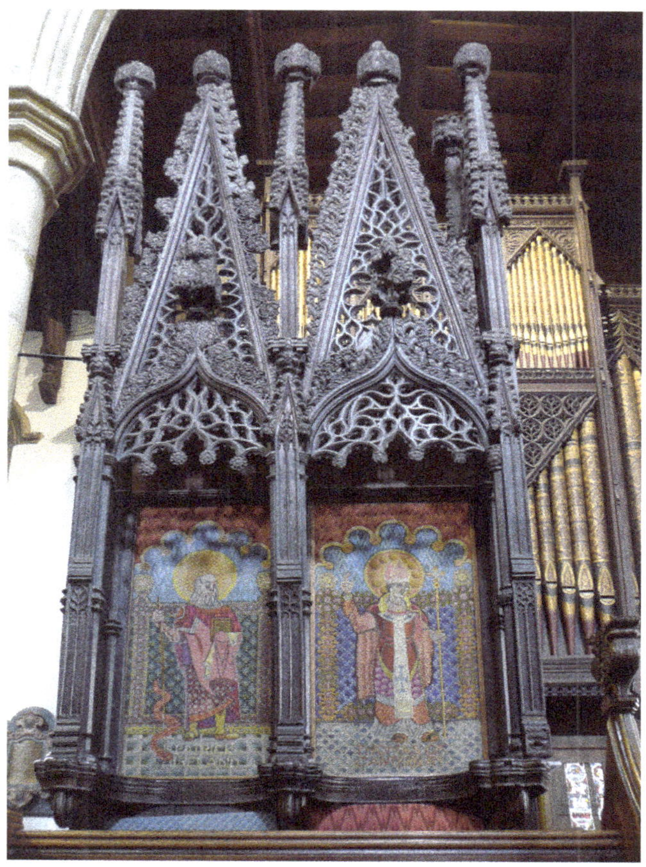

Photos of Lancaster Priory – clockwise from top left

Lancster Priory Church of St Mary
Statue of the patron saint with the infant Jesus
The luxuriant canopies of the choir stalls
Carved and highly detailed medieval misericords

Lytham Priory

St Mary & St Cuthbert • Benedictine 1190–1535

Lytham Hall, built between 1757 and 1764, now stands on the site of this small priory cell, founded in 1190, when a local knight, Richard fitzRoger, donated his manor at Lytham to the Benedictine monks of St Cuthbert of Durham. The founder is said to have experienced two miracles ascribed to St Cuthbert, resulting in his recovery and that of his son, both from serious illnesses, and had travelled to Durham where the saint was enshrined, to give thanks. Small parcels of land and the church of Appleby were later added to the endowments. The small number of monks, probably never more than three or four, supported themselves by farming. However, life at any time in their history was never peaceful. In 1243, the right of Durham Priory to the cell of Lytham was disputed by the abbot of Evesham, who eventually withdrew his claim upon payment of thirty marks. Disputed rights of pasture brought the monks into conflict with cantankerous neighbours, who expressed their hostility in acts of violence. These included an assault on the prior at Lytham Mill and threats to 'dowke' him in the sea, the theft of cattle by 200 armed raiders led by Sir William Clifton of Westby, and a mass riot by Layton tenants that left its name at Mad Nook. Relations with the mother house were also strained, with Prior Roger of Tynemouth (1316-25) charged by Durham with oppressing the tenants and selling stock to maintain an excessive household. But times were hard for the community, exacerbated by Scottish raids, which severely diminished the temporalities of the house. Between 1535 and 1540, Durham withdrew the monks from Lytham and let the property at a rent of £48 19s. After the Dissolution, the possessions were sold to the ruthless Sir Thomas Holcroft who had already acquired several monastic properties. Every trace of the priory has been obliterated.

Penwortham Priory

St Mary • Benedictine -1140–1535

This small dependent cell to the great Benedictine abbey of Evesham was founded in the reign of King Stephen, not long before 1140, by Warin Bussel, Baron of Penwortham, who gave a township and churches to Evesham, in return for Penwortham church being served by three monks and a chaplain. Further gifts were added by the founder before his death. The house remained totally dependent on Evesham throughout its history, of which little is known. It had no separate property, and had no say in the appointment of prior, who was sometimes given the more lowly title of custos (keeper). One prior stands out from the sparse records, although nothing good has been said about him. Formerly abbot of Canterbury and Evesham, Roger Norris became prior of Pentwortham in 1213 and, over a period of five years of oppression, reduced the monks to penury. His contemporary, Thomas of Marlborough, described him as "a glutton, wine-bibber, and loose-liver", who was able, unscrupulous, courtly in manner and whose eloquence gave him a show of learning. Thrust into Evesham as abbot by Richard I, Thomas continues, "he dissipated its revenues until the monks were reduced to a diet of bread and water, varied occasionally by bread and beer which differed little from water, and for lack of decent clothing many of them could not appear in choir and chapterhouse". It appears that Evesham withdrew its monks between 1535 and 1539, as in the latter year the priory buildings and possessions were leased to John Fleetwood, whose family retained the estate until 1749. A house named Penwortham Priory now stands on the site, but there are no medieval reminders.

Preston Grey Friars

-1260-1539

Nothing has survived from this house of Franciscan Friars who arrived at Preston before 1260, when Henry III granted the friars five oaks in Sydwood, Lancaster, for building on land given by the local Preston family. Edmund, Earl of Lancaster, younger son of Henry III, has been described as the "original and great builder of this house" and has also been credited as the founder. Apart from records of small bequests, and an unsuccessful attempt to wrest the custody of the house from Worcester, nothing is known of its history until the last warden, Thomas Todgill, was accused of having made away with goods in his custody. The record of the verdict has been lost. The house was probably surrendered in 1539, and, together with the priories of Lancaster and Warrington, came into the hands of Sir Thomas Holcroft in June 1540.

Tulketh Abbey

St Mary • Savignac 1124–1127

In 1124, Stephen, then Count of Boulogne and Mortain and Lord of Lancaster, granted to the abbot of Savigny the vill of Tulketh, which became the first Savignac foundation in England. However, after just three years, the community left for the more remote vale of Benkansgill, later to become known as Furness.

Photos of Upholland Priory - clockwise from top

Ancient doorway in priory church
Ruined west wall of dormitory range
Priory church of St Thomas the Martyr

Photos courtesy of John D Barton

Upholland Priory

St Thomas the Martyr • Benedictine 1319–1536

The priory of Upholland was founded in 1319 by Robert de Holland, who gave consent to Bishop Walter de Langton of Lichfield to replace the secular canons of a college established in 1310 with Benedictine monks. The founder re-assigned the small endowments of the college, which included land and two rectories, to the new priory. It is not known where the community of monks came from, and little is known of its history. Edward II stayed at the priory in 1323 and, in 1391, the community became involved in a violent quarrel with a local farmer over tithes. By 1497, the house was in a parlous state, with non-observance of the rule, the church and other building in a poor state of repair or ruinous, and their spiritual and temporal goods dilapidated or dissipated by negligence. To the credit of the community, charity was not altogether neglected and both aged persons and children were cared for. The net annual income of the house in 1535 was £53 3s, which brought it within the 1536 Act of Suppression. The last prior, Peter Preston, who had been described by the King's commissioners as having "exceedingly loose morals", surrendered the house in May 1536. There were then also five monks and twenty-six servants. Like so many of the Lancashire houses, Upholland ended up in the hands of Sir Thomas Holcroft.

The nave of the present parish church was the monastic chancel. No transepts or nave were ever built, but a small bell-tower was added in the fifteenth century. The ruins to the south of the church, now in private grounds, comprise the two-storey west wall of the dormitory range to the east of the cloister. It is approximately 21m (69ft) long, with a row of seven windows in the upper storey. It forms part of an enclosure measuring c19 x 8m (62 x 26ft). A chamber was mentioned in 1546 at the west end of the chancel, the roof corbels of which still remain. L-shaped ruins of an unidentified fourteenth or fifteenth century structure from the priory exist in Church Street. The walls stand to a height of 9m (30ft) and incorporate doorways and several blocked windows.

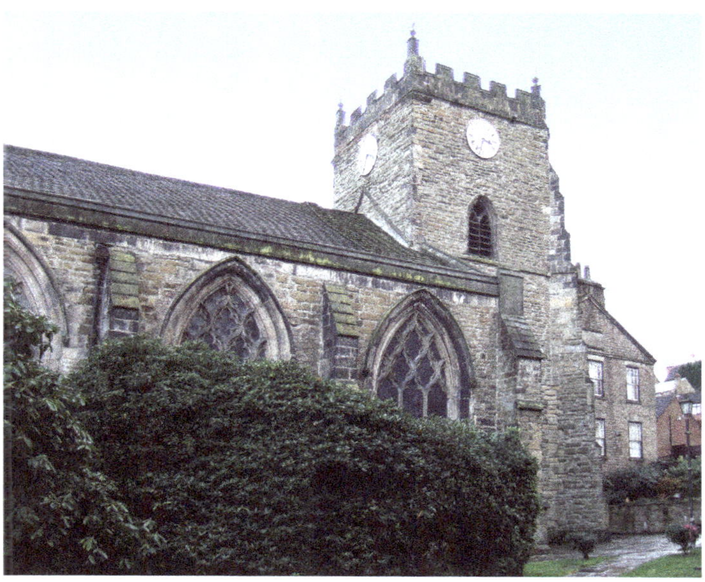

Warrington Austin Friars

-1308-1539

The hermit friars of the Order of St Augustine settled in Warrington before 1308, on land on which stood an old hospital, probably granted by William le Boteler, Lord of Warrington, who was buried in the friars' church after his death. Almost nothing is known of the history of the house, which appears to have been quite large, as many friars took holy orders here and several were appointed penitentiaries in the latter part of the fourteenth century. It was probably surrendered in 1539 and was sold by the Crown, along with the priories of Preston and Lancaster, to Sir Thomas Holcroft, in June 1540. Nothing visible has survived.

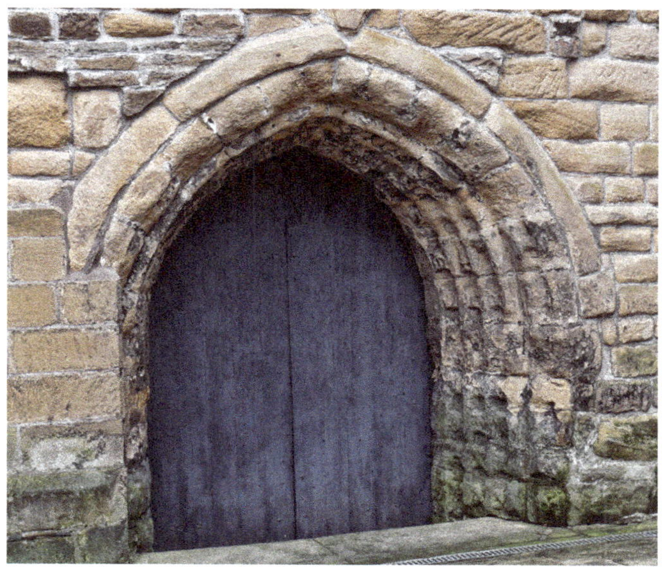

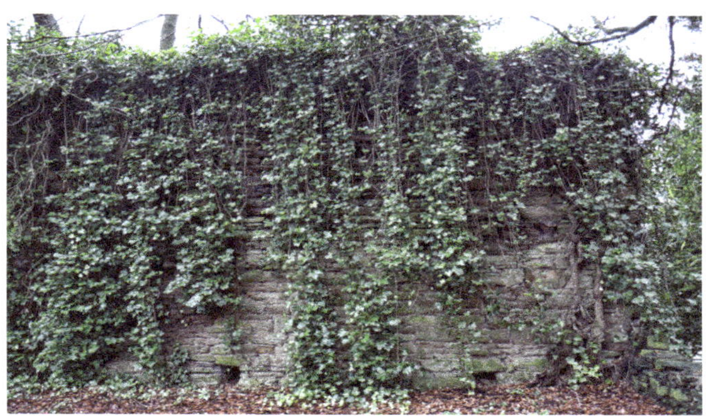

Whalley Abbey

St Mary • Cistercian 1172–1537

Very little now remains of Whalley Abbey, but its unusual history is worth recalling and may help the visitor to gaze upon its broken walls with greater understanding. It was first founded for the Cistercians in 1172 by John, Constable of Chester and Baron of Halton, at Stanlaw in the Cheshire lowlands near the shores of the Mersey. Although named in the charter of foundation as Benedictus Locus, the blessed spot, it was anything but. Often under water and inaccessible at spring tides, the site proved extremely unhealthy and greatly inconvenient, forcing the monks to obtain permission to move to what they thought was a more convivial site. This was provided at Whalley in Lancashire by Henry de Lacy, Earl of Lincoln, and the abbey was refounded in its new location in 1296. Surprisingly, within twenty years, the monks were anxious to move again and although they obtained a grant of land in 1316 at Toxteth and Smithdown in Liverpool, from Thomas, Earl of Lancaster, who had acquired the de Lacy estates through marriage, the move never happened. The monks had cited the bleakness of the country, absence of trees for timber and fuel, and bad roads, which made the transportation of corn difficult.

The new abbey did not have a happy start, nor a happy ending. Its foundation caused friction with Sawley Abbey, another Cistercian house, whose close proximity was considered by Sawley's abbot as contrary to the Cistercian constitution. He also complained that merchants took advantage of having two abbeys so close together to raise prices, causing the Sawley monks to travel further to obtain more favourable terms. A General Chapter was convened and the dispute was settled by a commission of Cistercian abbots in 1305, when the two agreed to cooperate, rather than confront. It was perhaps a very early example of joint purchasing power soon pushing down costs to the benefit of both. Nothing of note occurred over the next 200 years, but in March 1537, Abbot John Paslew, together with two of his monks, was hanged for high treason, having been wrongly implicated in the Pilgrimage of Grace insurrection against the Dissolution of the monasteries. By the end of the year, Whalley Abbey had been stripped bare.

The building of a church began immediately but, given the difficulties faced in the early years, progress was slow and the church was not completed until 1380, when the first mass was said. Only the wall of the south aisle and the south and west walls of the transepts are still standing to a fair height, but the outlines of the foundations give a clearer picture of the size of the church. This was 78m (255ft) long, with ten bays making up the nave, and the presbytery and choir taking up two more bays. The transepts, 43m (142ft) across, had three chapels in each wing. Above rose a central bell tower. On the south wall is an aumbry, which presumably held the books the monks used when reading in the adjacent cloister. The domestic buildings were completed sometime later. A royal licence was obtained in 1339 to enclose the precincts with a crenellated wall. Some walls remain standing of the east range, including the decorated arch with tracery and ogee arches above, which formed the entrance to the chapter house, but the refectory in the south range has gone. The west range is the most complete and is now used as a Roman Catholic church hall. It once was the house of the lay-brothers. A group of ruins to the east include the abbot's lodgings and infirmary. The present entrance to the abbey grounds is the north-east gateway, which was finished in about 1480, but the oldest part of the abbey is the north-west gateway, some 275m (900ft) to the west. The early fourteenth century structure with a large entrance for vehicles and a smaller one for foot passengers measures 23 x 11m (75 x 37ft). It is stone-vaulted throughout and has a large room above, which may have served as a chapel.

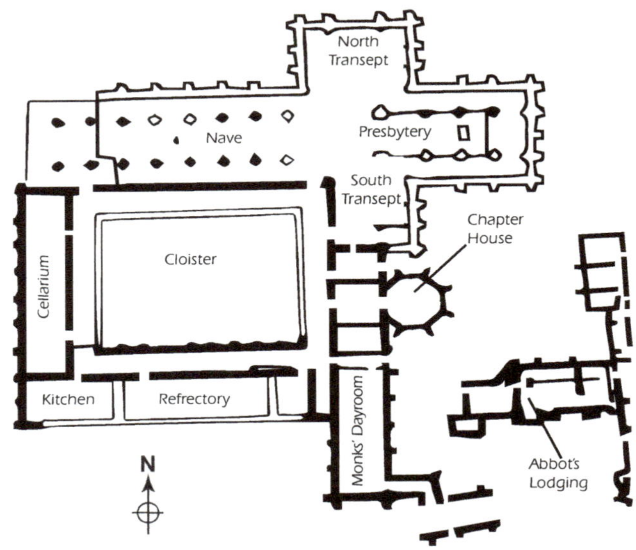

Wyresdale Abbey

St Mary • Cistercian c1193–c1204

This short-lived Cistercian abbey was founded towards the close of the twelfth century on land probably donated by Theobald Walter, Lord of Weeton and Amounderness who, between 1193 and 1196, appropriated to the new foundation the church of St Michael-on-Wyre. The monks came from Furness Abbey but soon crossed the Irish Sea, as only a few years later (before 1204) Theobald removed them to Wotheney, on his Irish lands in Munster, in the present county of Limerick. The site of the abbey in Wyresdale is not known, but may be indicated by the name Abbeystead in Over Wyresdale, near the confluence of Tarnbrook Wyre and Marshaw Wyre.

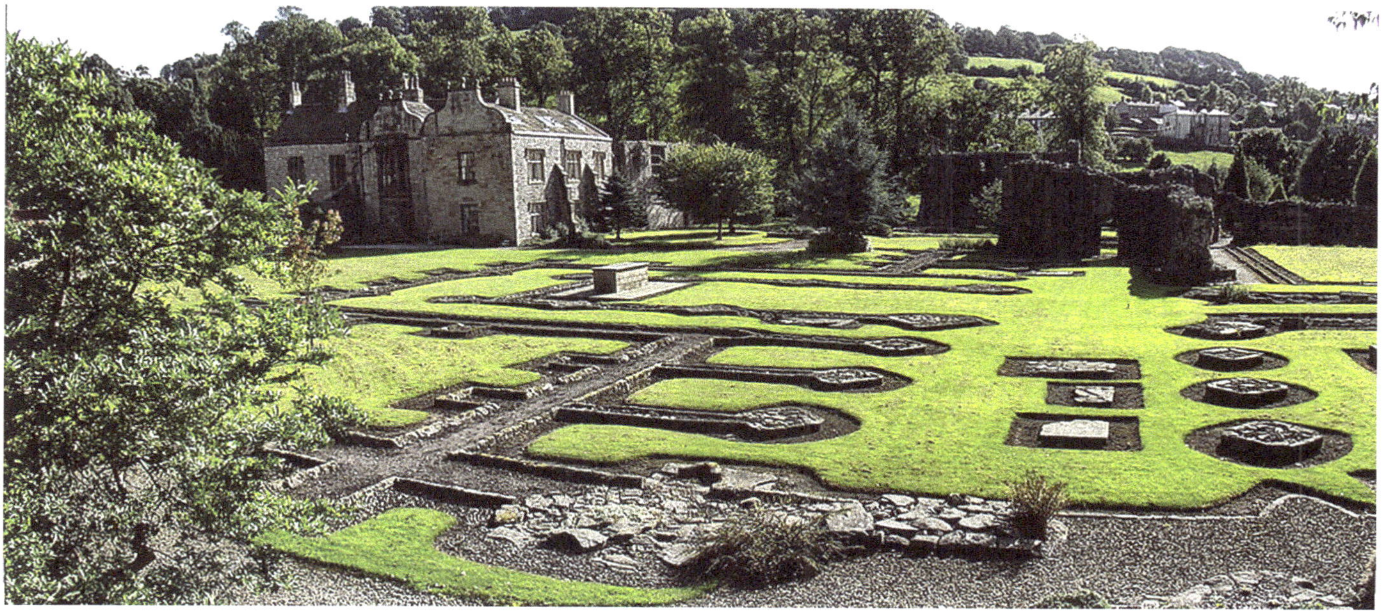

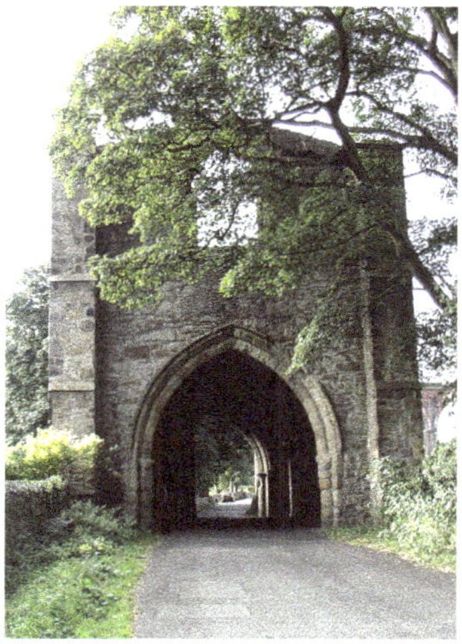

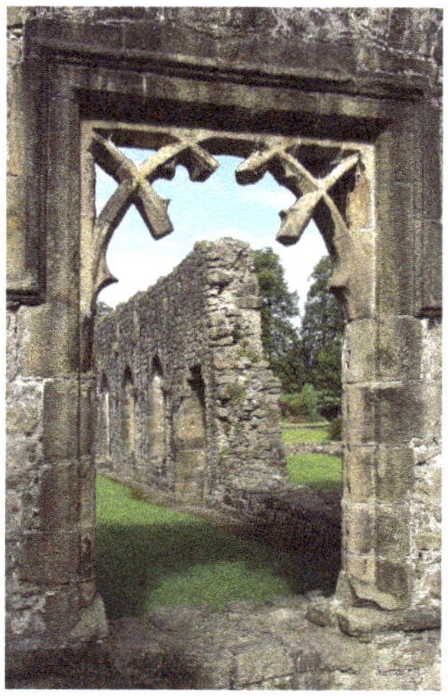

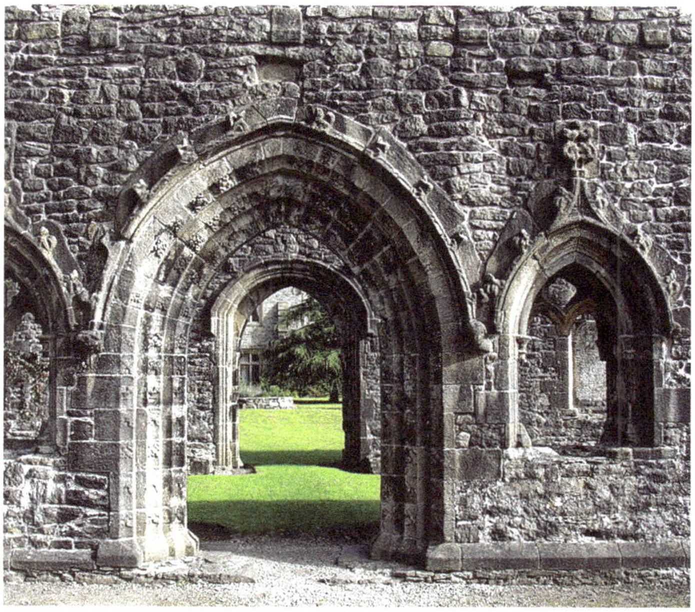

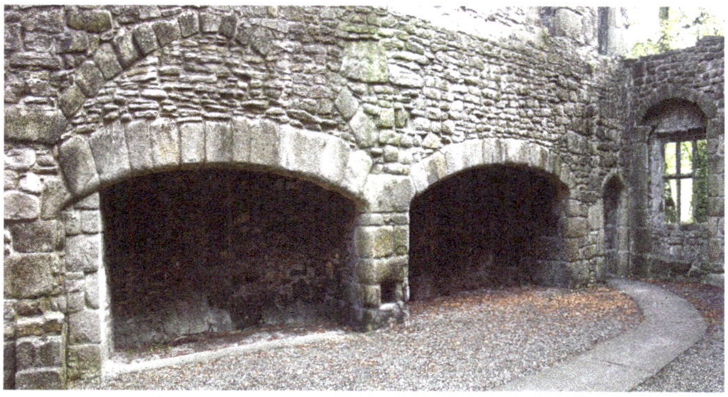

Photos of Whalley Abbey - clockwise from top

Foundations of transepts and presbytery of abbey church
Ornate entrance arch to chapter house with flanking windows
Lavatorium and entrances to refectory and day stairs
Double fireplace in the kitchen
North-east gateway
Square-headed window with remains of tracery

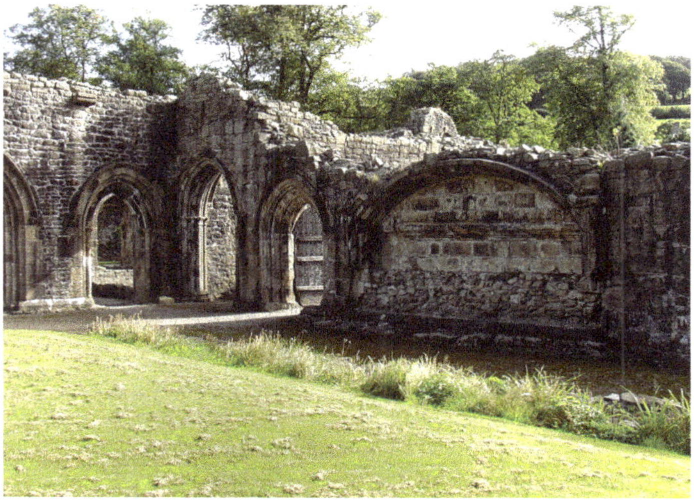

Lincolnshire

Fertile Ground

The county emerged from the consolidation of the territory of the ancient Kingdom of Lindsey and that controlled by the Danelaw borough of Stamford. It was still recorded as Lindsey in the Domesday Book of 1086. Following the Norman Conquest, the land was divided among the new Norman nobility, many of whom were responsible for founding monasteries, of which there were nearly ninety by the late thirteenth century. The prosperity of the county through sheep farming and wool production proved fertile ground for all the monastic Orders, although many abbeys and priories remained relatively poor and, disappointingly, very little has survived.

The word unique should not be used lightly, but the Witham Valley deserves such a description for the remarkable concentration of nine abbeys and priories, which were virtually within sight of one another. On the east bank of the River Witham there were six: Barlings Abbey, Stainfield Priory, Bardney Abbey, Tupholme Abbey, Stixwould Priory and Kirkstead Abbey, with three more: Nocton Park, Catley and Kyme, all priories, on the west bank. No definitive explanation for this phenomenon has been advanced by historians, although the fact that Lincoln enjoyed high ecclesiastical status and the river was a busy and vital route for the wool trade from Lincoln through the Fens to the port of Boston, may be closest to the truth. Today, only fragments of a few of these remain, but the visitor should make the pilgrimage to all nine sites, starting at Barlings in the north.

Lincolnshire can claim another unique position among England's counties. It was home to the only indigenous monastic Order established by Gilbert, son of a Norman knight, who was vicar of St Andrews at Sempringham and was later canonised. Known as the Gilbertines, these were largely mixed houses of canons and nuns, totalling some twenty-six. The mother house was at Sempringham, with other priories in Lincolnshire those at Alvingham, Bridge End, Bullington, Catley, Haverholme, Lincoln, Newstead-on-Ancholme, North Ormsby, Sixhills, and Tunstall. It was a popular Order, and in spite of the majority coming under the 1536 Act of Suppression of the smaller houses, Henry VIII allowed the Gilbertines to carry on until 1538, when they surrendered 'of their own free will'.

The most impressive extant ruins are those of Thornton Abbey in the north of the county, an Augustinian house founded in 1139 by William le Gros, Earl of Yorkshire. It became the most influential and one of the wealthiest abbeys in Lincolnshire. The oldest and richest was the Benedictine abbey of Croyland, which was established on the site of St Guthlac's hermitage in the mid-eighth century. The only surviving part now serves as the parish church, as does that of its Freiston Priory dependency. The church is all that remains of Bourne Abbey, founded for canons of the Arrouaisian Order, and of Deeping priory of St James, a Benedictine house, both founded by Baldwin fitzGilbert. Benedictine foundations were also established at Alkborough, Belvoir, Burwell, Covenham, Humberston, Lincoln, Partney, Stamford, and the pre-Conquest foundation of Stow. Stainfield Priory was a house of Benedictine nuns.

Given the predominance of the wool trade, it is surprising that the Cistercians were not more prominent, although the largest achieved reasonable wealth. The main foundation was that of Kirkstead Abbey near Woodhall Spa, founded in 1139 by Hugh Brito, Lord of Tattershall. It was colonised by monks from Fountains Abbey in Yorkshire, as was Louth Park Abbey, founded in 1139 by Alexander, Bishop of Lincoln. Revesby Abbey was founded in 1142 by William de Romara, Lord of Bolingbroke. Another large and important monastery was Swineshead Abbey, but nothing has survived. Early prosperity began to decline by the end of the thirteenth century at Vaudey Abbey. There were seven Cistercian nunneries at Greenfield, Fosse, Gokewell, Heynings, Legbourne, Nuncotham and Stixwould. Most were small and poor.

Augustinian canons settled at Elsham, Hirst, Hough, Kyme, Markby, Newstead by Stamford, Nocton Park, possibly Sandtoft, Thornholme, Thwaite, Torksey, and Wellow Abbey, the latter one of the few Augustinian houses with abbey status. Grimsby Priory was a house of Augustinian canonesses. The Premonstratensians had an abbey at Newsham, the first house of the Order in England, and at Hagnaby, Newbo and Tupholme, together with a house for nuns at Orford (Irford). Axholme Priory was the only Carthusian house in Lincolnshire, founded around 1395 by Thomas de Mowbray, later to become the first Duke of Norfolk.

There were a few alien cells, dependent on abbeys in France. These included Cammeringham Priory, which was dependent on the Premonstratensian abbey of Blanchlande in Normandy; Haugham Priory, which belonged to the Benedictine abbey of St Severus, also in Normandy; Long Bennington Priory, whose ownership was disputed; Minting Priory, a Benedictine house dependent on the abbey of Fleury; Spalding Priory, eventually a dependency of St Nicholas at Angers, before being denizised; Wenghale Priory, which belonged to the Benedictine abbey of Séez; West Ravendale, dependent on the Premonstratensian abbey of Beauport in Brittany; Willoughton Priory, a dependency of St Nicholas at Angers; and Wilsford Priory, a cell of the great Benedictine abbey of Bec-Hellouin in Normandy. Most were dissolved by Henry V in 1414.

With several large and important towns and cities, the mendicant friars had many houses in Lincolnshire, but have left few visible remains. The four principal Orders of Austin Friars, Dominicans (Black Friars), Franciscans (Grey Friars) and Carmelites (White Friars) were all present at Boston, Lincoln and Stamford, while Austin Friars also had a house at Grimsby, and Grey Friars at Grantham and Grimsby. Small houses of the Friars of the Penance of Jesus Christ, or Sack Friars, existed at Lincoln and Stamford, and there may have been a short-lived foundation of the order of the Holy Cross, or Crutched Friars, at Whaplode.

Gazetteer

Alkborough Priory College Farm, Back Street, Alkborough, 11km (7 miles) N of Scunthorpe, Lincolnshire (SE 881216). No visible remains

Alvingham Priory Abbey Road, Alvingham, 5km (3 miles) NE of Louth, Lincolnshire (TF 368913). Redundant church

Axholme Priory N of Owston Ferry, 11km (7 miles) SW of Scunthorpe, Lincolnshire (SE 806019). No visible remains

Bardney Abbey Bardney, 14.5km (9 miles) E of Lincoln, Lincolnshire (TF 113706). Minimal remains

Barlings Abbey Low Barlings, 11km (7 miles) E of Lincoln, Lincolnshire (TF089735). Minimal remains

Belvoir Priory Near Belvoir Castle, Woolthorpe, Lincolnshire (SK 820341). No visible remains

Boston Austin Friars Skirbeck Road, Boston, Lincolnshire (TF 331434). No visible remains

Boston Black Friars Blackfriars Theatre and Arts Centre, Spain Lane, off A 16 John Adams Way, Boston, Lincolnshire (TF 329439). Tel: 01205 363075. Web: www.blackfriarsartscentre.co.uk

Boston White Friars Fydell Crescent, Boston, Lincolnshire (TF 326438). No visible remains

Bourne Abbey A15 South Street, Bourne, Lincolnshire (TF 097200). Church in use; Tel: 01778 422412

Bridge End Priory Prior Farm, off B1177, Bridge End, 13km (8 miles) SE of Sleaford, Lincolnshire (TF 143362). Earthwork remains

Bullington Priory Off Shortwood Lane, Swinthorpe, 11km (7 miles) NE of Lincoln, Lincolnshire (TF 101767). No visible remains

Burwell Priory Off A16 London Road, Burwell, 8km (5 miles) S of Louth, Lincolnshire (TF 357797). No visible remains

Cammeringham Priory Off B1398, Cammeringham, 11km (7 miles) N of Lincoln, Lincolnshire (SK 949822). Minimal remains

Catley Priory Off Digby Road, Walcott, 10km (6 miles) SW of Coningsby, Lincolnshire (TF 119556). No visible remains

Covenham Priory Grange Lane, Grainthorpe, 6.5km (4 miles) N of Louth, Lincolnshire (TF 353957). Redundant church

Croyland Abbey Abbey Walk, Crowland, off A1073, 16km (10 miles) NE of Peterborough, Lincolnshire (TF 241103). Tel: 01733 211763. Web: www.crowlandabbey.org.uk

Deeping Priory Church Gate, Deeping St James, Lincolnshire (TF 158096). Church in use; Tel: 01778 346420. Web: www.dsj.org.uk

Elsham Priory Off B1206, Elsham, 13km (8 miles) E of Scunthorpe, Lincolnshire. Precise location unknown

Fosse Priory Near A156, The Elms, Saxilby, 10km (6 miles) Nw of Lincoln, Lincolnshire (SK 836782). No visible remains

Freiston Priory Church View, Freiston, Boston, Lincolnshire (TF 377437). Church in use; Tel: 01205 760480

Gokewell Priory Minor Lane, off B1207, Broughton, Scunthorpe, Lincolnshire (SE 941103). No visible remains

Grantham Grey Friars Off A52 Sankt Augustin Way, Grantham, Lincolnshire (SK 911358). No visible remains

Greenfield Priory Greenfield Lane, off A1104, Woodthorpe, 13km (8 miles) SE of Louth, Lincolnshire (TF 433780). No visible remains

Grimsby Priory Grimsby, Lincolnshire (TA 265079). No visible remains

Grimsby Austin Friars Off Victoria Street South, Grimsby, Lincolnshire (TA 269064). No visible remains

Grimsby Grey Friars Prince's Avenue, Grimsby, Lincolnshire (TA 264090). No visible remains

Hagnaby Abbey Hagnaby, 11km (7 miles) NE of Coningsby, Lincolnshire (TF 484806). No visible remains

Haugham Priory Haugham, 6.5km (4 miles) S of Louth, Lincolnshire. No visible remains

Haverholme Priory Off Park Lane, Ewerby, 5km (3 miles) NE of Sleaford, Lincolnshire (TF 109494). No visible remains

Heynings Priory Minor Road, off B1241, Knaith Park, 4km (2.5 miles) S of Gainsborough, Lincolnshire (SK 846853). No visible remains

Hirst Priory The Lincolnshire Golf Course, off A161, Crowle, Scunthorpe, Lincolnshire (SE 778102). No visible remains

Hough Priory High Road, Hough-on-the-Hill, 11km (7 miles) N of Grantham, Lincolnshire (SK 924463). No visible remains

Humberston Abbey Church Lane, off A1031 Humberston Avenue, Humberston, Grimsby, Lincolnshire (TA 310051). No visible remains

Kirkstead Abbey Abbey Lane, off B1192, Woodhall Spa, Lincolnshire (TF 189616). Minimal remains

Kyme Priory Church Lane, off B1395, South Kyme, 11km (7 miles) NE of Sleaford, Lincolnshire (TF 168498). Church in use; Tel: 01526 861746

Legbourne Priory Buston Lane, Legbourne, 5km (3 miles) SE of Louth, Lincolnshire (TF 360842). Earthwork remains

Lincoln Priory Derby Street, off A15 St Catherines, Lincoln, Lincolnshire (SK 970694). No visible remains

Lincoln Priory (Monks Abbey) Monks Road, Lincoln, Lincolnshire (SK 989713). Minimal remains

Lincoln Austin Friars Off Newport Road?, Lincoln, Lincolnshire (SK 976723). No visible remains

Lincoln Black Friars Abbey Street, Lincoln, Lincolnshire (SK 980715). No visible remains

Lincoln Grey Friars A15 Broadgate, Lincoln, Lincolnshire (SK 977712). Exhibition Centre; Tel: 01522 873479

Lincoln Sack Friars Conningsby Street, Lincoln, Lincolnshire (SK 806712). No visible remains

Lincoln White Friars B1262 High Street, Lincoln, Lincolnshire (SK 974707). No *in situ* remains

Long Bennington Priory Church Lane, Long Bennington, 10km (6 miles) NW of Grantham, Lincolnshire (SK 843438). No visible remains

Louth Park Abbey Abbey Lodge, Eastfield Road, Keddington, Louth, Lincolnshire (TF 354886). Private; minimal remains

Markby Priory Off A1111, Markby, 6.5km (4 miles) S of Maplethorpe, Lincolnshire (TF 487788). Earthworks only

Minting Priory Church Lane, Minting, 8km (5 miles) NW of Horncastle, Lincolnshire (TF 185734). Earthwork remains

Newbo Abbey Near Abbey Lane, Sedgebrook, 5km (3 miles) W of Grantham, Lincolnshire (SK 862379). No visible remains

Newsham (Newhouse) Abbey Near Newsam Lake, off B1211, Habrough, Immingham, Lincolnshire (TA 128132). Some earthwork remains

Newstead by Stamford Priory Newstead Lane, off A1175 Uffington Road, Newstead, Stamford, Lincolnshire (TF 046078). No visible remains

Newstead-on-Ancholme Priory Cadney, Brigg, Lincolnshire (TA 000044). Private

Nocton Park Priory Nocton Fen Lane, Nocton, 10km (6 miles) SE of Lincoln, Lincolnshire (TF 078648). No visible remains

North Ormsby Priory Minor Lane, North Ormsby, 8km (5 miles) NW of Louth, Lincolnshire (TF 282930). No visible remains

Nuncotham Priory Off Brocklesbury Road, Keelby, 10km (6 miles) W of Grimsby, Lincolnshire (TA 156112). Earthwork remains

Orford (Irford) Priory Country Lane, Stainton le Vale, 8km (5 miles) NE of Market Rasen, Lincolnshire (TF 197945). No visible remains

Revesby Abbey Off B1183 Boston Road, Revesby, 8km (5 miles) NE of Coningsby, Lincolnshire (TF 299609). Fragments in parish church

Sandtoft Priory Sandtoft, 16km (10 miles) W of Scunthorpe, Lincolnshire. No visible remains

Sempringham Priory Country lane, off B1177, Pointon, 11km (7 miles) N of Bourne, Lincolnshire (TF 106325). Earthworks and remains in church

Sixhills Priory Sixhills Road, Sixhills, 6.5km (4 miles) SE of Market Rasen, Lincolnshire (TF 163873). No visible remains

Spalding Priory Vine Street, off Bridge Street, Spalding, Lincolnshire (TF 248225). Uncertain remains

Stainfield Priory Stainfield, 13km (8 miles) E of Lincoln, Lincolnshire (TF 113732). No visible remains

Stamford Priory Off A43 Kettering Road, Stamford, Lincolnshire (TF 027066). No visible remains

Stamford Austin Friars Rutland Terrace, Stamford, Lincolnshire (TF 025069). No *in situ* remains

Stamford Black Friars Adelaide Street, Stamford, Lincolnshire (TF 034072). No visible remains

Stamford Grey Friars A1175 Uffington Road, Stamford, Lincolnshire (TF 036075). Surviving gateway

Stamford Sack Friars Stamford, Lincolnshire. Exact location unknown

Stamford White Friars Priory Road, Off A1175, Stamford, Lincolnshire. No visible remains

Stixwould Priory Duckpool Lane, Stixwould, 3km (2 miles) N of Woodhall Spa, Lincolnshire (TF 173661). Earthworks only

Stow Abbey Stow, 15km (9.5 miles) NW of Lincoln, Lincolnshire (SK 882820) Church in use;
Tel: 01427 788787
Web: www.stowminster.org.uk

Swineshead Abbey Swineshead, 10km (6 miles) SW of Boston, Lincolnshire (TF 250407). No visible remains

Thornholme Priory On country lane, off B1207, near Appleby, 6.5km (4 miles) NE of Scunthorpe, Lincolnshire (SE 965125). No visible remains

Thornton Abbey On minor road off A1077 at Thornton Curtis, 8km (5 miles) SE of Barton-on-Humber, Humberside (TA 115190). English Heritage;
Tel: 01469 541445

Thwaite Priory Thwaite Hall, off B1196 Hanby Lane, Willoughby, Lincolnshire (TF 467698).
No visible remains

Torksey Priory Abbey Park, A156 Main Street, Torksey, 16km (10 miles) NW of Lincoln, Lincolnshire (SK 837791). No visible remains

Tunstall Priory Of B1206 High Street, near Redbourne, 6.5km (4 miles) SW of Brigg, Lincolnshire.
Precise location unknown

Tupholme Abbey Off B1190, near Bardney, Lincolnshire (TF 144682).
Minimal remains, freely accessible

Vaudey Abbey Grimthorpe Castle, Grimthorpe, 5km (3 miles) NW of Bourne, Lincolnshire (TF 037215)
No *in situ* remains

Wellow (by Grimsby) Abbey Abbotsway, Grimbsby, Lincolnshire (TA 269087). No visible remains

Wenghale Priory On country lane, off B1205 Waddingham Road, Waddingham, 16km (10 miles) SE of Scunthorpe, Lincolnshire (TF 029969). No visible remains

West Ravendale Priory On country lane, off The Avenue, East Ravendale, 11km (7 miles) SW of Grimsby, Lincolnshire (TF 227997). Minimal remains

Whaplode Crutched Friars Near Gelder's Lane, Whaplode, 3km (2 miles) W of Holbeach, Lincolnshire.
No visible remains

Willoughton Priory Willoughton, 10km (6 miles) NE of Gainsborough, Lincolnshire. No visible remains

Wilsford Priory Wilsford, 6.5km (4 miles) SW of Sleaford, Lincolnshire. No visible remains

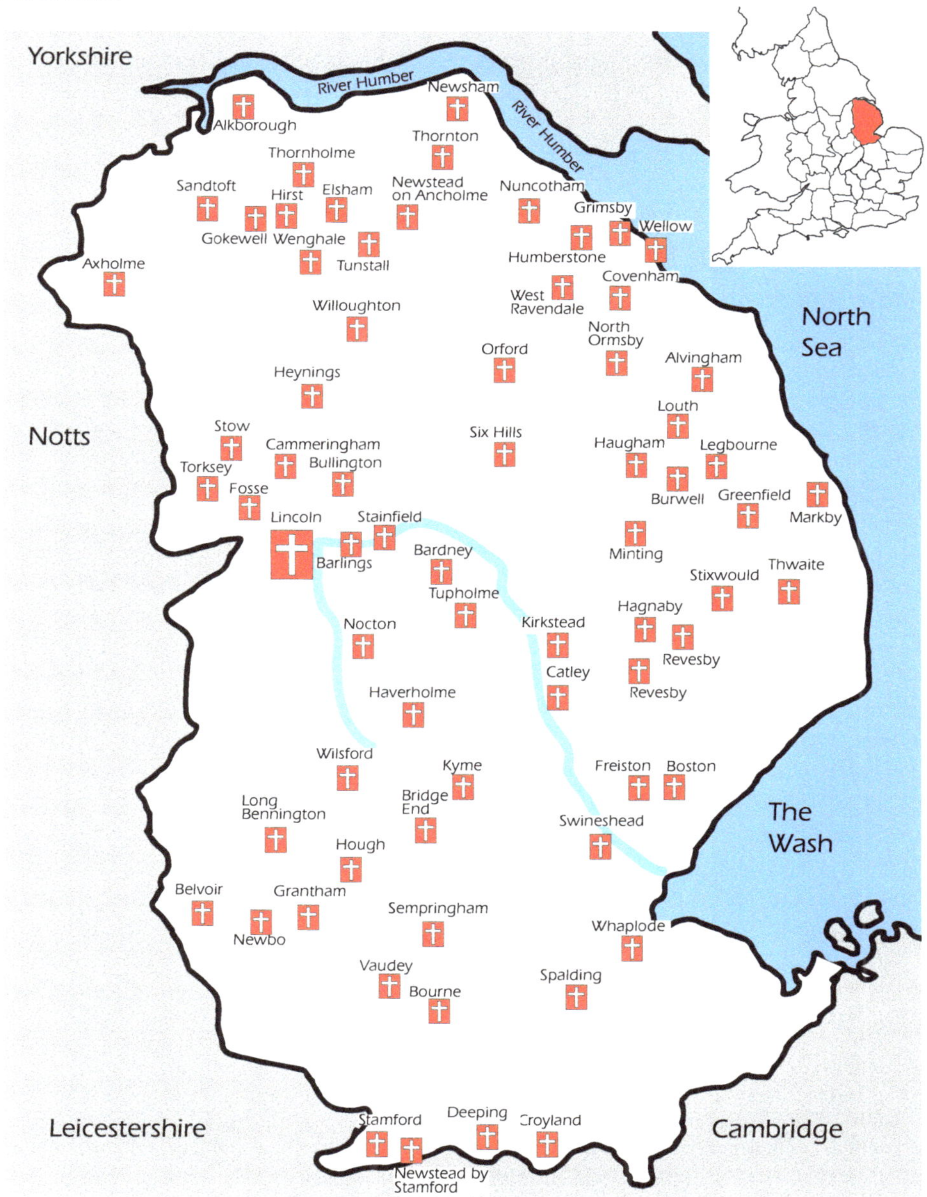

Alkborough Priory

St John the Baptist • Benedictine 1052–1220

A Benedictine priory, dependent on Spalding Priory, was founded here by Thorold of Buckenhale, Sheriff of Lincoln, in 1052 with just three monks, a secular chaplain and a prior. The site was carefully chosen for its strategic position overlooking the River Trent as it joins the Ouse to become the Humber. It also was and still is an area of outstanding natural beauty. The only reminder is the parish church of St John the Baptist, which was built before 1052 and was serviced by the monks. The church has been much altered in its long history, but contains several medieval features of interest. The most prominent is the unbuttressed west tower of Anglo-Saxon origin with a great selection of gargoyles but within, note should be taken of the cylindrical Norman font, albeit on a modern base, and an ancient free-standing holy water stoup, thrown out of the church during the reign of Henry VIII, but restored to its present position some years later. The arches in the nave were built with Caen stone in 1200. College Farm now stands on the site of the priory, which had a relatively short history. In 1074, the small cell became alien, but ceased to exist in 1220.

Alvingham Priory

St Mary • Gilbertine 1148/54–1538

The feeling that time has stood still in the small village of Alvingham, lying in the fertile area known as Middle Marsh, is enhanced by the presence of two ancient churches within one churchyard. Earthworks mark the foundations of the two cloisters, the fishponds and the internal moat, which, together with a high wall, surrounded the nuns' quarters. Many stones from the old priory can still be found in the fields around the village. The former priory church of St Mary has been much altered over the centuries and served as the parish church of North Cockerington, but is now redundant. The south arcade and two bays of the nave date from its original construction in the twelfth century, while the west end of the nave with the pointed window to the east was added c1300. The rather plain octagonal font was created in the thirteenth century. The restored chancel arch originated in the fourteenth century, and from the same time is a fragment of a stone coffin in the south aisle with the torso of an effigy of a knight with a long-tailed lion at his feet. There is a blocked-up window in the chancel, which may belong to the Saxon period.

Although the priory's history is well covered in ancient records, the exact date and identity of its founder remains open to conjecture. Alvingham Priory was founded as a Gilbertine double house between 1148 and 1154, possibly by Hugh de Scotney or one of his tenants, but William de Friston and Hamelin the Dean have also been suggested. What is clear is that within a very short time, the priory possessed many parcels of land and granges, the advowsons of several churches and houses or rents in a number of major townships. The roll of benefactors was considerable. Based on these endowments, the community was limited to eighty nuns and lay-sisters, and forty canons and lay- brothers. An interesting and eminently sensible pact was struck in 1174 with the nearby Cistercian house of Louth Park, whereby it was agreed that neither house should acquire land without the consent of the other. The aftermath of the Black Death, floods, sterile lands and pestilence among sheep and cattle plunged the community into heavy debt and prevented it from maintaining its famed hospitality. Its dire situation was eased in 1465, when it received some benefices following an appeal to Pope Paul II in 1465. Its clear annual worth was only £128 14s in 1535, but it survived until September 1538, when it was surrendered by Prior Robert Ingleby and seven canons. Prioress Joan Barket and eleven nuns also received pensions. The priory church was stripped of its roof, the chancel demolished and the conventual buildings left to decay.

Axholme Priory

St Mary, St John the Evangelist & St Edward • Arthusian 1395/6–1414

Not a vestige is left above ground of this Carthusian priory, founded in 1395 or 1396 by Thomas de Mowbray, Earl of Nottingham and Earl Marshall of England, who later became the first Duke of Norfolk. Three sides of the moat, which enclosed the conventual buildings and slight earthworks are now the only reminders. Thomas established the charterhouse in the Isle of Axholme at Low Melwood, where stood a twelfth century Premonstratensian chapel dedicated to the Virgin and known as the Priory in the Wood. Among the many endowments of the new foundation was the alien priory of Monks Kirby in Warwickshire, which had been founded in 1078 by one of the earl's ancestors as a cell to the Benedictine monastery of St Nicholas at Angers. Thomas planned to build a church, in which task he was aided by an indulgence granted by Pope Boniface IX, and cells for a prior and thirty monks, but it is unlikely that the community ever numbered more than a prior and twelve monks, in addition to a group of lay-brothers. However, in 1399, after Thomas' death in Venice following banishment after a quarrel with Henry of Bolingbroke, later Henry IV, the priory of Monks Kirby was restored to St Nicholas, depriving Axholme of a large part of its income. This situation was reversed in 1414 when Henry V confiscated all alien priories and Monks Kirby was returned to Axholme. This was the beginning of a recovery and, by 1449, the charterhouse was flourishing. Its internal history was without reproach until crassly disturbed when Prior Augustine Webster, together with the priors of Beauvale and London Charterhouse, refused to take the Oath of Supremacy and was executed for treason in 1535. Prior Mekeness and eight monks offered no resistance in June 1538, when the King's commissioners arrived to take the surrender. Its value in 1535 had been assessed at £237 15s.

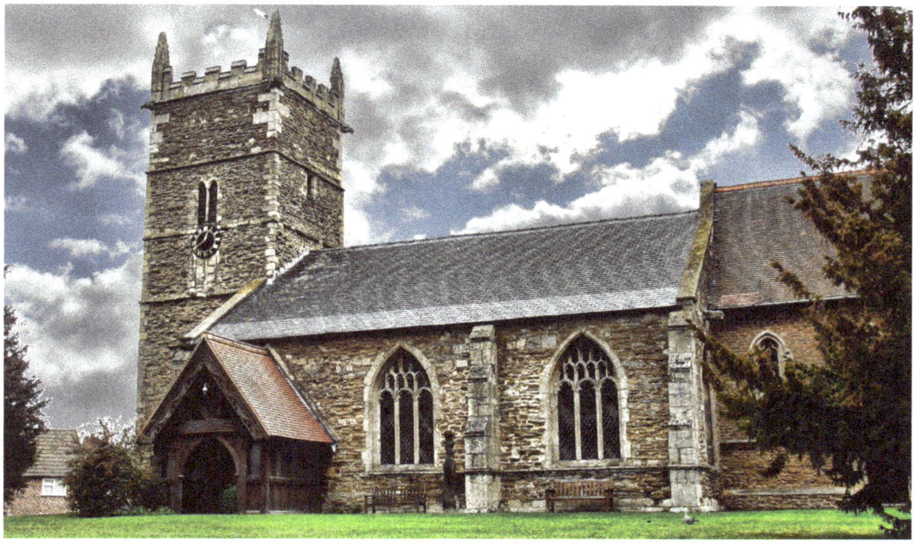
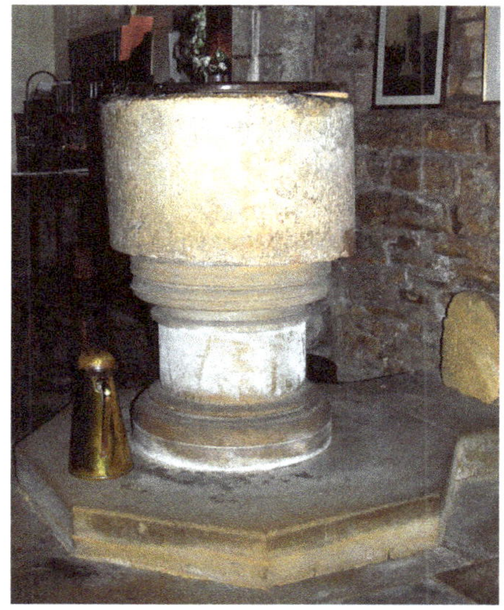
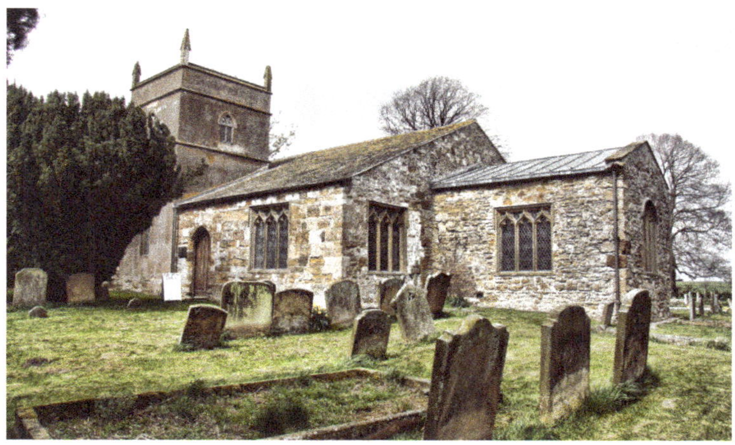
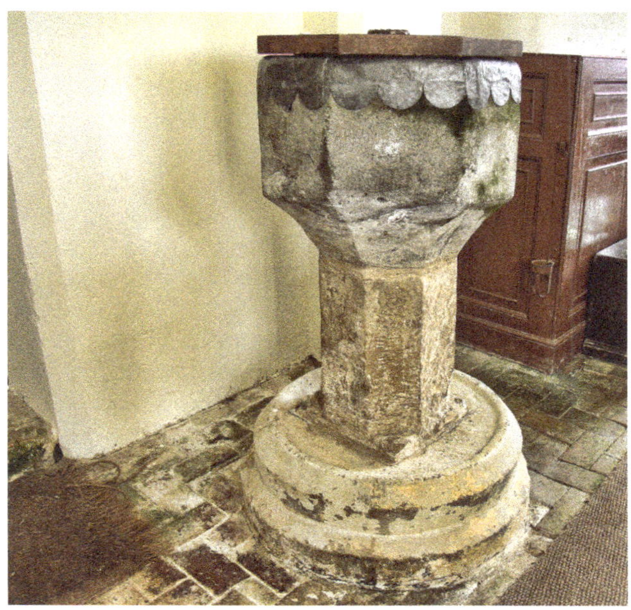
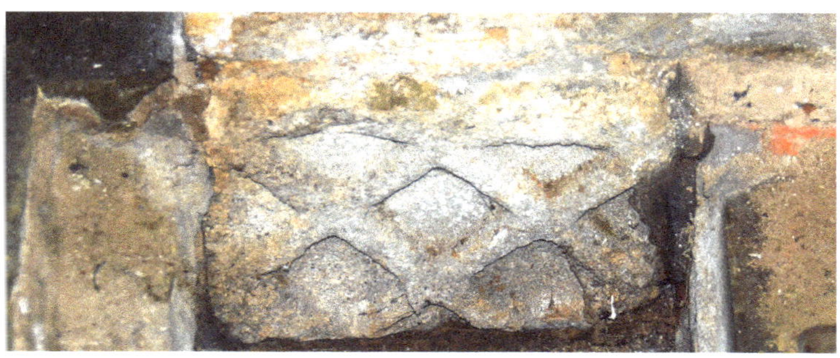
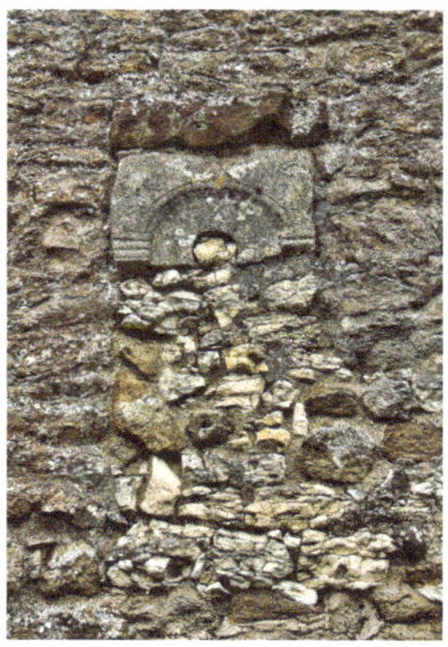
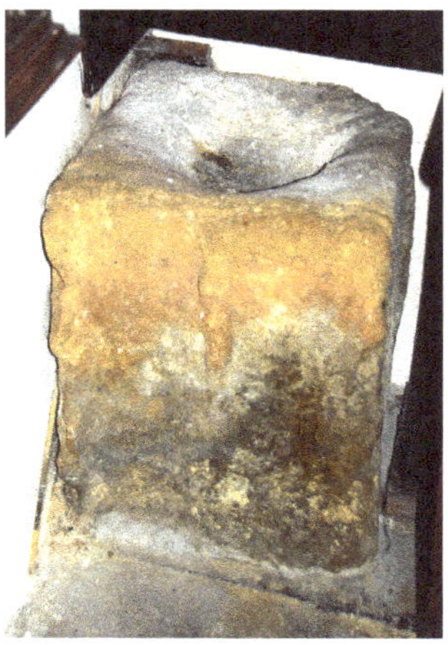

Photos - clockwise from top left

Alkborough church of St John the Baptist
ylindrical Norman font on modern base
ormer Alvingham priory church of St Mary, now redundant
3locked-up Saxon window in St Mary's
ylindrical Norman font in Alkborough St John the Baptist
3tone of Romano/British origin near base of tower
ree-standing holy water stoup

Bardney Abbey

St Peter, St Paul & St Oswald • Benedictine 1087–1538

What remained of this Benedictine abbey after its dissolution was first unearthed in 1909 by local vicar Charles Laing, but has since been covered up to protect the exposed ruins. However, it is still possible to discern the outlines of the buildings, enabling the visitor to appreciate the scale of the abbey and the location of the church, cloister and surrounding ranges. Information boards sponsored by English Heritage, the Countryside Commission, the Rural Development Commission and the Friends of Bardney Abbey are of great help. Standing within the abbey ruins, now reposing in its quiet rural environment, with creamy cattle grazing all around, it is difficult to imagine that when first built, this site was a small island in marshy ground surrounding the Witham. Until the river was straightened early in the nineteenth century, the abbey would also have been much closer to the water's edge than it is today. It is hard not to be disappointed that a monastic settlement that dates far back to Saxon times has been destroyed so thoroughly. Some stonework is beginning to peek through the earth mounds and a few decorated stones are being preserved, but it is to be hoped that the foundations will once again be exposed to enable visitors to fully understand and enjoy this ancient site.

Bardney Abbey is thought to have been founded by King Aethelred of Mercia and his Northumbrian Queen, Osthryd, probably before AD 675. It was then that it became a centre of pilgrimage after the relics of the Queen's uncle, King Oswald, later St Oswald who had been killed in battle in AD 642, were enshrined there. Oswald's head was sent to Lindisfarne, and his arms to Bamburgh. Legend has it that when the body of Oswald arrived at the abbey gates, the monks refused entry. A 'pillar of light' is said to have emanated from the cart and lit up the night sky, convincing the brethren that Oswald was indeed a saint. The abbey gates were left open permanently thereafter. Today's saying "Do you come from Bardney?" means that you have left the door open. The presence of Oswald's body made Bardney a prosperous religious centre, but the Danes destroyed the monastery in AD 870 as they rampaged through the country. The bones of St Oswald were taken to Gloucester in AD 909 for safe-keeping. Nothing is known of Bardney for the next two hundred years.

The monastery was refounded in 1087 as an alien priory cell of Charroux Abbey by Gilbert de Ghent, the new Norman lord, who endowed his foundation with various parcels of land. Bardney was elevated to abbey status in 1116 by his son Walter who added to the endowments. At the same time, the abbey also became independent. The abbey was favoured by many wealthy benefactors and as a result became prosperous, but poor administration and quarrels with a succession of Kings in the twelfth and thirteenth centuries prevented it from becoming a major force. What little is known of its subsequent history comes from records of visitations by the bishops of Lincoln in 1383 and 1435, which speak of lawsuits, dissension leading to fighting within the house, the presence of women visitors, and of adultery of one of the monks. These were probably isolated incidents, as the abbots enjoyed high standing and were summoned to Parliament in the fifteenth century. Henry IV visited the abbey in 1406. The last abbot, William Marton, acknowledged the King's supremacy in 1534, at which time the abbey was valued at £366. In October 1536, six monks from Bardney were implicated in the Lincolnshire Rising and were hung, drawn and quartered at Lincoln in March 1537. Bardney Abbey was surrendered in 1538 and its buildings and lands given to Sir Robert Tyrwhitt, who destroyed the church and converted other monastic buildings into a mansion house, long since demolished. The cloisters were turned into a walled garden.

Barlings Abbey

St Mary • Premonstratensian 1154–1536

The Abbey of Our Lady at Barlings was founded in 1154 by Ralph de Haye, and colonised by monks from the abbey at Newsham, the first Premonstratensian house in the British Isles, with Adam becoming its first abbot. But it was the last abbot, Matthew Mackarel, who is remembered for his alleged participation in the Lincolnshire Rising against the Dissolution and eventual martyrdom. Together with four of his canons, the abbot, who was also suffragan bishop, was hanged at Lincoln for his insurrection in 1537. The history of the house in the near four hundred years in between was one of wealth accumulated from agriculture and wool production on its extensive landholdings to the north and east of Lincoln, and from royal patronage. Edward III is known to have lodged at Barlings on three occasions, and the King's chaplain became abbot. The abbey was exempted from wool taxes for many years, which facilitated the large-scale rebuilding of the abbey church during the period 1334-1360. Visitations found little wrong with internal discipline, the brethren being admonished only for adopting new fashion, unnecessary ornamentation and for wearing slippers!

After the Dissolution in 1536, the rather grand 91.5m (300ft) long church was stripped of its lead and its walls demolished, along with the other abbey buildings, and its valuables carted away. The east window is said to have been 12.2m (40ft) high. In 1539, the abbey site was granted to the King's brother-in-law, Charles Brandon, Duke of Suffolk. The destruction was so complete that the site today is a mass of earthworks, with only an imposing arch and part of a wall of coursed limestone ashlar and limestone rubble still defying time and the elements. The surviving remnant is the eastern arch of the north arcade of the nave, and part of the north-west pillar of the tower base. In 1710, the tower was described as 12.2m (40ft) square and nearly 55m (180ft) high, but it fell in 1757. The arch is filled in, but on the western edge is part of an open arcade with early fourteenth century stiff-leaf capitals with acorns, abaci and the springing of a sexpartite filleted rib vaulting above. There are two roof corbels and a fragmentary string course. Some carved remnants are extant in a nearby cottage. It is thought that the canons first settled on higher ground at Barlings Grange some 0.6km (1 mile) away, but moved to the present site, then an island in Fiskerton fen. Although now in private hands, access is permitted, but when approaching, it is worth remembering that under the modern road lies the half-a-mile long causeway built by the canons to cross the fen to higher ground.

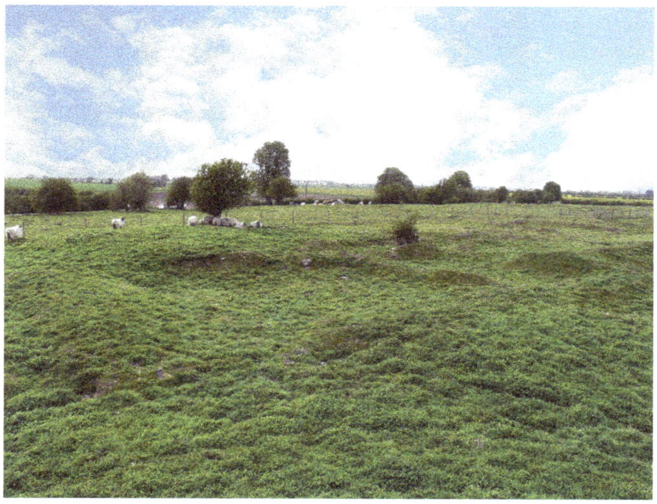

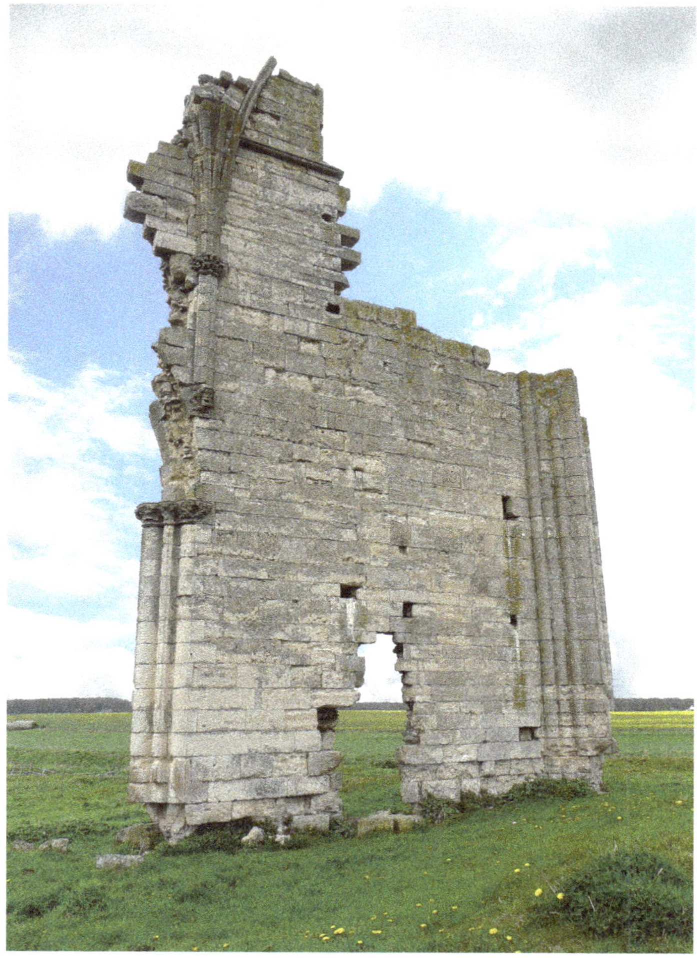

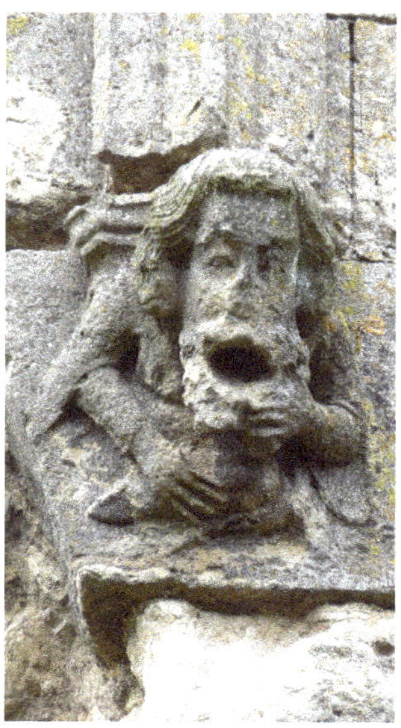

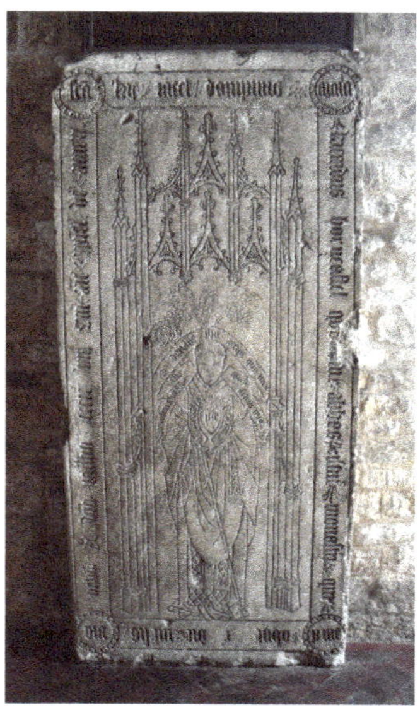

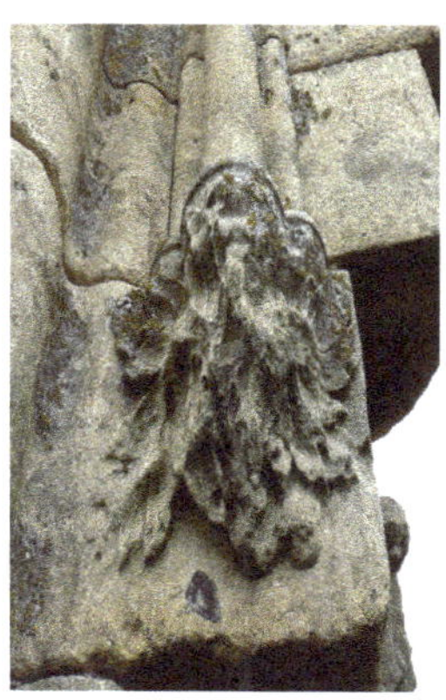

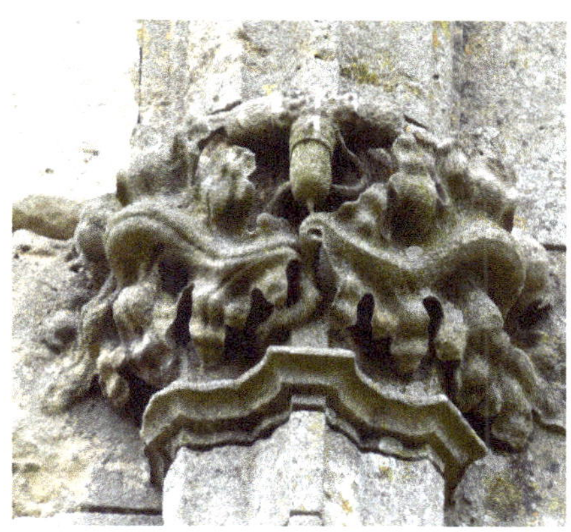

Photos - clockwise from top left

Clearly defined earthworks of Bardney Abbey
Eastern arch of the north nave arcade of abbey church of Barlings
Column capital carved with oak leaves and acorns
Foliated corbel and weathered carving of figure
Tomb slab of Abbot Richard Horncastle of Bardney Abbey in St Lawrence church

Belvoir Priory

St Mary • Benedictine 1087–1539

The priory was begun by Robert de Tosny (Todeni) on land near his own castle in 1076. It apparently was intended as an independent abbey, but before being completed became a cell to the Benedictine abbey of St Albans, which sent four monks to Belvoir. The founder was buried on his death in the priory's chapter house. Although it was never wealthy or important, it numbered several well-known persons among its benefactors who, like the founder, were buried in the priory church or chapter house. The cell's history was largely unremarkable, but its management was rather variable, with some priors, and there were many, dissipating its goods and presiding over a burden of debt. Only William Belvoir ruled the priory with great success during the difficult time of the Black Death, repaired the conventual buildings and left it in a good state.

By the beginning of the sixteenth century, the priory was unable to support even the four monks, and when it was surrendered with the parent house in 1539, only the prior, Thomas Hamtyll, and one monk were in residence. Earthworks only are now left and an inn, which is said to have been built on the site of the monks' cemetery. Some excavations were undertaken early in the twentieth century, which revealed fragmentary remains of the priory church and the inscribed tomb-slab of the founder, now resting in the chapel of the Duke of Rutland's Belvoir Castle. A plan drawn of the priory shows a polygonal chapter house in the unusual position in the centre of the cloister garth.

Boston Austin Friars

1316–1539

Nothing is left of this house, which stood near St John's Road and whose stones were probably used to reinforce the sea walls. The Austin friars received a licence from King Edward II in 1316 or 1317, to acquire land for the building of their house, but almost nothing is known of its history, other than a record of numerous benefactors in the early days, although these did little to keep the priory out of extreme poverty. By the time Richard Ingworth, Bishop of Dover, received their surrender in February 1539, the friars had nothing left but the lead on the roofs of their buildings. The site and other property was bought by the town in 1544-45 under the obligation to keep in repair the dyke and harbour frontage, and leased out to private tenants.

Boston Black Friars

-1288–1539

The Dominican friars arrived in Boston sometime before 1288, along with other Mendicant Orders, reflecting a strong religious revival in this then important trading port. The priory buildings stood on the east bank of the River Witham, but had to be rebuilt after 1288 when a fire swept through the town and destroyed the church and refectory. King Edward I gave the friars eight oaks of timber out of Sherwood Forest in 1290 and by 1309, they had rebuilt their church. The only building still standing today in Spain Lane is the rebuilt refectory, which after the Dissolution was used as a forge, warehouse, wine store and Baptist meeting house. It is now the home of the Boston Arts Centre, which stages many types of live arts activities, including theatre, music and dance. Stonework of other parts of the priory exists in nearby buildings. A part of the priory adjoining the custom house was used as a granary, but was pulled down in 1820.

Life within the strong community, which numbered thirty when Edward I came to Boston and gave them 19s 8d for two days' food in 1300, and had reached thirty-six in 1312, when Edward II sent them 12s for one days' food, was occasionally quite stormy. In 1376 at the burial of William, Lord of Huntingfield, the friars refused entry to the bishop, defending the choir with swords and arrows. When the bishop tried to say mass in the Blackfriars church the next day, the friars armed themselves with heavy stones, but bloodshed was avoided. Soon after, the friars were again in trouble, when rebellious friars and 'evil-doers' scaled the precinct wall and broke into the priory, assaulted Prior Roger Dymoke and friars in their beds, and carried away the prior's goods. Roger Dymoke, of Oxford, was afterwards elected head of the Black Friars Schools in London. No further problems were recorded thereafter. The priory was surrendered to the bishop of Dover in February 1539. It was a poor house, its annual value having been assessed at only 46s. The property was granted to the Duke of Suffolk in 1540 or 1541.

Boston Grey Friars

St Francis • -1168–1539

Nothing at all is left of this house of Franciscan friars in the south-east of the town, but the main building of the Grammar School is said to have been constructed with stone from the Grey Friars. According to Leland, it was founded by 'Merchants of the Steelyard' sometime before 1168, when one Luke de Batenturt complained that wine and other goods, which he had deposited in the priory church, had been removed. In 1300, Edward I gave them 20s 4d, and in 1328, Edward III gave a pittance of 11s 8d to the thirty-five friars then resident. With land granted in 1322, the friars were able to enlarge their dwelling-place, but in c1354, a sudden inrush of the sea caused the loss of some muniments. Little is known of its subsequent history, but it is clear that the friars suffered poverty throughout. The house was surrendered with the other Orders in the town in February 1539, valued at just 44s a year. The property was purchased by the town in 1544-45.

Boston White Friars

Blessed Virgin Mary • 1293–1539

The Carmelites were first mentioned in 1293, when they obtained a licence from Bishop Sutton for a chantry in the oratory at Boston, and consent from the papal nuncio and rector of the parish church of St Botolph, Master Giffred de Vezano, to build a church, houses and churchyard in his parish. Edward I gave the friars 12s for two days' food, which provided for eighteen friars. In 1307, William de Ros granted a new site on the west side of the river to the friars, who obtained a licence from Bishop Dalderby and Edward II, to transfer to the new location and construct a church and other buildings. Almost nothing is known of the history of the house, with the exception of several gifts of land in the first half of the fourteenth century, which facilitated an enlargement of the house, but it always remained piteously poor. Two friars attained eminence through their writings: John Hornby, whose works included a defence against attacks on his Order, and George or Gregory Ripley, author of the lives of St Botolph and St John of Bridlington. Another, John Viude, was provincial of the English Carmelites. The priory was surrendered in February 1539 and the site was purchased by the town, subject to the obligation of keeping in repair 40m (130ft) of the dyke towards the wharf. Nothing at all has survived to this day. The site lay between West Street and Liquorpond Street.

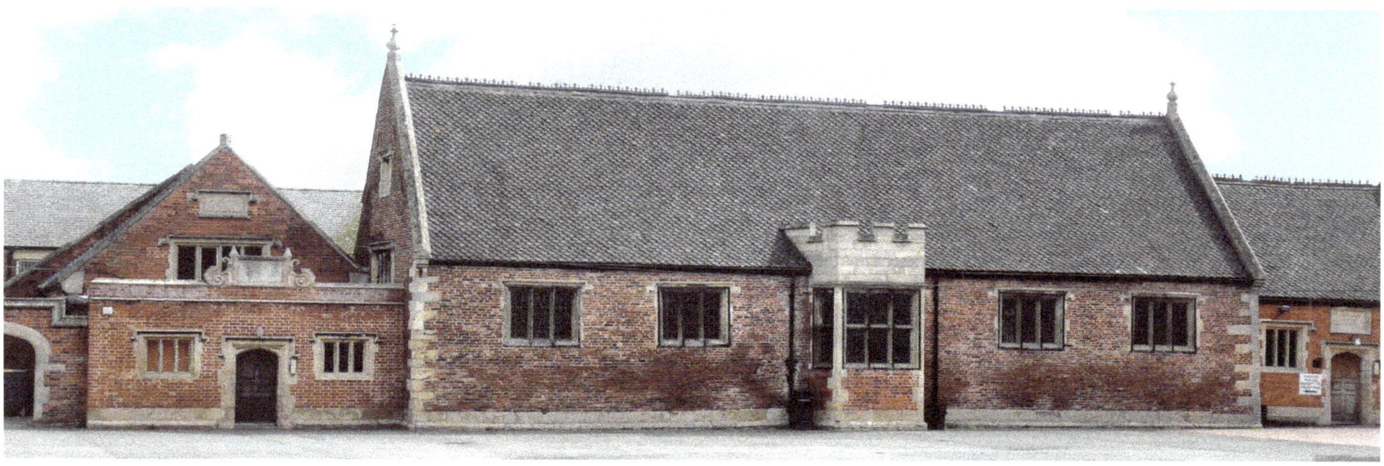

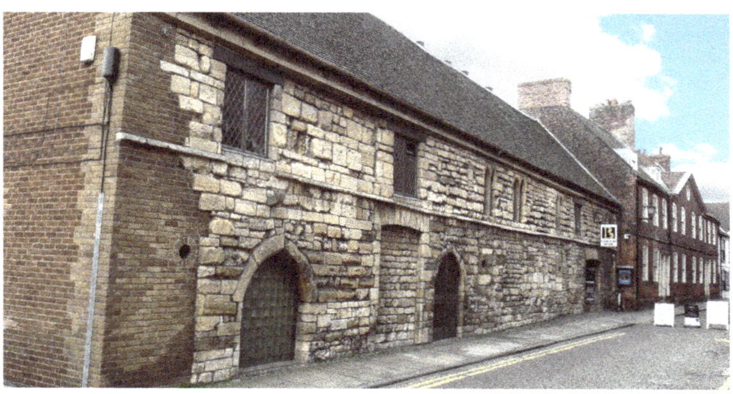

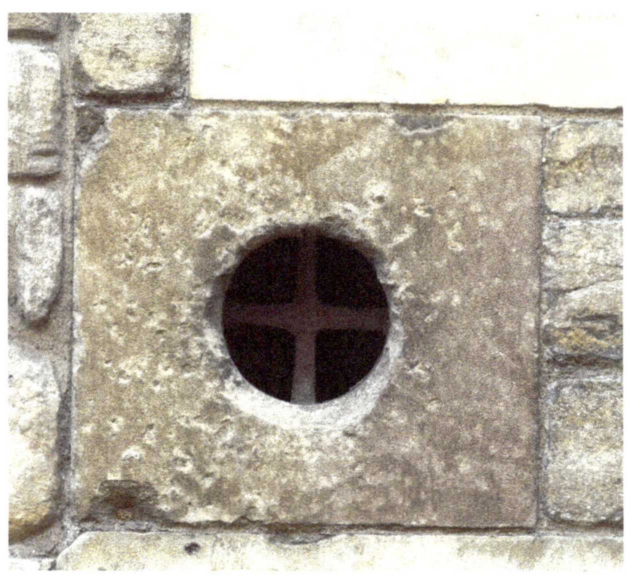

Photos - clockwise from top

The Grammar School is said to have been built with stone of the Grey Friars
Porthole stone with iron cross built into wall of Black Friars building
Surviving Black Friars building in Spain Lane

Bourne Abbey

St Peter & St Paul • Arrouaisian 1138–1536

The four bay nave which now forms the parish church, together with the west front, which was partially rebuilt c1200 when the south-west tower was erected, is all that remains from this abbey for Arrouaisian canons. The north-west tower was never built. A stone stairway in the south-east corner of the present organ chamber could once have been the night stairs from the dormitory into the church. None of the claustral buildings to the north have survived, their existence being referenced only by the blank arcading where the west range joined the church.

The abbey was founded in 1138 for canons of the Arrouaisian Order, a sub-division of the Augustinians, by the lord of the manor, Baldwin fitzGilbert, who also founded nearby Deeping Priory the following year. Baldwin was a younger son of Gilbert de Clare and brother of the first Earl of Pembroke. The patronage of the house passed through the marriage of the founder's daughter to Hugh Wake to the lords of Liddell, with whom it continued until the fourteenth century. The abbey was colonised by canons from St Nicholas at Arrouaise, but was always an independent house. It was never a wealthy or important abbey, and its history was largely uneventful, interrupted only by unsuccessful attempts in 1311 and 1324 by the King's escheator to claim the abbey as a royal foundation, the imprisonment of the abbot of Missenden at Bourne in 1359, for tampering with the coinage, and some minor infringements of the rules reported after visitations in the fifteenth and sixteenth centuries. The *Ormulum*, an important work, which bridged the gap between Old English and Middle English in the development of the language, is said to have been written in 1175 at Bourne Abbey by Orm the Preacher. In 1401, Bourne acquired the small Wilsford priory cell through purchase from the abbot of Bec-Hellouin.

In 1534, the clear annual revenue of the abbey was assessed at £167 14s, which brought it within the Dissolution of the lesser monasteries in 1536, when the last abbot, John Small, the prior and nine canons signed the surrender.

Bridge End Priory

St Saviour • Gilbertine 1199–1538

This small priory of Gilbertine canons, of which only earthworks remain, has had a troubled history since being founded in or before 1199 by Godwin the Rich of Lincoln. In addition to the meagre endowments of land and tenements, the canons were also bound to keep in good repair the Holland Bridge causeway through the fens and the thirty bridges over it as far as the new dike near Donington. The community's income was clearly not sufficient to fulfil its obligations, which proved a great burden and led to many disputes. When the causeway was damaged by floods in the mid-thirteenth century, the canons used what little money they had to buy more land, rather than repair the damage. In 1366, the prior received an indulgence from the bishop of Lincoln, and in 1379, Richard II granted a licence to the prior to beg for seven years throughout England. Before then, Edward III had granted the right to hold a weekly market and a yearly fair, which somewhat ameliorated their plight, which had been further exacerbated by the ravages of the Black Death. In 1445, a serious fire devastated the church and monastic buildings, after which the priory became a cell to the mother house of Sempringham. There were probably never more than three or four canons and a few lay-brothers at Bridge End and in 1535, its annual value was only £5 1s. It was dissolved with Sempringham in September 1538. By 1770, all buildings had been demolished.

Bullington Priory

St Mary • Gilbertine 1148/54–1538

This Gilbertine priory was founded as a double house between 1148 and 1154 by Simon de Kyme, who granted his foundation lands, woods, pasturage for 600 sheep and several churches. His son, Philip, and the convent of Sempringham added more land to the endowments, as did Alexander de Crevequer who also transferred c1189 to Bullington a small Gilbertine priory, which his father had founded on the island of Tunstall. By the fourteenth century, the canons and nuns presided over a thriving wool trade, which was aided by the acquisition of more land. However, the presence of many nuns and lay-sisters, as well as the demand for hospitality, drained its resources. Its income was boosted through the appropriation of further churches, but after the Black Death, such revenues dwindled alarmingly. The house further suffered in 1449, when the prior reported trespass and damage to ten of its granges. The house was surrendered in September 1538, with only Prior Richard Bretton, nine canons, Prioress Mary Sutton, and fourteen nuns then present. In 1535, its annual value had been assessed at £158 7s. Bullington Priory was one of thirty monasteries and their lands granted to the Duke of Suffolk by Henry VIII. The last wall standing fell in 1962, and only earthworks now indicate its location, including a moat, which may have enclosed the precincts of the nuns, and, attached on the northern side, an elaborate water management system of channels and ponds.

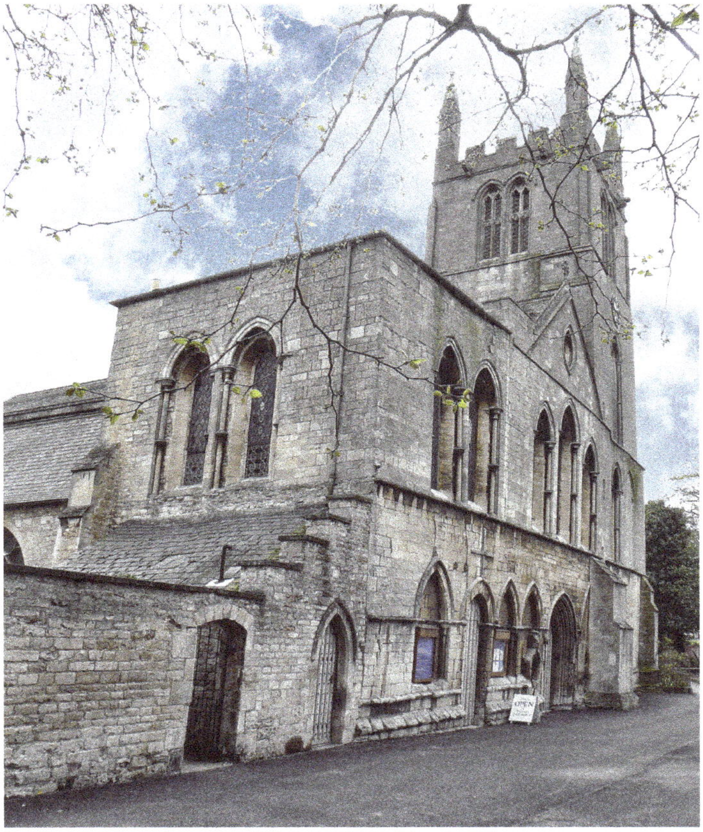

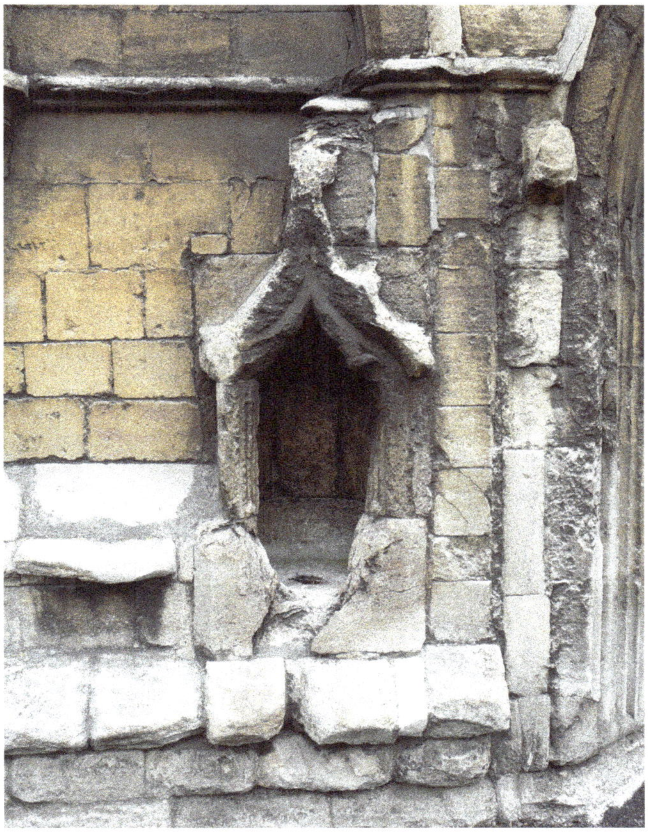

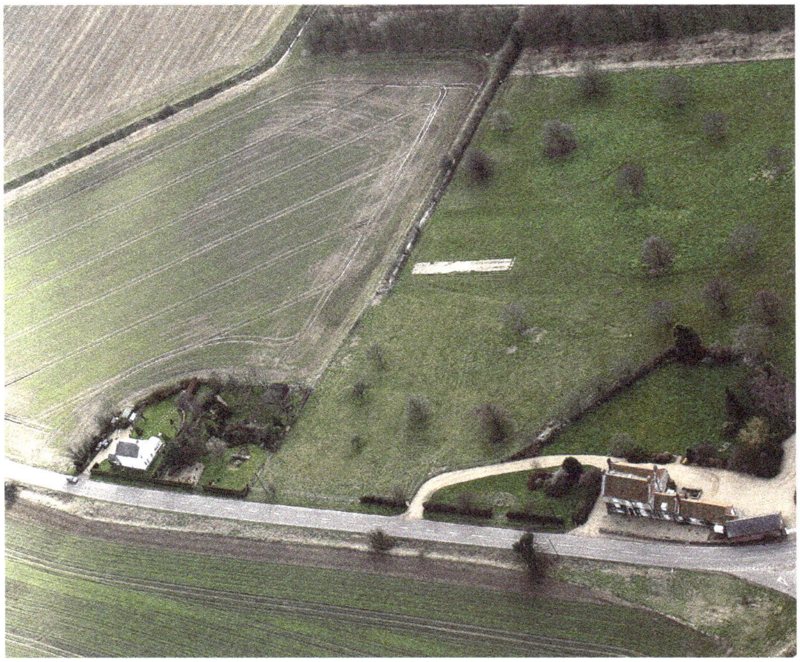

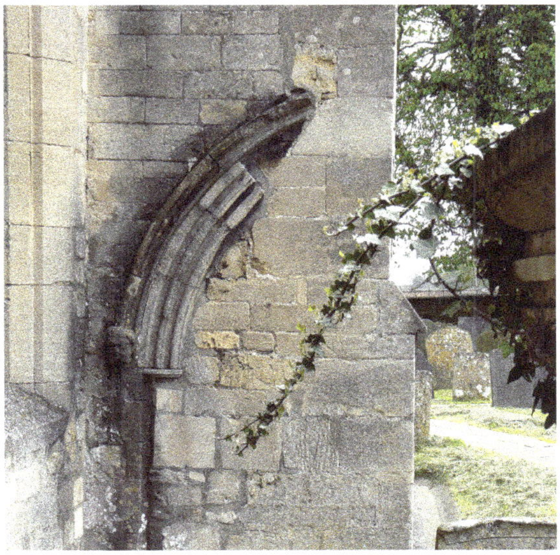

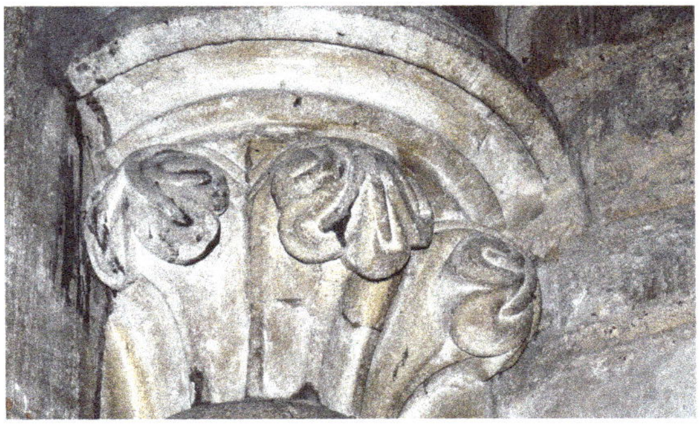

Photos - clockwise from top left

West front of Bourne Abbey Church
Water stoup beside west door
Remnant of arched doorway with carved head
Stiff-leaf decoration on column capital
Aerial view of Bridge End Priory site by Simon Erskine Crum

Burwell Priory

St Saviour • Benedictine c1110–1414

This Benedictine priory was founded very early in the twelfth century by John de Haye, but c1110 was granted by Ansgot of Burwell to the Abbey of La Sauve Majeure near Bordeaux, where he had received great hospitality. Its initial endowment comprised several churches and land, added to later by several other benefactors, but it was never wealthy. Although it was treated as an alien cell, being seized twice by Edward III and Richard II during the French wars, it did not strictly fall into that category as the Duchy of Aquitaine, to which the parent abbey belonged, was then ruled by the Kings of England. Upon the conclusion of the Hundred Years' War, however, Burwell was rightly considered an alien cell, but for unknown reasons survived the closure by Henry V in 1414. When Prior Peter de Monte Ardito died in 1427, the priory buildings were in a dilapidated state and worth nothing, and were granted to Tattershall College. Upon the Dissolution of the monasteries by Henry VIII, the King gave its possessions to Charles Brandon, first Duke of Suffolk. The earthworks did survive into the twentieth century but have been ploughed out.

Bytham Priory

• Cistercian 1147

An abbot and twelve Cistercian monks settled here in 1147 but found the site unsuitable. Within the year, they moved to a new location they called Vallis Dei, now known as The Vaudey. Well worth a visit is the church of St Medardus and St Giraldus, two sixth century French saints, and particularly the finely carved tympanum over the Priest's Door.

Cammeringham Priory

• Premonstratensian 1126–1383

This small alien priory cell had an uncertain beginning. In 1126, the church of Cammeringham was granted by Robert de Haye to the abbey of L'Essay in the diocese of Coutances, but also appears to have been given to the Premonstratensian abbey of Blanchlande in Normandy, early in the reign of Henry II. The resulting dispute between the two houses was settled in 1192 in favour of Blanchlande. The priory was probably built that same year. Its recorded history is sparse, but it is known that the advowson passed to Alice, Countess of Lancaster, and from her to Hugh le Despenser in 1325. Thereafter, it was taken into the King's hands during the wars with France, and in 1383 was leased out by Richard II to various farmers. In 1396, the abbot of Blanchlande sold all his rights to the abbot of Hulton in Staffordshire. There were two canons in residence at that time, and its annual worth was around £37. A mid-twelfth century now blocked-up undercroft said to have formed the cellars of the priory, has survived under the present manor house. The north wall of the parish church of St Michael and All Angels is plain, except for the outline of one and a half round-headed arcades of the twelfth century, believed to have been part of the cloister walk of the priory. There are no other visible remains above ground.

Catley Priory

St Mary • Gilbertine 1146/54–1538

In between Nocton and Kyme lay the Gilbertine priory of Catley. Like most Gilbertine houses, Catley was a double community of canons and nuns, with the house limited to sixty nuns and lay-sisters and thirty-five canons and brethren. Alas, nothing now remains, except a few mounds in a field, a moat and fishponds. Where canons and nuns once strolled in quiet contemplation, coming close to each other only in the church, albeit separated by a dividing wall, sheep, pheasants, rabbits and other wildlife now enjoy the rural solitude. The priory was founded between 1146 and 1154 in the reign of King Stephen by Peter de Billinghay, who endowed it with the island of Catley, the site of a grange, arable land and the chapel at Walcott, the church at Billinghay, pasturage for 400 sheep, and fishing rights on Walcott marsh. The priory attracted many other grants but these were mostly small and scattered and, although the value of its holdings increased through the excellent land management of the canons, it was never rich.

The internal life of the large double community appears to have been harmonious, with no troubles recorded. No contact was allowed between the sexes, with canons and nuns accommodated in separate buildings with a cloister for each. They shared the church, but this was divided by a wall high enough to ensure no visible contact was possible, but enabled both to hear and celebrate mass together. The nuns could only communicate with the canons by two turntable windows covered by an iron plate, which permitted only a thumb and two fingers through the gap. The nuns were responsible for all sewing and laundry, while the canons brewed their own ale, any excess of which was sold at the inn in Digby village. If the nuns ran out of ale, the

Photos – clockwise from top left

Church of St Mary and All Angels at Cammeringham
Priest's door of Bytham church of St Medardus and St Giraldus
Redundant church of St Bartholomew at Covenham
Carving of a bishop's head above church doorway

canons also had to drink water. By 1338, the house was in serious financial straits and petitioned King Edward III to be excused from taxes. It descended further into difficulties following the loss of tenants and sheep as a consequence of the Black Death. In 1535, it was valued at only £34 18s but survived until September 1538, when Prior William Swift and two canons surrendered the priory to Dr William Petre. Prioress Margaret Gastwek and four nuns were also pensioned.

Covenham Priory

- Benedictine 1082–1536

This small alien priory in a quiet backwater of the Lincolnshire Wolds was founded by William, Bishop of Durham, in 1082, on land granted by William the Conqueror to the abbey of St Carileph at Le Mans. William, a Norman, had been a Benedictine monk at St Carileph. The advowson remained with the bishops of Durham. There were probably never more than one or two monks looking after the estate of the mother house, but this is mere conjecture as almost nothing has been recorded about its history. It is clear, however, that the estate proved unprofitable for the Norman abbey, which sought and received permission from the King in 1303 to sell it to Kirkstead Abbey, with which it remained until the Dissolution in 1536, when it was granted to William Skypwyth. It has been surmised that the now redundant church of St Bartholomew once served as the chapel for the priory. Originally cruciform in shape, it lost its north transept when it was destroyed. The fabric of the church dates mainly from the fourteenth century, but was heavily restored in 1863 by Rogers and Marsden of Louth, only to be abandoned a hundred years later. Of medieval interest is a blocked thirteenth century pointed doorway in the north wall, a fourteenth century inner doorway to the porch, several three-light windows of the fourteenth and fifteenth centuries, some with cusped ogee trefoil heads, chamfered square surrounds and moulded hoods. Above the outer doorway is a large carved corbel head of a bishop.

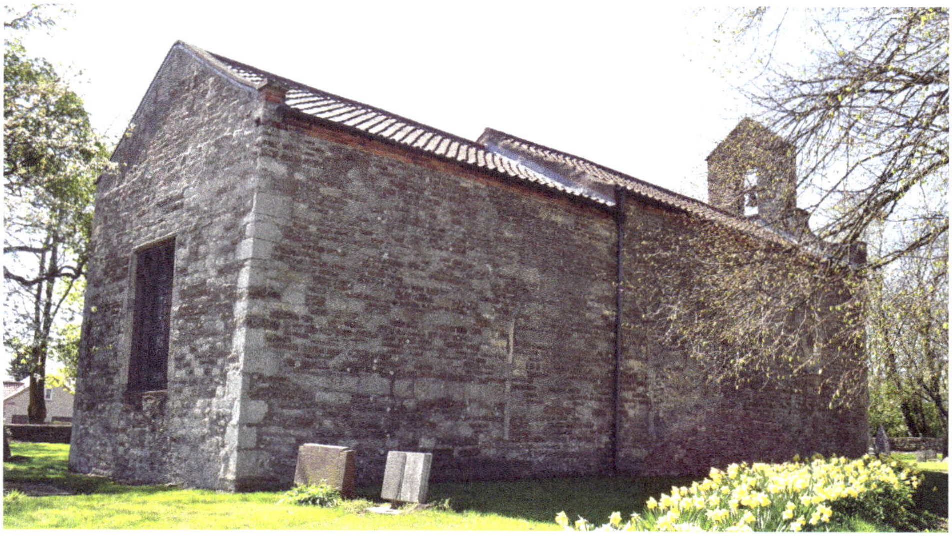

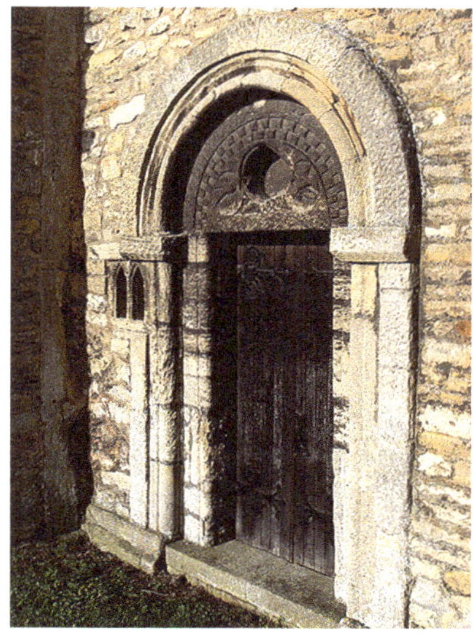

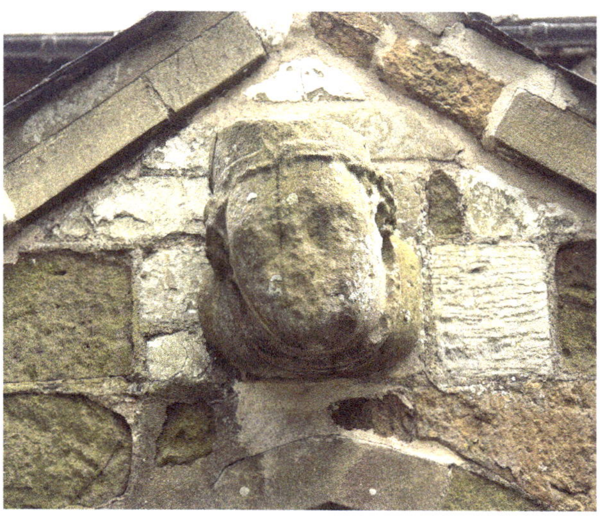

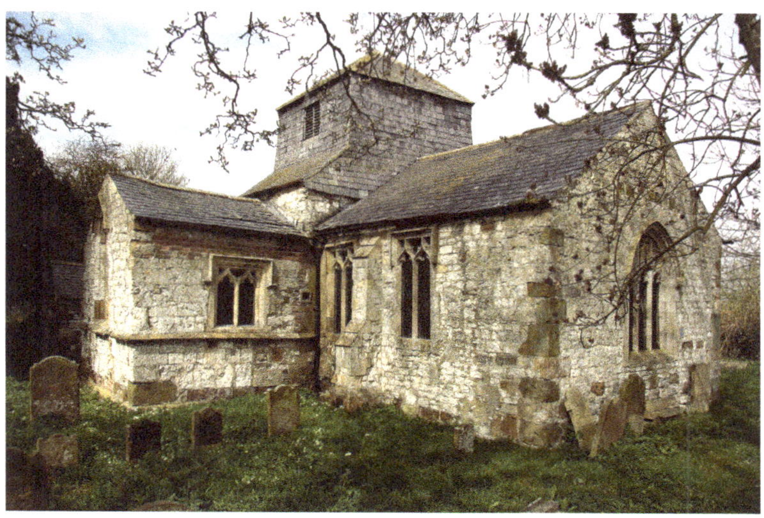

Croyland Abbey

St Mary, St Bartholomew & St Guthlac • Benedictine AD 948-1539

The magnificent west front of this partially ruined abbey can be seen from miles around in the flat landscape. Yet, this same location was once one of the many wet and remote Fenland islands that could be reached only by boat. It was this total isolation that persuaded Guthlac, a youth of royal birth, to seek a life of solitude among the Lincolnshire fens. Guthlac, together with two companions, landed at Crowland in AD 699 and lived as a hermit until his death in AD 714. On the site of Guthlac's hermitage, Ethelbald, King of Mercia, laid the foundations of a monastery, which developed into the great abbey of Croyland. Kenulph, a monk from Evesham, became the first abbot. In AD 827, Egbert, King of Wessex, defeated Witlaf, King of Mercia, who fled to Croyland, where he was concealed for three months. His Kingdom was restored to him after he paid homage to Egbert.

Tragedy struck in AD 870, when, after 200 men from the monastery had joined battle with the ravaging Danes at Kesteven, the victorious pagan hordes pursued the survivors to Croyland and slaughtered Abbot Theodore and thirty monks. They then proceeded to set fire to the bodies of the murdered monks and to the buildings, leaving behind little more than a heap of ashes. If there was one blessing in this carnage and destruction, it was that the body of St Guthlac, together with his psalter and whip, had been safely hidden in Ancarig Wood. The monastery was revived when King Eadred granted much of Wellingborough to the new foundation in AD 948.

A more peaceful reign ensued, during which the abbey was led by a succession of notable abbots, among them Ingulphus, who ruled from 1075 to 1109. His pseudo-chronicle was long thought to provide the definitive early history of the abbey, but is now acknowledged as a fifteenth century compilation. Fire again consumed the abbey in 1091, a result of negligence, destroying the church and most of the other buildings, but in 1114, Abbot Joffrid laid the foundation stone for a new church, which was dedicated to St Mary, St Bartholomew, and St Guthlac, whose relics were transferred to Croyland in 1136. Fire again brought suffering to the community of monks. In 1170, the greater part of the Benedictine abbey and church was once more burnt down, but rebuilding was put in hand by Abbot Edward immediately and completed in 1195. The relics of St Guthlac had been saved from the fire and were re-dedicated in the new church the following year.

From then on, Croyland enjoyed unbroken prosperity, being richly endowed by royal and noble visitors to the shrine of St Guthlac. Its remote location in the heart of Fenland country also insulated it from national events and ensured a peaceful existence throughout. During the Wars of the Roses, Henry IV stayed in Croyland for three days in 1460, and repaid the hospitality of Abbot John Lytlington by granting exemptions for its tenants and residents from "all fines for all kinds of transgressions, offences, misprisons, negligences, falsifications, contempts, deceits, concealments, and all other kinds of lapses whatsoever, ransoms, payments and penalties incurred or to be incurred ..." In 1467, Edward IV visited with 200 horsemen and was entertained by the abbot.
The abbey came into the hands of Henry VIII in 1539, when Abbot John Welles (or Bridges) and his twenty-seven monks signed the deed of surrender. The King granted it to the Clinton family. The annual value was estimated at over £1,093. Most of the buildings were dismantled, but the north aisle was saved as the parish church and is still in use today. The remains of the abbey were fortified during the Civil War in 1643, but besieged and taken by Cromwell's army in May that same year. In 1720, the nave roof collapsed, possibly the result of a weakening during bombardment in the Civil War, and in 1743, the south aisle was demolished and the stone used to repair the north aisle and tower.

The abbey church was 56m (183ft) long and 26.5m (87ft) wide and comprised a nine-bay aisled nave, a 27.4m (90ft) long five-bay apsidal choir, a central tower, and a detached bell tower at the east end was begun in 1427. In 1470, Abbot John Lytlington gave five bells, whose clear ringing tone could be heard far and wide across the empty expanse of the fen. The present ruins consist of a few piers and Norman arches of the nave, and the splendid west front. This retains its great, now empty window, completed in 1370, and is elaborately decorated with five tiers of sculpted images of St Guthlac and other saints, apostles and persons associated with the abbey. The interior of the church is a long, graceful space highlighted by its tierceron ribbed vault, with the ribs springing directly from the piers, uninterrupted by capitals. Worth looking out for is an odd font, or holy water stoup, set into one of the piers, and a rare memorial to a church mason, William de Wermington, who died in 1427.

Photos - clockwise from top

The partially ruined abbey church is a famous landmark
Ruined nave with Norman arch from old crossing
Detail of Norman arch
Delicate blind arcading around doorway
Lower west front with St Guthlac's relief
Upper part of west front still retaining its statuary

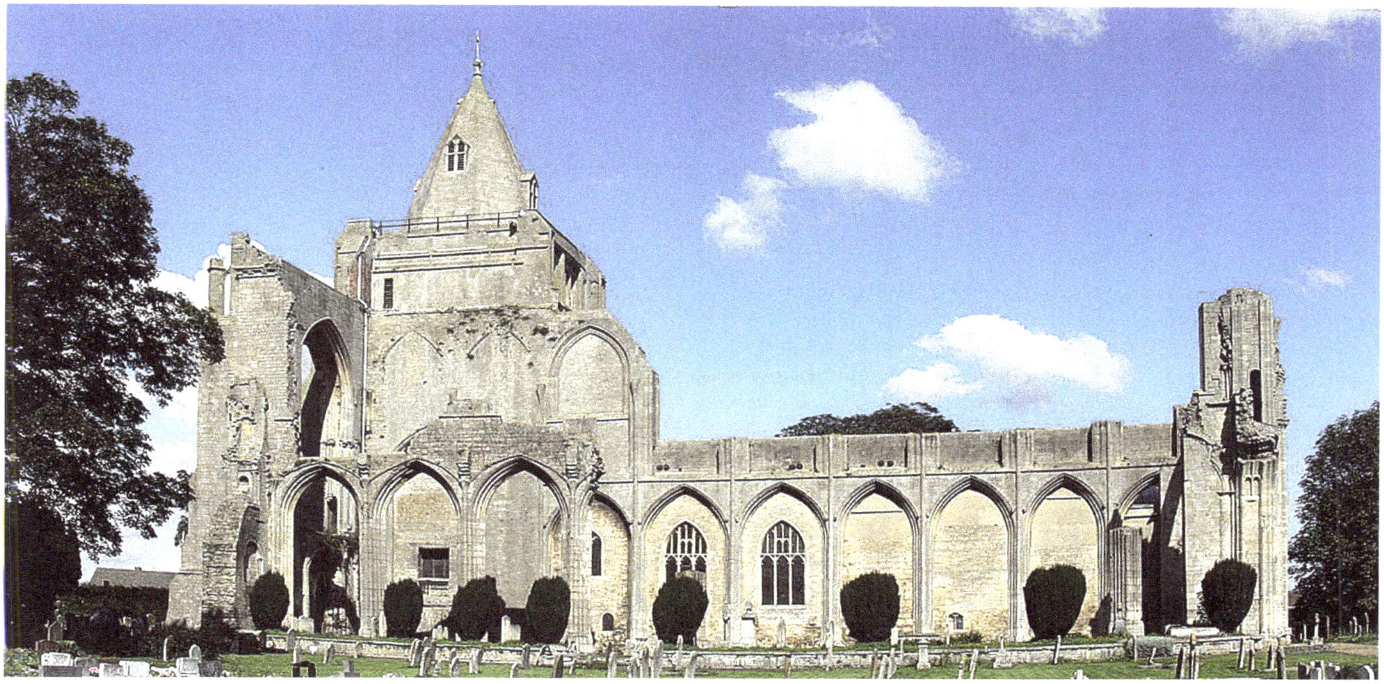

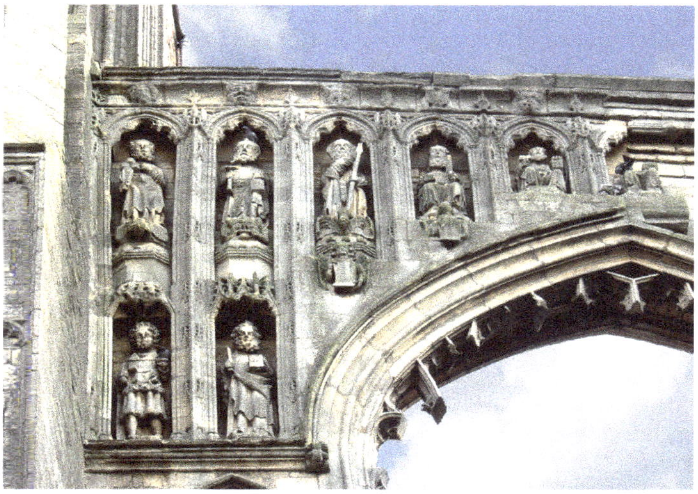

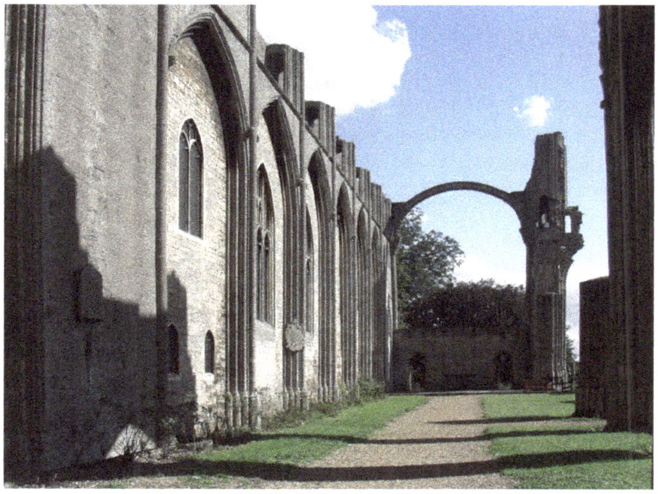

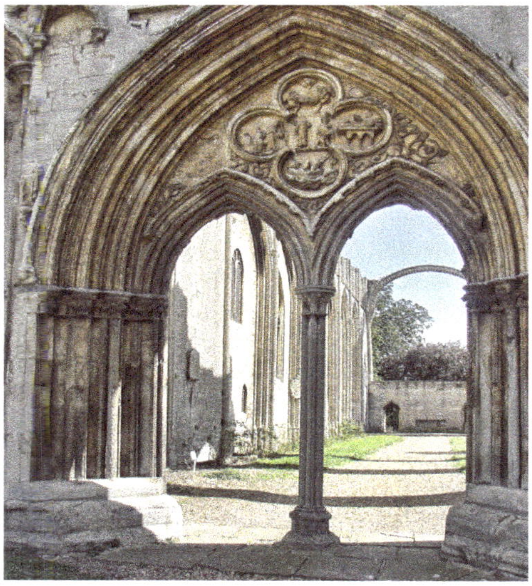

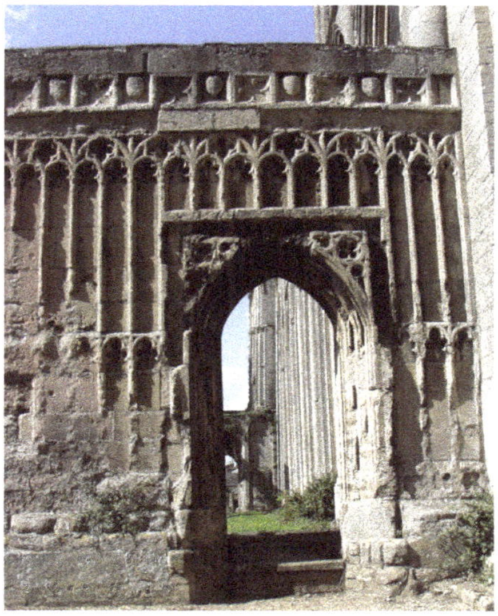

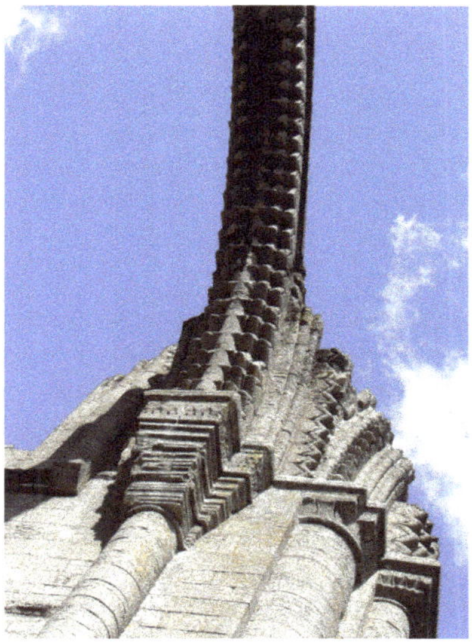

Deeping Priory

St James • Benedictine 1139–1539

The Priory Church of Deeping St James is all that is left of this priory cell of the Benedictine abbey of Thorney in Cambridgeshire, but there is much still to be admired from its medieval existence. In spite of the cell probably never having housed more than three or four monks, the church is of an impressive size, measuring 55m (180ft) in length. The tower, although it blends well with the older fabric of the church, is an eighteenth century replacement of the original, which fell in 1717, having been undermined by centuries of flooding. After passing through the thirteenth century south porch with its hoodmould and dogtooth decoration, the first item of great interest is the twelfth century tub-shaped font with interlaced Romanesque arcading. In the baptistery, nebule moulding above and traces of chevron and lozenge string course below suggest that this section marked the outside wall of the smaller, earlier building. The south aisle was extended and its roof raised between 1250 and 1349.

The impressive twelfth century nave arcade of seven bays is topped by a triforium made up of thirteen pointed arches. These originally continued further east and are Early English. The broken springers on two of the nave arcades may indicate a division of the church between monastic and lay areas. A blocked-up archway past the choir stalls on the left is known as the 'Prior's Door'. Also on the south side of the sanctuary is a twelfth century four-arched sedilia, with a double piscina alongside, the latter dating from the mid-thirteenth century. The two-light window above with foliated capitals is said to have been donated c 1230 by Prior David, who later became abbot of Thorney. The three perpendicular windows on the north side date from 1408.

Deeping St James Priory was founded by Baldwin fitzGilbert, a junior member of the de Clare family, which was much favoured by Henry I. After acquiring much land in the south of the county, which became known as the Honour of Bourne and Deeping, Baldwin extended his estate eastwards, through reclamation of the fens. The endowment of religious foundations came next with the founding of a house for Arrouaisian canons at Bourne in 1138, followed a year later by Deeping, where Baldwin favoured the Benedictine Order. The church was consecrated on St James' day in 1139 by Alexander, Bishop of Lincoln. The original church was much smaller, but as it also served as the parish church, it had been enlarged within fifty years to take account of population growth. Like all small cells of the greater abbeys, the priory cell has little independent history over the four hundred years of its existence and the only event worthy of note was some trouble about the tithes of the two churches belonging to the priory in the early years, and its association at the end of the fifteenth century with Lady Margaret Beaufort, mother of King Henry VII. Lady Margaret took a particular interest in the priory, after she inherited the manors of Bourne and Deeping, granting it the right to have its own mill, which proved a major source of income. In return, she was mentioned in the monks' prayers. Deeping Priory was dissolved with the final surrender of Thorney Abbey in December 1539 and its lands sold to the Duke of Norfolk. The last prior, William Lee, was pensioned off.

Elsham Priory

St Mary & St Edmund • Augustinian -1166–1536

This small priory began life as a hospital for the poor, founded before 1166 by Beatrice d'Amundeville for one or two Augustinian canons. Her three sons, Walter, William and Elias, increased the endowment, and c1200, Jocelyn d'Amundeville, son of Elias, confirmed the gifts of his predecessors, having first supported attempts by the Knights Hospitallers to lay claim to the endowments. No mention was then made of a hospital, and it is believed that it had become an Augustinian priory. Little is known of its history, but a visitation in 1440 found standards among the small community to have fallen far short of the religious rule and canons 'unlearned' and prone to eat and drink to excess, thus depleting the priory's income. Discipline improved in later years. The last prior, John Baxter, six canons and one novice, surrendered the house under the first Act of Suppression in 1536. Its annual value had been assessed two years previously at £70. The only trace of the priory is the old fishpond in the grounds of the eighteenth century Elsham Hall, which now occupies the site.

Fosse Priory

St Mary • Cistercian nuns -1184–1539

Nothing is left of this small and extremely poor Cistercian nunnery, which was apparently founded before 1184 by the men of Torksey. Nothing is known about its history until 1341, when Edward III granted the nuns exemption from taxes on their wool, because their endowment was not sufficient to maintain themselves without alms and help from friends. When Bishop Alnwick visited in 1440, he found nothing amiss but poverty. The prioress and five nuns then in residence appeared to bear their burden with dignity and without complaint, other than pointing out the difficulty in keeping their house in good repair. In 1534, the house was valued at a paltry £7 3s, causing the King's commissioner, Dr London, to call it "a beggarly poor house" when he accepted the surrender of Prioress Agnes Marr and seven nuns in July 1539. It probably survived the earlier Act of Suppression because there were no material gains from closing it down.

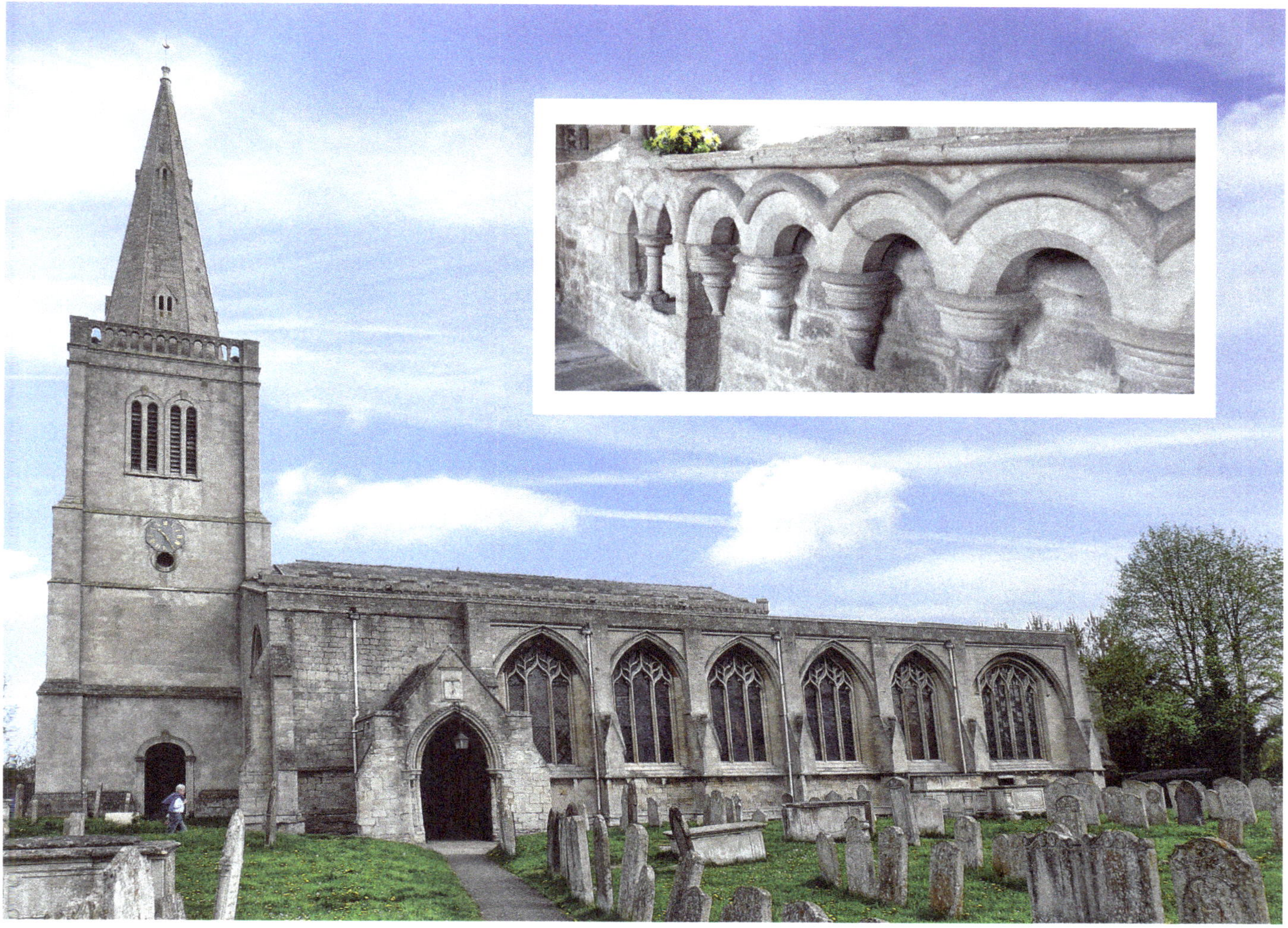

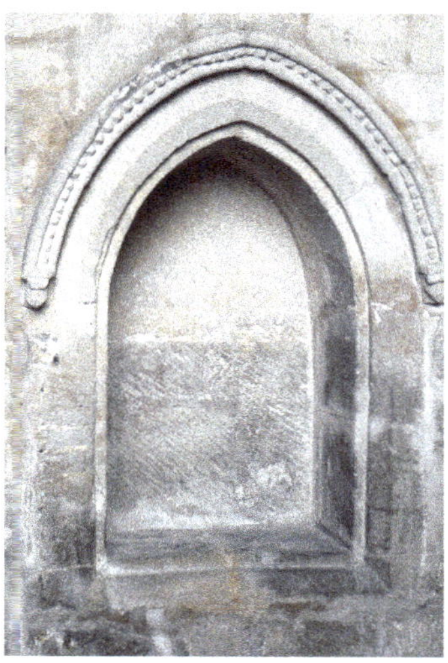

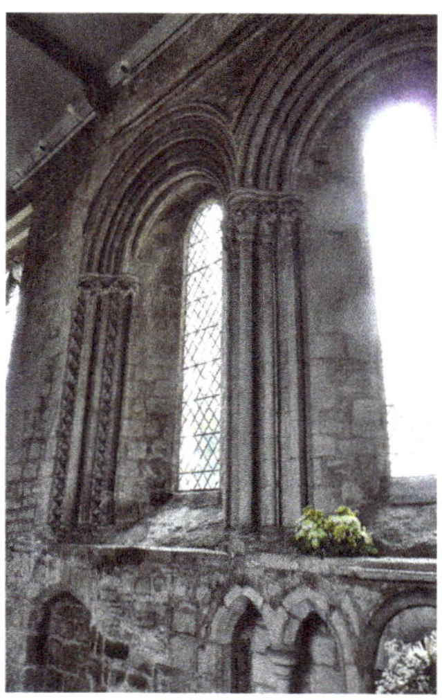

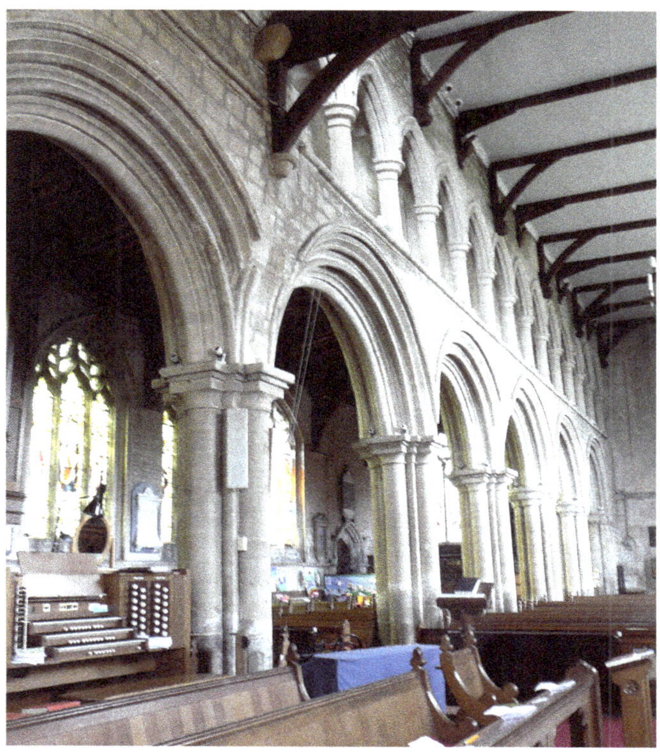

Photos – clockwise from top

Priory Church of Deeping St James
Inset - Four-arched sedilia with double piscina alongside
Impressive seven-bay nave arcade with triforium
Medieval aumbry in chapel
Prior David's window

Freiston Priory

St James • Benedictine +1114–1539

This Benedictine priory was founded soon after 1114, when Alan de Creoun gave the church of Freiston to Croyland Abbey, which sent a prior and probably twelve monks to Freiston. The new priory received further endowments, which eventually included several churches and diverse parcels of land. Little independent history has been recorded, the only upheaval appearing to have incurred in 1283 when several people broke through the doors and consumed the victuals provided for the household. They also stayed for some time at the expense of their unwilling hosts. When Bishop Gray visited in 1431, he found that the number of monks had dwindled to seven, and that all were aged and infirm and unable to maintain daily services. He ordered the abbot of Croyland to bring the community up to the original numbers with young men, but this had not been implemented when Bishop Alnwick came to the priory in 1440, seriously endangering the continued existence of the house, further exacerbated by the negligence and absence of the prior. It may be assumed that the required reform was soon effected, as the cell continued until the dissolution of the mother house in December 1539. Its value in 1534 had been assessed at £167 8s.

The parish church incorporates the nine-bay nave of the conventual church, but the transepts and presbytery to the east were demolished after the Dissolution. Strong evidence of this can be seen in the great pointed arch with Norman decorations above the altar, now in-filled, and on the outside the presence of 'interior' pillars of Norman style, partly supporting the arch. There are six pairs of simple round arches supported by stubby circular piers and plain square capitals in the nave, and three pairs of more slender piers with pointed arches and carved capitals, confirming that the nave was extended westwards in the thirteenth century. Further changes were effected in the fourteenth and fifteenth century by raising the roof to provide more light, and aisles and the tower were added. The stone font, with its kneeling stones, is of a delicate design, while the cantilevered cover is particularly fine, with delicate tracery reflecting the designs in the windows. It was carved, so the story goes, by an apprentice, and when the master saw how beautifully it was made, he flew into a jealous rage and killed the lad. Considerable restoration of the church took place in 1871. Nothing at all has survived of other priory buildings. Four stone coffins, all dating from before 1300, were discovered in 1900. Of interest in the churchyard is a medieval stone cross, of which the base and part of the shaft have survived.

Gokewell Priory

St Mary • Cistercian nuns +1154–1536

This was another exceptionally poverty stricken house of Cistercian nuns, whose endowments were barely enough to provide food and clothing. It was probably founded in the reign of Henry II by William de Alta Ripa who, together with other benefactors, provided the nuns with only small parcels of land in the neighbourhood. A school for boys up to eight years of age and girls up to ten years of age supplemented their income, but when Bishop Alnwick visited in 1440, he found the house very poor, but in good order. Throughout most of its history, a warden or steward took charge of the temporalities, as in other small nunneries. Its annual value was a mere £16, and the house was surrendered in 1536 by the last prioress, Anne Castleford, and seven nuns. Not a vestige is left of this priory, which stood in a quiet wooded valley, but there is slight evidence of thirteenth century masonry in the now derelict farm buildings.

Grantham Grey Friars

St Francis -1290–1539

The Friars Minor established a house in Grantham by 1290, when Pope Nicholas IV granted indulgences to penitents visiting the church. Not much is known about their daily lives. In about 1300, there were apparently twenty friars in residence and there are records of grants of corn and land from John de Warenne, Earl of Surrey, and his descendants. In 1314, Richard Kellew, Bishop of Durham, authorised the friars to build a leaden conduit to bring water to their house, on condition that they make good any disturbance to the ground and keep the pipes in good repair.

In 1339, a murderer took sanctuary in the church of the friars and when a similar incident happened in the next century, the friars came into dispute with the town but maintained the right of sanctuary after an appeal to the King. A Provincial Chapter of the Premonstratensian Order was held in the church in 1492. Richard Ingworth, Bishop of Dover, received the surrender of the house from Warden Richard Hopkins and an unknown number of friars in February 1539. The site, which included the church, cemetery, aqueduct, gardens and several tenements, was sold to Austin Porter of Belton in 1542. The house stood at the west side of Market Place but there are no remains.

Greenfield Priory

St Mary • Cistercian nuns -1153–1536

Very little history is known of this house of Cistercian nuns founded before 1153 by Eudo de Grainsby and his son, Ralf de Aby. Ranulf, Earl of Chester, was also a benefactor and, while the endowment included land and churches, the nuns always struggled against poverty. In 1303, Bishop Dalderby found that the prioress had been absent for two years and that the house was in danger of serious financial loss, causing the bishop to permit a remission of tithes in 1312. No other visitations have been recorded until that of Bishop Atwater in 1519, during which he found few complaints. However, in 1525, two nuns were found guilty of moral lapses and were required to lie prone on the chapter house floor twice a week, for the nuns to walk over them as they entered. The annual income of the house was assessed in 1534 at £63 4s, leading to its suppression in 1536. In residence then were the prioress, Agnes or Anne Guderyk, and nine nuns. Only earthworks and a moat remind of the existence of the house, although the moat may have served a post-Dissolution house. The farmhouse on the site may incorporate some early carved stones.

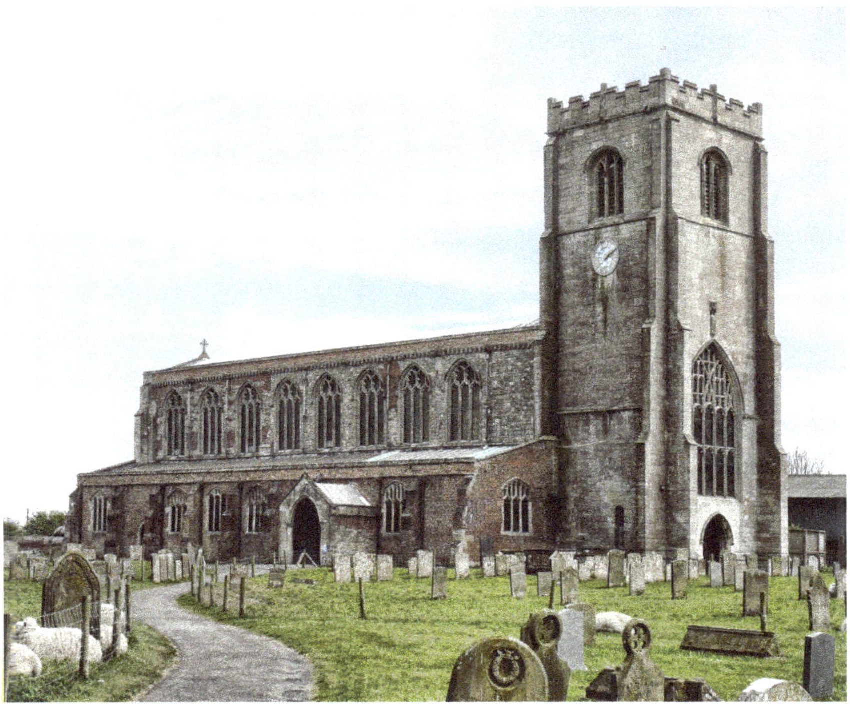

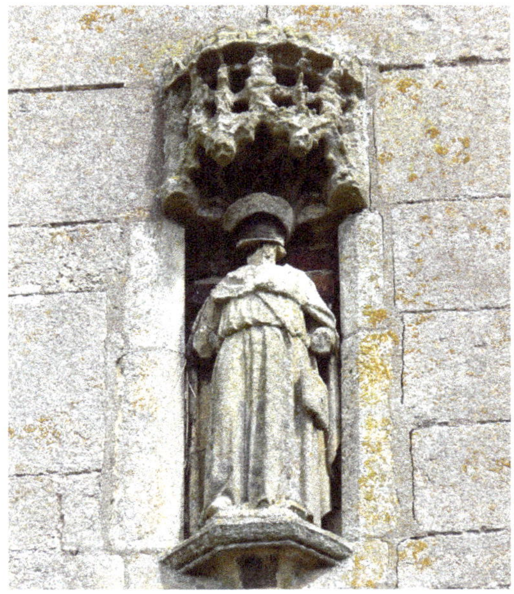

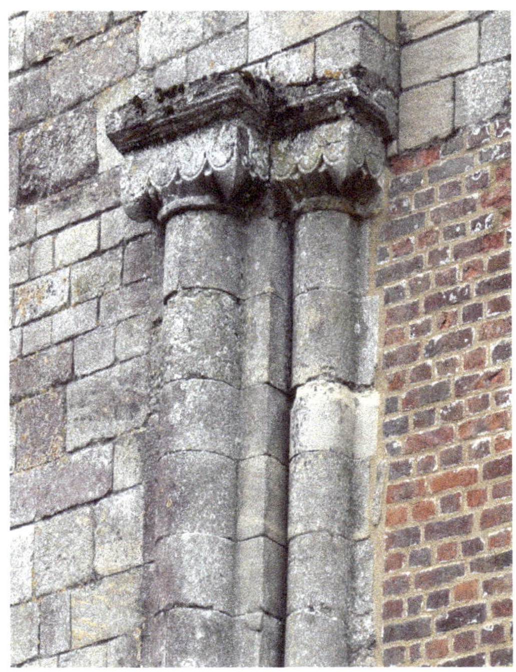

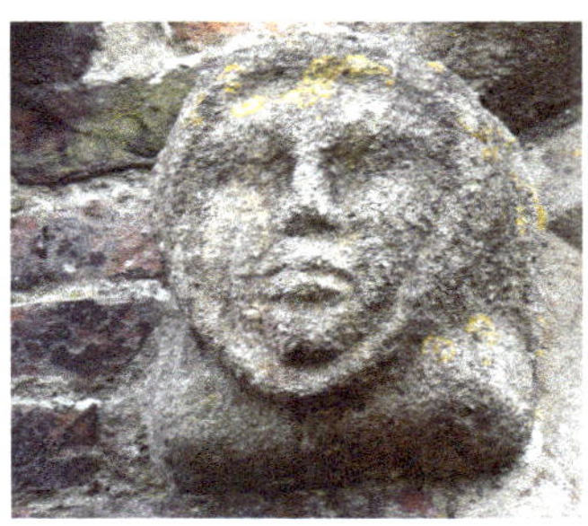

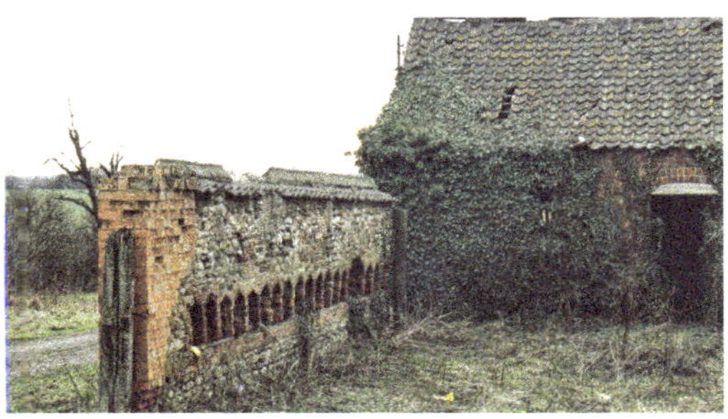

Photos - clockwise from top left

The large parish church of Freiston incorporating the nave of the conventual church

Defaced stone statue under an ornate baldachin over the east window

Former interior columns with scalloped capitals on external face of the church

Sandstone carving of hooded head

Remains of Gokewell Priory, now believed demolished

Grimsby Priory

St Leonard • Augustinian canonesses +1154–1539

This poor and obscure house of Augustinian canonesses was probably founded during the reign of Henry II, but the identity of the founder remains unknown. In 1184, the house was placed under the protection of the Austin canons of Wellow. At various times in their long history, the nuns had to beg for alms and were excused taxes, on account of poverty. This was due to insufficient endowments, and great damage by fire, which, in 1311 and 1459, consumed their buildings and corn. Their lands were also inundated by flood waters in the latter year. No episcopal visitations have been recorded and the only information about the internal state of the house dates from 1337, when absolution was granted to a nun for apostasy, with another absolved in 1356 for a breach of chastity. In spite of its minute annual income of £9 14s, the priory was not suppressed in 1536, but lingered on until September 1539. The last prioress, Margaret Riddesdale, and an unknown number of nuns received pensions. There are no visible remains.

Grimsby Austin Friars

1293–1539

Founded in 1293 by William Fraunk with a messuage in Grimsby, the friars were always poor, in spite of several additional bequests over the years. Few historic details are available. The only events of note were an attack on one of the friars by townsfolk in 1339, which resulted in the friars being awarded a one-year protection, and another unjust assault in the fifteenth century. The attackers were ordered by the King to desist. In 1536, the prior of the house, together with the warden of the Grey Friars, became involved in the Lincolnshire Rising, but appears to have survived retribution. When an agent of Thomas Cromwell visited the house in October 1538, he found that most friars had deserted. The prior surrendered the house to Richard Ingworth, Bishop of Dover, in February 1539. In 1542, the site was granted to the Dean and Chapter of Westminster. Nothing is left.

Grimsby Grey Friars

-1240–1538

Apart from bequests and small legacies, little has been recorded of the history of this house of the Friars Minor. It was founded before 1240, but the founder's identity is not known. In 1255, Henry III granted the friars twenty oaks in Sherwood Forest for the enlargement of their house. In 1313, Edward II authorised them to build a subterranean conduit from Holm to the priory, which in part went through the King's land. The warden, Adam Howeton, rode out to the rebels of the Lincolnshire Rising and gave them money borrowed from the prior of the Austin Friars. In October 1538, John Freeman, Cromwell's agent, accepted the surrender from the warden and six friars. There are no visible remains.

Hagnaby Abbey

St Thomas the Martyr • Premonstratensian 1175–1536

This Premonstratensian house is said to have been founded as a priory in 1175 by Agnes de Orreby, widow of Henry de Orreby, and colonised by canons from Welbeck Abbey. The original endowments consisted of small parcels of land and the church of Hagnaby, with apparently little added in subsequent times. The house was elevated to abbey status in 1250, but very little else is known. The abbot was appointed visitor of the English province at least once in the fourteenth century. Several visitations by Bishop Redman between 1475 and 1503 resulted in good reports, both in spiritual and temporal matters, with only a lapse in the rule of silence in the cloister and refectory remarked upon. In 1478, the house was free of debt and money was owed to the canons. With a clear annual value of £87 11s, the abbey was suppressed in 1536. Abbot Edmund Toft and six canons received pensions. It was reported that that there was local indignation, which helped to bring about the Lincolnshire Rising, about the irreverent manner in which the King's officers took down the pyx, containing the Blessed Sacrament, which hung above the altar.

Haugham Priory

• Benedictine +1080–1337

The alien priory cell of Haugham was built upon land granted by Hugh d'Avranches, first Earl of Chester, towards the end of the eleventh century, to his Benedictine abbey of St Severus in the Normandy diocese of Coutances. It probably never had more than a prior and one or two monks, to manage the abbey's estate and to pray for the soul of the founder. As with all alien cells, the wars with France caused great difficulties and Haugham was seized by the King in 1337 and then let out to farm. By 1385, it was alleged that the various farmers had wasted much of the property of the house and, in 1397, it was granted to the Carthusian priory of St Anne at Coventry. The value of the house in 1380 was just £19. Not a vestige from the priory has survived.

Haverholme Priory

St Mary • Gilbertine 1139–1538

In 1137, Alexander, Bishop of Lincoln, offered to Abbot Gervase of Fountains a marshy island in the river near Sleaford for the establishment of a Cistercian abbey. The offer was accepted and, although two years were spent on erecting the monastic buildings and monks arrived from Fountains, the site was considered unsuitable and the bishop gave them a new site at Louth Park in 1139. The bishop then turned to his former confessor, Gilbert of Sempringham, who sent nuns, lay-sisters and lay-brothers, to take possession of the existing buildings. The community soon fell into severe poverty, but a gift of land from Simon Tushett in 1140 eased their plight, which improved further later with benefactions from Henry II, Roger de Mowbray and Roger de Lacy. Gilbert added canons to the community in 1148 and then limited the numbers in the house to 100 nuns and lay-sisters, and fifty canons and lay-brothers. In 1164, Thomas, Archbishop of Canterbury, found shelter at Haverholme, among other houses of the Gilbertine order, when he fled abroad from the Council of Northampton. The needs of the community were met by various benefactions and the sale of wool, which at the beginning of the fourteenth century amounted to fifteen sacks a year.

The time of Edward II was not a happy one for the community. Complaints were made that the prior refused to repair the water course to Kyme, and failed to provide a boat 'by day and night' to carry foot passengers at the Bothe near the Wathe mouth over the Kesteven crossing. Men broke into the priory's property, stole fish and goods and assaulted the canons and manservants. In 1330, some knights broke the banks of the fishery and flooded 300 acres of meadows. At the same time, they assaulted two canons, one lay-brother and a servant, imprisoned one canon and robbed the other of money. There is no record of reprisals. The later history is obscure. The priory was surrendered in September 1538 by Prior William Hall and six canons. Also then in residence were Prioress Margaret Woodhouse and seven nuns. In 1535, the clear annual value of the property was £70 15s. The present ruin on the site is the remains of a nineteenth century Gothic house.
(see photo below courtesy of Colin Brammer).

Heynings Priory

St Mary • Cistercian +1134–1539

This Cistercian house was founded early in the reign of King Stephen by Rayner de Evermue for 'brethren and sisters', but the brethren were probably priests serving as chaplains and the house was ruled by a prioress. Its well-documented history is one of impoverishment due to diverse misfortunes, including meagre endowments, barrenness of land, 'multiplication of guests and corrodies', and costly repairs, and several injunctions for negligence of religious rules and the admission of children and seculars to the cloister and dormitory. When Bishop Atwater visited in 1519, there was nothing to correct. On account of their poverty, the nuns were from time to time absolved of payments to the King, and various grants in the fourteenth century, including the advowson of Knaith and the church of Wormersley in Yorkshire, provided some relief. As its annual income in 1534 was only £49 5s, it should have been dissolved with the lesser monasteries in 1536, but was somehow spared. It was eventually surrendered in July 1539 by Prioress Jane Sanford and eleven nuns, all of whom received pensions. Nothing has survived.

Hirst Priory

St Mary • Augustinian c1300–c1540

The tiny Augustinian cell of Hirst in Axholme was built on land granted by Nigel d'Albini to Nostell Priory, probably early in the twelfth century. It was never conventual and supported just one resident canon, who managed the grove and marsh of Hirst, and collected tithes of corn, malt and fish from the neighbourhood. It still belonged to Nostell in 1534, when it was worth just £7 11s.

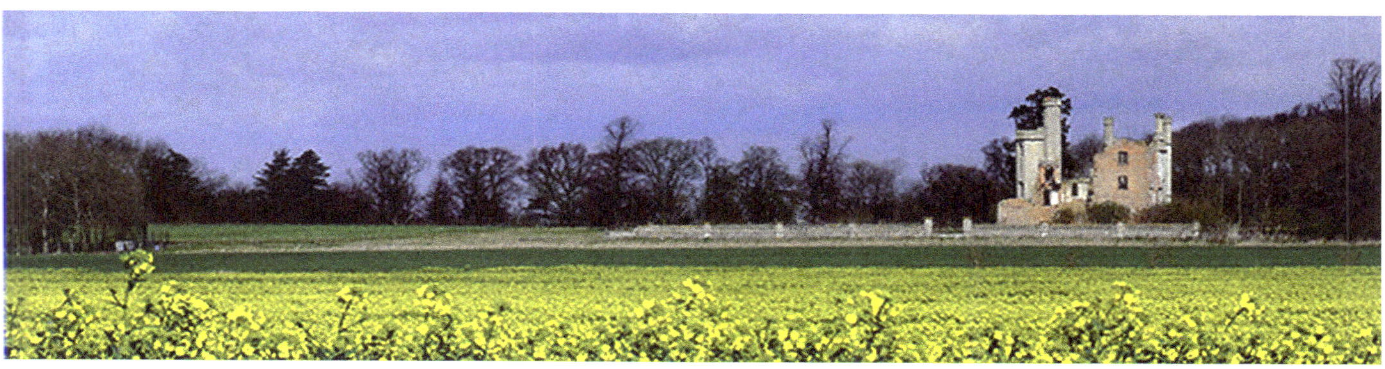

Site of Haverholme Priory

Hough Priory

St Mary • Augustinian c1164–1414

An Augustinian priory cell was founded at Hough-on-the-Hill about the year 1164, when Henry II gave the manor and church to his abbey of St Mary de Voto at Cherbourg in Normandy. The endowment was barely enough to support the prior and single chaplain, who were to maintain divine service for the King and his family. When the small income derived from the manor was transferred to the Exchequer during the wars with France, the chaplain was withdrawn, and in 1340, even the prior, now the sole occupant, was reduced to beseeching the King for remission of his arrears. By 1349, everything of value had been sold to pay the Exchequer and most of the chantries in the priory church had lapsed. Its revenue was valued in 1388 at £38 8s. The priory was restored by Henry IV to the abbey of Cherbourg in 1399, but finally granted to the Carthusians of Mount Grace by Henry VI in 1432, and confirmed to them by Edward IV in 1462.

Humberston Abbey

St Mary & St Peter • Benedictine c1160–1536

Not a vestige is left of this house of Benedictine monks, said to have been connected to the Normandy Hambye Abbey of the Order of Tiron, although there is no documentary evidence that it was so. It certainly was not considered an alien house and was never taken into the King's hands during the wars with France. It was founded in c1160 during the reign of Henry II by William fitzRalph, but its endowments were probably never enough to support more than twelve monks and the community dwindled over the centuries. In 1305, a fire reduced the monastic buildings to ashes, forcing the monks to sell the advowson of one of their churches, and beg for alms, to enable them to rebuild. Not all was well within the community. The abbey was regularly visited by the bishops of Lincoln who found much to be remedied. In 1358, a commission was issued for the correction of the house, on account of the daily 'crimes, excesses, and other insolences'. Although there was some improvement, a visitation by Bishop Alnwick in 1440 found the community again disobedient, unruly, quarrelsome and rebellious, most likely because of the frequent absence of a superior in the chapter. Four years later, the house was described as in "a state of collapse, spiritual and temporal". Mismangement also plunged the house into debt. Its annual value in 1536 was assessed at only £34 and the abbey was suppressed in 1536. The last abbot, Robert Coningsby, received a pension. There were also four monks and a lay-brother.

Kirkstead Abbey

St Mary • Cistercian 1139–1537

One startling remnant of masonry at Kirkstead Abbey continues to point defiantly to the heavens. Sparse as the remains are, some broken detail of window arches and vaulting of the south transept of the abbey church remind the visitor that this was one of the greater abbeys of Lincolnshire. The moat that enclosed the abbey and the outline of the buildings within can still be roughly recognised from the prominent mounds. Several large depressions in an adjacent field were probably the monastic fishponds. Also of great interest is the chapel of St Leonard's Without, which was built c1230 outside the abbey's gates, most probably for lay-brothers, although it has also been described as a chantry chapel in memory of Robert de Tattersall, who died in 1212. Fortunately, it was spared when the abbey was surrendered at the Dissolution, and remains open for worship. The chapel measures only 12.8 x 5.8m (42 x 19ft), but has the feel of a mini cathedral and is an Early Gothic gem. The west doorway is adorned with stiff-leaf capitals and dogtooth decoration, which is repeated in the blind arcading above. The interior is lit by six lancet windows on each side and a triple lancet at the east end, highlighting an abundance of stiff-leaf foliage and dogtooth decorations on bosses of the vaulted roof, and on capitals, corbels and arches. A screen with simple trefoiled arches could be one of the oldest wooden screens in England. Not to be missed is the monument to an early thirteenth century knight with an ancient 'coal-scuttle' helmet but no facial features. His identity will never be known.

Kirkstead Abbey was founded by Hugh Brito, Lord of Tattersall, in 1139 and colonised by monks from Fountains Abbey in Yorkshire. Robert of Sudholme became the first abbot. The original site, a level plain surrounded by marshland, was not only said to be "a place of horror like a vast solitude", but it was also too small. In 1187, therefore, Hugh's son Robert granted leave to the monks to move to a more amenable location nearby. Through the patronage of the Brito family and considerable grants from other benefactors, the abbey became quite wealthy, benefiting from the wool trade, agriculture and the ownership of four iron forges. The alien cell of Covenham was given to the abbey in 1303. Not all was well, however. The abbey later suffered impoverishment through the failure of its flocks of sheep from murrain, and from mismanagement and 'unthriftiness' of a succession of abbots. The house was also not without scandal. In 1275, the abbot was accused of claiming the right to erect a gallows at Thimbleby, for which he could not present a charter, and was also accused of buying wool and selling it to

Flemish merchants. In 1404, an unruly monk ejected the abbot to whom he objected, but the abbot regained control and the monk was condemned to perpetual silence. Other minor misdemeanours were also reported. In 1534, the abbey's clear annual value was assessed at £286 2s, which was a goodly amount given its earlier state of poverty. The last abbot, Richard Harrison, and three of his monks were implicated, probably unjustly, in the 1536 rising at Lincoln and were put to death in 1537. The abbey was attainted and deliberately destroyed.

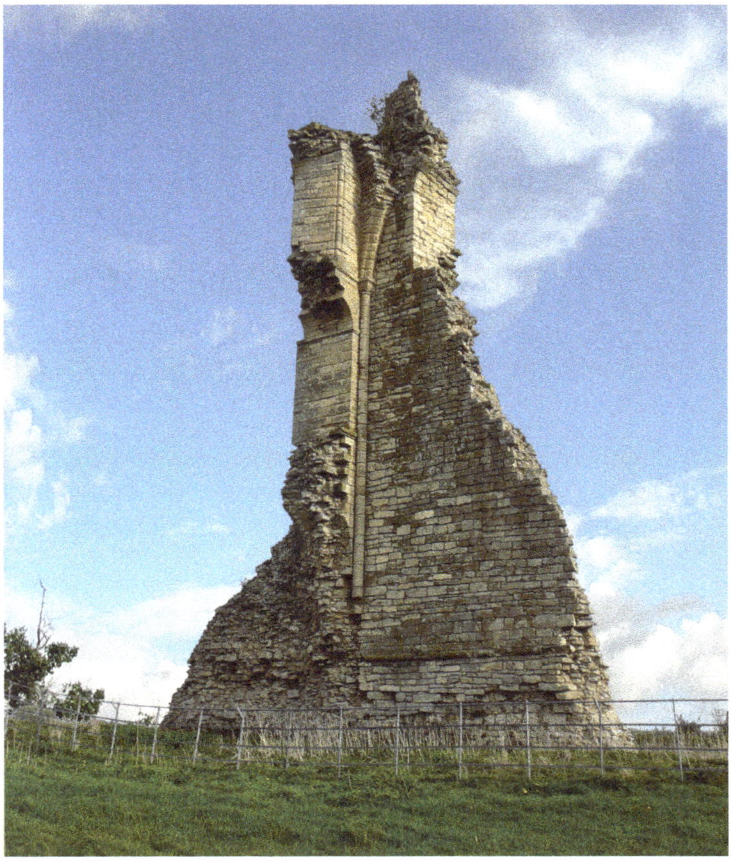

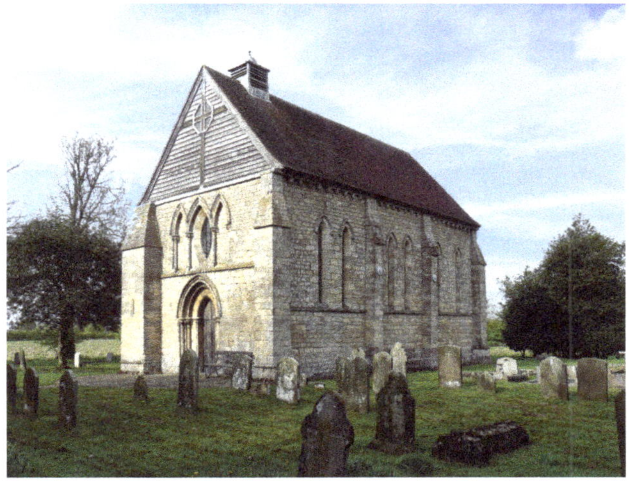

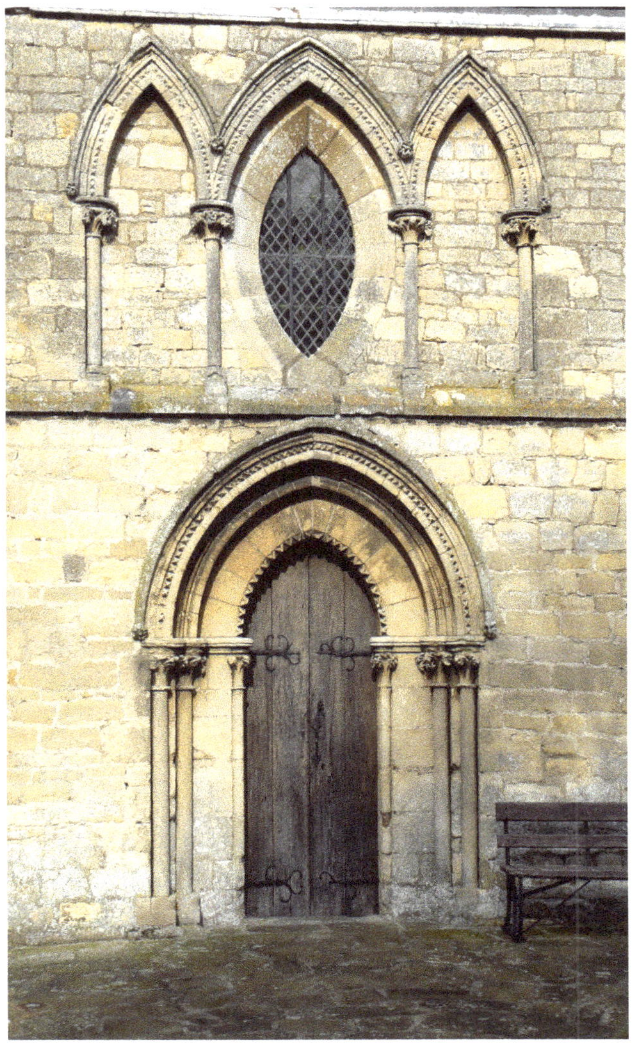

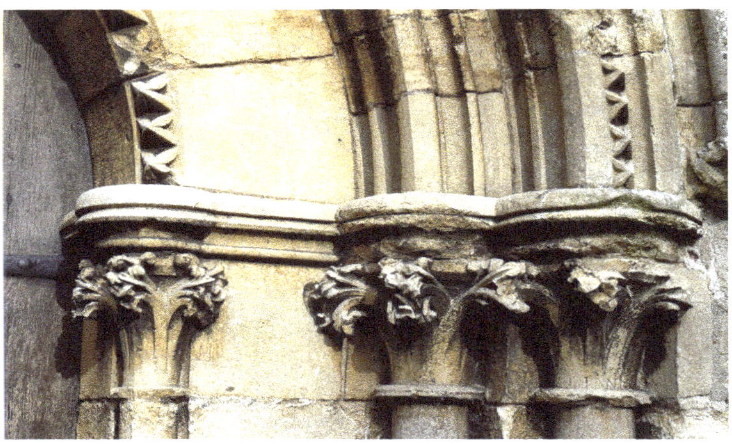

Photos of Kirkstead Abbey – clockwise from top left

Fragment of south transept with remnants of vaulting
Chapel of St Leonards Without
West door of chapel with unusual window above
Columns with stiff leaf capitals supporting west door arch

Kyme Priory

St Mary • Augustinian -1169–1539

The Augustinian Priory of Kyme was founded in honour of the Blessed Mary by Philip of Kyme, steward to Gilbert, Earl of Lincoln, sometime before 1169. It was located on the north bank of the River Slea within the wider Witham Valley and never had more than a dozen canons and remained poor. Its endowments comprised only the demesne land and smaller benefactions with several churches in the neighbourhood. A lengthy period in the fourteenth and fifteenth centuries was marked by visitations, which found a disturbing flouting of the rules, including a lack of contemplation and study time. In 1377, Bishop Bokyngham forbade the wearing of swords or any other weapons, or have the habits unnecessarily ornamented. There were injunctions against canons eating and drinking outside the monastery, or entertaining friends too liberally. Similar injunctions were issued by Bishop Flemyng in 1422. The visitation by Bishop Alnwick in 1440 is preserved in full and makes interesting reading. The prior complained that his canons were too fond of idle sports, with one canon hunting for his own profit, there was too free access of seculars to choir and refectory, too many boys in the choir disturbing divine service, the infirmary was in disrepair, and the obedientiaries ate in the town of Kyme while there on business. The bishop dealt with all these points, particularly demanding that time spent on games should be given to contemplation, reading and study. Apart from these none too serious misdemeanours, the priory appears to have been an admirable religious establishment. With a clear annual value of £101 0s, it survived the first Act of Suppression in 1536 after the canons paid a hefty fine for being allowed to continue. It was finally surrendered by Prior Ralph Fairfax and nine canons in July 1539. Site and possessions were granted to the earl of Rutland and Robert Tyrwhitt.

The west end of the south aisle, together with the southern section of the adjacent nave and porch of the conventual church is incorporated in the present parish church of South Kyme, which was much altered in 1890. Of particular note is a Norman doorway of c1140 and water stoup, enclosed by the original south porch, above which is a worn and headless statue of the Coronation of the Virgin. There are several interesting items within the church, including fragments of Saxon stone in the north wall with knotwork and carving of a cross, which probably dates from the seventh or eighth centuries, and pieces of fifteenth century glass within the fourteenth century widows. The congregation has dwindled over the years and only two services a month are now held in the church. This lack of use contributes to its slightly worn and neglected look, but its picturesque setting on the edge of the village is sublime.

Legbourne Priory

St Mary • Cistercian nuns c1150–1536

A house occupies the site of this former priory for Cistercian nuns founded c1150 by Robert fitzGilbert. There are no visible masonry remains among the extensive earthworks that mark the site. The priory was originally located at Keddington, north of Louth, but the nuns moved to Legbourne shortly before 1199. The nuns were granted some land, mills and crofts, but had difficulties securing their churches, leading to several disputes. It appears to have been a quasi-double house, as masters were recorded between 1294 and 1343, who may have been Premonstratensians. Little else is known of its early history and there are no records of visitations by the bishops of Lincoln before that of Bishop Alnwick in 1440. The bishop found the buildings ruinous on account of poverty, but also some irregularities, mainly concerning the prioress who was said to have been too fond of entertaining her relatives, and partly supporting them from the convent's revenues. A secular boarder brought her pet birds into the dormitory at night and caused much disturbance to the nuns due to their 'jargoning'. Bishop Atwater found nothing to correct in 1519. Having been valued at only £38 8s in1534, the priory fell within the 1536 Act of Suppression and was duly dissolved. Prioress Joan Missenden and nine nuns received pensions. The King's commissioners, Millicent and Bellow, were still at work in the priory at the outbreak of the Lincolnshire Rising that same year and were 'dragged out of the priory by an excited mob'. There is a possibility that the insurgents may have restored the nuns to the house, but this is not at all certain.

Of interest is a letter to Thomas Cromwell from the prioress, after the news came to Legbourne of the passing of the Act of Suppression in 1536, which caused great distress and consternation to the nuns. As Cromwell himself happened to be patron of their house at that time, they thought perhaps he might be able to use his influence on their behalf. "Please yt your goodnes," wrote the prioress to him, "to understonde that whereas almyghty God hath indued you with just title of Founder . . . to the great comfort of me and all my systers, we doo and shall alweyes submit oure selfes to youre most rightuouse commaundement and ordre, oonly puttyng oure comfort in your goodnesse. And whereas we doo here that a grete nombre of abbyes shalbe punysshid, subprest and put downe, bicause of their myslyvyng, and that all abbyes and pryoryes under the value of cc be at oure moste noble prynces pleasure to subpresse and put downe, yet if it may pleas your goodness we trust in God ye shall here no complayntes agaynst us nother in oure lyvyng nor hospitalitie kepyng." She promises him, if he will be a suitor for his own poor priory, "you shalbe a more higher Founder to us than he that first foundid our howse." Her petition was unheeded.

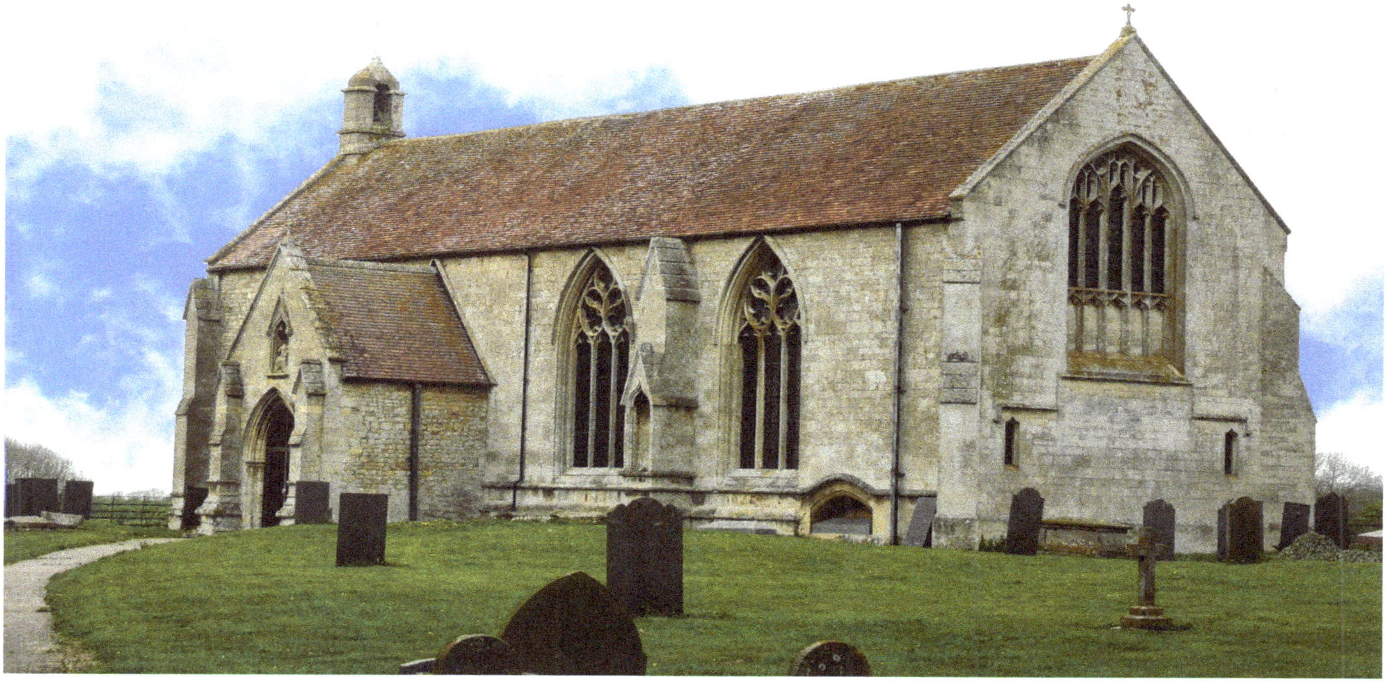

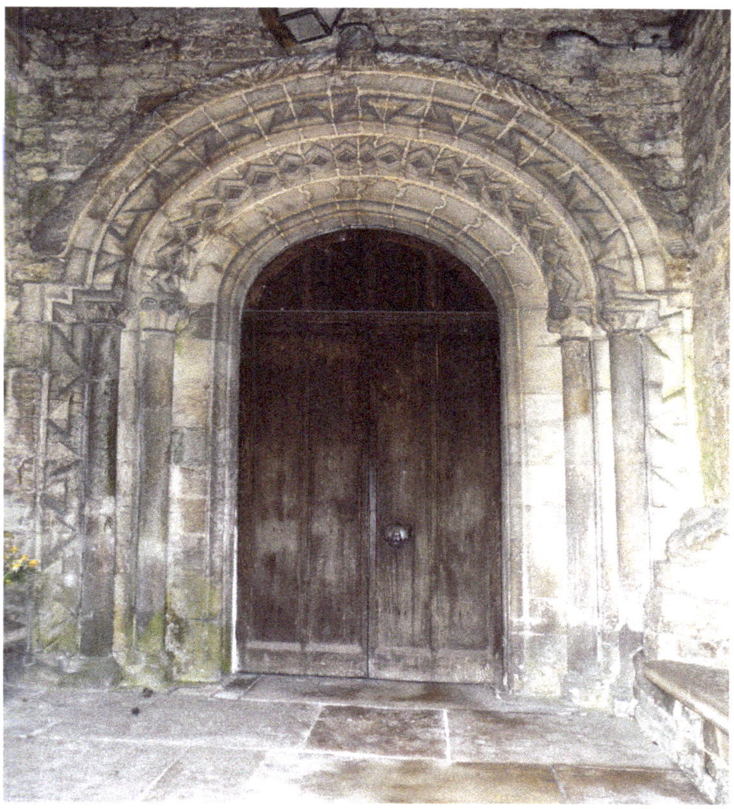

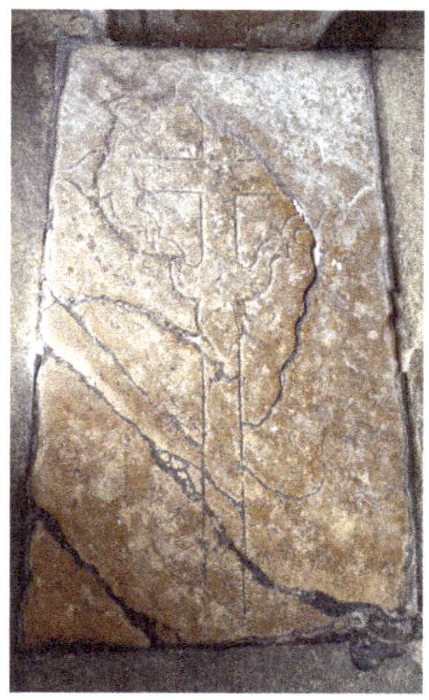

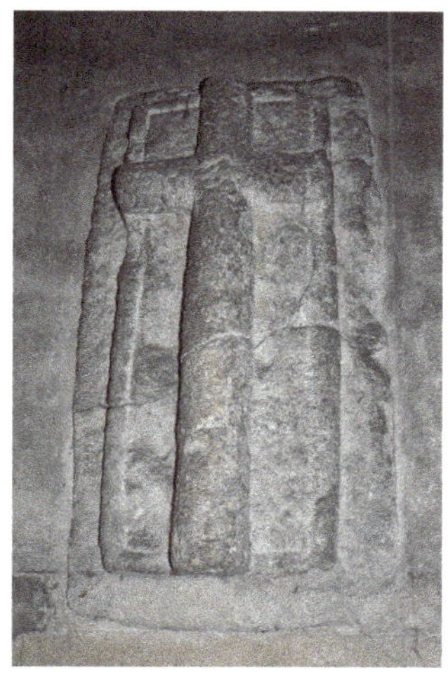

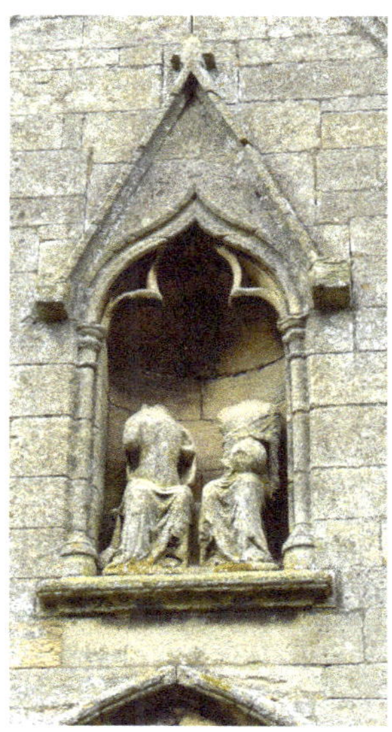

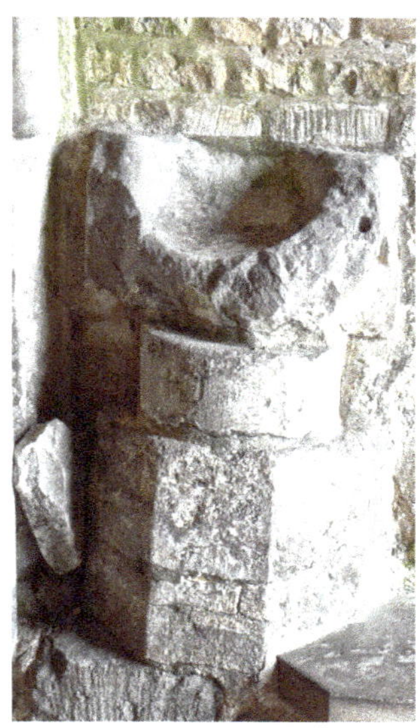

Photos of Kyme Priory – clockwise from top

The much restored former priory church of St Mary
Ancient Saxon stones with knotwork and carvings of a cross
Medieval water stoup in the south porch
Badly worn and headless statue of the Coronation of the Virgin
Norman doorway with typical decorations

Lincoln Priory

St Katherine • Gilbertine +1148–1538

Nothing at all has survived *in situ* from this Gilbertine house founded outside Lincoln by Bishop Robert de Chesney, but stone from the priory was used to construct a gateway to Castle Villa in Drury Lane. The exact date of the foundation is unknown, but probably took place soon after the confirmation of the Order of Sempringham by Pope Eugenius III in 1148. The bishop endowed the priory with several churches and land, and also handed over to the canons the older hospital of St Sepulchre, which had been established by another bishop of Lincoln, Robert Bloet (1094-1123). Although the house was founded for canons, lay-sisters were also accommodated to undertake the care of the sick. The number of canons was limited to sixteen, with lay-sisters numbering twenty. It is believed that there were no nuns in the house. The night before St. Hugh of Avalon was entered as bishop of Lincoln (1181), he stayed with the prior at St Katherine's and it later became the custom for a new bishop elect of Lincoln to spend the night before his enthronement at St Katherine's and hence go to his cathedral barefoot. The streets were draped with cloth, which was then distributed to the poor. St Hugh died in 1199 in London and his body was carried back to Lincoln and rested overnight at the priory. The funeral procession, which included King John of England, King William of Scotland, archbishops, bishops, earls and barons, carried the coffin up the hill from St Katherine's to the cathedral. In 1285, the prior obtained a licence to build a windmill to the east of the priory gate, and later was able to add land for enlargement, and built an aqueduct for a water supply. The body of Edward I's much loved Queen Eleanor rested in the priory church in November 1290, on the first night of the journey from Harby to London. Soon after the grieving King ordered the building of the first of the Eleanor crosses on Swines Green, opposite the priory gates.

Endowments and later benefactions were considerable, and the priory's profits from the sale of wool early in the fourteenth century, when the average was 35 sacks a year, were substantial. However, the financial demands from caring for the sick and poor, reckless speculation in lands and wool, and the loss of a large number of sheep when intruders assaulted the prior's men and servants at Scopwick, plunged the priory into financial difficulties. The Black Death also affected its fortunes and by 1391, the house was greatly in debt. The priory had an ignominious end. Robert Holgate, who was installed as prior in 1529 and later became the last master of the Order, robbed it of a chalice and other valuable goods, and his successor, William Griffiths, forcibly took the priorship and maintained his position until the surrender of the priory in July 1538. Griffiths and thirteen canons received pensions, but the lay-sisters got nothing. In 1535, the annual revenue of the priory had been assessed at £202 5s, derived from property in three counties.

Lincoln Priory (Monks Abbey)

St Mary Magdalene • Benedictine +1154–1539

Little is left of this priory for Benedictine monks, now described as Monks Abbey, and not much more is known of its history. The identity of the founder is still a mystery, and the date of foundation, said to have been in the reign of Henry II, is speculative at best. What is certain is that it was established as a cell to St Mary's Abbey at York and supported a prior and one or two monks, to look after the estates belonging to the abbey. St Mary's had an obligation to ensure the celebration of daily services in the chapel for the souls of people who had provided land for the priory, but in 1393 when farm animals were found in the chapel, the priory site came, for a short time, into the possession of the King. In 1312, the abbot asserted that some men had assaulted one of the monks at St Mary Magdalene's, but otherwise, its history was largely uneventful. It came to notice only in the last years, when an exchange of confusing letters between the abbot of York, King Henry VIII and Thomas Cromwell, variously calling for the withdrawal of the prior and monks who 'had brought the abbey into great expense and trouble', but no details were given. Complaints were also made that there were but one or two monks, sometimes none, 'no hospitality kept, nor Almighty God served, nor any religious order'. St Mary Magdalene Priory was dissolved in late 1539, at which time it was valued at just £23 6s, consisting mostly of small rents and a few pensions in diverse churches. Fenced in alongside a children's playground in a small park, stand the remains of the chapel, consisting of three walls, with some surviving window tracery. Close by is one surviving wall of an unidentified domestic building with a doorway.

Lincoln Austin Friars

c1269-1539

In the sixteenth century, Leland noted the ruins of the house of Augustinian friars on the south side of 'the suburb to Newport Gate', but not a vestige has survived to this day. The friars settled here under royal protection about 1269-70 and obtained licence from Bishop Sutton to have their church and area consecrated in 1291. Gilbert de Stratton granted them a messuage in the suburb of Lincoln in 1292 and the friars received a similar gift next year in Grimsby, where a new priory was founded. Further bequests were made by citizens over the next two hundred years, but it is not known if these were sufficient to support the house, which contained thirty-six friars in 1335. A Provincial Chapter of the Order was held here in 1307, and another in 1332, but little else has been recorded of its subsequent history. That it was a poor house can be seen from reports at the time of its surrender to the bishop of Dover in February 1539, when only four friars were left and their buildings were in ruins.

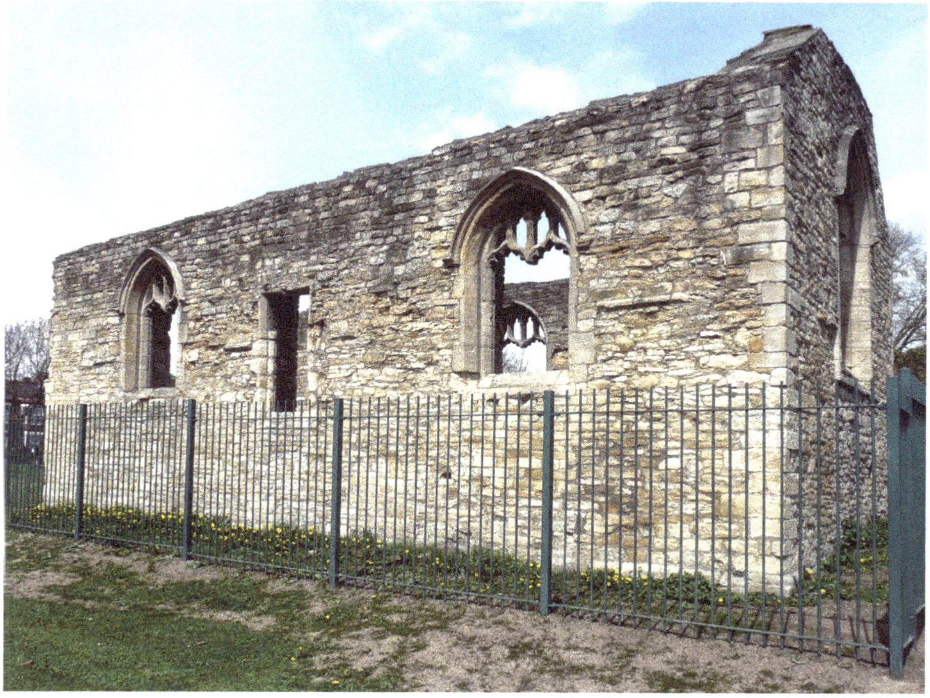

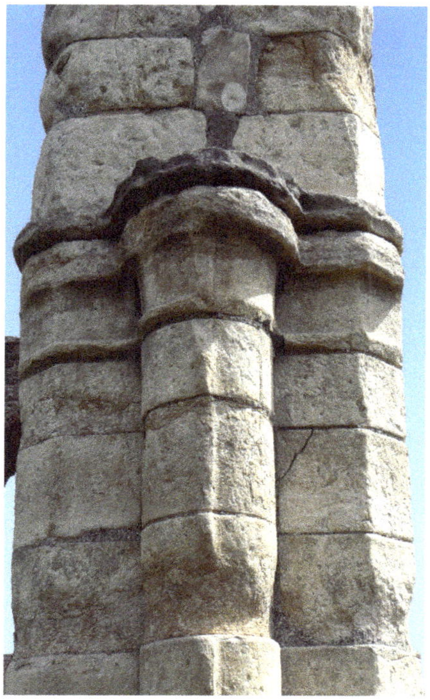

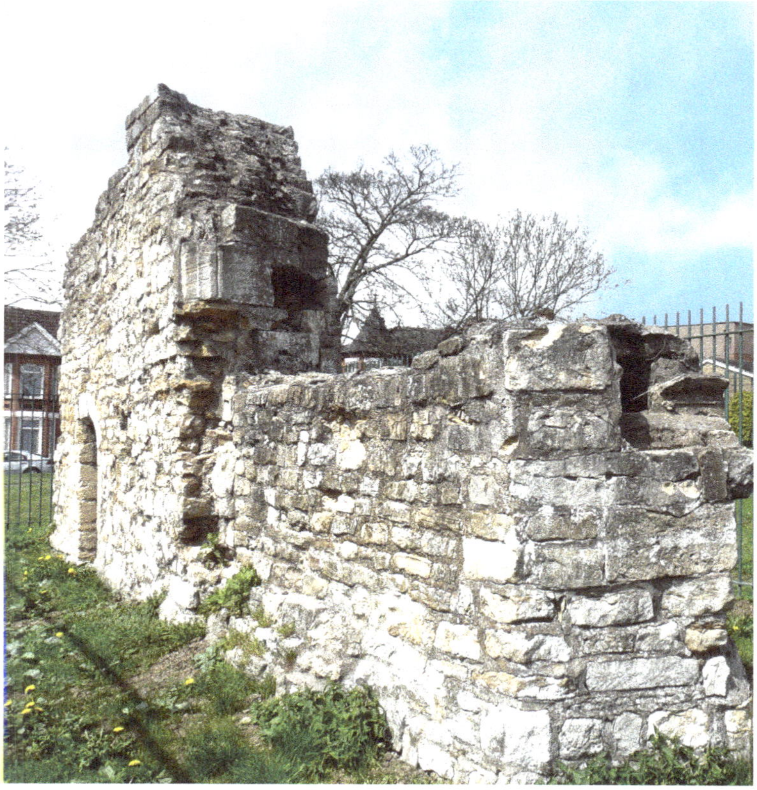

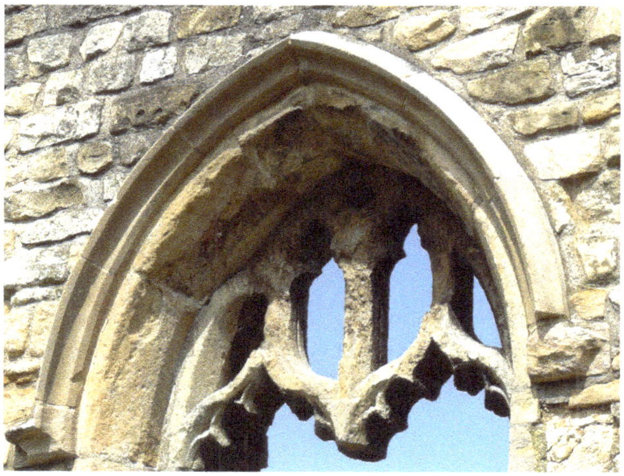

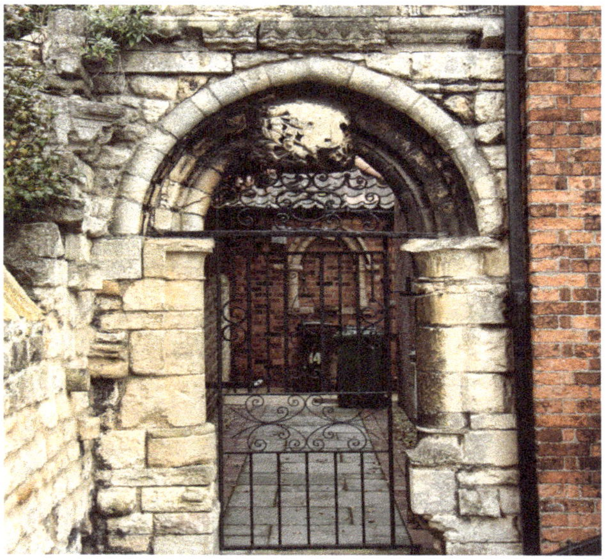

Photos of Monks Abbey – clockwise from top left

Remains of chapel of Monks Abbey
Clustered columns in chapel
Arched chapel windows with tracery remains
Reconstructed archway with stone from St Katherine's
Surviving wall of unidentified building of Monks Abbey

Lincoln Black Friars

St Dominic -1238–1539

The Dominican friars settled in Silvergate outside Pottergate before1238. In that year, Henry III gave them timber and 100s towards the expenses of their Provincial Chapter. Provincial Chapters met here on several more occasions over the next 150 years. A royal grant of ten oaks in 1255 indicates that building was still going on and, after acquiring more land and oaks from Edward I in 1284 and 1290, the friars began rebuilding their church, which was consecrated in 1311. It was perhaps the largest of all the Dominican priories. In 1260, the friars had obtained leave to build a conduit along the highway to their house from a spring belonging to a cell of St Mary's Abbey at York. Edward I gave them alms in 1300, which were sufficient for forty-seven friars. The house clearly was of some importance. Friar Walter Jorse, Archbishop of Armagh, made the Black Friars of Lincoln his residuary legatees in 1320, and was buried in the church, and in 1330 the prior was one of the papal commissioners appointed to arbitrate on a dispute about the bishop of Durham's jurisdiction in Osmotherly. There was some local friction and a few misdemeanours, but the house was generally in good order. Of note is the statutes passed at the Provincial Chapter in 1388, which regulated the promotion of friars to degrees in the universities, and appointed a number of friars to lecture on the sentences at Oxford and Cambridge. Almost nothing has been recorded in the fifteenth century, but by then it appears to have suffered poverty. It was surrendered to the bishop of Dover in February 1539.

Lincoln Grey Friars

St Francis c1230–1539

The surviving building in Broadgate of the Franciscan friars, comprising an undercroft and, unusually, the church above, is said to be one of the earliest surviving Franciscan priory churches in Europe and the oldest priory building in England. Like many monastic buildings that were not destroyed after the Dissolution, it has had many uses. In 1568, Richard Monson opened a Freeschool and in 1574, the building was granted to the city, which established the Corporation Grammar School on the upper floor. It was used as such until 1900. A House of Correction was set up in the undercroft in 1612, but this soon gave way to the Jersey School, for the teaching of spinning and knitting of wool, replaced in 1833 by the Mechanics' Institute. In 1862, the Grammar School expanded into the undercroft. After closure of the school in 1900, the building was restored, later housing the City and County Museum, and later still becoming an exhibition centre.

The Franciscans arrived in Lincoln in c1230 and began building their house in 1237 on a site near the Guildhall, granted to the friars by William de Beningworth, subdean of Lincoln. The area of the priory was small, bounded on the east by the line of the Roman defences running down the western side of Broadgate. Priory and church were completed after 1283/84 when Edward I gave them timber for their church, but not before the friars were accused of having built too close to the wall, thus endangering the defence of the city. Nevertheless, and in spite of the usual quarrels with the parish priests, the Franciscans proved popular in Lincoln and received numerous grants and gifts from all sections of the community. The Order's Provincial Chapters were held here in 1288, 1293 and 1295, and even the Premonstratensian Order met at the priory for its Provincial Chapters on three occasions in the fifteenth century. Edward I provided 100s towards expenses in 1293, and when he gave the friars 35s 4d towards two days' food in 1300, the house would appear to have supported fifty-three friars. The number of friars gradually fell from then onwards.

In 1534, the warden received permission from the city to take as much stone as he wanted for the repair of his house and church from the ruinous churches of St. Augustine and Holy Trinity, and received a similar licence the following year to appropriate the timber roof of St 'Bathe' Church - perhaps St Peter ad Fontem - for the same purpose. But it was to little avail. The house surrendered to the bishop of Dover in February 1539 and the site was let on a yearly tenancy to William Monson of Ingleby.

Lincoln Sack Friars

-1266-c1307

The Friars of the Penance of Jesus Christ or Friars of the Sack settled here before June 1266, when Henry III granted them a vacant place next to their house, which was situated in Thornbridgegate Street in the suburb of the city. In1268, the King gave them thirteen oaks towards the fabric of their church, but their tenure was short-lived, as the Order was suppressed and forbidden to admit new members, by the Council of Lyons in 1274. At least four friars were still in residence in 1300, when Edward I gave them 2s 8d for two days' food. The house was no longer occupied by 1307, when the abbot of the Premonstratensian convent of Barlings sought to acquire the site for use as a storehouse. He was not successful, but a meeting of the abbots of the Premonstratensian Order in England was held in this church in 1310. Secular chaplains served the chapel in 1327 and a chantry was founded here in 1359. In a deed of 1455, mention is made of 'a stone wall lately belonging to the friars', but nothing at all is left today.

Lincoln White Friars

Blessed Virgin Mary 1269–1539

What was left of this house of Carmelite friars is now buried beneath St Mark's Railway Station. It was bounded by the High Street to the east, the River Witham to the west, St Edward's Church to the south and St Mark's Church to the north, covering an area of 70 by 95m (230 x 310ft). Excavations have discovered the plan of the church, which was at the southern end with the cloister to the north, west range, and the location of other buildings. The church was demolished in the fifteenth century and rebuilt. The conduit head of an elaborate water system survives in the churchyard of St Mary-le-Wigford. The White Friars house was founded in 1269, believed by Odo of Kilkenny, in the year when Henry III granted the friars six beech trees for a kiln. Edward I gave the friars leave in 1280 to acquire land to increase their precinct. In 1287, probably at a Provincial Chapter, the Order agreed to adopt the white habit. The highest number of friars recorded was thirty-four in 1335. A Provincial Chapter was held here in 1343, at which the general, Peter Raymond, was present. The priory had a valuable library of which one volume has survived the appropriation by Henry VIII and can be found in the Royal MSS in the British Library. This contains the Roman histories of Eutropius and Paulus Diaconus, besides other works. The priory was surrendered to Richard Ingworth, Bishop of Dover, in February 1539.

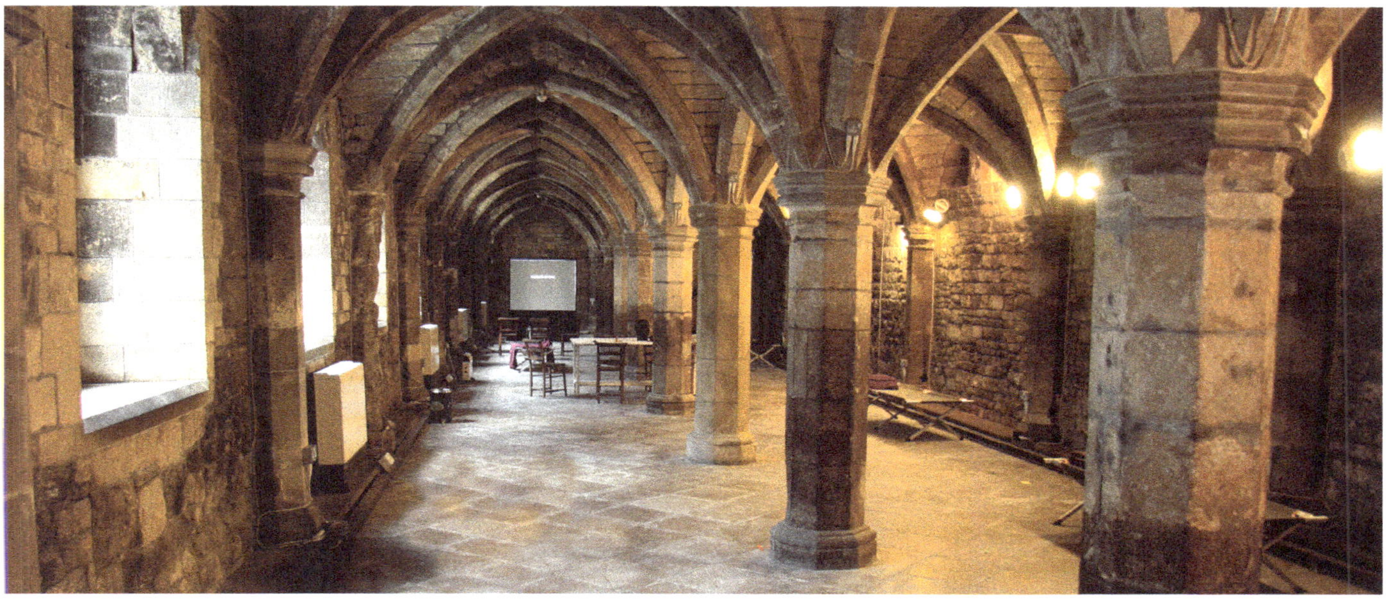

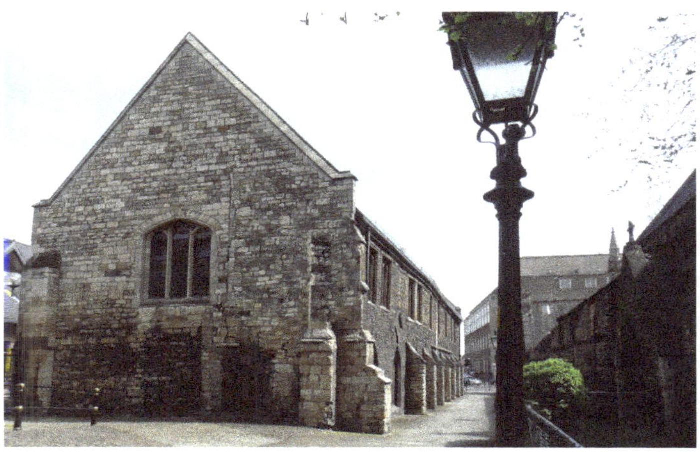

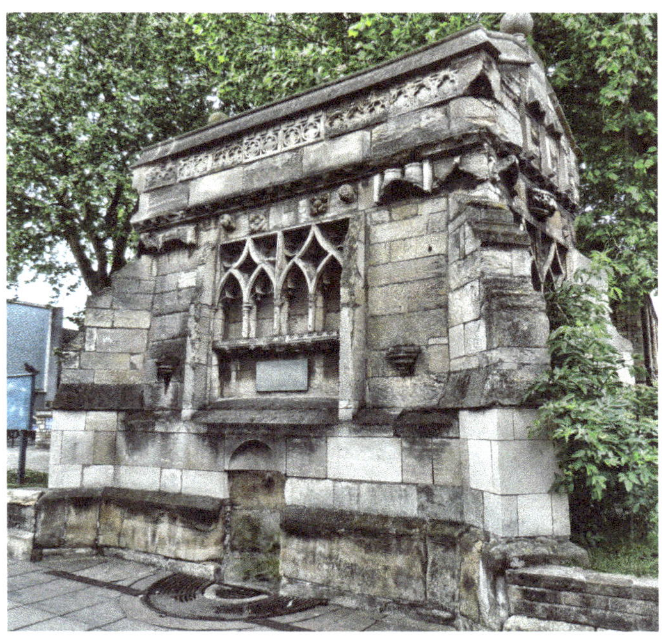

Photos - clockwise from top

The splendid undercroft in the Greyfriars building
The ornate conduit-head built with stone from the White Friars
Greyfriars is said to be the oldest priory building in England

Long Bennington Priory

-1275-1414

The church of Long Bennington was granted by Ralf de Fougères to the abbot of Savigny in 1163, and confirmed by Henry II and Pope Alexander III, although Savigny was involved in a long dispute over the church with the abbey of St Serge, Angers before then. Exactly when the priory was founded has not been recorded, but one monk was certainly resident there in 1275. A warden, later styled prior, was mentioned on the Patent Rolls of 1319 and 1323 and is thought to have been the only incumbent of this alien priory, which was taken into the hands of the King on a number of occasions. In 1401, the priory was farmed for the Crown, but was granted to Mount Grace Priory in Yorkshire by Edward IV in 1462. Its worth in 1384 had been assessed at £51 8s. Nothing has survived.

Louth Park Abbey

St Mary • Cistercian 1139–1536

This Cistercian abbey was founded in 1139 by Alexander, Bishop of Lincoln, as a dependency of Fountains Abbey in Yorkshire. The monks from Fountains, led by Gervase, were initially presented with a site at Haverholme, but settled themselves at Louth Park instead, because, it has been suggested, the park was more suitable for cultivation than the swamps of Haverholme. The abbey received considerable additional endowments from notable benefactors, which brought in a substantial income, worth more than £200 at the end of the thirteenth century. However, legal suits to secure the profits of the abbey's wool, and a great loss of sheep, exacerbated still further in 1336 when Thomas of Lissington is said to have carried off horses, oxen and 300 sheep, hunted in the abbot's free warren, set cattle to depasture his grass, and assaulted his servants, halved its income. By 1344, the abbey was in debt and was taken under the King's protection. An inquisition was held in 1345 into the ownership of the manor of Cockerington, which had been made over to the abbot on his deathbed by Henry le Vavasour, but was disputed by his widow. The Black Death carried away the abbot and many monks a few years later, adding to the difficulties of the house. There are no records of episcopal visitations, but there were no complaints and the community appears to have led a spiritually healthy life. With a value of £147 in 1536, the monastery was dissolved under the first Act of Suppression in September 1536. By that time the community, which was said in the thirteenth century to have comprised sixty-six monks and 150 servants, had shrunk to just the abbot, George Walker, and ten monks. One of the monks, William Moreland, became involved in the Lincolnshire Rising and was executed in March 1537, along with the abbot of Barlings and others. All that has survived *in situ* from the abbey is a large fragment of the south wall of the chancel and other church walls, standing in a private field. A re-erected archway in The Priory Hotel garden is made up of a fourteenth century traceried window and piscina, and twelfth century round piers and scalloped capitals. Other fragments are dotted around elsewhere in the grounds.

Markby Priory

St Peter • Augustinian -1204–1536

This small priory of Augustinan canons was founded by Ralf fitzGilbert in the reign of Henry II, although its first mention was not made until1204. Early endowments included lands and the churches of Mumby in Lincolnshire and Wycliffe in Yorkshire. The community does not appear to have enjoyed a happy existence. In 1300, the prior laid a complaint against certain persons, said to have besieged the priory, prevented the delivery of food to the brethren, and beaten up any servants found outside the gates, and a quarrel between the prior and cellarer led to an appeal to the pope. This was settled by the death of the prior from the Black Death that same year. When Bishop William Alnwick visited in 1438, he found 'not even a shadow of religion, but debts, drinking, and suspicion of even worse sins', with one of the canons suspected of sinful intercourse with a woman at Markby. The priory was also in debt. The appointment of the prior as a visitor for the Order early in the sixteenth century would indicate an improvement in the house, backed up by a visitation in 1519 by Bishop Atwater, who found no grave faults. With a clear annual value of £130 13s, the priory was dissolved in 1536. The community then comprised the prior, John Penketh, and eight canons. In the thatched parish church is a north doorway, chancel arch and font, which came from the lost priory.

Minting Priory

• Benedictine 1129–1414

There are no standing remains and only prominent earthworks recall this alien Benedictine priory, which appears to have been founded in 1129, when Ranulph le Meschines, third Earl of Chester, made a grant of land to the abbey of Fleury on the banks of the Loire. It is not certain when the priory was actually established, as the earliest mention of a prior was in 1213. By all accounts, this English cell was an embarrassment to the mother house, which also seems to have taken little interest in the conduct of the small community, except as a source of revenue. A letter to the abbot of Fleury in 1238 by Bishop Robert Grosseteste requested a prior 'who knew the way of truth', but this was ignored, as was a follow-up letter, where the bishop exhorted the abbot to send only men, long tried and faithful, as those at Minting had been 'wont to live luxuriously with harlots, known no obedience to rule, and had been given to much eating and drinking'. Many other complaints of sinful behaviour were made, but there is no evidence that matters improved. As an alien house, Minting was taken into the King's hands in 1337, 1344 and 1346 during the wars with France and, in 1403, was being farmed by a clerk. Its value in 1384 had been assessed at £41 11s, and probably supported no more than one or two monks. It was dissolved by Henry V in 1414 and given to the Carthusian priory of Mount Grace in Yorkshire in 1421.

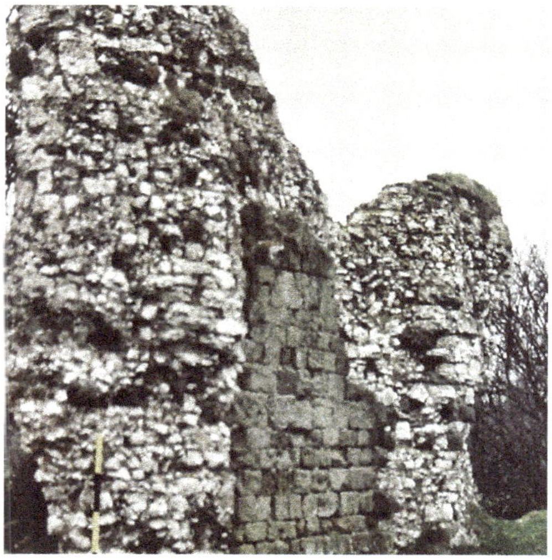

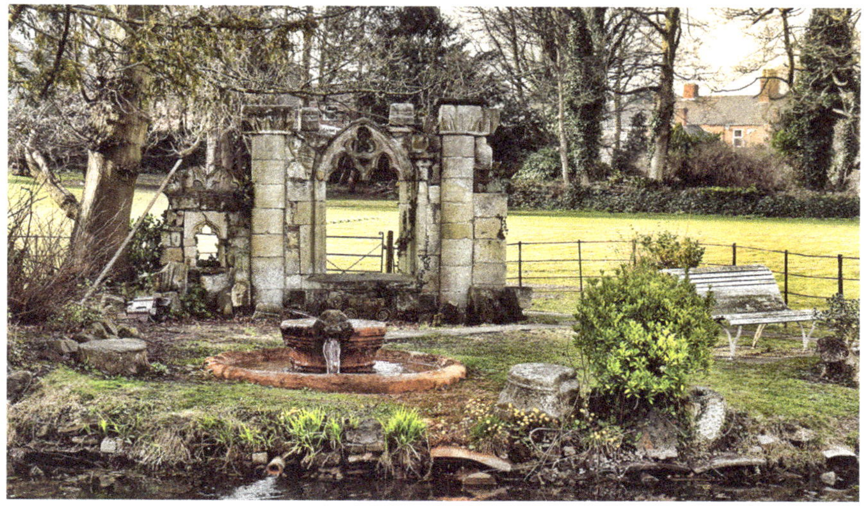

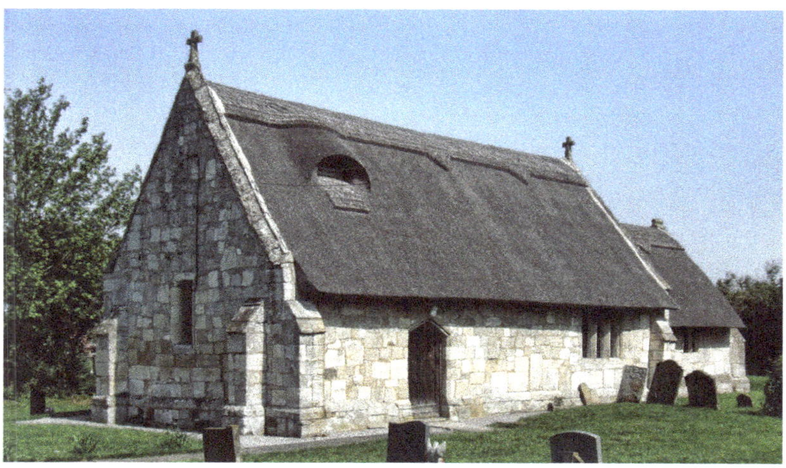

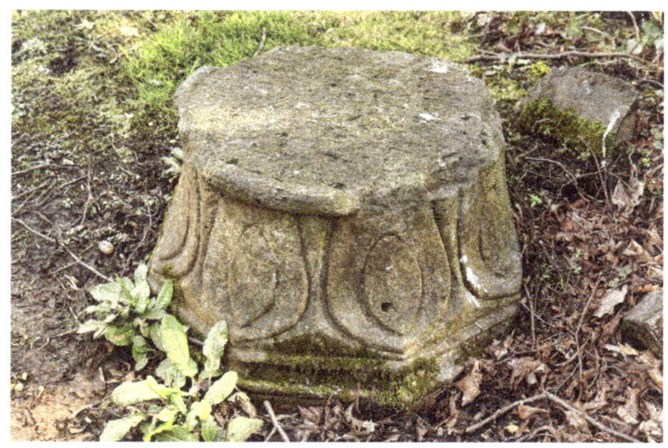

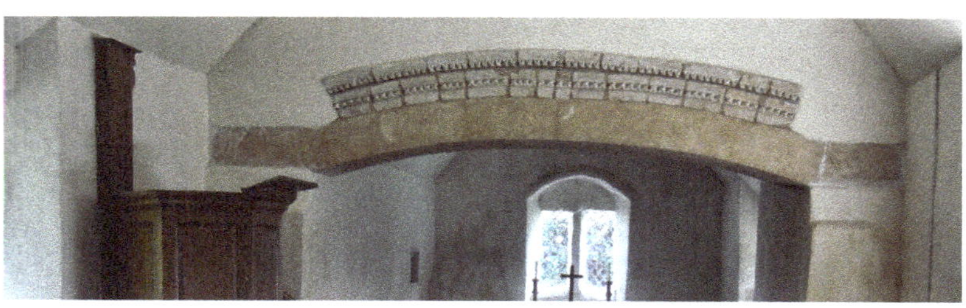

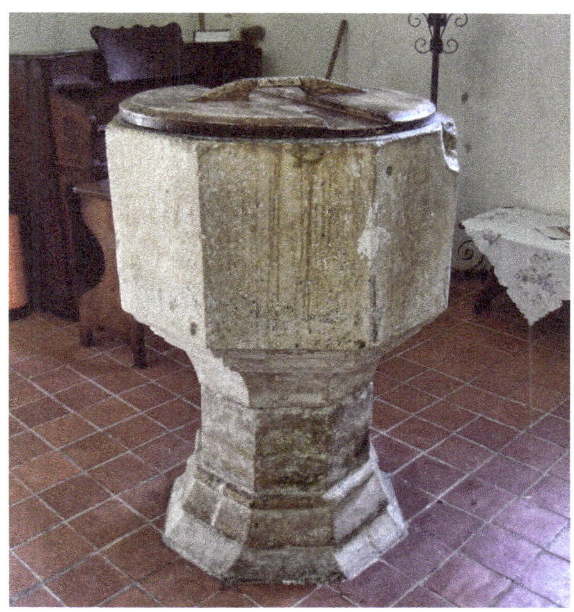

Photos – clockwise from top

South wall of chancel of Louth Park Abbey church
Recreated archway from elements of the abbey. Trefoil-headed piscina on left and capital re-used as springhead in foreground
Lotus leaf capital
Font from Markby Priory in the parish church
Surviving chancel arch from Markby Priory
Markby Church of St Peter

Newbo Abbey

St Mary • Premonstratensian c1198–1536

This is yet another of the county's many monasteries where nothing at all remains visible. It was founded for Premonstratensian canons about 1198 by Richard de Malebisse, most probably in expiation for his part in the massacre of the Jews in York. It was a cell of Licques Abbey near Calais. The early history records a number of suits over advowsons of churches, but life within appears to have been in good order, as a general chapter was held in the abbey in 1336. However, poverty and pestilence had reduced the community to very few canons, and a licence was granted for either twelve canons or seculars to bring the house back up to strength, but it is not known if this was achieved. An indulgence was also granted to anyone visiting the church and contributing to its repair. Poverty continued to afflict the abbey, which found itself greatly in debt in 1482. However, by 1491 debt was much reduced and all was well within the monastery. Bishop Redman visited on a number of occasions between 1475 and 1503 and, while issuing minor injunctions against the use of hunting dogs, drinking after compline, canons absenting themselves without permission, and games played for money, the bishop praised the abbot's administration in 1500. It is amusing to learn that one canon was 'sharply rebuked for wearing slippers'! In 1534, the abbey's net annual income was given as £71 8s and it was duly suppressed with the lesser monasteries in 1536. The last abbot, Richard Carre, six canons and a novice were paid off.

Newsham (Newhouse) Abbey

St Mary & St Martial • Premonstratensian 1143-1536

This, the first Premonstratensian house in Britain, was founded in 1143 by Peter de Goxhill, who held Newsham of Ralf de Bayeux, who is also considered the co-founder. The abbey was colonised by canons from the abbey of Licques, between Calais and Boulogne, mother house of three other Lincolnshire monasteries at Barlings, Tupholme and Newbo. It is believed that the relics of St Martial were transferred to Newsham c1163 from the abbey of Limoges, with which the founder was associated. The early history of the house was marked by a lengthy dispute with the nuns of Elstow over the advowson of the church of Halton-on-Humber, but this was eventually resolved when Pope Alexander III ordered the nuns to 'molest the canons no further'. By 1385, pestilence and poverty as the result of barren lands and heavy demands on hospitality had blighted the abbey, and heavy storms had brought the monastic buildings to near ruin. Age and infirmity by the abbot towards the end of the fifteenth century resulted in an unsatisfactory state within the community, with canons excommunicated for incontinence and apostasy, one canon on three occasions. Injunctions referred to a lack of keeping silence, 'the very key of the religious life', drinking after compline, poor attendance in choir, and leaving the precincts of the monastery without permission. However, by 1500, under the guidance of Bishop Redman, there was a marked improvement and it was declared in excellent order, with the buildings also in a beautiful state. In 1534, the clear annual value of the house was £99 2s, which led to its surrender in 1536. In residence then were the abbot, Thomas Doncaster, and ten canons. Nothing visible has survived.

Newstead by Stamford Priory

St Mary • Augustinian -1247–1536

Nothing has survived of this house of Augustinian canons, which began its existence before 1200 as a hospital for seven poor and infirm persons, founded by William d'Albini III, 'at the bridge of Wass between Uffington and Stamford'. The founder later increased the endowment to provide thirteen beds, but his son appears to have changed the endowment for a prior and canons before 1247. Although small and poorly provided for, it nevertheless played host to a general chapter on two occasions, in 1340 and 1362. When Bishop William Alnwick visited in 1440, he found the house in debt and much ruined. The community had shrunk to the prior and three canons, with one too ill to appear before the bishop, and another living at Ulverscroft priory. Some later difficulties were due to its poverty, but there were no complaints about the community, which, on its dissolution in 1536, consisted only of the prior, John Blakyth, two canons and one novice. Two years earlier, the clear annual value of the priory had been assessed at £37 6s.

Newstead-on-Ancholme Priory

Holy Trinity • Gilbertine 1164–1538

The Gilbertine priory was founded by Henry II and endowed with the island of Rucholm, on which the priory was built, and other lands nearby. Although it was first recorded in 1171, its foundation may date back to 1164, when a foundation agreement was signed by Gilbertine priors. As the endowment was small, the community was limited to thirteen. It derived its income principally from the sale of wool, which at the beginning of the fourteenth century averaged ten sacks a year. The effects of the Black Death impacted severely on the priory's economic health, which seems to have continued to deteriorate. In 1397, an indulgence was granted by Pope Boniface IX to anyone assisting with the repair of the church and, in the later fifteenth century, Edward IV released the priory from high rents being charged. In 1535, the net valuation of the priory amounted to £38 14s, but it survived the closure of the lesser monasteries. It was finally surrendered by Prior Richard Hobson and five canons in October 1538. The post-medieval farmhouse, now used for weddings and entertainment, incorporates fabric of the priory, the most prominent being a 6.1m (20ft) square vaulted room, which may have been part of the refectory. The groin vault has typically round arches and is supported on the walls on corbels and by two octagonal piers with simple capitals in the centre. Also of note in an upstairs room is a three-light Perpendicular window with hoodmould and reset label stops. Earthworks and fishponds provide another reminder of the priory, as are stones dotted around the grounds and gardens.

Nocton Park Priory

St Mary Magdalene • Augustinian +1135–1536

On the west bank of the River Witham was the priory for Austin canons of St Mary Magdalene at Nocton Park, its site remembered only by the rising ground to the east of the village. Founded by Robert d'Arcy, probably in the reign of King Stephen, its peaceful existence was marred by an uneasy relationship between d'Arcy and the church, leading to frequent disputes over the appointment of priors and trespasses by the patrons, as well as the presence of a canon from Thornton Abbey, who created a scandal when he was suspected of a sexual relationship with a woman from Bardney. The canon from Thornton was banished to a cell of St Osyth's Abbey. Little is known of the internal history and only one visitation report survives, which confirmed that the house was generally in good order. The priory never comprised more than a prior and four canons and was one of the poorer houses in the county, being valued at just £43 at the time of its suppression in 1536.

North (Nun) Ormsby Priory

St Mary • Gilbertine 1148/54–1538

The rural site of this Gilbertine house remains an area of natural beauty but, alas, no upstanding remains have survived. It was founded as a double house between 1148 and 1154 by Gilbert fitzRobert of Ormsby, with the consent of William, Earl of Albemarle. The endowments were considerable and were intended to support 100 nuns and lay-sisters and fifty canons and lay-brothers, but these numbers were probably never reached. The main income came from seven or eight granges, producing an average of eight sacks a year at the beginning of the fourteenth century. After the Black Death, the revenues of the house were greatly diminished, and remained so, as attempts to appropriate the valuable church of Ludborough, in spite of a royal licence, never succeeded. In 1399, an indulgence was granted by Pope Boniface IX for the fabric and maintenance of the Lady Chapel. The net valuation of the house in 1535 was only £80 11s but, along with other houses of the Gilbertine Order, it survived early closure and was not surrendered until September 1538. The much reduced community then comprised the prior, Christopher Cartwright, five canons, and Prioress Joan Stokwith and nine nuns.

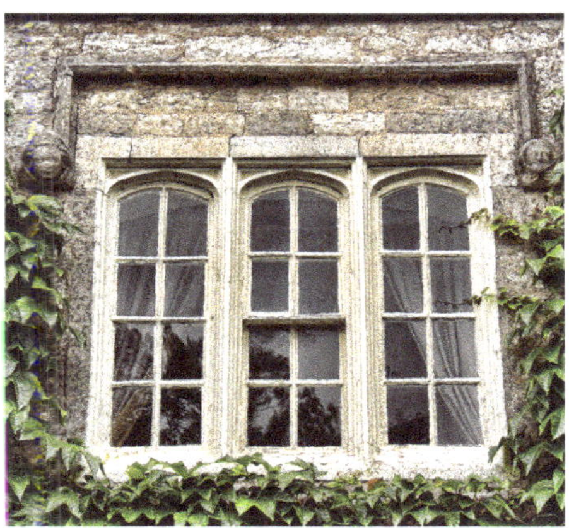

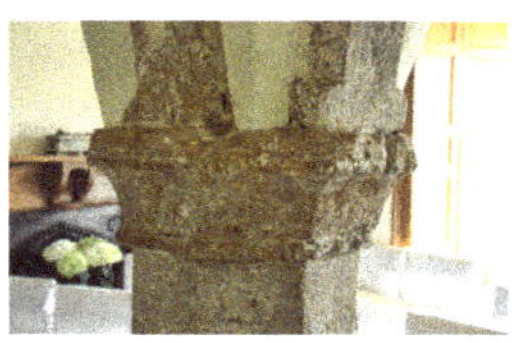

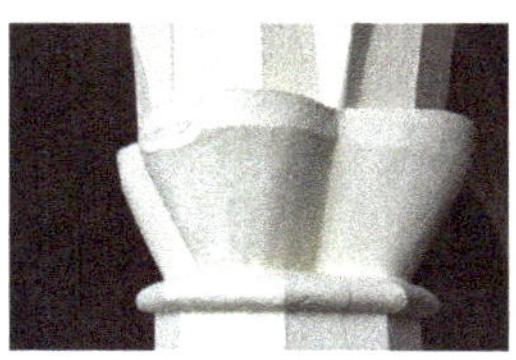

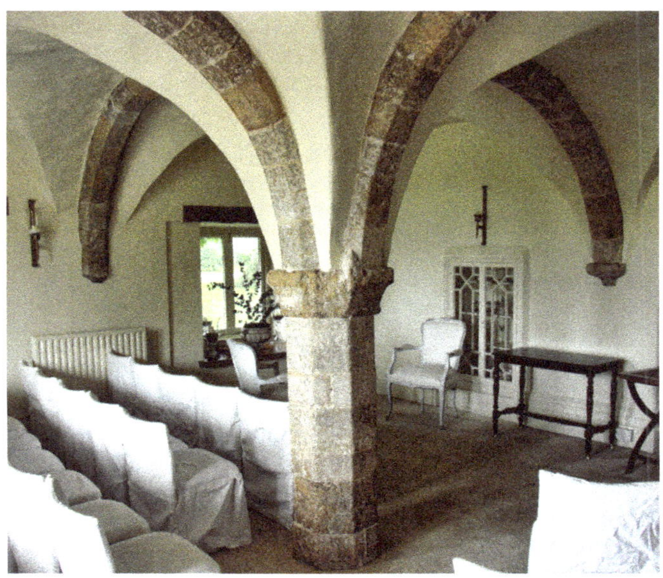

Photos of Newstead-on-Ancholme – clockwise from left

Sixteenth century three-light perpendicular window

Simple capitals on octagonal piers

Square vaulted room probably part of the former refectory

Nuncotham Priory

St Mary • Cistercian nuns c1150–1539

This priory for Cistercian nuns was founded in c1150 in the reign of King Stephen by Alan de Muncells, who endowed the community with the vill of Cotham, the church of Cuxwold and various parcels of land. In spite of receiving three more churches from other benefactors, the priory's possessions were not extensive and considered by Bishop Hugh of Lincoln at the end of the twelfth century to be sufficient only for thirty nuns. In fact, the bishop drew up a constitution limiting the size of the community, apparently because the nuns had been living beyond their means. The nuns suffered severely at the time of the Black Death and were forced to take in lady boarders, which provided much needed income, but they also 'brought the world into the cloister'. Injunctions by visiting bishops to cease this practice proved to no avail and, while the bishops said that "the conversation of seculars disturbed the contemplation of religion", Bishop Alnwick, in his visitation in 1440, found no breaches of rules, nor evidence of luxurious living. Poverty continued to stalk the community and the poor quality of bread and beer became a frequent complaint. In a visitation by Bishop Longlands in 1531, the last prioress, Joan Thompson, was admonished for treating the house as if it was for her exclusive use, and for allowing her kinsfolk to lodge there at the convent's expense. With a net annual income of only £46 17s, the priory should have been dissolved under the first Act of Suppression, but it survived until July 1539, when Dr London took the surrender. Apart from the prioress, there were then twelve nuns in residence. There are no standing remains.

Orford (Irford) Priory

St Mary • Premonstratensian nuns +1154–1539

There is nothing left and scarcely anything is known of the history of this insignificant house of Premonstratensian nuns, nor is there certainty about its foundation. It was probably founded in the reign of Henry II by Ralf d'Albini, but, in the absence of a charter, the original endowment is unknown. There was poverty in 1391, when the nuns were allowed to appropriate the church of Wragby, and in 1491, Bishop Redman excommunicated a nun for breaching her vow of chastity with a canon of Newsham Abbey! The bishop also stipulated on one of his visitations that no nuns were to be admitted unless they could read and sing. The house was valued in 1534 at a paltry £13 19s but survived until the final surrender by the prioress and seven nuns to Dr London in July 1539. An interesting episode took place during the Lincolnshire Rising, when the prioress was required to provide a horse for William Morland, a former monk of Louth Park. Morland was executed for treason in March 1537. The priory site was granted to Robert Tyrwhitt.

Partney Priory

St Mary Magdalene • Benedictine -1318–?

There was a monastery here in the seventh century, which was probably destroyed by the Danes in cAD 870 and never rebuilt. At the beginning of the twelfth century, Gilbert of Ghent gave a chapel to the monks of Bardney Abbey, and Gilbert's son, Walter, founded a hospital after 1115. By the fourteenth century, the hospital ceased to exist and was regarded as a Benedictine cell to the abbey, providing occasionally a home for former abbots. Nothing is now visible.

Revesby Abbey

St Mary & St Laurence • Cistercian 1142–1538

The Cistercian abbey of Revesby was founded in 1142 by William de Romara, Lord of Bolingbroke, who ended his days as a monk and was buried in the house of his foundation. The first monks under Abbot William were sent from Rievaulx by St Ailred. The abbey was well endowed with lands and many churches in the area and this, together with a sizeable wool production, made it one of the richer houses in the county. Its history was largely uneventful. In 1216, a monk of Revesby was arrested for having taken part in the Baron's War against King John, but was released when it was found that he had taken the habit before the rebellion began. In the fourteenth century, the abbey suffered from having to support unwelcome ex-royal servants, and a plea to Edward II to provide some relief from taxes on account of prolonged barrenness of their lands and the death of nearly all the livestock, fell on deaf ears. His successor, Edward III, also added to the abbey's distress in 1340 by buying £115 worth of wool, but failing to pay. Only a small fraction of this was recovered later. In 1382, the abbot received a licence to acquire the manor of Mareham to aid its recovery.

Nothing further is known until 1527, when a suit was brought against the abbot for failing to repair the causeway and bridge of Northdyke. A witness claimed after the Lincolnshire Rising that monks of Revesby, as well as those of Bardney and Kirkstead, were seen in the field among the insurgents, but none were brought to trial. A note by the Duke of Norfolk in 1538 stated that the abbey was in great ruin and decay, but found nothing amiss with the moral standards of the house, although there was some mismanagement of revenues. Nevertheless, the clear annual value of the abbey had been assessed in 1534 at a substantial £287 2s. The house was most likely surrendered by Abbot John in 1538 and the site and possessions were granted to Charles Brandon, Duke of Suffolk. Nothing *in situ* has survived, but various fragments are incorporated in St Lawrence parish church, including a tile pavement, various carved stone fragments, and a free-standing piscina, now used as a font.

Sandtoft Priory

- Benedictine 1174/1186–c1291

Whether or not there was an actual priory at Sandtoft remains open to conjecture. What is known is that between 1174 and 1186, Roger de Mowbray granted the island of Sandtoft in Axholme to the abbot of St Mary's at York, for the support of one monk. Other small parcels of land and the churches of Nocton and Dunston were granted by Thomas d'Arcy and Hamelin, Earl of Warenne, but the churches became involved in a lawsuit by the prior of Nocton Park, who claimed ownership. Sandtoft appears as a separate cell in 1291, but was probably annexed soon after to St Mary Magdalene's at Nocton Park.

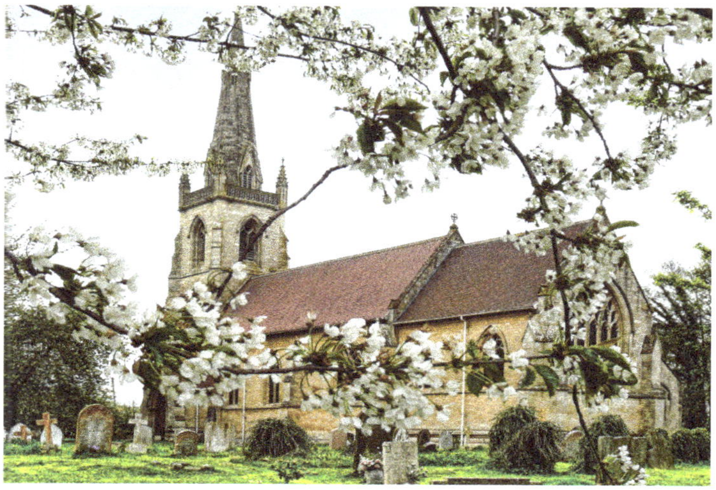

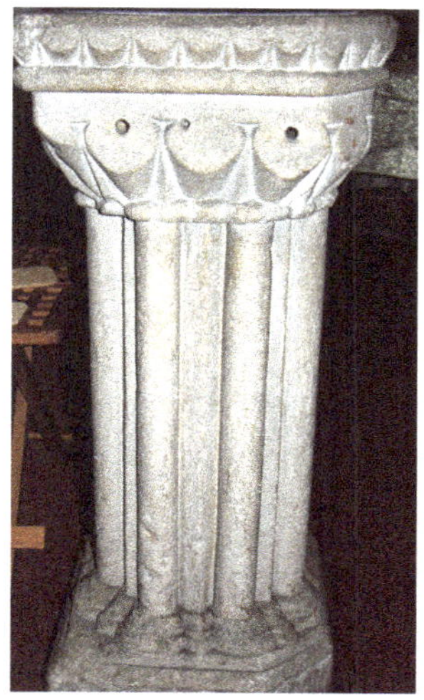

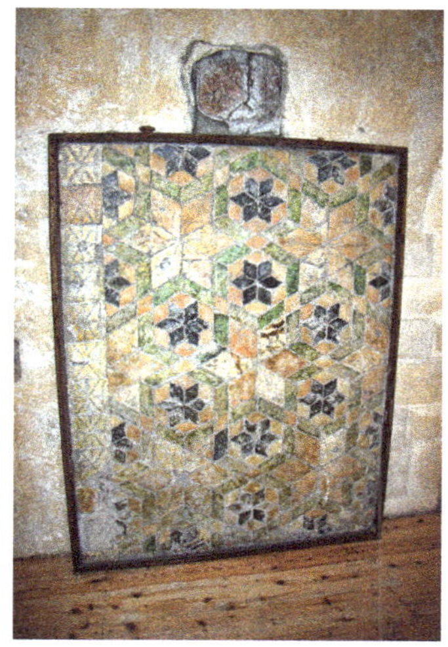

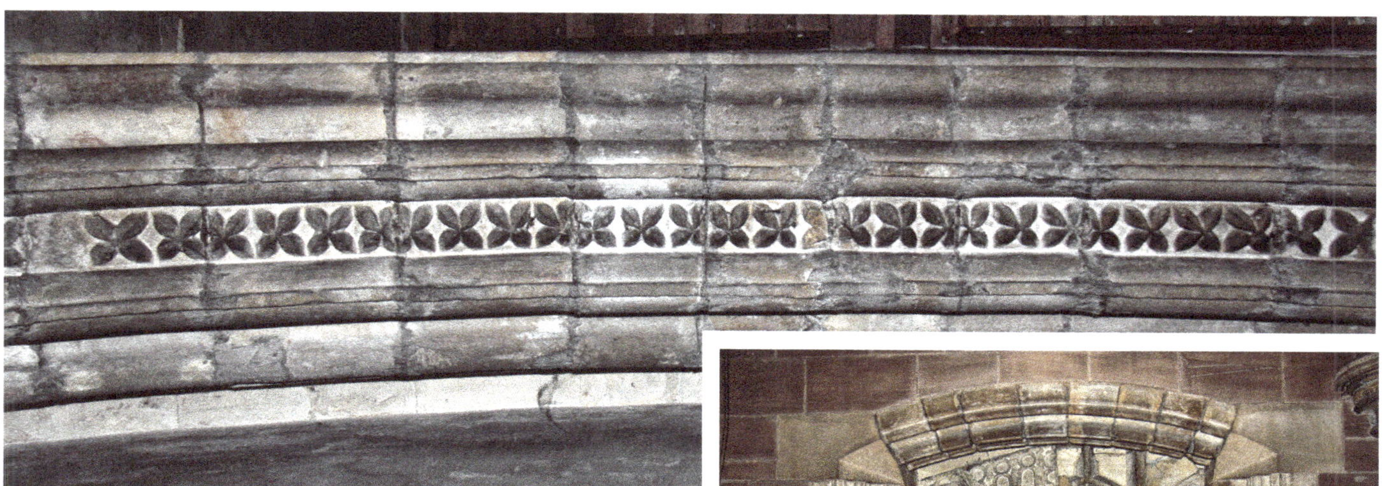

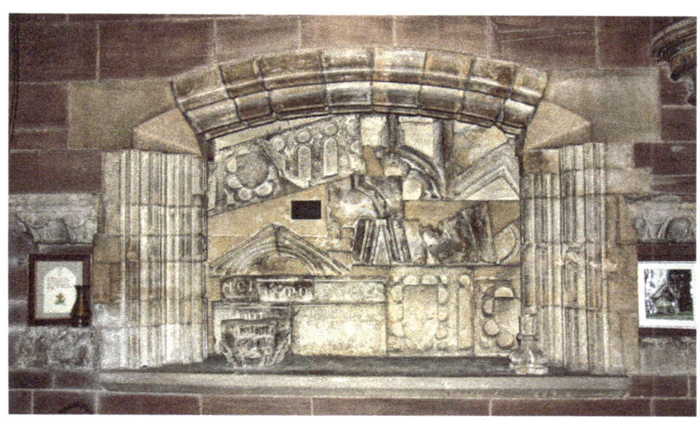

Photos of Revesby Abbey – clockwise from top left

Revesby parish church of St Lawrence
Pillar piscina now used as a font
Floor tile panel with heraldic shield in tower
Section of large radius arch with dogtooth decorations
Fragments of carved stone from the abbey

Sempringham Priory

St Andrew / St Mary • Gilbertine 1131–1538

The largely Norman church of St Andrew with the crocketed pinnacles on its tower is today a lonely landmark on rising ground near the village of Pointon, surrounded in springtime by a swathe of luminous yellow rape. It is believed to have been the site of the first monastery established in 1131 by Gilbert of Sempringham, who had been instituted as vicar of St Andrews two years before and who later founded the only English monastic Order and was canonised in 1202. Since early in his life, Gilbert had worked to 'win souls for Christ', and when he was unable to find men who wished to serve God, he turned to seven maidens, whom he had previously taught and who had a desire for a strict religious life. With the help of Bishop Alexander of Lincoln he built a small cloistered enclosure on the north wall of the church for the new community. This small group of nuns attracted much attention and brought many others into the community to serve as lay-brothers and lay-sisters. The latter lived and worked the land given by Gilbert de Ghent, whose sister was married to William the Conqueror. De Ghent was granted a hundred and five lordships by William, of which the chief lordship was at nearby Folkingham. The nuns quickly outgrew the little priory and a new house was built some 320m (1,050ft) to the south-west. With several periods of rebuilding, including the north wall of the northern aisle, any evidence of this first priory has been destroyed, but there are several features of note in the church, which is said to have been built c1100 by St Gilbert's father, Jocelin de Sempringham, on the site of an ancient Saxon church. Of particular interest is the Norman priest's doorway, now set inside the southern porch, although the doors with wonderful medieval iron scrollwork probably date from the thirteenth century.

Work on a vast new priory was begun in 1139 and by virtue of his gift of land, Gilbert de Ghent was considered the founder. Gilbert of Sempringham also sent some nuns to the marshy island of Haverholme, given by Bishop Alexander, but he did not himself want to rule the nunneries. He, therefore, travelled in 1147 to the General Chapter of the Cistercians at Citeaux in Burgundy, but failed to persuade the abbots to accept his nuns into their Order. This led Gilbert to draw up the Institutes of the Order of Sempringham, reviving the double monasteries, which had been normal in Anglo-Saxon times. The canons followed the rule of St Augustine, while the nuns kept the rule of St Benedict. Gilbert tried to limit the number of canons to sixty and nuns to one hundred and twenty, but a hundred years later there were two hundred nuns. Sempringham eventually owned land in seventy parishes, most of these close to the priory, but in spite of its possessions, papal protection and royal favour, especially from King Henry II and Edward I, II and III, the priory was never wealthy.

It suffered severely in 1193, when all the wool of the Order was seized for the ransom of Richard the Lionheart. There were also problems with a relaxation of the rules, complaints of its harshness, and in 1312, the priory was attacked by several local knights, the canons and servants assaulted, and the goods carried away. The canons retaliated by raiding the park of Roger de Birthorpe, one of the attackers, and recovering their animals. Further deprivation followed in 1349, when a great storm and flood destroyed the priory's books and damaged many sacks of wool. The Black Death also grievously reduced the numbers of lay-brothers and sisters, and the death of sheep from the pestilence, made it impossible to carry on farming and trading. The priory never fully recovered. In 1535, the clear annual value of the mother house was £317 4s, one of only four Gilbertine houses to have revenues in excess of £200. Master Robert Holgate, Prior Roger, and sixteen canons surrendered Sempringham Priory to Dr William Petre in September 1538. Prioresses Agnes Rudd and Margery Marbury, and sixteen nuns also received pensions. The site was granted in 1539 to Edward Fiennes, Lord Clinton and Saye.

The original layout of the priory church remains unknown, but in 1301, Prior John de Hamilton began to build a massive new church, as the earlier one had fallen into disrepair. Excavations by the Lincolnshire Architectural Society in 1938/39 proved the existence of a church 100m (325ft) long by 28.3m (93ft) wide, with a dividing wall through the middle, which ensured the physical separation of the canons and nuns, and two cloisters, one on each side of the church. Excavations also uncovered a substantial medieval building, probably the kitchen, the domestic range and prior's lodging, as well as painted window glass, pottery and tiles. Further investigation appears to have discovered walls of not one, but two churches. The site later began to be used for agricultural purposes and was ploughed on a regular basis. All that is now visible in the midst of the fields are the earthworks.

A nearby memorial stone commemorates Welsh princess Gwenllian, daughter of Llywelyn, the last Prince of Wales. After the death of her mother while giving birth to her, and the murder of Lywelyn in 1282, the orphaned Gwenllian was sent by Edward I to Sempringham to ensure that she would never marry and produce a claimant to the Welsh throne. Edward III stayed at Sempringham in 1327 and granted Gwenllian a yearly pension of £20 for life. She died in 1337 at the age of 54.

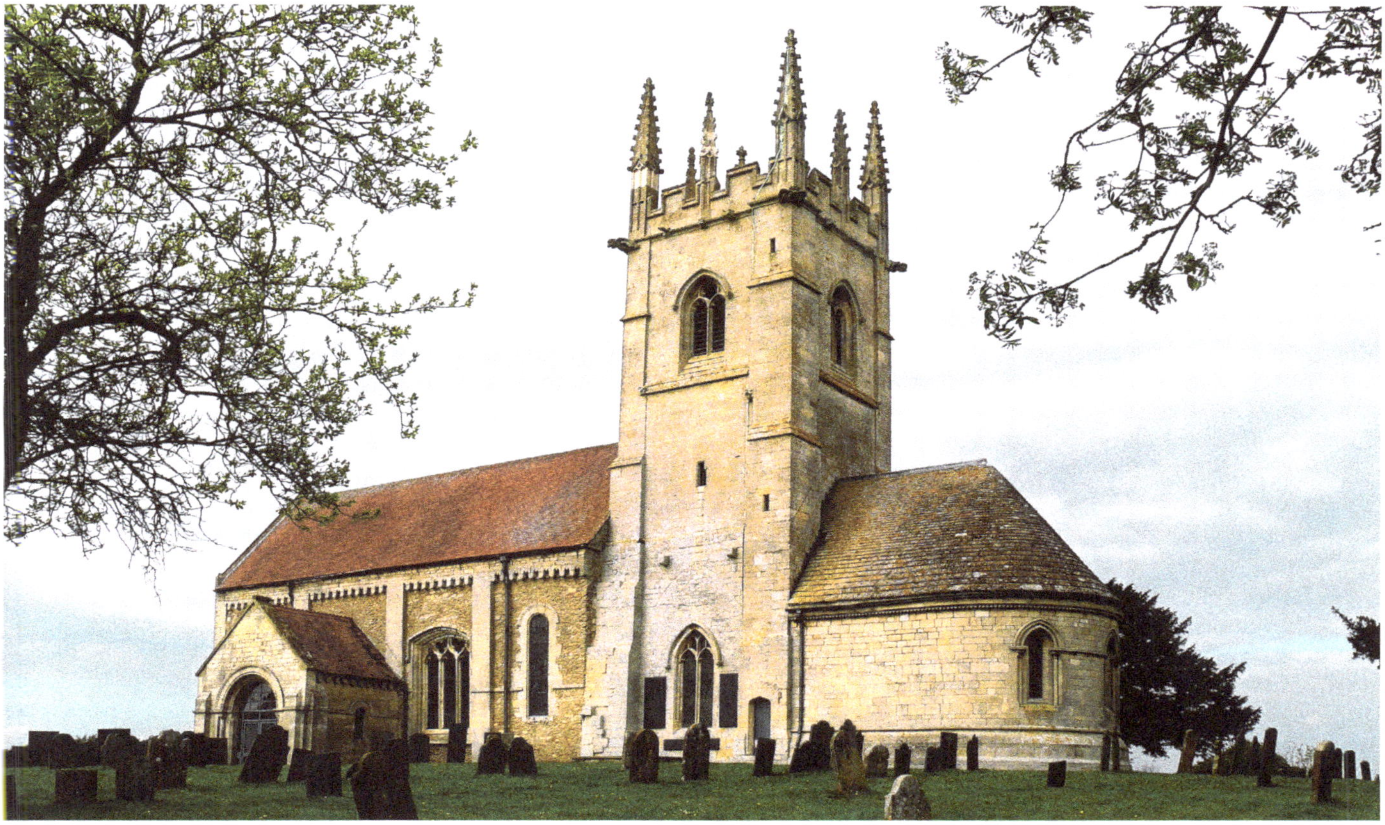

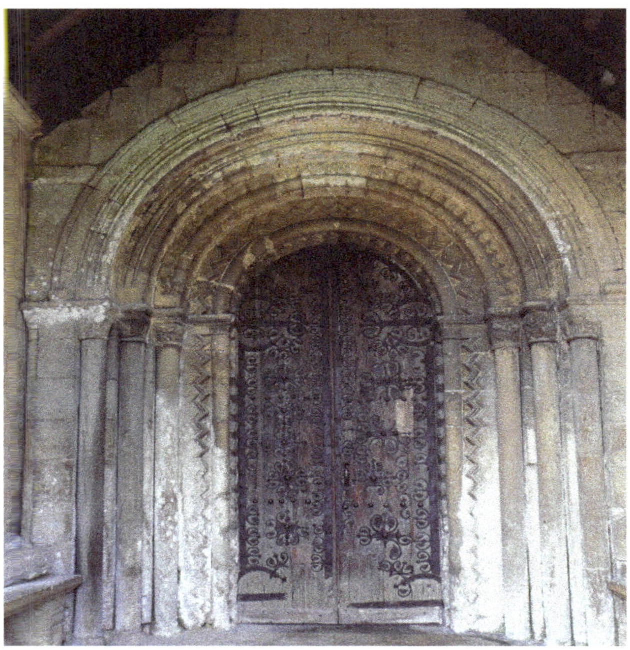

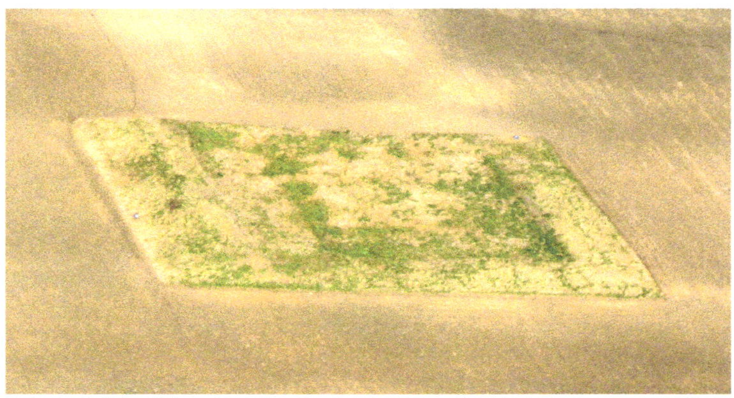

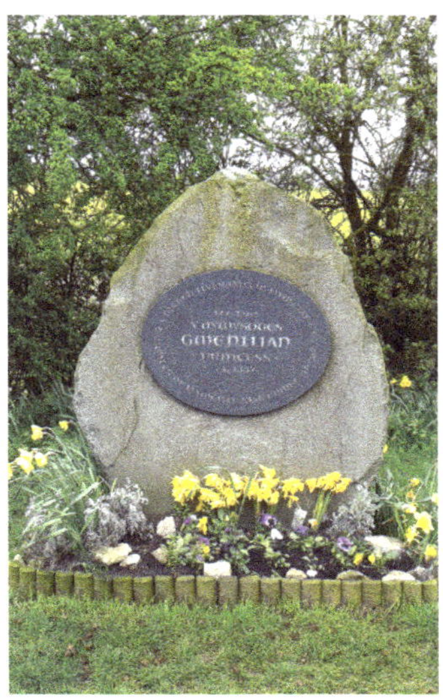

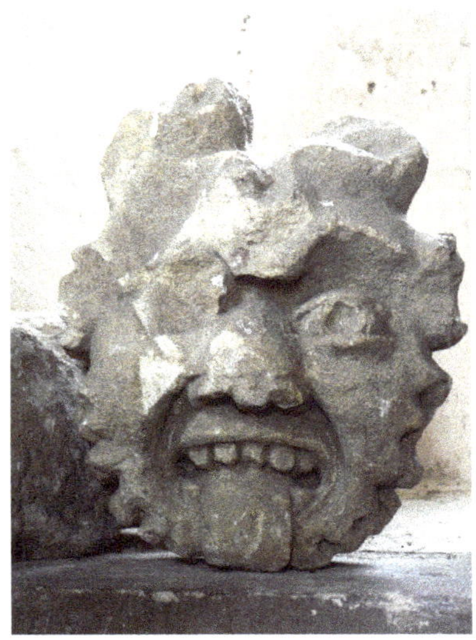

Photos – clockwise from top

St Andrew's was the birthplace of the Gilbertines
Aerial view of priory site by Simon Erskine Crum
Carved face found during excavations
Memorial to Welsh Princess Gwenllian
The wonderfully ornate priest's doorway

Sixhills Priory

St Mary • Gilbertine 1148/54–1538

This double house of Gilbertine canons and nuns was founded between 1148 and 1154, most probably by Robert de Gresley, the founder of Swineshead Abbey. The community owned considerable spiritual and temporal possessions, which, together with rents, a weekly market and a yearly fair on the vigil and feast of St Peter ad Vincula, provided a comfortable living. The canons developed a lucrative wool trade, being able to sell eighteen sacks a year at the beginning of the fourteenth century. Following the execution of David, Prince of Wales, Edward I sent David's small daughter, Gladys, to the convent to be veiled, and made an allowance for her upkeep. Gladys stayed at Sixhills from 1283 until her death in 1336. Edward I confined Christina Seton, sister of Robert de Bruce, here following her husband's execution. Robert Manning of Bourne wrote *The Story of England* while living at the priory in 1338. Great impoverishment by the middle of the fifteenth century had substantially diminished the community to twenty-eight, which, at its foundation, probably numbered fifty-five canons and lay-brothers, and 120 nuns and lay-sisters. Shortly before the Dissolution, the community suffered further from an epidemic sickness, so that on the surrender in September 1538, only Prior James Wales and seven canons, and Prioress Joan Manby and fourteen nuns were left. Its net annual value in 1535 had amounted to £135 0s. Nothing *in situ* is left and the only reminder of its existence are four stopheads, three of women and one of a man in a cap, built into the walls of a farmhouse, which stands on the site.

Spalding Priory

St Mary & St Nicholas • Benedictine 1074–1397

Conflict and associated difficulties marred the early history of this Saxon foundation, said to have come into existence in 1051, when Thorold of Buckenhale, Sheriff of Lincoln and a special benefactor of Croyland Abbey, granted the manor of Spalding to the Benedictine monks. Further lands and the wooden chapel of St Mary were gifted in 1059 by Earl Algar. But when Ivor Tailbois, who had been standard bearer at Hastings, came to live in Spalding in 1071, it ushered in a difficult period for the community. According to the Croyland chronicle, Ivo despised the monks for their Saxon origin, says Ingulf, so much so that he was roused to such an extremity of hatred and fury, which drove him to kill their cattle and swine, and to browbeat all their tenants. The monks soon succumbed to this onslaught and returned to the mother house, leaving a single monk to celebrate the divine office. When this monk died in a great storm, Ivo offered the manor of Spalding to the abbot of St Nicholas at Angers who, in 1074, sent a prior and five monks to occupy the vacated house. Ivo's charter was confirmed by William I. The community obtained additional lands and churches of a considerable value during the twelfth century from notable benefactors, which involved the monks in many lawsuits, but did not prevent it growing in wealth and importance. Attempts by the abbot of Croyland to have the original lands returned proved fruitless, but a settlement was reached in 1332.

During the wars with France, the monks were accused of various misdemeanours and the priory was taken into the King's hands on a number of occasions. In 1397, it became denizen and was freed from all dependency on the Norman abbey. Mismanagement plunged the priory into debt in the middle of the fifteenth century, but a recovery ensured that it was one of the richest monasteries in Lincolnshire in 1534. Some injunctions were issued by visiting bishops, but the house was generally in good order. Cardinal Wolsey's attempt to get his hands on the priory's property in 1526 came to nothing. Spalding Priory was surrendered in 1540. There is some doubt about the remains. The fifteenth century brick Abbey Buildings in Priory Street are said to have been the dormitory, and the provenance of a small stone building known as the Prior's Oven is also uncertain but dates from 1230 and may have been used as the monastic prison. Near Weston, to the south of Spalding Marsh, stands the ruined Wykeham Chapel of St Nicholas, which dates from 1311 and was built for Prior Hatfield as a private chapel for his country house.

Stainfield Priory

St Mary • Benedictine nuns +1154–1536

Nothing at all is left of Stainfield Priory, a house for Benedictine nuns founded after1154, in the reign of Henry II, by William de Percy, fourth Baron de Percy, who was a prolific patron of religious establishments. It was the only Benedictine nunnery in Lincolnshire and remained small and poor, never housing more than twenty nuns, its poverty exacerbated by a demand to maintain one of Edward II's servants for the rest of her life. Early in the thirteenth century, the nuns sold twelve sacks of wool per year, and the appropriation of the church at Quadring helped to keep the community afloat. There is little known history, and religious life proceeded without great upheaval but, in 1392, Bishop Bokyngham forbade merchants to sell their wool in the conventual church, which was a most unusual occurrence. Bishop Alnwick found the priory in good order in 1440, but some later laxity in obeying the rules incurred the wrath of the bishops. Nuns were found to be late coming to choir, dozing instead of singing, and gathering in groups and chattering over their meals. The house also had no proper infirmary. In 1534, it annual value was assessed at £98 8s. After at first being granted a licence to continue following the Act of Suppression of the smaller monasteries, Henry VIII changed his mind and installed the nuns in Stixwould Priory, with one of them, Mary Missenden, becoming prioress.

Saint Gilbert of Sempringham

The Order of Sempringham was established by Gilbert, son of Norman knight, Jocelin de Sempringham, and an unknown Saxon lady. Sometime before her child was born, she dreamed that the moon came down and settled in her lap, which she interpreted as a sign of her child's coming greatness. Gilbert was born c1083 with a physical deformity, thought to have been a curvature of the spine, which led to much ridicule. His mother's affection helped him to become good, pure, gentle and considerate towards women, and imbued him with a 'great desire to gain souls for Christ'. Gilbert was ordained vicar of St Andrews at Sempringham and, in 1131, with the help of Bishop Alexander of Lincoln, built accommodation against the north wall of the parish church of St Andrew for 'seven maidens', whom he had taught and who desired to lead a strict religious life.

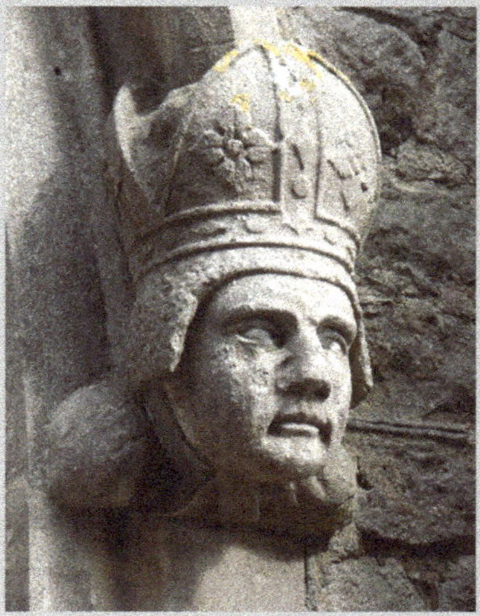

However, Gilbert was reluctant to rule the houses himself, but had little success in persuading the Cistercians to accept the nuns into their Order. With the help of St Bernard, Abbot of Clairvaux, and in agreement with the pope, Gilbert drew up the Institutes of Sempringham in 1147, thus establishing the only English monastic Order, while also reviving the double houses of canons and nuns that had existed in Anglo-Saxon times. The canons followed the Rule of St Augustine, while the nuns and sisters kept the Rule of St Benedict. The new Order was led by the Master of Sempringham who presided over the General Chapter, which was held at Sempringham every year in April on Rogation Day. Gilbert died in 1189 and was canonised by Pope Innocent III in 1202.

On Gilbert's death, there were thirteen houses in England belonging to the Order, with 700 canons and 1300 nuns. Nine of these were double houses, with four for canons only. He had also built hostels for the poor, the sick, orphans and widows. By the time of the Dissolution in 1538, these had grown to twenty-six Gilbertine houses, of which only three remained double communities. However, numbers had shrunk to just 143 canons, 139 nuns, and fifteen lay-sisters.

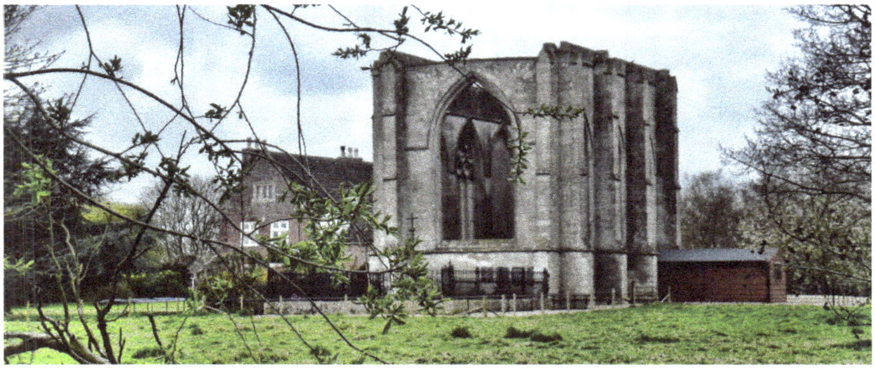

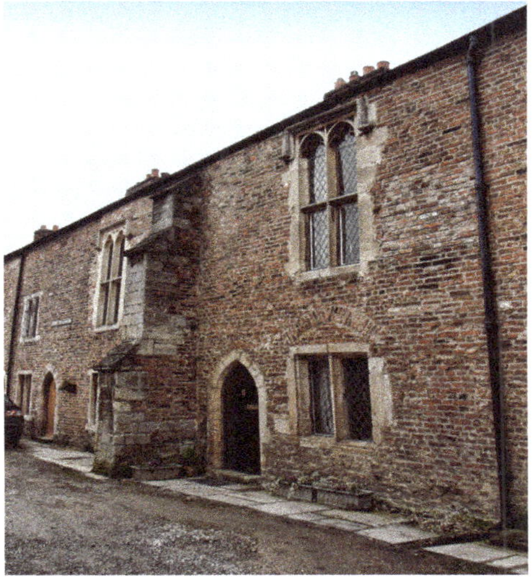

Photos of Spalding Priory – clockwise from above

Ruined Wykeham Chapel built for Prior Hatfield
Fifteenth century brick Abbey Buildings believed to have been the dormitory

Stamford Priory

St Leonard • Benedictine 1082–1538

What little remains of this ancient Benedictine priory is, nevertheless, Stamford's finest medieval building. Standing in a little grassy enclave on the north-eastern edge of the city are the part remains of a substantial twelfth century priory church, comprising the five open bays with round arches of the north arcade of the nave, which originally opened into the north aisle, now disappeared. There was no south aisle. The two eastern bays are slightly lower than the remaining three and exhibit characteristics of the early twelfth century, which would suggest that the church was extended westwards, probably c1150, when the ornate Transitional west front was built. The central arch is decorated with zigzag and rope carvings and is supported by four orders of single and twin-colonettes with foliated capitals. On each side there are smaller arched windows, both now blocked up. Above is a colonnade of seven arcades with three slender lancet windows in alternating positions. The lozenge-shaped design in the gable end above may have held a statue.

Archaeological excavation between 1967 and 1972 revealed that the church comprised a six-bay nave, crossing tower, transepts, each with an apsidal chapel, and a long apsidal presbytery, which was later squared off, probably in the thirteenth century. The cloister abutted the south wall of the nave, with a small chapter house and refectory probably in the typical locations in the east and south ranges. Unusually, the dormitory was above the cellarium and reredorter in the west range. Among the finds during the excavations were metallic mercury, crucibles and glassware, strongly suggesting that scientific experiments were taking place at the priory in the later fifteenth century. Finds are displayed in the Stamford Museum.

Local legend has long associated the site with the land given by Alcnfrid, son of King Oswy of Northumbria, to St Wilfrid, who is said to have established a monastery there in AD 658, which was destroyed by the Danes in the ninth century. The uncertainty of this early foundation also persists over the re-establishment of the house in the eleventh century. A manuscript of the fifteenth century states that it was refounded in 1082 by William de St Carileph, Bishop of Durham, with the co-operation of William the Conqueror, but historians now believe that it was founded c1100 as a cell of Durham to administer its southern properties. The priory cell has little independent history, but Edward I is known to have stayed at the priory when passing through the town. The priors were frequently changed, and when Bishop William Alnwick visited in 1440, there were only the prior and one monk resident. Prior Robert Barton gave the low income of the house, which was insufficient to meet its liabilities, as the reason why the priors never wanted to stay. In 1534, its value was assessed at just £25 1s, and the house was surrendered in 1538. After the Dissolution, the priory buildings came into the hands of the Cecil family who leased them out. The site became a farm and the church was converted into a barn. Much of the remaining stone was removed and the church eventually deteriorated. The west front collapsed in 1833 but was carefully reconstructed by the Marquess of Exeter.

Stamford Austin Friars

1343-1538

The founder of this house of Augustinian friars was Robert de Wodehouse, Archdeacon of Richmond, who obtained leave from the King and the pope to build a house for twelve friars in the western suburb of the town near St Peter's Gate, on land formerly occupied by the Friars of the Sack. The bishop of Lincoln gave his consent in 1343. The founder was buried in the priory church after his death soon after and willed all his goods to the friars. The prior of Sempringham granted ten acres of adjacent land, but otherwise, almost nothing is known of its history. Among the brethren was Thomas Winterton of Oxford, who was provincial prior in 1382. The house was surrendered to Dr John London by Prior Richard Warnar and five friars in October 1538. The site was granted to Edward, Lord Clinton, in 1548 and the buildings were soon destroyed and the stone removed. Nothing of the priory remains *in situ*, and although the priory site was excavated in 1712 by local antiquarians Forster and Peck, it has not been possible to obtain a clear picture of what the buildings looked like. A gargoyle above medieval windows on the almshouse next to the site on St Peter's Street is thought to have come from the priory, but the finest surviving piece is a late medieval head in a carved fifteenth century octofoil surround, thought to be a panel from a tomb chest or vault-boss. It was recovered in the 1980s from a building in the High Street and was displayed in Stamford Museum.

Photos – clockwise from top

Part remains of the priory church of St Leonard
Ornate transitional west front
Central arch with zigzag and rope carvings
Late medieval grotesque in carved surround from Austin Friars (Lincolnshire County Council)

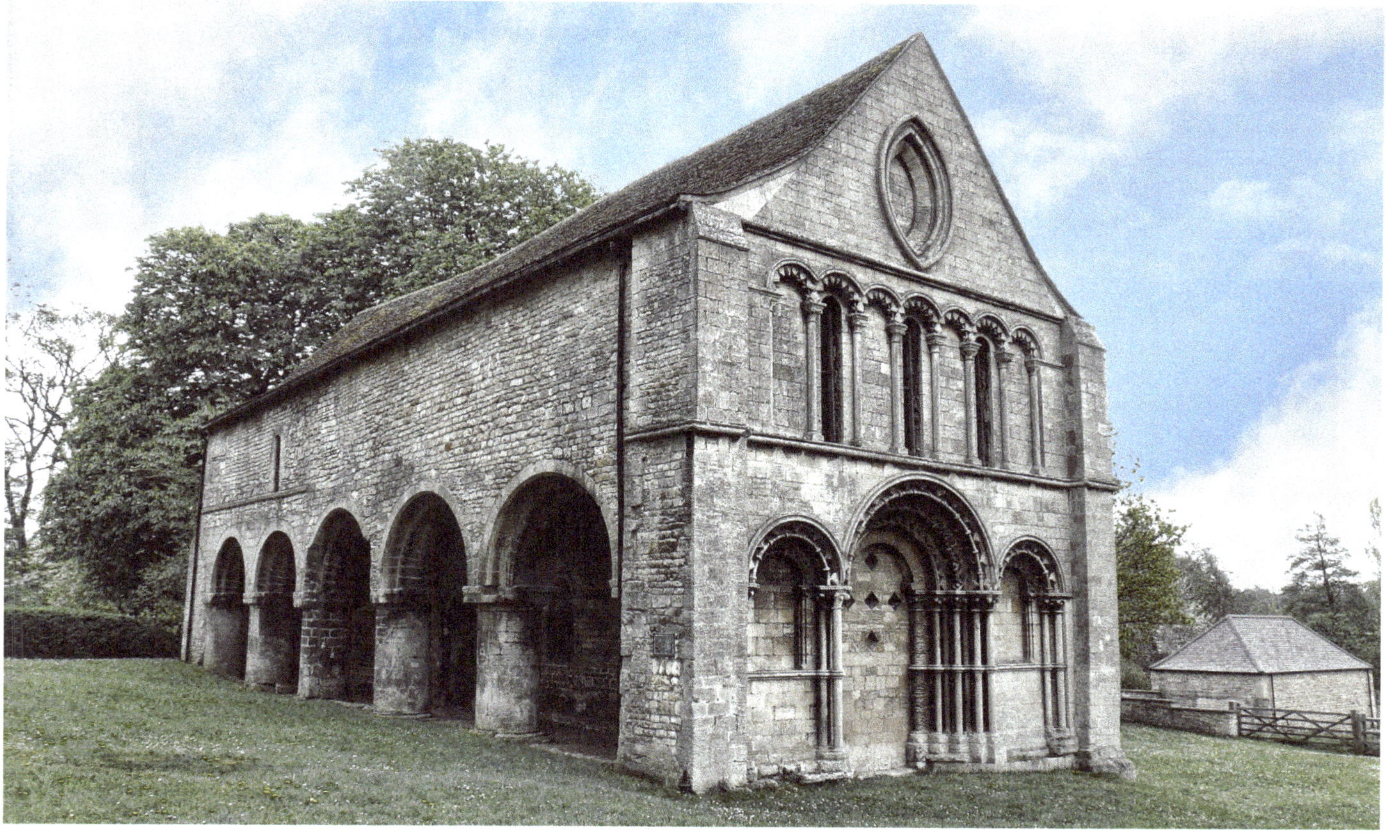

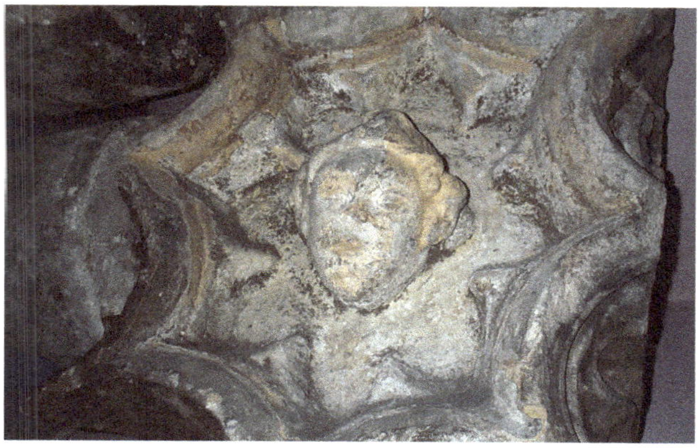

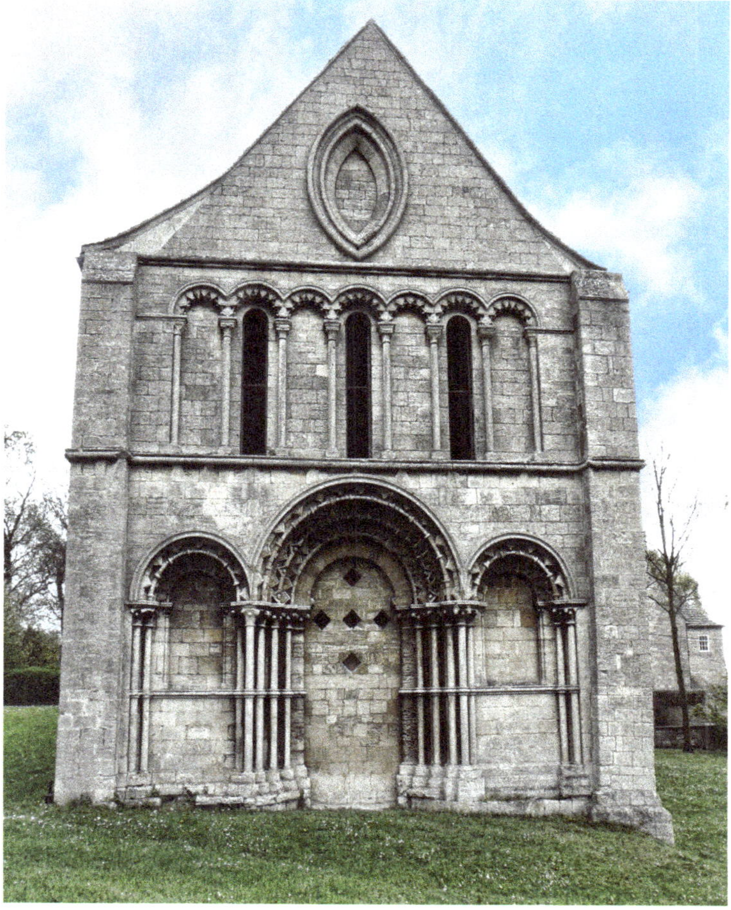

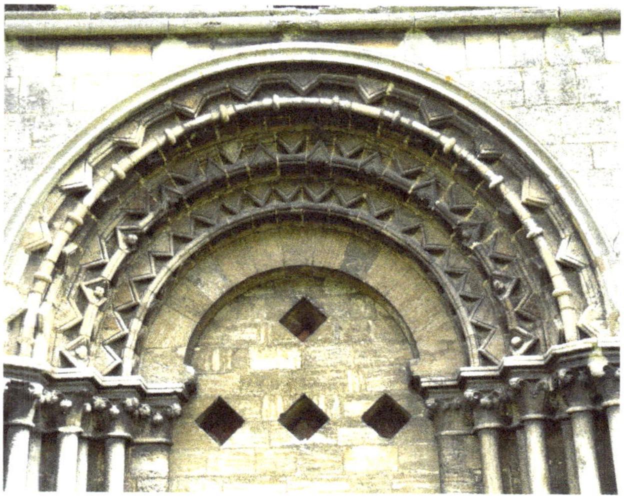

Stamford Black Friars

-1241-1538

There has been no physical evidence of this house of the Dominican Order, which stood between the city walls and the water gate by the River Welland, since the last fragment disappeared around 1727. This sad state of affairs is rather disappointing, as the friars enjoyed huge royal support and patronage throughout their early existence. The house was first mentioned in 1241, but was founded sometime before that date. The identity of the founder is unknown. In 1243 or 1244, Henry III gave them ten oaks for their refectory, and fifteen marks for making a conduit, which ran from a spring in Northamptonshire and must have crossed the River Welland. Henry III and Edward I ensured that the friars were supplied with food, and wine at one time, for the Provincial Chapters of the Order, which were held at Lincoln on several occasions over the next century. When Edward I passed through Stamford, he gave them alms for food, which was of an amount that suggested that there were at least forty friars present at that time. When the court was at Stamford, the Crosses of St. Neot and the Holy Thorn were kept in the Black Friars' church, and attracted worshippers and oblations. The church was rebuilt before 1310. Edward II and III both stayed at the priory, and in 1315, Queen Isabella made an offering of a cloth of gold at the high altar. Some interruptions to the tranquillity of the community occurred, including the imprisonment of one friar for a carnal sin, for which he was later sent to Cologne, where he did his penance. He was re-instated to Stamford in 1396. In 1416, three Stamford inhabitants were charged with assaulting and beating two friars. Apart from royal favour, the house had many influential benefactors, including the Despensers, who had a chapel in the church. The house was surrendered to Dr John London in October1538 by Prior William Stafforde, and eight brethren. The site was valued at 40s.

Stamford Grey Friars

-1230-1538

At the junction of Ryhall Road and Uffington Road stands what is believed to have been the infirmary gateway entrance of the Franciscan Friars Minor. Historians from the end of medieval times have left much confusion about the exact site of this priory, generally confusing it with that of the White Friars. Although historians in the 1970s have tended to favour the above site, no conclusive evidence has been produced. The gate at the west end of the site is the only surviving element of the original structure. It was built in the second quarter of the fourteenth century in Barnack limestone, with repairs and alterations made in a similar stone. The friars must have settled in Stamford before 1230, as it was at the beginning of that year that Henry III made them a grant of fuel. The friars later received several more royal grants of timber for their church and money to help with expenses for the several Provincial Chapters held at Stamford. At one such chapter held in 1249, the Franciscans formally welcomed the Austin Friars to England. When passing through Stamford several times in 1299 and 1300, Edward I gave alms to the friars, which then appeared to have numbered between thirty-nine and fort-six. In 1337, all friaries in the custody of Oxford met here, possibly in an attempt to establish a university in the town. The Grey Friars attracted many notable benefactors and a 'sumptuous chapel' in their church was a favoured burial place. Thomas Holland, Earl of Kent, was buried here in 1360, as later was his wife, Joan, the 'Fair Maid of Kent', who after his death had married the Black Prince and became the mother of Richard II. Blanche, daughter of Henry, Earl of Lancaster, was also laid to rest in the chapel. In the early fifteenth century, a friar was implicated in treasonable practices against Henry IV, and another maintained in a sermon at Stamford in 1424 that 'a religious might lie with a woman without sin'. Three Observant Friars were sent to the priory at Stamford and treated as prisoners after the suppression of the Observant houses in 1534. The priory was surrendered to Dr. London in October 1538 by John Schewyn, the warden, and nine other friars, and granted to the Duke of Suffolk in 1541.

Stamford Sack Friars

-1274-c1300

Nothing at all is known of the house of the Friars of the Sack, or Friars of the Penance of Jesus Christ, nor has anything survived from the short period of its existence. It must have been founded here before 1274, when the Council of Lyons decreed the suppression of the Order. The house was still occupied by four friars in 1300, when Edward I gave them a pittance. The site was conferred on the Austin Friars in 1342.

Stamford White Friars

Blessed Virgin Mary -1268–1538

The Carmelite priory is said to have been a magnificent structure, famous for its beautiful church and steeple, and the grounds appear to have been nearly a mile in circumference. Alas, only some indistinct earthworks have survived, although some historians, having long confused the site of the White Friars with that of the Franciscans, contend that the surviving gateway on the junction of Ryhall Road and Uffington Road had belonged to the Carmelites. However, it is almost certain that the priory was situated immediately east of the town walls on land sloping down to the River Welland. The Carmelites established themselves in Stamford before 1268, when Henry III gave them six oaks for the construction of their church. Although the house claimed to be a royal foundation, the founder is more likely to have been Henry de Hanna, the second provincial prior of the Order (1254-71). The priory acquired many parcels of land at the end of the thirteenth and early fourteenth century, and appears to have been of special importance during that period, with several Provincial Chapters held here. The royal alms granted to these friars between 1298 and 1314 by Edward I and Edward II indicate that there were from twenty to twenty-six brethren in the house. There seems to be very little evidence to support the tradition that the educational eminence of Stamford in the early part of the fourteenth century was mainly owing to the Carmelites, but they managed a school and several eminent scholars were inmates at the priory. Dr John London received the surrender of the house in October 1538, the deed being signed by Prior John Kyrtun and six friars. Richard Cecil seems to have promptly taken possession of the house and site, but it was granted to Edward, Lord Clinton, in 1552.

Stixwould Priory

St Mary • Cistercian nuns/Premonstratensian c1135–1539

Stixwould was probably the first of seven Cistercian nunneries to be founded in Lincolnshire, although no exact date has been established. It was founded by Lucy, Countess of Chester, probably in the reign of Henry I, and was later endowed by her son, Ranulf, and Ralf fitzGilbert, the founder of Markby. The priory became involved in several disputes about certain advowsons, most of which the prioress won, and complaints about trespass and even cattle-rustling by the King's men! With an annual income of less than £200, it was dissolved in 1536, and the nuns pensioned off. But the King ordered the buildings to remain standing to provide accommodation for the nuns of Stainsfield. In July 1537, in a most baffling move, Henry VIII re-founded Stixwould under the Premonstratensian rule, but this was of short duration. In September 1539, Mary Missenden surrendered the priory to the King's commissioner. Both Stainfield and Stixwould served for a time as double monasteries, with nuns and canons living side by side. Nothing is left standing, although some parts of the original structures were incorporated into the respective parish churches.

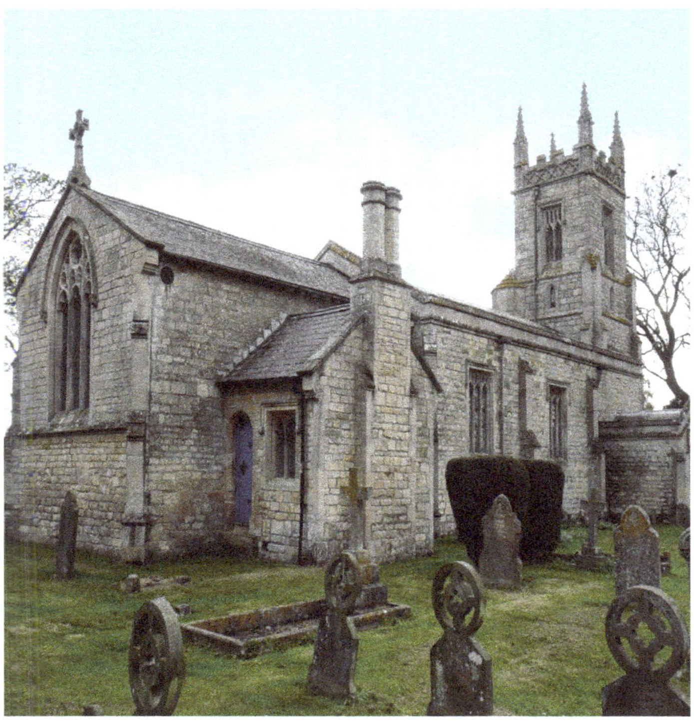

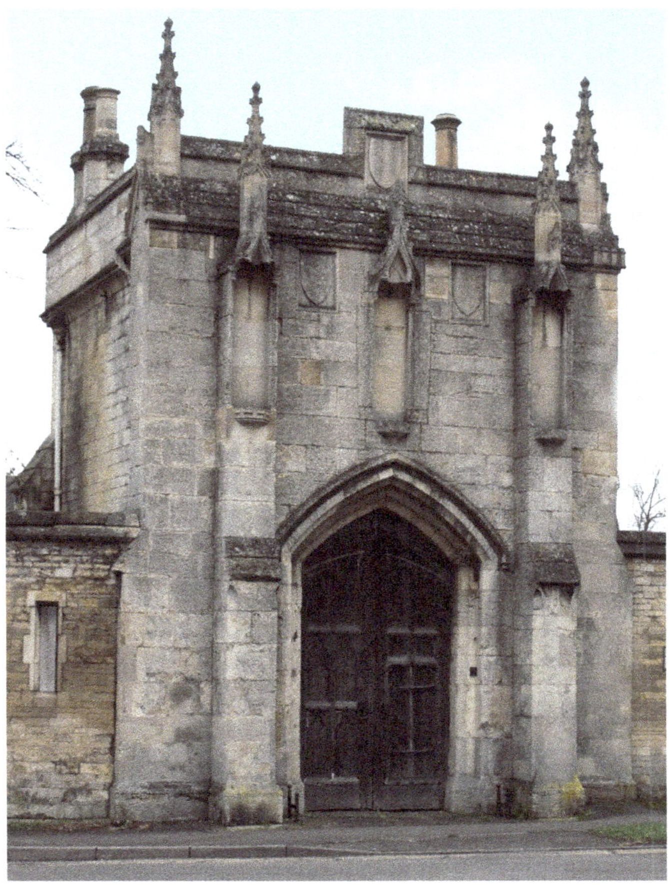

Photos - from left

The parish church of Stixwould may incorporate fragments of the priory

The surviving gate of the Franciscan priory at Stamford

Stow Abbey

St Mary • Benedictine 1091–1109

The abbey of Stow was founded initially as a collegiate church in c1040, probably by Eadnoth II, Bishop of Dorchester, and enriched later in an agreement between his successor, Ulf, and Leofric, Earl of Mercia, and his wife Godiva. King Edward the Confessor confirmed the gift of the earl and countess. After the Conquest, Bishop Remigius de Fécamp (1067-92) found the house desolate and determined to convert it into a Benedictine abbey. The lands and revenues of the abbey of Eynsham in Oxfordshire were annexed in 1091 to the new house at Stow, which was populated by a number of monks from Eynsham under Abbot Columbanus. This arrangement was confirmed by a charter of William II (Rufus), but was not to last. In 1109, Henry I issued a new charter for the restoration of the abbey of Eynsham, and the monks of Stow were transferred there soon after. The estates of their church were annexed to the See of Lincoln, which had been removed from Dorchester by Remigius.

The conventual church has survived as the parish church. It is large and one of the oldest parish churches in England and is often referred to as the "Mother Church of Lincolnshire". Although the church was extensively, but apparently sensitively restored by John Loughborough Pearson in 1865, it retains its Anglo-Saxon appearance, with some parts dating back to AD 950 and others to the Normans who added a grand nave and chancel. There is much still to admire, both from the outside, including the south doorway with its zigzag decoration, and the interior, which is commanded by the mighty Saxon arches of the crossing. However, the insertion of later Gothic arches to support the fifteenth century tower built within the Saxon one detracts from the overall pleasing impression.

On the east wall of the south transept are some charming fifteenth century heads, while a bracket in the north transept is supported by musicians playing a double pipe and perhaps a harp or psaltery. Set into the south transept wall is a mix of windows, representing round-headed Saxon, circular Norman and Decorated Gothic designs. Behind the altar are the remains of a painting of the murder of St Thomas Becket dating from the twelfth or early thirteenth century. The reworked but impressive chancel arcades, window surrounds and vault ribs are carved with zigzag and crenellations. Also of note is the magnificent octagonal Early Gothic font with its pagan symbols.

Swineshead Abbey

St Mary • Cistercian 1134–1536

This was a large and important Cistercian abbey with an apparent high standard of monastic life, at least in early years, yet so little is known of its history and nothing at all is left to form a clear picture. It was founded in 1134 by Robert de Gresley and colonised by monks from Furness. It was endowed with 240 acres of demesne land with mills and fisheries, and attracted a large number of benefactors of high standing. But the house is remembered principally as a resting place for the dying King John. In October 1216, the King had forded the Wash, at low tide, from Crosskeys to Fossdyke, but the return of the tide suddenly swept away the carriages and horses that conveyed all his baggage and treasures. The irritated King proceeded to Swineshead, where he was gripped by a violent fever that same night. He left the following day on horseback, first to his castle at Sleaford, and then to Newark, where he died four days later. One writer has asserted that rather than having died of fever, John was poisoned by a monk at Swineshead! Internal life was disrupted in 1329, when three monks deserted the monastery with some of its goods, and in 1401, when an abbot was attacked and a monk imprisoned. A monk later fled the house because of the severity of the discipline. No complaints were made against the community in 1536, when Abbot John Haddingham and ten monks surrendered to the King. Its value in 1534 was given at £167 15s. The site of the abbey was granted to Edward, Lord Clinton, in 1551. The present building on the site, known as Swineshead Abbey, retains parts of a house built out of the abbey remains by Sir John Stockton in 1607.

Thornholme Priory

St Mary • Augustinian -1154–1536

Nothing is now visible of this house of Augustinian canons, thought to have been founded before 1154 by King Stephen or John Malherbe. It was never a large house and, in spite of holding various parcels of land and several churches, it fell into debt from time to time. There were disputes with local families over property rights, and in 1280, the prior complained of violence to his property and brethren. Episcopal visitations in the fifteen century exhorted the community to desist from strife, and the prior was accused of harshness of correction. Little else is known. In 1534, the clear annual value of the priory was £105 13s, which led to its suppression in 1536, when Prior George Clayton, or Rotherham, and nine canons signed the deed of surrender.

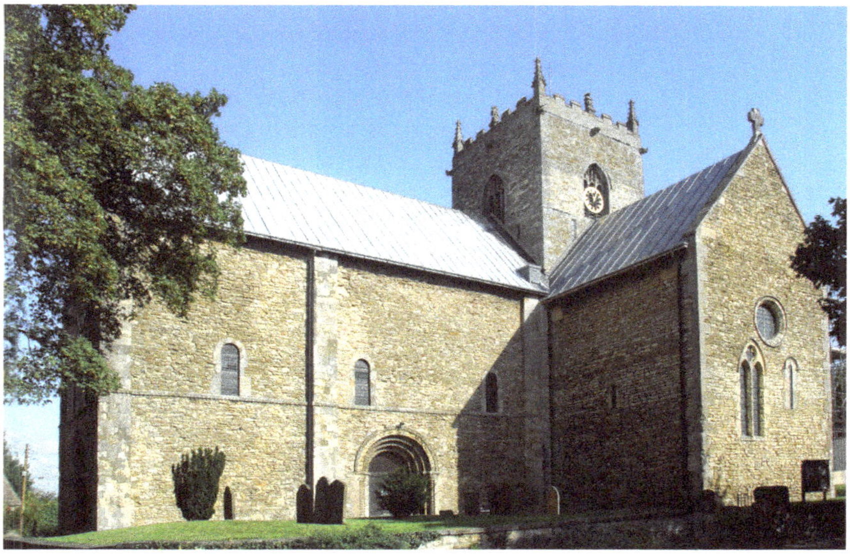

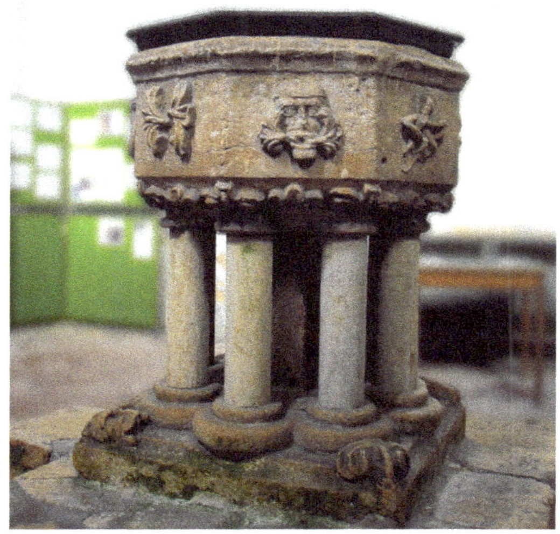

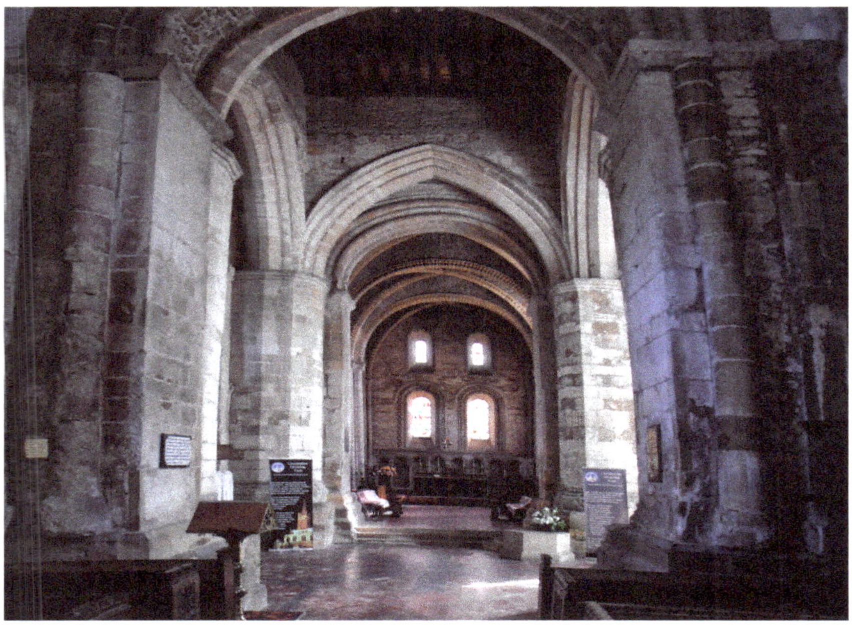

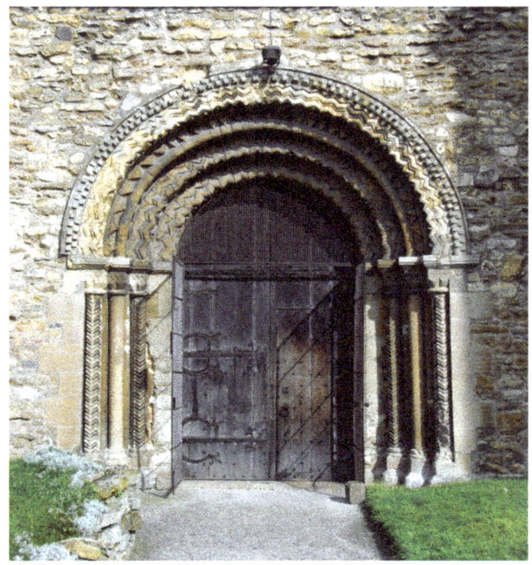

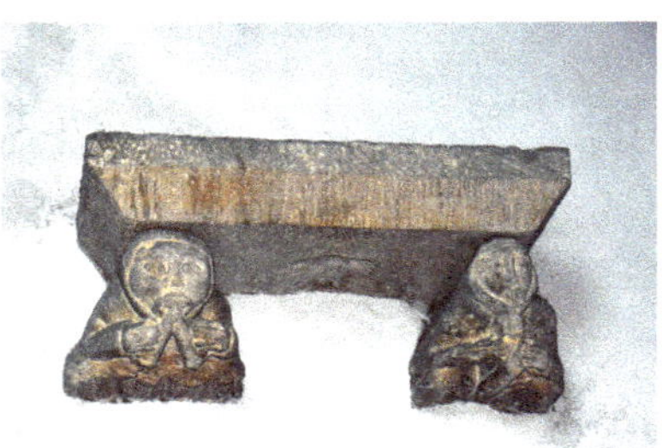

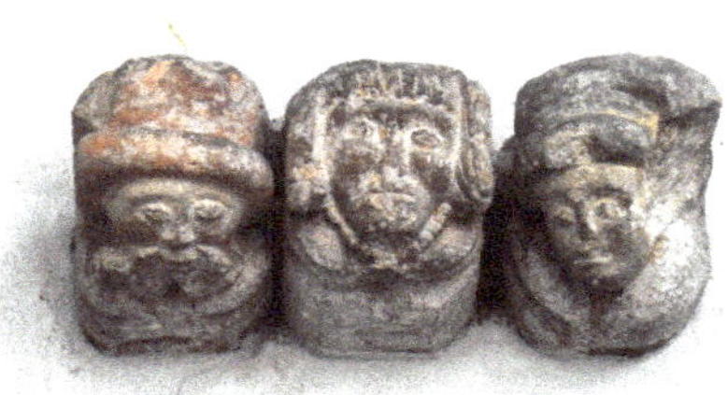

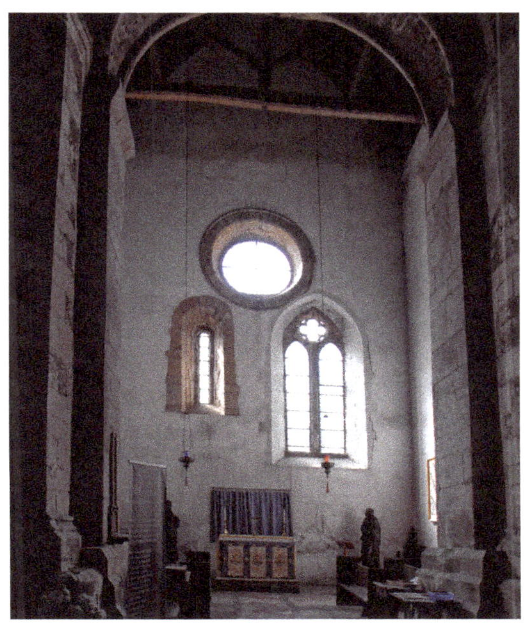

Photos of Stow Abbey - clockwise from top left

Stow parish church of St Mary
Early Gothic font with pagan symbols including the Green Man
South doorway with zigzag decoration
A history of windows in the south transept wall
Fifteenth century heads and musicians
The mighty Saxon arches of the crossing

Thornton Abbey

St Mary • Augustinian 1139–1539

Travelling through the Fenland from the west and through Thornton Curtis, one is quite unexpectedly met by an imposing and beautifully decorated monastic gatehouse, which somehow seems to have been misplaced. The storage tanks and pipework of the Immingham refineries and docks on the desolate south shore of the River Humber provide a surrealistic backdrop to such a beautiful building, which should be hidden away in lush green pastures. Yet this holy place remarkably retains the quiet solitude of the days when its horizon was filled with nothing more than grazing livestock, fertile crops and the meandering river. The massive brick-built gatehouse, the largest in the country, is a curious mixture of religious decorations and symbolism and sturdy fortress-like defences guarding the entrance, which could only be reached via a bridge over a deep moat. The abbot received a licence to build the gatehouse and add some defensive work in 1382, clearly to protect the abbey site from an unspecified threat. One of the speculative reasons advanced for this unusual move was as a response to the Peasants' Revolt led by Wat Tyler in 1381, a repeat of which could well have concerned the abbot of a rich and isolated establishment.

Between the four tall turrets above the central vaulted archway, the façade is a mass of niches and canopies, which once contained statues of saints, fragments of which still remain *in situ*. The crenellated parapets, on the other hand, were adorned with soldiers, tradesmen and scientists. The main purpose of the gatehouse appears to have been to provide opulent accommodation for the abbot, appropriate to his standing as head of a well-endowed abbey. Several fireplaces and garderobes can be found throughout the building. Nothing has survived from the original church, and only foundations remain of later rebuilding, with the exception of one of the south transept walls, which stands to almost full height. Alongside the wall are two complete sides of the elegant octagonal chapter house, dating from the twelfth century. The magnificent false arcading and highly decorative tracery are telling examples of the abbey's prosperity. The vaulted parlour is also notable, as is the quarry-tiled walkway around the cloister. Traces of other monastic buildings are, however, sparse.

Thornton Abbey was founded in 1139 as an Augustinian house by William le Gros, Earl of Yorkshire, and colonised by monks from Kirkham Priory in North Yorkshire. Its wealth and influence grew rapidly, and already in 1148, it was elevated to abbey status. William was buried in the abbey after his death. Henry II made some gifts to the abbey during his reign. Life at Thornton Abbey appears to have been largely uneventful and, while the abbey's chronicle gives considerable detail of the construction and decoration of the gatehouse, it says nothing about why such a grand and fortified building was erected. The abbey was dissolved in 1539, when it was valued at the considerable sum of £591. The last abbot remained as guardian for the next two years, after which the abbey was re-founded by Henry VIII as a college for secular canons. This had a short life, being dissolved just six years later and given to Henry Randes, the bishop of Lincolnshire. Subsequently passing through many hands, it was partially dismantled and its stone used for new buildings nearby.

The ghostly figure of the fourteenth abbot of Thornton, Sir Thomas de Gretham, may be seen wandering through the abbey grounds late at night looking for his lost love. Sir Thomas fell in love with one of his students, Heloise, the beautiful daughter of Sir William Wellam, but paid dearly for his sin. Accused and convicted of witchery, black magic and lax living, he was walled up alive in a secret chamber in the abbey. In the 1830s, workmen found his skeleton sitting at a table, with a candlestick and book by his side.

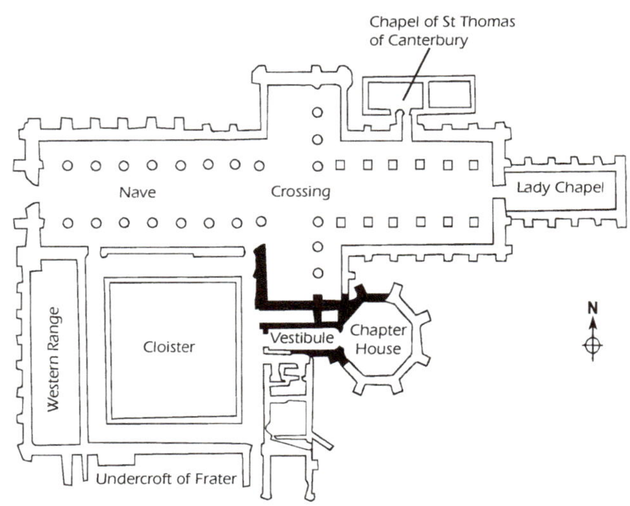

Photos – clockwise from top

The beautiful turreted gatehouse protected by a formidable barbican
South transept with remains of chapel
Two walls remaining of the elegant octagonal chapter house
Detail of carved figures above main front of gatehouse
Blind arcading and delicate tracery of the chapter house

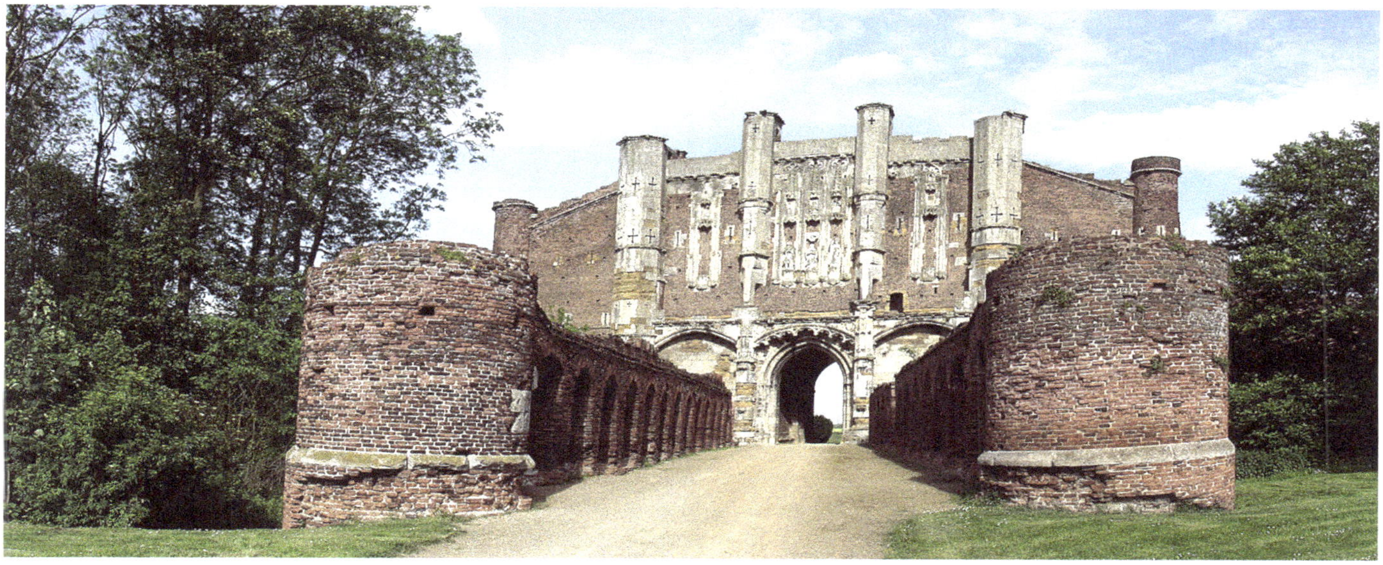

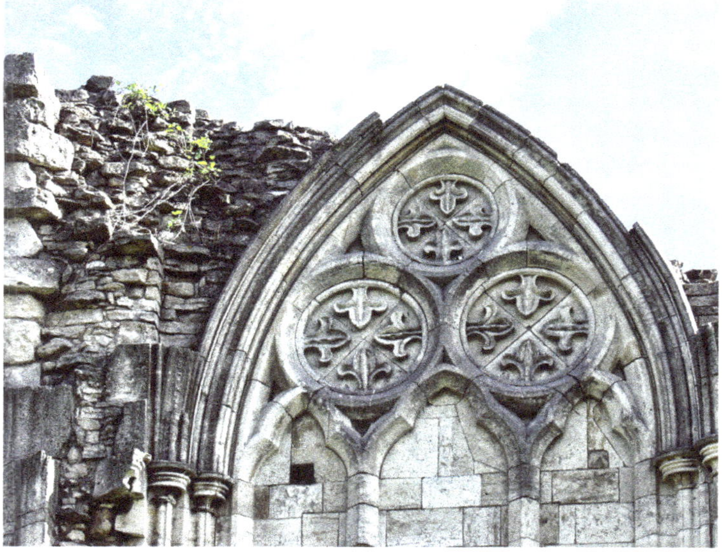

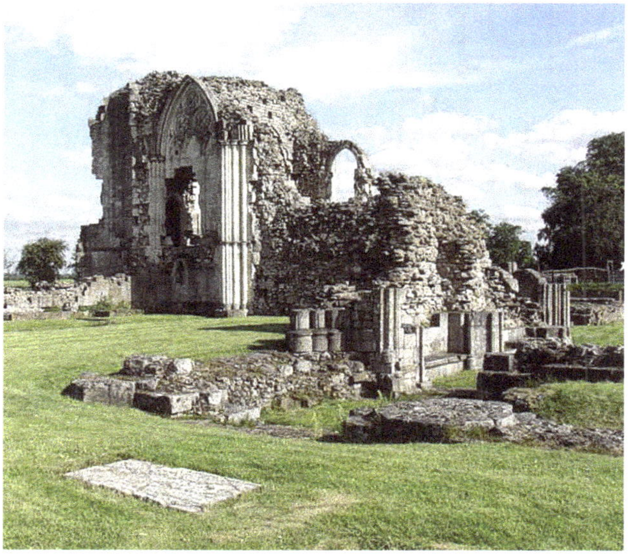

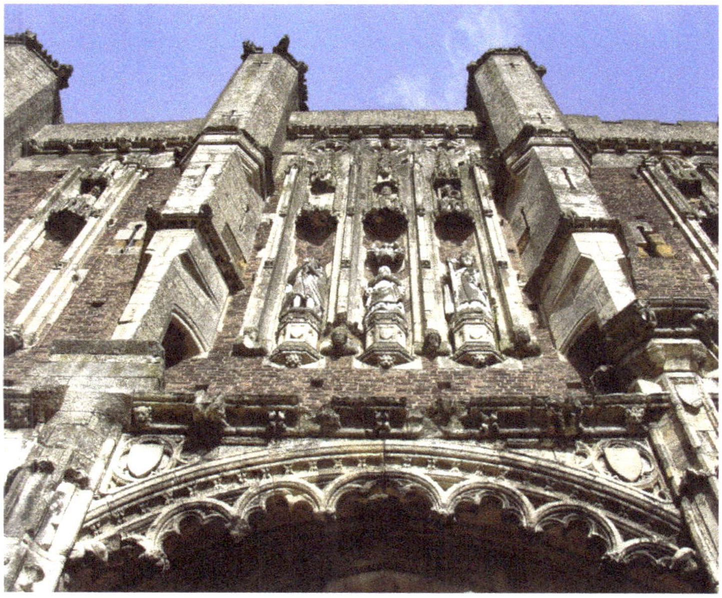

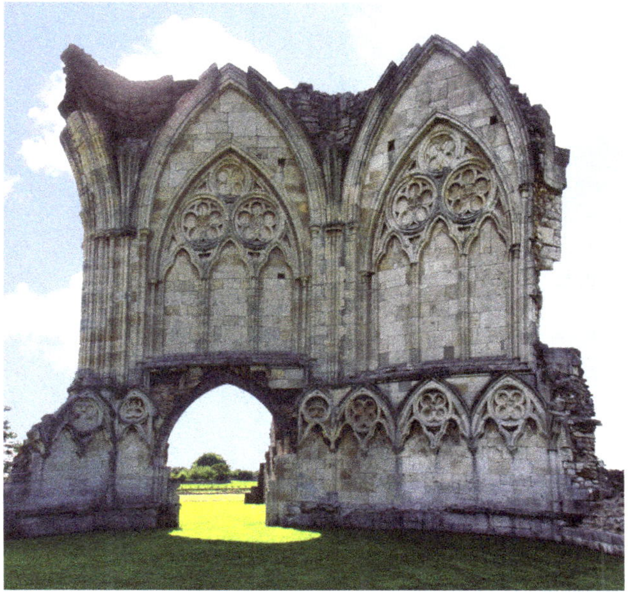

Thwaite Priory

• Augustinian ?–1536?

The earliest record of this small priory cell to the Augustinian abbey of Thornton appears to be 1440, when a single canon was present. Its income under Thornton was a mere £15, and it may have been suppressed in 1536. Nothing else is known.

Torksey Priory

St Leonard • Augustinian +1154–1536

This small priory of Austin canons was founded during the reign of Henry II, and possibly by the King himself. What little has been recorded of the history of the house does not reflect well on the community, and particularly on some of the priors. In 1275, the prior was accused of setting up a court for himself, to the prejudice of the King's court at Torksey, appropriated the assize of bread and ale, and enclosed more than two feet of the King's highway. The community pleaded poverty in 1319, and in 1323, the prior was accused of burning houses in Wold Newton and committing robberies and trespasses. In 1342, the house was said to be 'greatly wasted by misrule'. Nothing is then known until 1440, when Bishop Alnwick made a visitation and found no fault with the morality of the community. Injunctions were issued for a few minor transgressions, such as non-attendance at choir and drinking in Torksey, but in 1444, the bishop deposed the prior for bringing the house almost to ruin. When Bishop Atwater visited in 1519, he found everything satisfactory, except for the utter poverty of the house, which was without cloister and dormitory. In 1534, the clear annual value of the house was only £13 1s, and John Coyell and five canons signed the Deed of Surrender in 1536. Not a vestige is left.

Tunstall Priory

St Mary • Gilbertine -1164—1189

The double Gilbertine house of Tunstall was founded before 1164 by Reginald de Crevequer, who endowed it with the 'Island of Tunstall near Redburn', his fee in the island of Hade, the meadow between the islands, and rights of common. His son, Alexander, united the house with the Gilbertine priory of Bullington, sometime before 1189. The monastery's short existence was most likely due to insufficient endowments to support a community of canons and nuns. Nothing has survived to remind of this short-lived priory.

Tupholme Abbey

St Mary • Premonstratensian c1155–1536

The most prominent remains of the monasteries in the Witham Valley are at the remote Tupholme Abbey, where the south wall of a thirteenth century refectory still stands to two-storey height, with graceful Early English lancet windows lighting the upper level, and small square windows letting light into what was a lower vaulted undercroft. A fine reader's pulpit has also survived, although it has been substantially altered. Other surviving foundations are hidden below ground, which would have included the cloister, church and other buildings to the north. The mounds and hollows are overlaid by the foundations of a Tudor mansion. Several monastic fishponds have also been preserved to the south, and the moated area is thought to be the remains of a water-surrounded arbour. It is rather fitting that a flock of Soay sheep is now gracing on the 'island of sheep', which is the ancient meaning of Tupholme, also reminding that the production of wool was the principal income for the abbey. The visitor can enjoy the wildlife and learn about the abbey from the interpretation panels on the site, while having a picnic.

This Premonstratensian abbey was founded around 1155 on land given by Gilbert and Alan de Neville, and populated by an abbot and twelve canons from Newsham Abbey in North Lincolnshire. In the thirteenth century, it was granted a charter, confirming the abbey's right to build a canal linking it with the River Witham. In 1329, the Earl of Lancaster granted the manor of Burreth to Tupholme Abbey, which was further endowed in 1342 with the manor of Ranby by Ralph de Neville. By 1347, however, the abbey was heavily in debt, with an enterprising abbot accused of 'forgery and counterfeiting of the coin of the realm', apparently using the proceeds to buy wine and corn, which he sold for profit. The loss of the abbot, probably through the Black Death the following year, brought added hardship. By the late fifteenth century, discipline at the abbey began to slide. Bishop Redman visited the house regularly from 1475 to 1503 and found much to be corrected among the community, which numbered some twenty-four canons, including novices. In 1497, one canon, Thomas Pynderwelle, was banished to Croxton Abbey in Leicestershire for having fathered a child with a local woman called Philippa, while several others were forbidden to leave the precinct of the monastery. The situation improved, as a visitation by the bishop in 1501 found nothing wrong. Tupholme Abbey was valued at £100 14s, which brought it within the closure of the lesser monasteries in 1536. The last abbot, John Acaster, and eight canons were pensioned off. The abbey and its possessions, which included the church, bell tower and churchyard, were granted to Sir Thomas Heneage of Hainton, who adopted it to build a grand Tudor mansion for his daughter Elizabeth and her new husband, William Willoughby. In the process, he demolished the church and converted the other ranges to domestic accommodation. The mansion was demolished after being sold in 1661 and replaced by Tupholme Hall, which was torn down in the twentieth century.

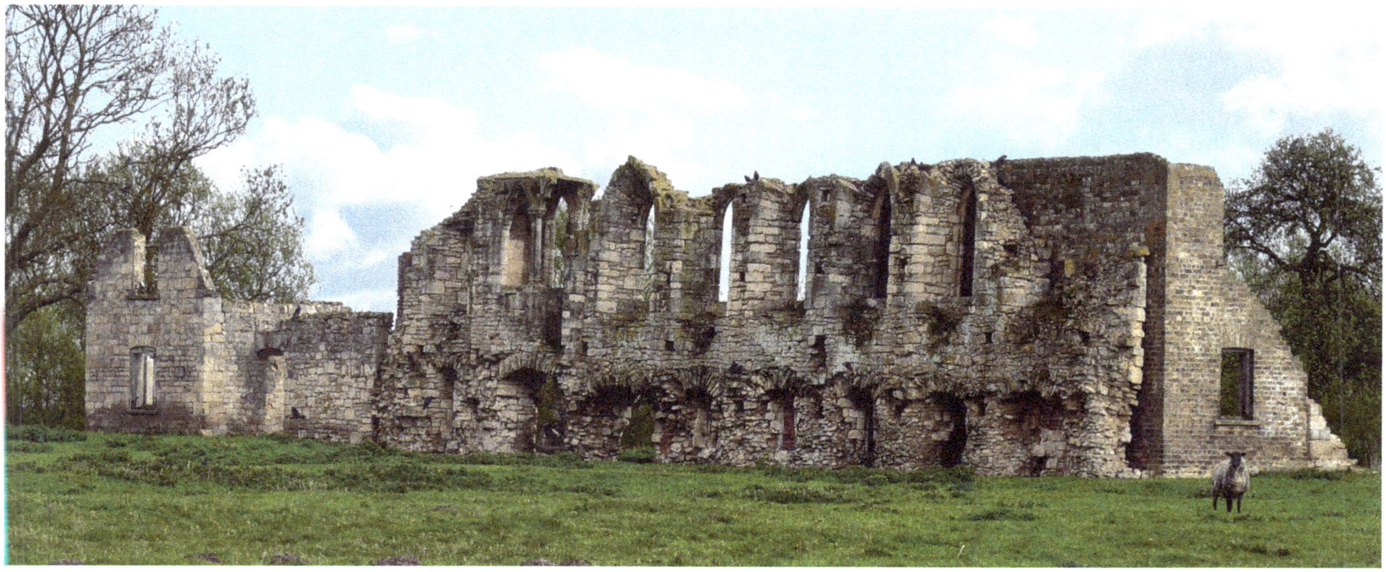

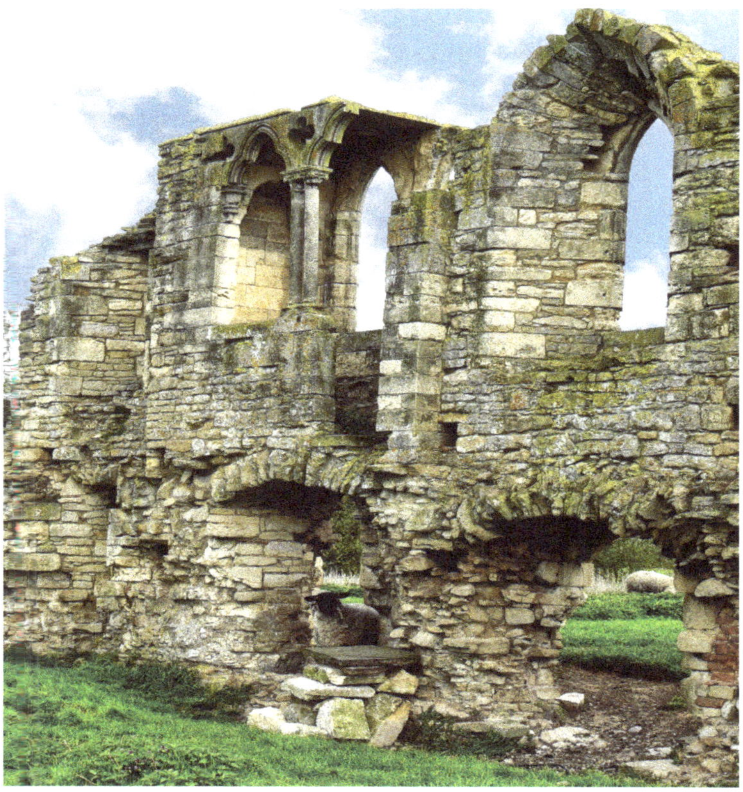

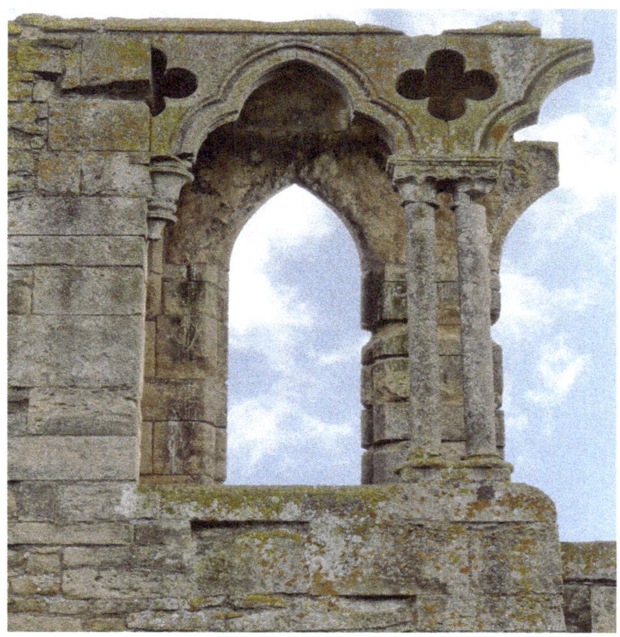

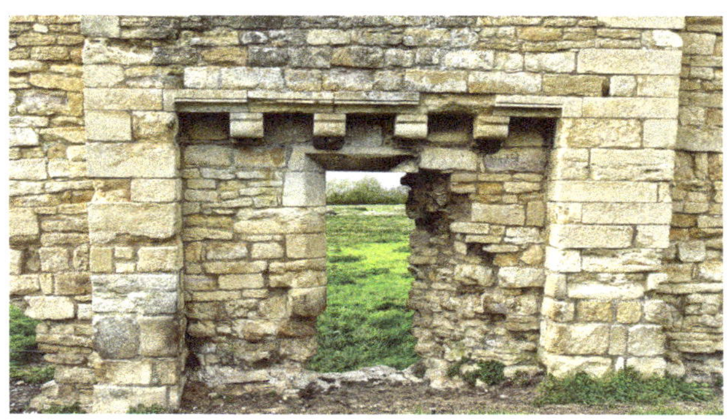

Photos of Tupholme Abbey - clockwise from top

South wall of refectory with remnants of Tudor house
Fine reader's pulpit
Remains of fireplace against refectory wall
Reader's pulpit, lancet windows and undercroft

Vaudey Abbey

St Mary • Cistercian 1149–1536

Abbot Warin and twelve Cistercian monks first settled near Castle Bytham in 1147, on land granted by William, Count of Aumale and Earl of York, but found the site unsuitable. Just two years later, Geoffrey de Brachecourt, a tenant of Gilbert de Ghent, offered the monks a new site in nearby Grimsthorpe, then still covered in dense woodland. The monks cleared the land, created fishponds and erected their monastic buildings. They called their new home Vallis Dei, meaning Valley of God, known today as The Vaudey. Geoffrey granted all his lands to the abbey, which obtained further parcels of land in Lincolnshire and Leicestershire from a number of other benefactors, which enabled the community to build a flourishing wool trade. It also appears to have been a house of some importance, with the abbot sent in 1229 in the King's name to bear messages to Llywelyn, Prince of Wales. In 1280, the abbot was empowered to arrest all vagabond Cistercians, monks or lay-brethren, with the help of the secular arm, and to inflict punishment upon them according to the needs of the case.

Early prosperity began to decline rapidly by the end of the thirteenth century. The abbey was taken under the King's protection in 1292 and by 1347 its debts were such that there was not enough income to support the monks. Some remission of taxes through the King's compassion, and a promise to repay a small sum of money lent to him for the French wars, will have helped a little, but the Black Death added further to its difficulties. Nothing further is known until 1532 when, following a joint visitation by the abbots of Fountains, Woburn and Pipewell, Abbot Henry Saxton was accused of mismanagement and of neglecting the divine office. The abbot was deposed but, after a plea to Cromwell, was advised to offer his resignation to qualify for a pension.

With an annual value of £124, the abbey was dissolved in 1536 under the first Act of Suppression. The community then comprised Abbot William Stile and ten monks. In 1539, Henry VIII granted the abbey and its possessions to Charles Brandon, first Duke of Suffolk, who used its stone as building material for his new house. Local antiquarian, William Stukely, noted in 1736 that 'foundations of the ruins of the abbey generally remain from the gatehouse to the dovecote'. Only earthworks within Grimsthorpe Castle Park now recall the abbey's existence. Stone remains at Scottlethorpe, now used as a barn, may be of a chapel from Vaudey Abbey.

Wellow (by Grimsby) Abbey

St Augustine & St Olaf • Augustinian c1132–1536

This was one of the few Augustinan houses with the status of abbey. It was founded c1132 by Henry I, who provided the community with land, mills, and the church of St James. The endowments were enlarged with more lands and churches granted by Ranulf, Earl of Chester, Gilbert de Turribus and the burgesses and knights of Grimsby. The house was situated on a hill in the centre of the town and was supplied with fresh water from a nearby spring, which was of sufficient strength to power a watermill at the bottom of the hill. During the Scottish wars of Edward II, the abbot was required to supply the King with wheat, malt and sheep and, although he was recompensed by Edward III, the house was seriously in debt and was managed for a time by a secular clerk. In 1368, the canons were rebuked for visiting Grimsby taverns and gossiping, and Abbot John Utterby was deposed in 1374 for having 'sold, alienated, and dissipated the goods of the house and brought it almost to ruin'.

Episcopal visitations in the fifteenth century resulted in few complaints and, when Bishop Atwater visited in 1519, the house appeared to be in better condition as some others of the Order. In 1518, Abbot Richard Kyngson had been made one of the definitors at the general chapter held at Leicester under the presidency of Cardinal Wolsey. With a clear annual value in 1534 of only £95, the abbey fell within the first Act of Suppression and was dissolved in 1536. Abbot Robert Whitgift received a pension, and nine canons were also paid off. Apart from a few worked stones in the grounds of Abbey House, nothing else has survived.

Wenghale Priory

• Benedictine -1115–1414

Date of foundation and the name of the founder of this small priory are unknown, but it was probably founded before 1115, when the monks of Wenghale held land in Owersby of the Earl of Mortain. It was a cell of the Benedictine abbey of Séez in Normandy, and the earliest appointment of a prior is dated 1223. In 1400 it was in the hands of a secular clerk in recompense for services rendered to the King. As the other alien houses, Wenghale was dissolved by Henry V in 1414 and granted by his successor, Henry VI, to the college of St. Nicholas, Cambridge, in 1441. It was later transferred to the college of St. Michael (Trinity College) in exchange for other lands. The value of its revenue in 1380 was just £12 18s.

West Ravendale Priory

• Premonstratensian 1202–1414

This small priory is said to have been founded by Alan, son of Henry, Earl of Brittany, who gave the manor and church in 1202 to the Premonstratensian abbey of Beauport in Brittany. There are several references of a prior looking after the estate, but it is not known if canons were also resident. The possessions were taken into the King's hands during the wars with France, but were released in 1340 and 1343 on the grounds that Brittany was not under the power of France. Some years before the dissolution of the alien houses in 1414, Henry IV granted the lands of West Ravendale to his Queen, Joan of Navarre, in dower, and when she died without issue, they were finally assigned to the Dean and Capter of Southwell in 1452. In 1380, the revenue of the priory was £22 19s. Nothing has survived.

Whaplode Crutched Friars

c1246–c1260

There is a report about the short-lived existence of a house for Crutched Friars at Whaplode, but nothing at all is known. Its foundation has been given as c1246 and it appears to have been abandoned by 1260.

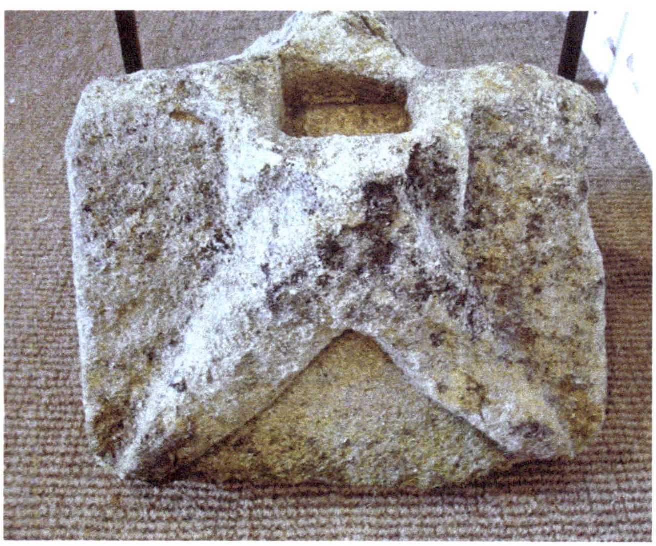

Photos of Vaudey Abbey

Stones believed to have come from the abbey. Stone on left may have been fixed to the top of a column, and the three pieces of carved stone (right) may have formed an archway

Photos courtesy of Grimthorpe Castle

Willoughton Priory

Benedictine ?–1414

The manor and the moiety of the church of Willoughton were granted by the Empress Matilda, daughter and heir of Henry I, to the Benedictine Abbey of St. Nicholas at Angers. The priory was probably built during the mid-twelfth century and, as an alien priory, it was recorded as being in the King's hands in 1390, and again in 1403, when it was being farmed by a clerk. Its revenue in 1387 was given as £18 6s. Nothing else is known

Wilsford Priory

Benedictine • 1135/54–c1401

The priory was founded in the reign of King Stephen by Hugh Wake, who presented the manor to the Benedictine Abbey of Bec-Hellouin in Normandy. The endowment was sufficient for only two or three brethren, but in 1380, the net income of the house was found to be too small to provide the prior, then and probably always the only representative of the mother house, with food and clothing. The scant revenue of the house diminished still further under the losses sustained by the recurrent seizures of alien cells during the French wars, and payments to the Exchequer. Sometime during the reign of Edward III, the priory was granted to Thomas of Holland, Earl of Kent, a descendant of Hugh Wake, and, through his influence, its property was finally secured to the abbey of Bourne in 1401. Its revenue in 1371 was valued at £18 2s

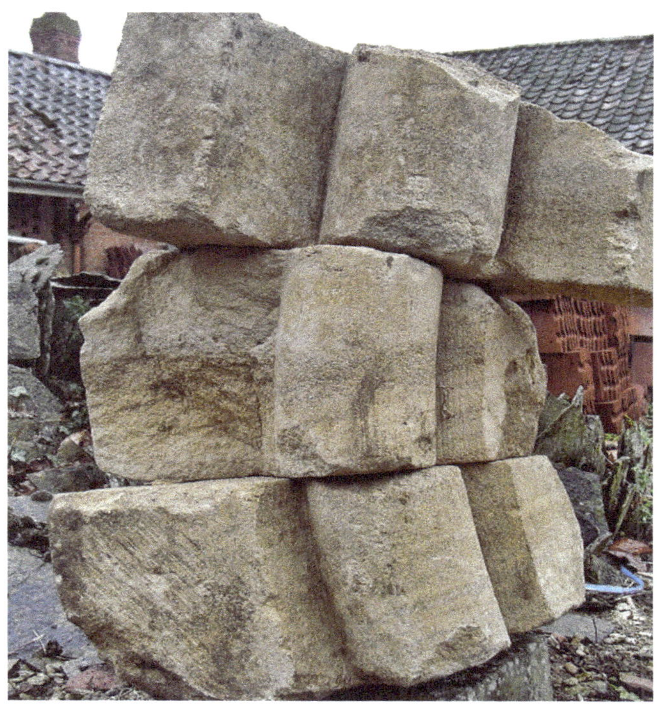

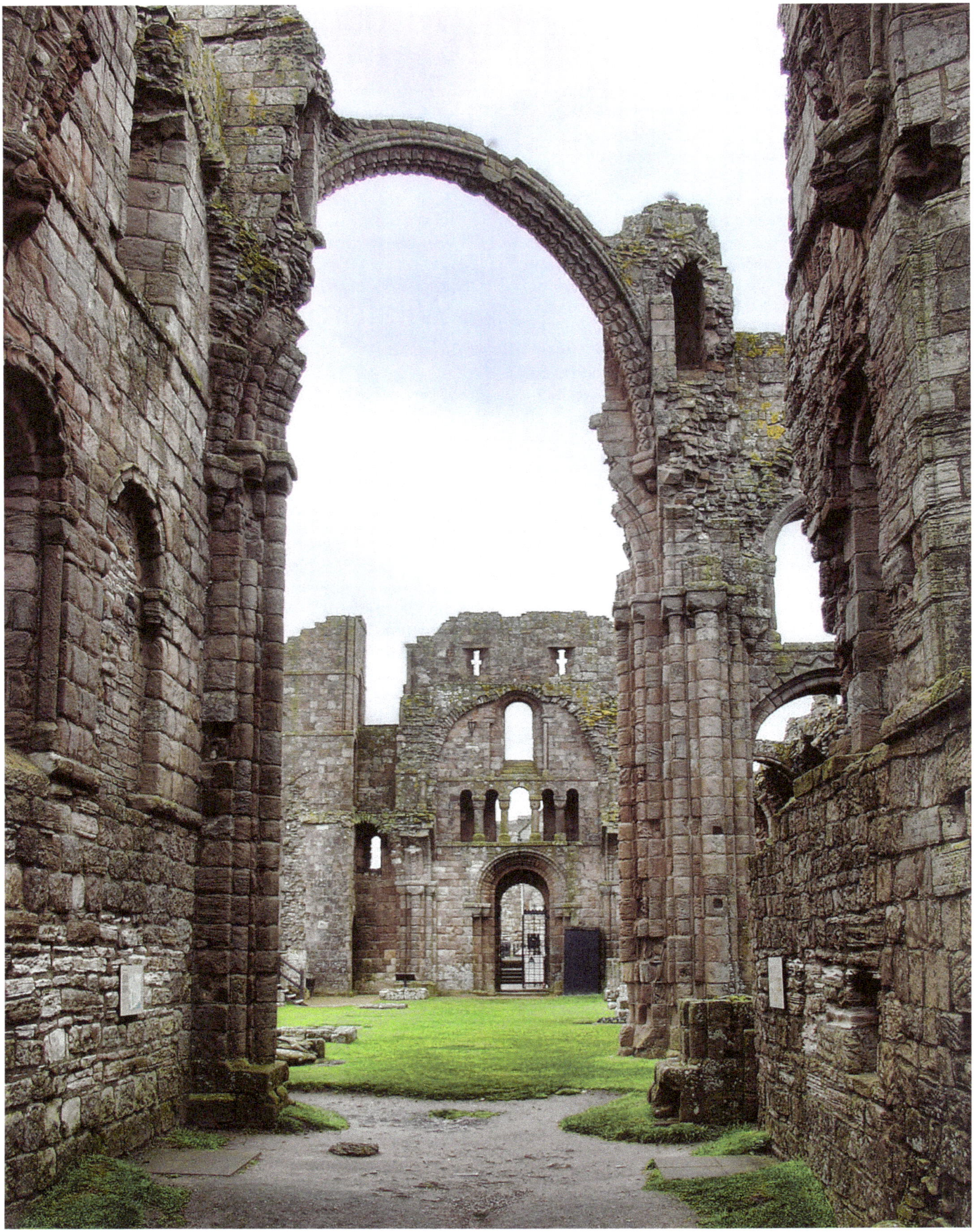

Lindisfarne Priory

Northumberland

Inspirational Spirituality

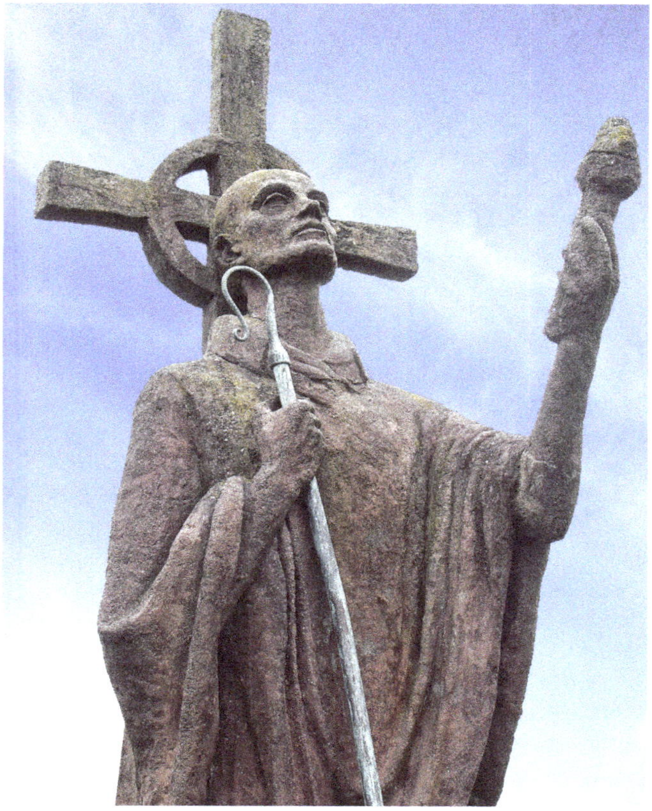

This northern region once formed the core of the Anglian Kingdom of Bernicia, which was united with Deira south of the river Tees in AD 654 to form the Kingdom of Northumbria, which in AD 944 became an earldom within the united Anglo-Saxon Kingdom of England. The name of Northumberland was first recorded in the *Anglo-Saxon Chronicle* in 1065 and officially came into being as a shire county in 1089. It became involved in many conflicts between the English and the Scots and Berwick-upon-Tweed on its northern border changed many times between the two. Durham, a liberty under the control of the Bishops of Durham was considered part of Northumberland, but this was disputed by the bishops who, in 1283, won a concession from the Crown to appoint their own sheriff, effectively becoming a private shire. Durham eventually became a County Palatine

Northumberland's Christian heritage is deeply rooted in what has been called 'inspirational' spirituality, as attested to by the shrines of several venerated saints and scholar-monks, whose writings have illuminated history in the early Anglo-Saxon period. Christianity arrived both from Rome and the Celtic lands in a two-pronged foray into the pagan minds and souls in this remote Kingdom, then known as Northumbria. Paulinus, a monk at St Andrew's Monastery in Rome, was sent by Pope Gregory I to join Augustine and other missionaries in Kent, where he stayed until accompanying Ethelburga, sister of King Eadbald of Kent, to Northumbria in AD 625 where she was to marry King Edwin. Two years later, Paulinus became the first Archbishop of York and proceeded to baptise many Northumbrian people in the River Glen. His missionary work was crowned with the baptism of King Edwin that same year.

The King's heir and successor, Oswald, then summoned Aidan, a monk from Iona, to re-affirm and consolidate the Christian message among his peoples. Aidan was created Bishop of Northumbria in AD 635 and founded a monastery at Lindisfarne. Aidan was succeeded by Finan and, in AD 664, by Cuthbert, who is regarded as the most spiritual of the English saints. But in AD 676, he sought greater solitude and retired to a cave on the Inner Farne Island, where he died in AD 687, having had a short spell as Bishop of Hexham.

In parallel with the Celtic traditions, Wilfrid and Benedict Biscop built on the more orderly Roman monasticism that had been introduced by Paulinus. Wilfrid became Abbot of Ripon in AD 664 and Archbishop of York a year later and, in AD 678, built the first Christian church at Hexham, which became a bishopric and monastery. Wilfrid's church was said to have been the most magnificent north of the Alps. Wilfrid was later driven from his homeland and is credited with having introduced Christianity to Sussex in AD 681. In AD 674, Northumbrian nobleman, Benedict Biscop, founded a monastery at Wearmouth, on the north bank of the River Wear, on land given by Ecgfrith, King of Northumbria, several fragments of which still survive in the present church building.

Biscop, who traveled widely in Europe, also established a European centre of learning with books brought back from Rome, and in AD 682 founded a sister monastery at nearby Jarrow under Abbot Ceolfrid. Much of the building work was undertaken by the monks from Wearmouth, including the church, which was completed in AD 685. Above the chancel arch is the oldest surviving church inscription in England, which records in Latin the dedication to St Paul, and the date, 23 April 685. More than 600 monks lived in the twin foundations of Jarrow and Wearmouth.

That same year, a 12-year old boy, Bede, entered the monastery at Jarrow, where he spent the remaining 50 years of his life. Confined to his tiny cell, Bede achieved a prodigious output of books on many scientific, historical and theological subjects and became the greatest scholar in Christendom. He wrote the earliest English version of the Gospel of St John, Life of St Cuthbert, and his Ecclesiastical History of the English People told the story of England from Roman times. It was justifiably described by Sir Arthur Bryant as "...immensely learned ...a monument to his age, his Faith and his country". The Venerable Bede, as he is known, died at Jarrow in AD 735, and his huge tomb-chest of local marble now resides in the Galilee Chapel in Durham Cathedral.

The start of Danish raids on the north-east coast in AD 793 proved an unwelcome interruption and led to the burning of the settlement at Lindisfarne and the death of many monks. The community recovered and rebuilt its church, but the fear of a second major incursion led to a wholesale exodus from Lindisfarne in AD 883. For over a century, the peripatic Lindisfarne community, known as the 'Congregation of St Cuthbert', wandered far and wide across Northumbria, always carrying the body of their saint, from time to time settling at Norham, Chester-le-Street, Ripon and, finally, in AD 995, at Durham, where they built a wooden church for Cuthbert's relics on a rock high above the River Wear. It is said that the guardians of St Cuthbert were guided to that spot by a maiden searching for her lost cow. After the building of the great monastic Romanesque cathedral at Durham, St Cuthbert's relics were placed in their present position behind the High Altar in 1104.

It was monks from Durham who refounded the monastery at Lindisfarne as a Benedictine priory in 1082. Although now in ruins, the dark red sandstone remains of the church and other monastic buildings are still hauntingly beautiful, highlighted by the 'rainbow' arch across the transept and the exquisite Norman carving of the west front. In 1085, monks from St Albans, led by Remigius, refounded Tynemouth Benedictine Priory, which had been plundered and burnt by the Danes on several occasions in the eighth century. Only the beautiful chancel has survived to almost original height, and there remain some elaborate decorations on the west front. Tynemouth later established a tiny cell on Coquet Island. A short-lived cell dependent on Durham was said to have existed at Warkworth. Aldwin, prior of Winchcombe, and two monks from Evesham may have settled at Newcastle c1073, but moved on to Jarrow the following year.

Hexham, which had been utterly ruined when plundered and burnt by Halfdene the Dane in AD 875, was rebuilt and became an Augustinian priory. It also had a cell at Ovingham. Augustinian canons occupied Brinkburn Priory, which lies secreted away in a beautiful wooded valley along the River Coquet, but its location did not stop the Scots plundering it in 1419. Founded c1135 at the end of the reign of King Henry I, it was never a wealthy foundation. The beautiful carved Norman gateway to the largely restored priory church is worth the long journey north.

The Premonstratensians had houses at Alnwick and Blanchland. The latter was initially founded as a priory by Walter de Bolbec II in 1165, as a daughter house of Croxton Abbey in Leicestershire, but was elevated to abbey status in the later thirteenth century. Only the impressive gatehouse has survived from Alnwick Abbey, founded in 1147 by Eustace fitzJohn, then owner of nearby Alnwick Castle, as a daughter house of Newhouse Abbey in Lincolnshire. Founded in 1137 by Ranulph de Merlay, Lord of Morpeth, Newminster Abbey was one of the largest foundations for Cistercian monks in the north and the only one in Northumberland. Once of some importance, the abbey ruins are now very neglected and their existence almost forgotten.

With few towns of any size in this remote and largely wild part of Britain, the mendicant friars were thin on the ground. Only Newcastle, the largest and most important town in the region, boasted all four of the major Orders – Augustinian, Dominican, Franciscan and Carmelite – as well as the lesser house of the Friars of the Sack. Probably the first Carmelite priory to be founded in England was Hulne, whose extensive remains repose deep in the huge estate of the dukes of Northumberland near Alnwick. Carmelites were also present at Berwick. Benedictine nuns were established at Newcastle and Lambley, with Augustinian canonesses having a small house at Holystone, and Premonstratensian canonesses at Guyzance. A Cistercian nunnery dedicated to St Leonard is also said to have been in existence on the outskirts of Berwick.

Gazetteer

Alnwick Abbey In Hulne Park, off B6346, 2.5km (1.5 miles) NW of Alnwick, Northumberland (NU 177140). Public access to park

Bamburgh Blackfriars Friary Farm, off Radcliffe Road, Bamburgh, 32km (20 miles) SE of Berwick-on-Tweed, Northumberland (NU 174348). Private

Bamburgh Priory On B1342, Church Street, Bamburgh, 32km (20 miles) SE of Berwick-on-Tweed, Northumberland (NU 178350). Church in use; Tel: 01668 214748

Blanchland Abbey On B6306, Blanchland, 13km (8 miles) E of Consett, Northumberland (NY 966503). Minimal remains

Brinkburn Priory Off B6334, 6.5km (4 miles) SE of Rothbury, Northumberland (NZ 116983). English Heritage; Tel: 01665 570628

Carham Priory Carham village, 6.5km (4 miles) NE of Kelso, Northumberland (NT 797384). No visible remains

Coquet Island Priory On Coquet Island, 1.5km (1 mile) offshore from Amble, 13.5km (8.5 miles) SE of Alnwick, Northumberland (NU 294045). Private

Guyzance [Brainshaugh] Priory By Branshaugh Bridge, near Guyzance village, 11km (7 miles) S of Alnwick, Northumberland (NU 208031). Private, but visible from road

Hexham Priory Abbey Grounds, Beaumont Street, Hexham, Northumberland (NY 935641). Tel: 01434 602031. Web: www.hexhamabbey.org.uk

Holystone Priory Holystone, 13km (8 miles) W of Rothbury, Northumberland (NT 955027). Remains uncertain

Hulne Priory In Hulne Park, from end of Ratten Road, Off B6346, 3km (2 miles) NW of Alnwick, Northumberland (NU 164157). Public access to park. Unattended

Lambley Priory Lambley, 6.5km (4 miles) SW of Haltwhistle, Northumberland (NY 674594). No visible remains

Lindisfarne Priory S end of Holy Island, accessible only at low tide from minor road off A1, 13km (8 miles) SE of Berwick-on-Tweed, Northumberland (NU 126418). English Heritage; Tel: 01289 389200

Newcastle Austin Friars City Road, Newcastle-upon-Tyne, Tyne and Wear (NZ 252642). Reconstructed tower

Newcastle Black Friars Friars Street, Newcastle-upon-Tyne, Tyne and Wear (NZ 244 642). Houses shops and a restaurant

Newcastle Grey Friars Near Market Street, Newcastle-upon-Tyne, Tyne and Wear (NZ 249644). No visible remains

Newcastle Sack Friars Near Forth Street, Newcastle-upon-Tyne, Tyne and Wear (NZ 249368). No visible remains

Newcastle White Friars Near Forth Street, Newcastle-upon-Tyne, Tyne and Wear (NZ 255641+ NZ 249368). No visible remains

Newcastle Priory Near Nun Street, Newcastle-upon-Tyne, Tyne and Wear (NZ 248643). No visible remains

Newcastle Priory Newcastle-upon-Tyne, Tyne and Wear (NZ 255641). No visible remains

Newminster Abbey Off B6343 Mitford Road, 1km (0.5 miles) W of Morpeth town centre, Northumberland (NZ 189858). Off footpath, unattended

Ovingham Priory West Road, Ovingham, Prudhoe, 24km (15 miles) W of Newcastle, Tyne and Wear (NZ 085636). No visible remains

Tynemouth Priory Near the North Pier, Tynemouth, Tyne and Wear (NZ 374695). English Heritage; Tel: 0191 257 1090

Warkworth Priory Warkworth village, 12km (7.5 miles) SE of Alnwick, Northumberland (NU 247062). No visible remains

Warkworth Hermitage On N bank of River Coquet, 1km (0.5 miles) W of Warkworth, 12km (7.5 miles) SE of Alnwick, Northumberland (NU 241059). English Heritage; Tel: 01665 711423

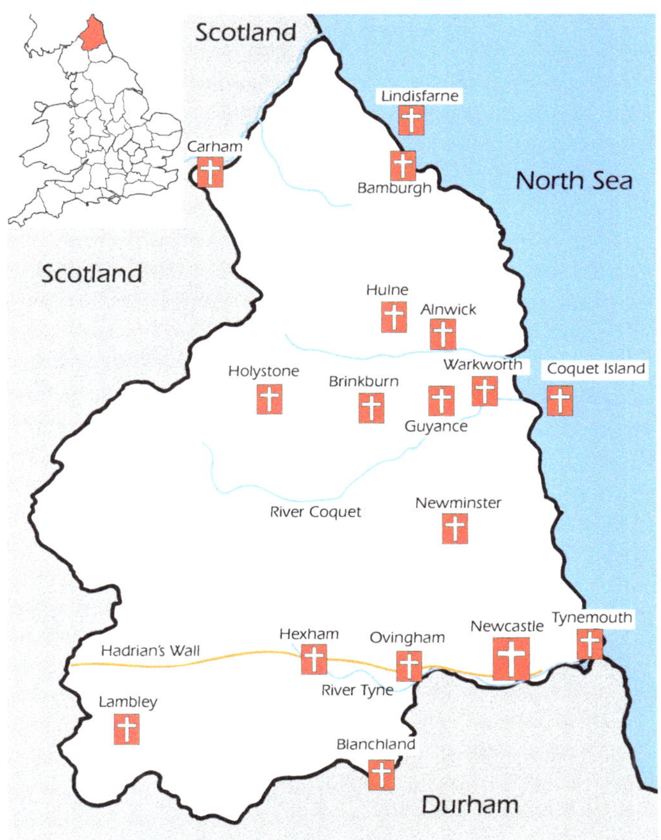

Alnwick Abbey

St Mary & St James • Premonstratensian 1193/1216–1539

The gatehouse is all that remains standing of this Premonstratensian abbey, one of three houses of the Order to have been established in Northumberland. Apart from minor alterations and restoration in the late eighteenth and early nineteenth century, this two-storey structure with four taller machicolated corner turrets and a vaulted passageway has survived much as constructed in the late fourteenth century. Of note are the armorial shields of the Percys high above the central arch and window, several crosses, and a richly canopied niche with open Gothic work. It now stands alone along the River Aln and gives access only to beautiful parkland, the other monastic buildings having long since vanished. The fortified abbey was secured by a precinct wall, which defined a protective screen around three sides, with the southern flank covered by the river. Exacavations have revealed the location of the church and claustral buildings, which are outlined on the ground. The cruciformed, aisled church had two chapels each in the north and south transepts, with the slype, chapter house, warming house and dormitory to the south. An outer court to the west included the cellarer's range, guest house, kitchen, bakehouse and ovens. The infirmary was housed in a separate block to the south-east of the church.

Nearby are the ruins of the medieval St Leonards Hospital, which was annexed by the abbey in 1376 and had fallen into decay before the Reformation. It was probably founded by Eustace de Vescy between 1193 and 1216 as an independent hospital. The chapel consists of nave and chancel, while some domestic buildings to the south also survive as ruins. All were reconstructed in the mid-nineteenth century, although the lower courses were left unaltered. Another hospital, founded in memory of Malcolm III of Scotland, who was killed nearby in 1093, was also annexed by the abbey in 1376. It was reported as ruinous in 1535 and nothing has survived. Alnwick Abbey also owned St Margaret's Grange and chapel, now ruined, which was established between 1157 and 1185. On a commanding position three miles north of Alnwick stands the curious ruined shell of the ashlar-faced Hefferlaw Tower, which belonged to the abbey and appears to have served as a look-out post, to provide early warning of a raid. Two carved panels depict the abbot's crozier and the arms of the fourth Percy Earl of Northumberland (1469-89). The three-storey tower has a plan area of 8.8 x 7.4m, is 6.2m high and has 1.1m (3.6ft) thick walls. It stands on private land and is not accessible to the public.

Alnwick Abbey was founded for Premonstratensian canons in 1147 by Eustace FitzJohn and his wife Beatrice, then owner of nearby Alnwick Castle, as a daughter house of Newhouse Abbey in Lincolnshire. It was dedicated to St James and the Blessed Virgin. According to the *Genealogia Fundatorum et Advocatorum Abbatiae de Alnewyk*, written in 1380, the abbey remained under the de Vescy family until the barony and castle of Alnwick, to which it was attached, was acquired in 1309 by Henry, Lord Percy, whose descendants continued the patronage of the abbey until the Dissolution. In the time of Edward I and Edward II, the abbot was summoned to Parliament. The abbey continued to flourish until the Dissolution, when its revenues were estimated at £194 7s. It was dissolved in 1535, refounded in 1536 and finally dissolved in 1539 when Abbot William Harrison and twelve canons surrendered the house. It became the property of the Brandling and Doubleday families until acquired by the Duke of Northumberland.

Amble (Coquet Island) Priory

St Mary • Benedictine 1090–?

A close look at the base of the lighthouse on this island, a mile off the mouth of the River Coquet at Amble, will reveal that it was built upon the tower of a monastic cell, which once belonged to the Benedictine Priory of Tynemouth. Other medieval work includes a vaulted chamber under the adjacent cottages. Amble and Coquet Island were granted to the monks of Tynemouth in 1090 by Robert de Mowbray, who died in 1125. It became famous as the retreat of St Henry of Coquet, a Danish nobleman, who sought solitude among the seabirds of the island. However, his reputation as a holy man and prophet spread far and wide, and his advice was sought by rich and poor alike. He was enshrined at Tynemouth after his death in 1127. Another hermit, Martin, later took his place and records show that he was involved in a curious dispute with Roger fitzRoger, second Baron of Warkworth. The lord of the manor objected to the building of a windmill by the eccentric hermit and sent his men with mattocks and axes to destroy it. It is likely that monks from Tynemouth continued to serve a chapel on the island, and in 1415, the tower was listed as a fortalice belonging to the prior of Tynemouth. The island's attraction as a place of peace and contemplation had been recognised long before St Henry's tenure. It was here in AD 684 that Abbess Elflaeda of Whitby visited St Cuthbert and persuaded him to accept the Bishopric of Lindisfarne.

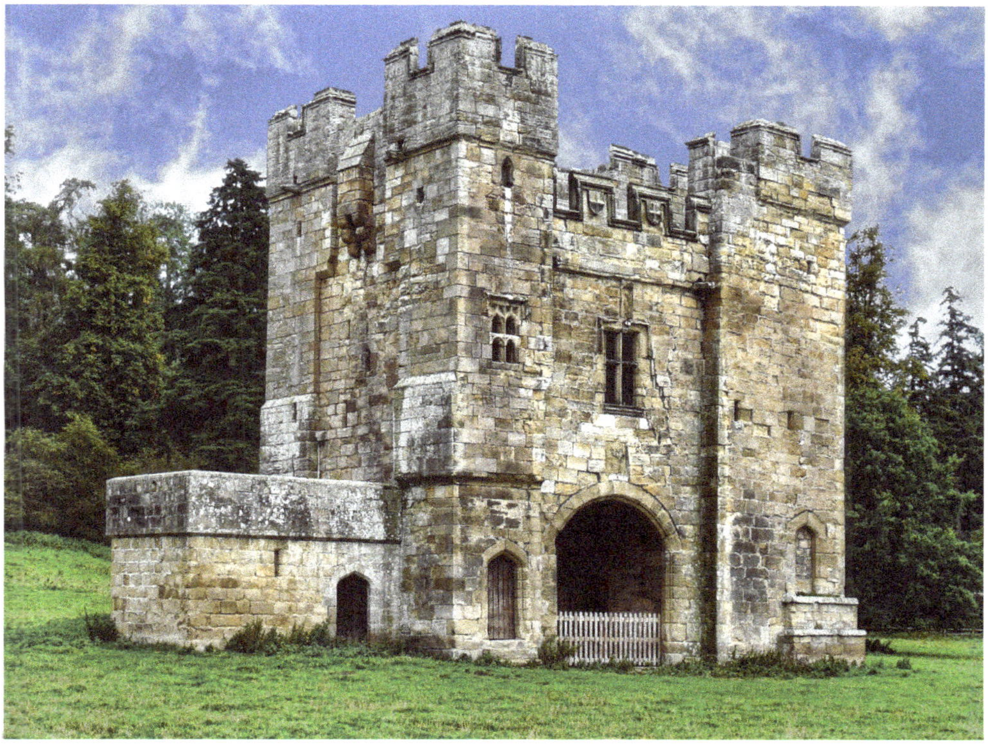

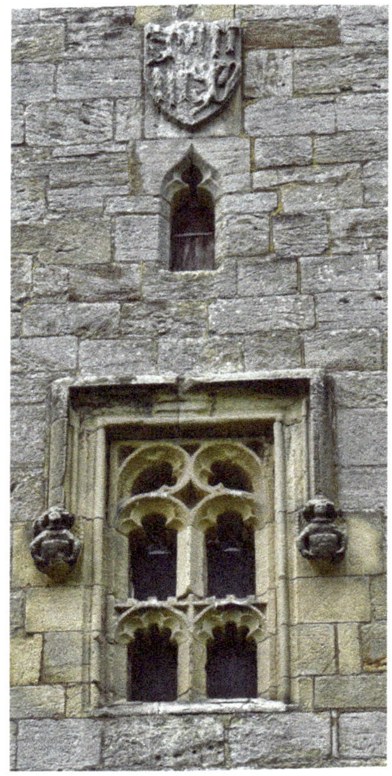

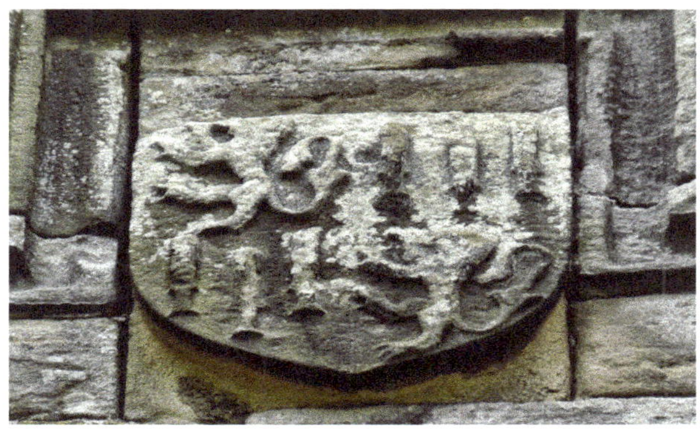

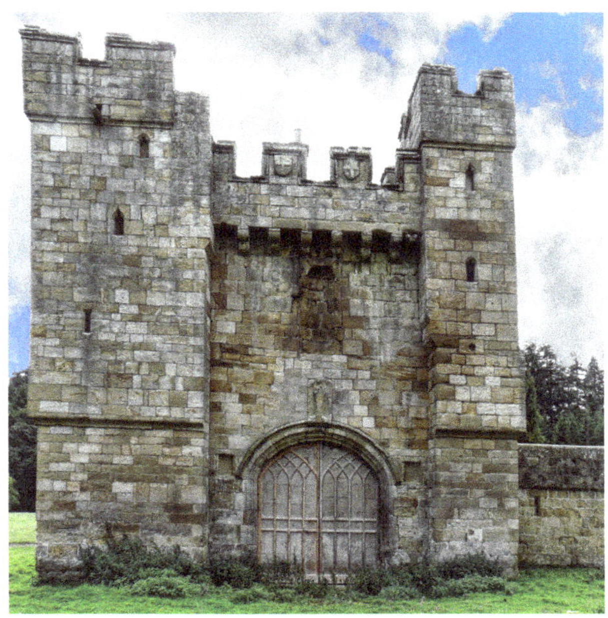

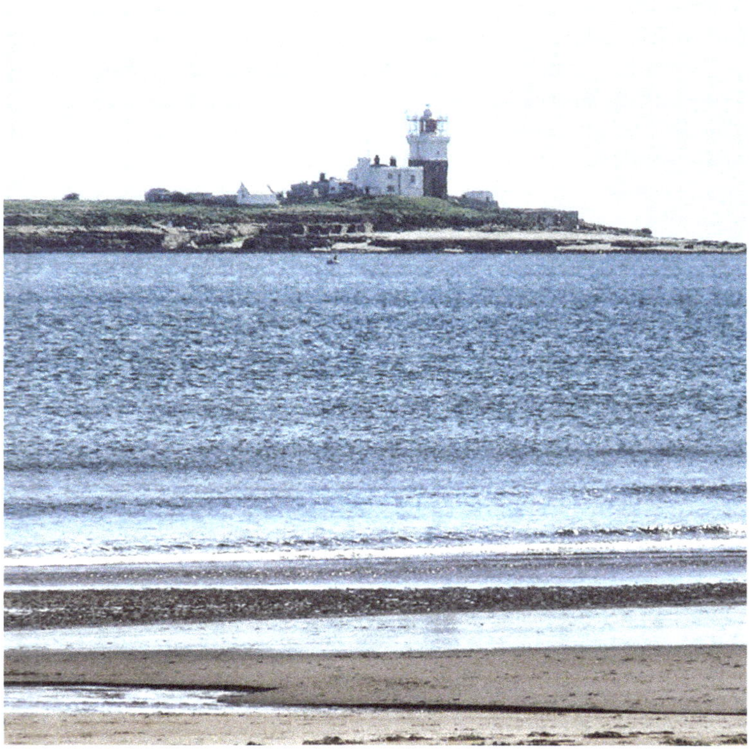

Photos - clockwise from top left

Rear view of Alnwick abbey gatehouse
Ornate traceried window with square head
Percy coat of arms
Main entrance gate with machicolations above
Coquet Island lighthouse

Bamburgh Priory

St Aidan • Augustinian 1121–1537

A place of worship was founded on the site of the present parish church in AD 635 by St Aidan, an Irish-born missionary, who was called to Bamburgh from Iona by King Oswald to establish Christianity in his newly united Kingdom of Northumbria. No trace has survived from this early wooden building, although tradition has it that the beam over the font in the baptistery is the very one St Aidan was leaning against when he died in AD 651. The beam, which serves no structural function, is said to have miraculously survived two fires. Mention of this beam is made by the Venerable Bede. The site of St Aidan's death is marked by a simple shrine within the church, although his body was laid to rest at nearby Lindisfarne Priory.

The present church dates from the end of the twelfth century but has been extensively reconstructed. Construction of the greater part of the church was begun in 1270 and the earliest feature may be a window in the east wall of the north transept, which has a round-headed internal splay. The north aisle was added in 1190, and the north transept was enlarged at the same time. The present chancel, which, in relation to the nave is unusually long, measuring 18.3 x 6.4m (60 x 21ft), superseded the Norman chancel in 1230. Of note within the chancel is the recumbent effigy of a knight, reputed to be of Sir Lancelot du Lake, dating from 1320 or later. Both transepts were lengthened in the fourteenth century to provide space for new altars, and the north transept was turned into a chantry chapel, now known as St Oswald's Chapel. The remarkable crypt was re-discovered in 1837 but, alas, is not open to the public. Used as a burial place for the canons and later the Forster family, the crypt comprises two chambers, the larger of which has a vaulted roof and appears to have been used as a chapel, as the presence of an altar, piscina and aumbry would indicate. Although created in the late nineteenth century out of Caen stone, the reredos should not be ignored. It is carved with sixteen Northumbrian and other saints, with the two principal figures being Saints Aidan and Oswald.

Following the granting of the churches of St Oswald and St Aidan, and large tracts of land by Henry I to Nostell Priory in 1121, a number of Augustinian canons were settled here to administer the land as a cell to the Yorkshire house. It is likely that the cell became conventual under a prior after 1228. At that time, there are said to have been five or six canons, although this appears to have been reduced as a result of Scottish raids in the fourteenth century. The clear annual value of the priory cell in the *Valor* of 1535 was given as £64 19s and the priory was dissolved in 1537. The priory and its tithes in Northumberland were given to Sir John Forster in 1546 and lay neglected for some time. In 1611, it was recorded that 'the steeple was only half covered with lead and the other half utterly decayed and open. The church was thatched and indecently kept and defiled with doves. The windows thereof not sufficiently glassed…'. It was only after the estates, including the church, came into the possession of Lord Crewe, Bishop of Durham, whose wife was the aunt of Tom Forster, that the gradual restoration of the church was begun.

Bamburgh Black Friars

1265–1539

A Dominican priory was founded in 1265 in what is now the western part of the village, but apart from some masonry, including the northwest corner of the chancel of the church incorporated in later buildings, nothing has survived. Evaluation prior to the conversion of farm buildings has ascertained that the north wall of the farm block incorporates the north wall of the conventual church, which was 37.3m (122ft) long and 6.5m (21ft) wide, with a short, three-bay north aisle measuring 19.5 x 3m (64 x 10ft). The cloister to the south was approximately 16m (53ft) square. The Black Friars acquired extensive lands and flourished at first, but the frequent attacks by the Scots caused a great deal of damage to the land. As a result, the friars and burgesses petitioned the King several times to provide relief from rents and taxes. When a Scottish invasion was expected in 1330, Friar John hid ecclesiastical goods, but was loath to part with them when the danger had passed. In 1300, there were ten friars. Among the friars' charitable activities was the running of a lepers' hospital, but this closed in the fourteenth century, and its site remains uncertain. The priory was dissolved in 1539 and its property sold to Sir John Forster, who converted the entire complex into a defendable domestic dwelling, with the cloister forming a courtyard. In the eighteenth century, this was demolished and replaced by a farmhouse, now known as Friary Farm.

Photos of Bamburgh Priory – clockwise from top

The church of St Aidan overlooking the North Sea
View towards altar and reredos
Ancient crypt used as burial chamber for the canons
Effigy thought to be of Sir Lancelot du Lake
Attractive column capital with floral designs

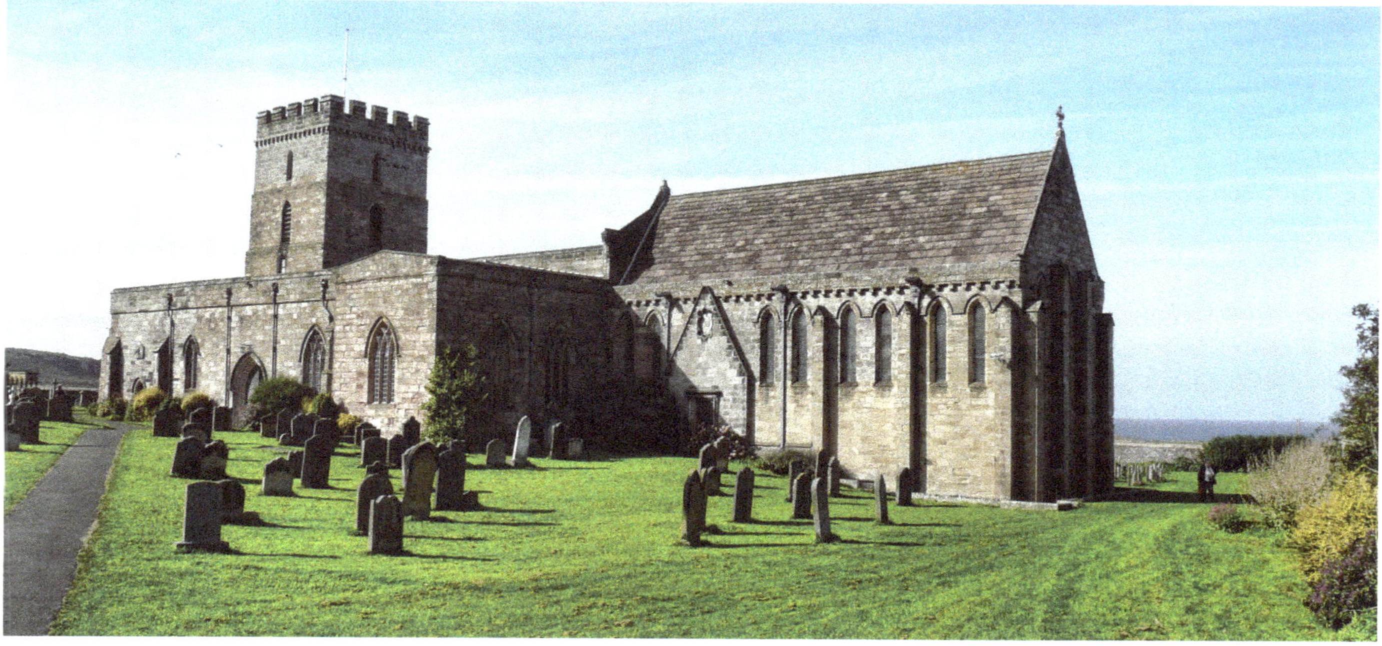

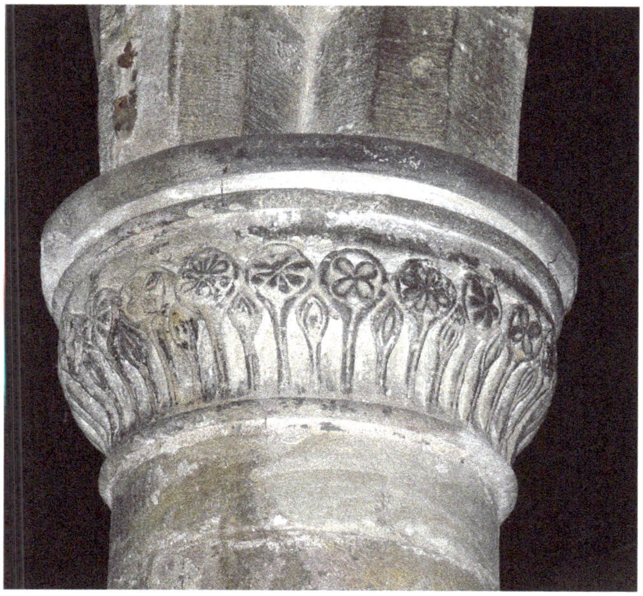

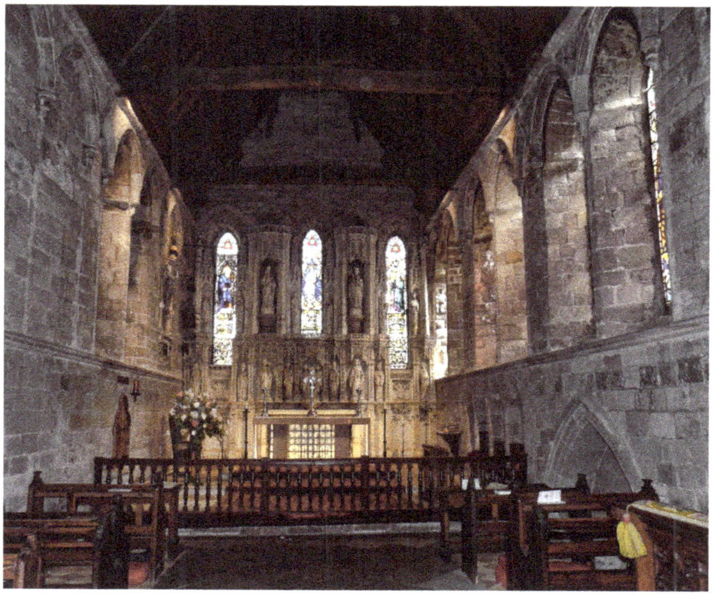

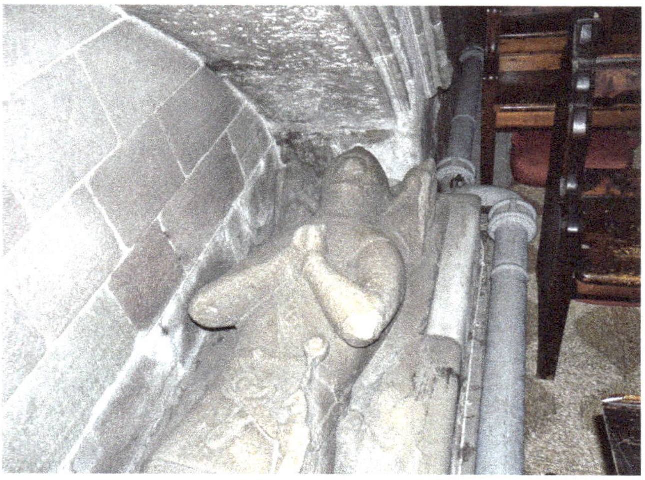

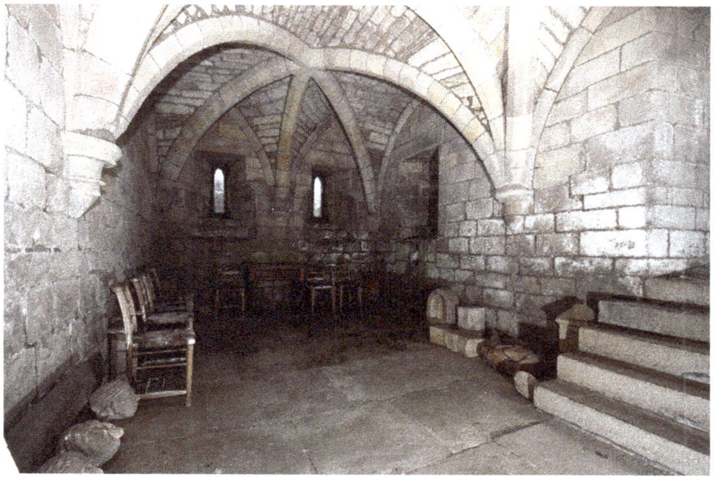

Blanchland Priory/Abbey

St Mary • Premonstratensian 1165–1536

Little may have survived from this Premonstratensian house, initially founded as a priory in 1165 by Walter de Bolbec II as a daughter foundation of Croxton Abbey in Leicestershire, but the visitor will still be entranced by its atmospheric location in the North Pennines, set as it is beneath magnificent fells in a wooded part of the secluded upper Derwent Valley. Village and abbey almost certainly took their name from the white habits worn by the Premonstratensian canons. When the priory was gifted more land in 1214, it was elevated to abbey status.

During the Anglo-Scottish wars, the abbey granges were pillaged, but the abbey itself was apparently left unscathed, at least for a brief while. Legend has it that, following prayers by the canons, a mist shielded the valley and monastery during one Scottish foray in the area, and was consequently missed by the raiders, who passed by. Foolishly, upon realising that they had been saved, the canons rang the bells in celebration. The raiders followed the sound and returned to ransack the monastery. Another version tells of Henry VIII's commissioner who came to inspect the abbey prior to the Dissolution. Apparently, the commissioner was unable to find Blanchland in the mist, but was guided when the canons rang the bells in celebration. He thanked them profusely for signalling their whereabouts.

Edward III stayed at the abbey in summer of 1327 to make his confession before the impending battle, which, in the end, never happened. It is said that the abbot had a cousin on the Scottish side and kept him informed of the movements of the English army. So, after a week of watching each other across the valley, both armies went home. However, the army caused a lot of damage to the village and abbey and diminished their food stocks, for which the King later compensated the abbot. The abbey was fortified, although what these defensive measures comprised of is unclear. The Black Death in 1349 decimated the community to no more than five, making it difficult to farm the land and repair the crumbling abbey buildings. The chapter house was almost completely in ruins. The bishops of Newcastle or Durham, who were responsible for regular visitations, requested the abbot to increase the number of canons, but this clearly proved impossible in the remote and rugged Derwent Valley.

Life at the abbey also became lax. Against church rules, the canons kept a pack of hounds to hunt deer, and were found drinking with nearby tenants after night prayers. Their appearance also left much to be desired, and the abbot was ordered to find a washerwoman, tailor and barber to make them more presentable. The abbey had also fallen into debt. In the *Valor* of 1535, its net annual income was assessed at just £40, resulting in its suppression in 1536 as a lesser monastery. It was refounded under a new charter the following year, for reasons yet to be determined, only to be finally dissolved in 1539. The abbot, sub-prior, five canons and two novices received pensions. Blanchland Abbey was granted to the Bellow and Broxholm families and eventually came into the hands of Nathaniel Lord Crewe, Bishop of Durham, in 1708.

The north transept and chancel were retained when the original abbey church dedicated to St Mary the Virgin was altered in the nineteenth century to serve as the parish church, and is believed to be the only intact example of a church built by Premonstratensian canons. It was begun in 1255 and added to later in the thirteenth and fourteenth centuries. Inside the church are some fine medieval tomb covers of abbots, canons and foresters, as well as rare medieval stained glass of around fifteenth century date. In the chancel windows are two panels with figures of Premonstratensian canons. Also of note is a plain twelfth or thirteenth century font. The fourteenth century abbey gatehouse is also extant, as is the former sixteenth century abbot's lodging, guest house and kitchen, which later became a manor house and is now the Lord Crewe Arms Hotel. The garden of the hotel was the abbey's cloisters and incorporates a large archway, which formed part of the lavatorium. The row of cottages running down the side of the garden incorporates parts of the refectory walls. The two-storey embattled rectangular gatehouse, dating from the late fifteenth century, has been much remodelled and comprises a single vaulted north-south gate passage with a parallel chamber on the ground floor. A single large chamber with fireplace formed the upper floor. The stone houses surrounding the village square were partly constructed using stone from the abbey.

Photos – clockwise from top left

The ground floor chamber of the gatehouse, now a shop
Gatehouse with stair leading to first floor
The former abbey church of St Mary
Medieval fireplace in the Lord Crewe Arms
Sign of the Lord Crewe Arms
Trefoiled piscina in abbey church
The former abbot's lodging, guesthouse and kitchen

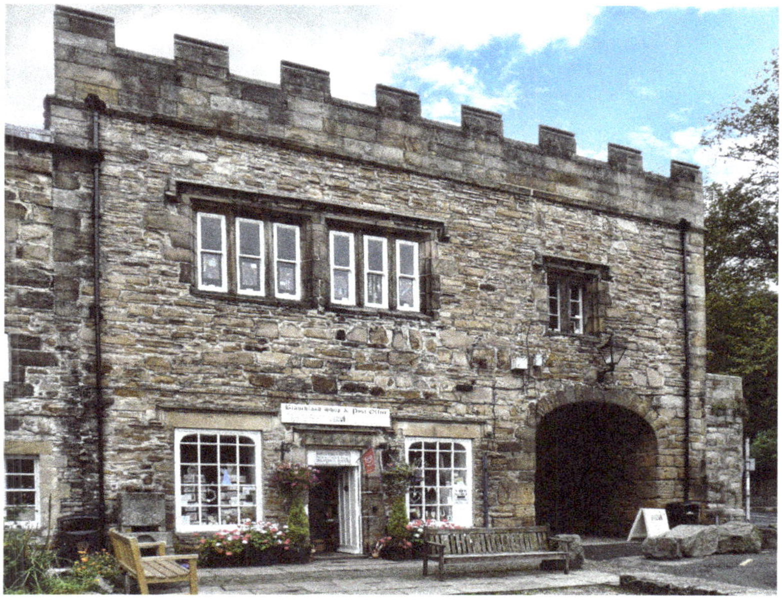

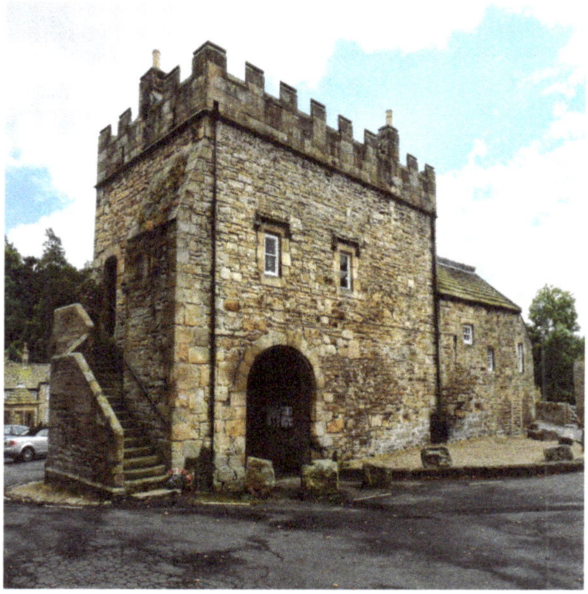

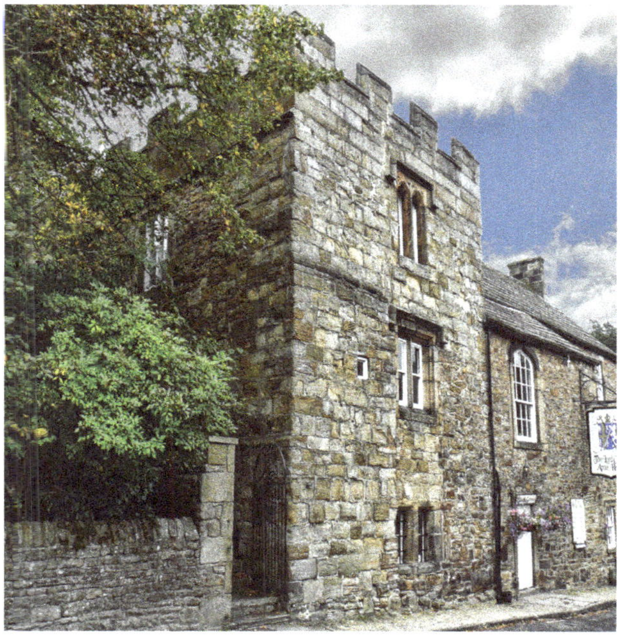

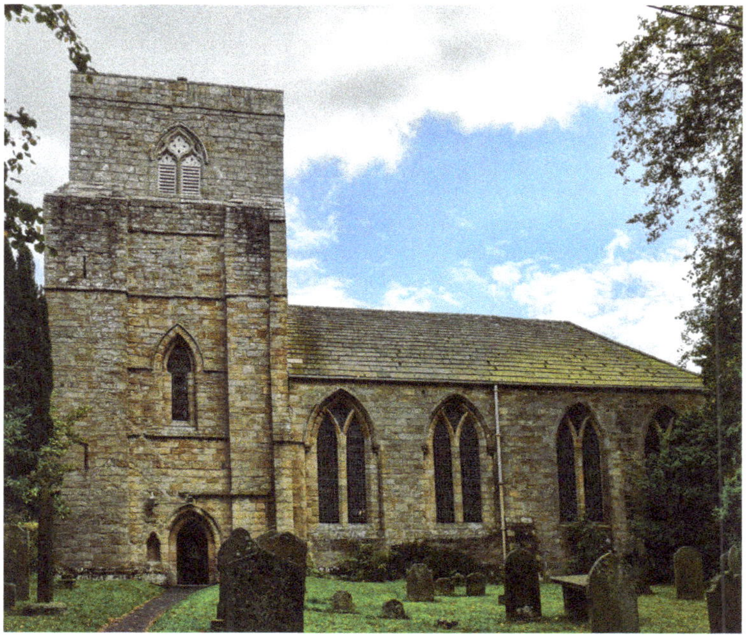

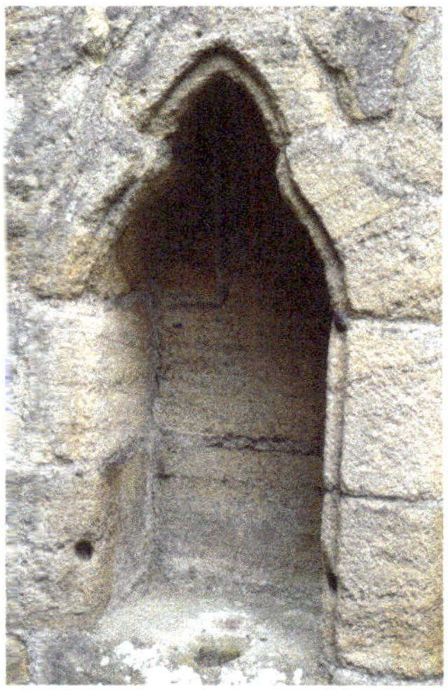

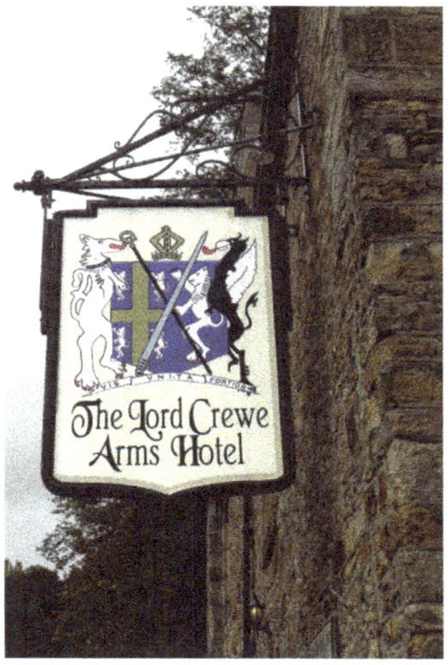
The Lord Crewe
Arms Hotel

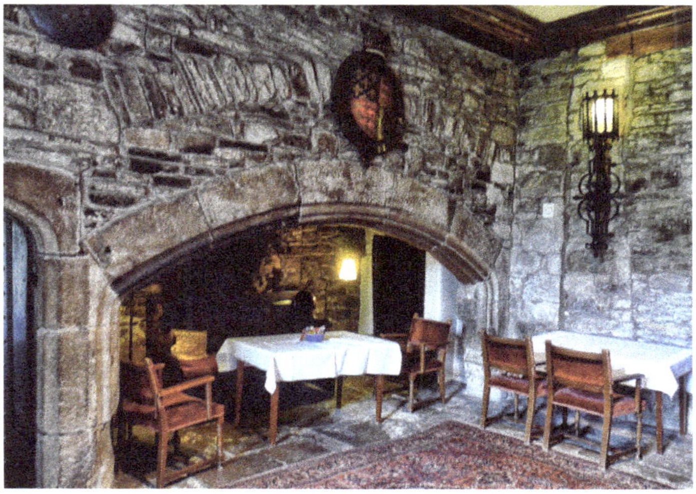

Brinkburn Priory

St Peter & St Paul • Augustinian -1135–1536

This former house for Augustinian canons lies in a beautiful wooded river valley by a small loop in the River Coquet, almost hidden by the dark foliage of mature trees. A pleasant ten-minute stroll down a rough winding track leads to the sudden appearance of the small north door of the restored priory church. It is likely the visitor will encounter few other likeminded souls, a testament to the priory's isolation rather than a scarcity of interest. The eyes are drawn immediately to the beautifully decorated and carved Norman doorway, which is surmounted by a gable with three trefoil niches that would once have held statues of saints. Within the cruciform church, some of the original fabric has survived, including a few medieval tiles beside the high altar and a richly carved gravestone dating from 1484 of then Prior William, who also was suffragan bishop of Durham, as alluded to by the mitre and crozier. Outside, there is a fine arcade of trefoiled arches in the south wall of the nave, and there are a few remains of the claustral buildings, including the restored Monk's House. A mutiliated stone arch is still recognisable as the laver recess in the refectory, whose undercroft forms the cellars of the adjacent mansion.

Founded in the reign of Henry I, probably shortly before the King's death in 1135, by William Bertram, Baron of Mitford, the priory acquired scattered lands in Northhumberland and Durham, but never became wealthy. Its relatively unremarkable history was, nevertheless, punctuated by troubled times. In 1419, it was raided and plundered by marauding Scots, a criminal act that gave rise to an interesting, if unsubstantiated tale. It is said that the raiding party came close but was unable to find the secluded priory among the dense woodland and started to head home, when the sound of bells, which the monks rang in joy, made them turn back. The bells duly led the Scots to the priory, which was relieved of its treasures and burnt. A deep nearby part of the river is known as Bell Pool, because, the story goes, the raiders flung the priory bells into the water at this spot. Whoever recovers the bells, so the tale continues, will be rewarded with untold treasures. According to another legend, the Northumbrian fairies were buried within the priory precincts. In 1535, Brinkburn Priory was valued at only £69 and along with other minor houses was dissolved the following year. Although church services continued, by 1602, the church was reported in a state of decay, which continued to accelerate until major restoration was undertaken in the mid-nineteenth century.

Carham Priory

St Cuthbert • Augustinian +1131–1539

A small priory for two or three Augustinian canons was founded sometime after 1131 as a cell to Kirkham Priory in Yorkshire. It was located close to the River Tweed at the west end of this small town and the 'Black Canons' made their living from sheep grazing and fishponds, having been granted the vill and manor of Titlington, as well as other property nearby. The priory's history is a virtual blank, but it is known that it was burnt down in 1296 by the Scots under William Wallace and continued to suffer frequently as a result of being so close to the border with Scotland. It was suppressed in 1539, at which time its value was £31 10s. Not a vestige of the priory has survived.

Farne Islands Priory

St Cuthbert • Benedictine 1255–1540

St Aidan and St Cuthbert spent much time on the isolated rocky Farne Islands off the Northumberland coast in prayer and meditation. St Cuthbert, who had built himself a small hermitage on Inner Farne, returned there to die in AD 687. A succession of hermits followed, but it was not until 1255 that Durham Cathedral Priory established a small priory cell for one monk and a warden. These served primarily to look after Durham's interests and serve as a retreat for monks seeking seclusion. Nothing of note has been recorded. The cell was suppressed along with Durham in December 1540. At the Dissolution, the income was estimated at £12 17s and in 1541, Henry VIII granted the islands to the newly established Dean and Chapter of Durham. A small single-room chapel built in about 1370 on top of an earlier building is probably all that has survived from monastic times. Foundations exist at the west end of a galilee porch, which was typical of churches dedicated to St Cuthbert. It has been suggested that the chapel may have been fortified, as the north wall is solid with no openings. The chapel was restored in the 1840s by Archdeacon Thorp.

Guyzance (Branhaugh) Priory

St Wilfred • Premonstratensian nuns 1147/52–1350

The ruined Norman church of this Premonstratensian nunnery dedicated to St Wilfred of Gysnes, from which its name has been derived, makes a romantic feature in a green field grazed by sheep and surrounded by a ring of mature trees. Tate family members are interred in the medieval burial ground alongside, which is still in use. The chapel displays building work dating from the twelfth to the fourteenth century, and a fluted pillar and medieval grave stone can be found outside. The undulating ground to the south may indicate buried foundations of other priory buildings. Guyzance Priory stands on private land close to Branshaugh Bridge over the River Coquet, but can be easily seen from the nearby road. The small priory was founded sometime between 1147 and 1152 by Richard Tison and was possibly abandoned in 1350 after the devastation wrought by the Black Death. However, it may then have become a cell of Alnwick Abbey. As written in Tanner's *Monastica*, the nunnery was endowed with a portion of the tithes of the nearby village of Guyzance, and two bovates of land, but no other information is known of its history.

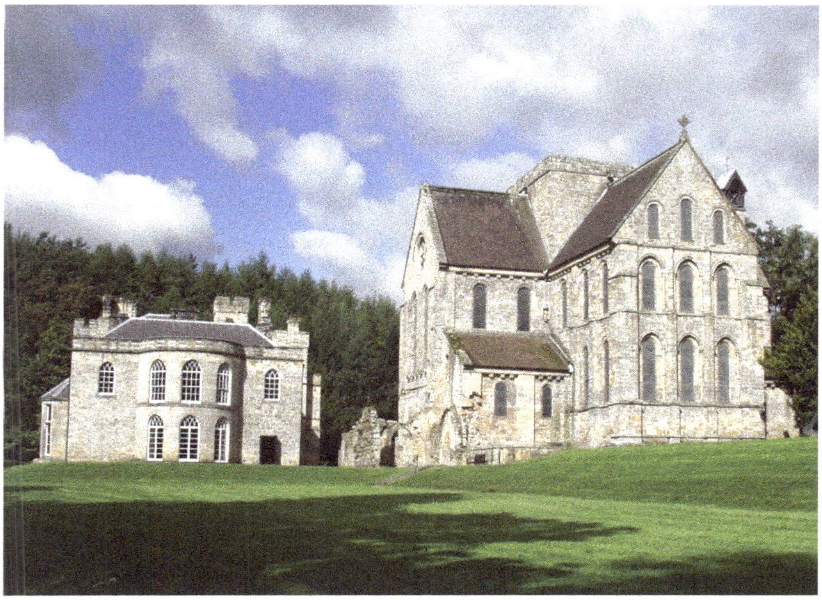

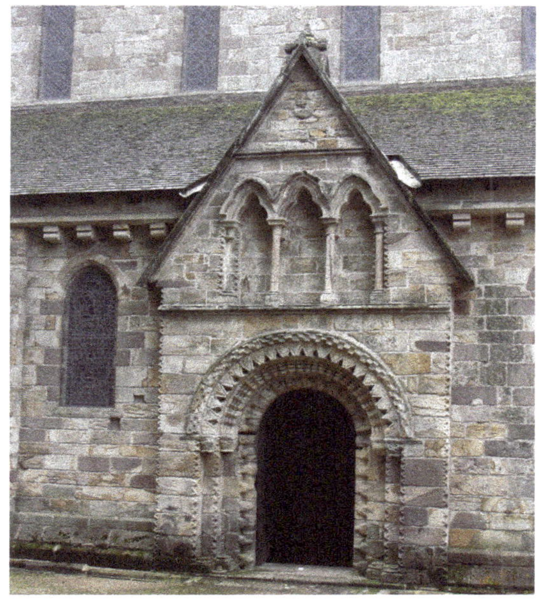

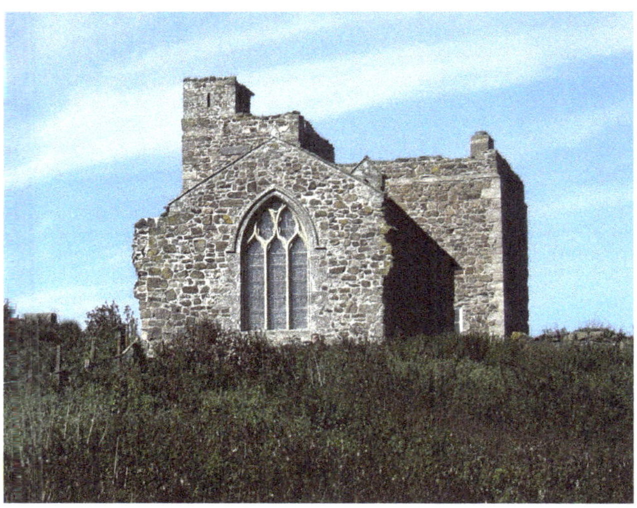

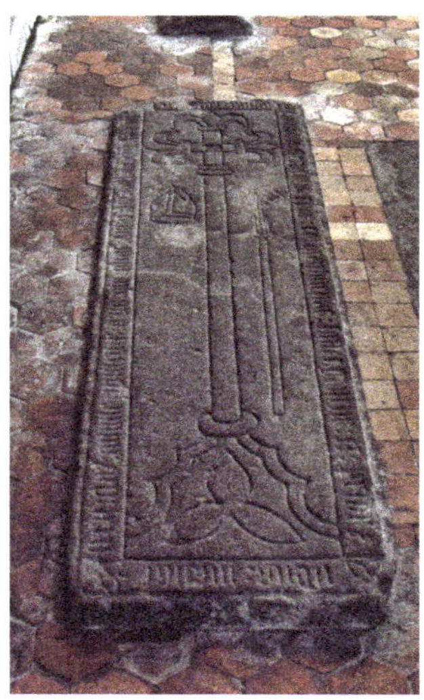

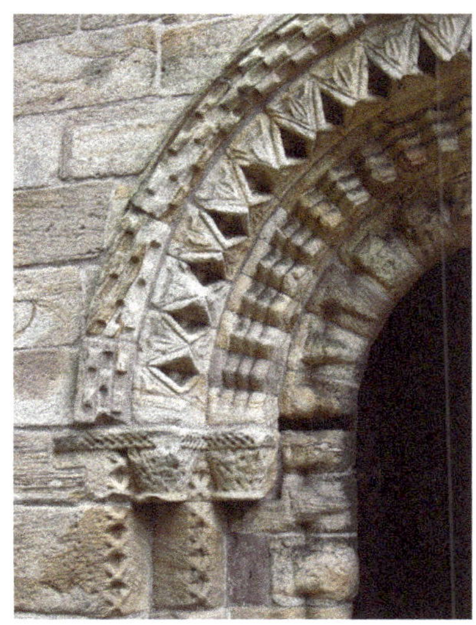

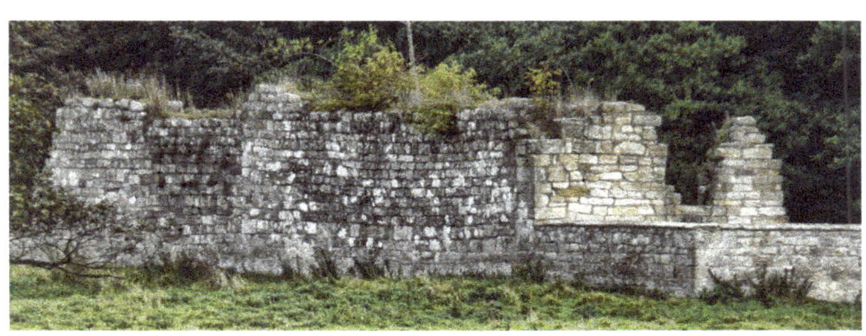

Photos – clockwise from top left

Former priory church of Brinkburn with adjacent mansion
Norman south door with trefoiled niches above
Beautifully carved arch of doorway
Carved gravestone of Prior William
Sparse remains of Guyzance Priory
St Cuthbert's Chapel on Inner Farne Island

Hexham Priory

St Andrew • Augustinian 1113–1537

A first glance at the imposing parish church of St Andrew, which looms large over the market square, will reveal little of its long history of more than 1,300 years, dating back to the late seventh century. The reason for this is that the east end was rebuilt in 1858 and the nave in 1908. Yet, once inside, the visitor will find a rich treasure trove of Anglo-Saxon and medieval features and artefacts, which survived the plunder and frequent wanton destruction during several turbulent periods of British history. A wonderful place to start is the south transept, which is dominated by the famous stone night-stairs, once used by the canons to come into church from their dormitory above. It is one of only two such features extant in England and is still used on a daily basis. At the bottom stands an inscribed sculpted stone slab of Flavinus, a Roman standard-bearer from Gaul. The north transept is arcaded with elaborate detail, and both transepts retain their fifteenth century roofs with intact bosses. Monastic buildings include the chapter house vestibule, lavatorium in the west cloister walk, cellarium, and ruins of the gatehouse.

Beneath the chancel arch is a wonderful sixteenth century rood screen, whose panels depict sixteen bishops of Hexham and Lindisfarne, the Visitation and a rather poignant representation of the Annunciation. The screen is the work of Thomas Smithson, who was prior between 1491 and 1524. On the sanctuary wall in the north of the chancel is another painted screen of oak, whose centrepiece are four small panels depicting the Dance of Death, considered the best preserved in England, featuring a Cardinal, King, Emperor and Pope. A lower screen in front is made up of traceried panels with faded paintings of Our Lord, the Blessed Virgin and the Twelve Apostles. As it projects in the centre to form a pulpit, the screen is thought to have come from the former refectory. In the north choir aisle is the chantry chapel of Prior Rowland Leschman, who died in 1491. Its almost primitive stone carvings, which include a Border Reiver, a fox preaching to geese, a jester, and several others, require close inspection and provide food for thought.

Also of great interest is the frith stool, or bishop's throne, in the centre of the choir, one of only two dating from the Saxon period and carved from a single block of stone, probably in the seventh century, and the font bowl, which was fashioned from the base of a Roman pillar and was part of St Wilfrid's church. Of similar antiquity is the Anglo-Saxon crypt, reached via a steep stone stair from the nave. The crypt is the only remaining structure from the church as first built in the seventh century. There are many other treasures housed in various parts of the church, including the remains of two eighth century crosses and a tiny copper chalice, only 64mm (2.5 inches) high, thought to have been used by St Wilfrid.

Hexham Priory was founded around AD 674 by Wilfrid, Bishop of York, on lands given by Queen Etheldreda. The priory was constructed entirely from material salvaged from nearby Roman ruins. When the York diocese was divided in AD 678, Tumbrith was consecrated as the first bishop. In AD 681, the priory church became a cathedral, and in AD 709, Wilfrid died as incumbent Bishop of Hexham and was canonised. After Halfdene the Dane landed and raided the countryside surrounding the River Tyne in AD 875, Hexham, along with the monasteries at Jarrow and Wearmouth were plundered and burnt to the ground. Eilaf, treasurer at Durham, was instructed in 1050 to rebuild the ruined church, but nothing remains from that work.

In 1113, Thomas II, Archbishop of York, refounded the church at Hexham as a priory for Augustinian canons. Work on the church in the Early English architectural style was begun c1170 and completed by around 1250. The choir, transepts and cloisters all date from that period. Low points in the abbey's history came in 1296 when Scottish raiders burnt the priory, its books and relics of the saints, leaving only the walls standing. It was sacked again and again, plunging the monastic community into financial straits. The nave was completely destroyed and probably never rebuilt. When the King's commissioners arrived in September 1536, the twenty canons barricaded themselves within the church, saying they would rather die than surrender house. This defiance led to the Pilgrimage of Grace, which was brutally suppressed the following year. Edward Jay, the last prior, was hanged from the priory's gateway, and five canons of Hexham are also believed to have been executed for their part in the rebellion. Hexham was suppressed in February 1537 and its lands and buildings granted to Sir Richard Carnaby.

Photos – clockwise from top

The former priory church dominating the market square
Attractive arcading in cloister area
One of only two Saxon frith stools surviving in England
Carving of sheep stealer in Prior Leschman's chantry chapel
Carving of fox preaching to geese
Famous stone night-stairs in south transept

Photos courtesy of Adrian Fletcher

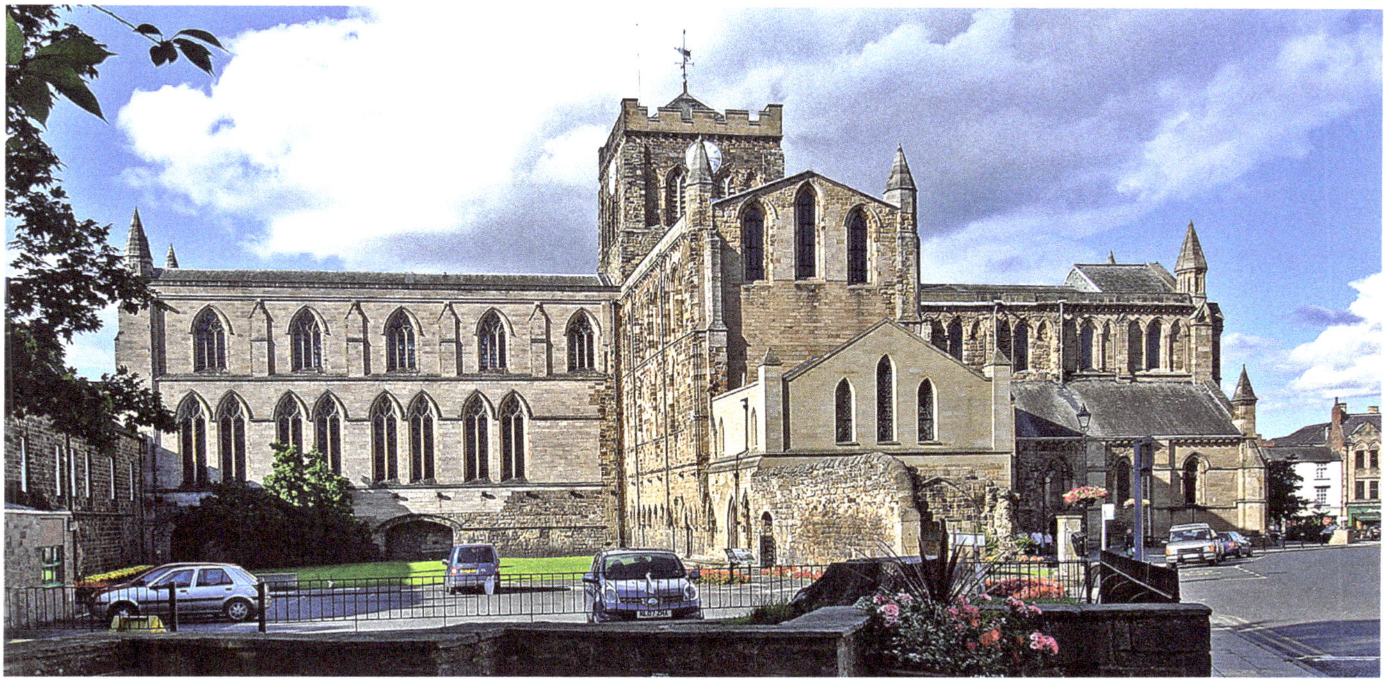

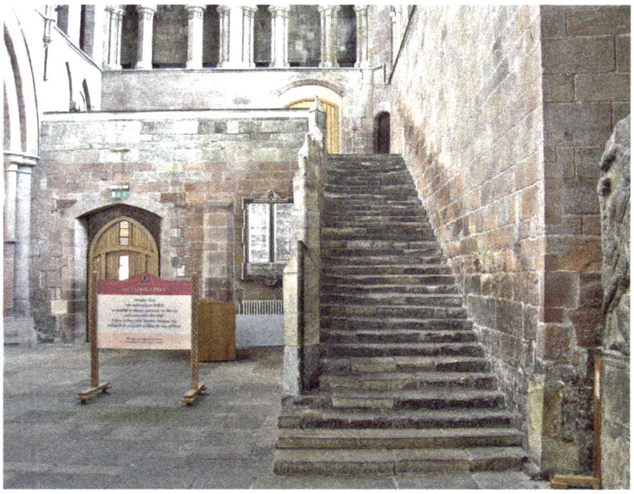

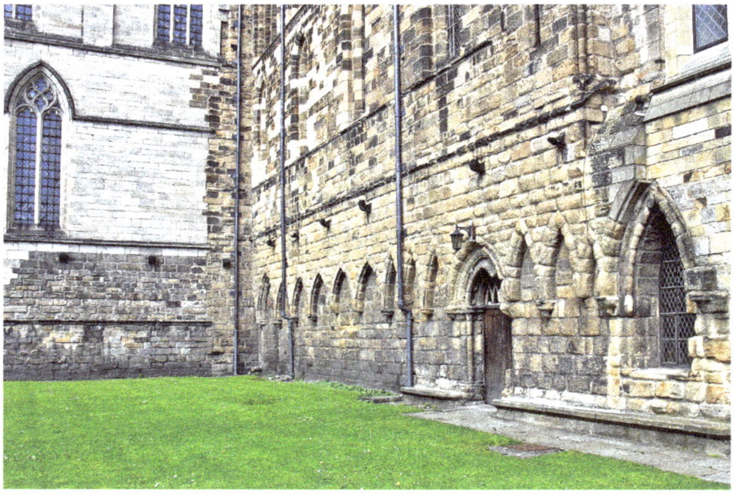

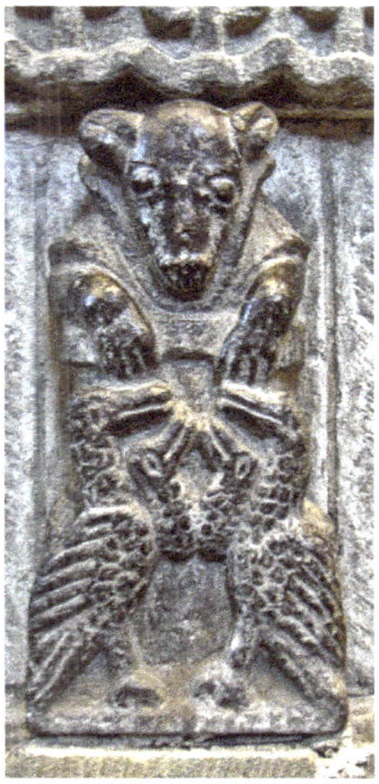

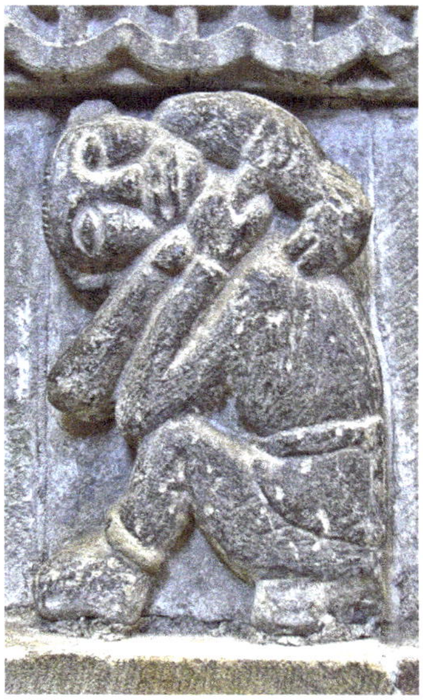

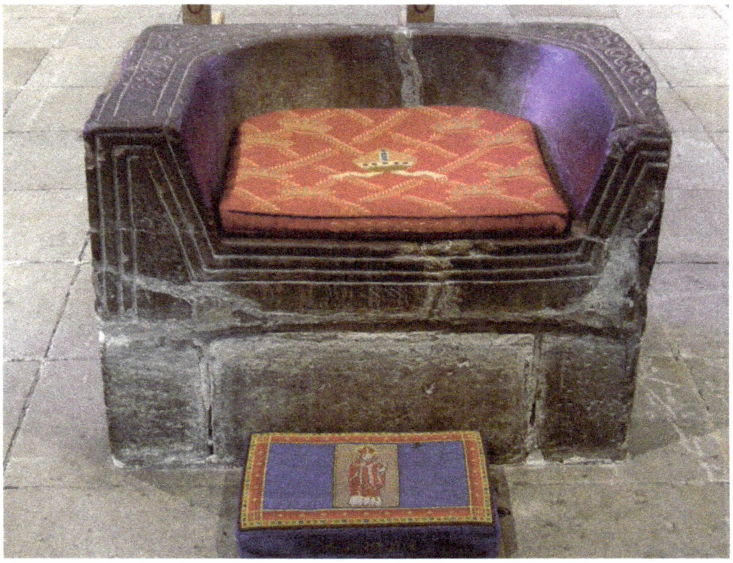

Holystone Priory

St Mary • Augustinian nuns -1124–1539

So little has survived of this minor religious establishment for Augustinian nuns in this sleepy village by the River Coquet that much of what has been written is in great part speculative. It is believed that the church served the monastic community, as well as the parish, and was incorporated in the priory complex. The nave of the church as it stands today is likely to have been the chancel of the former priory church, but the only visible evidence is a moulded capital at the south-west corner of the building. This is now only one metre above ground, which shows that the ground level in medieval times must have been considerably lower. A case can also be made for Priory Farm, before the additions in the seventeenth century, having formed part of the priory complex. Alas, only some carved stonework, grave covers, window surrounds and columns, which survive in the south wall of Mill House, can be associated with the priory.

Holystone Priory was founded by either Odinel de Umfraville I, Lord of Redesdale, or his predecessor Robert, sometime before 1124 during the latter years of the reign of Alexander I, King of Scotland, who is said to have endowed the priory with land and other property. In spite of its royal origins and patronage, the community remained relatively poor and was driven deeper into poverty, ironically as the result of Scottish raids in 1312 and 1320. To balance these deprivations, the nuns were granted several churches and smaller gifts. The nuns also benefited from the pilgrims who visited the nearby holy well, now known as The Lady's Well, said to have been the place where St Paulinus baptised 3,000 people in AD 627. They tended the clear pool, which now lies silent among a small grove of trees, and are said to have added the cross that is now reflected in the pure spring water. In 1499, the patronage passed from the Umfravilles to the Tailbois, but this did not improve its financial situation. Although its income, assessed at only £11, brought it within the scope of the closure of lesser monasteries, it escaped suppression in 1536-7, but had to surrender in 1539, when the prioress and six nuns were granted pensions.

Hulne White Friars

St Mary • 1242–1538

The extensive priory ruins now stand undisturbed within the enormous walled estate of the dukes of Northumberland, a location which comprises stretches of farmlands, woods and moors. It has preserved the peaceful environment of medieval times, although the occasional hunting party may interrupt the quiet slumber of the spirits of the White Friars among its jagged walls. Its close proximity to the Scottish Borders forced the friars to protect themselves against the constant threat from marauding Scots by enclosing the church and main claustral buildings within a stone wall. Its defences were further strengthened in 1488 with the erection of a pele tower, which was a gift from Henry Percy, fourth Earl of Northumberland. The tower with its attractive oriel window still stands to full height. Other focal points are the long, narrow church, now roofless, with an unusually stepped triple sedilia, and parts of the chapter house and cloister. A unique feature is the Carmelite infirmary, which is built on the standard hospital plan of the medieval period. The old infirmary and attached chapel have been converted into a dwelling for the estate's gamekeeper. Among the remains are attractive Victorian sculptures, including praying friars.

Hulne Priory was founded in 1242 for twenty-four friars and was probably the first Carmelite house to be established in England. It was founded by Ralph Fresborn, a young Northumbrian soldier, who visited the monastery on Mount Carmel during the Crusades and stayed. When William de Vescy found him there on a later Crusade, he persuaded him to return to England to establish a sister monastery and allowed him to choose the site. The site on a bluff rising steeply from the River Aln is said to have been chosen by Fresborn for its slight resemblance to Mount Carmel where the Order originated.

The priory grew and prospered and became an important seat of learning, with a library of more than a hundred manuscripts. The famous fourteenth century *Poppleton Manuscript,* now in the Bibliothèque Nationale in Paris, which contains numerous works including seven consecutive documents concerning medieval Scotland, is likely to have been compiled by Robert of Poppleton, who was prior of Hulne. The priory was dissolved in 1538 and the church was destroyed the following year. The claustral buildings were left to fall into ruin, with the exception of the west range, which was reconfigured by Sir Robert Ellerker, forming the 'Lordes great chamber'. In the 1560s, Hulne Priory came into the possession of the seventh Earl of Northumberland.

Photos - clockwise from top left

Hulne Priory standing on a bluff above the River Aln
Praying friar facing the church
Remains of medieval infirmary
Roofless church with unusual stepped sedilia
Pele Tower built to aid the defence of the priory
Holystone St Mary may have been part of the priory church

Lambley Priory

St Mary & St Patrick • Benedictine nuns -1190–1537

This Benedictine nunnery was founded before 1190 and was situated in wild and picturesque countryside near the well-wooded banks of the Tyne. It was granted pannage and common of pasture by Adam de Tindale, whose gift was later confirmed by King John. The community remained small and probably never supported more than six nuns, who struggled to make ends meet. In 1296, the nunnery was burnt by the Scots, who plundered and laid waste to the neighbourhood. Although the buildings were restored and life at the nunnery continued, it remained poor. Its value was assessed at a mere £5 15s and it was dissolved in 1537. The six nuns in residence all fled before the arrival of the receiver. Only earthworks and fragments of medieval stonework in the garden of Lambley Farm have survived. The very thick walls in the farmhouse may also indicate that parts of the priory could have been used in its construction.

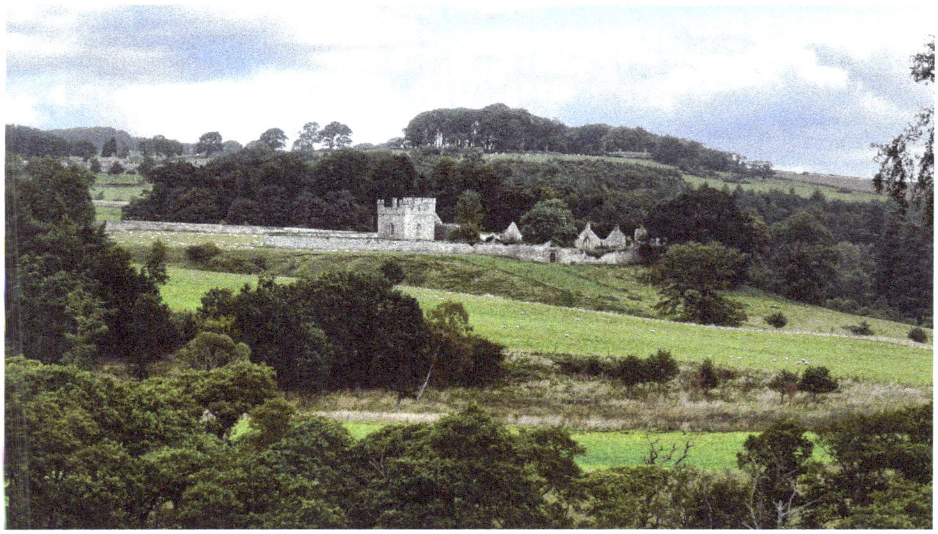

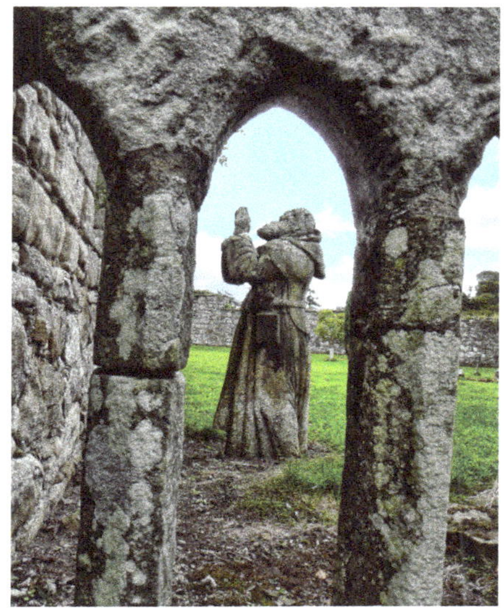

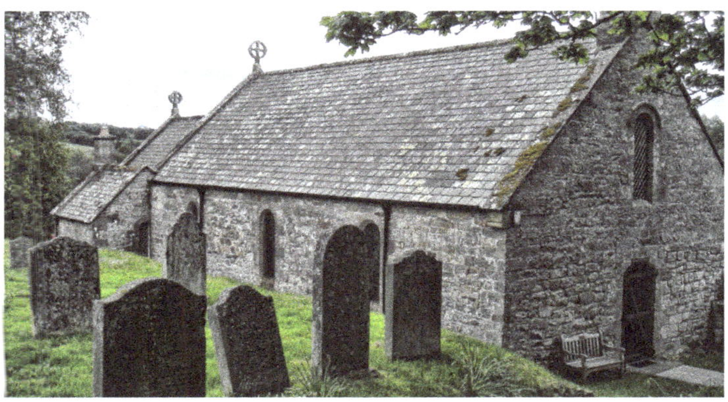

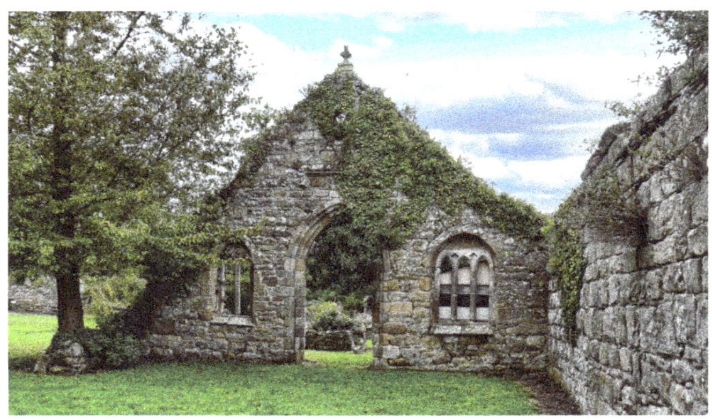

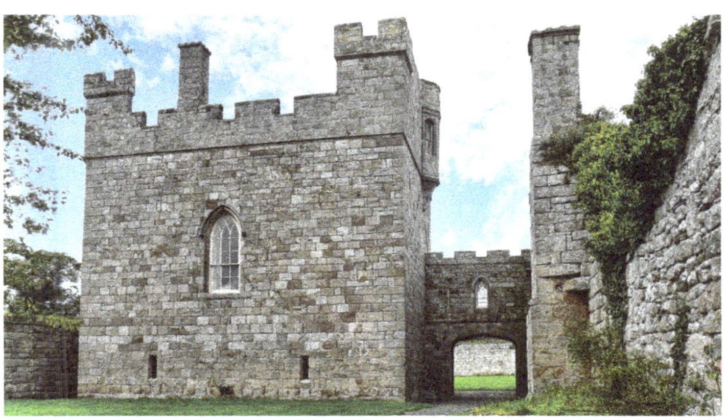

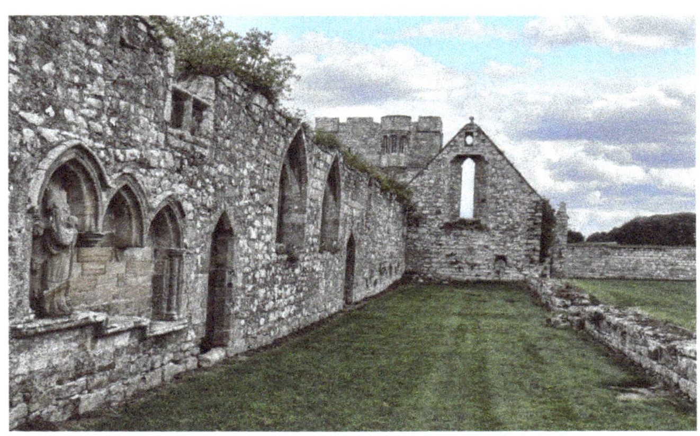

Lindisfarne (Holy Island) Priory

St Peter • Benedictine 1082–1537

Time and tide waits for no man, so the saying goes, and Holy Island can only be reached by causeway when the tide is out. So, the timing for a visit is important and as the mainland is left behind, the journey across what was once a dangerous ridge of sand used by monks and pilgrims should be one of anticipation and reflection. Standing on the headland looking down on the ruins of the priory, the realisation that the eyes are focused on the cradle of Christianity in Anglo-Saxon England will leave few unmoved. That the present day remains bear little resemblance to the original monastery will not detract from that experience, since they confirm the return of religious worship after the reign of terror and destruction by Danish raiders in the late eighth century. Indeed today, Lindisfarne is still a place of pilgrimage for believers and non-believers alike. Miracles may be rare occurrences in this modern age, when compared to those ascribed to the time of St Cuthbert, but hope springs eternal, especially when treading hallowed ground. At the very least, a visit to Lindisfarne will linger long in the memory.

Two saints are associated with the priory. The first, St Aidan of Iona, drawn to the island for its peace and remoteness, founded the first religious community at the invitation of King Oswald of Northumbria as long ago as AD 635, probably building simple wooden huts grouped round a thatched church. The fame of Lindisfarne spread after the arrival in AD 685 of St Cuthbert, who was persuaded to give up his life as a hermit on the Farne Islands further offshore and become bishop of the monastery. He died two years later, and lay buried beneath the church for over a decade, before being disinterred for enshrinement in AD 698. It is told that St Cuthbert's body showed no signs of decay and this miracle most likely proved the inspiration of the *Lindisfarne Gospels*, a beautiful manuscript of 258 illuminated pages created by Bishop Eadfrith, now in the British Museum and one of the great works of art. Pilgrims began to arrive from all corners of the land and the wealth and power of the monastery grew. In AD 793, Danish raiders landed on Lindisfarne and eventually forced the monks to flee, taking the body of St Cuthbert and other relics with them. After a long odyssey, they finally settled in Durham.

In 1082, Benedictine monks from Durham, determined to follow in the footsteps of the saint, came back to Lindisfarne, which they called Holy Island, and immediately began building the priory church. The red sandstone and carved pillars of the church, and especially the surviving parts of the west front remind one strongly of the great Romanesque Cathedral at Durham. Lindisfarne Priory became a cell of Durham, and remained of modest size, supporting a maximum of ten monks. From 1200 onwards, other buildings were added, completing the standard monastic layout. Life at Lindisfarne proceeded without upheaval, but its isolated position made it extremely vulnerable during the Scottish border wars, forcing the small community to fortify the priory's walls and towers. Arrow loops above the carved decorations of the great west door of the church strike a discordant note in the holy surroundings. The number of monks declined, but the priory somehow survived until it was dissolved in 1537. Upon the death of the last prior, Thomas Sparke, the property passed to the Dean and Chapter of Durham. The exposed position of the site and the soft sandstone contributed to its swift decay. Some of the priory's stones were used in the building of the nearby castle.

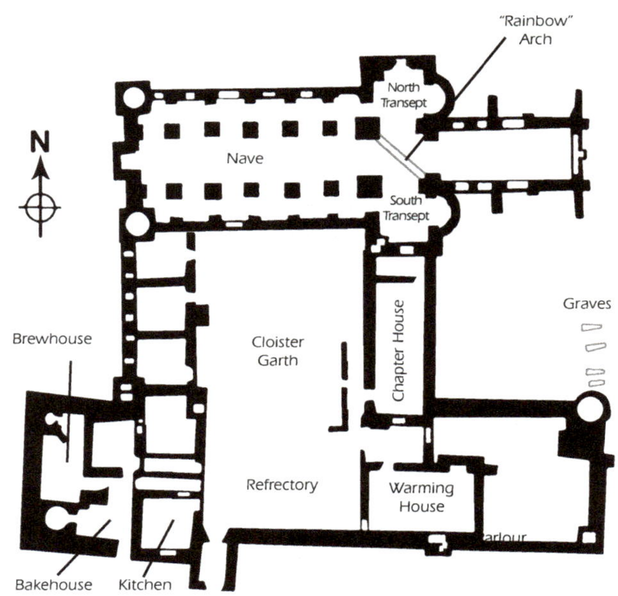

Although few walls stand to any great height, there is still much to admire among the ruins. None more so than the striking 'rainbow' arch, a single vault rib from the crossing that has survived against all the odds, and the solid pillars and rounded Norman arches of the nave arcade. The cruciform church was 45m (150ft) long and the tower was still standing in 1728. A well in the nave is most unusual. Also of interest are surviving ovens in the kitchens and bakehouse, remnants of a cellar, and a drain that runs from the kitchen through the cloister. The priory is enclosed by a wall, much of which has survived the depredations of the post-Dissolution years.

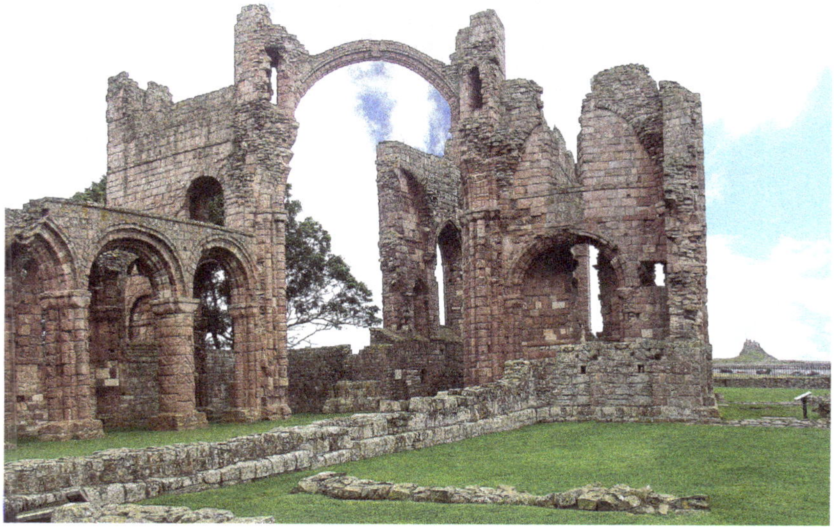

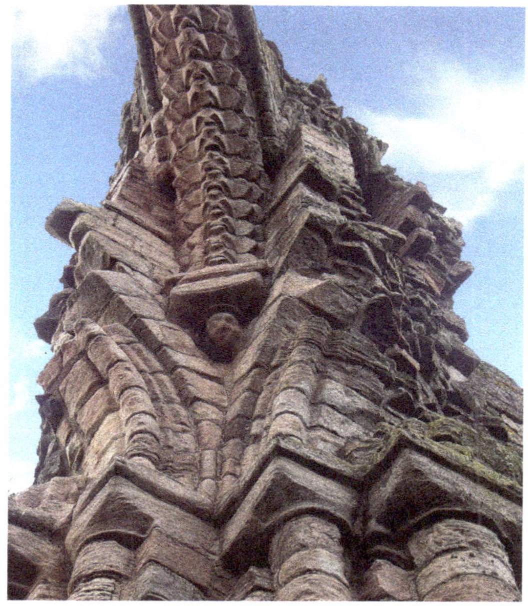

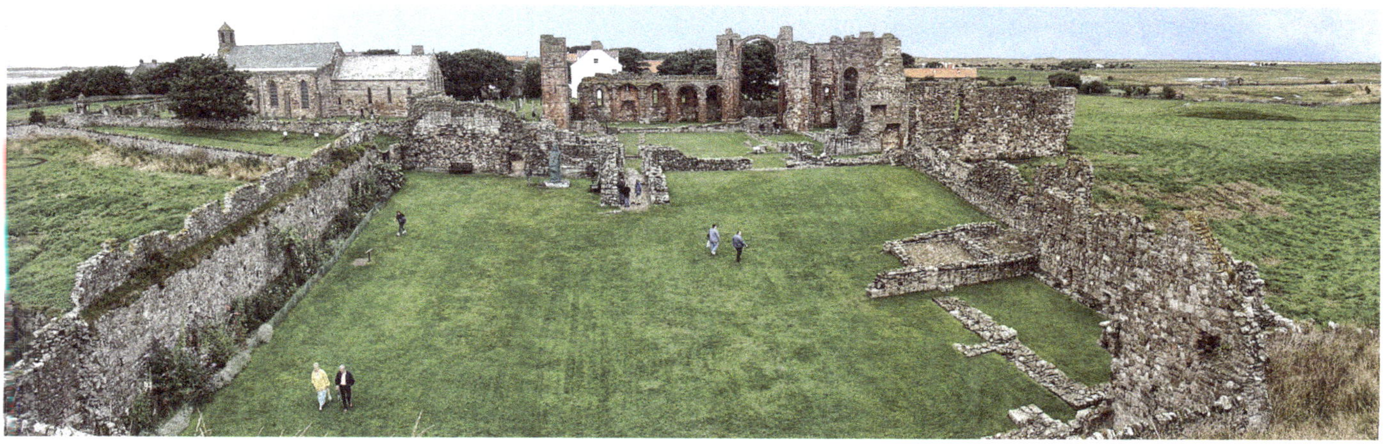

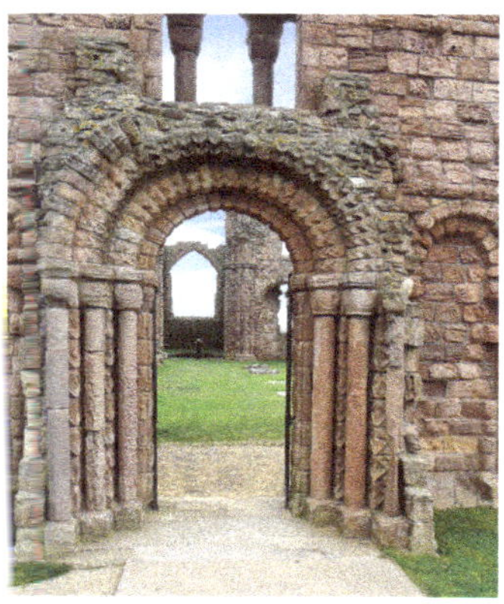

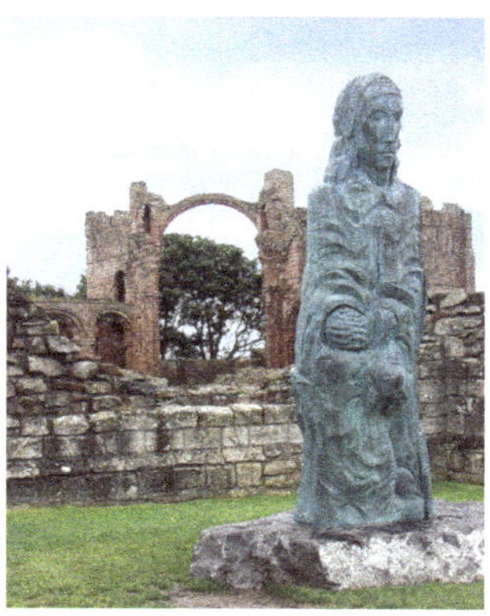

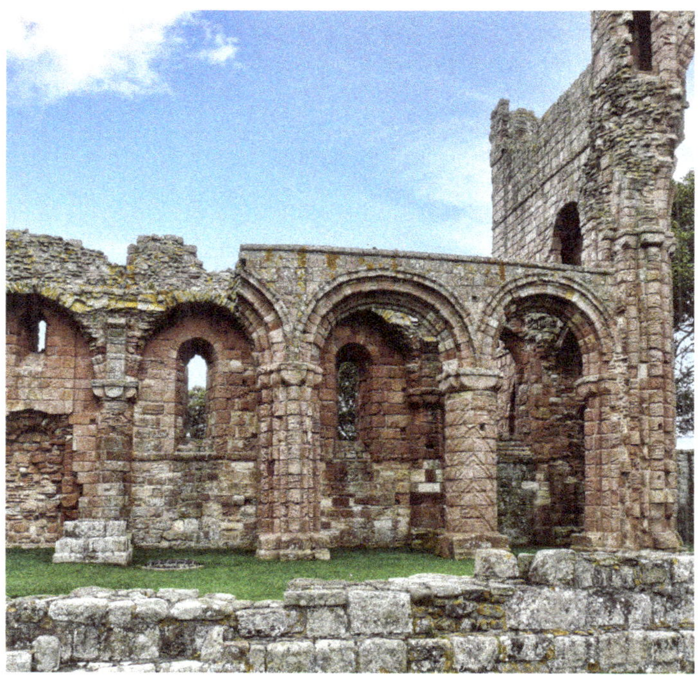

Photos – clockwise from top left

'Rainbow' arch at crossing with Lindisfarne castle in background
Detailed carvings at base of 'Rainbow' arch
Panoramic view looking across the cloister to the church
Pillars and Norman arches in nave arcade
Statue of St Cuthbert by Fenwick Lawson
Beautiful west door

Newcastle Austin Friars

c1290–1539

No certainty pertains to the date when the Augustine Friars arrived in Newcastle, but it is generally assumed that this house was founded c1290 by William Lord Ros, Baron of Wark upon Tweed. When King Edward I passed through Newcastle in 1299, the friars received 8s 4d for a pittance of one day, suggesting that there were twenty-five friars then present. The friars received several grants of land over subsequent decades, which enabled them to extend their premises, said to have included several buildings, a fair church and cloisters. In 1503, Princess Margaret, eldest daughter of Henry VII, was entertained at the priory on her way to Scotland. The last prior, Andrew Kel, seven friars and three novices surrendered the house in January 1539. It remained for the use of the King for sometime thereafter and used by the Council of the North. The only remaining feature above ground is a thirteenth century tower with fourteenth and eighteenth century additions, situated at the back of what was the Holy Jesus Hospital, now converted into the John George Joicey Museum. The tower measures 6.8 x 6.2m (22 x 20ft).

Newcastle Black Friars

c1239–1539

The Dominican priory is the only one of six houses of mendicant friars to have survived the Dissolution and ravages of time. Although heavily restored, the remaining buildings in the city centre, close to the town wall, are grouped around what was the 21m (69ft) square cloister garth, and now house craft shops, exhibition space and a well-known restaurant. The church to the north of the cloister was demolished in the sixteenth century, but its outline can be made out in the grassy area that remains.

The Dominican priory is said to have been founded by wealthy merchant Sir Peter Scott, and his son Sir Nicholas, in about 1239, on land donated by three pious sisters. The friars, who probably numbered close to forty, busied themselves with organising their community, starting in 1264 with building an aqueduct from a nearby fountain into their monastery. In 1280, the friars obtained a royal licence to cut a postern gate through the town wall, which had split their property in two, and in 1312, Edward II gave permission for the building of a wooden drawbridge over the new fosse, to provide access to the priory garden. Royal permission was granted under the condition that the drawbridge be removed at any sign of immediate danger to the town. The community continued to enjoy the ear of the King, who granted further land for the enlargement of the monastery. A highlight occurred in 1334, when, in a grand ceremony in the priory church, Edward Baliol, King of Scotland, paid homage to Edward III for the Kingdom of Scotland. Prior Rolande Hardynge and twelve friars surrendered the house in June 1539. Its annual value was just £2 19s. The buildings and lands were granted in 1544 to the mayor and burgesses of Newcastle, who leased it to nine of the town's craft guilds for use as their headquarters. The buildings later fell into disrepair but were restored by Newcastle Corporation some thirty years ago.

Newcastle Grey Friars

St Francis • -1237–1539

This house for Franciscan friars was established in Newcastle by the Carliols, who were wealthy merchants in the time of Henry III. The exact date is unknown, but the friars are believed to have arrived in the town before1237. The importance of this foundation can be acknowledged by the fact that at a general chapter of the Order, held in Narbonne in France in 1258, Newcastle was one of seven custodies in England. Its wardenship included eight other convents, namely Richmond, Hartlepool, Carlisle, Berwick, Roxburgh, Dundee, Dumfries, and Haddington. The community comprised thirty-four friars in 1299, when Edward I passed through Newcastle and gave them 11s 4d for their pittance of one day, but this had shrunk to twenty-four by 1322. The friars were expelled in 1498 by Henry VII and replaced by the stricter Observant branch of the Franciscans, which enjoyed his particular patronage. However, when the Observants supported Elizabeth Barton, the Holy Maid of Kent, who was executed for treason in 1534, they were removed. The house was again taken by the Conventuals, but their renewed occupancy was short-lived. In January 1539, Prior John Cragforth, eight friars and two novices were forced to surrender to the King's commissioners. According to Tanner, the priory was granted to James Rokeby, Earl of Essex, and others. Nothing is left of the priory buildings, but the Sevenhead Well at Lork Burn, from which the friars took a conduit to supply their water, and also gave the public leave to use it, is still in existence.

Photos - clockwise from top right

Reconstructed tower of the Austin Friars

The Black Friars buildings grouped around the cloister garth is a rare survival

Newcastle Sack Friars

1267–1307

This short-lived house was established near the White Friars Tower in Newcastle in 1267, but was given additional land at Stable Garth by Henry III, on the insistence of Robert de Bruce, that same year. In 1299, when Edward I passed through Newcastle, the three remaining friars were given a pittance of 2s for two days. By 1307, Walter de Charlton was the only surviving member and the King granted the site to the Carmelites, on the condition that they should take in this brother and support him in the manner appropriate to his rank.

Newcastle White Friars

c1240–1539

The Carmelites were settled on the Wall Knoll in Newcastle around 1240, but when their premises were being squeezed by the encroaching town wall, King Edward I granted them the house of the Friars of the Sack in 1307. Records contend that there were thirty-eight friars resident in 1310. The site was enlarged in 1337, and in1361, the friars vacated their original property on Wall Knoll, which was granted to the Trinitarians. The sparse history recalls a breach of sanctuary in 1312, when several persons were taken from the church and beheaded. The house, which extended between Westgate and the River Tyne, was surrendered by Prior Gerald Spor, seven brethren and two novices in 1539. Its value was assessed at a mere £9 11s. The priory was granted in 1546 to Richard Gresham and Richard Billingford. Nothing at all now remains.

Newcastle Priory

St Michael • Trinitarian 1361–1539

The Trinitarians moved into Newcastle in 1361, when they were given the site on Wall Knoll, which had been vacated by the Carmelite friars in 1307. The first warden, William Wakefield, came from Berwick, after his attempts at establishing the Order in the town were frustrated by the Bishop of Durham. Founder William de Acton was more kindly disposed to the friars, but stipulated that the hospital in honour of the Holy Trinity, as it was called, was to have a warden, two priest brothers, three clerks to teach in the school and instruct in the chapel, and three beds were always to be kept prepared for 'incidental guests', such as the poor and infirm. The house was suppressed in 1539, when only a 'prior was left'. Nothing has survived, after the last vestiges were demolished at the end of the eighteenth century to make room for the construction of City Road. Even the exact location is no longer known, nor is any information on how much of the Carmelite priory was left for the use of the Trinitarians, and what they may have built themselves.

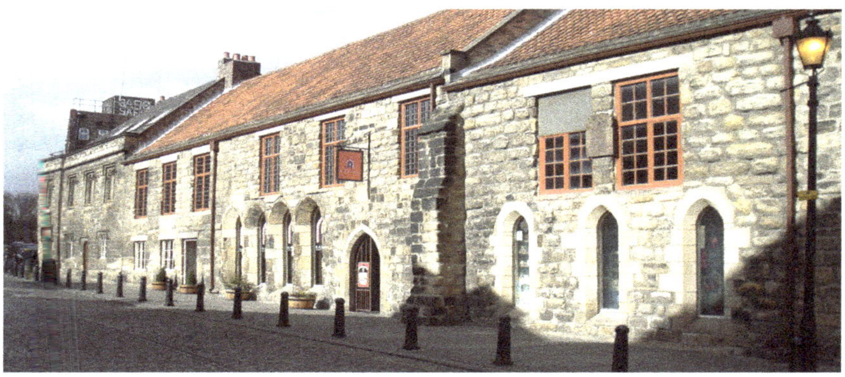

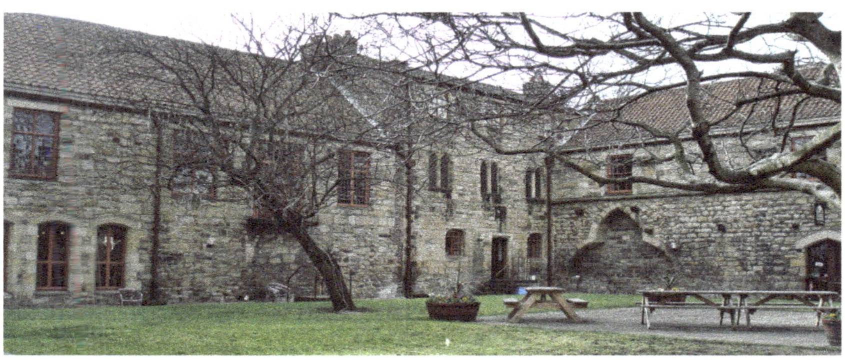

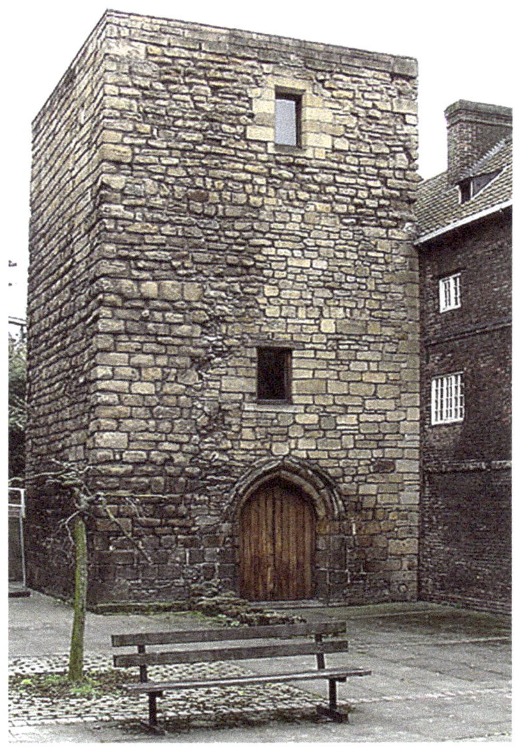

Newcastle Priory

St Bartholomew • Benedictine nuns c1135–1539

Nothing remains of this, the oldest of Newcastle's religious foundations. According to a manuscript in the Bodleian Library in Oxford, this house of Benedictine nuns was founded by a Baron Hilton, probably before 1086. In that year, Agar, mother of Margaret, Queen of Scotland, and her sister, took the veil after the death at Alnwick of King Malcolm. It has been suggested that the nunnery may have been refounded c1135, as both, King Henry I of England, and David I, King of Scotland, have been cited as founders. It is certainly true that both were great benefactors to the nuns. The nuns also received gifts and lands from the bishops of Durham and many landowners in Newcastle and immediate surrounds, and as far away as Hartlepool. On the arrival of King Edward II in the town in 1322, the community was apparently some twenty-strong.

In spite of the great many possessions, the priory seems to have fallen into poverty, while discipline is also said to have degenerated to such an extent that, in 1363, Bishop Hatfield of Durham appointed a commission to visit the nunnery. Fire damage and non-payment of pension forced the prioress to petition Robert Nevill, Bishop of Durham, for relief in 1448. The priory's parlous financial state was eased somewhat through the leasing out of several parcels of unused land. The nunnery survived the Dissolution of the lesser monasteries, but was finally suppressed in January 1539. According to Dugdale, its value had been assessed in 1535 at £36 10s, which included the dependent St Edmund's Hospital in Gateshead. The Deed of Surrender was signed by the prioress, a retired prioress, and nine other nuns. The priory buildings were destroyed by one Robert Anderson who, says Bourne, "pulled down all the houses therein; it being a receptacle for Scots and Unfreemen".

Newminster Abbey

St Mary • Cistercian 1137–1537

Given the fact that this was one of the largest Cistercian houses in the north, it is rather surprising that no effort has been made to preserve and display its remains, which are hidden in a wooded enclosure and strangled by the vigorous growth of vines and shrubbery. Although located on the edge of the town of Morpeth, there is no signage that might assist the visitor and only the most determined will find their way across a field to reach the abbey remains. While it is almost impossible to gain an insight into the extent and layout of the abbey, sufficient, and in parts decorated standing masonry, will reward the effort of running the gauntlet of bulls and cows grazing along the way.

The most visible remains, all built in local sandstone, include large parts of the cloister, which has been re-erected. This displays a mix of pointed and round arches supported on slender twin colonettes with waterleaf capitals. The round-headed doorway to the square chapter house, with its two orders of columns and waterleaf capitals, has also been re-erected and makes for a romantic gateway amidst the rampant greenery. The remains of the church lie to the north and include standing parts of a large north widow, and vestiges of a fifteenth century screen with cinquefoil heads in the north transept. Fragments of stone walls lie around and among the many low foundations of unidentified stone walls. Also hidden is the thirteenth century tiled floor of the abbot's chapel.

Ranulph de Merlay, Lord of Morpeth, founded this Cistercian monastery dedicated to the Virgin Mary in 1137 and endowed it with extensive lands that eventually extended to the Scottish border. The abbey was located by a small stream in a secluded valley sheltered by the rising hills. It was colonised by monks from Fountains Abbey in North Yorkshire, and St Robert became its first abbot the following year. During his energetic leadership, which ended with his death in 1159, three communities of monks were sent out to found new monasteries, which would suggest that the house had a large complement of brethren in the early years. The three Cistercian monasteries were established at Pipewell (1143), Roche (1147) and Sawley (1148). By the late thirteenth century, the abbey also had two dependent hospitals, at Mitford and Allerburn.

Its location made it vulnerable to border raids by the Scots and almost as soon as the abbey had been established, it was burned in a Scottish attack and was not completely rebuilt until 1180. It would appear that its subsequent history was uneventful and allowed the abbey to accumulate some wealth through gifts of succeeding lords of Morpeth, the barons of Bolam and Bolbec, and several families in surrounding villages, together with lands that yielded a plentiful supply of corn. The abbot was often summoned to the Parliaments of Edward I, Edward II and Edward III. In the *Valor Ecclesiasticus* of 1535, the net annual income of the abbey was assessed at just £100, although in the following year, it was returned as £265. This did not, however, save it from the first round of closures and it was dissolved in 1537. The estate was leased by the Crown to the Grey family, which proceeded to use the abbey as building materials for its own dwellings, leaving few upstanding remains. In 1609, ownership passed to Robert Brandling.

Ovingham Priory

St Mary • Augustinian 1378–1537

The Augustinian priory of Ovingham was established in 1378 by one of the Umfravilles of Prudhoe for a master and three canons as a cell to Hexham Priory. The annual value assessed in the *Valor* of 1535 amounted to only £11 2s, leading to its early suppression in 1537. At that time, there were four canons in residence. The priory stood opposite the church, but not a trace can now be found above ground.

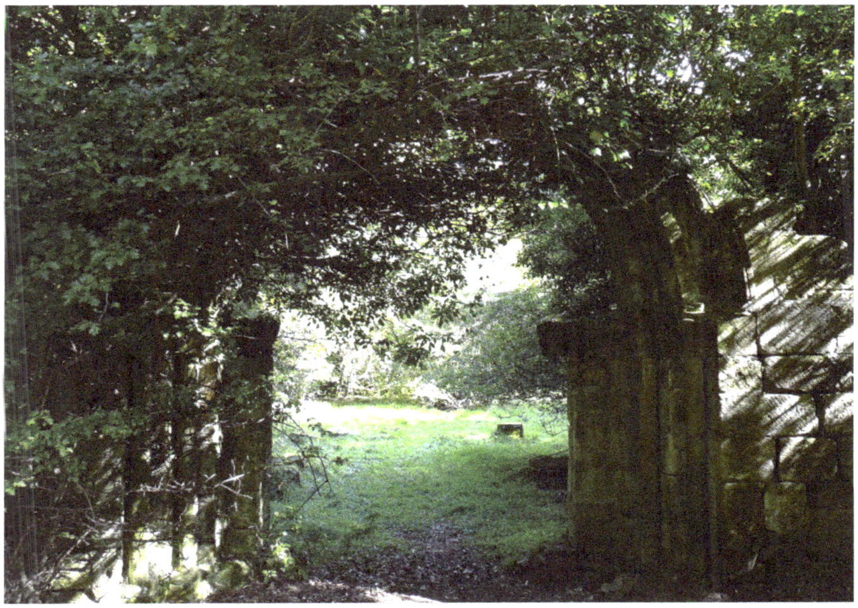

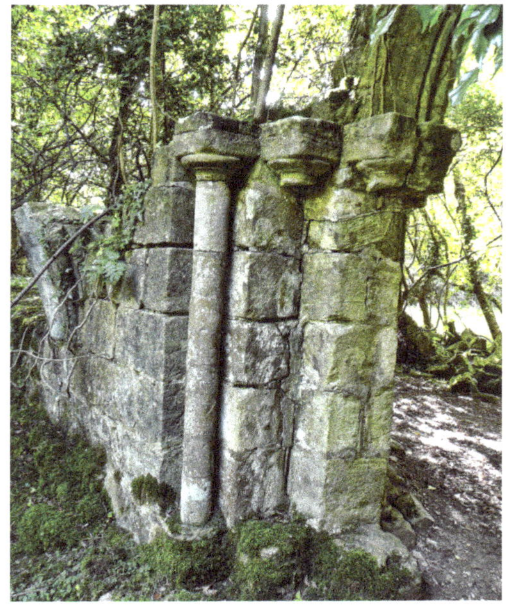

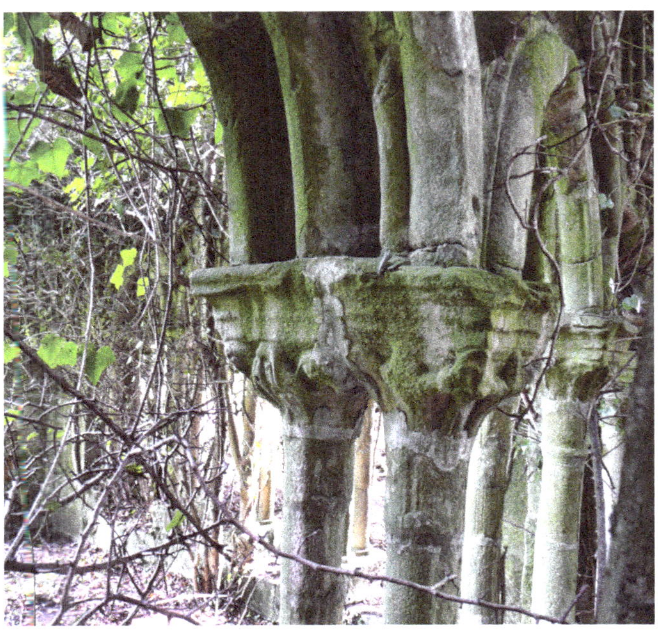

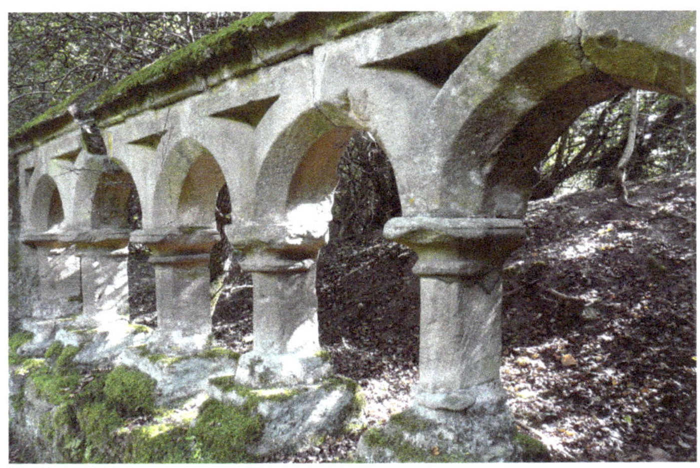

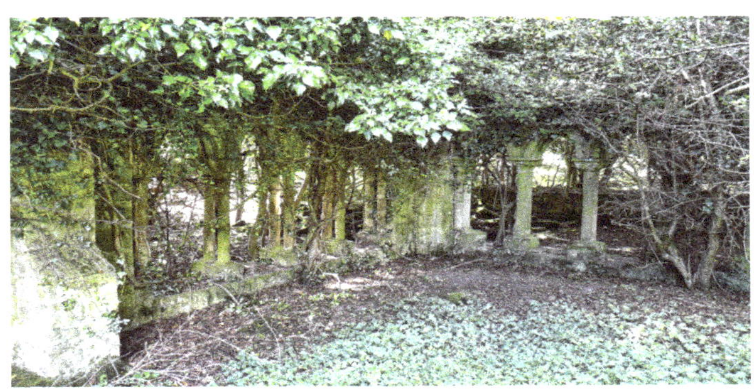

Photos of Newminster Abbey - clockwise from top left

Arched chapter house doorway
Unidentified doorway with colonette
Re-erected cloister arcades
Badly weathered corbels supporting arches

Tynemouth Priory

St Mary & St Oswyn • Benedictine 1085–1539

The steep and rocky headland at Tynemouth is unique in that it combines ruins of both sacred and military significance. Within the confines of the castle, which commanded the northern approaches of the river, the stark remains of Tynemouth Priory look out to the open sea and continue to serve as a landmark to passing ships. It occupies the site of an earlier Saxon monastery, which was plundered and burnt several times by the Danes. Its fame as the burial place of the martyred King St Oswyn spread far and wide. In 1074, the site was granted to the Benedictine house at Jarrow, but was re-founded by Robert de Mowbray, Earl of Northumberland, in 1085, with monks from St Albans, led by Remigius, who became the first prior. Building of the great Norman church of St Mary and St Oswyn was begun in 1090 and took nearly a century to complete.

The church was later greatly enlarged, with a 41m (135ft) long choir with aisles added to the Norman apse, while the nave was also lengthened. About 1320, a Lady Chapel was built east of the chancel, attributed to the Percy family, which had acquired the vast Northumberland estates. The wealth of the abbey was derived from the coal industry, but a large income was needed, for the prior of Tynemouth was also responsible for the upkeep of the castle. Although Henry VIII retained the castle as a royal stronghold, he did not spare the monastery. In 1539, the last prior, Robert Blakeney, together with fourteen monks and four novices, signed the deed of surrender. In the *Valor Ecclesiasticus* of 1535, the priory had been valued at a very respectable £397.

Only the beautiful chancel has survived to almost original height, all the claustral and domestic buildings having been razed to the ground under the stewardship of Colonel Villars, Governor of Tynemouth Castle. It is probable that the extremely thick walls of the church defied the attempts to flatten it. The west front still displays some elaborate ornamentation, while the impressive east end rises to 22m (70ft), almost the original height. It has an unusual elongated oval window, which is flanked by two smaller lancet windows and topped by a single lancet above. The south wall of the presbytery is particularly fine, with two rows of lancet windows sitting above a panel of blind arcading, inset with a tomb recess, aumbry, piscina and sedilia. Beneath the east front is the small, heavily restored fifteenth century Percy Chapel, which once housed the relics of St Oswyn. The headstones of the former parish graveyard add to the feeling of solitude and desolation.

Warkworth Priory

• Benedictine c1241–?

Bishop Ranulph Flambard of Durham founded a chantry at Warkworth early in the twelfth century, and one of his successors, Nicholas de Farnham, provided for the maintenance of two Benedictine monks from Durham during the reign of Henry III. Of this cell, which appears to have existed only for the eight years of the bishop's reign (1241-1249), nothing now remains. It has been conjectured that a nunnery existed in the eighth century in the village, then known as Wercewode, as it has been recorded that an abbess, named Werce, gave a sheet of fine linen to the Venerable Bede to be used as his shroud.

Warkworth Hermitage

• Benedictine c1350–?

A pleasant stroll along the Coquet River from Warkworth, followed by a short crossing on a little rowing boat by the ferryman custodian, will bring the visitor to this former hermitage, which is almost hidden above the wooded river bank. Hewn out of solid rock in c1350, the surprisingly large and extraordinary two-storey cave contains a little chapel, complete with carved rib vaulting, an altar, sacristy and two small rooms, which are believed to have been the hermit's original living quarters. The badly worn carving to the right of the altar is officially described as a nativity scene, but appears more like the grave slab of a lady, probably of the legendary Lady Isabel. The ruined remains of a fourteenth century hall, chamber and kitchen outside the original cave attest to a later, less austere lifestyle.

The building of the hermitage has traditionally been ascribed to Sir Bertram of Bothal, one of Earl Percy's knights who mistakenly killed his own brother and lover, while trying to rescue the latter from the Scots. The story goes that having been badly wounded in a battle against the Earl of Douglas, Sir Bertram sent a message to his betrothed, the Lady Isabel, daughter of Lord Widdrington, to come to his side. She didn't arrive and when he was later informed that Lady Isabel was held captive in the tower of a remote castle, he rushed to her aid. Seeing her leaving the tower with a figure in Highland costume, he attacked his opponent with his sword, inadvertently killing them both, only to find that the slain adversary was none other than his own brother. Sir Bertram gave away everything he owned and built the hermitage, where he lived in solitude for the rest of his life. It is said that he built an altar-tomb with the effigy of a beautiful lady, her hands raised in prayer. At her feet kneels the figure of a hermit, his left hand pressed to his heart, as if in sorrow. A description over the doorway reads: "My tears have been my meat day and night". The hermitage became a popular place of pilgrimage and later hermits benefited greatly from the patronage of the earls of Warkworth. As a result, they largely forsook their austere lifestyle and, in exchange for saying prayers for the nobles listed by the earls, received pasture for twelve cows, a bull, two horses, twenty loads of firewood, fish every Sunday, plus a cash sum of £13.33!

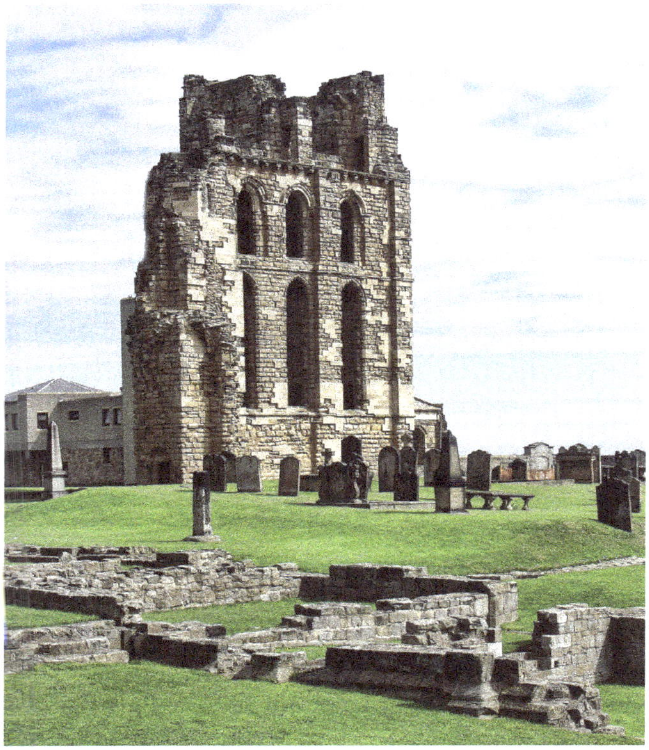

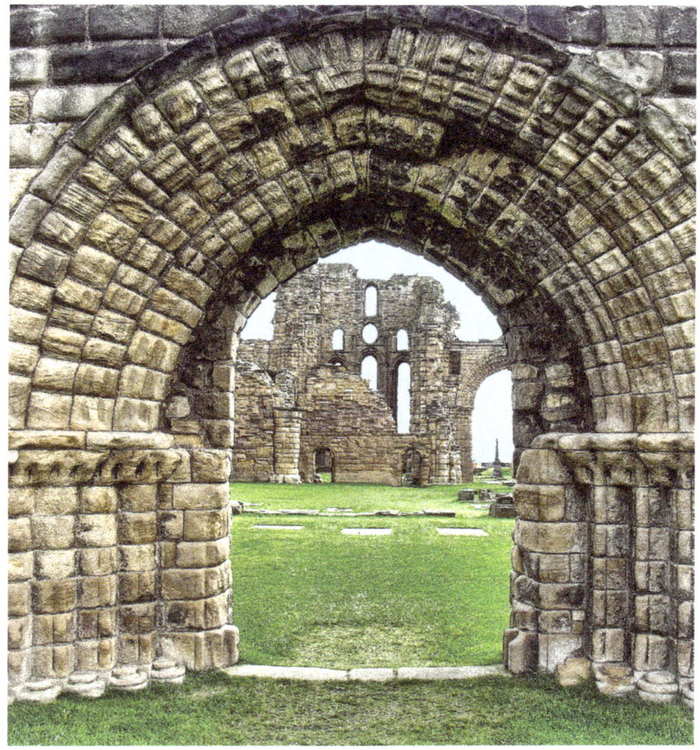

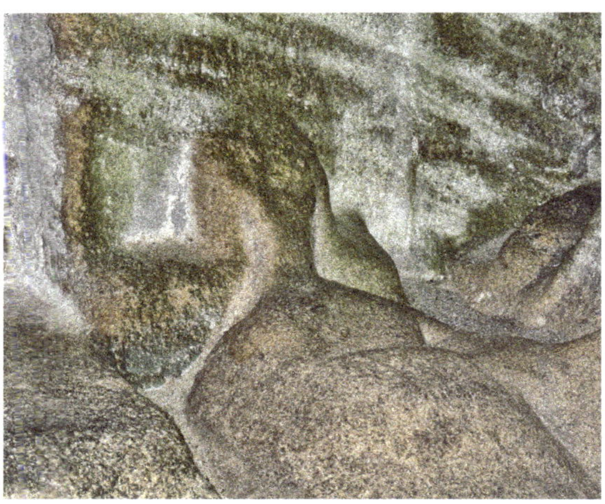

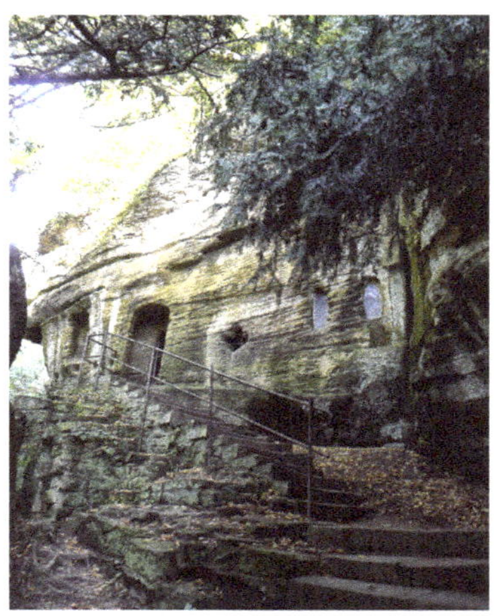

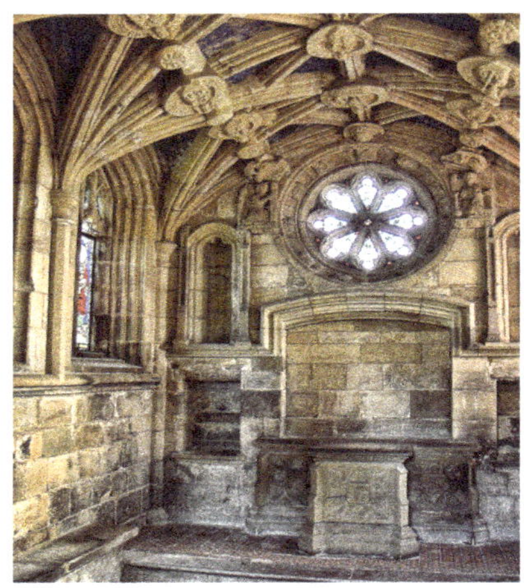

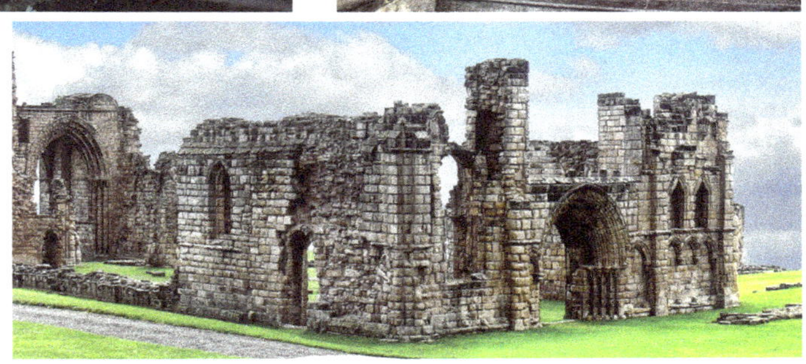

Photos - clockwise from top left

East end of Tynemouth priory church
Doorway with five orders and hoodmould
Percy Chapel with elaborately carved roof bosses
Standing remains of priory church
Warkworth hermitage hewn out of solid rock
Badly worn carving of a lady

Nottinghamshire

Post-Conquest Monasticism

The area was settled by Angles around the fifth century, and became part of the Kingdom, later Earldom of Mercia. The name of Nottinghamshire first occurs in 1016, when it was harried by King Cnut. At the time of the Domesday Survey in 1086, Nottinghamshire was divided into eight wapentakes, whose divisions remained in place until 1610. Apart from the King, the Archbishop of York and the Bishop of Lincoln, major landowners were William Peverel, a favourite of William the Conqueror, who was rewarded with 162 manors in central England and who built Nottingham Castle, and Roger de Busli, tenant-in-chief of eighty-six manors in the county, and many more elsewhere. Until the end of the medieval period, Nottinghamshire was administratively united with Derbyshire under a single sheriff, entitled the High Sheriff of Nottinghamshire, Derbyshire and the Royal Forests.

Nottinghamshire had eleven monastic houses for monks and canons, and two nunneries. Of these, only one stood east of the Trent, and one to the south of the river, with all the others located north of the Trent. It appears strange that the religious Orders, which usually settled on the most productive lands, were not to be found in the Vale of Belvoir. Presumably the reason lies to some extent with the generosity, or otherwise, of the benefactors. Furthermore, there were no monastic houses in the county before the Norman Conquest.

The post-medieval mansion of Rufford Abbey incorporates the best-preserved remains of a west cloister range of a Cistercian abbey in England, dating mainly from the mid-twelfth century, when it was founded and populated by monks from Rievaulx Abbey in North Yorkshire. With a large number of generous endowments, which included mills and lands for twenty-one granges, the abbey became prosperous, and its history was generally uneventful, until trumped-up charges against the abbot forced an early closure in 1536. A late twelfth century doorway is probably the only identifiable survival from Welbeck Abbey, founded for Premonstratensian canons after 1154 by Thomas de Cuckney, but the land belonging to the Welbeck Estate is still a potent reminder. It became a large and noted house, sending out canons into distant parts of England and Wales to found seven daughter houses.

Several reminders from the Augustinian priory of Felley, established in 1156, can be found in the gardens of a magnificent mansion, which also incorporates some worked masonry and the tombstone of a prior. It was dependent on Worksop Priory but obtained its independence in 1260. Worksop was one of the great Augustinian priories, whose wealth kept growing after being founded sometime after 1119. It was also a well-ordered house, free from scandal and, in later years, became a famous centre of learning. The principal survivals are a fine gatehouse and the former, but reconstructed priory church, now serving the parish.

The parishioners of Thurgarton still worship in the former priory church of another wealthy Augustinian house, founded in the reign of Henry I. Three of the original seven bays of the nave and a wonderful Norman west doorway have survived from the conventual church. The ruined, yet exceptionally beautiful and impressive west front is the dominant feature of another Augustinian house, that of Newstead Priory in Sherwood Forest, founded c1170 by Henry II. After its suppression in 1539, it became the ancestral home of the romantic poet, Lord Byron. The small Augustinian priory of Shelford stood on the south bank of the River Trent, but nothing has survived.

Very little is left of the small and compact Gilbertine priory at Mattersey, hidden away in the rolling countryside. Founded in 1185, it suffered destruction by fire in 1279, from which it never fully recovered. The most substantial remains are those of the thirteenth century refectory. Benedictine nuns led a blameless life at Wallingwells, from its foundation in the time of King Stephen to its dissolution in 1539. The small and remote Premonstratensian priory of Broadholme was one of only two nunneries of the Order in England. It was probably founded in the reign of King Stephen and struggled through to the Dissolution, but nothing now remains. The last house to be founded in Nottinghamshire was Beauvale, a Carthusian priory, when Nicholas de Cantilupe of nearby Greasley Castle gave land and twelve cells for the monks in 1343.

Alien houses were established at Blyth, when Roger de Busli gave the church to the Benedictine abbey of La-Trinité-du-Mont near Rouen, sometime after 1087, and at Lenton, the only Cluniac house in the county, although there is said to have been a small dependency in Nottingham (Roche). Blyth Priory was founded c1109 by William Peverel who provided rich endowments. Only the nave of the priory church has survived, but the medieval mural of the Last Judgment on the east wall is of greatest interest.

Mendicant Orders settled friars in Nottingham and Newark in the mid-thirteenth century. Franciscan (Observant) and Austin Friars found homes in Newark, while Franciscans and Carmelites preached in Nottingham. The existence of a Carmelite house at Lenton is disputed.

Gazetteer

Beauvale Priory Beauvale Abbey Farm, New Road, Moorgreen, 13km (8 miles) W of Nottingham, Nottinghamshire (SK 492490). Tel: 01773 710682. Web: www.beauvalepriory.co.uk

Blyth Priory Priory Close, Blyth, 8km (5 miles) NE of Worksop, Nottinghamshire (SK 624873). Church in use

Broadholme Priory Manor Lane, Broadholme, 8km (5 miles) NW of Lincoln, Lincolnshire (SK 895735). Earthwork remains

Felley Priory On minor lane, off A608 Mansfield Road, Nottinghamshire (SK 483513). Tel: Web: www.felleypriory.co.uk

Lenton Priory Priory Street, off A6005 Abbey Street, Nottingham, Nottinghamshire (SK 552387). Minimal remains

Mattersey Priory East of Mattersey village, off B6045, 10km (6 miles) N of Retford, Nottinghamshire (SK 704896). English Heritage; Tel: 01604 735400

Newark Austin/Grey (Observant) Friars Friary Road, off Queens Road, Newark, Nottinghamshire (SK 802540). No visible remains

Newstead Priory Ravenstead, Nottinghamshire (SK 542538). Tel: 01623 455900. Web: www.newsteadabbey.org.uk

Nottingham Grey Friars Off A6008 Maid Marian Way, Nottingham, Nottinghamshire (SK 572395). No visible remains

Nottingham (Roche) Priory On A6005 Castle Boulevard, Nottingham, Nottinghamshire (SK 563392). No visible remains

Nottingham White Friars Friar Lane, off A6005 Maid Marian Way, Nottingham, Nottinghamshire (SK 571398). No visible remains

Rufford Abbey Off A614 Old Rufford Road, 3km (2 miles) S of Ollerton, Nottinghamshire, England (SK 645648). English Heritage; Tel: 01623 821338

Shelford Priory Main road, off A6097, Shelford, 8km (5 miles) E of Nottingham, Nottinghamshire (SK 672434). No visible remains

Thurgarton Priory Priory Road, Thurgarton, 5km (3 miles) S of Southwell, Nottinghamshire (SK 692492). Church in use

Wallingwells Priory Wallingwells, 5.5km (3.5 miles) N of Worksop, Nottinghamshire (SK 572841). No visible remains

Welbeck Abbey Off A60, near Belph, 6.5km (4 miles) SW of Worksop, Nottinghamshire (SK 564742). Private

Worksop Priory Priorswell Road, off B6040, Cheapside, Worksop, Nottinghamshire (SK 590789). Church in use. Web: www.worksoppriory.co.uk

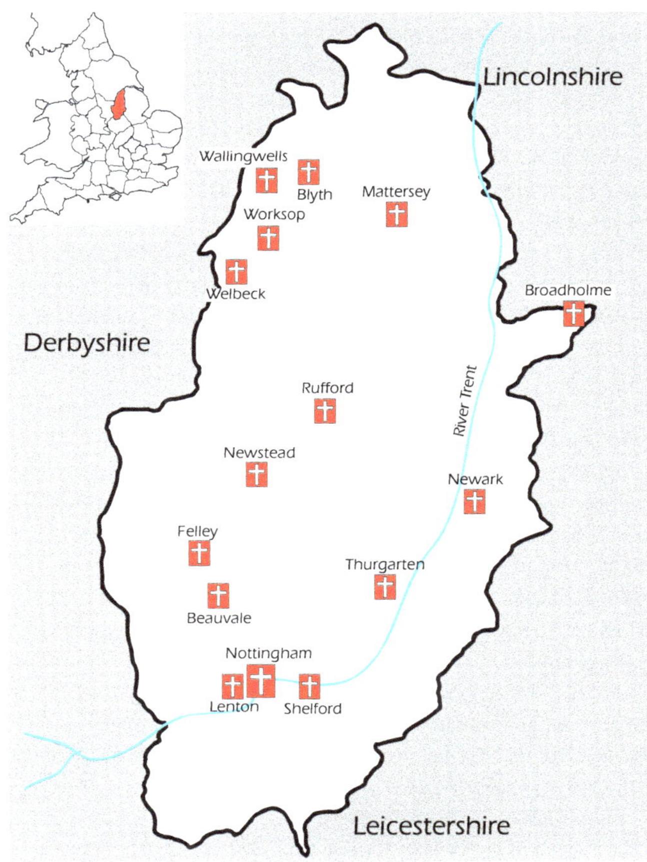

Beauvale Priory

Holy Trinity & St Mary • Carthusian 1343–1539

The Carthusian priory of Beauvale, or Pulchra Vallis in Parco de Gressley, was, as its name implies, situated in a park in the lovely valley of Beauvale in the parish of Greasley. It was the last monastic house to be founded in Nottinghamshire when, in 1343, Nicholas de Cantilupe of nearby Greasley Castle obtained permission from Edward III and endowed the new foundation with land and properties in the villages of Greasley and Selston. Nicholas provided twelve cells for the monks, and at a later date at least two more were added. The foundation charter was witnessed by the Archbishop of York, the bishops of Durham, Lincoln and Lichfield, the earls of Derby, Northampton and Huntingdon, and other persons of high standing. The monks eventually owned property in Nottinghamshire, Lincolnshire and Derbyshire, and also obtained the right to mine coal at Selston, but the income was insufficient to sustain the community, and by 1370, the house was said to be ruinous. When the founder's grandson died without heirs in 1375, the de Cantilupe patronage came to an end. The monks leased some of the pits out to others, and in 1403 were granted the alien grange at Bonby in Lincolnshire, but the struggle for survival continued.

A Beauvale monk jailed in a monastery prison at Grenoble had by all accounts wrought destruction in several prisons he was confined in, forcing the governor to write to Beauvale to ask that he be repatriated at a cost of one year's maintenance, or the cost of a new prison. The outcome is not known. Not much else has been recorded of the internal history of the priory, but what transpired towards the end of its existence provides a vivid picture into the murky world of Henry VIII's vendetta against the Catholic faith. Prior John Houghton, formerly of Beavale but now head of the London Charterhouse, had several times refused to take the Oath of Supremacy and accept Henry VIII as head of the Church of England. In spring 1535, he, Prior Robert Lawrence of Beauvale, and Prior Augustine Webster of Axholme petitioned Cromwell to be exempt from taking the oath, but all three were found guilty of treason in a trial at Westminster Hall and executed at Tyburn in May 1535 in barbarous fashion. All three were hung, drawn and quartered. At least one of the three was still alive when the quartering was begun. The execution of these martyrs was the first of many, with more than one hundred condemned to die at Tyburn for their religious convictions in the years to come.

The priory, which was valued at £196 6s in 1535, just below the threshold value for the lesser monasteries, avoided early closure on payment of a large fine. It was finally surrendered by the last prior, Thomas Woodcock, to Dr London in July 1539. The prior and eight monks received pensions, as did two aged lay-brothers, whose presence at such a late date was unusual. Two years later, the site was acquired by Sir William Hussey of London.

The remains of Beauvale Priory are now incorporated in Abbey Farm, but the owners, with co-operation from English Heritage, have been undertaking major restoration and have made them accessible to the public. The surviving structures include the former gatehouse, south wall of the church, a fragment of the north wall, the prior's house that faced the great cloister, and a stretch of low precinct wall from the fourteenth century. Some stained glass from the priory is now in Greasley Church.

The most substantial and best preserved structure is the prior's house, which has two arched doorways with hood moulds, and two barrel-vaulted rooms, two fireplaces, and vestiges of a spiral staircase within. The gatehouse is also relatively complete, but no longer exhibits its one-time splendour. Two sets of gate pillars have been partially exposed, which would suggest that it once had at least a double arched entrance. There are two rooms flanking the entrance, with the western room still with its original wooden wind brace. The south wall of the church incorporates a blocked doorway to the cloister with segmental head and remains of a fifteenth century lancet window. The only other survival from the church is a short stretch of the north wall, although this is in a precarious condition. In the place where the altar once stood is a modern memorial stone to the Beauvale Martyrs. The founder's tomb was not used, as Sir Nicholas was buried in Lincoln Cathedral. The boundary wall, running northwards from the gatehouse is up to 2.45m (8ft) high in places and incorporates a postern gate, and putlog holes, indicating that other priory buildings once abutted the wall. The cloister area is now an orchard, and nothing is visible above ground of the chapter house and refectory.

Photos – clockwise from top left

Surviving north and south walls of priory church
Memorial stone to Beauvale Martyrs
The well preserved prior's house
Arched doorways from prior's house and church into cloister
Remains of gatehouse
Lancet window in the south wall of the church

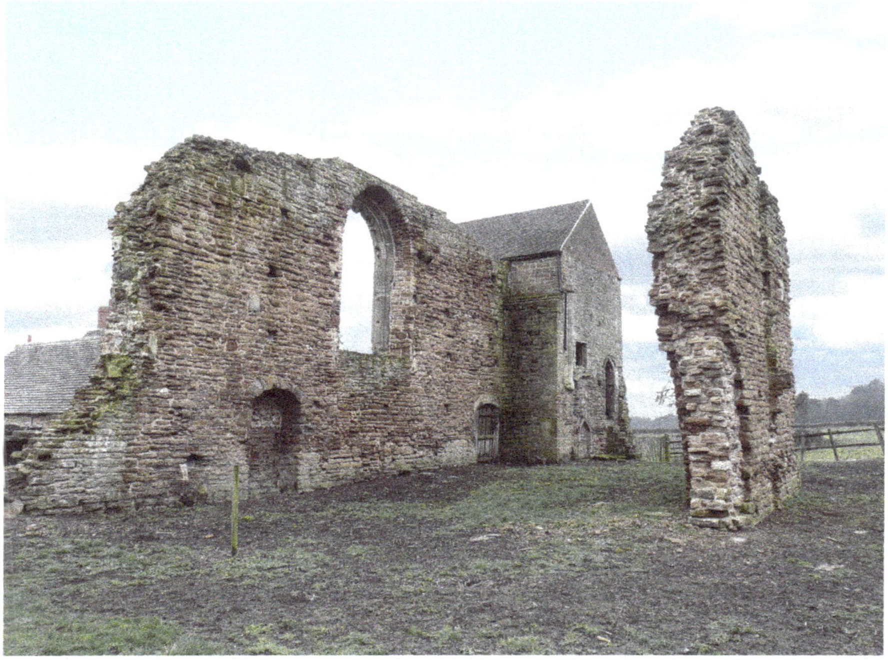

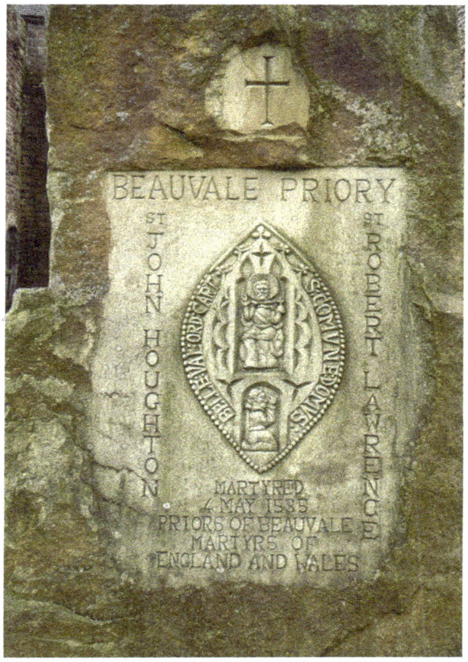
BEAUVALE PRIORY
ST JOHN HOUGHTON
ST ROBERT LAWRENCE
MARTYRED
4 MAY 1535
PRIORS OF BEAUVALE
MARTYRS OF
ENGLAND AND WALES

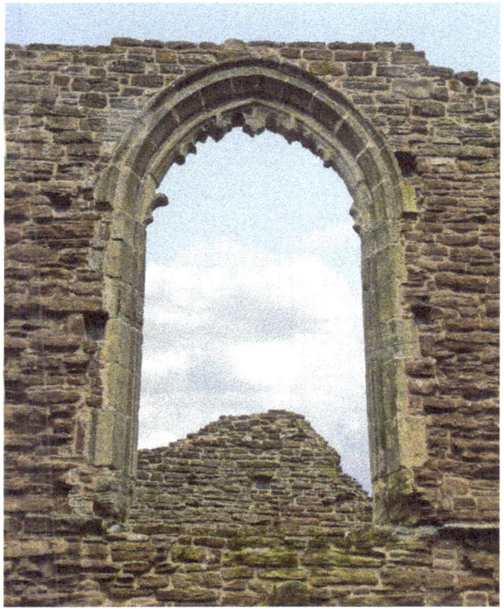

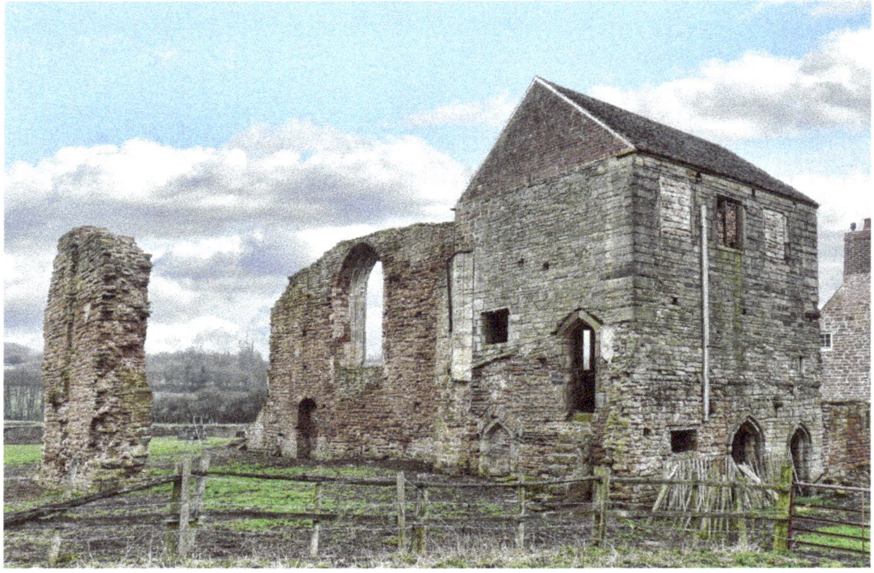

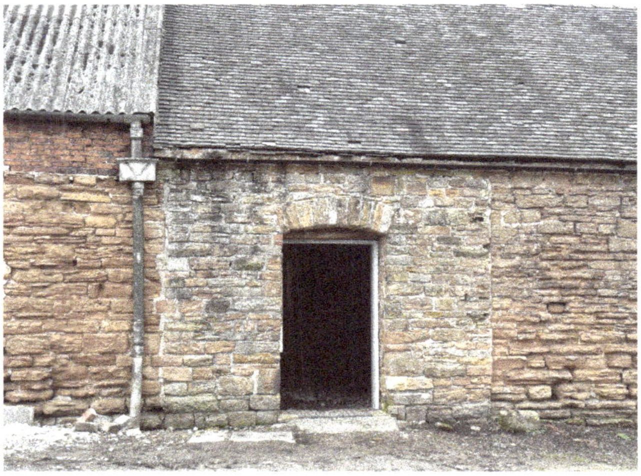

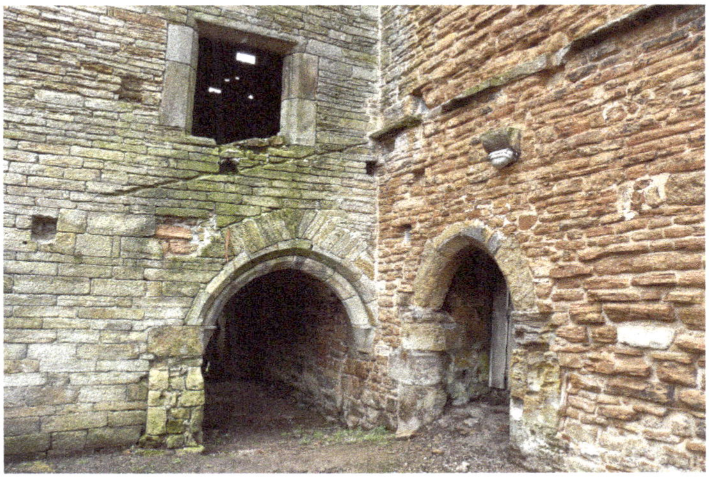

Blyth Priory

St. Mary • Benedictine 1087–1536

Roger de Busli, a generous benefactor to the Benedictine abbey of La-Trinité-du-Mont near Rouen, and his wife Muriel gave the Saxon church at Blyth for the foundation of a priory dependent on the Norman abbey. The date was most likely 1087, as no mention of it is made in the Domesday Survey of the previous year, but the deed of the founders implies that it took place before the death of William I. It was the first monastic foundation in Nottinghamshire. Roger's large holdings in England in 1086 included the manor of Tickhill, where he built his castle, and more than 230 other manors in five counties, principally in Nottinghamshire and Yorkshire. The prior was granted the manorial rights of the village, together with tolls from a market and fair. Roger may also have established a jousting site between the priory and his castle, and one of the duties of his priory may have been to tend to the injured knights. Building work began on a substantial scale almost immediately, but the only survival from the priory today is the nave of the original priory church, which retains its austere Norman appearance so aptly described by Pevsner who wrote "there is nothing like Blyth to get a feeling for early Norman grimness". Indeed, the construction is rather crude and a simple scroll and the occasional monster's head are the only remaining decorations on the capitals, yet this very simplicity has a powerful resonance of the asceticism of early monastic houses. Of interest is the lack of symmetry and slight variations at the bases and of opposing columns, which has been attributed to a merging of Anglo-Saxon and Norman style of architecture.

The visitor must look beyond the nave arcade to the east wall, which was inserted by the crossing at the beginning of the fifteenth century to separate the priory from the parish, where the Last Judgment is one of the largest and most complete medieval murals in the country. It served not only to decorate the hastily erected wall, but also as a teaching aid for parishioners who could not read. The painting, which had been plastered over after the Dissolution, was rediscovered and cleaned in 1985. Unsurprisingly, the mural has faded somewhat and it requires careful study to understand its features. These include a red-haired Christ at the top, sitting on a rainbow, angels with flowing wings on each side and haloed apostles below. In the centre, the dead rise from coffins, all naked with the exception of the King who wears a crown. The King's coffin is decorated, but all others are plain. The work is unsophisticated and, as suggested in the guide, may have been carried out by travelling artists. The fifteenth century screen in the south aisle is painted with figures of saints, including, from the left, St Stephen, St Agatha, St Edmund, St Helena, St Barbara and St Ursula. There are several green men to be discovered, including one in wood high up on the cross beam in the south aisle. Of the chapter house and refectory grouped around the cloister to the north, nothing has survived.

The priory had a chequered history, which was not helped by the fact that the priors were Frenchmen appointed by the mother house and, reputedly, were sent to Blyth as a form of punishment. The cold and wet climate also was not appreciated and it was suggested that five years should be the limit of their stay. Laxity in the observance of the religious rules also added to the general disorder. Henry I and II probably stayed at the priory during visits to Blyth, and the latter monarch bestowed the Honour of Blyth upon Ranulph de Blundeville, sixth Earl of Chester, after the de Busli line had died out. The prior had the right to hang on the gallows at Emmeslowe (now Blyth Law Hill) robbers arrested within the liberty of Blyth, but this probably never took place. In 1274, the prior was found to have built a dyke, which for four years had rendered the highway impassable after heavy rain. The priory became involved in several court cases over tolls, tithes and other privileges.

As Blyth was at a major crossroads connecting Newark with York, the community incurred heavy hospitality costs, which, following a visit by Edward II in the fourteenth century, brought the house to the brink of ruin. In1278, the priory was partially destroyed by fire, and Edward I made grants of 'oaks fit for timber' from Sherwood Forest towards its repair. As an alien priory it was seized by the Crown at various times during the wars with France, and the prior became one of the victims of the Black Death in 1349. After the priory became denizen in 1409, its history was unremarkable until it was surrendered by the last prior, George Dalton, in 1536, when its declared annual value was £180. It was granted to Sir Gervase Clifton in July 1538. The church owes its survival to the widening of the south aisle of the nave for parochial use, which now comprises five of the original seven-bay nave, and the west tower of c1400. The crossing, transepts and chancel, which had three apses, were demolished.

Photos – clockwise from top

Blyth Priory Church dating back to Norman times
Early fifteenth century mural of Last Judgement
A red-haired Christ sitting on a rainbow
Unusual double-head sculpture thought to be of the founder and his wife
Crude carving of head on column capital
Wooden carving of the Green Man, high up on the cross beam in the south aisle

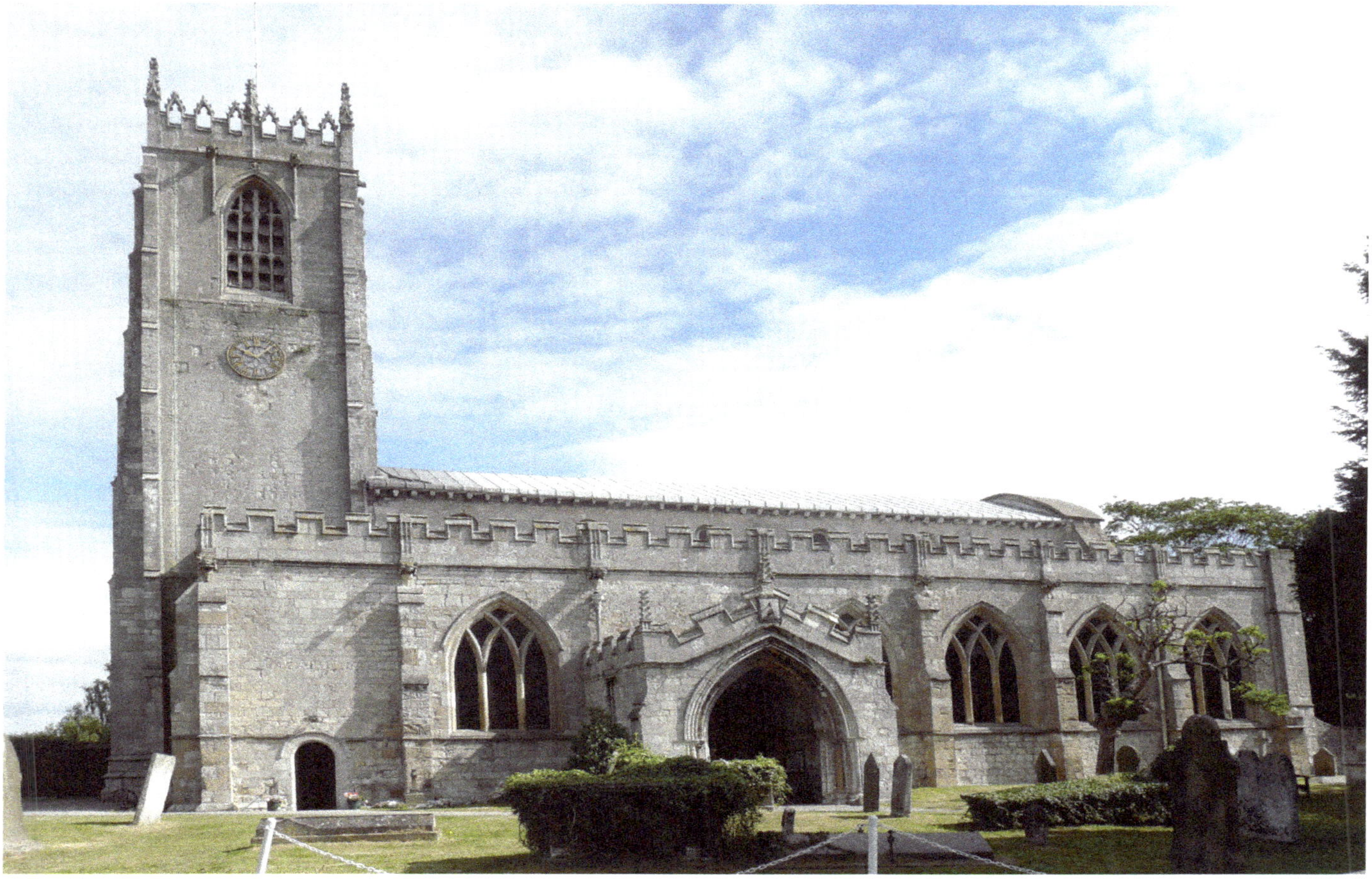

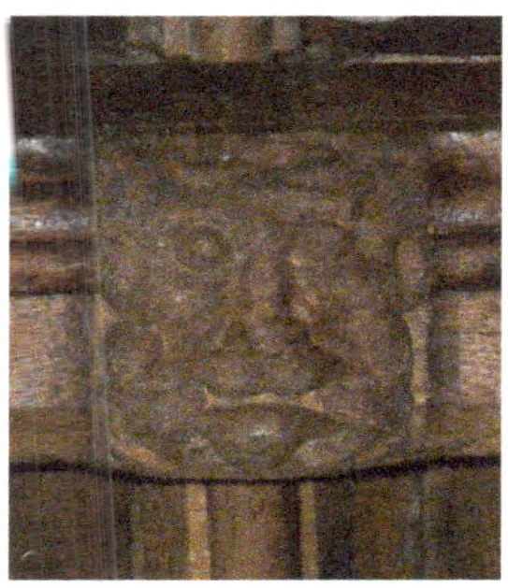

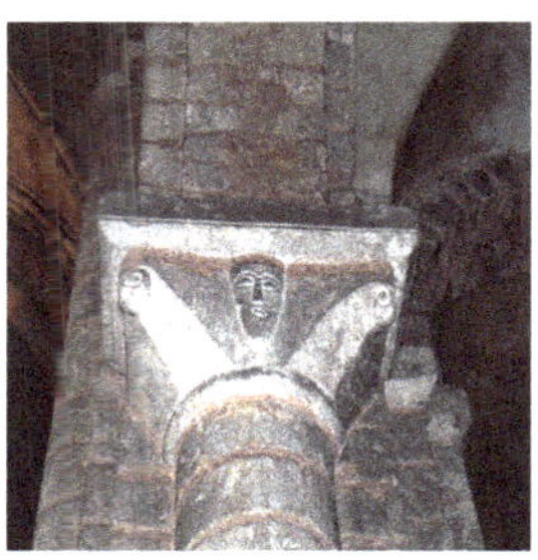

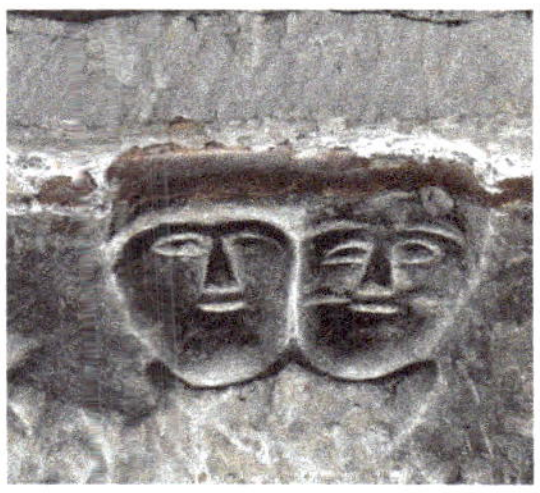

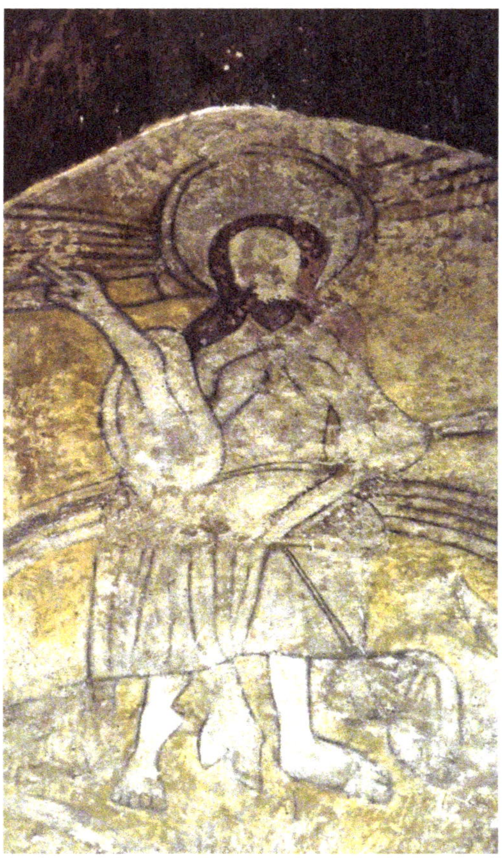

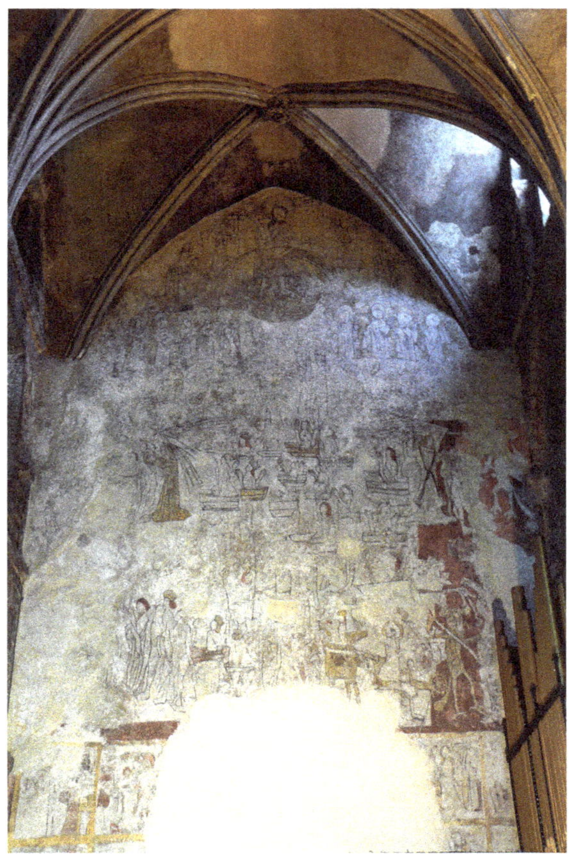

Broadholme Priory

St Mary • Premonstratensian canonesses 1135/54–1536

This small and remote Premonstratensian house on the border with Lincolnshire, one of only two nunneries of the Order in England, had an uncertain beginning. According to Leland, it was founded in the latter part of the reign of King Stephen (1135-1154) by Agnes de Camville, wife of Peter de Gousley, founder of Newsham Abbey, and a confirmation charter by Edward II appears to suggest that it was originally a house for both sexes with close connections to Newsham. By 1319, it contained only canonesses. The community's possessions included lands, pastures, meadows, a mill and rents in Nottinghamshire and Lincolnshire, with the d'Aubigny family being generous benefactors, as was Queen Isabella who provided land and rents in Norfolk. The peace and serenity of the nuns was disturbed twice in the fourteenth century. In 1349-50, a nun, Margaret Everingham of Laxton, was forcibly abducted, stripped of her habit, clothed in a green gown, and relieved of goods to the value of forty shillings. The leader of the abductors was the Reverend William Fox, vicar of Lea near Gainsborough, assisted in his nefarious project by two Franciscan friars. In 1383, a body of men attacked the priory, besieged the prioress and her canonesses and threatened them with death. They then broke into the priory and dragged out a married woman named Isabella de Kent whom they found crouching in the belfry. In both instances, the outcome has not been recorded.

In 1534, the net annual value was only £16 5s, which was barely enough to sustain the nine or so canonesses then left. The priory was duly suppressed with the lesser monasteries in 1536 and the last prioress, Joan Angevin, received a pension. In 1537 the site and buildings were alienated by the Crown to Randolf Jackson, Chester Herald, and nothing now remains except some worked stones in a neighbouring farmhouse and traces of the fishpond.

Felley Priory

St Mary • Augustinian 1156–1536

The magnificent house that stands on the site of the priory incorporates some worked masonry in the central part and has a tombstone of one of the priors in an upstairs room. But this is strictly private and can be admired from the outside only, its setting being particularly pretty in late winter when an abundance of snowdrops paints the lawn at the front in brilliant white. The seeker of evidence from medieval times should not despair, however, and head for the lovely gardens, where four solid pillars with carved capitals flank the entrance gates and a stretch of garden wall incorporates an aumbry and a trough. Other carved stones surrounding a stone coffin make a feature near the pond, and a statue of a scholar or bishop reading a book tucked away in a corner may also date from the time of the priory.

Alas, none are *in situ* but are the only reminders of this small priory for five or six Augustinian canons founded in 1156 by Ralph de Brito of Annesley. The founder endowed the priory with the church and hermitage of Felley, but as the church had apparently already been given to Worksop Priory in 1151, Felley Priory became subject to Worksop. It remained so until 1260, when the prior of Worksop agreed to Felley's independence upon an annual payment of twenty shillings. The agreement for this release was witnessed by the Archbishop of York and six abbots and priors. That there remained at least cordial relations in spite of the odd dispute, can be seen by the fact that two priors of Felley became priors of Worksop. The priory's possessions also included the church of Annesley, a mill, and several parcels of land in Nottinghamshire and Derbyshire, which provided a reasonable income, although a visitation by Archbishop Giffard in 1276 found that wastage of resources had led to the house becoming dilapidated, and that some canons had become involved in theft and immorality. The prior was deposed for mismanagement. A long-standing dispute with Henry, Lord Grey of Codnor, over the ownership of Attenborough Church was the only other major incident that diverted attention away from the normal life of the community. The prior died of the Black Death in 1349, but may not have been the only victim within the priory and the locality.

When the infamous royal commissioners, Legh and London, visited in 1536, the house was valued at £40 19s, leading to its immediate closure. The last prior, Christopher Bolton, received a pension and was appointed to the living at Attenborough. The possessions of the priory, including a watermill, passed to William Bolles, but must have reverted to the Crown soon afterwards, as Queen Mary sold it in 1551 to Sir Anthony Strelley.

Photos of Felley Priory - clockwise from top

Central part of house incorporating medieval worked stone
Statue of bishop or scholar with book
Decorated column capital
Solid pillars at the entrance to the gardens
Much weathered carving believed to be of a lion and unicorn
Stone arch of window set into garden wall

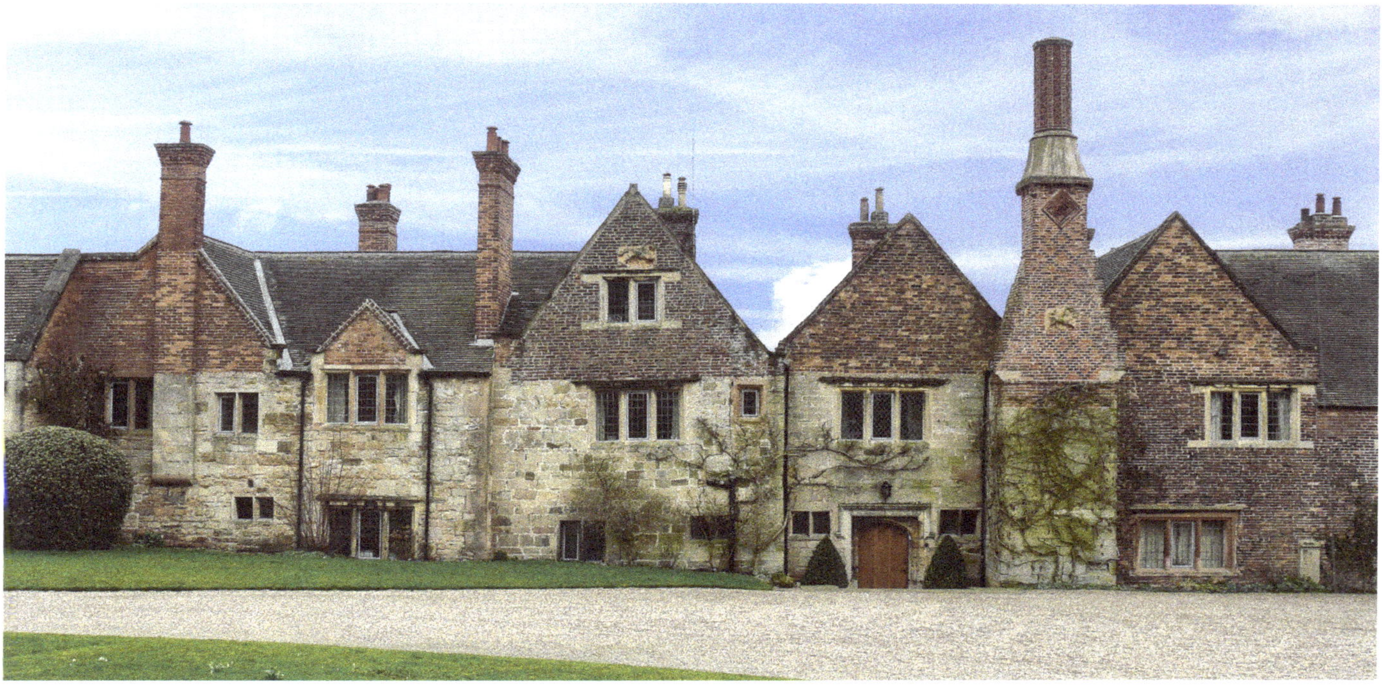

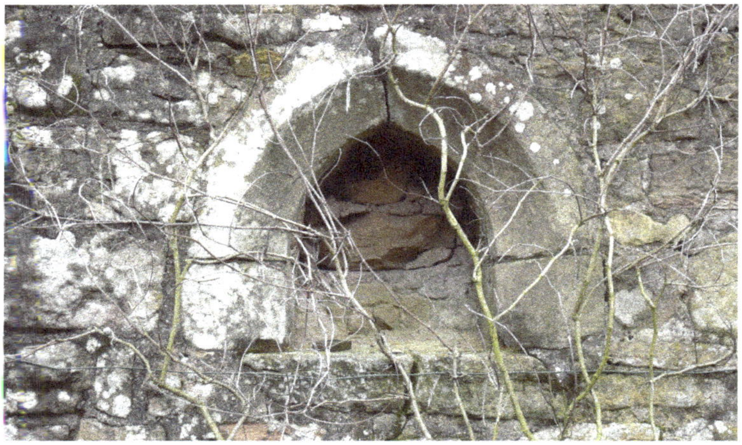

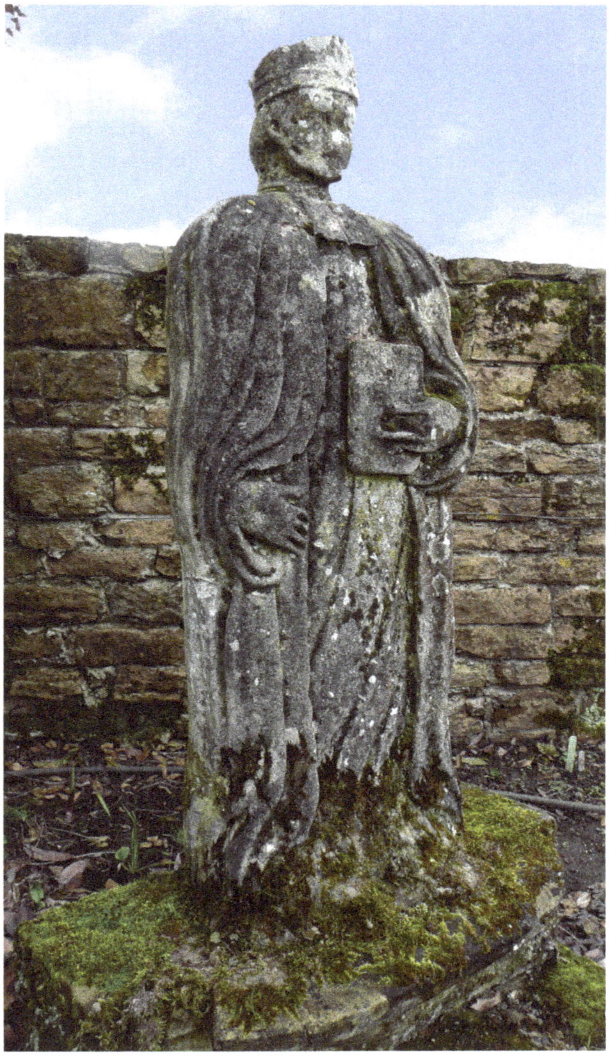

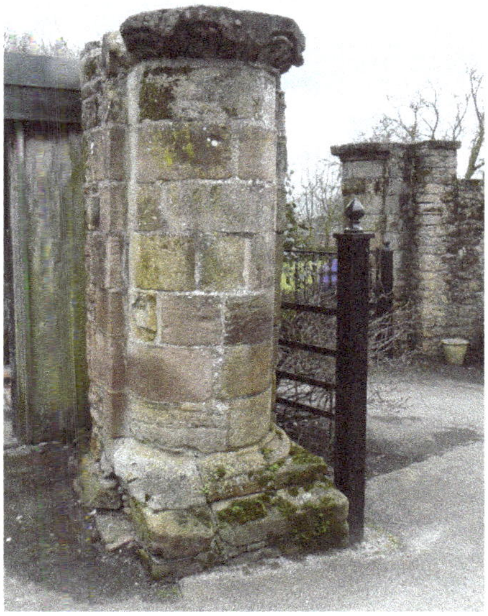

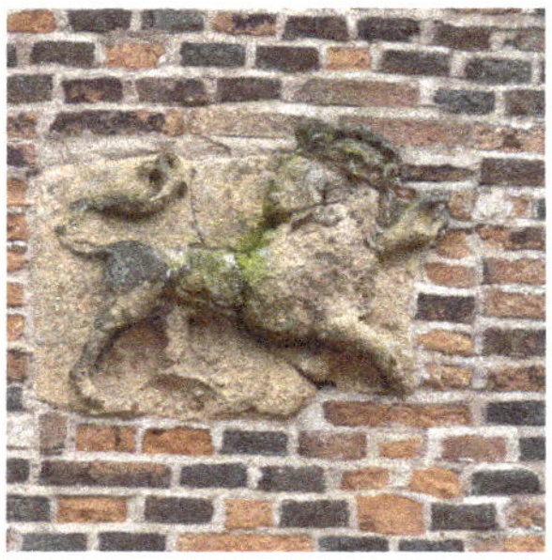

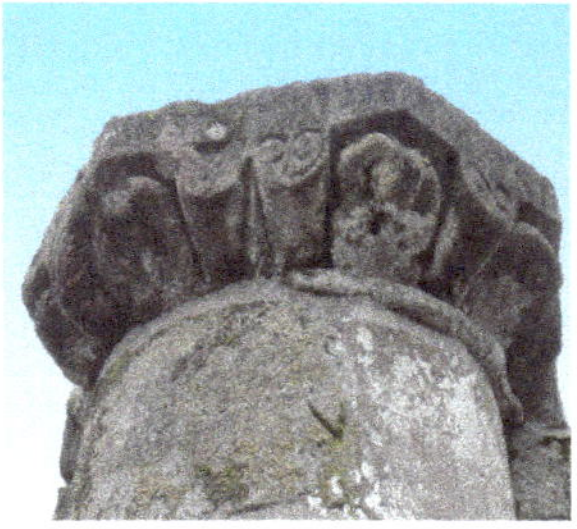

Lenton Priory

Holy Trinity • Cluniac c1109–1538

The Alien Priory of the Holy Trinity on the western outskirts of Nottingham was the sole Cluniac monastery in the county, but also had the distinction of being the most powerful and wealthiest in Nottinghamshire. It is, therefore, rather disappointing that so little has survived. Two column bases excavated in 1936, some masonry built into the nineteenth century church in Gregory Street, and a rather splendid font, now in Lenton parish church, are the only items that are left to recall its former glory. It was founded c1109 by William Peverel who provided rich endowments, which, together with those of other benefactors, ensured a high annual income. Among other privileges enjoyed was the right to hold an annual twelve-day fair at which a toll was levied by the monks on most goods sold, and the right to the first catch of fish at Chilwell. The monks also benefited from a right to have complaints against the priory heard by the King himself or his Chief Justice.

The normal existence of the community was disrupted from time to time by some extraordinary events. In 1263, William, son of Nicholas de Cantilupe of Greasley Castle, was born in the priory, when William's mother was most likely accommodated at the priory while the Cantilupe home was being rebuilt. The monks gained a reputation for being litigious, with one dispute with the Chapter of Lichfield dragging on for three hundred years and, in 1250, resulting in bloodshed in Tideswell Church, when the rector's proctor was killed during a brawl in 1263. The priory and its lands were seized from time to time during the wars with France, but it became denizen in 1392 after paying a large sum to the Crown. Four Kings visited Lenton Priory including Henry III in 1230, Edward I in 1302 and 1303, Edward II in 1307 and 1323, and Edward III in 1336 and on several other occasions. In 1415, Prior Thomas Elham, who was supervisor of all Cluniac houses in Britain and a royal chaplain, was present with King Henry V at the Battle of Agincourt in 1415. The last prior, Nicholas Heath, eight monks and four labourers were charged with high treason in 1536, and he and two of the monks, as well as the labourers, were executed in March1538. The priory site and adjacent lands thereafter changed hands frequently, contributing to its almost total destruction.

Lenton White Friars

According to Tanner, a Carmelite house was supposed to have existed at Lenton, but it is doubtful if it was established.

Mattersey Priory

St Helen • Gilbertine 1185–1538

There is very little left of this small and compact Gilbertine priory, and for much of the long approach over mostly rough farm tracks, it appears to hide away behind the rolling country. It comes as almost a surprise when the grey ruins come into view behind a low wall, adjacent to Abbey Farm. Its location was well chosen amid fertile lands stretching towards the distant hills with good access to the nearby river. The most substantial and interesting remains are those of the thirteenth century, twin-aisled refectory and its undercroft, where parts of the window wall remain intact. There are also fragments of walls and the west entrance of the church, but the cloister walks have been almost completely robbed of stone. An oven can be discerned in the north-west angle of the kitchen, probably flanking a large fireplace in the west wall. Some low masonry in the east indicates the location of the canon's dormitory. A fifteenth century tall remnant of a tower overlaps part of the north wall of the nave. At the north end of the east range, where the chapter house would normally have been, are two curiously positioned altars, suggesting that this area served as the church until rebuilding could begin after a devastating fire. The ditch under the reredorter, where water from the River Idle would have flowed, is still extant.

The priory was founded in 1185 by Roger fitzRanulph de Maresay, who endowed it with property in the immediate vicinity and built a single-aisle church dedicated to St Helen. Religious life began with a small group of six regular canons who followed the Order of the Gilbertines, the only entirely English Order. With the help of ten lay-brothers who worked as labourers in the fields, the priory had a reasonably comfortable existence, and the prior became a man of some importance. However, a fire in 1279 destroyed the priory buildings and documents, and, in spite of being granted the income of Mattersey Parish Church in 1280, the priory never really recovered. A generous bequest by a descendant of de Maresay, Isabell de Chauncey, to the priory, provided some relief from the financial burden of re-building the priory, but it was probably not enough to complete the work. Financial deprivation also meant that the priory eventually had to let the lay-brothers go. In 1403, Henry IV granted the canons a weekly fair in the village to raise money from selling produce, and three years later, the pope granted an indulgence, but the struggle continued. The priory survived the initial suppression of the smaller monasteries, but in October1538, Prior Thomas Woodcock and four canons signed the Deed of Surrender. Mattersey Priory was valued at just over £55 2s, and was granted to Anthony Nevill.

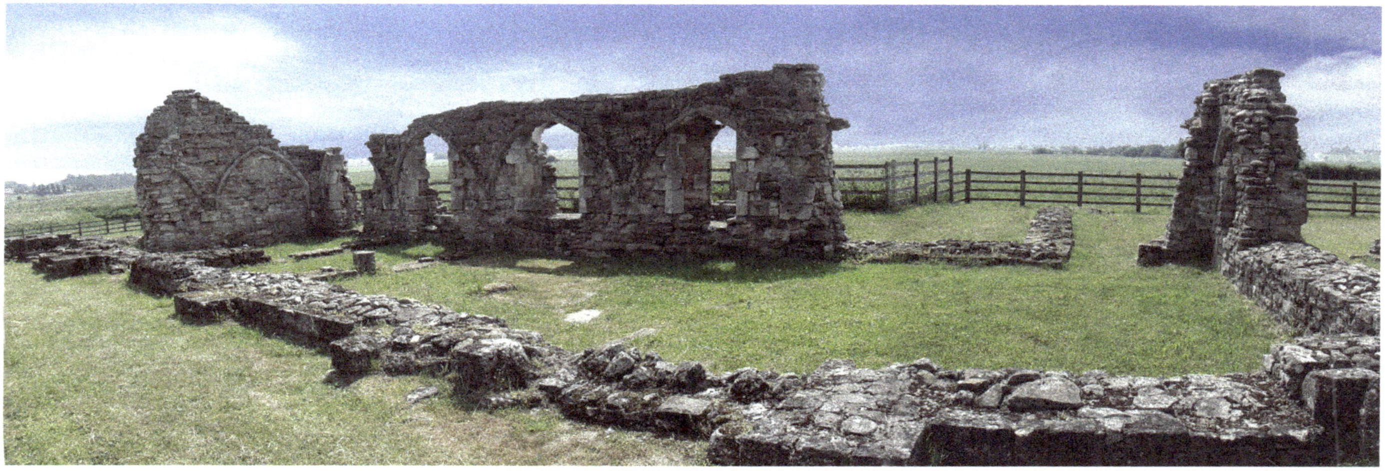

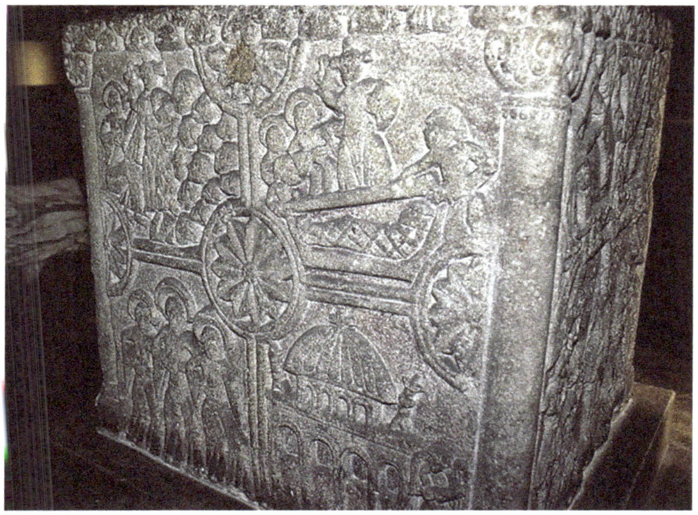

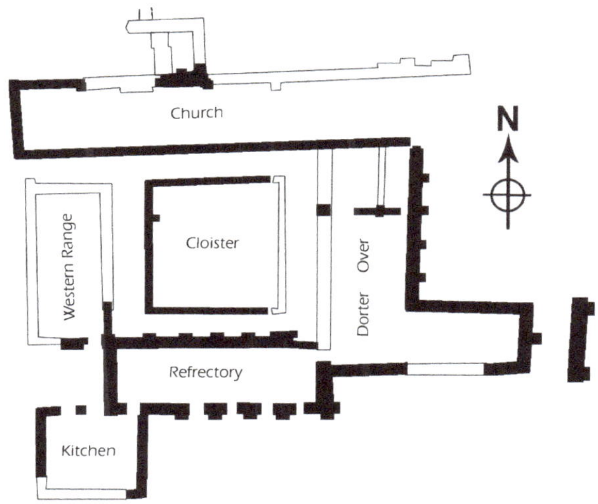

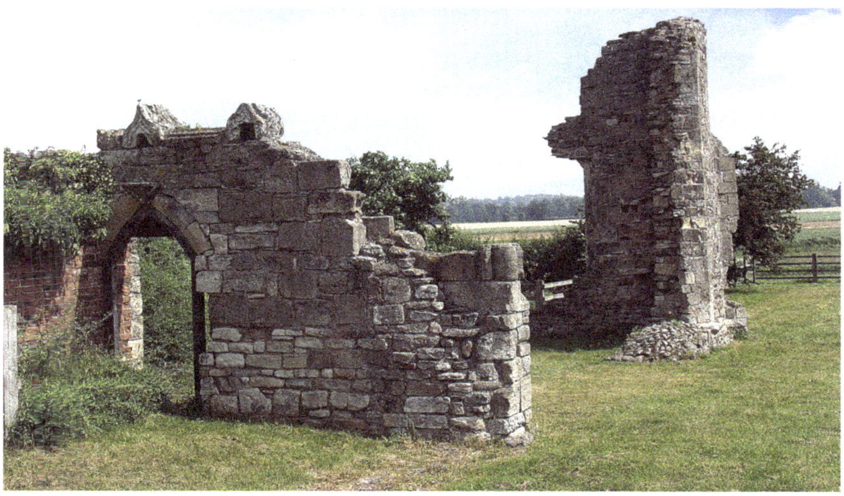

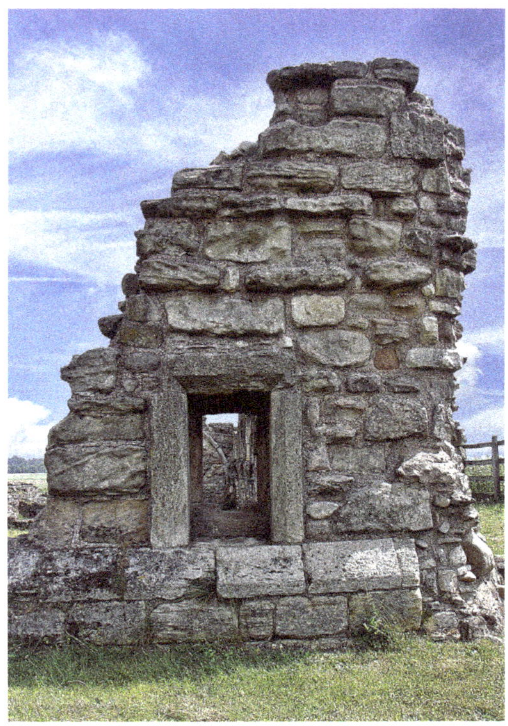

Photos – clockwise from top

View of twin-aisled refectory of Mattersey Priory
Layout of Mattersey Priory showing standing walls
Serving hatch from kitchen
Sparse surviving elements of church including nave and tower
Splendic font from Lenton Priory now in the parish church

Newark Austin Friars

1534–1539

When the Observant Franciscan friars were evicted in 1534, Augustinian friars occupied the house, but nothing has been recorded of their brief existence in the town. Richard Ingworth, Bishop of Dover, wrote to Thomas Cromwell in March 1539 that he had received 'to the king's use' twelve poor houses of friars, one of which was that at Newark. In July 1543, Richard Andrewes of Gloucestershire and Nicholas Temple were granted much monastic property in the Midlands, including the site, churchyard and gardens of the Augustinian house at Newark. A house known as The Friary in Appleton Gate stands on the site and may incorporate some medieval masonry.

Newark Grey (Observant) Friars

c1499–1534

This reformed and stricter branch of the Franciscans settled in Newark around 1499, at a time when Henry VII became a special patron and in a codicil to his will in 1509 left the considerable sum of £200 to the convent 'that by his succour and aid was newly begun in the town of Newark'. Nothing is known about its income or about the number of friars, but it was a small house, which ceased to exist when the Order was suppressed in 1534 and the friars evicted. The site was then apparently taken over by Augustinian friars.

Newstead Priory

St Mary • Augustinian c1170–1539

The former Augustinan priory of St Mary of Newstead (De Loco Novo) is now called Newstead Abbey and is best known as the ancestral home of the romantic poet Lord Byron. On approach to the lodge gates, the visitor should stop briefly to look at and touch the well-known Pilgrim's Oak, which was first planted in medieval times and whose trunk of enormous girth and still virile foliage reminds of days when the Austin canons were still at Newstead. The long drive through the extensive parkland dotted with mature trees heightens the anticipation of setting eyes on the priory buildings, which do not disappoint. Of the priory church, all that remains is the exceptionally beautiful west front of 1274, whose graceful shape is outlined against the sky. This retains fine tracery and carved panels of birds, animals and foliage, crowned by a statue of the Blessed Virgin and Child, a sceptre held in her right hand to indicate her place as the Queen of Heaven. Her smiling presence has been immortalised by Byron with the words: *But in a higher niche, alone, but crown'd, The Virgin Mother of the God-born Child, With her Son in her blessed arms, look'd round, Spared by some chance when all beside was spoil'd.* All beside her were the statues of twelve saints, which were destroyed during the Civil War. The great west window has lost its tracery, but still gives a hint of the original design, while below it, the double doorway has survived in a good state, although the doors themselves have long since disappeared. The front is largely symmetrical, even though there was no south aisle, but curiously, a row of small windows above the west window is offset from the centre.

Many of the claustral buildings, including the south transept of the church, chapter house, warming room, refectory, kitchen and prior's lodging survive intact in the adjoining mansion, which has been transformed into a museum. Little of the monastic origins can be discerned externally, but much is visible from within the house and cloister. Of particular note is the chapter house, which has been used as a chapel since Byron's days.

The priory in Sherwood Forest was founded c1170 by Henry II. The foundation charter, which conferred upon the community a site near the centre of the forest, the church and mill at Papplewick, meadows, rents and other lands in Nottinghamshire, was witnessed by Geoffrey, Archdeacon of Canterbury, in 1174. King John confirmed the grants in 1206 and added gifts of his own. In spite of many further bequests, the priory found itself heavily in debt by 1274, a situation that was eased temporarily in 1279, when the prior obtained leave to sell timber. But the community failed to extricate itself from poverty, a position that was not helped by expenses incurred through extension and re-building, and from frequent royal visits from the hunting lodge in nearby Clipston. Edward I visited in 1280 and 1290, followed by Edward II in 1307 and again in 1315. Its financial difficulties persisted when Edward III came to the throne, but thereafter, additional grants and gifts later assisted a partial recovery and enabled the construction of a prior's lodging, great hall and new dormitory in the fifteenth century.

On a visitation in 1252, Archbishop Gray found the prior and canons 'fervid in religion and lovers of peace and concord', but only seven years later, Archbishop Geoffrey de Ludham issued injunctions to the prior,whom he compelled, considering the evil days in which they were living, to do his best to obtain grace and favour with patrons, and to receive guests with a smiling countenance. In this and subsequent visitations, the community was urged to observe the rules, many of which appear to have been ignored, including silence in the church, cloister, dormitory and refectory and the selling of corrodies. Infirm canons were to be better fed and the presence of seculars within the abbey was also to be discouraged. Very little is known of internal life from the late fourteenth century to the Dissolution. By the time of the *Valor* of

1535, the clear annual value of the priory was assessed at £167 16s, which brought it within the Act of Suppression of the minor houses in 1536. However, upon payment of a hefty fine to the Crown of £233 6s, a sum the community could ill afford, the prior managed to stave off the closure of the house for a few more years. The King's commissioner, Dr London, accepted the surrender from Prior John Blake and eleven canons in July 1539 and custody of the house was immediately handed over to Sir John Byron of Colwick, ancestor of the poet, who converted the priory into a family home.

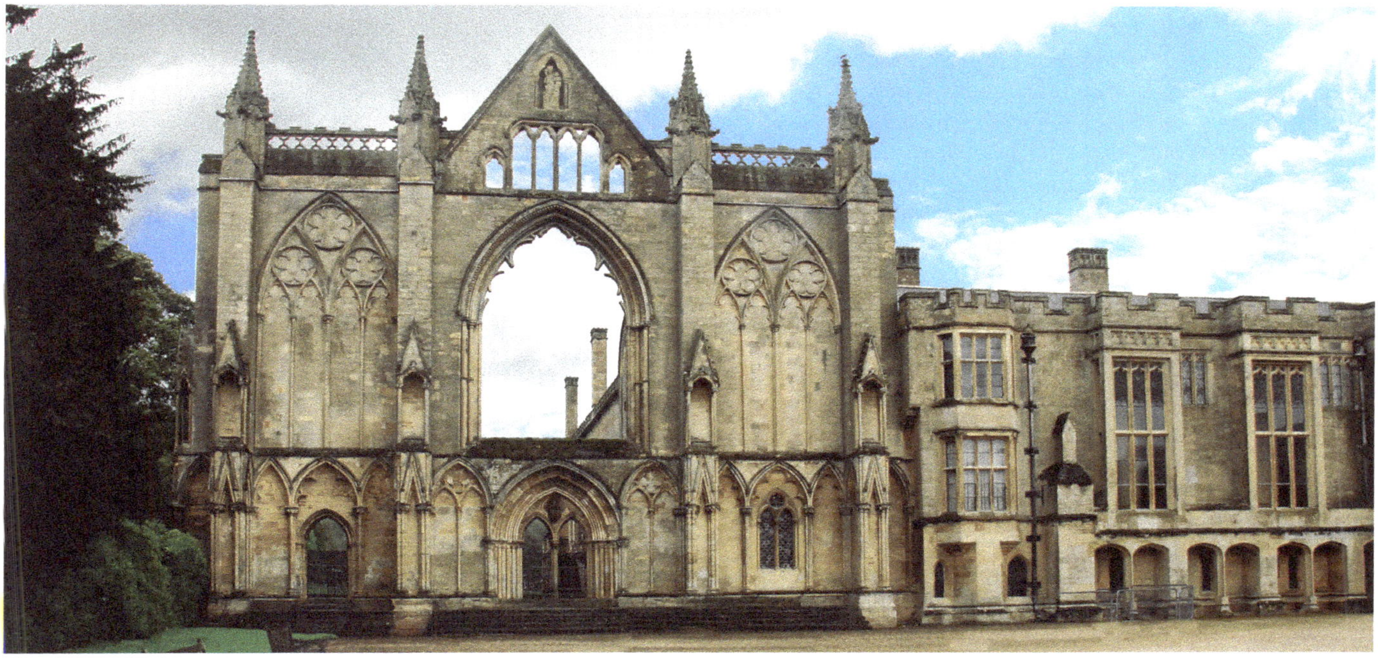

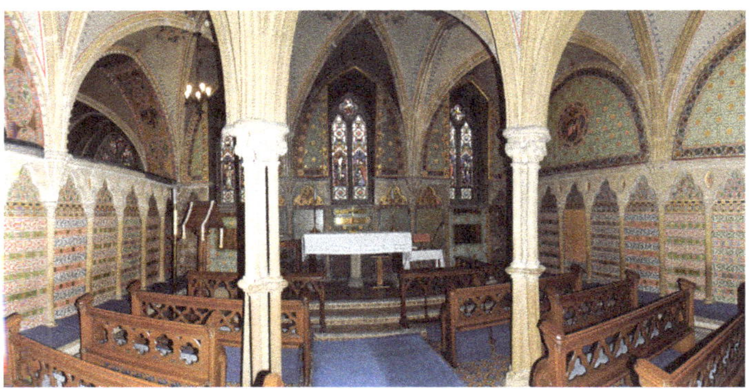

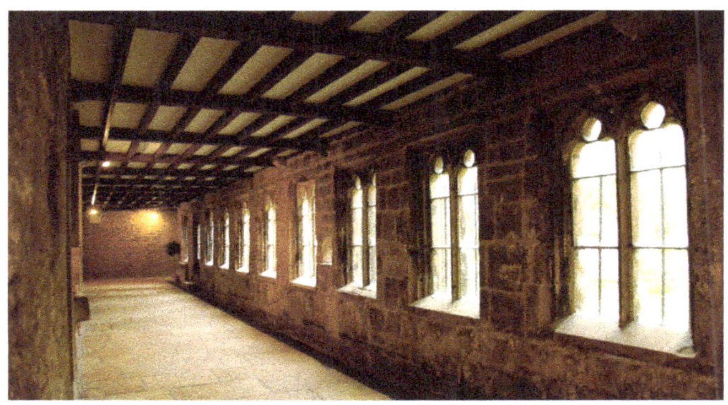

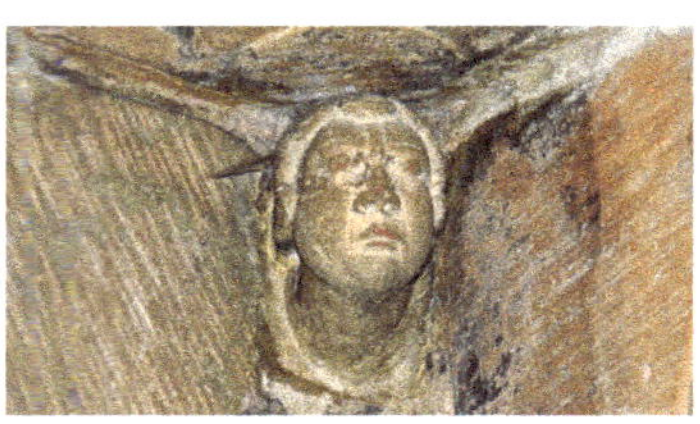

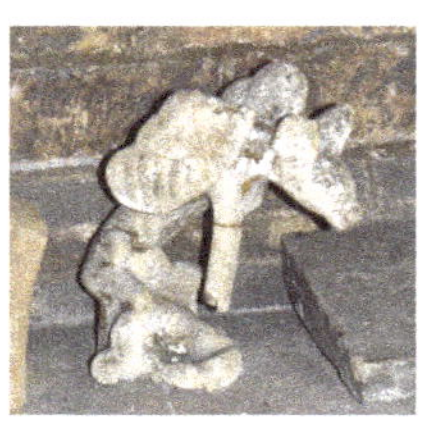

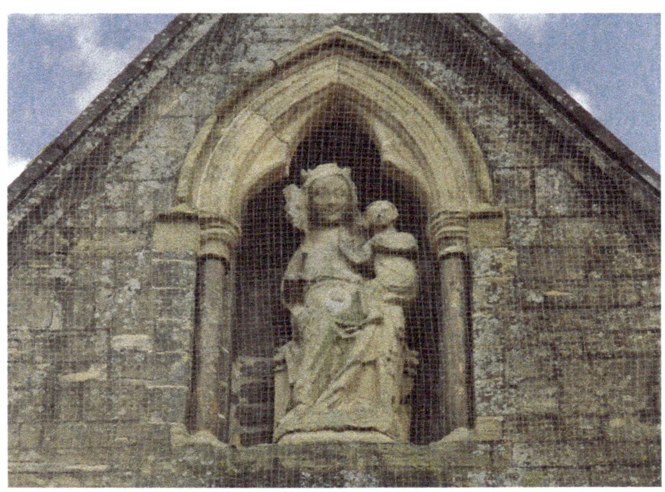

Photos of Newstead Priory - clockwise from top

Magnificent west front of the priory church
Remodelled cloister arcade
Statue of the Virgin and Child
Carving of winged animal
Carved face with traces of paint
Former chapter house, now serving as chapel

Nottingham Grey Friars

+1224–1539

The exact date of the foundation of the house of Franciscan friars in Nottingham is not known, but is likely to have occurred soon after the arrival of the Order in England in 1224. The first mention dates to 1230, when Henry III is recorded as having granted the friars twenty tie-beams for the construction of their chapel. Over the next forty years, further grants of timber were made for the construction of the chapter house, dormitory and infirmary, as well as for a quay on the river. The friars also obtained a licence to take stone from Nottingham quarry to rebuild their church in stone. The warden was ordered in 1291 to supply friars to preach on the Crusades. In 1303, permission was granted to build an underground conduit from a spring in Atherwell to their house within the town. Several felons sought sanctuary in the church, and in the reign of Henry IV, one friar was hanged at Tyburn in 1402 for preaching that Richard II was still alive, but otherwise, life for the community appears to have been unremarkable. The last warden, Thomas Basford, and seven friars surrendered the house to the King's commissioner, Dr London, in February 1539. In 1548, the site was granted to Thomas Heneage. Regrettably nothing is left of this priory, which stood in the south-west corner of Broad Marsh, but Grey Friars Gate provides a reminder. This stands on the site of the Grey Friars Cross, first mentioned in 1359 and demolished in 1571.

Nottingham Priory

Holy Sepulchre

Augustinian canons founded a hospital c1170, but whether a conventual establishment existed alongside remains unproven. The Order of the Holy Sepulchre lapsed in 1188, but the hospital continued, at least until 1307, the date of the last record. Nothing else is known.

Nottingham (Roche) Priory

St Mary • Cluniac -1409–?

What limited knowledge exists of this Cluniac house is confusing. The earliest record dates from a visitation in 1405, which noted that this establishment was a cell to Lenton Priory and consisted of a prior and one monk. Yet, the *Archives de la France Monastique* give the name as Rockchapel, and records it as dependent on Montacute Priory in Somerset. Not surprisingly, there are no remains.

Nottingham White Friars

c1272–1539

Nothing at all is left of the house of Carmelites in Nottingham, which stood between Moothall Gate and St James's Lane. Its beginnings are somewhat uncertain, but it is reputed to have been founded c1272 by Reginald, Lord Grey of Wilton, and Sir John Sturley, although it has also been said that the friars were present in Nottingham before that date. Its early history is sparse, but numerous small bequests of parcels of land and tenements attest to the high esteem the Carmelites enjoyed in the town. Two friars, both natives of Nottingham, achieved distinction in the fourteenth century as poets and orators. In later times, the peaceful existence of the community was disturbed on several occasions. In 1393, a certain Henry de Whalley, having killed his wife, fled to the priory church for sanctuary, and as he could not be taken, the town seized his goods. Towards the end of the fifteenth century, the priory twice suffered forced entry by local vandals, resulting in some damage and theft. The prior was himself later accused by a mason for insufficient payment for work carried out on the east window of the church. Henry VIII visited Nottingham in 1511 and made an offering at the Rood of the White Friars. In 1532, Prior Richard Sherwood obtained a pardon from the King for having killed a friar during a drunken quarrel. When the priory was surrendered in February 1539, only the prior, Roger Cappe, and six friars were in residence. In November 1541, the Crown granted the priory and its gardens and land to John Sturley, probably a descendant of the joint founder of the same name.

Rufford Abbey

St Mary • Cistercian 1146–1536

The seventeenth century and later mansion incorporates the best-preserved remains of a west cloister range of a Cistercian abbey in England, dating mainly from around 1170. The largely ruined house now forms a picturesque entrance to a large and popular country park with its lake, woodlands and gardens on the edge of Sherwood Forest. The principal survival from the abbey is the cellarium, whose vaults are supported on three circular piers, the outer parlour and lay-brothers' refectory with traces of the day-stair, and a medieval wall, suggested to have been part of the west wall of the church. All other monastic buildings are covered by the east lawn. Surviving relics include a narrow oak table, which runs the whole length of the hall, together with the benches used by the monks at mealtimes, and a tombstone in the chapel aisle bearing the Latin inscription 'Robert Markham a monk of this house who died in 1309'. Of interest within the abbey precinct are faint traces of ridge and furrow cultivation, believed to relate to the medieval villages, which were abandoned to make way for the abbey.

The abbey was founded by Gilbert de Gant, later Earl of Lincoln, in 1146 and populated with Cistercian monks from Rievaulx Abbey in the North Riding of Yorkshire. The first community comprised Abbot Gamelius and the traditional twelve monks. The English Pope, Adrian IV, gave his blessing to the new foundation in 1156. The clearance of land for the building of the abbey involved the flattening of the villages of Cratley, Rufford, Grimston and Inkersall and the relocation of the villagers in neighbouring settlements. The villagers were well compensated by the founder for their forced upheaval. With a large number of generous endowments, the abbey became prosperous and by 1285, had acquired most of the town of Rotherham, including 'five mills under one roof'. It also owned twenty-one granges and pasture for more than 1,300 sheep. Between 1262 and 1287, 7,000 oaks and 1,000 saplings were felled to clear the land for farming.

Little has been recorded of its history, which was largely without incident and life within the community appears to have been orderly and unremarkable. The monks held a weekly market and fair and as the abbey was situated within Sherwood Forest, the community had the right to cut and sell timber from the forest. The only notable events occurred in 1290, when Edward I and Queen Eleanor visited Rufford just before her death, and in 1359, when Abbot Robert de Mapelbek was charged with overzealous felling and laying waste an entire wood of nearly 60 acres! Although the abbey's net income in 1535 had been assessed at £254 6s, it was surrendered to the King's commissioners, Legh and Layton, in the first wave of the Dissolution of the lesser monasteries in 1536, following trumped up charges against the abbot, Thomas of Doncaster, and several monks. In addition to the abbot, there were about fifteen monks and several paid servants. The abbey church was demolished but most of the other buildings and its lands were slowly transformed into an impressive country house estate, owned first by the Talbots and later the Savile families. One of the most famous owners was the Elizabethan aristocrat George Talbot, sixth Earl of Shrewsbury, whose wife 'Bess of Hardwick' later built Hardwick Hall in Derbyshire.

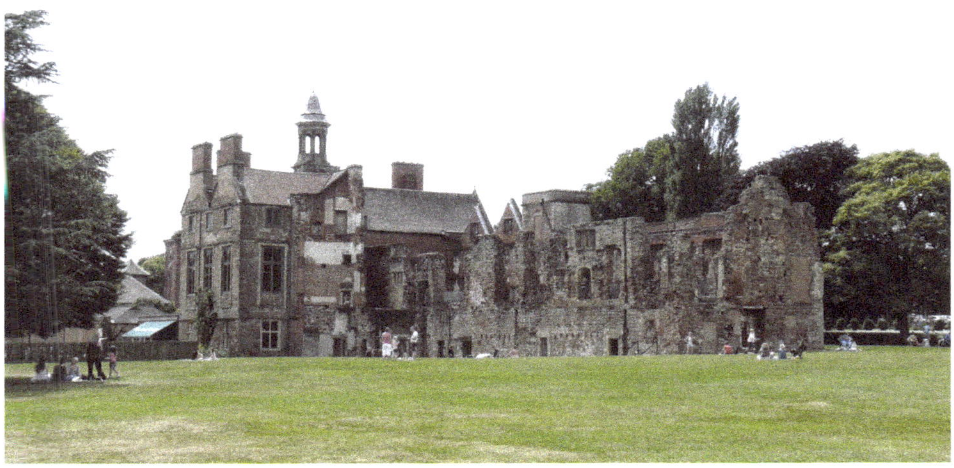

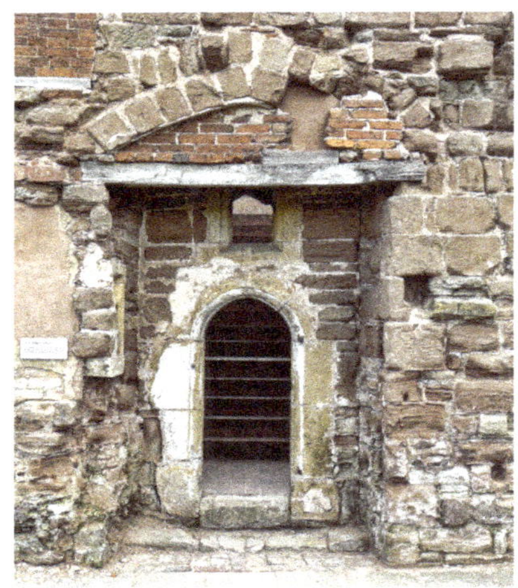

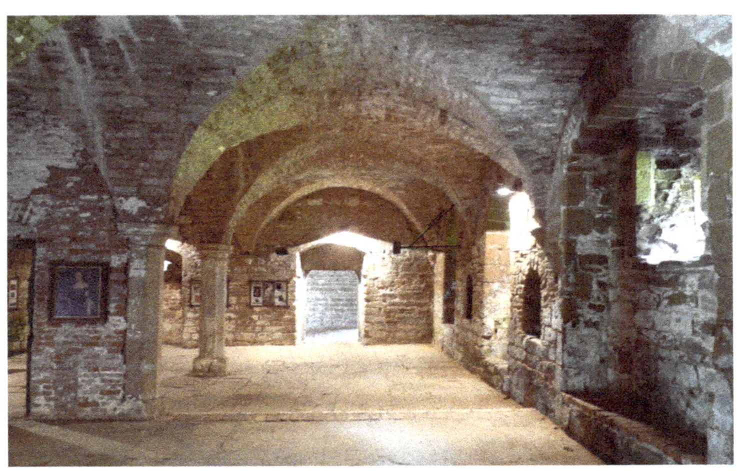

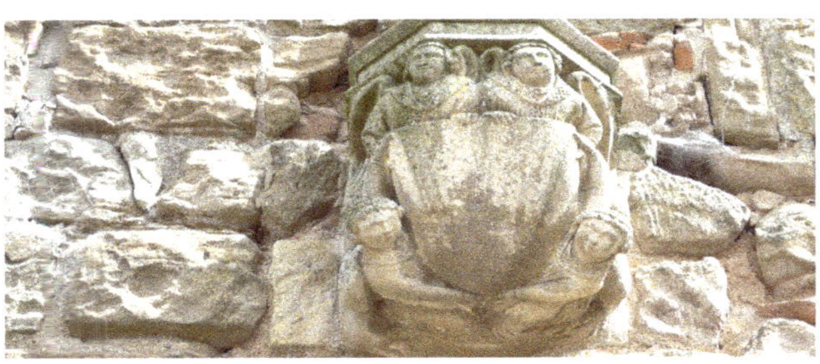

Photos of Rufford Abbey – clockwise from top left

Seventeenth century mansion with west range
Night stairs into lay-brothers refectory
Vaulted cellarium
Carving on refectory wall

Shelford Priory

St Mary • Augustinian 1154/89–1536

This small house for Augustinian canons stood on the south bank of the River Trent to the north-east of the City of Nottingham. Shelford Manor House now stands on the site, no doubt incorporating stone from the priory, but every other trace has been obliterated. The priory was founded in the reign of Henry II (1154-1189) by Ralph Haunselyn or Hauselin who granted the canons all his lands and the advowson of several churches. Additional bequests of pasturage later enabled the community to derive a fair income from the sale of wool, but it found itself in debt during its later, largely unremarkable history. The only event of note was a visitation by Archbishop Romayne in 1280, following which he issued several injunctions banning worthless persons from eating and drinking in the refectory, forbidding the prior to sell corrodies without a licence, to cease his indulgence in drink, to observe silence at the appropriate times, and many more for minor misdemeanours. These injunctions were to be read in the chapter house three times a year, 'in a distinct and intelligible voice'. Entries in the Patent Rolls of 1317 and 1319 appear to indicate that Edward II made brief visits to the priory during those years. Additional information on the priory was provided in 1536 by the royal commissioners, Legh and Layton, who estimated the annual net value at £70 and stated that the community venerated a girdle and milk of the Virgin and part of a candle she is said to have carried at her purification, and that it possessed some of the oil of the Holy Cross and St Katherine. The commissioners also accused, most likely without foundation, three canons of unnatural sin and three others of incontinence. The last prior, Robert Dyxson, was forced to surrender the priory in the same year.

Thurgarton Priory

St Peter • Augustinian 1100/35–1538

The splendid Early English north tower of the priory church rises above this charming village, lying between two hills and watered by a little stream that runs through its heart to join the broad waters of the Trent. Its twin tower has long since fallen, as has the central tower, but the cruciform church must then have been an impressive structure. Only three of the original seven bays of the nave and a wonderful Norman west doorway have survived from the conventual church and now form part of the parish church. Of the original Norman buildings nothing has survived and the part of the church now standing is from a thirteenth century rebuilding. The two decorated two-light windows above the altar, the carved statue niche and canopy and many of the carved stones about the village are examples of fourteenth century work or later. An old altar slab marked with six crosses, found in 1854 during restoration, now forms the top of the present altar.

The central doorway demands closer attention. Eight pillars on each side of the doorway enrich its deep jambs, and the recessed archway with its numerous mouldings is particularly beautiful. There are three rows of dogtooth ornament on the face, two on the soffit, and one on the label mould. The smaller doorway in the lower stage of the tower has similar characteristics and is almost as beautiful. The tower is well proportioned and the arcade around the staircase buttress in the north-west corner is a fine example of Early English work. There is also a rare display of carved detail in the lancet window under the belfry, which appears to be a zigzag development of early Norman design. The present mansion on the site was built in 1777 by John Gilbert Cooper, of Southwell, who swept away all the older work that was left in his time, with the exception of the plain undercroft, which still exists in good preservation below the present house.

The Augustinian priory was founded in the reign of Henry I by Ralph de D'Aincourt, son of Walter, who inherited vast possessions, which included sixty-seven lordships. Ralph acted on the advice and request of Archbishop Thurstan, and bestowed upon the new community all of Thurgarton and Fiskerton, and eleven of his churches. The manorial rights enjoyed by the canons included the contribution of a cock and hen by the cottagers beside their rents. The natives had also to contribute three pence each in reaping time, cleanse the mill-dam, plough and reap for their religious superiors, and each 'she native' had to pay five shillings and four-pence when she was married, while the fine upon the daughter of a cottager was half that sum. The prior also had the right to a stall in the choir of the great collegiate church of Southwell. These curious customs prevailed throughout the priory's existence. Henry III granted the priory a weekly market and annual fair in 1270. There were several disagreements over tithes with St Catherine's Priory in Lincoln and that at Kyme, but these were settled amicably. A visitation by Archbishop Wickwane in 1280 called for silence, no drinking after compline, and the opening of the lockers of the canons three times a year, so that 'the vice of private property might be obliterated', as well as some minor corrections. Nothing was reported after another visitation in 1293, and it must be assumed that all was well by then, although one of the canons had caused a scandal in 1290, when he violently assaulted a clerk in the church.

The priory attracted a constant stream of

benefactors and royal gifts, until it owned considerable property in all parts of the county, as well as in neighbouring Derbyshire and Lincolnshire. By the time of the *Valor* of 1535, its clear income had risen to £259 9s. The King's commissioners, Legh and Layton, visited the house in 1536 and surpassed themselves in the wholesale character assassination of the community. Not only did they claim that ten of the canons were guilty of unnatural offences, six of whom were also accused of having been incontinent with married and single women, they wrote that the prior had also been incontinent with several women. These lies, of course, sealed the priory's fate and John Berwick, the last prior, and his ten canons surrendered the house in June 1538. The King granted the priory and its possessions partly to Trinity College, Cambridge, and partly to William Cooper, who was in royal service.

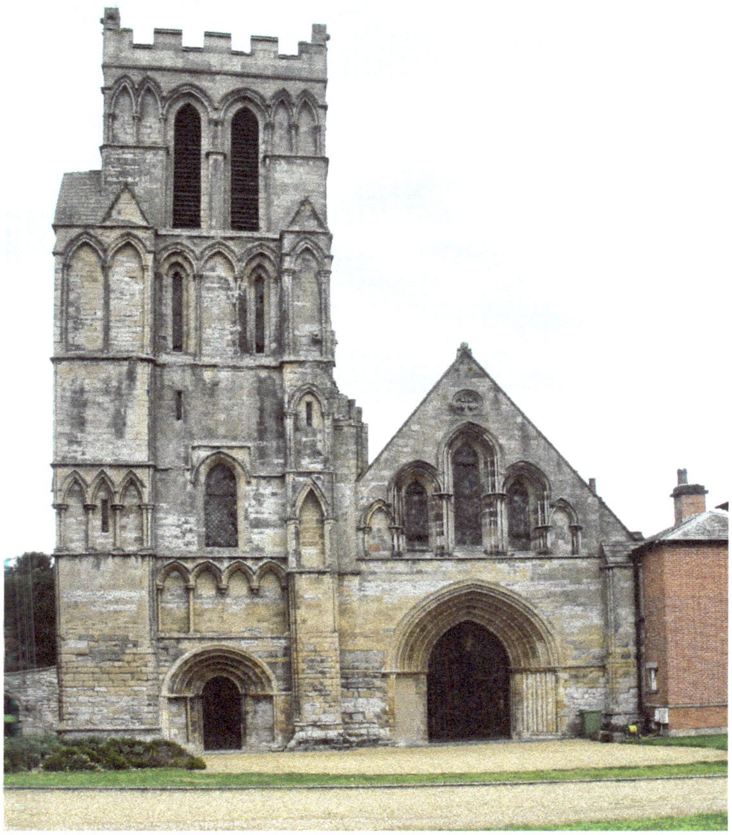

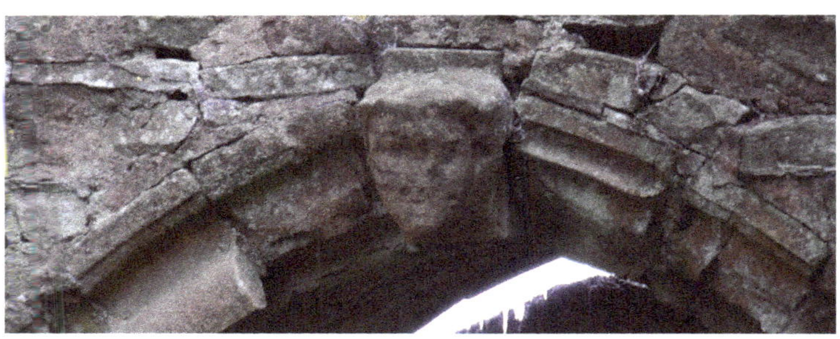

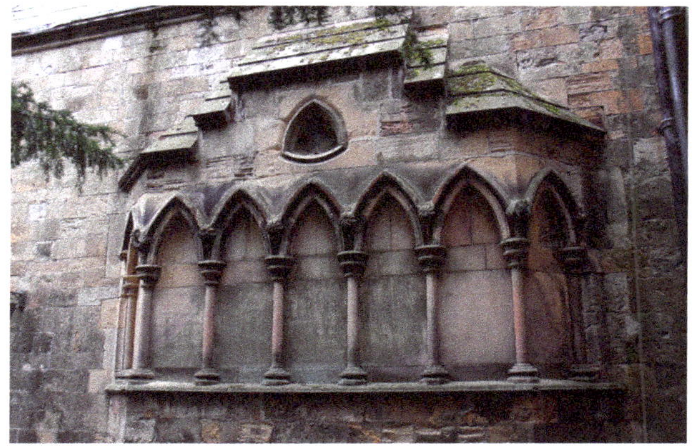

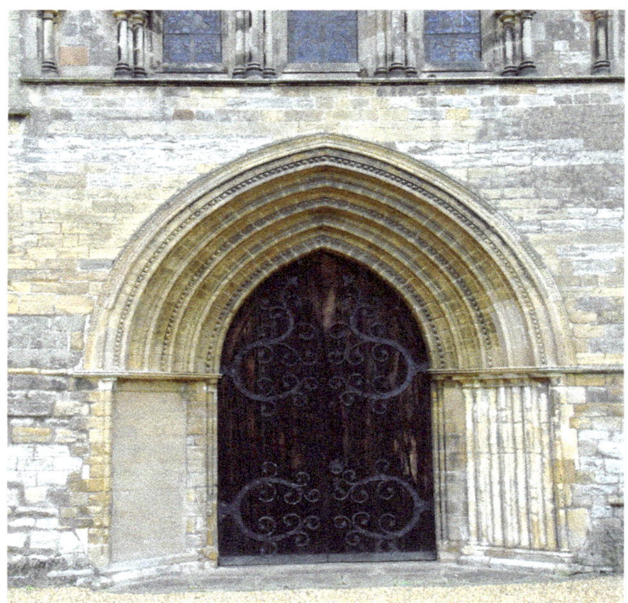

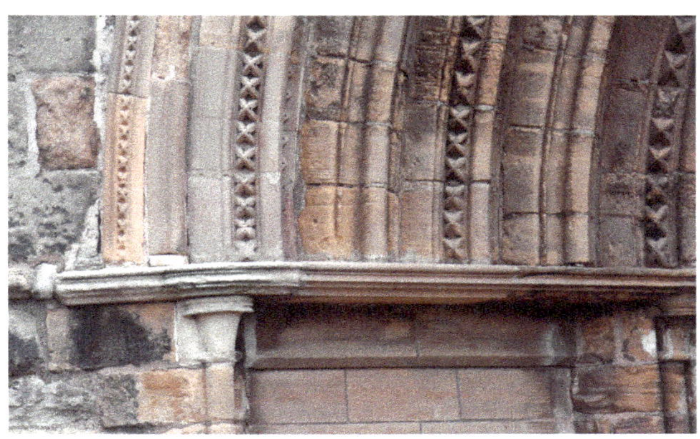

Photos of Thurgarton Priory - clockwise from top left

North tower and nave of former priory church
Projecting oriel with blind arcading
Splendid recessed west doorway
Close-up of west doorway dog-tooth decorations
Weathered face on stone arch

Wallingwells Priory

St Mary • Benedictine nuns 1135/54–1539

Not a vestige is left of this small priory for Benedictine nuns beautifully situated in a park on the north-west border of the county, adjoining Yorkshire. The handful of nuns led a blameless life and even the evil royal commissioners, Legh and Layton, when visiting in 1536, found it impossible to lay any scandal on the small community. The priory was founded in the reign of King Stephen sometime between 1135 and 1154 by Ralph de Chevrolcourt, who provided the nuns with a place in his park at Carlton-in-Lindrick by the Wells and gave them pasture in the park, pannage for ninety swine, right of way through the park, various parcels of land and pasture, and advowsons of a number of churches. Interestingly, the foundation charter included a curse on all who would disturb or diminish these benefactions. Four times a year, alms were distributed in memory of the founder. In 1262, on account of the priory's great poverty, Archbishop Godfrey gave corn and freed the community of all tithes on its land at Carlton. With an annual net value of £58 9s, the priory should have been surrendered in the first wave of the Dissolution, but Prioress Margaret Goldsmith paid a hefty fine of £66 13s for a licence to continue and, in 1537, demised the nunnery estates, but not the conventual buildings, to Richard Oglethorpe, on certain terms for twenty-one years. The end came in December 1539, when the prioress, sub-prioress and seven nuns were forced to surrender their house and were pensioned off. The site was granted to R Pype and Fran. Boyer in 1563-64. A house now stands on the site of the nunnery.

Welbeck Abbey

St James • Premonstratensian +1154–1538

The land in rural Nottinghamshire belonging to the Welbeck Estate is still a potent reminder of the former wealth of this Premonstratensian abbey of St James. The noble mansion that replaced the abbey following the Dissolution now has no monastic appearance and has been modified and enlarged so much over successive centuries that it is difficult to distinguish the old from the new. Much of medieval interest was concealed by these later developments and what remained of the lowest level of the abbey's 'old wing' was then adapted for use as servants' and domestic quarters. One bay of the medieval vaulted undercroft was adapted as a service room in 1903, a date indicated on its small fireplace, but the largest part of the undercroft and its vaults are no longer accessible. Perhaps the most interesting and identifiable survival from the ancient monastic buildings is the west cloister arched doorway, which dates from the late twelfth century.

The abbey was founded after 1154 in the reign of Henry II by Thomas de Cuckney in fulfilment of his father's wishes on land first owned by a Saxon named Sweyn and then by Norman lord, Hugh fitzBaldrick. The foundation was liberally endowed by several prominent families in the county and also later benefited significantly from the largesse of Edward I. The abbey was colonised by canons from Newhouse Abbey in Lincolnshire. Its possessions soon extended throughout Nottinghamshire and into Derbyshire and Lincolnshire, and included large swathes of agricultural land and pastures, woodlands, mills and the advowson of several churches. It flourished under the first abbot Berengarius and quickly became a large and noted house, being able to send out large numbers of canons into distant parts of England and Wales to found seven daughter abbeys. These included Dureford in Sussex, Hagnaby in Lincolnshire, Leiston in Suffolk, Beauchief in Derbyshire, West Dereham in Norfolk, Torre in Devon, and Halesowen in Salop.

Welbeck's history was generally unremarkable, its serenity being interrupted on a few occasions by minor disputes. In 1334, Abbot John de Nottingham and several of his flock were accused of having broken into the park of Elizabeth de Furnival and hunted and carried away her deer, and in 1393, some canons of Welbeck were pardoned by Edward III for having assaulted the keeper of the rolls, who was taking the rolls by cart from York to Nottingham. Although the canons and other evil-doers "shot and pierced the books in the carriage and took the horses, and would have carried the same away but that by the grace of God and their help they made too good a defence". When the zealous Richard Redman, abbot of the small house of Shap in Westmorland, was appointed visitor of all Premonstratensian establishments in the British Isles, he subjected Welbeck to a total of eleven visitations between 1462 and 1500. With the exception of a short period of 'grievous decline, when Abbot William Burton was dismissed because he had "squandered the abbey's goods, allowed the buildings to fall into disrepair and let out the land and tithes to local rich men", the abbey was ruled well. This was recognised in 1512 when, under Abbot Thomas Wilkinson, all Premonstratensian houses in England were placed under its control. However, trumped-up charges against several canons following a visit by the notorious royal commissioners, Legh and Layton, in 1536, heralded the end. In June 1538, the last abbot, Richard Bentley, along with the sub-prior and sixteen other canons, signed the surrender of his house. Its net annual value in 1536 had been assessed at £240. The monastic property was granted to Richard Whalley of Shelford in February 1539.

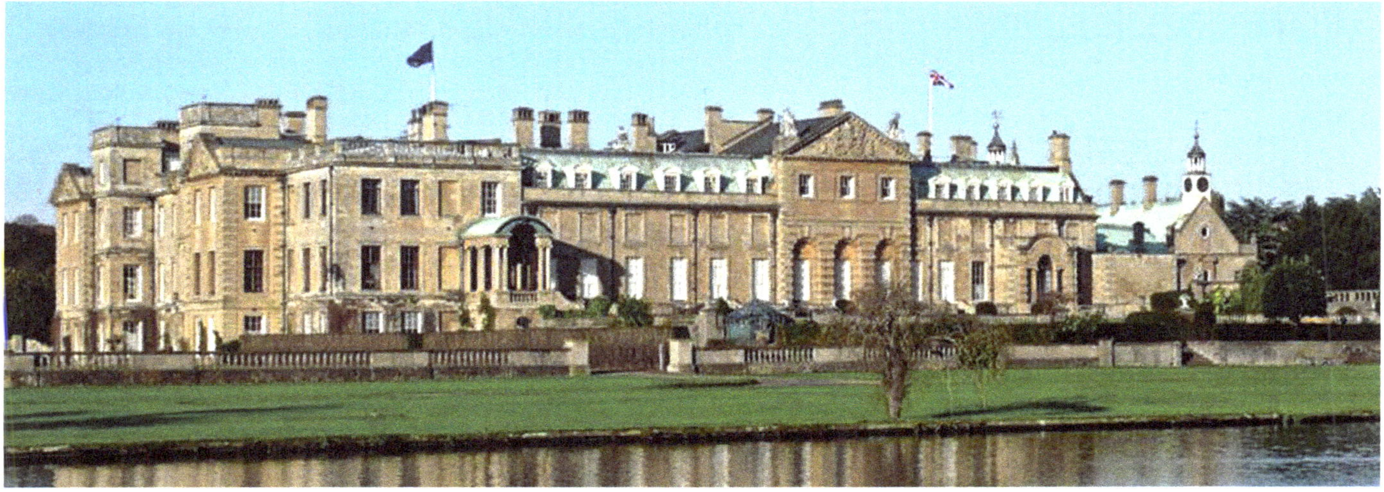

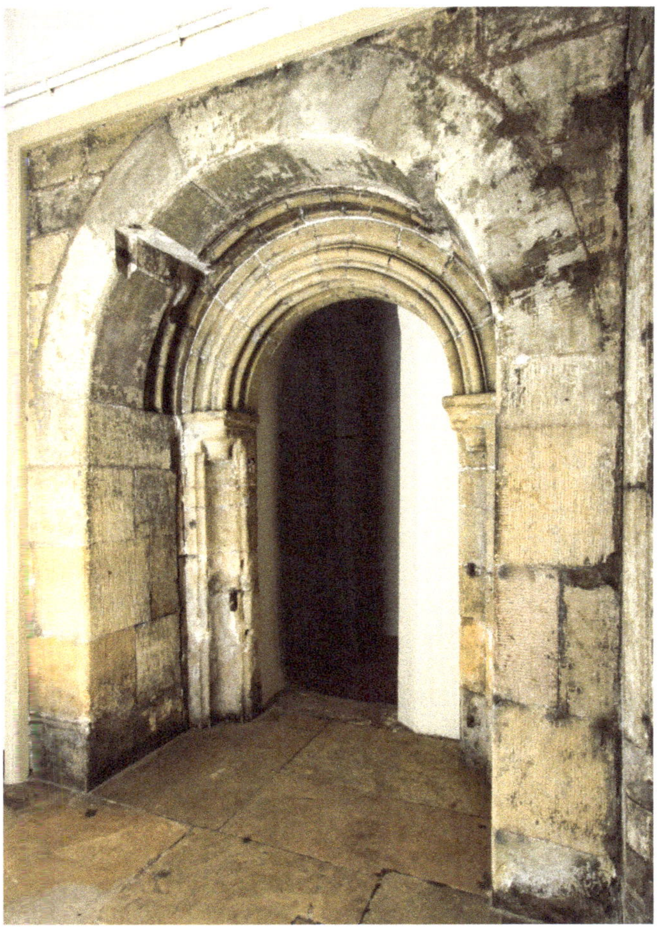

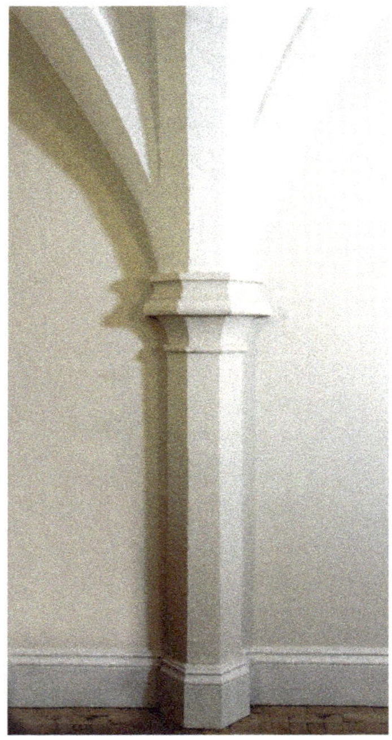

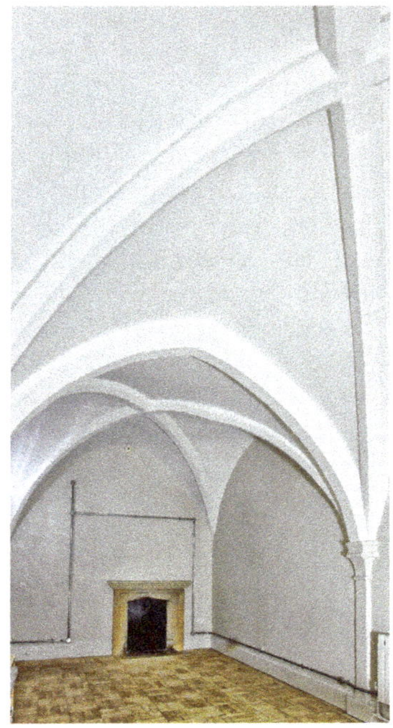

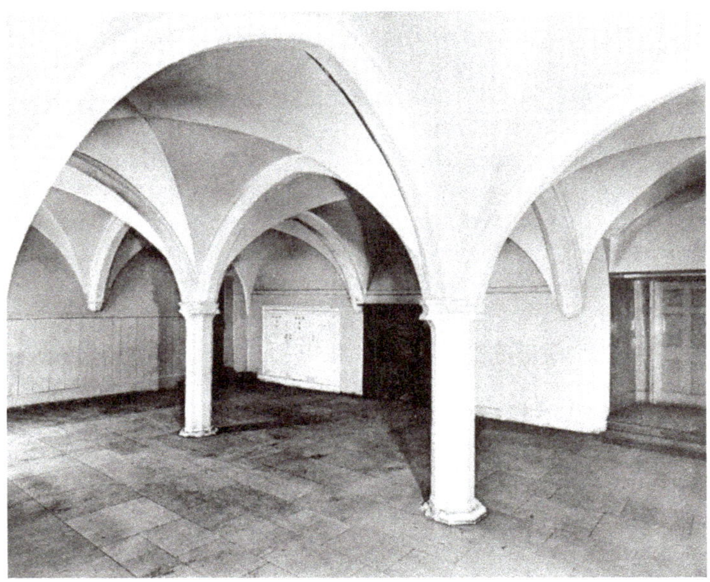

Photos of Welbeck Abbey - clockwise from top

The grand post-medieval mansion that rose from the abbey
Small vaulted room adjacent to undercroft
Undercroft column and springing of vault ribs
Medieval undercroft
Late twelfth century west cloister doorway

Photos courtesy of Portland Collection/Derek Adlam, FSA, Curator Emeritus

Worksop Priory

St Mary & St Cuthbert • Augustinian +1119–1539

The two bold battlemented and pinnacled towers of the parish church rising above the industrial town, together with a fine west front, long Norman nave and restored Lady Chapel, are a potent reminder of a once great medieval priory. The crossing tower and east end are modern, and whether or not the integration with the ancient church has been achieved in a pleasing manner, is open to personal interpretation. Be that as it may, there is much of interest within, starting with the extravagantly long and imposing nave of ten bays with alternating round and octagonal piers, whose arches are ornamented with late Norman dogtooth design. The capitals feature primitive stiff-leaf decorations. The aisles are vaulted, although the original vaulting appears to have fallen c1567, as evidenced in the churchwarden's accounts. Behind a modern screen in the south transept stands the Lady Chapel, of which only the wall and the late Gothic lancet windows with moulded capitals are original. A small glass-covered opening in the north wall houses part of an ancient skull with an arrowhead embedded in it, which, according to local tradition, is that of a Sherwood Forester. Of note in the south porch is a superb Sherwood Forest yew door with Norman ironwork.

The cloisters and living accommodation were to the north of the great church, served by water from the River Ryton via the priory mill on the Canch. Fish ponds were maintained on what is now Bracebridge. But the first glimpse travellers had of the grandeur of the priory church was the fine gatehouse, which incorporates medieval statuary and an unusual projecting wayside shrine to house an image of the Virgin Mary. It was built in the first quarter of the fourteenth century, most probably with the consent and financial support of Thomas de Furnival, a descendant of the founder, William de Lovetot.

The pleasing principal elevation of this two-storey structure demands closer inspection. Above the 3.65m (12ft) wide gateway arch is a large flat-arched transomed window of six lights, surmounted by quatre-foiled tracery. This is flanked by two richly canopied niches containing statues, the one on the east representing St. Cuthbert, the patron saint of the priory, the other probably St. Augustine, whose rule was observed at Worksop. In the central gable above is another similar niche, filled with a statue of the first person of the Holy Trinity, holding a crucifix between his knees. Above this is a pretty little perforated circlet. The little chapel, where they would offer prayers of thanksgiving after surviving a journey through Sherwood Forest with its thieves and outlaws, still exists. All visitors were received in the upstairs main hall, which runs the whole length of the building.

A grant of land and monies in 1103 by William de Lovetot, a local landowner living at Worksop Manor, led to the founding of this Augustinian priory at Radford sometime after 1119. It was a large house with a prior and eighteen canons. Under the continued patronage of the de Lovetots and their descendents, the Furnivals and Talbots, Earls of Shrewsbury, two of whom were buried in the church, the priory's fortunes grew. In the *Valor Ecclesiasticus* of 1535, Worksop Priory was shown to have a net income of £239 15s, derived from lands, mills, bequests of money and property. King Henry III allowed the canons to take two cartloads of heather daily from Sherwood Forest in recompense for his eldest son, Prince Edward, having taken the canons' timber 'to make engines of war'. Apart from a series of injunctions issued to tighten discipline following a visitation in 1280, the priors appear to have maintained a well-ordered house throughout its history.

In later years, the priory became a famous centre of learning, with a superb library, which included sumptuously illustrated bibles, a bestiary given to the prior by the Bishop of Lincoln, and the *Tickhill Psalter*, so called because it was produced by John de Tickhill who was prior in the early fourteenth century. It is said to be one of the finest of all surviving English manuscripts but rather than being enjoyed by the people of Nottinghamshire, it is today kept in the New York Public Library.

Worksop was surrendered by the prior, William Stokes, and sixteen canons in November 1539. Much of the 1,000 acres of land and treasures went to Francis, fifth Earl of Shrewsbury, in exchange for the manor of Farnham Royal in Buckinghamshire, and on condition that he and his successors as lords of the Manor of Worksop provided a fine glove for the right hand of the Sovereign at the Coronation – an obligation still in force today. The townspeople were allowed to keep the nave as the parish church and the gatehouse as the vicarage. The gatehouse later became the first elementary school in England. All the monastic buildings were plundered for stone and lead and fell into ruin.

Photos – clockwise from top

The parish church, once the heart of a great monastery
The fine gatehouse still standing complete
Carved capital on octagonal pier
Long nave of ten bays
Statuary on the gatehouse elevation

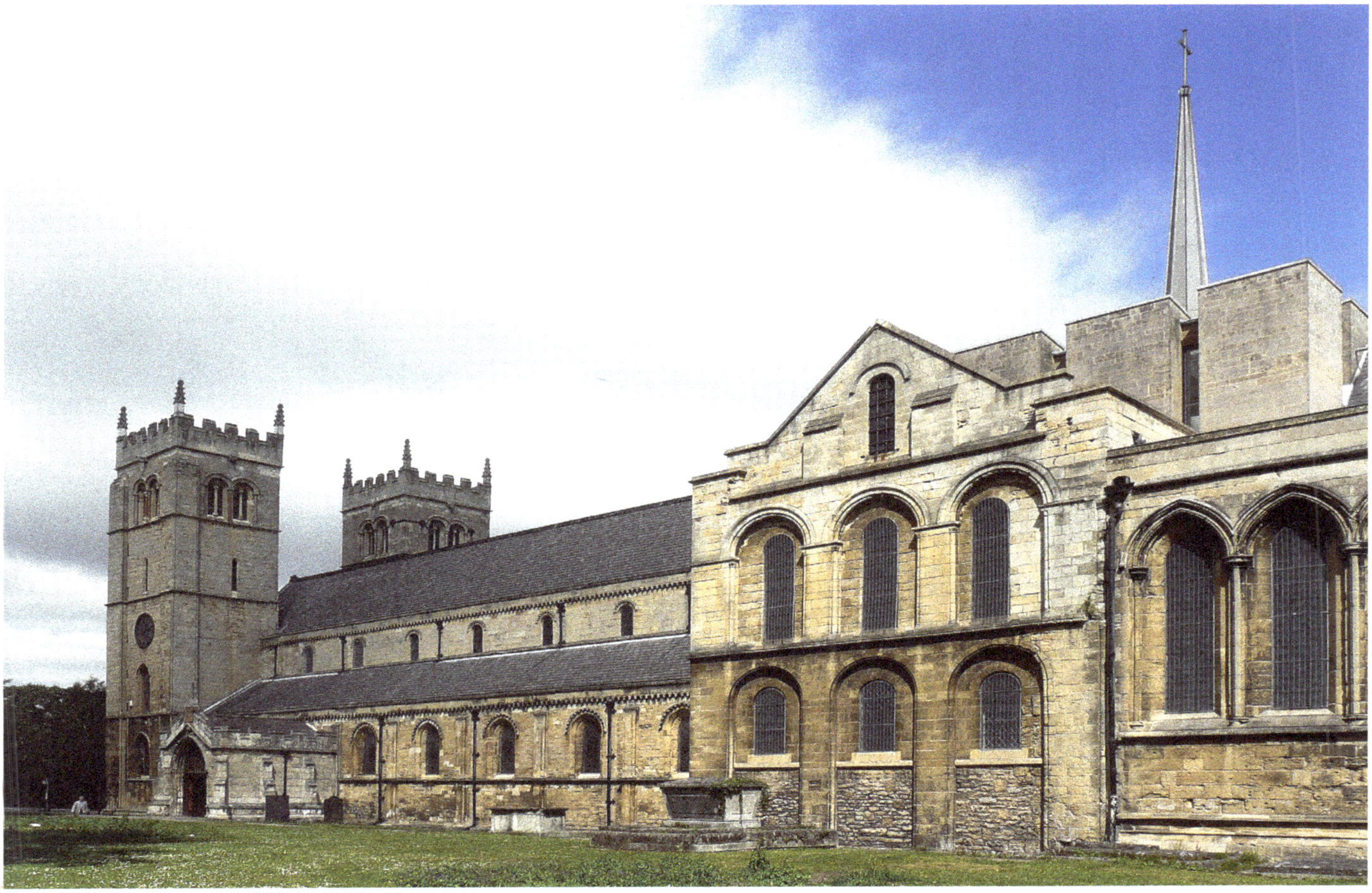

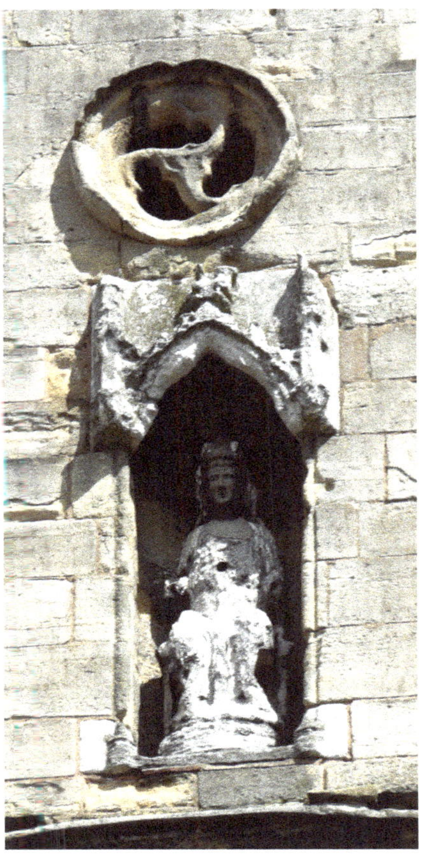

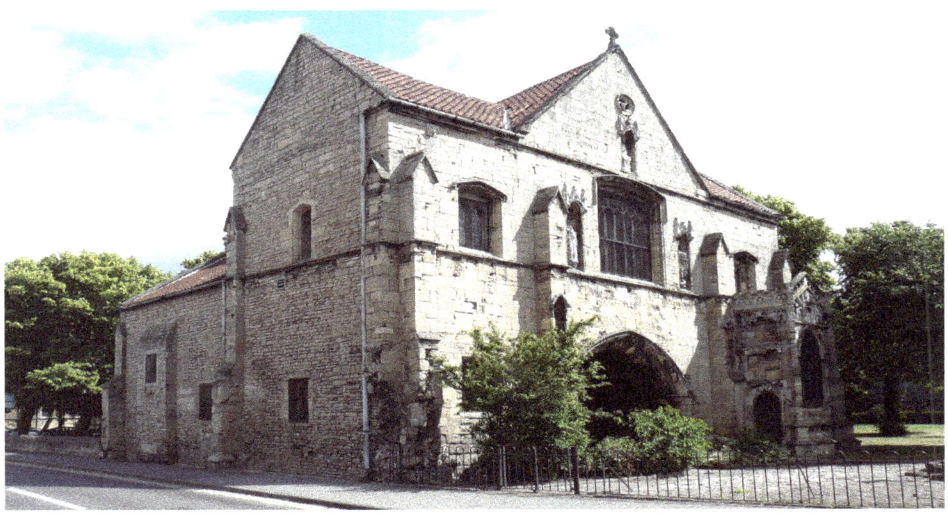

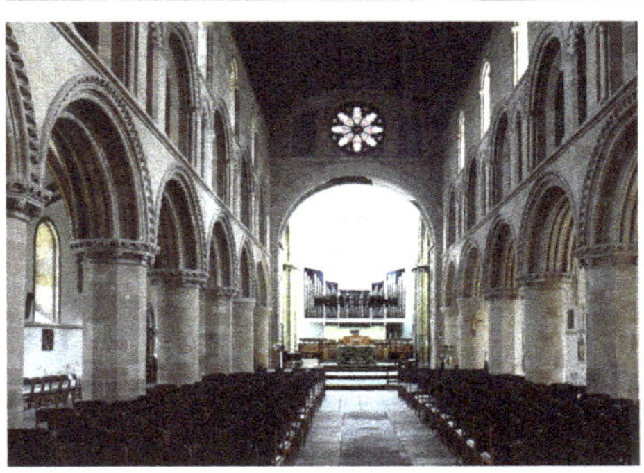

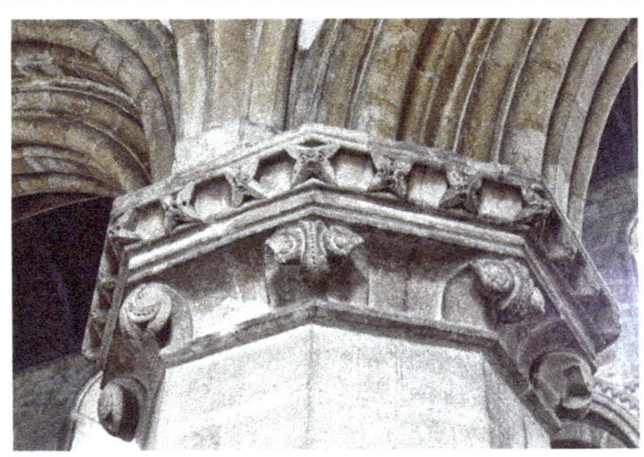

Westmorland

Remote Wilderness

At the time of Domesday in 1086, certain areas were considered either to form part of Yorkshire, or to lie within the then separate Kingdom of Scotland. After the Normans wrested the area from Scotland in 1092, they created the baronies of Kendal and Westmorland, which were formed into a single county of Westmorland in 1226/7. Considering the extreme remoteness and wilderness, later marked by lengthy conflicts with the Scots, it is not surprising that monastic foundations were thin on the ground. Shap Abbey was the last abbey to be founded in England, having been established on the present site by Premonstratensian canons in 1201. The canons also maintained a hospital for three lepers at the county town of Appleby, which was also home to a Carmelite house, one of only three monasteries in the county. The third, which is surrounded by some uncertainty, was that at Ravenstonedale, said to have been a cell to the large Yorkshire Gilbertine foundation of Watton.

Gazetteer

Appleby White Friars Off B6542 Battlebarrow, Appleby-in- Westmorland, Cumbria (NY 684208). No visible remains

Ravenstonedale Priory Ravenstonedale, 7km (4.5 miles) SW of Kirkby Stephen, Cumbria (NY 722043). Minimal remains

Shap Abbey On minor road off A6, 2.5km (1.5 miles) W of Shap village, 16km (10 miles) SE of Penrith, Cumbria (NY 548153). English Heritage; unattended

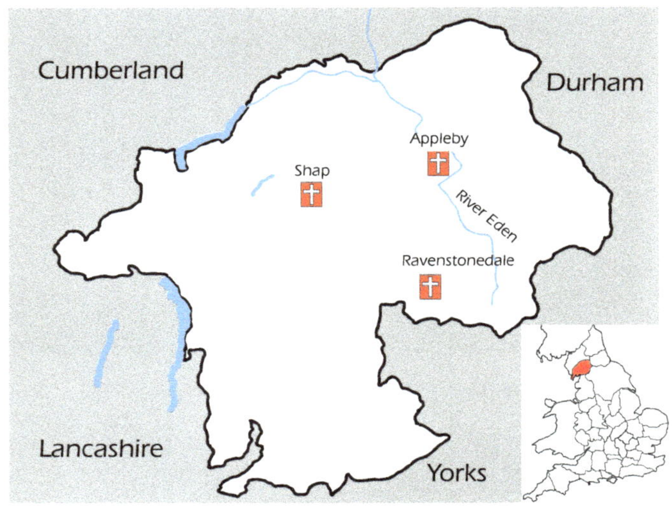

Appleby White Friars

St Mary • 1281–1539?

History has swept away most references to this Carmelite house, which, according to the *Chronicle of Lanercost*, was founded in1281 by the Lords Vesey, Percy and Clifford. According to Nicholson & Burns in the *History of Westmorland and Cumberland* of 1777, a house on the west side of Battlebarrow was "built out of the ruins of an ancient friary that stood behind the opposite row of houses". A barn at The Friarage has part of a fourteenth century window in its southern end, but its provenance cannot be confirmed. The friars existed largely through voluntary alms from the local population, but these generally proved insufficient and were topped up from gifts in recognition of the hospitality shown to the Kings or members of the royal family on their progresses through the country. Edward I stayed at the priory in 1300 on his way back south. Their roving commission often brought them into conflict with the secular clergy, resulting in a bull of Pope Boniface VIII in 1300 that partially restricted the friars from intruding too much. The house was suppressed by Richard Ingworth, Bishop of Dover, in 1539.

Ravenstonedale Priory

• Gilbertine -1300-?

The sparse ruins and buried foundations immediately north of the parish church of St Oswald are believed to be those of a small cell of the Gilbertine canons of Watton in Yorkshire, to whom the vill of Ravenstonedale was given in the latter half of the twelfth century, probably in the reign of Henry II, by one Torphin, son of Robert, son of Copsus. It was intended to be managed by a master and three canons and probably remained at that level. The canons would have looked after the spiritual well-being of the local parish, while also managing the priory's possessions, with the lay-brothers responsible for farming the land.

The canons also had a fishpond, which has completely disappeared but may have been located at the bottom of Ash Fell, and possibly rabbit warrens to the north of Scandal Beck, as well as pasture near Tebay.

Few historical references to life in the small community have survived. It is known that there was a dispute over lands with Bishop Robert Chause of Carlisle (1258-78) and that the local church was appropriated in 1336. An enquiry of 1405 claimed that no canons had been in residence for some time. Records also show that the Gilbertine Order declined after the death of the founder and it is known that the settlement at Ravenstonedale was often well below strength and that the buildings were probably converted to a smaller house to more closely match the reduced circumstances. A new wing was added much later, which included a fireplace and garderobe, but it has not been possible to accurately date this domestic accommodation. It could well have been constructed in the post-Dissolution period. At the closure of Watton Priory in 1539, Ravenstonedale passed to the archbishop of York, and from him to the Wharton family of Wharton Hall near Kirkby Stephen. Following the sequestration of the Wharton estate in 1729, the lands were bought by the Lowther family.

The ruins were first mention in writing by George Fothergill in 1677, and in 1681, Thomas Machell, vicar of Kirkby Thore and antiquarian, visited the site and described a cloister court some 18.3m (60ft) square, with rooms up to 6.4m (21ft) wide, some with vaulting on the ground floor. By the time Bishop Nicholson wrote about them in 1703, the ruins had largely disappeared, but he did note a vault, which, he said, had been used as a prison. Excavations by E P Frankland in 1928-9 confirmed the presence of this Gilbertine cell. The visible ruins have since been consolidated and are believed to be of the east range of the cloister, probably dating from a remodelling in the late thirteenth/early fourteenth century. The upstanding remains are some 1.8m (6ft) high and represent unknown rooms divided by internal walls. The foundations of a pele tower have also been identified. This may have been built by the Whartons to protect their estate. A drain leads to the beck on the east side. The church of St Oswald dates from 1744, but was probably built on the site of the original church and incorporates some worked masonry, likely to have come from the ruins.

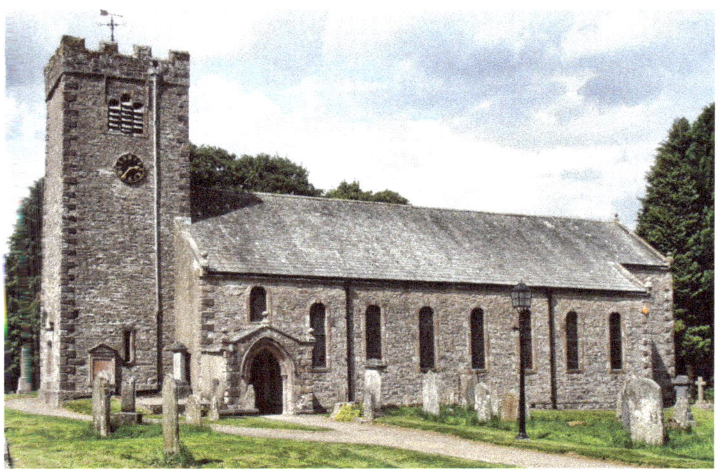

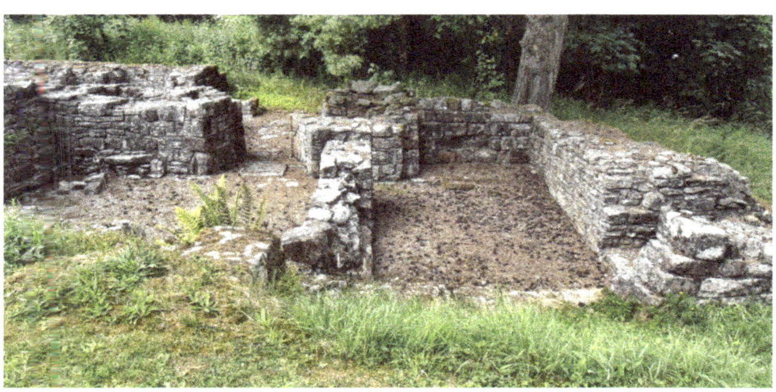

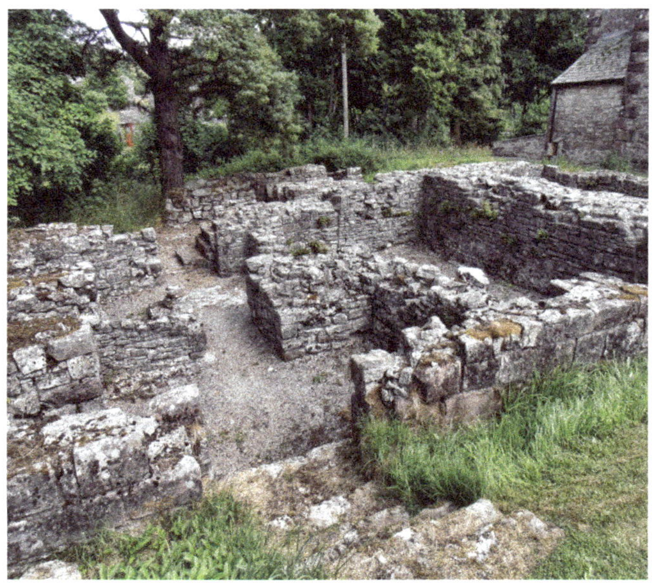

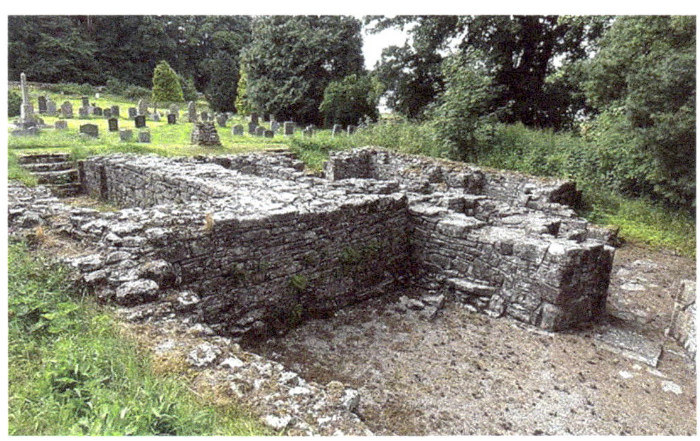

Photos of Ravenstonedale Priory - clockwise from top left

Church of St Oswald
Foundations of east range of cloister

Shap Abbey

St Mary Magdalene • Premonstratensian 1199–1540

There can be few more remote places to build an abbey than the wilderness of Westmorland, which probably is not much different today as it must have been in the twelfth century when Shap Abbey was built. Set on the western banks of the River Lowther, it reposes in splendid isolation, with stunning views of the bleak grass moorland all around. Founded in 1199 by Thomas, son of Gospatrick, at Preston Patrick, some 32km (20 miles) south of the village of Shap, he moved the abbey in 1201 to the present site, which he considered more suitable for religious seclusion. It was the last abbey to be founded in England. Premonstratensian canons came over from France and dedicated the abbey to St Mary Magdalene. It was endowed by the founder with land and many privileges, including permitting the abbot to take wood from his forests, and grinding toll-free at his mills. Thomas was buried in the abbey church, and all gifts and privileges were confirmed by his successors. The canons also maintained a hospital at Appleby dedicated to St Nicholas or St Leonard for three lepers.

The abbey's lands were spread throughout Westmorland, and extended as far as Craven in Yorkshire. Another possession was the rectory at Annandale in Scotland, which was given in 1332 by Edward Balliol. While tilling the land, the monks of Shap Abbey, believed to have numbered never more than twenty, were also renowned for their teaching and scholarship. Although its annual worth in the *Valor* of 1535 was assessed at only £154, it escaped the closure of the lesser monasteries in 1536. The last abbot, Richard Evenwood, eventually surrendered Shap Abbey to the King in 1540. The abbey and its lands were granted to Sir Thomas Wharton, Governor of Carlisle.

The most prominent feature at Shap is the striking west tower at the end of the nave, which still retains its beautiful Gothic doorway and window at the upper level. The tower was one of the last additions in a continuous improvement programme, and was probably built by one of the greatest religious reformers of his time, Richard Redman, who was abbot of Shap for some fifty years until his death in 1505. He also held successive posts as bishop of St Asaph, Exeter and Ely. The 60.6m (200ft) long church, which comprised a six-bay nave, a north aisle, two chapels in the transepts and a plain, narrow chancel, is now much ruined, as are the chapter house, dormitories and cloisters. Many monastic buildings were incorporated in a working farm. A pillar of an ancient bridge has survived in the river to the south of the abbey. After the abbey was abandoned, the plain grey stone was used to build Shap Market Hall, while much of the carved and decorated stonework was used in the building of Lowther Castle and can still be seen in the gardens. The huge solid tower proved more difficult to destroy. A path from the abbey leads to the small sixteenth century Keld Chapel, once a chantry chapel belonging to the monks of Shap Abbey. A key can be had in the village to visit the chapel.

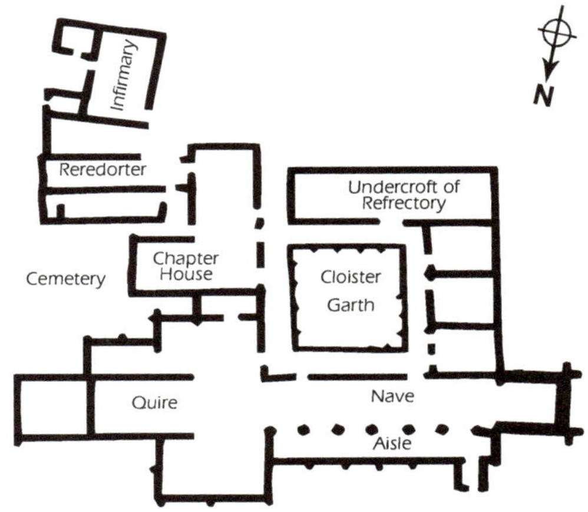

Richard Redman

Born to a noble Westmorland family, whose main seat was at Levens, near Kendal, Richard Redman achieved high office, but was never far from controversy. Almost nothing is known of his early life and education, nor when he was born or why he chose a religious life. He was clearly an able man, being elected as abbot of Shap, probably before 1458, but it was his appointment as commissary-general of the abbot of Prémontré in the British Isles that caused much controversy and led to ten years of friction between himself and Abbot Thomas Shoreham of Bayham, who held this post at the same time. Redman spent more than four decades as visitor of all the Premonstratensian houses in Britain, gaining a reputation as a tireless enforcer of monastic standards. He remained abbot of Shap in commendam after he was made bishop of St Asaph in 1472. Edward IV appointed him as one of the commissioners of Flint and Chester in 1474, 'to approve all the castles, manors and other properties' and to consider the appointments of all ministers and officials. In 1482, he became a trier of petitions for Gascony, but his 'political' career took a dive when Richard III came to the throne. In yet another twist of fate, Redman was translated to the bishopric of Exeter in 1495 and Ely in 1501. In spite of his heavy workload, Redman frequently visited Shap and was able to maintain good order and ensure continued prosperity. He died in 1505 and is buried in Ely cathedral.

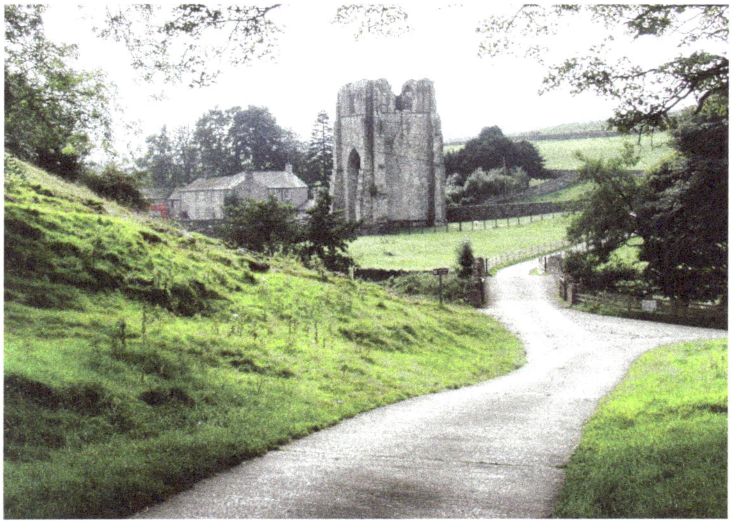

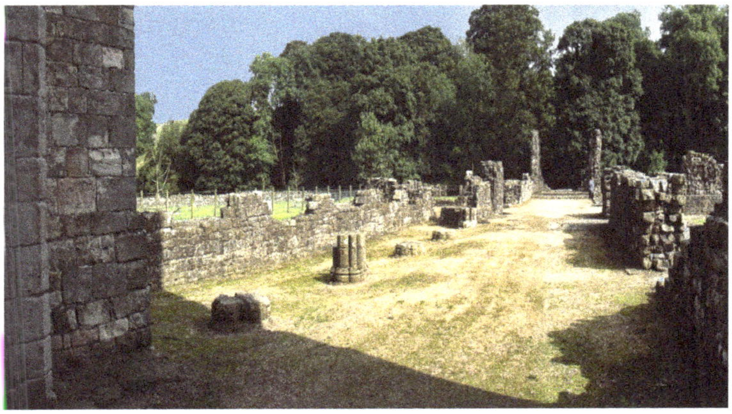

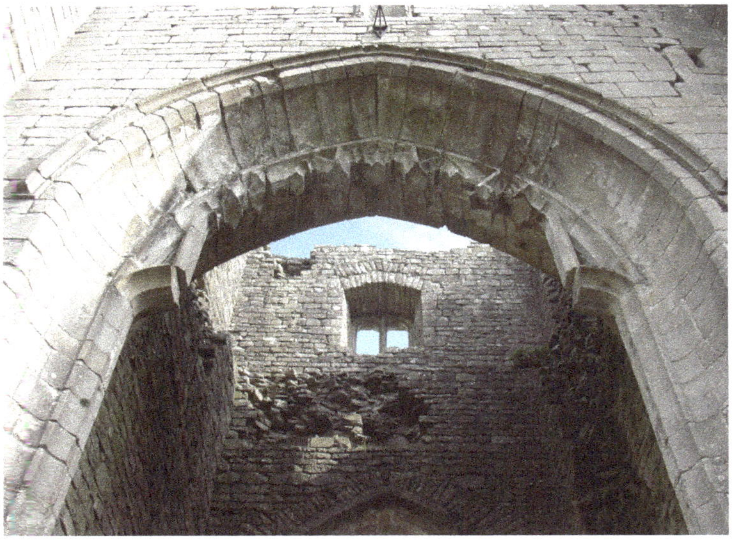

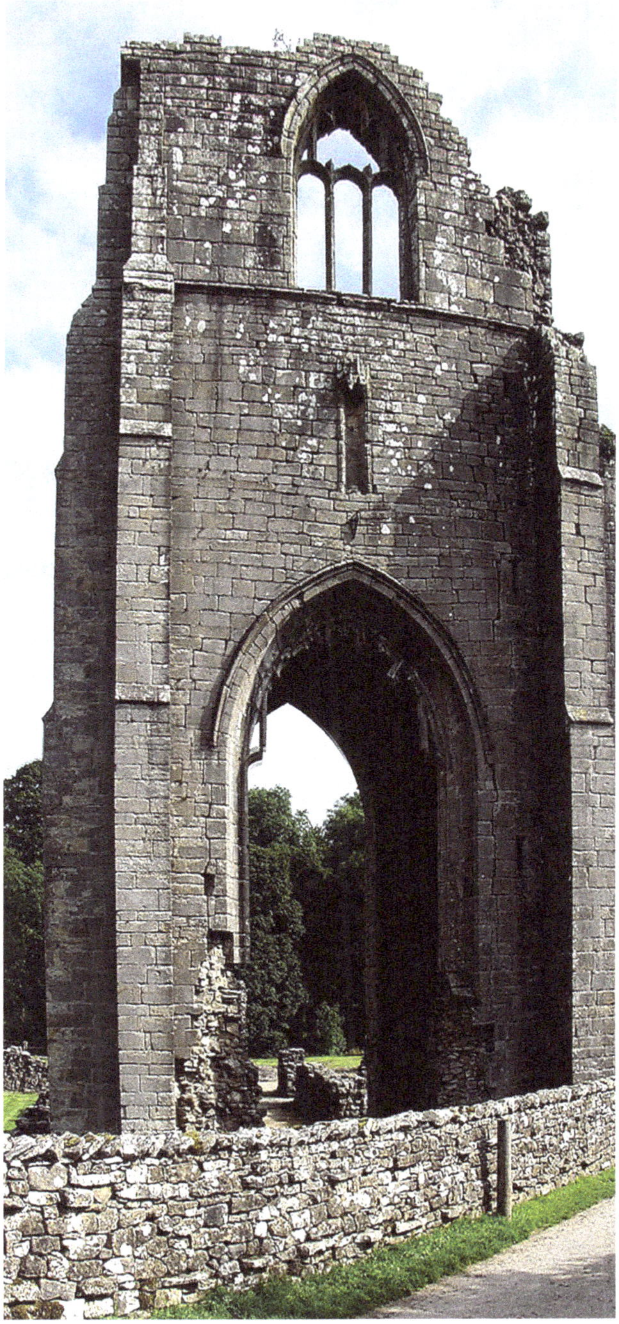

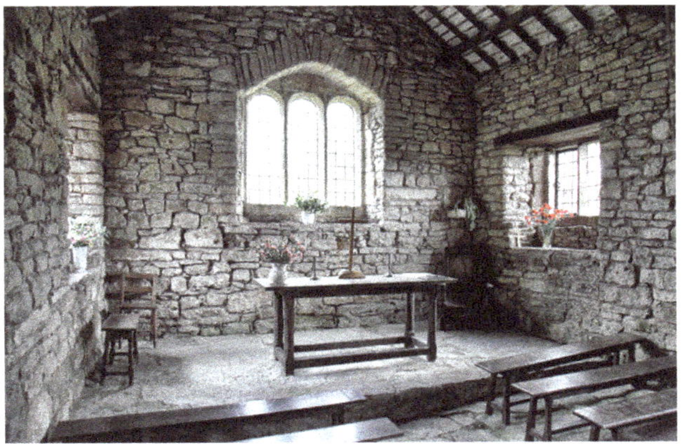

Photos – clockwise from top left

Shap Abbey standing in wonderful isolation
The striking West Tower
Keld Chapel, once belonging to the monks
Great Gothic doorway in the tower
Looking towards nave and quire

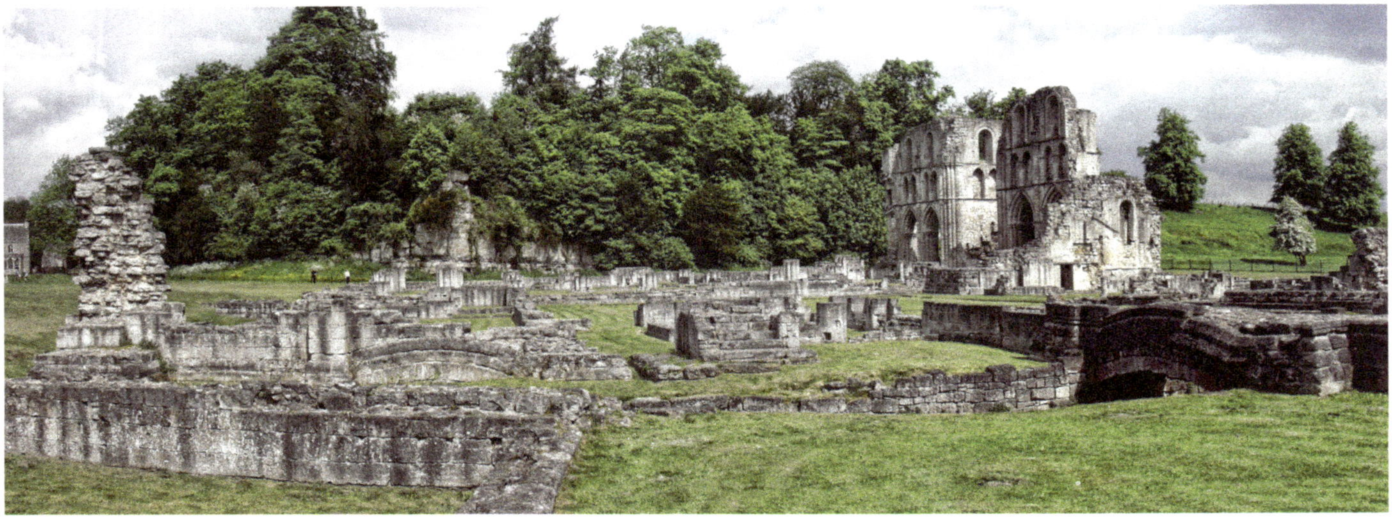

Roche Abbey

Yorkshire

God's Own Country

The stunning landscape of the northern moors and dales, sparsely populated and isolated from much of the rest of the country, proved irresistible to the monastic Orders, which swept like wildfire through the British Isles after the Norman Conquest. It is not surprising therefore that Yorkshire boasts some of the most magnificent reminders of an age of religious devotion, still remarkably remote in a landscape that has been touched little by modern life.

Christianity reached Yorkshire, then part of the Saxon Kingdom of Northumbria, early in the seventh century when Roman monk Paulinus was sent by Pope Gregory the Great, to first assist St Augustine in the south of England. However, in AD 625, he accompanied Ethelburga, daughter of King Ethelbert of Kent, on her journey north to marry the pagan Northumbrian King Edwin of Deira. In accordance with the Pope's wishes, Paulinus was consecrated Bishop of York and immediately began his missionary work. On Easter Day in AD 627, King Edwin and many of his nobles were baptised in York. Paulinus also consecrated Hilda, who presided over the monastery at Heretu (now Hartlepool) and in AD 657 became the founding abbess of Streonshalh, later to become known as Whitby. Hilda ruled a double community of men and women and considerably increased the abbey lands. Here the great Synod of Whitby was held in AD 664, which settled the controversy over the observance of Easter in favour of the Roman form of Christianity. Hilda also founded a convent for nuns at Hackness shortly before her death in AD 680.

St Hilda's abbey was a place of great learning and piety and produced many eminent men, including St John of Beverley and St Wilfrid, both of whom were raised to the See of York. St John founded a Benedictine monastery at Beverley around AD 700, and was buried therein when he died in AD 721. St John ordained Bede, later to become known as the Venerable Bede, a monk at the Northumbrian monastery of Wearmouth, from whose famous *Historia ecclesiastica gentis Anglorum* (The Ecclesiastical History of the English People), completed about AD 731, much has been learned of early Christianity. St Wilfrid's life was a turbulent one, which eventually led to his banishment from the north and new missionary work in Sussex. The crypt at Ripon Cathedral is almost certainly a relic of St Wilfrid's early monastic church. Other early monasteries were founded at Lastingham and Middlesbrough.

Many Saxon religious and secular establishments in the north-east were left in ruins by Danish raiders in AD 867, and many were subsequently abandoned. It was not until after the Norman Conquest in 1066, encouraged by Thurstan, Archbishop of York, that a monastic revival was initiated in the north. Many of the great abbeys came to own and dominate vast areas of the northern landscape for more than four hundred years, until their ruthless destruction by Henry VIII in the 1530s. Yorkshire boasted the greatest concentration of monastic settlements in England, totalling some 98 in the East, North and West Ridings of Yorkshire, including forty-six abbeys and priories, twenty-five nunneries, twenty-one houses of mendicant friars, and six alien houses.

Among the foundations for Benedictine monks were the great houses of Selby, Whitby and St Mary's in York. In 1073, three monks were despatched from Eavesham to revive the destroyed religious establishment of Whitby, one of whom, Reinfrid, refounded the monastery as a Benedictine priory, later elevated to abbey status. Another early foundation was Selby Abbey, whose history began in 1069 when Benedict, a monk from Auxerre, arrived in Selby with the dried finger of St German. He received a charter and land from William the Conqueror the following year, and Benedict became the first abbot, but his tenure was cut short when he was forced to resign on the grounds of cruelty. Monastic life continued and flourished under his successor, Abbot Hugh, who began an extensive rebuilding in stone, including the wonderful cruciform church. The most influential and wealthiest Benedictine house in the north, however, was St Mary's at York. The abbey was founded by King William II, in atonement for the terrible deeds his father and he had committed in York. The monks came from Whitby via Lastingham. But St Mary's was by no means the only monastery in the city. Another eight foundations of different Orders of regular monks and canons, as well as mendicant friars, were clustered within the city walls. The Priory of St Clement for Benedictine nuns was located outside the walls.

Other Benedictine houses existed at Hackness, Headley, Lastingham, Middlesbrough, Rosedale, and York All Saints and Holy Trinity. There were also ten Benedictine nunneries at Arden, Foukeholm, Marrick, Nunburnholme, Nunkeeling, Nun Monkton, Thicket, Wilberfoss, Yedingham and York.

It was the search for a stricter form of religious life, which led a group of dissatisfied Benedictine monks from St Mary's Abbey in York to a remote and wild North Yorkshire valley by the River Skell to establish Fountains Abbey on land given by Thurstan in 1132. However, after St Bernard of Clairvaux sent over a holy man in 1135, *Sancta Maria de Fontibus* (Our Lady of the Springs) became a Cistercian house. Fountains became very rich and many of its abbots sat in Parliament. The first Cistercian foundation in the north was Rievaulx Abbey, which dates back to 1132 and is one of the most spectacular monastic survivals in the country. Its most celebrated abbot was St Aelred, under whose abbacy Rievaulx achieved great repute and grew in size to 140 monks and probably up to 500 lay-brothers and servants. St Aelred was a renowned scholar and the most prominent religious figure in the twelfth century who, among others, was responsible for the *Genealogia Regum Anglorum,* written to instruct Prince Henry, later King Henry II, in the history of Saxon Kings. Other notable Cistercian abbeys were those at Byland, in the shadows of the Hambleton Hills and founded in 1177 within the sound of bells from Rievaulx, and Jervaulx in the Ure Valley, established in 1156. There were six other Cistercian monasteries at Barnoldswick, Hampole, Kirkstall, Meaux, Roche and Sawley (now in Lancashire), and nunneries at Basedale, Ellerton, Esholt, Handale, Keldholme, Kirklees, Nun Appleton, Sinningthwaite, Swine and Wykeham.

Augustinian houses were the most numerous in Yorkshire. Bridlington Priory was founded by Walter de Gant in 1113 and was the first Augustinian house to be established in the North of England. With several endowments, it soon grew to become one of the wealthiest monastic settlements in the county. The priory church survived for the parish. Kirkham Priory was founded in 1122 for Augustinian canons by Walter l'Espec, Lord of Helmsley, who ten years later also founded the Cistercian abbey at Rievaulx, much closer to his estate. Bolton Priory was established in a delightful setting overlooking the River Wharfe, when a group of canons removed from their harsh abode on higher ground at nearby Embsay in 1154. Gisborough Priory was founded in 1119 by Robert de Brus, Lord of Cleveland, who, along with other wealthy benefactors, endowed the new foundation with much land. Augustinian canons also formed communities at Drax, Haltemprice, Healaugh Park, Marton (a unique double house), Newburgh, North Ferriby, Nostell, Richmond, Skewkirk, Warter and Woodkirk. The only Augustinian nunnery was at Moxby.

Mount Grace Priory was one of only two Carthusian houses. It was founded in 1398, and is unique in that it is the most complete and only Charterhouse accessible to the public. The other was situated in Hull. The Premonstratensians were established in three locations, headed by the abbey of St Agatha at Easby on the riverside in quiet Swaledale. On the border with the County of Durham is Egglestone Abbey. It was founded by the Multon family in 1195, but with few endowments struggled against poverty throughout its history. The other house of this Order was at Coverham. The Cluniac Order also failed to establish itself in Yorkshire, with houses only at Monk Bretton and Pontefract in the south of the county, together with the nunnery at Arthington, one of only two in England. A single Trinitarian house was established at Knaresborough, while the Priory of St Mary at Old Malton was one of four monastic houses of the Gilbertines, the only British monastic Order. It was founded in 1150 by Eustace fitzJohn, and the church is the only surviving example where worship continues to this day. Other Gilbertine double houses were founded at Ellerton on Spalding Moor, Watton and York. Alien monasteries were the Benedictine cells at Allerton Mauleverer, Burstall and Ecclesfield, the Cistercian house of Beggar near Richmond, and Grosmont of the Grandmontine order.

Mendicant friars settled in the major conurbation in the thirteenth century, with the greatest distribution in the City of York, which had houses of the four main Orders of Dominican (Black), Franciscan (Grey), Austin and Carmelite (White) Friars, as well as of the Friars of the Sack and Crutched, or Crossed Friars. The last-named also had a short-lived house at Kildale. Black Friars were also present at Beverley, Scarborough and Yarm, with Grey Friars at Beverley, Doncaster, Richmond and Scarborough. Austin Friars also settled at Kingston upon Hull, Northallerton and Tickhill, and White Friars at Doncaster, Kingston upon Hull, Northallerton, Scarborough and Sutton.

Economic and political grievances, together with Henry VIII's attack on the Roman Catholic Church encouraged the northern abbots to participate in a strong resistance movement against a King hell-bent on vengeance against Rome, through the Dissolution of all monastic houses in the Kingdom, while plundering their treasures to satisfy his greed and to finance the wars against his enemies from across the English Channel.

The abbots of Fountains and Jervaulx were among the leaders of the so-called Pilgrimage of Grace, which started in October 1536, when barrister Robert Aske led nine thousand insurgents into York where he drove out the King's tenants and arranged for the expelled monks and nuns to return to their houses to resume religious observance. In his Narrative to the King, Aske had declared: "In all parts of the realm, men's hearts much grudged with the suppression of the abbeys, and the first fruits, by reason the same, would be the destruction of the whole religion in England." Henry VIII, reneging on promises made during negotiations with the leaders, ruthlessly crushed the rebellion and Aske and the abbots and priors of Fountains, Jervaulx, Bridlington, Sawley, and Barlings in Lincolnshire were among those hanged at Tyburn in July 1537 for their insurrection. The ex-abbot of Rievaulx and ex-prior of Gisborough suffered the same fate. Whitby Abbey was the last religious establishment in Yorkshire to be dissolved.

Gazetteer

Allerton Mauleverer Priory Near St Martin's Church, Allerton Mauleverer, 12km (7.5 miles) NE of Harrogate, North Yorkshire (SE 4157). No visible remains

Arden Priory Arden Hall, Arden-with-Ardenside, Hawnby, 10km (6.5 miles) NW of Helmsley, North Yorkshire (SE 520906). Private

Arthington Priory The Nunnery, on A659, Arthington, 6 km (4 miles) E of Otley, West Yorkshire (SE 288451). Private

Barnoldswick Abbey W of Barnoldswick, 14km (9 miles) NE of Clitheroe, Lancashire (SD 872466). Private

Basedale Priory Baysdale Abbey, 10km (6 miles) SE of Stokesley, North Yorkshire (NZ 622056). Minimal remains

Beverley Black Friars Friars Lane, Beverley, East Riding (TA 038393). Youth Hostel Association

Beverley Grey Friars near Albert Terrace, Beverley, East Riding (TA 030394). No visible remains

Bolton Priory Bolton Abbey Estate, on B6160, 11km (7 miles) NE of Skipton, North Yorkshire (SE 074541). Tel: 01756 718009; Web: www.boltonabbey.com

Bridlington Priory Church Green, Bridlington, East Riding (TA 177680). Tel: 01262 601938; Web: www.bridlingtonpriory.co.uk

Burstall Priory S of Skeffling, 32km (20 miles) SE of Kingston upon Hull, East Yorkshire (TA3518). No visible remains, site submerged

Byland Abbey On minor road near Coxwold village, 3km (2 miles) W of Ampleforth, North Yorkshire (SE 549789). English Heritage; Tel: 01347 868614

Coverham Abbey Off Coverham Lane, in centre of Coverham, 6.5km (4 miles) W of Middleham, North Yorkshire (SE 106863). Private

Doncaster Grey Friars N of the Sheffield & South Yorkshire Canal, Doncaster, South Yorkshire (SE 572036). No visible remains

Doncaster White Friars Minor road off A630, Doncaster, South Yorkshire (SE 574032). No visible remains

Drax Priory On farmland, Long Drax, 11km (7 miles) SE of Selby, Yorkshire (SE 667284). Minimal remains

Easby Abbey Off B6271, 1.5km (1 mile) SE of Richmond, North Yorkshire (NZ 185003). English Heritage; Tel: 0870 333 1181. Unattended, free access

Ecclesfield Priory Suburb of City of Sheffield, 6.5km (4 miles) N of city centre, Sheffield, South Yorkshire (SK 188397). Private

Egglestone Abbey On minor road off B6277, 1.5km (1 mile) S of Barnard Castle, County Durham (NZ 062151). English Heritage; Tel: 0870 333 1181. Unattended, free access

Ellerton Priory Alongside B6270, 5km (3 miles) SE of Reeth, North Yorkshire (SE 079973). Private, but visible from road

Ellerton Priory In Ellerton village, 16km (10 miles) SE of York, North Yorkshire (SE 701399). Church in use

Embsay Priory In Embsay village, 3km (2 miles) NE of Skipton (SE 010543). No visible remains and exact location uncertain

Esholt Priory At Esholt Hall, near Apperley Bridge, Shipley, 2.5km (1.5 miles) S of Guiseley, Leeds, West Yorkshire (SE 188397). No public access

Foukeholme Priory Nun House, near Thimbleby, 6.5km (4 miles) E of Northallerton, North Yorkshire (SE 446940). No visible remains

Fountains Abbey On minor road off B6265, 6.4km (4 miles) SW of Ripon, North Yorkshire (SE 278703). National Trust; Tel: 01765 608888

Gisborough Priory Close to Guisborough town centre, North Yorkshire (NZ 618163). English Heritage; Tel: 01287 633801

Goathland Hermitage Abbot's House, on minor road off A169, Goathland, 13km (8 miles) SW of Whitby, North Yorkshire (NZ 841006). No visible remains

Grosmont Priory In Grosmont village, 9km (5.5 miles) SW of Whitby, North Yorkshire (NZ 828058). Private

Hackness Priory Storr Lane, Hackness, 10km (6 miles) NW of Scarborough, North Yorkshire (SE 969905). No visible remains

Haltemprice Priory Abbey Lane, 3km (2 miles) S of Cottingham, North Yorkshire (TA 042309). Private

Hampole Priory Village Green, off A638, Hampole, 10km (6 miles) NW of Doncaster, South Yorkshire (SE 506104). Private

Handale (Grendale) Priory In Handale village, 11km (7 miles) E of Guisborough, North Yorkshire (NZ 725157). Private

Headley Priory Headley Hall Farm, Spen Common Lane, 5km (3 miles) SW of Tadcaster, West Yorkshire. No visible remains

Healaugh Park Priory Off minor road near Healaugh village, 4km (2.5 miles) NW of Tadcaster, North Yorkshire (SE 484464). Private

Jervaulx Abbey Close to A6018 at East Witton, 5km (3 miles) SE of Middleham, North Yorkshire (SE 173856). Private, but public access

Keldholme Priory In Keldholme village, Kirkbymoorside, 9km (5.5 miles) NW of Pickering, North Yorkshire (SE 710863). Private

Kildale Crutched Friars Kildale, 5km (3 miles) SE of Great Ayton, North Yorkshire. No visible remains

Kingston upon Hull Austin Friars On A63 Castle Street, Kingston upon Hull, East Riding (TA 101284). No visible remains

Kingston upon Hull Priory Off A165, Kingston upon Hull, East Riding (TA 099293). No visible remains

Kingston upon Hull White Friars Off Beech Hill Road, Kingston upon Hull , East Yorkshire (TA 098129). No visible remains

Kirkham Priory Beside minor road off A64, 8km (5 miles) SW of Malton, North Yorkshire (SE 735657). English Heritage; Tel: 01653 618768

Kirklees Priory In Kirklees Estate, off A62 Leeds Road, Mirfield, 6.5km (4miles) NE of Huddersfield, West Yorkshire (SE 175221). Private

Kirkstall Abbey On A65, 5.5km (3.5 miles) W of Leeds city centre, West Yorkshire (SE 297338). Tel: 0113 2305492; Web: www.leeds.gov.uk/kirkstallabbey

Knaresborough Priory On edge of Knaresborough, 5km (3 miles) NE of Harrogate, North Yorkshire (SE 357557). No visible remains

Lastingham Abbey In Lastingham village, 5km (3 miles) NE of Kirkbymoorside, North Yorkshire (SE 728904). Church in use

Malton Priory Old Malton, 1km (0.5 miles) N of Malton, North Yorkshire (SE 799726). Church in use

Marrick Priory Near Marrick hamlet, 11km (7 miles) SW of Richmond, North Yorkshire (SE 670 978). Private; outdoor education centre

Marton Priory Marton Abbey Farm, on B1363, Marton-cum-Moxby, 5km (3 miles) E of Easingwold, North Yorkshire (SE 585696). Private

Meaux Abbey Near Meaux village, 6.5 km (4 miles) E of Beverley, East Riding (TA 092394). Private

Middlesbrough Priory Off Ferry Road, Middlesbrough, North Yorkshire (NZ 496211). No visible remains

Monk Bretton Priory Abbey Lane, off A633, 1.5km (1 mile) E of Barnsley, South Yorkshire (SE 373065). English Heritage; unattended, free access

Mount Grace Priory Staddle Bridge, on A19 just NW of Osmotherley, 10km (6 miles) NE of Northallerton, North Yorkshire (SE 449985). National Trust; Tel: 01609 883494

Moxby Priory Moxby Hall Farm, off B1363, Moxby, 8km (5 miles) SE of Easingwold, North Yorkshire (SE 597668). No visible remains

Newburgh Priory Near Coxwold village, 8km (5 miles) N of Easingwold, North Yorkshire (SE 543765). Private, but open to the public. Tel: 01347 868372; Web: www.newburghpriory.co.uk

Northhallerton Austin Friars On site of Fleece Inn, Northallerton town centre, North Yorkshire (SE 369940). No visible remains

Northallerton White Friars In Friarage Field, E of Northhallerton town centre, North Yorkshire (SE 370942). No visible remains

North Ferriby Priory North Ferriby, 11km (7 miles) SW of Kingston upon Hull, East Riding (SE 987257). No visible remains

Nostell Priory Off A638 Doncaster Road, 8km (5 miles) SE of Wakefield, Yorkshire (SE 407172). National Trust; Tel: 01924 863892

Nun Appleton Priory Nun Appleton Hall, Appleton Roebuck, 10km (6 miles) SE of York, North Yorkshire (SE 556399). Private, no visible remains

Nunburnholme Priory In the village of Nunburnholme, 5km (3 miles) SE of Pocklington, East Riding (SE 853485). No visible remains

Nunkeeling Priory Nunkeeling, 3km (2 miles) W of Bewholme hamlet, 10km (6 miles) NW of Hornsea, East Riding (TA 145501). Free access

Nun Monkton Priory Nun Monkton, 10km (6 miles) NW of York, North Yorkshire (SE 512578). Church in use

Pontefract Priory In Monk Hill area of City of Pontefract, West Yorkshire (SE 463226). No visible remains

Richmond Grey Friars Friary Gardens, off Victoria Road, Richmond, North Yorkshire (NZ 171010). Free access

Richmond Priory On A6136, Richmond, North Yorkshire (NZ 177007). Private, but visible from road

Rievaulx Abbey On minor road off B1257, Rievaulx village, 4km (2.5 miles) W of Helmsley, North Yorkshire (SE 577849). English Heritage; Tel: 01439 798228

Roche Abbey Off A634, 2.5 km (1.5 miles) SE of Maltby, Rotherham, South Yorkshire (SK 544898). English Heritage; Tel: 01709 812739

Rosedale Priory In Rosedale Abbey village, 13km (8 miles) NW of Pickering, North Yorkshire (SE 724959). Church in use

Sawley Abbey Sawley, off A59, 5.5km (3.5 miles) NE of Clitheroe, Lancashire (SD 776464). English Heritage, free access

Scarborough Black Friars Friar's Way, Scarborough, North Yorkshire (TA 043889). No visible remains

Scarborough Grey Friars Near St Sepulchre, Scarborough, North Yorkshire (TA 046889). No visible remains

Scarborough White Friars Near Queen Street Chapel, Scarborough, North Yorkshire (TA 044887). No visible remains

Selby Abbey The Crescent, Selby, 20km (13 miles) SE of York, North Yorkshire (SE 616324). Tel: 01757 703123; Web: www.selbyabbey.org.uk

Skewkirk Priory Skewkirk Hall, off Ness Lane, near Kirk Hammerton, 13km (8 miles) W of York, North Yorkshire (SE 472541). Private

Snaith Priory Gowdall Lane, Snaith, 10km (6 miles) S of Selby, West Yorkshire (SE 641222). Church in use

Swine Priory In Swine village, 13km (8 miles) NE of Kingston upon Hull, East Riding (TA 132358). Church in use

Syningthwaite Priory Syningthwaite Priory Farmhouse, off B1224, Bilton in Ainsty, 13km (8 miles) SW of York, North Yorkshire (SE 462487). Private

Thicket Priory Near Thorganby village, 16km (10 miles) SE of York, North Yorkshire (SE 697435). Private Carmelite community

Tickhill Priory The Friary, Tickhill, 11km (7 miles) S of Doncaster, South Yorkshire (SK 586928). Private

Warter Priory Warter, off B1246, 6.5km (4 miles) E of Pocklington, East Riding (SE 869504). No visible remains

Watton Priory Watton, 10km (6 miles) N of Beverley, East Riding (TA 024498). Private

Whitby Abbey On cliff top above Whitby town on E side of River Esk, Whitby, North Yorkshire (NZ 904115). English Heritage; Tel: 01947 603568

Wilberfoss Priory N of St John the Baptist Church, off A1079, Wilberfoss, 13km (8 miles) E of York, North Yorkshire (SE 733510). No visible remains

Woodkirk Priory On A653 Dewsbury-Leeds Road, Woodkirk, Leeds, West Yorkshire (SE 272250). Church in use

Wykeham Priory Wykeham Abbey, 10 km (6 miles) SW of Scarborough, North Yorkshire (SE 960820). Private

Yarm Black Friars The Friarage, on A67, Yarm, 13km (8 miles) SE of Darlington, North Yorkshire (NZ 420125). Private

Yedingham Priory Abbey Farm, Yedingham, 14km (9 miles) NE of Malton, North Yorkshire (SE 897798). Private

York Clementhorpe Priory Off Nunnery Lane, City of York, North Yorkshire (SE 603511). No visible remains

York Fishergate Priory Off Fishergate, City of York, North Yorkshire. No visible remains

York Holy Trinity Priory S side of Micklegate, City of York, North Yorkshire (SE 599515). Church in use

York St Andrew's Priory Off Fishergate, City of York, North Yorkshire (SE 606511). No remains

York St Mary's Abbey In Museum Gardens, City of York, North Yorkshire (SE 599522). York Museum's Trust; Tel: 01904 687687. Web: www.yorkstmarys.org.uk

York St Olave Priory Marygate, adjacent to Museum Gardens, City of York, North Yorkshire (SE 599522). Church tower extant

York Austin Friars Near York Museum Gardens, City of York, North Yorkshire. No visible remains

York Black Friars Off Queen Street, City of York, North Yorkshire. No visible remains

York Crutched Friars Off Scarcroft Road, City of York, North Yorkshire. No visible remains; exact location unknown

York Grey Friars N of Tower Street, City of York, North Yorkshire. No visible remains; exact location unknown

York Sack Friars N of York Museum Gardens, , North Yorkshire. No visible remains; exact location unknown

York White Friars Stonebow Lane, N of Foss Bridge, City of York, North Yorkshire. No visible remains

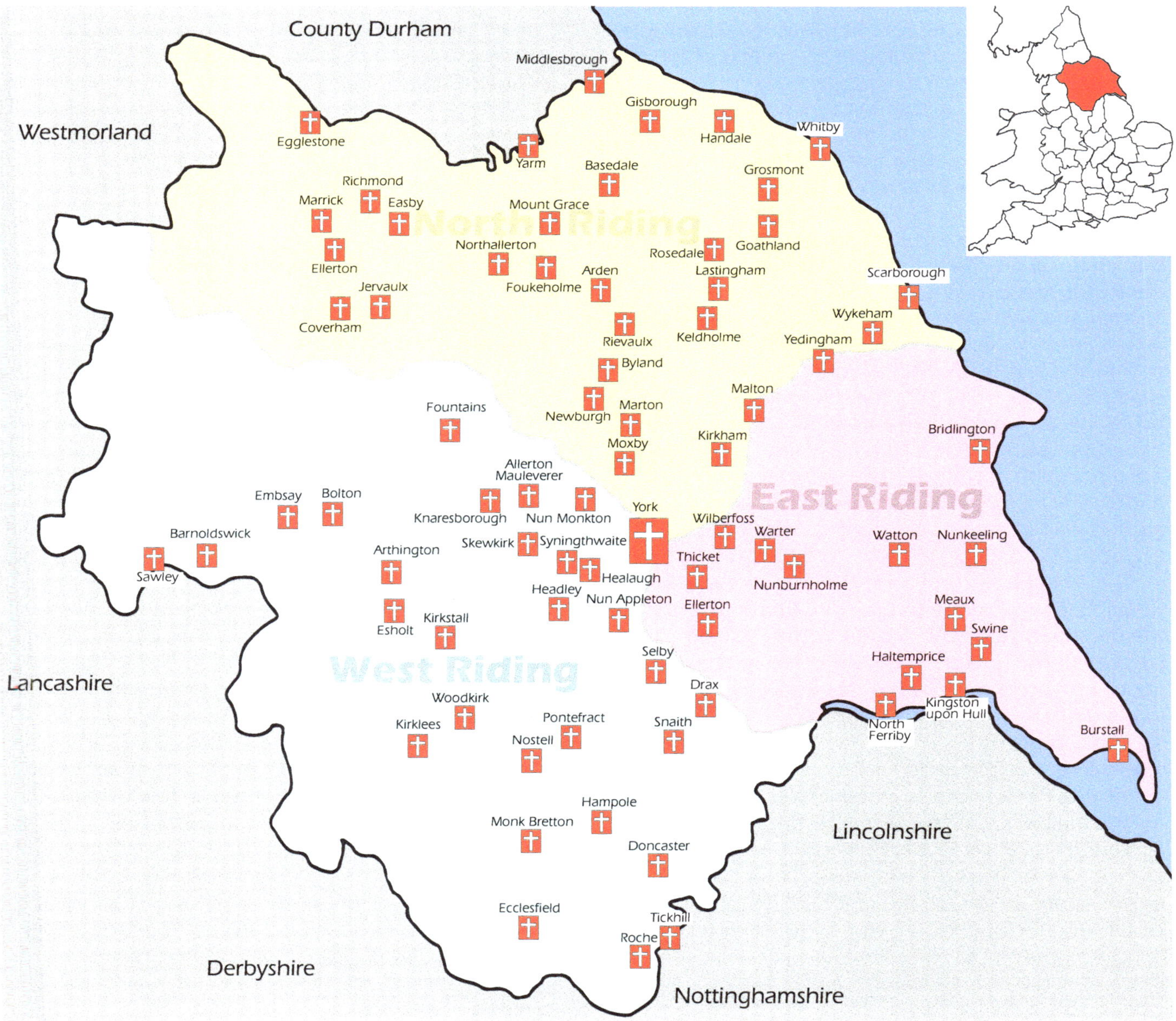

Beverley Black Friars

-1233–1539

Urban developments have destroyed most of the medieval houses of the preaching friars, but one building of the Dominicans, or Black Friars, has been rescued from a dilapidated state in Beverley and restored by the Friary Trust. This rare survival is now a Youth Hostel. It probably was the dormitory and library, which had been damaged by fire in 1449, restored by Henry VI, and then left to fall into decay after the Dissolution. The surviving building is a complex structure largely of two phases, with the eastern walls with dressed limestone blocks dating from the rebuilding after the fire and standing on fourteenth century footings, and the western part added much later in thin, probably Flemish bricks. The south doorway behind the porch is of the fourteenth century. Affixed to the exterior of the south wall is a remarkable but much eroded stone sculpture of a lady (c1300), which may have been a tomb cover.

Of note within is a portion of recently excavated medieval floor tiles, but the most interesting are the wall paintings in the Great Hall and the ante-room, which date from the fifteenth or early sixteenth centuries and are said to be the most important in the East Riding. The vigorous floral design in the hall is in charcoal on chalk and includes a large floral motif interspersed with small fruits and flowers, and a chain and lozenge pattern, laid horizontally within which are stylised acanthus leaves flanking a pattern of thin strap work. Further acanthus scrolls fill in the spaces between the links. The foundations of other buildings, including the church and cloister, now lie buried beneath the nearby railway line, which was cut through the priory in 1846. A sixteenth century gateway from the priory is incorporated in the garden wall of the old vicarage. It once stood on the opposite end of Eastgate.

The Dominicans arrived in Beverley before 1233, when Stephen Goldsmith provided land close to the great minster and beyond Eastgate for the construction of a large priory complex taking up about forty-two acres (17ha). The Provincial Chapter was held here in 1240, with the King contributing 10 marks towards expenses. The foundation is also claimed by the town and the Crown. Henry III granted fifteen oaks from royal forests in 1263 for the building of a large church. The community apparently reached its zenith in 1304 when there were forty-two friars in residence and continued to prosper until the severe fire of 1449. The priory was dissolved in February1539 and let to Richard Faircliff and then granted to John Pope. It later came into the ownership of the Wartons, a well known and wealthy Beverley family.

Beverley Grey Friars

-1267–1539

The origin of the priory is obscure, but it was in existence by 1267 when one Franciscan friar preached at Beverley on the feast of St John. Its founder may have been John de Hightmede. The priory may originally have been within the town walls, but was later given a site outside Keldgate, together with additional land and many other goods. Some thirty-eight friars were in residence in 1300, when Edward I gave 38s for food. This was probably the largest number of friars, but the community was devastated by the Black Death later that century, which threw it into great poverty, with the result that its buildings fell into ruin. However, many bequests enabled a restoration and rebuilding programme soon after. The priory was threatened when a rebellion broke out in autumn 1536 on Westwood Green outside the priory, but it was spared. Richard Ingworth, Bishop of Dover, accepted the surrender by Warden Thomas Thomson in February 1539. The house, which covered some seven acres (2.8ha) was valued at only £5 6s and was granted to Thomas Culpeper in 1540. The site changed hands several times later in the sixteenth century. Nothing at all is left.

Burstall Priory

• Benedictine 1115–1395

The Priory of Burstall was an alien cell of the Benedictine abbey of St Martin d'Auchy near Aumale in the diocese of Rouen, which in 1115 was given a large amount of land and several churches and tithes in Holderness and North-east Lincolnshire by Stephen, Earl of Albemarle. Several monks were sent over to England and formed a small monastic establishment centred on the chapel of St Helen. In the wars with France, the priory was frequently seized by the Crown and its revenues withheld. In 1381 Richard II granted it to Durham, with the intention that the prior and all foreign monks were to be replaced by as many English monks or secular canons. This did not come to pass, as with the assent of the Prior of Durham, the King granted the custody of the priory to the Prior of Burstall, John de Harmesthorp, in 1382. It was, however, a short-lived reprieve. The priory had become so impoverished by the seizure of its revenues that the abbey of Aumale sold its property to Kirkstall Abbey in 1395, marking the end of the Burstall cell. The last traces of the priory disappeared under a sea of mud during floods of the River Humber in the 1900s. A stone doorway from the priory is now in Easington Church, and a lavishly decorated fourteenth century tomb, probably of William de la Mare, Provost of Beverley Minster, reposes in the south aisle of St Mary's church at Welwick.

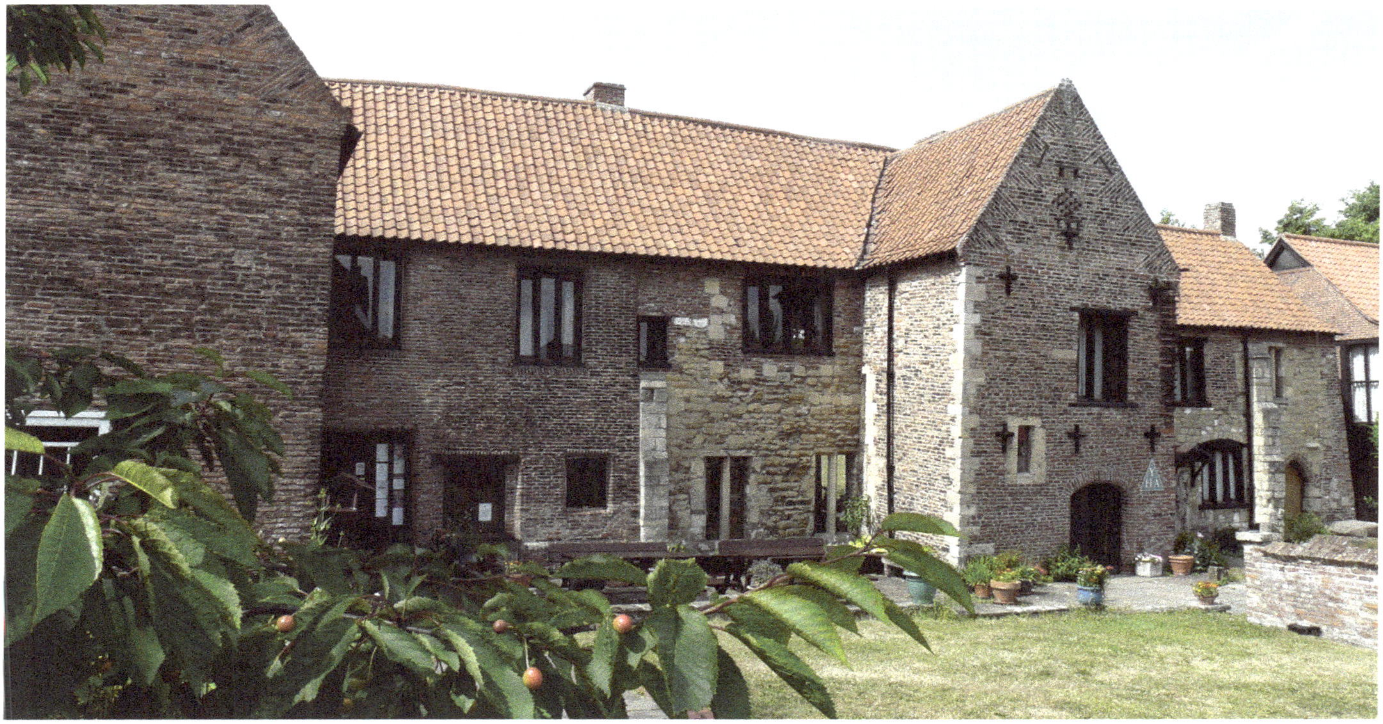

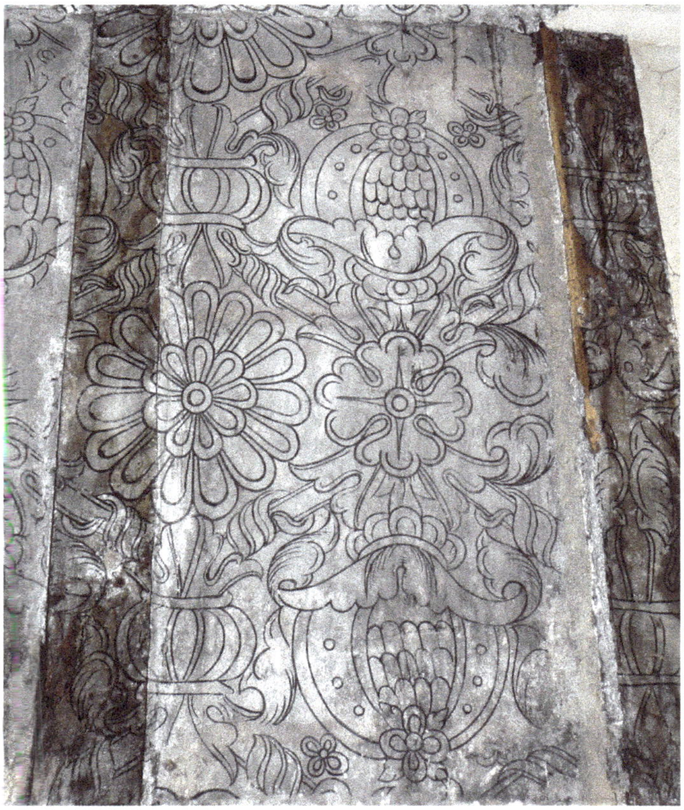

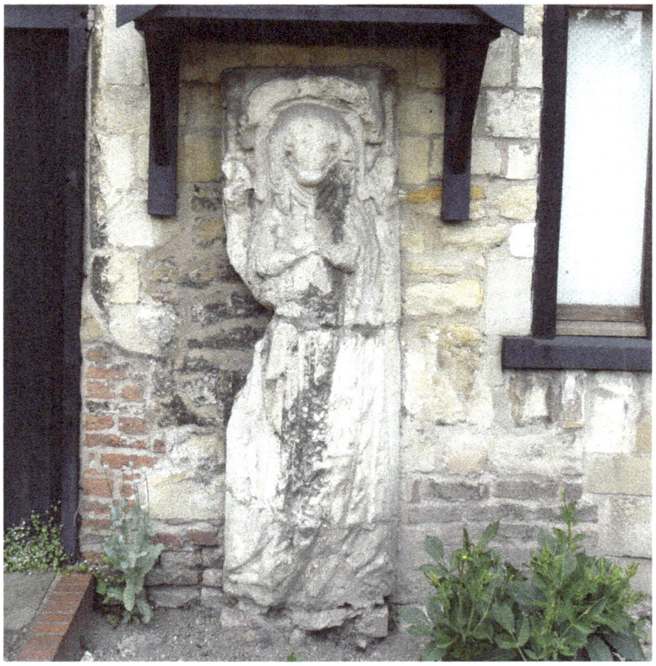

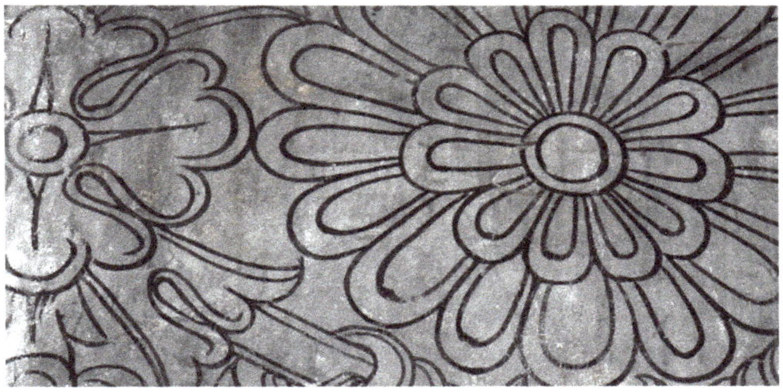

Photos of Beverley Black Friars- clockwise from top

Surviving Black Friars building, now a Youth Hostel
Stone sculpture of lady from c1300
Large floral motif in charcoal on chalk
Vigorous floral design interspersed with fruits

Bridlington Priory

St Mary • Augustinian 1113–1537

The nave of the church of St Mary and the repaired gateway known as the Bayle, from the French Baille meaning enclosure, are the only surviving parts of this Priory of Augustinian canons. The impressive church escaped destruction after the Dissolution only because it was then already the parish church. The church is a mixture of old and new, but the mighty nave easily recalls the great days of the priory. It is a large and airy space with ten bays of arcading, particularly notable in the north arcade with its clustered columns, triforium and clerestory in the Decorated style, and an unusual triforium with tracery in two planes on the south side. There are several features to admire within, the most precious of which is the Founder's Stone, richly carved in black Tournai marble, which is incised with the outline of a Byzantine church. It is believed to be the tomb cover of founder Walter de Gant. The reconstructed cloister arcading in the north isle dates from between 1175 and 1200, and full details of the cloisters, octagonal chapter house and other monastic buildings, as they would have been c1535, can be seen in the nearby model. Adjacent is the fourteenth century font of Frosterly marble from County Durham, but the wooden canopy dates from 1955 and was made by Robert Thompson and bears his trade mark – the mouse. Not to be missed is the north porch with stone carvings of Henry III, Queen Eleanor and Archbishop de Gray of York. The altar stands on the pre-reformation base with its five consecration crosses.

Externally, the church is dominated by its western aspect, and especially the two towers, whose upper storeys were added by George Gilbert Scott in the 1870s as part of a complete rebuilding programme. One of the towers has been squared off above the bell enclosure, while the other rises to a pinnacled and battlemented crown. The richly carved central doorway is surmounted by an ogee arch and finial set against the lower part of the great west window, said to be the largest Perpendicular window in Yorkshire. The earliest part of the priory is the lower section of the wall between the north-west tower and the north porch, while the south side shows traces of the cloister and prior's lodging, which were built against the church wall. The east end marks the site of the crossing between the nave and the vanished choir and transepts.

The Bayle was the priory's main entrance and was built as part of the fortifications licensed in 1388. The passage gives access to small wings, each with its own garderobe. One room was used as the porter's lodge and the other as a prison. A large first floor chamber accessed via a spiral stair was used as the prior's court. Although it has been much altered and since the Dissolution used a school, garrison, town hall and much more, its original form has been retained.

Bridlington Priory was founded on the site of a Saxon church by Walter de Gant in 1113 and was the first Augustinian house to be established in the North of England. With several endowments, it soon grew to become one of the wealthiest and most important monastic settlements in the county. In 1148, during the troubled reign of King Stephen, the priory was fortified but to no avail. It was seized by William le Gros, Count of Aumale, who expelled the prior and canons and used the priory as his base. In 1200, King John granted a licence to hold an annual two-day fair and a weekly market. As Bridlington was always vulnerable to attacks by Norsemen and the Scots, Richard II granted it a licence to crenellate in 1388, but its defences were never tested. The community acquired much land in Yorkshire and Lincolnshire, where it undertook sheep farming on a grand scale, the wool trade being its chief source of income. The priory also became a centre of literary culture.

Frequent visitations, however, discovered a lack of sound financial management and lax discipline, but its history was otherwise uneventful. Exempt from these negative revelations was John of Bridlington, who was prior in the mid-fourteenth century and was credited with many miracles. In 1401, John was the last Englishman to be canonised before the reformation. Henri IV and Henry V both came to Bridlington to worship at his shrine. In 1409, Pope Gregory XII conferred on the prior the privilege of wearing mitre and ring, an honour shared north of the Trent only by the Benedictine abbots of Selby and St Mary's at York.

The priory was dissolved in 1537 and its last prior, William Wode, was executed at Tyburn for his part in the Pilgrimage of Grace. As a result, the priory suffered savage destruction. The shrine of St John was publicly burnt in the market place of the Old Town. Bridlington was a wealthy monastery, its annual value having been assessed in the *Valor* of 1535 as £547 6s. Apart from the prior, there were twenty-six canons in residence at that time.

Photos – clockwise from top

The priory church is a major landmark in this seaside town
The Baille was the main gateway into the priory
Richly carved Founder's Stone in black Tournai marble
Stone carvings of Henry III, Queen Eleanor and Archbishop de Gray
Quatrefoil and vine leaf decorations on arch

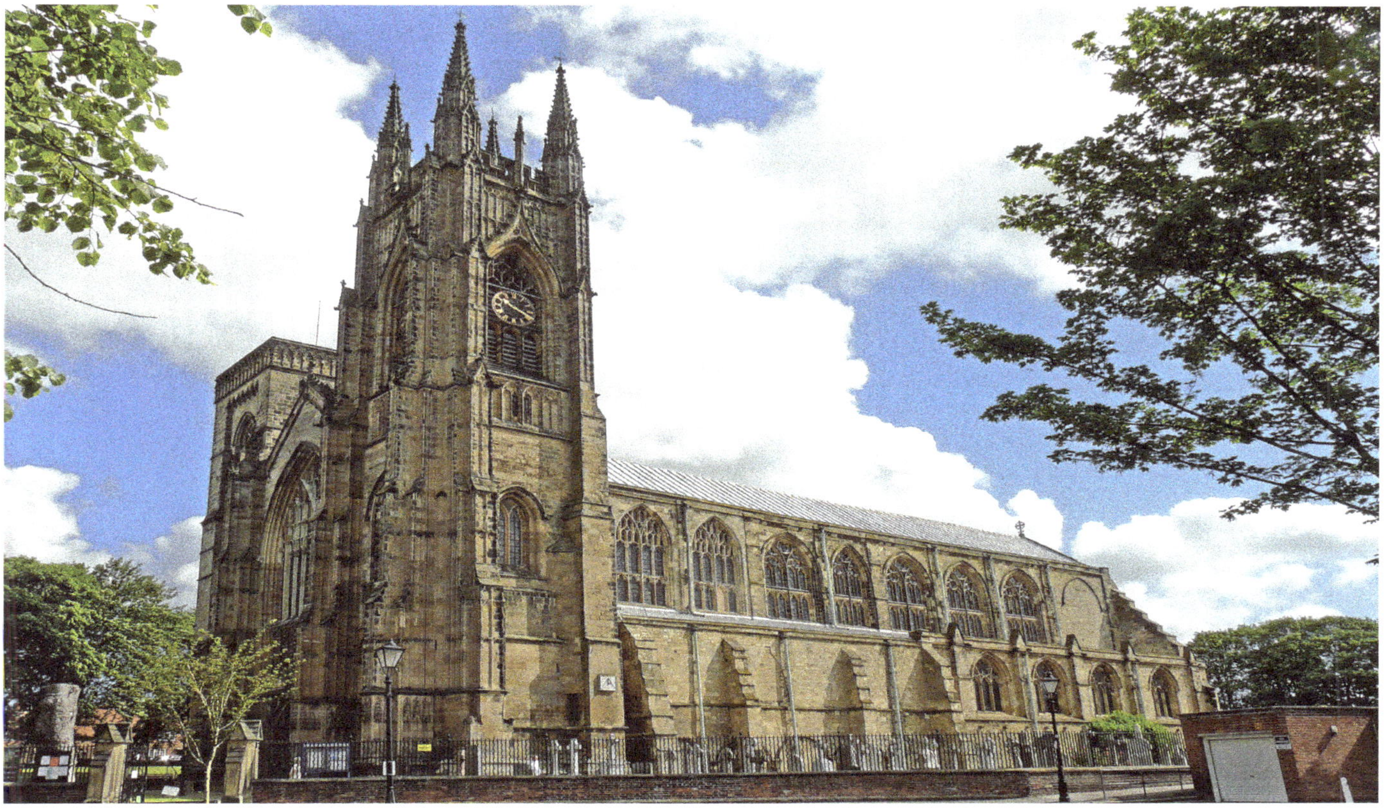

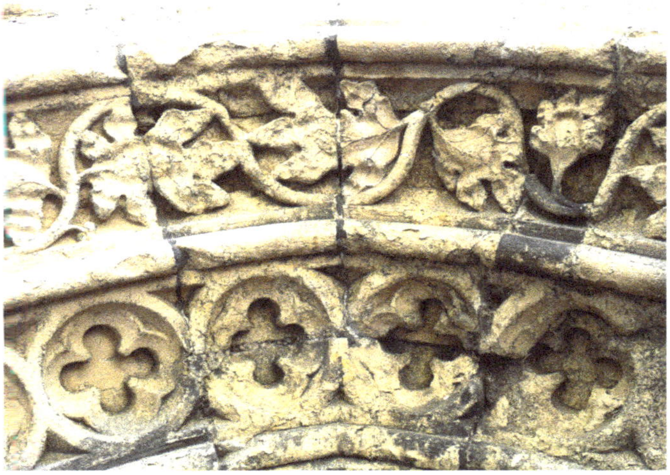

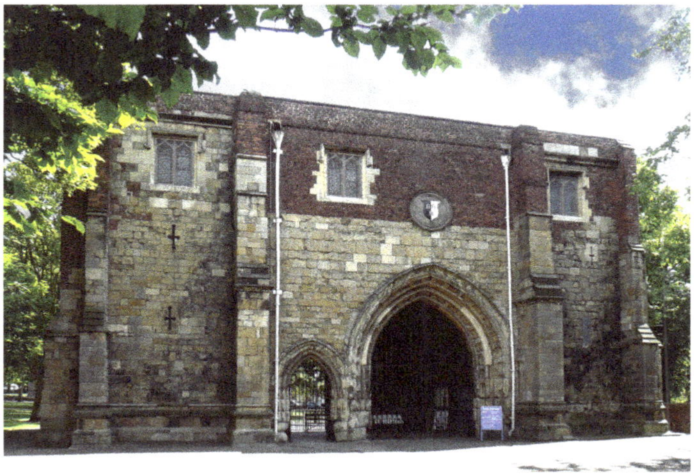

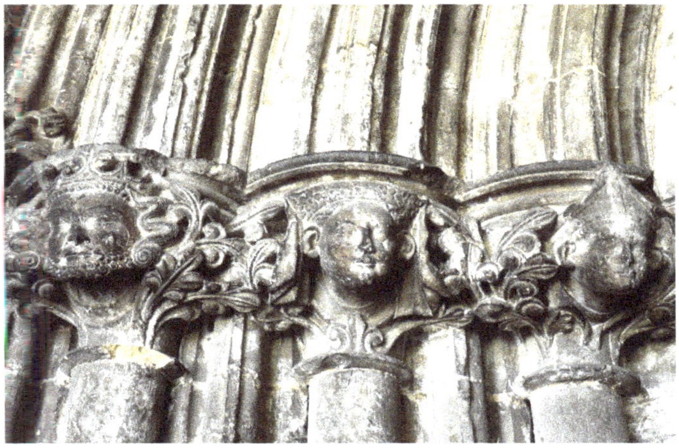

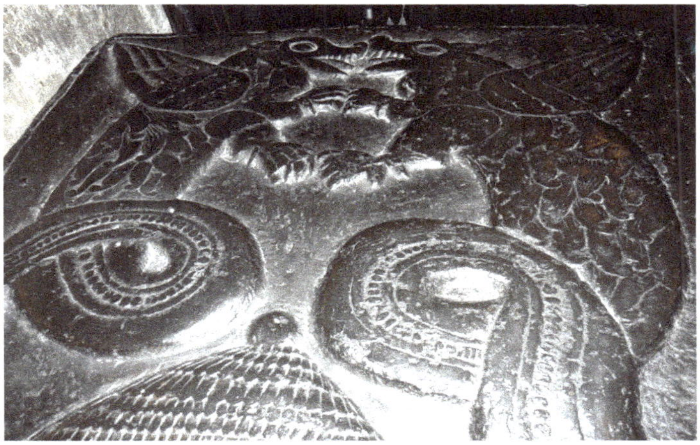

Ellerton Priory

St Mary and St Lawrence • Gilbertine 1199/1212–1538

High on Spalding Moor, on the eastern side of the Vale of the Derwent, overlooking the vast spaces of the Derwent Ings flood meadows, once stood a small priory dedicated to God, the Blessed Mary and St Lawrence. It was founded sometime between 1199 and 1212 by William fitzPeter for canons of the indigenous order of St Gilbert of Sempringham, and for the support of thirteen poor persons of the district. The endowment included lands in Ellerton and neighbourhood, as well as other possessions. Alan de Wilton later became a major benefactor, granting lands and twelve skeps of salt from his works at West Coatham, for a light at the altar of St Lawrence in the canons' church, and for the maintenance of a chaplain. In 1387, it was agreed that patron German Hay and his successors, lords of Aughton, should nominate eight of the poor supported by the priory. Little else of note is known of its history.

The house was surrendered in December 1538 by Prior John Golding and four canons. Its annual value was assessed at £78 0s. All that has survived are earthworks clustered around the church, whose nave is that of the old priory. There is also some evidence of fishponds. The church was made redundant in 1978, but was saved from demolition by the Ellerton Church Preservation Trust and has been restored. While little of medieval interest remains, a visit will reward with some exquisite modern stained glass windows, with the two west windows containing the last fragments of medieval glass at the top.

Haltemprice Priory

St Mary & Holy Cross • Augustinian 1322–1536

Sections of medieval ashlar and decorative brickwork built into a farmhouse, is all that remains of this Augustinian monastery dedicated to Mary the Virgin and the Holy Cross. The farmhouse itself is in an advanced state of decay and unless some restoration is carried out, all traces of Haltemprice Priory will vanish. Records suggest that Sir Thomas Wake, Lord of Liddell, who had inherited the manor of Cottingham in 1300, founded an Augustinian priory there in 1322 but due to legal complications moved it two miles away to Newton and founded Haltemprice Priory, or *Alta Prisa* in Latin, in 1325. He richly endowed the new foundation, which at its peak controlled a large swathe of land. However, it soon fell into debt and after Sir Thomas' death in 1349 the canons were unable to keep the priory in good repair. In a report to the pope in 1411 it was stated that the bell-tower had fallen into the church causing substantial damage, and a fire had destroyed the gatehouse. On the grounds of 'notorious poverty', the priory was exempt from royal taxation, but it never fully recovered. It was dissolved in August 1536. In residence were Prior Robert Colynson, nine canons and forty servants and boys.

Kingston upon Hull Priory

St Mary, St Michael, All Angels & St Thomas the Martyr • Carthusian 1378–1539

The priory had a difficult gestation. According to local historian Tickell, a small college of six secular priests was first established on land granted by Edward I to William de la Pole. After some disagreements, the priests were replaced by Franciscan friars, a move that also proved unsuccessful. William then pulled down all the buildings and determined to found a large monastery for nuns of the Order of St Clare. This did not come to pass and, after William's death, his son and heir, Michael de la Pole, obtained a licence in 1377 from Edward III, to change his father's proposal to a Carthusian priory for a prior and twelve monks, as well as thirteen poor men and an equal number of poor women, as had been his father's wish. The Charterhouse was founded on land outside the town walls the following year, and Walter de Kele was appointed the first prior. A cell for an additional monk was added before 1412. Michael also proceeded with the hospital, which, although a distinct entity, maintained a close connection with the priory and was commonly known as Charterhouse Hospital.

In spite of grants of land and advowson of a church, the priory found it difficult to maintain the community, but this was ameliorated by additional appropriations early in the fifteenth century following a petition to the pope, supported by King Richard II. In dispute was the appropriation of the church at Hogsthorpe in the Lincoln diocese, which after petitions and annulments was finally confirmed to the priory in perpetuity in 1406. Although its clear annual value assessed in the *Valor Ecclesiasticus* at £174 18s was below the £200 stipulated in the 1536 Act of Suppression, the priory survived until finally surrendered by Prior Ralph Mauleverey, together with ten monks, one novice, and one lay-brother, in 1539. Not a trace of the priory is left. It did not survive the Siege of Hull in 1643 during the Civil War and the last remnant, the East Gate, was demolished in 1805.

Kingston upon Hull Austin Friars

1317–1539

The Austin Friars of York founded a house in Hull in 1317, on land granted by Geoffrey de Hotham and John de Wetwang. Little is known about the friars, who are said to have numbered eighteen at the end of the fifteenth century, and were probably entirely dependent on alms. At the time of the Dissolution, their site and garden in Blackfriars Street measured only 45 x 30m (150 x 100ft) and was worth just 5s a year. Prior Alexander Ingram surrendered the house to the Bishop of Dover in March 1539. Nothing is now visible, as at the end of the eighteenth century, what little remained was demolished, with some buildings converted into the Tiger Inn. Excavations in 1994 revealed the plan of the church and cloister, the east and west ranges, and three ovens. The church had north and south aisles, and a tower at the west end.

Kingston upon Hull White Friars

St Mary • 1289/90–1539

This Carmelite priory was founded in 1289 or 1290, so it is said, by Edward I, Sir Robert Ughtred, and Sir Richard de Pole, within the town walls, on the south side of Monkgate, later Blackfriargate. The earliest mention of the house is contained in a petition by Master Robert of Scarborough, Dean of York, in 1289. There were thirteen friars in 1298, but their numbers appear to have increased rapidly, as in 1307, the friars moved to a new site at Milncroft near Beverley Gate, then outside the walls, on land given by Edward I, in return for the site at Monkgate. The friars built a new church, which was consecrated in 1311. They also benefited from further plots of land, and several bequests were made by women to the image of the Virgin Mary in the new church. Prior John Wade surrendered the house to Richard Ingworth, Bishop of Dover, in March 1539.

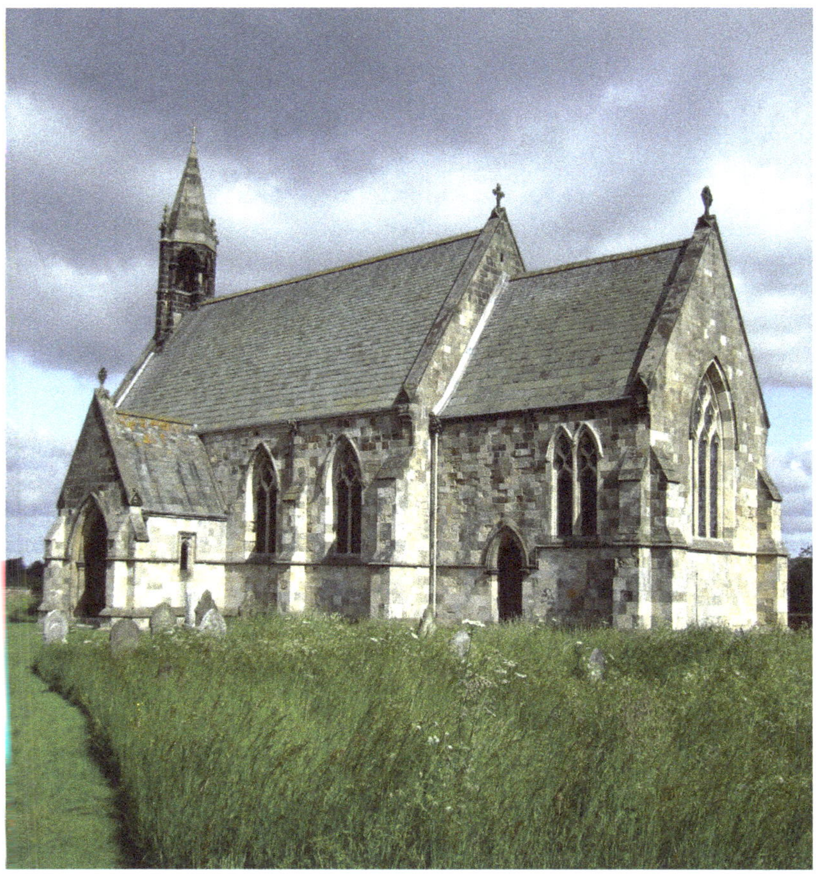

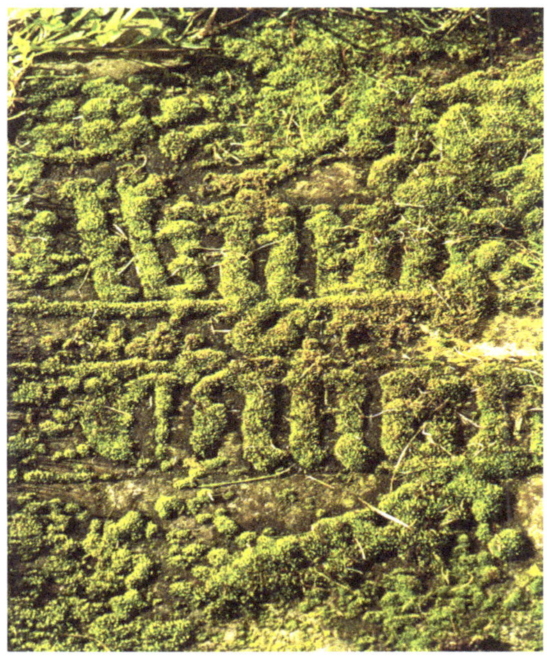

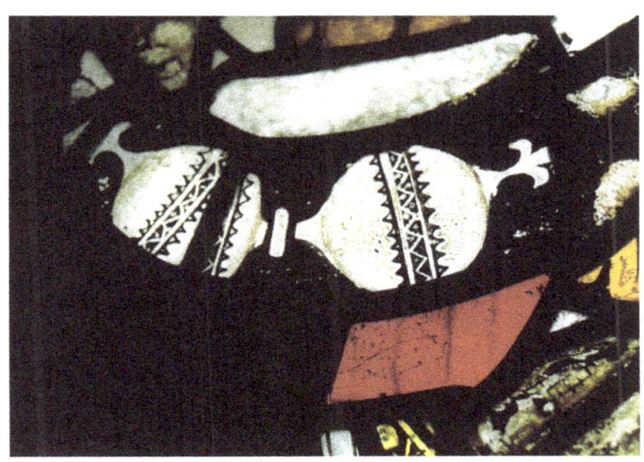

Photos of Ellerton Priory – clockwise from above

The restored Priory Church of St Mary the Virgin
Fourteenth century grave slab cover of John de Wyntringham
Medieval stained glass in the west window of the church

Kirkham Priory

Holy Trinity • Augustinian 1122–1538

The priory ruins, which are scattered along the River Derwent, meander peacefully along this beautiful Yorkshire Dale. The busy road above is screened by a dense growth of Norwegian firs, which blankets the slopes and preserves, most of the time, the site's tranquil ambience. But the priory layout can also be appreciated on the ground, even though much of the monastic buildings barely extend above the wide expanse of grass. The outstanding surviving feature at Kirkham is the late thirteenth century gatehouse, which is of rare quality and is adorned with beautiful carvings over the whole of its remaining façade. On each side of the huge ribbed entrance arch, framed by an ornately carved gable, the figures of George and the Dragon and David and Goliath have been fashioned out of the mellow sandstone. The empty trefoil niche above the apex of the arch once held a carving of the Crucifixion. In niches between the lancet windows, their elaborately embellished tracery still in place, are the figures of Christ, St Philip and St Bartholomew. Filling in other spaces are the heraldic shields of the benefactors.

Once through the impressive doorway, head for the foundations of the priory church, which shows evidence of all three churches built and rebuilt over a period of one hundred years. The first church, a plain aisle-less cruciform shape, was erected c1140, and rebuilt with thicker walls thirty years later. The final version extended the church in the early thirteenth century to a length of 91m (300ft), and, although two piers were added to carry the eastern arch of a new central tower, this was never built. An arched window at the east end of the church stands tall and displays fine architectural detail and the high-quality ashlar blocks used in the later building. An arched Norman gateway leads from the cloister to the refectory. Alongside, the west cloister wall incorporates two splendid thirteenth century arches forming the laver, while on the rear of the wall the outline of vaulting is clearly marked. The gable wall of the dormitory shows the upper doorway and lamp niches. The large reredorter and excavated drainage channels nearby are also worth noting. At the west end of the church stands the vaulted outer parlour, which formed the main entrance to the cloister.

The priory was founded in 1122 for Augustinian canons by Walter l'Espec, Lord of Helmsley, who ten years later also founded the Cistercian abbey at Rievaulx, much closer to his estate. It is said that Kirkham Priory was founded in memory of l'Espec's only son, who had died in the vicinity after a fall from his horse. The first prior was William, the founder's uncle, and the community probably numbered around twenty-six. The priory had an uncertain start, with many of the black canons soon leaving Kirkham, being attracted to the more austere Cistercian way of life. It somehow survived this upheaval and remained faithful to the Augustinian creed. Kirkham Priory never reached the heights of Yorkshire's great abbeys of Fountains and Rievaulx, but was sustained in the twelfth and thirteenth centuries by endowments from the de Roos, who had acquired the lordship of Helmsley. Under their patronage, Kirkham Priory embarked on an ambitious expansion programme, employing craftsmen to provide its buildings with elaborate decorations, some of which can still be admired today.

The priory got involved in several legal actions over hunting rights against William de Roos in 1257 and 1261, and when the archbishop of York visited in 1280, he found the priory heavily in debt, in spite of the sale of sixteen corrodies to help finance the rebuilding of the great choir and presbytery. By 1357, the debt had grown to £1,000, forcing the dispersal of some of the canons to other houses to reduce the size of the community. Visitations also found that the canons lived a 'colourful' life, keeping company with undesirables and being lax on celibacy. The priory, valued at £269 5s, escaped the first round of monastic closures, but was finally dissolved in December 1538, when the last prior, John Wilson, and seventeen canons signed the deed of surrender. The priory was stripped of all valuables and partially demolished before being sold to Henry Knevett in May 1540.

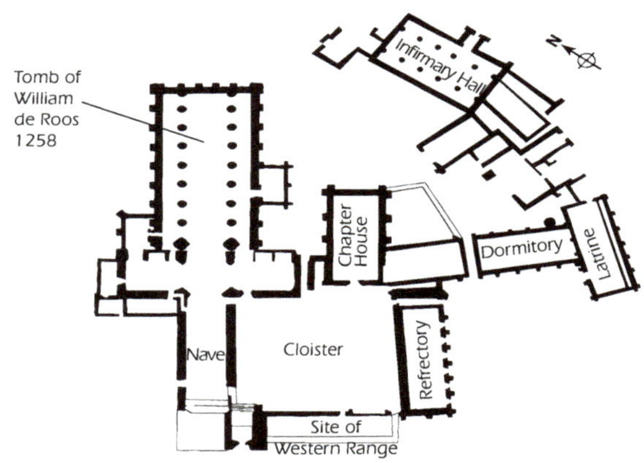

Photos - clockwise from top left

Ornate late thirteenth century gatehouse
Arched window of east end of church
Carving of St George and the Dragon
Remains of laver in cloister wall
View of priory site across the River Derwent
Decorated Norman archway to refectory

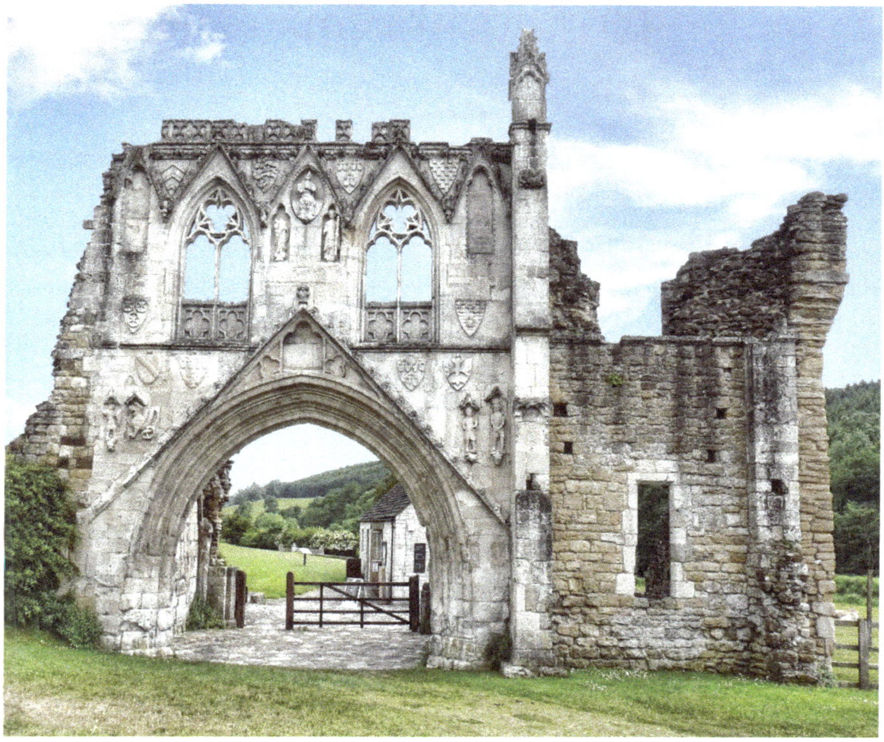

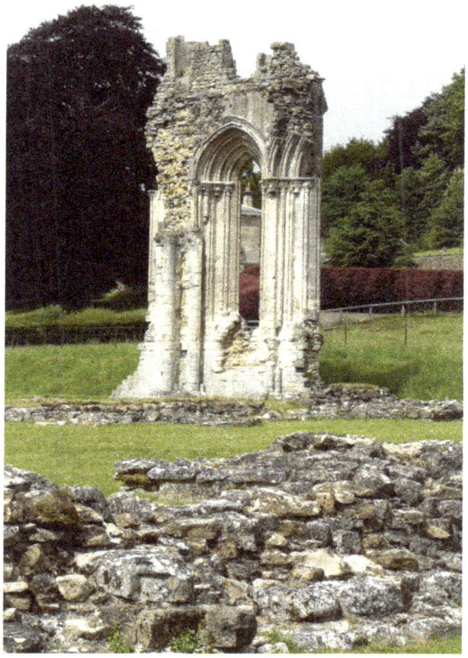

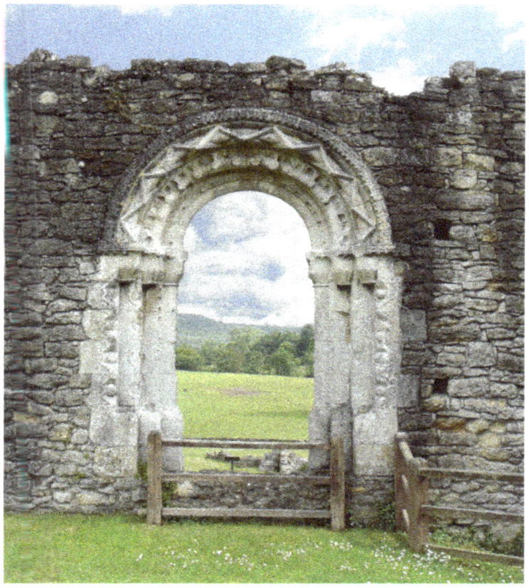

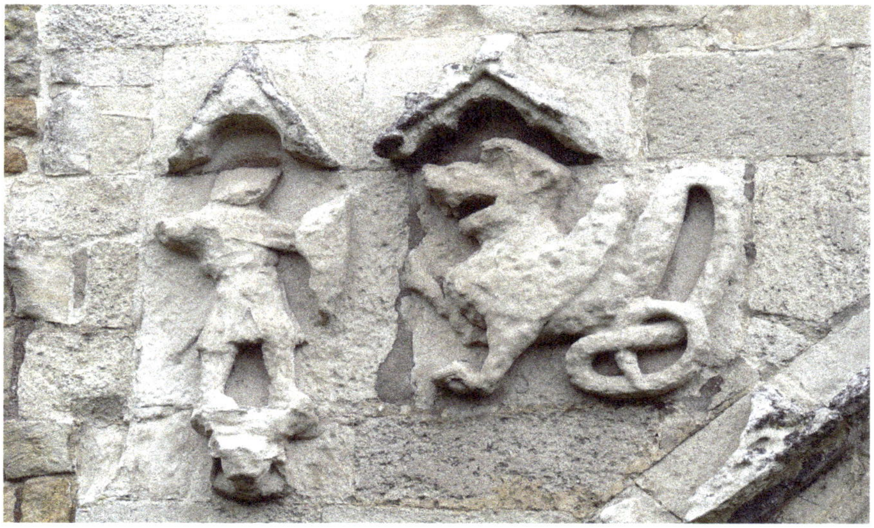

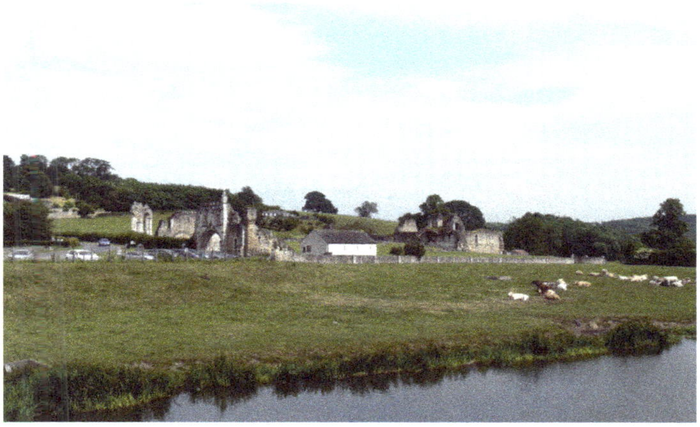

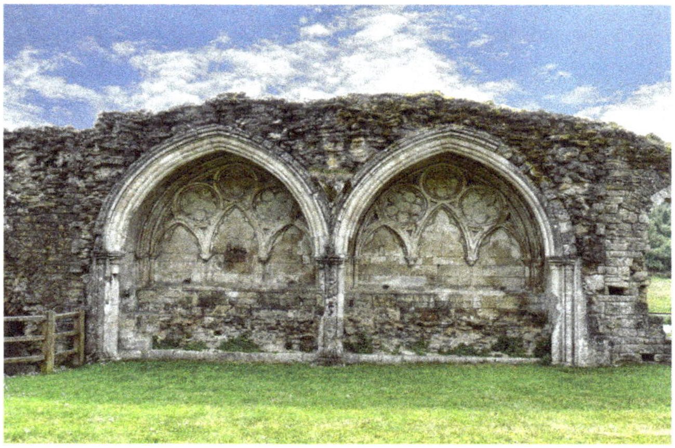

Meaux Abbey

St Mary • Cistercian 1150–1539

This great Cistercian abbey was so thoroughly demolished and its stone carted off to Kingston-upon- Hull for use in Henry VIII's fortifications that nothing of any substance has survived above ground level. The outline of the site can only be seen from the air. Meaux Abbey was founded in 1150 by William le Gros, Count of Aumale, in atonement for failing to honour his vow of going on pilgrimage to the Holy Land, and colonised by monks from Fountains Abbey. The building of the abbey was led by Abbot Adam who has become known as a 'monk-mason'. The site, in the flood plain of the River Hull, was prone to flooding, but this was only one of the problems faced by the community. A chronicle of its history, written by Abbot Thomas Burton (1396-9) recalls that the abbey was rarely free from debts, litigation, raids and internal rebellion, and suffered heavily in 1349 when the Black Death claimed thirty-two monks and seven conversi, leaving just ten monks in residence. Richard Draper, the last abbot, surrendered Meaux to Henry's commissioners in 1539. Three years later, its buildings were razed to the ground.

North Ferriby Priory

St Mary • Augustinian 1312–1536

Every trace of this small priory for six Augustinian canons, believed to have been located in the New Walk area of the village, has disappeared. It was first established c1200, in the reign of King John, by Eustace de Vesci as a commandery of the Knights Templars and was by all accounts a magnificent establishment. On the disbandment of the order in 1312, it was converted into an Augustinian priory dedicated to St Mary. The monks provided hospitality for pilgrims en route from the ferry to the shrine of St John of Beveley, where 'miraculous cures' were said to happen. It is said that one such miracle happened in 1321, when the ten-year old son of William de Ferriby was struck dumb, but was cured after a blessing by the prior of North Ferriby and a visit to St John's shrine. It was dissolved along with the lesser monasteries in 1536, its clear annual value having been assessed at £60 1s. The site was granted to Thomas Culpepper, but is said to have been in the possession of 100 different persons in the space of 130 years. If true, it is probably not surprising that without due care and attention, it fell into ruin and was eventually completely demolished.

Nunburnholme Priory

St Mary • Benedictine nuns c1254–1536

It may have been the smallest and poorest Benedictine house in Yorkshire at the time of its dissolution, but it had an illustrious beginning, being founded c1254 by no less a man than Richard, Earl of Cornwall and King of the Romans, who was the second son of King John and a great warrior and crusader. Small endowments from Richard and Roger de Merlay provided the nuns with a reasonably comfortable living, which appears to have progressed with little or no upheaval. Historic records of life at the nunnery are scarce. It was surrendered by the last prioress Elizabeth Kylburne and five nuns in August 1536, when its net income was just a fraction over £8. The site was granted to Sir Arthur D'arcy, but soon after came into the hands of Thomas Manners, first Earl of Rutland, who had also been given Warter Priory.

The conventual buildings and church were razed to the ground and only mounds of earth indicate the site, which can be reached via a track alongside Manor Farm. A few minutes pause in Nunburnholme church will reward with the arch of the original west tower, which rises from carved capitals and is ornamented with chevron surmounted by grotesque faces. In the churchyard, the shaft of an Anglo-Danish cross, carved on all four sides, should most definitely not be missed. Among the carvings are the Madonna and Child, a centaur, saint, lamb, dragons and a seated warrior. A visit to the nearby Lady's Well, whose sacred waters may have been guarded by the nuns of Nunburnholme, will also be rewarding.

Nunkeeling Priory

St Mary Magdalene & St Helena • Benedictine nuns 1152–1540

The ruined priory church reposes in splendid, almost forgotten isolation in the East Riding but comes alive once a year in autumn when a church service is held among its broken walls. After its suppression in September1540, when the prioress and eleven nuns signed the Deed of Surrender, it was granted to Sir Richard Gresham. It quickly fell into disrepair and soon only the nave and chancel were left standing. However, it was rebuilt in 1810 to serve as the parish church, only to be abandoned once again when the long walk from the centre of the hamlet of Bewholme proved too strenuous for the inhabitants. At that time, two thirteenth century effigies of Sir Andrew Fauconberg and his wife were removed to Hornsea Church, while the original font can be found in St Mary's Church in Hull. Nunkeeling Priory for Benedictine nuns was founded in1150 by Agnes de Arches, widow of Herbert de St Quintin, who bequeathed much of her late husband's estate, including Nunkeeling Church and land at Nunkeeling and Bewholme Wood. The prioress and twelve nuns lived a quiet life, but came to prominence in 1316 when the prioress was named the sole lord of Nunkeeling and one of the lords of Bewholme. The house was valued at only £35 in 1535 but survived the closure of the lesser monasteries.

Sutton White Friars

According to Burton, a house for Carmelites was founded at Sutton on Hull in the reign of Edward I. Nothing further is known and it is believed that the White Friars soon moved to the house in nearby Kingston-upon-Hull.

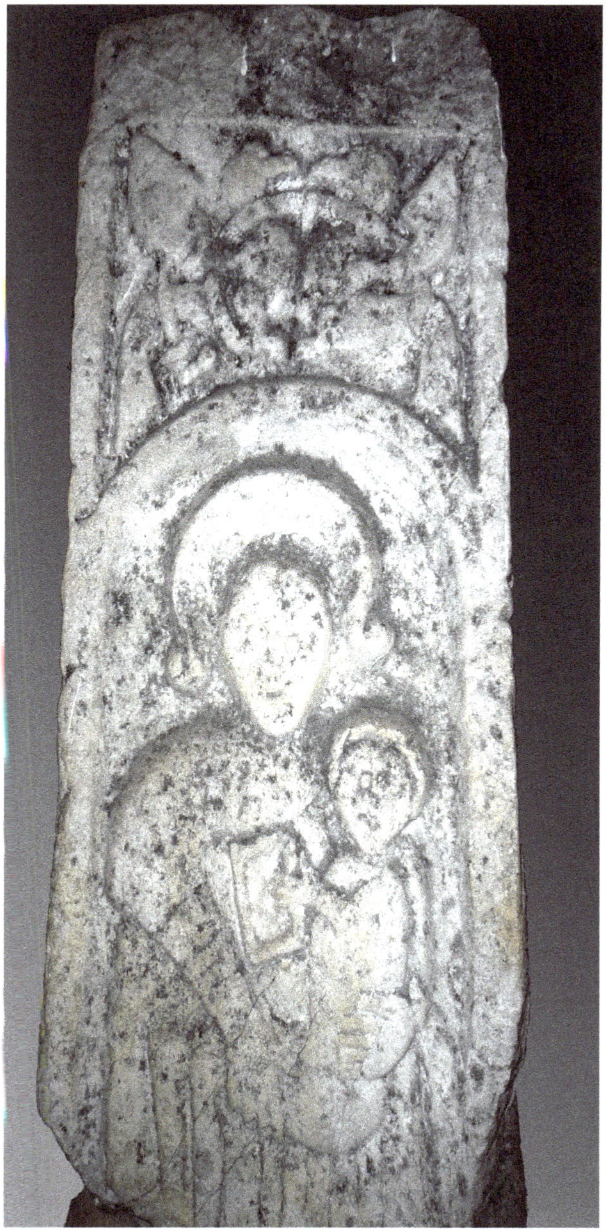

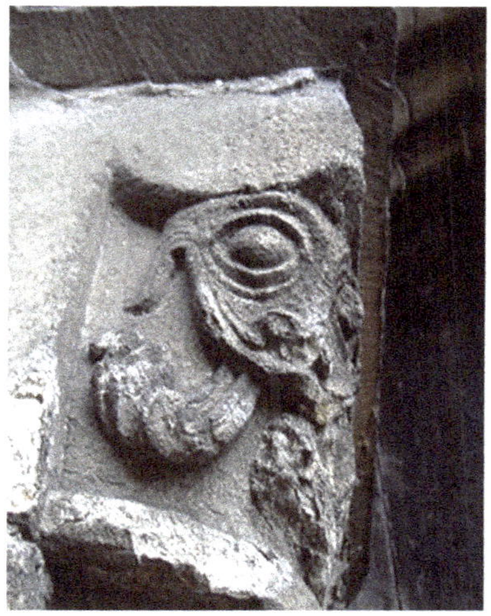

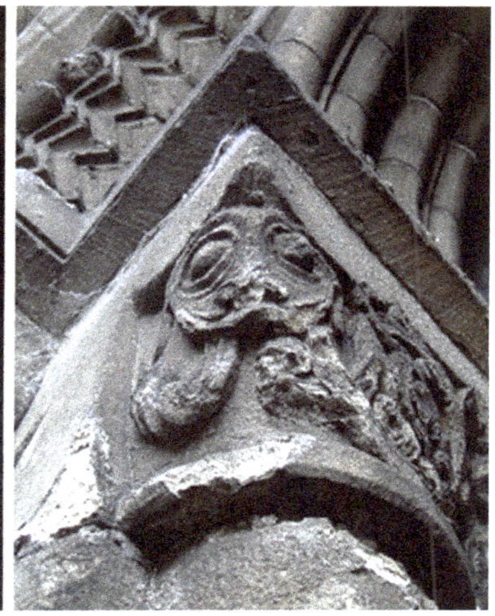

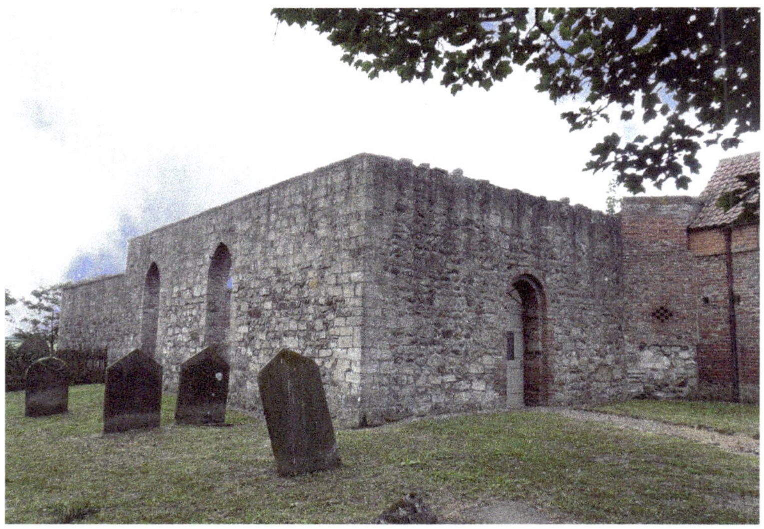

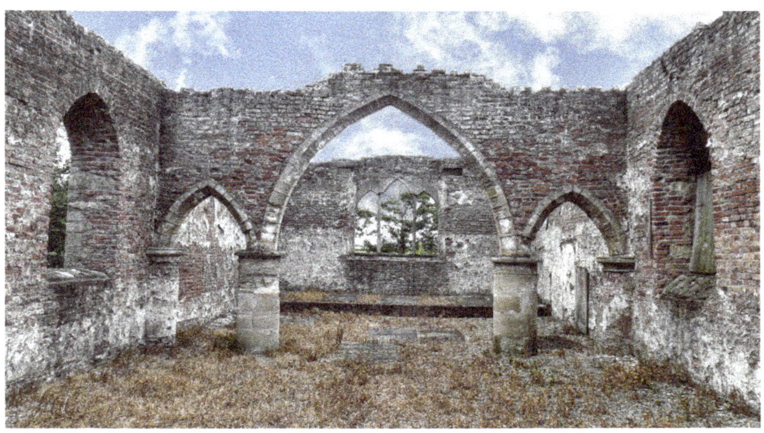

Photos - clockwise from top left

Anglo-Danish cross in Nunburnholme Church
Carvings of green man in Nunburnholme
Simple rectangular church of Nunkeeling
Looking towards altar at Nunkeeling

Swine Priory

St Mary • Cistercian nuns 1150–1539

The present parish church dedicated to the Virgin Mary is the chancel of the original priory church, which was always used by the parishioners. Missing are the transepts and the nave where, contrary to the usual custom, the nuns worshipped. Nothing else is left of the priory buildings, whose site is now overlaid by farm buildings, with only traces of fishponds and other earthworks faintly reminiscent of this Yorkshire house for Cistercian nuns. It was founded for a prioress and fourteen or fifteen nuns by Robert de Verli in 1150 and endowed with the parish church. Various parcels of land were given by Nicholas de Chevincourt and Thomas Riston, which the nuns used to derive income from the wool trade. There is some evidence, however, that the house was a double monastery in the early years as, in 1268, the nuns apparently complained that the canons were "daintily provided for", while they were given only bread, cheese, ale and water. Records also suggest that the canons were so terrorised by a local knight that they gave him a barn full of corn, which was intended for the support of the house. This act may have led to the removal of the canons and the lay-brothers, the latter being last mentioned in 1335. The nuns themselves failed to manage an ordered house and the buildings were in a ruinous state by the fourteenth century. For some unknown reason, the small priory escaped the suppression of the lesser monasteries in 1536, but was dissolved in 1539, when Prioress Dorothy Knight and some fourteen nuns were pensioned off. The priory site and its lands were granted to Sir Richard Gresham.

The isolated church is located in flat, featureless country to the north-east of Hull, but a journey through the quiet roads will not be wasted. The church is airy and light and the keen-eyed will notice the declining angles of pillars, a rare and symbolical feature of Norman architecture, which is said to represent the bowing of Christ's head on the Cross. The two arcades with pointed arches on round stumpy pillars with multi-scalloped flat capitals are twelfth century, with two arches on the north side ornamented with zigzag decoration. The great seven-light east window with Perpendicular tracery, known as 'The Pride of Holderness', is of late fifteenth century date. The tower, which stood on four large arches, collapsed in 1787, but was rebuilt using much of the original stone.

Particularly noteworthy is the beautiful oak screen of 1531 and a number of monumental effigies in a fine state of preservation, primarily of the Hilton family, who were descended from the ancient barons of Hilton in the County Palatine of Durham and became lords of Swine and Winestead. Among the three alabaster monuments is a fourteenth century tomb of a Sir Robert de Hilton in plate armour and his wife in horned head-dress. The stone monument of a knight and his lady in the wall of the south aisle may also belong to the Hiltons. Under a trap-door in the floor is an unusually large stone coffin. A close look should also be taken of the fifteenth century iron chest with an elaborate lock of eight bolts, and the ancient canon seats with carved fifteenth and sixteenth century misericords, of which eight remain out of an original total of sixteen. On the north side, these depict a bearded man lying prostate, looking through his legs, a man's head with forked beard, a griffin biting its tail, and a knight's head. The four misericords on the south side comprise a nun's head in a wimple, a grotesque with human face, long ears and wearing a bishop's mitre, a female head in long dress of the period, and a male head with foliage emanating from his mouth. The last-named is most likely the green man of Saxon times.

Thicket Priory

St Mary • Benedictine nuns -1180–1539

A Carmelite community now occupies the large secluded manor house built in the sixteenth century, probably out of a medieval priory for Benedictine nuns, although no obvious detail can now be discerned. Founded by Roger fitzRoger before 1180 near the River Derwent and endowed with land in surrounding villages, the Priory of St Mary soon fell into debt, a situation not helped by a lack of discipline among the small community of nuns. There is evidence of a devotion to 'Our Lady of Thicket' dating from that time. Several visitations resulted in injunctions for a catalogue of misdemeanours, although few were serious and did not generally reflect too badly on the nuns' religious life. The priory suffered particularly heavy losses from the death of its cattle when, in 1484, its pastures were inundated by floods. At the time of its surrender by Prioress Agnes Beckwith in August 1539, the priory was valued at just £20 18s, but was recorded to have comprised a church, chapter house, cloister, hall, two parlours, bakehouse, buttery, kitchen and various chambers. These were either razed to the ground or converted into a mansion by the Robinson family.

Warter Priory

St James • Augustinian 1132–1536

An empty field behind Warter parish church in the picturesque Yorkshire Wold denotes the location of the medieval Augustinian Priory of St James, founded in

1132 by Norman nobleman Geoffrey fitzPain. Not even ruins have survived from the Dissolution in 1536, when the prior and twelve canons surrendered the house to Henry VIII's commissioners. It had a respectable net value of £143 7s. The following year the site was granted to Thomas Manners, first Earl of Rutland. The founder's son, William Trusbut, and grandson, Geoffrey, were munificent donors to the priory, whose possessions included the hospital at St Giles, Beverley, land and the churches at Warter, Lund, Nunburnholme and Middleton-on-the-Wolds. Henry III granted a charter for an annual fair and weekly market, but this was withdrawn in 1328 in consequence of the murders that took place during its continuance. Some indiscipline appears to have crept into the community, with one visitation noting that the canons were sleeping away from the priory, as well as wearing gold and silver rings. One prior, William York, was removed from office in 1457 after complaints of financial irregularities and neglect of the monastery buildings. A visit to the Church of St James will reward with a view of an Anglo-Saxon cross, dating from before AD 900, which was discovered during restoration in 1872.

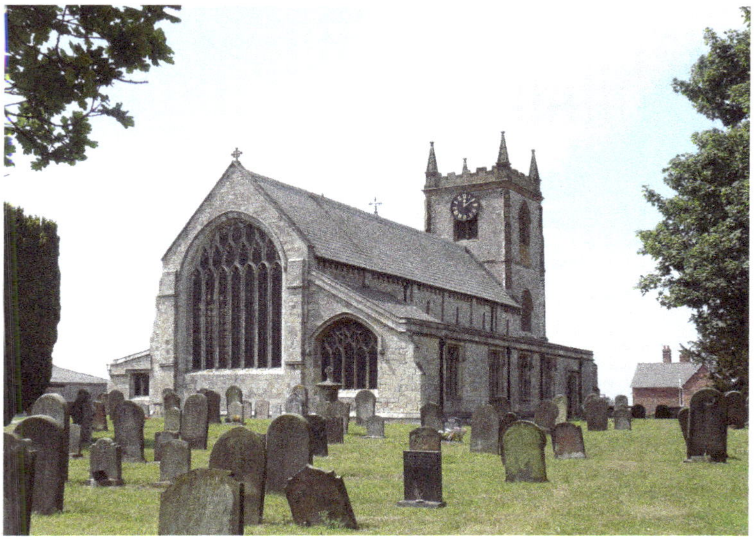

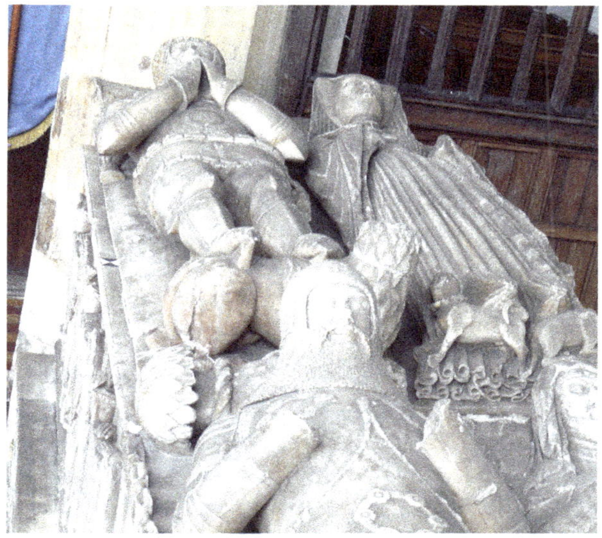

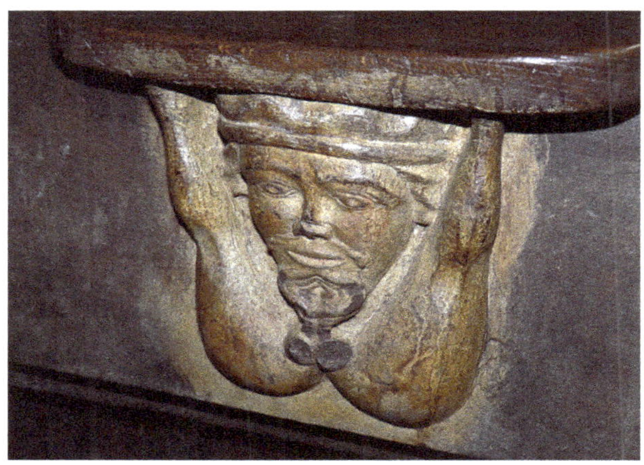

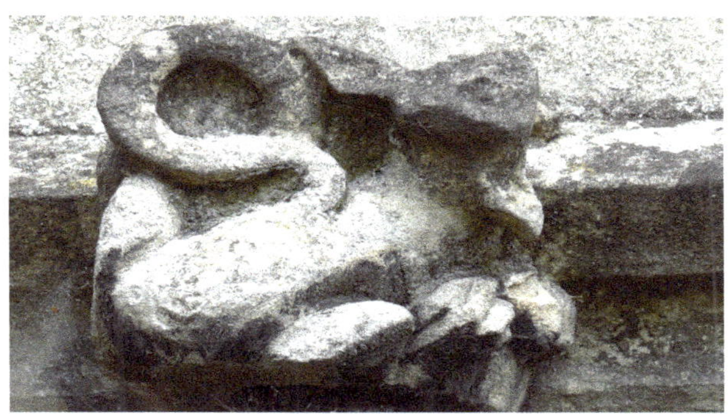

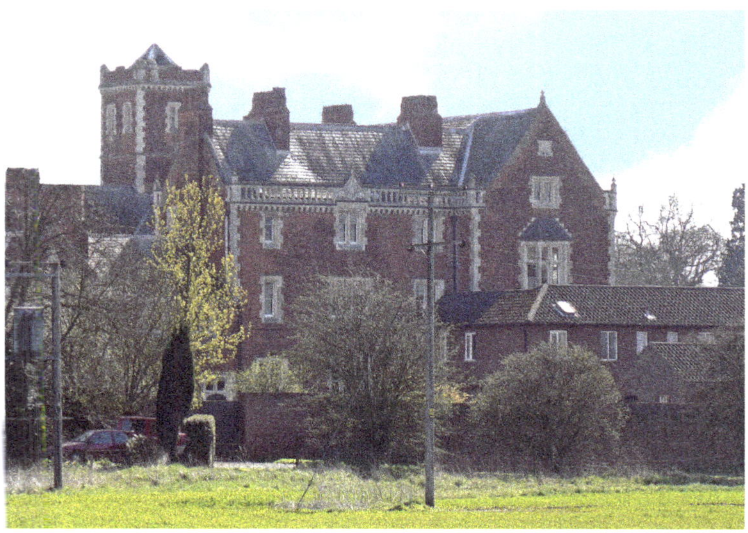

Photos - clockwise from top left

Swine Priory Church
Alabaster monumental effigies of the Hilton family, lords of Swine
Medieval misericords - a bearded man looking through his legs
Stone carving of mythical animal
Remodelled Thicket Priory, now home to Carmelite nuns

Watton Priory

St Mary • Gilbertine 1150–1539

Almost nothing is now visible above ground of this Gilbertine double house, the richest in England, but what has survived is worthy of note. Still in existence is the prior's lodging, which dates back to the fourteenth century and, together with fragments of masonry on the sites of the cloisters, is now incorporated into a private mansion. Extensive earthworks are also visible. Of particular interest is the semi-octagonal oriel with a moulded plinth, two two-light, square-headed windows in each side, one above the other separated by a band of panelled ashlar. Slender buttresses of five stages at the angles end under a parapet, which is enriched by a continuous series of traceried panels and carved figures projecting as gargoyles on the four free angles. Some ruined stone walls project from the house, and there are carved architectural fragments set into a wall.

Also of interest is the now much ruined brick-built Tudor barn, which belonged to the canons. The oldest survival is a carved stone tomb slab of Prior William de Malton, dated 1279, which reposes in the present parish church. Excavations of 1893 by the East Riding Antiquarian Society, later reburied, discovered the nuns' and canons' courts and the 63m (206ft) long cruciform church of about 1190, with an internal wall dividing the nuns from the canons, An interesting turntable was constructed in the choir wall to enable things to be passed from the canons to the nuns, without either being seen. Both courts comprised a cloister, chapter house, refectory, warming house, dormitory, infirmary and kitchen.

According to the Venerable Bede, a sisterhood of nuns was established in AD 686, but the community appears to have been destroyed by the Danes cAD 870. It was not until 1150, that Eustace fitzJohn, Lord of Knaresborough, and his wife Agnes, founded a priory of Gilbertine canons and nuns on the site, in penance for having fought on the Scottish side in the Battle of The Standard. The Priory of St Mary initially housed thirteen canons and fifty-six nuns, which were accommodated in a 183m (600ft) long building, but separated by dividing walls. According to Bede and other chroniclers, many miracles were wrought within its walls, especially by St John of Beverley. The priory obtained several endowments, including the manor and church of Ravenstonedale in Westmorland, and maintained a cell of three canons and a master. However, it was perpetually in debt and had to seek royal protection on several occasions to prevent thievery and other depredations. In the latter years of its existence, its fortunes improved, showing a clear annual value in 1535 of £360 16s, an amount exceeded by only seven other Yorkshire houses. In December 1539, Prior Robert Holgate, Bishop of Llandaff, who held the office *in commendam*, along with the sub-prior, seven canons, Prioress Joan Warcoppe and thirty-three nuns and nine sisters, surrendered the priory to the King's commissioners. Involvement by several canons in the Pilgrimage of Grace contributed to its severe destruction.

Unfortunately, Watton is remembered for an episode that is almost too gruesome to relate in detail. Suffice it to say that a young girl of four was brought by the Archbishop of York to Watton, where she grew up and fell in love with a young canon. When their illicit affair was discovered, the then pregnant nun was locked in a dungeon and the child taken away after birth. The canon was also brutally attacked. The nun now haunts the grounds near the old priory looking for her newborn child.

Wilberfoss Priory

St Mary • Benedictine nuns 1153–1539

So thoroughly has this priory been removed that not a single physical reminder exists of this Benedictine nunnery in a small village in an agricultural area east of York. As its end is embroiled in uncertainty, so is its beginning. Two alternatives have been advanced as to its foundation, but the truth may never be unravelled. One opinion is that it was founded in 1153 by Helias de Catton and endowed with land and the church of Wilberfoss, but another is that the founder was Jordan fitzGilbert, who granted a chapel at nearby Newton. In the first two centuries the Priory of St Mary appears to have had adequate income to enable it to live in an acceptable manner, but by 1397, it had descended into poverty, so much so that that there were insufficient funds to sustain the community. Bad management and a gradual slide into immorality appear to have had major influences on this decline. In 1283, the nuns were forbidden to take in secular women, and were reproved in 1308 for wearing red dresses 'like secular women'. In 1539, eleven nuns, including Prioress Elizabeth Lord, signed the Deed of Surrender. It was valued at just £12.

Photos of Watton Priory – clockwise from top

Mansion built from Abbot's lodging of Watton Priory
Beautiful semi-octagonal oriel window
Carved stones built into mansion wall
Band of panelled and decorated ashlar

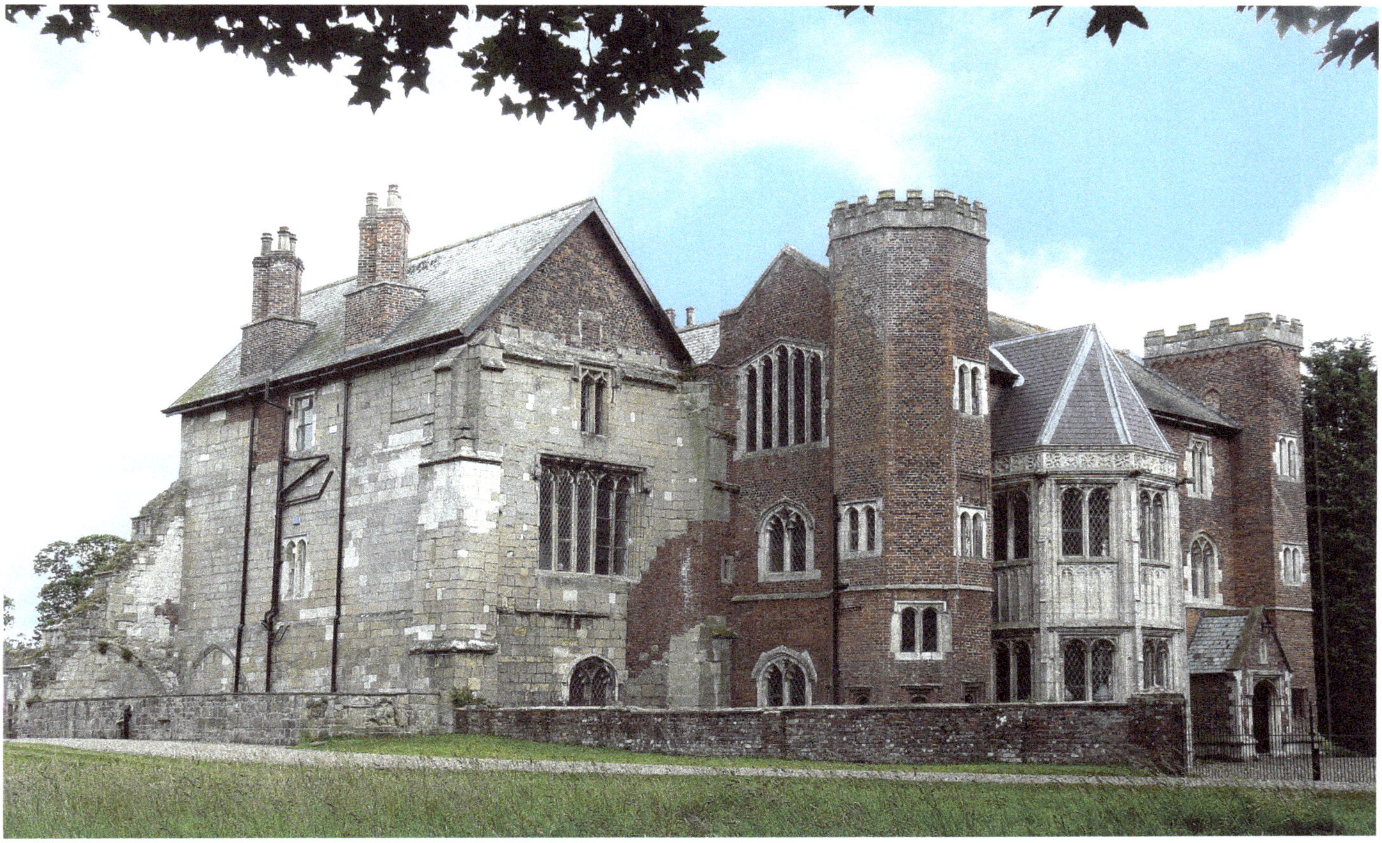

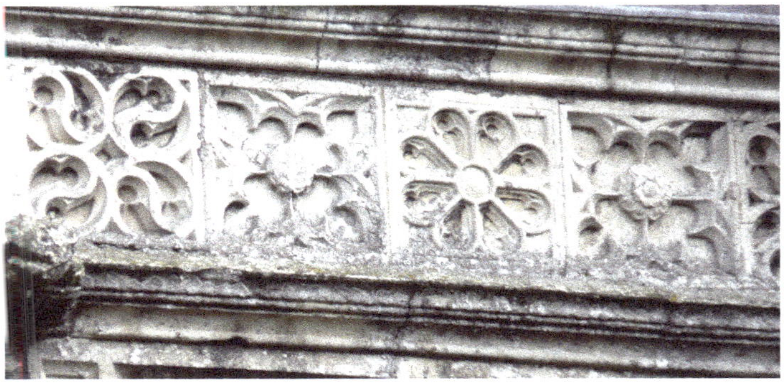

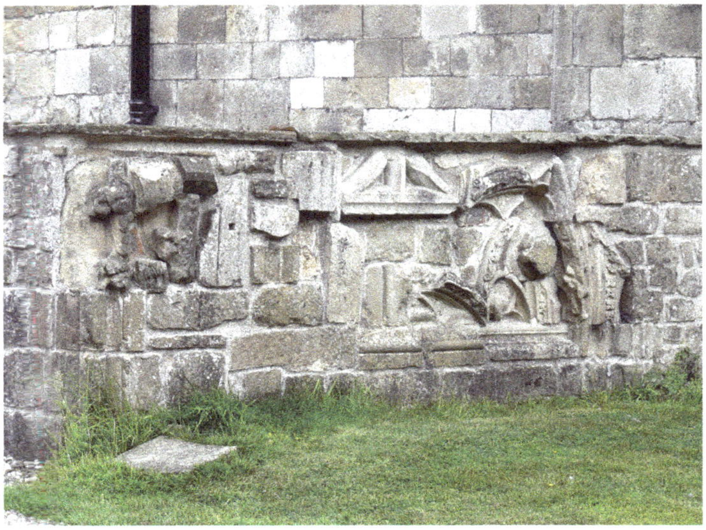

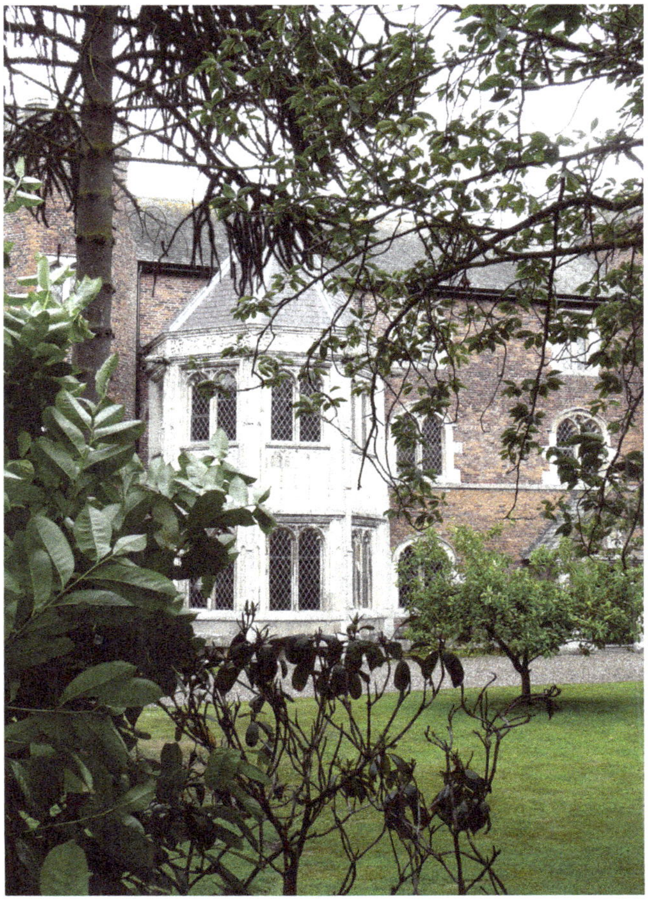

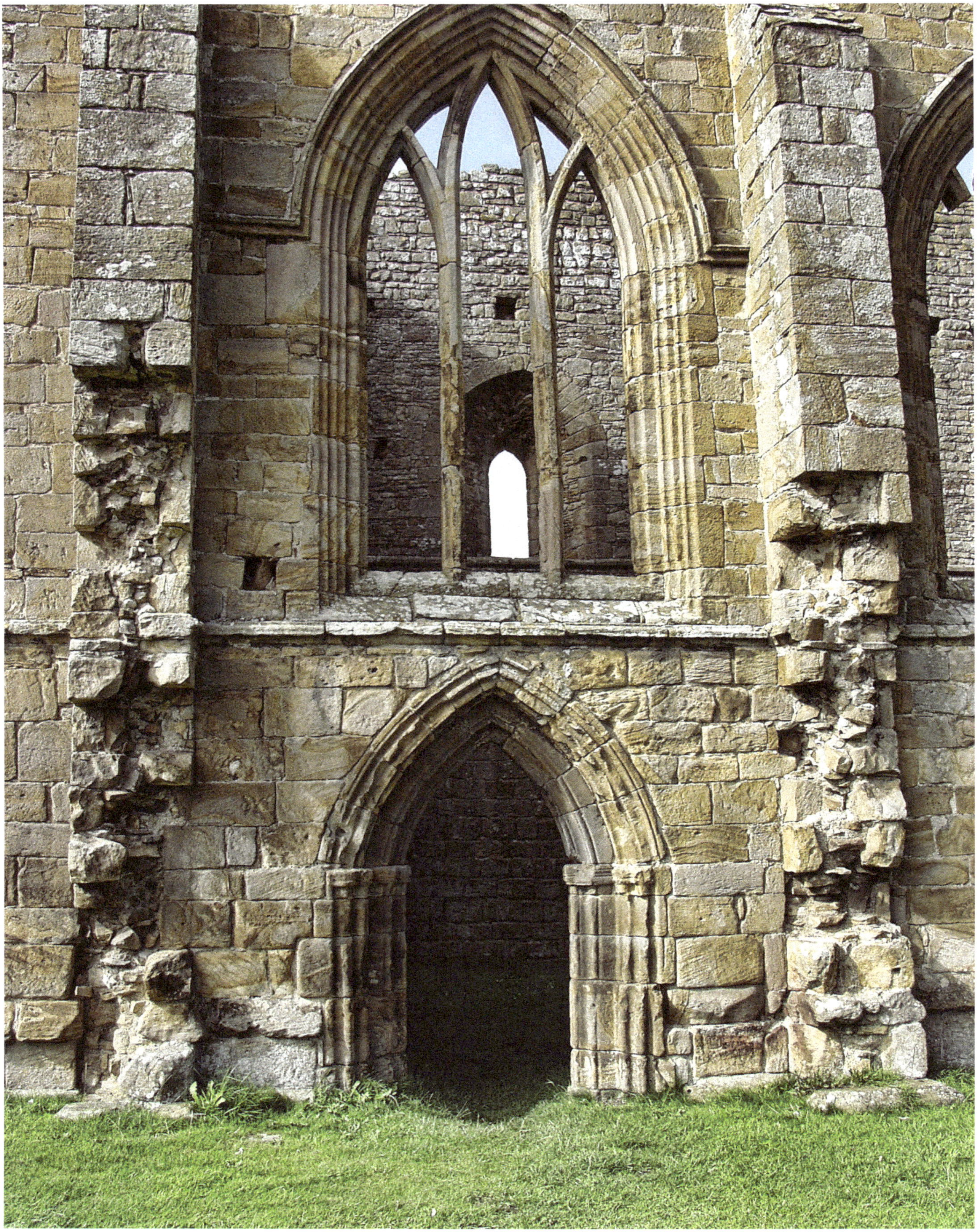

Egglestone Abbey

Arden Priory

St Andrew • Benedictine nuns c1150–1536

Poverty, mismanagement and secular activities marked the history of the Benedictine nunnery of St Andrew, founded c1150 by either Peter de Hoton or Roger de Mowbray, with the various gifts and grants confirmed by King John in 1201. Soon after its foundation, the nuns got involved with the monks of Byland over transiting each other's lands, but this was solved amicably. Several prioresses were found wanting in managing the administrative affairs and plunged the priory into debt from which it never recovered. It became so poor that there was nothing left to tax and the buildings fell into disrepair. In 1444, Archbishop Kemp granted an indulgence for two years to anyone helping to repair the nunnery, but this is not thought to have had much effect. Six nuns and fourteen servants and boys were in residence when the priory was surrendered in August 1536. Its value assessed in the *Valor Ecclesiasticus* was a mere £12 0s. The only remains of the priory include an old chimney rising through three floors within Arden Hall, two stone coffin lids set into a pavement in the yard, and a 2.4m (7.9ft) circular stone basin, into which flow the spring waters from the Nun's Well at the nearby hillside.

Basedale Priory

St Mary • Cistercian nuns 1189–1536/37

The remote Baysdale is one of the hidden gems of the North Yorkshire Moors and would still be a beautiful setting for a Cistercian nunnery that once stood among its green fields. Alas, the only surviving medieval structure from the priory is a narrow, ribbed bridge over Grain Beck, often referred to as Abbey Bridge, which dates from the thirteenth century and led to the gatehouse. The priory was founded in 1189, and while it is now referred to as Baysdale Abbey, it never acquired abbey status. Although the priory was surrounded by peace and tranquillity, there was no such within its walls. Records suggest a succession of unsuitable prioresses led to dubious and disreputable behaviour among the nuns, which appears to have continued throughout the history of the house. At least one prioress, Joan de Percy, was dismissed in 1307 for her excesses and perpetual and notorious misdeeds.

The nuns had first established themselves at Hutton Lowcross near Guisborough in 1162, but moved in c1166, when they were given two pieces of land and a mill at Thorp, later to become known as Nunthorpe, probably in the grounds of the present Nunthorpe Hall. The nuns acquired a reputation for dissolute behaviour and mismanagement, which clearly continued after the move to Baysdale, facilitated with a grant from Guy de Bovingcourt. The clear annual value in the *Valor Ecclesiasticus* of 1535 was a mere £20 1s. Basedale Priory was surrendered to the King's commissioners, Dr Legh and Dr Layton, in 1536 or 1537 by Prioress Elizabeth Raighton and ten nuns. According to the commissioners, the nuns were supposed to have the milk of the Blessed Virgin in veneration. The priory's stone was used to build private dwellings. While in the vicinity, the visitor should seek out Baysdale Cross on nearby Ingelby Moor. This stands alongside a moorland track, known as The Flagged Road, which led south from the priory.

Beggar Priory

Cistercian c1158–1414

Almost nothing is known of either the history or location of this alien priory. It was probably established c1158 to administer the estates in Yorkshire and Lincolnshire of the Breton Cistercian Abbey St Mary of Bégard. Its English cell may have been situated at Moulton, a small village lying in a secluded valley near Richmond, but this has not been confirmed. After the suppression of all alien houses in 1414, it was first granted to the chantry of St Ann at Thirsk, then to Eton College and the Carthusian priory of Mount Grace, before finally coming back to Eton.

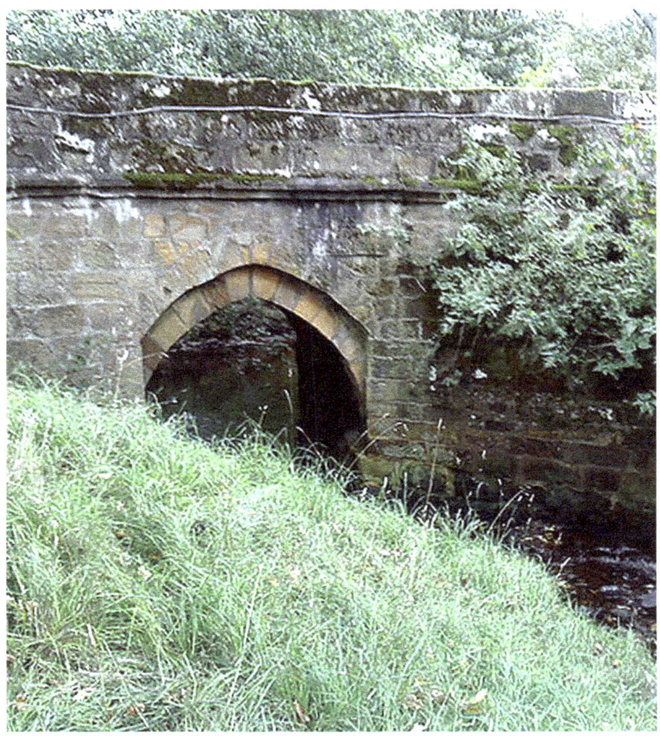

The Abbey bridge at Baysdale

Byland Abbey

St Mary • Cistercian 1177–1539

Set in quiet meadows in the shadow of the Hambleton Hills, the impressive west front of the abbey church, with its broken rose window and slender lancets, is one of the most recognisable monastic landmarks in the country. Its appeal is enhanced still further by the mellow tones of the honey-coloured sandstone, which imbue the ruins with extra warmth, especially in early morning or late afternoon sunlight. While the church is now little more than a three-sided empty shell, the soaring west gable of the 100m (330ft) long edifice, and the surviving curvature of the 8m (26ft) diameter wheeled rose window, provide a spectacular reminder of the glory days of life at Byland. The three large, but slender lancets would have directed the gaze upwards to the rose window, and beyond to the sky above. Substantial sections of the aisle walls remain standing, with the carved waterleaf mouldings on many capitals particularly noteworthy, as are the green and yellow medieval floor tiles with geometrical patterns, which were used throughout the church and can still be found in parts of the south transept and crossing. There is also an attractive piscina in the south transept.

Few of the claustral buildings have survived to any great height, but their outline and extent can be easily traced. Of note are a series of well-preserved stone staircases, of which the semi-circular night stairs from the cloister are especially graceful, a book cupboard in the chapter house, and a large fireplace in the warming house. The lay brothers' accommodation in the west cloister range was extensive and included a dedicated cloister and a lane, which gave access from the day stairs in the dormitory to the church. Along the lane are a remarkable series of thirty-five niches with stone seats. Set apart towards the south of the site lie the remains of the large abbot's lodging, notable for a fireplace in the hall and vaulted undercroft below the solar.

The monks, who originally came from Furness Abbey, had to endure many vicissitudes and tribulations before finally reaching this beautiful part of Yorkshire and settling here in 1177. The Savignac monks first colonised Calder Abbey in Cumbria in 1135, but were forced out by Scottish raiders. Unable to return to Furness, Abbot Gerald and his twelve companions travelled across the Pennines to enlist the help of the Archbishop Thurstan of York, and were eventually granted land by Roger de Mowbray at Hood near Thirsk in 1139. Gerald died in 1142 on his way back from the general chapter in Savigny and was replaced by Roger, who was sub-cellarer at Calder. As the community at Hood grew, its facilities became too small, and in 1143, Roger de Mowbray granted the monks his vill at Old Byland, where they started building within earshot of the bells of Rievaulx Abbey. This led to a squabble with their powerful Cistercian neighbours, who complained that the ringing of the church bells from the new monastic settlement caused too much confusion. The monks were left with no choice but to move further south on to land at Coxwold, elsewhere known as Stocking, where they built a small stone church, cloister and other conventual structures. The monks remained at Stocking for thirty years before settling on the present low-lying site, where they finally established Byland Abbey under the Cistercian rule.

Thickly wooded and swampy, the new site required extensive drainage before the commencement of any building work. But once accomplished, construction proceeded rapidly on one of the most beautiful abbey churches in the land and an extensive monastic complex. With further grants of more arable land and a growing community of lay-brothers to undertake the farming, the abbey soon prospered and it was not long before it was hailed as one of the three great monasteries of the North, alongside Fountains and Rievaulx. Life at the abbey appears to have proceeded in a relatively calm and undisturbed fashion, except for one occasion in 1322, when it was attacked and pillaged by the Scots, following the defeat of Edward II at nearby Shaws Cross. Its end came in 1538, when Abbot John Ledes and twenty-five choir monks were forced to sign over the abbey to the commissioners of Henry VIII. Its annual revenues at the time were estimated at £295. The abbey was quickly stripped of its assets and neglect accelerated its decay.

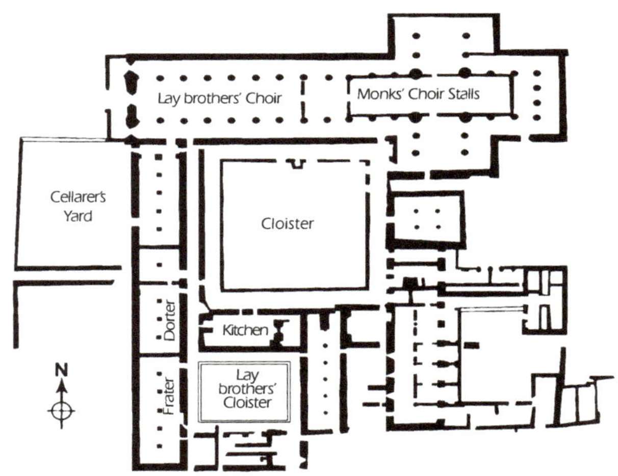

Photos - clockwise from top left

Stairs from cloister into the retrochoir
West front, now alas without its once magnificent rose window
Attractive tile design in the south transept
Medieval tile floor in the presbytery and re-erected arcading
Unusual refectory with vaulted undercroft

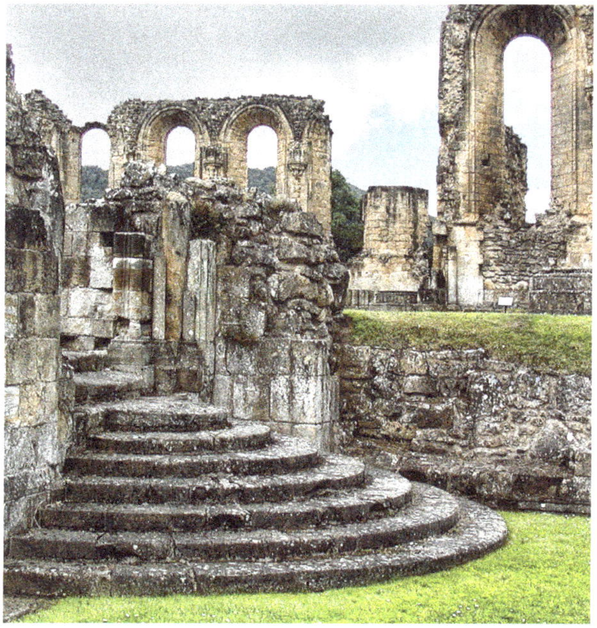

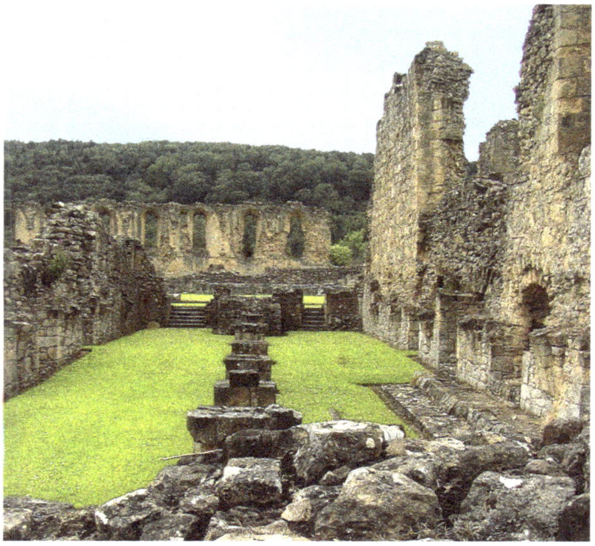

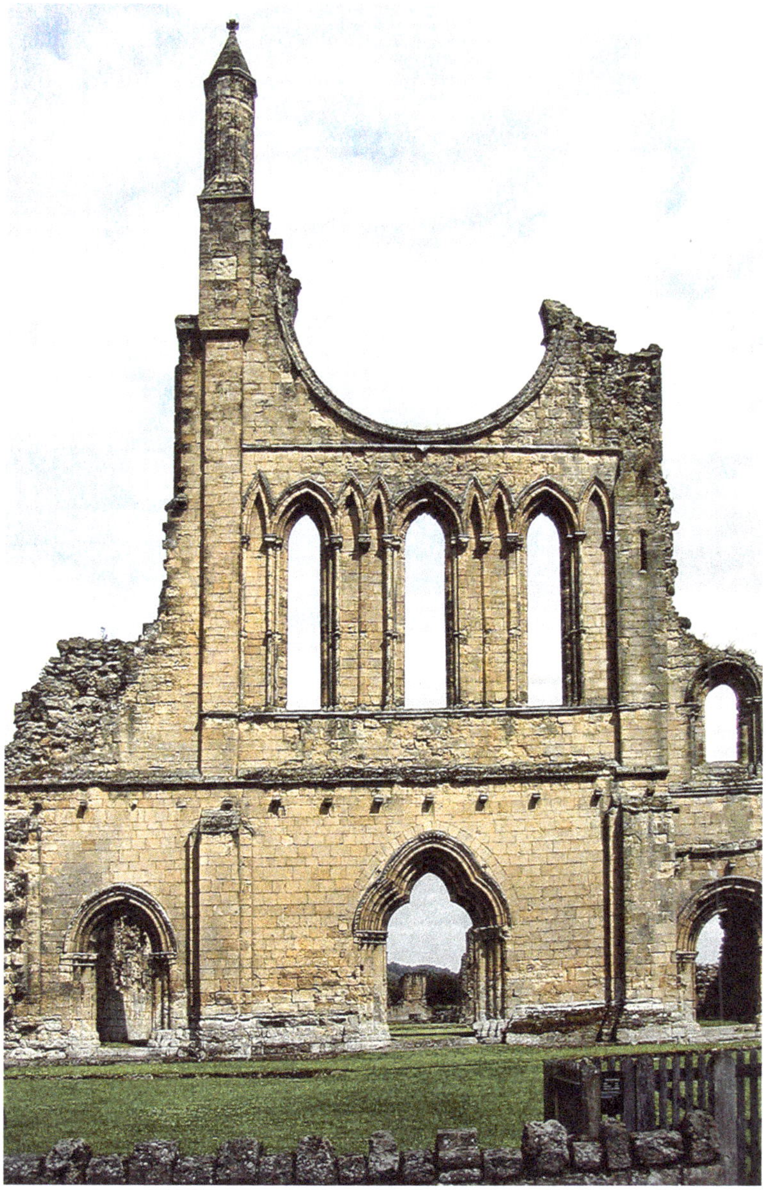

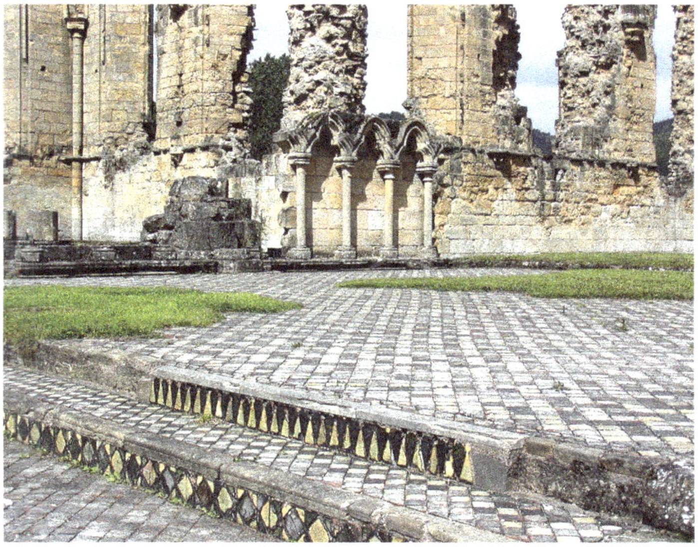

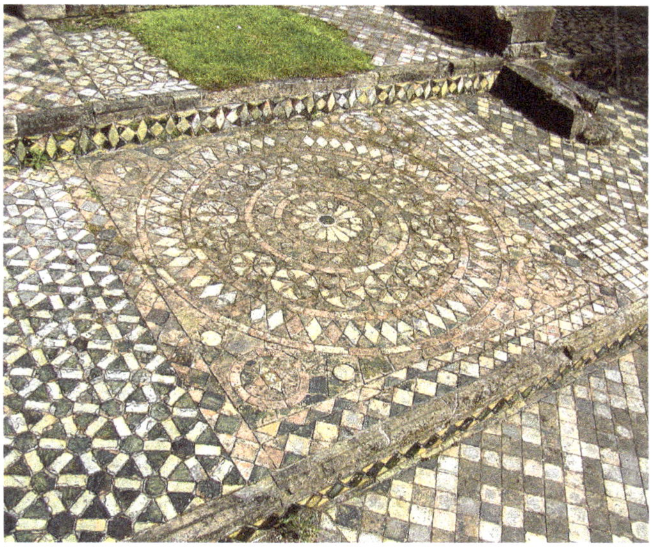

Coverham Abbey

St Mary • Premonstratensian -1190–1536

On a terrace above the north bank of the fast flowing brook of Cover, after which the dale is named, stand the sparse remains of this abbey for Premonstratensian canons dating back to 1212. Its stunning location below the now redundant medieval parish church, surrounded by high moorland rising sharply from each side of the brook, makes the short journey from nearby Middleham an experience to be savoured. A great disappointment is the fact that the site is strictly private and the lack of public access make it possible only to view the remains from afar. The incorporation of much of the abbey fabric into a modern mansion also challenges any attempt at discerning the layout of its buildings. Few features remain *in situ* and upstanding, but the richly carved stonework built into the house, outbuildings and garden walls provide a reminder of the original beauty the abbey, which was never wealthy, nor particularly large.

One of the main features still standing and visible from the nearby road is the partially dismantled inner precinct gatehouse, from the early sixteenth century, which stands about 125m (410ft) to the west of the cloister buildings. The gatehouse was about 5.2m (17ft) wide and 5.1m (16ft 9in) deep and comprised large three-centred entrance arches of two chamfered orders. Only the rear arch, flanked by tunnel-vaulted wings, remains. The church was relatively small, being only about 48m (157ft) in length, and appears to have comprised an aisled presbytery, north and south transepts, aisled nave and probably a central tower. Standing are two lofty arches of the nave arcade, which now make a romantic feature in a well-kept formal garden. Little is left of the east wall, but parts of the north transept include the much decayed west jamb of the doorway and two pointed single-light windows in the west wall. The lower part of the west wall of the church is also still standing. While the arches of the nave date from c1340 and are probably the result of a rebuilding after destruction by the Scots, the other fragments are of much earlier date. What was probably the abbey's guesthouse is now incorporated in the mansion, which retains an original stone fireplace, a fine sixteenth century doorway reset into the east wall of the house, and a large and interesting square-headed window with nine low trefoiled lights in the west wall. Several inscribed stones are built into the walls of the mansion, one of which states that "the abbot happily finished this house in 1508".

Among the fragments of masonry preserved are two larger-than-life stone effigies, which are now propped up against a wall, but were originally in a recumbent attitude. Both are habited in armour and cross-legged and thought to be of the founder, Ranulph fitzRobert, and of Robert fitzRanulph, Lord of Middleham Castle. The better preserved has his hands folded in prayer, with his shield on his left side and a long sword suspended from the belt. His broken feet rest on the back of a mutilated animal. Over the head of the other figure is a much fractured cusped and crocketed canopy, while on his left side are the broken remains of a long sword and shield. On his right are three dogs, two of which are chasing a stag, with the other playfully biting the scabbard of the knight's sword. There are also the remains of a number of tomb slabs with foliated and plain crosses, and many other fragments of carved stonework.

The monastery had first been founded at Swainby in the Vale of Mowbray sometime before 1190 by Ranulph's mother Helewise, daughter of Ranulph de Glanville, Lord Chief Justice of England under Henry II, but moved to the present site probably so that Ranulph fitzRobert could hear the sound of the abbey bells in his castle at Middleham. Helewise died in 1195 and was buried at Swainby, but her remains were later re-interred in the chapter house at Coverham. Ranulph fitzRobert, who gave the canons the church at Coverham, together with various lands and tenements, died in 1251 and was buried in the abbey church. The abbey later acquired further possessions, much from the Scrope lords of Castle Bolton, however, by the early fourteenth century, it faced near collapse through loss of income, fire and, between 1314 and 1316, severe destruction by hostile Scottish raiders. The abbey buildings were rebuilt soon after, and there is evidence that further reconstruction or enlargement was undertaken at the beginning of the sixteenth century. With a net income in 1535 assessed at a respectable £160 18s, it nevertheless was included among the lesser monasteries targeted for Dissolution in 1536. After being leased out, the abbey was sold in 1557 to Humphrey Orme and quickly fell into ruin.

Photos – clockwise from top

The surviving nave arcade making a romantic feature in the formal garden

Larger than life stone effigies of the founder and lord of Middleham Castle

Only the rear arch surviving from the gatehouse

A wealth of carved stonework set into a wall

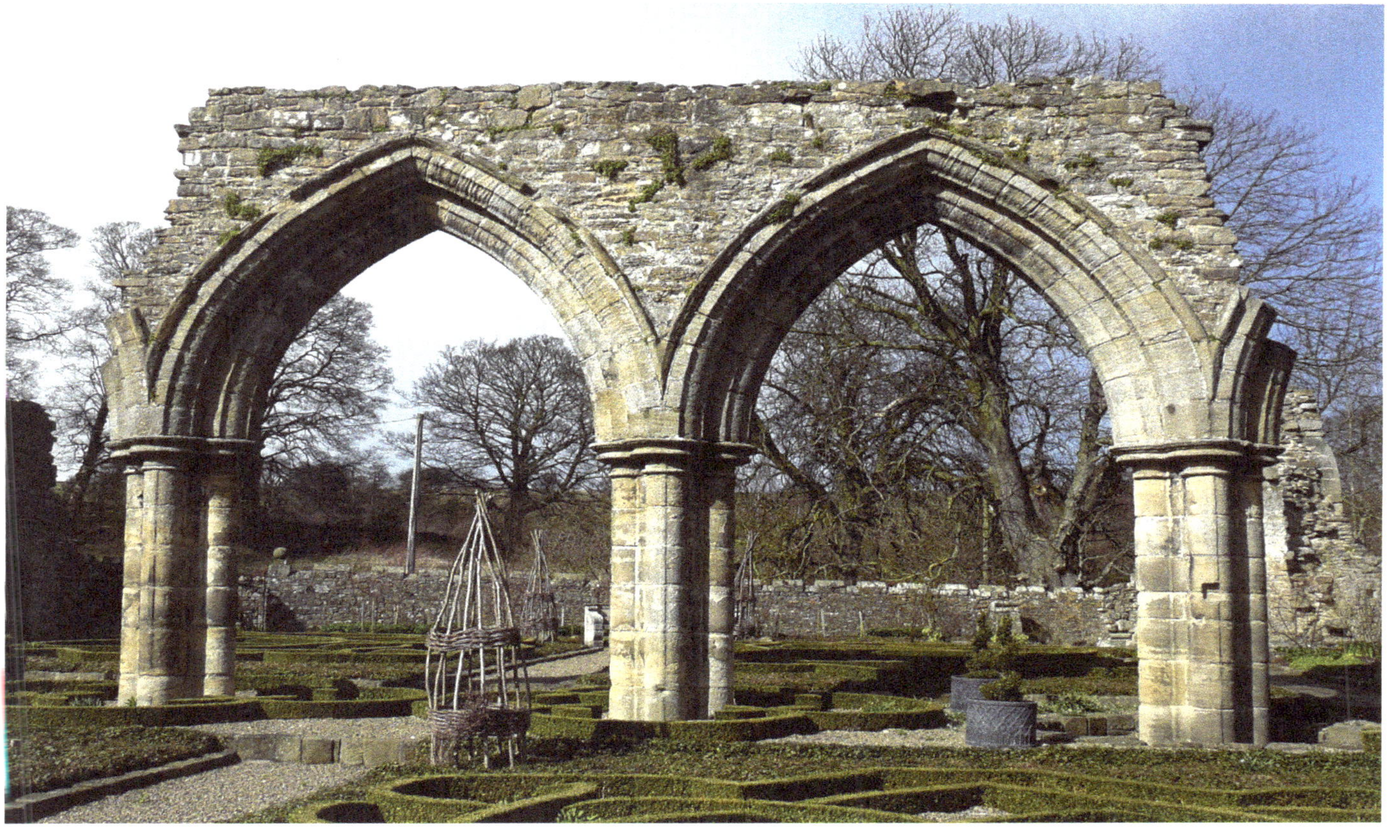

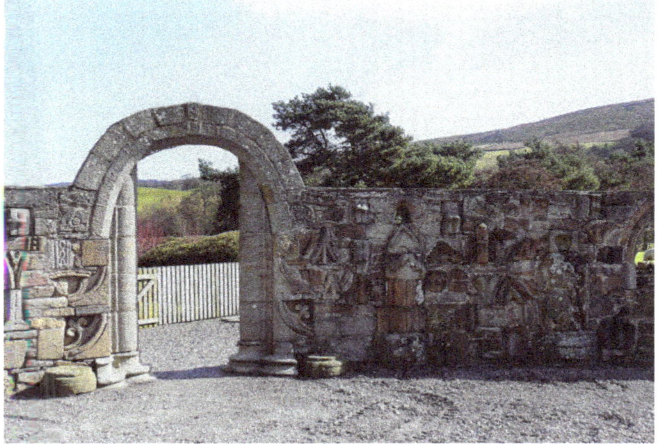

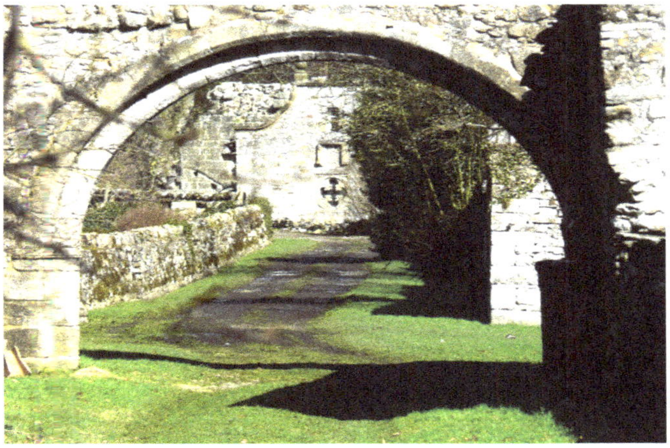

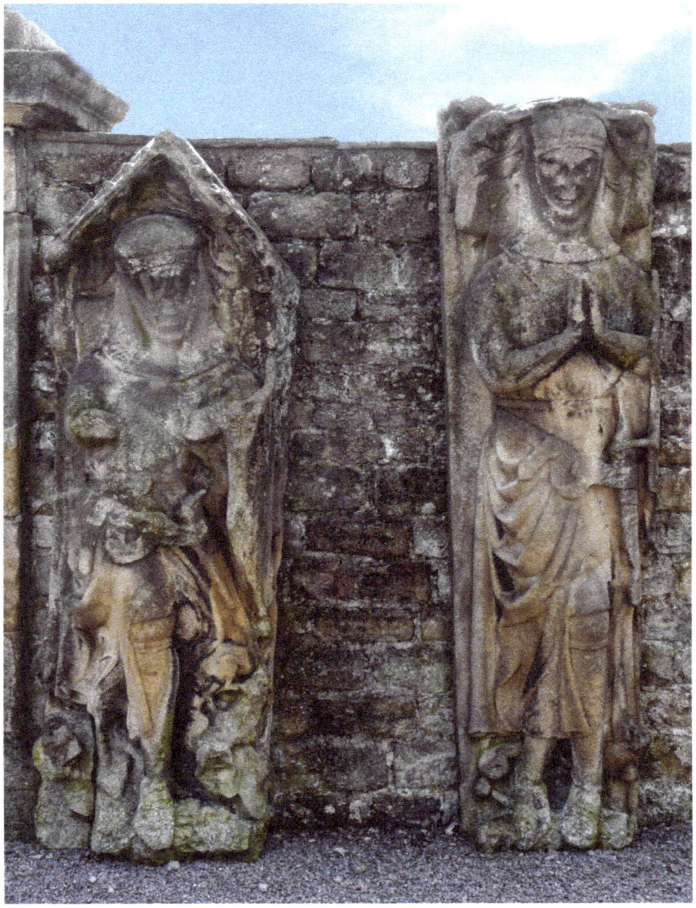

Easby Abbey

St Agatha • Premonstratensian 1152–1537

Taking the riverside walk from Richmond through quiet Swaledale, green wooded hills on either side, considerably heightens the anticipation of seeing the ruined abbey buildings in a setting that would have changed little from the time the canons from Pentney in Newcastle arrived in this lovely spot in 1252. When entering the abbey, the first detail that registers is the unusual aspect of the monastic buildings, at first a somewhat disorientating experience. The church of St Agatha, which predates the abbey and is still in use today, stands where one would normally find the infirmary, here located to the north of the ruined abbey church. The dormitory is on the west, rather than the usual east, and more memorable still is the oddly skewed cloister. But the realisation soon dawns that this imaginatively different layout was forced upon the community by the position of the River Swale and the existence of St Agatha's church. But while the white canons had to adapt to this new arrangement, it surely was but a minor inconvenience more than made up for by the beauty and tranquillity of the valley, from where they went forth preaching and ministering to the surrounding communities.

The Abbey of St Agatha at Easby was founded in 1152 by Roald, Constable of nearby Richmond Castle, for the Premonstratensian Order, although there is evidence of an earlier Anglo-Saxon community living at the site. The abbey prospered under Roald's patronage, and particularly that of the Scrope family of Castle Bolton in the early fourteenth century. Like most northern monasteries, Easby Abbey suffered from frequent Scottish raids during the Middle Ages, but it was the English army that caused the most damage, when it was billeted there in 1346 on its way to the Battle of Neville's Cross. Richard Scrope provided further funds in 1393 to support more canons. The abbey's fortunes declined somewhat thereafter, and at its dissolution in 1537, it was valued at just £111. In the year before, the abbey had become embroiled in the Pilgrimage of Grace rebellion, causing Henry VIII to instruct his northern commander, the Duke of Norfolk, to "without pity or circumstance cause the monks to be tied up [hung] without further delay." The fate of the Easby canons is not known.

Access to the abbey ruins was once via a well preserved gabled gatehouse, which today stands somewhat apart. The most striking feature is the refectory, which was rebuilt at the beginning of the fourteenth century and retains a series of magnificent windows, one of which still has much of its fine tracery. Arches along the wall and foundations of pillars along the centreline indicate that it once had a vaulted undercroft, probably used for storage. Very little remains of the church, beyond the outline of its foundations. Of interest are the numerous tomb slabs in the floor, and two large niches, which may have housed tombs of the Scrope family. Between the church and the refectory lies the fragmented chapter house, flanked by two rooms, probably the sacristy and parlour. The three-storey west range incorporates a number of buildings, including the reredorter and dormitory on the upper level, reached through a decorated Romanesque archway from the cloister. A visit to the church of St Agatha will delight with beautiful thirteenth century frescoes in the chancel, depicting the life of Christ on the south and Adam and Eve on the north wall. Also worth noting are the Holy Water stoup cut from solid stone, the carved font, trefoiled piscina and sedilia.

If, during your journey towards the abbey you hear the muted sound of a distant drum near a carved stone memorial, it is probably that of the drummer boy. Legend has it that there is an underground passage between Easby Abbey and Richmond Castle, constructed in medieval times to provide an escape route for the abbot and canons. It is said that at the end of the eighteenth century, soldiers discovered the opening to the tunnel under the castle keep, but it being rather small, a regimental drummer boy was told to crawl through. Guided by the sound of the drums, the soldiers were able to plot the tunnel's course above ground. The sound of the drum led along the River Swale towards Easby Abbey, but when reaching Easby Wood, half a mile from the abbey, the drumming ceased and the boy was never seen again.

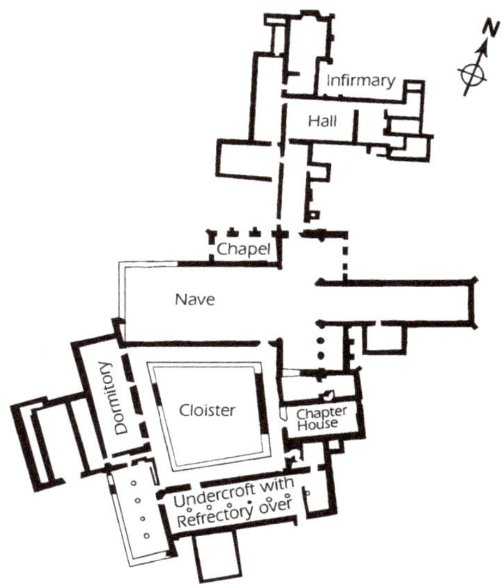

Photos - clockwise from top left

Easby Abbey ruins reposing serenely in wooded Swaledale
Decorated Romanesque archway to the chapter house
The refectory still standing to its full height
Well preserved gabled gatehouse
Interlinked arcading in the three-storey west range
Some refectory windows retaining their beautiful tracery

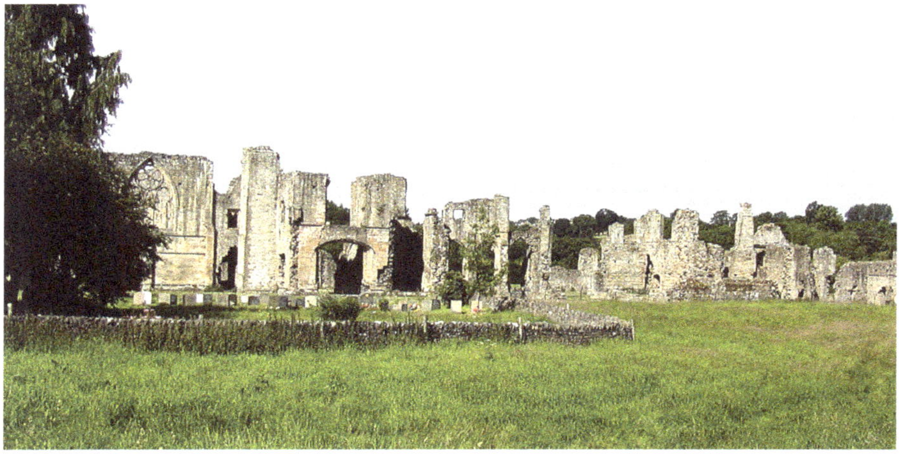

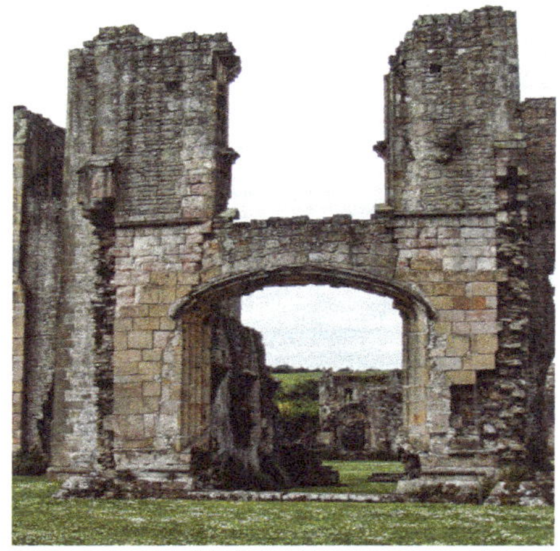

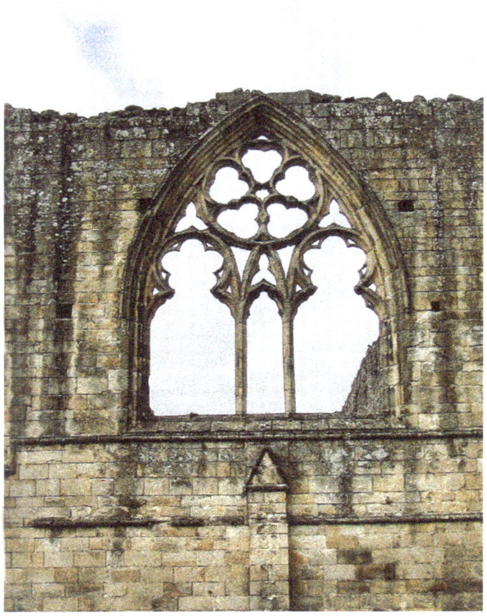

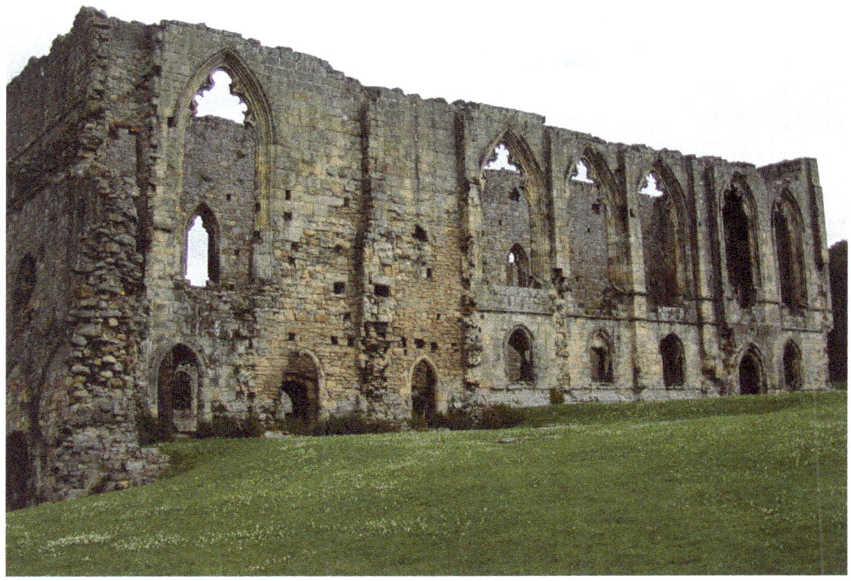

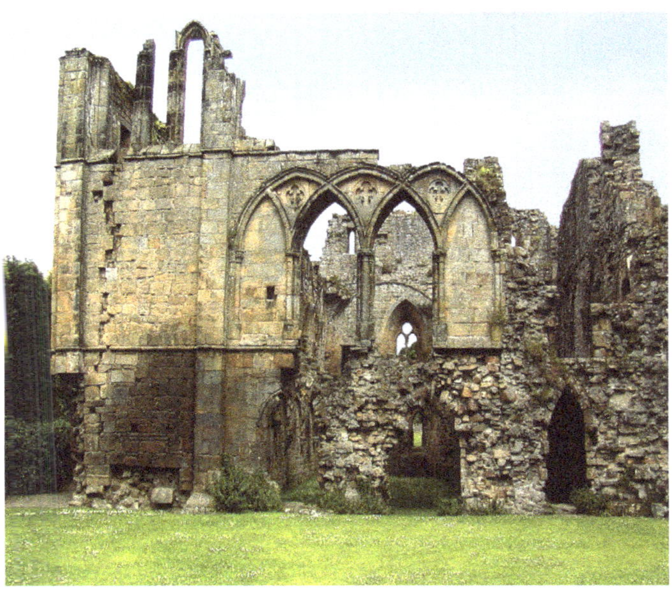

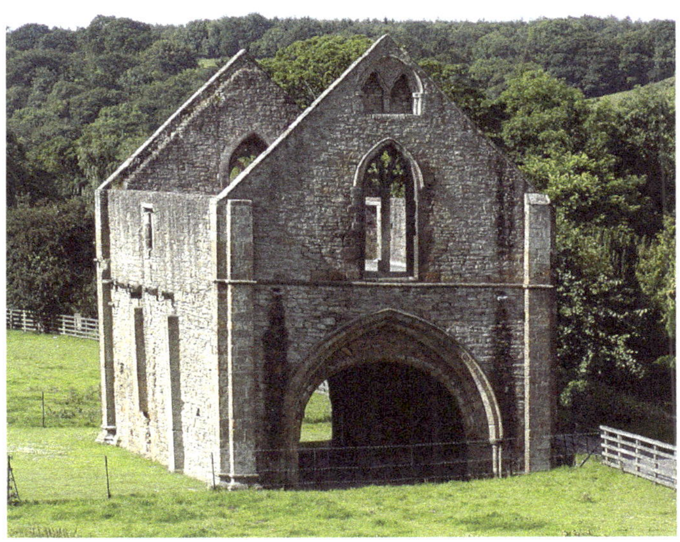

Egglestone Abbey

St Mary & St John the Evangelist • Premonstratensian -1198–1540

The ruins of Egglestone Abbey are perched high above Thorsgill Beck, a tributary of the River Tees. When the weather is fine, they present an idyllic picture, but in winter, the exposed position makes for a bleak landscape, and life for its small community of Premonstratensian canons would have been harsh and unproductive, the main income being derived from pasturing sheep. In the absence of generous endowments, the abbey was barely able to keep above subsistence level. In the mid-thirteenth century, the abbey managed to resist moves to demote it to a priory. Its history was punctuated by troubled times, from an attack by raiding Scots in 1315, to damage inflicted by the English Army in 1346 on its way to the Battle of Neville's Cross. Egglestone was also not without its share of scandals. Measures were later implemented to reverse the abbey's parlous financial state, including exemption from taxes, but these did not save it from the Dissolution in 1540, when the abbot, sub-prior and seven canons surrendered the house. It was valued at a mere £36. The land was granted in 1548 to Robert Strelly, who converted some domestic buildings into a manor house, in the process also demolishing the church tower for spoiling the view.

The abbey of St Mary and St John the Evangelist was founded by the Multon family in 1195, and although not much now remains, the scale of the thirteenth century church is still impressive. Some of the walls stand to a good height and retain some fine carved mouldings and window tracery in the slender twin lancets. The focal point is the east end of the church with its great five-lighted mullioned window. Within the church, there are a number of tombs to abbots and benefactors, including those of Sir Rafe Bowes and Thomas Rokeby, but the effigies are missing. Beside the high altar, two aumbries and two piscine have been preserved. Unusually, the cloister, chapter house and refectory, of which nothing remains, were ranged to the north and west, while the domestic buildings formed the north-eastern range. Some evidence of these still exists in the ruins of the manor house.

Ellerton Priory

St Mary • Cistercian nuns 1227–1537

The remains of this small Cistercian nunnery in Swaledale, comprising the fifteenth century west tower of a simple 30m (100ft) long rectangular church with a narrow aisle-less nave and parts of the eastern gable, are shaded by huge trees, but can still be seen from the adjacent road. Now situated on private land, few will have an opportunity for a closer look at these evocative runs in a stunning setting along the River Swale. The three-storey restored tower measures some 2.75m (9ft) square internally and is crowned by an embattled parapet. At the southeast corner is a small stair turret lit by three slits on the western face and one on the south. The tower arch is semi-circular. Light into the bell chamber comes from two-light trefoiled windows on each side. There are several gravestones carved with foliated crosses in the nave, most dating from the fourteenth century. There is also a huge stone slab, measuring 2.1 x 0.95 x 0.30m (6ft 11in x 3ft 2in x 12in), which is thought to have been used as an altar slab, although no crosses have been cut on the surface.

Ellerton Priory was founded in 1227 in the reign of Henry III by Warner, steward of the earls of nearby Richmond, or his son Wymar. It was always a poorly endowed house and little is known of its history. Apart from some trouble with an excommunicated nun in 1274, the only other major event at the priory appears to have been in 1347 when the Scots made their way into Swaledale and relieved the nunnery of seven charters and writings, including a grant from Robert de Wicliff to Margaret, the prioress at the time, of an annual rent of 6s 8d. Ellerton Priory was surrendered in 1537 by the last prioress, Joan, and granted to Robert Aske of Aughton in 1542, who sold it to John Palmes in 1579. Its value was a little over £15.

Fors Abbey • Savignac/Cistercian 1145–1156

The foundations of a Cistercian abbey were laid in 1145, when Akarius fitzBardolph bequeathed land at Fors in Upper Wensleydale to Peter Quinciano, a monk of Savigny. Fors came under the authority of Byland Abbey, which supplied John de Kinstan as abbot and twelve monks. The sterility of the land made it untenable, however, forcing the community to give up the unequal struggle in 1156 and relocate to found Jervaulx Abbey.

Foukeholm Priory

St Stephen • Benedictine nuns +1199– +1349

Little is known of this poorly-endowed Benedictine nunnery near Northallerton, and nothing at all has survived above ground to shed some light into its distant past. It was first mentioned in the time of King John, when Maud, widow of William de Colville, who was a benefactor and probable founder, brought an action against the prioress of St Stephen. A few events have been recorded, including an indictment of William, chaplain of Yarm, for the abduction of a nun, but the house was last mentioned in 1349, when Alice Gower was confirmed as prioress. It may well have succumbed to the ravages of the Black Death.

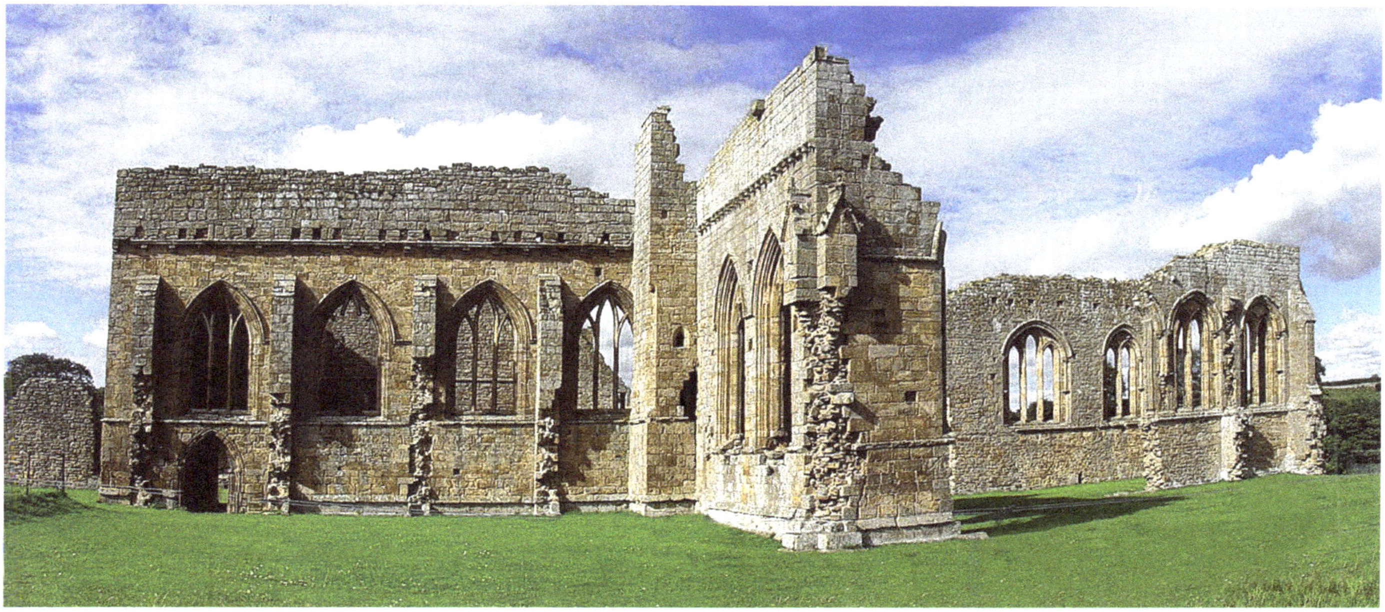

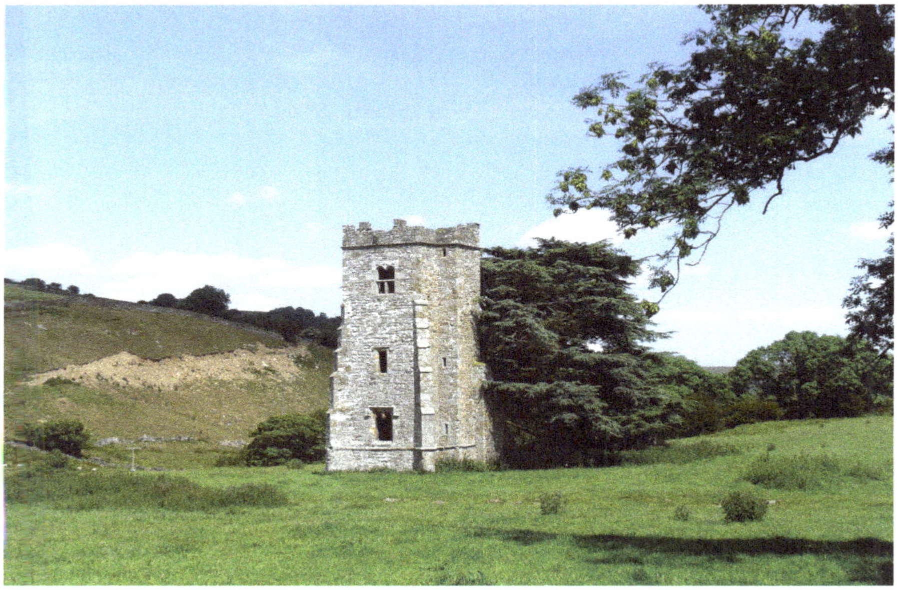

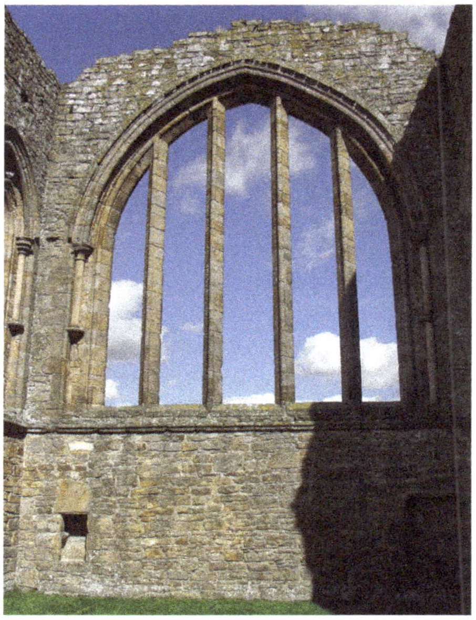

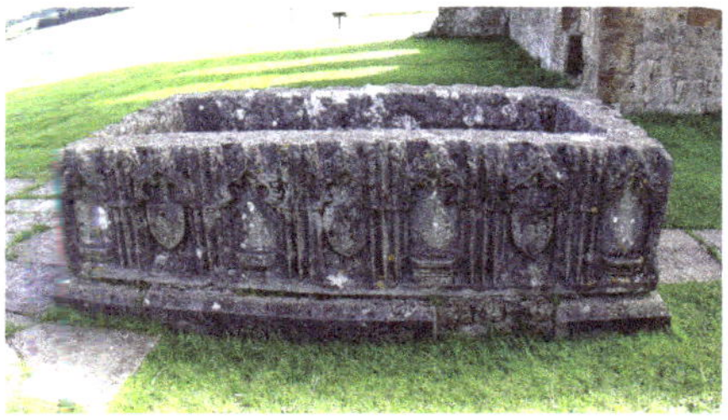

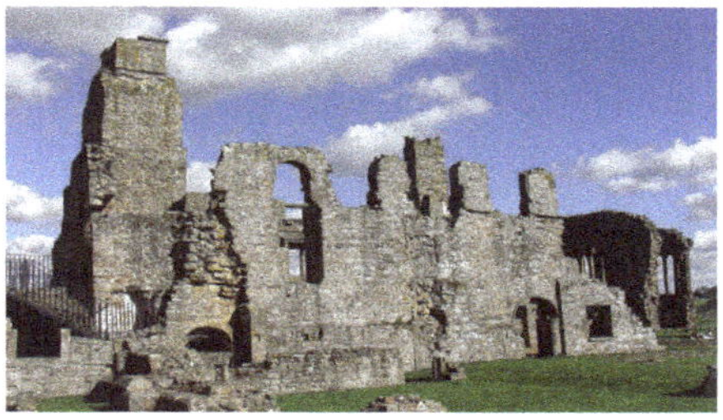

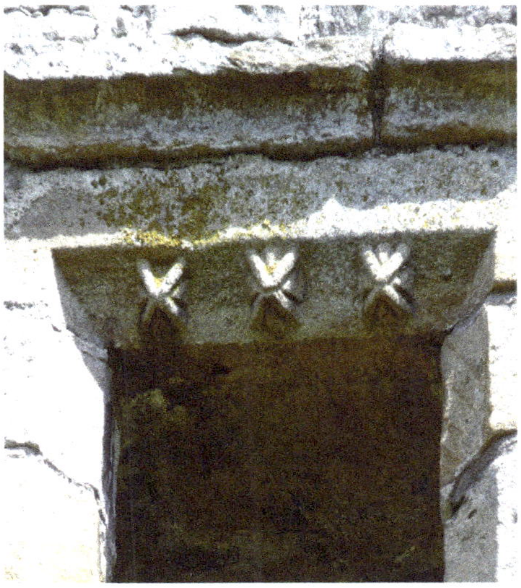

Photos - clockwise from top

Remains of the Egglestone Abbey Church
Great five-light east window
Ornamental carvings above tower window at Ellerton Priory Church
Ruins of sixteenth century manor house at Egglestone
Empty tomb with heraldic designs at Egglestone
The ruined tower of Ellerton Priory Church in Swaledale

Fountains Abbey

St Mary • Cistercian 1132–1539

The great tower, 49m (160ft) tall, soars above the surrounding hills, showing the way to what is the most complete and extensive monastic site in England. Standing on high ground looking down into the deep valley, the ruins of Fountains Abbey are a delight to the eye, both in terms of their picturesque setting and architectural diversity and excellence. The search for a stricter form of religious life led a group of dissatisfied Benedictine monks from St Mary's Abbey in York to this remote and wild North Yorkshire valley by the River Skell. Described as a place "more fit for wild beasts than men", this piece of land given by Thurstan, Archbishop of York in 1132, was everything Prior Richard and his twelve monks desired. Life in the first three years, however, was extremely harsh, the small group of brethren being forced to shelter in a thatched hut and survive on a diet of woodland fruits. St Bernard of Clairvaux sent over a holy man, Geoffrey, who taught them the rules of the Cistercian Order, and in 1135, *Sancta Maria de Fontibus* (Our Lady of the Springs) became a Cistercian house.

Hardship came to an end when Hugh, Dean of York, brought with him books and the monetary means to start construction of the grandest abbey of its time. The destruction of some early buildings in 1146 by followers of William, Archbishop of York, failed to halt the abbey's progress. The sale of wool, quarrying of stone, horse breeding and involvement in iron and lead mining, brought in substantial income. These activities, together with impressive endowments and good management of its estates, made the abbey very rich. Many of its abbots sat in Parliament. Of great importance was the introduction of lay-brothers, who looked after the vast flocks of sheep and carried out all manual work necessary on the abbey's huge estates, which stretched as far west as the Lake District and northwards to Teesside. During the thirteenth century, Fountains suffered raids by warring Scots, and its fortunes declined following failed harvests, and the decimation of lay-brothers by the Black Death. The abbey flourished once again under the abbacy of Marmaduke Huby, and the last abbot, Marmaduke Bradley, but this revival was cut short when it was dissolved in 1539. Its annual income was more than £1,000.

There is so much to see at Fountains Abbey, but the church has to be the first port of call. The great tower, built above the north transept, still looks down upon the desecrated church, which is an impressive 107m (351ft) long and 20m (65ft) wide at the aisle-less nave. Fragments of the Galilee porch that sheltered the beautiful arched doorway into the church can be discerned. In the south transept are the remains of two side chapels and the night stairs by which the monks came from their dormitory to Matins. In the sanctuary, the base of the high altar is still extant, as are some medieval tiles, but the most striking feature is the additional transept at the eastern end of the church. This highly decorated addition is named the Chapel of the Nine Altars, for the nine altars that once stood side by side along the wall. Two identical recesses in each were the aumbry and piscina.

Substantial remains of claustral buildings and living quarters ensure the completeness of the layout. Among the most impressive is the magnificent vaulted cellarium, which is an incredible 107m (350ft) long. One part was used as a refectory for the lay-brothers. The Chapter House opens out from the cloister and is accessed via three arched doorways. At each side are stone benches, while tombs of past abbots can be found within. Also accessed from the cloister is the splendid monks' refectory flanked by kitchen and warming room. Straddling the river are the remains of the infirmary, which had its own chapel and kitchen. The river is spanned by a series of small stone arches. A stone bridge over the Skell leads to the remnants of the abbey's workshops on the hillside.

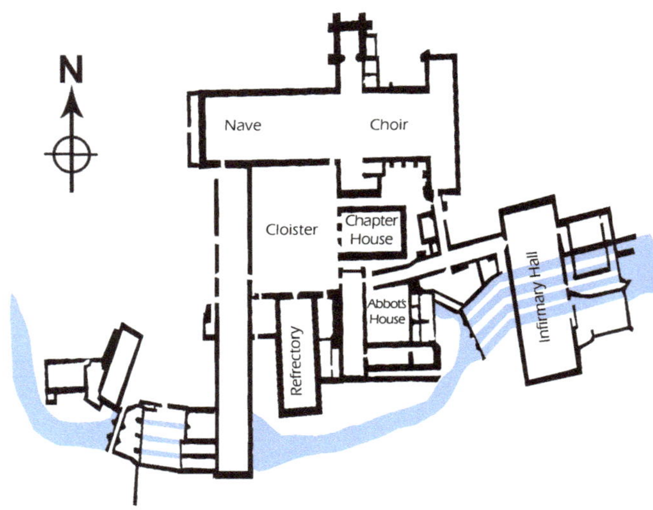

Photos - clockwise from top left

The great tower looking down upon the ruined church
Aiseless nave with its impressive line of Norman pillars
Entrance to chapter house from the cloister
Colourful medieval tile pavement in the sanctuary
The magnificent vaulted cellarium has no equal
Night stairs used by monks to attend Matins

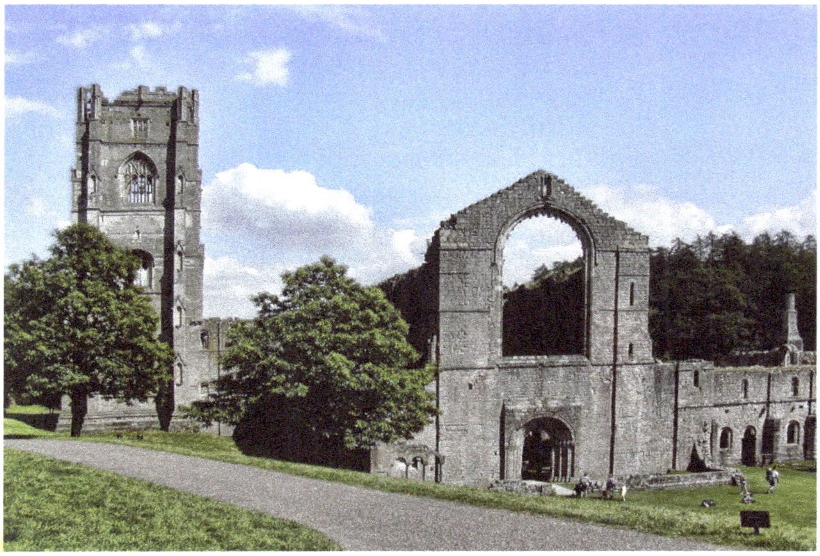

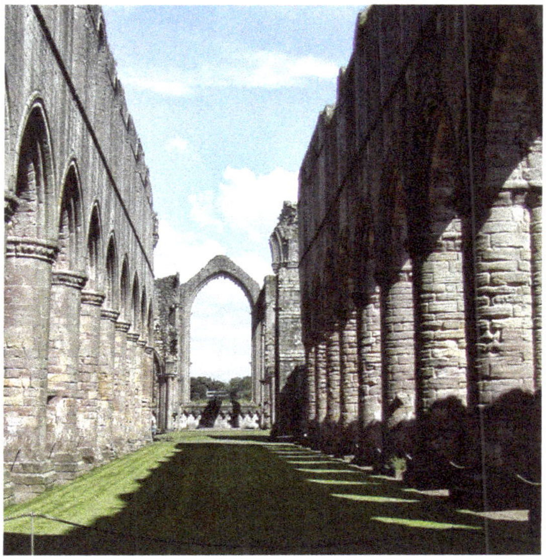

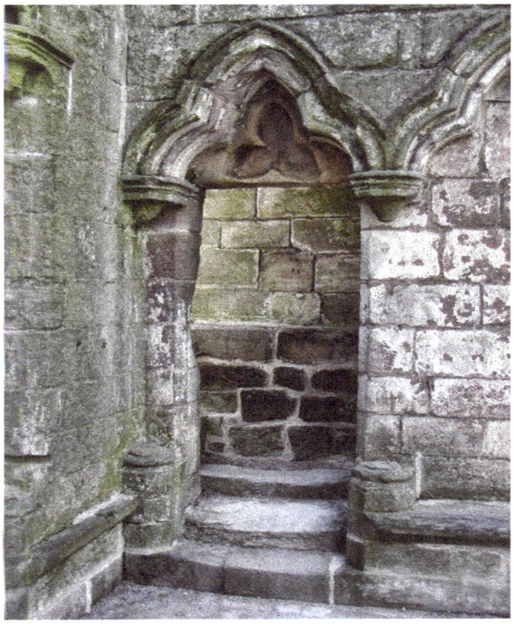

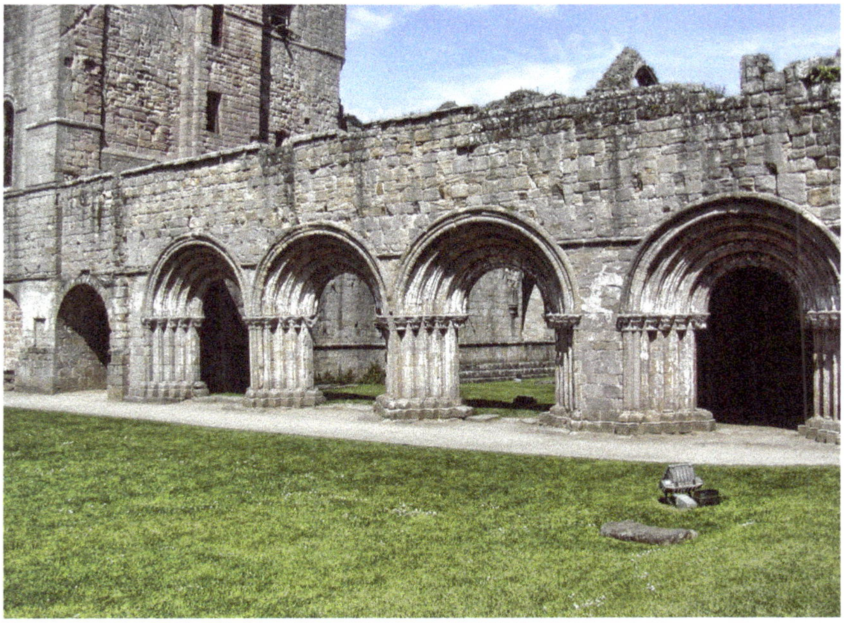

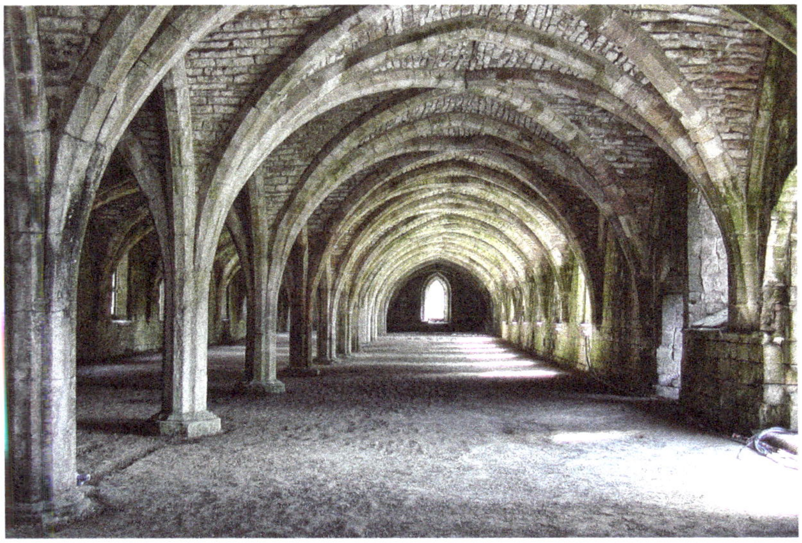

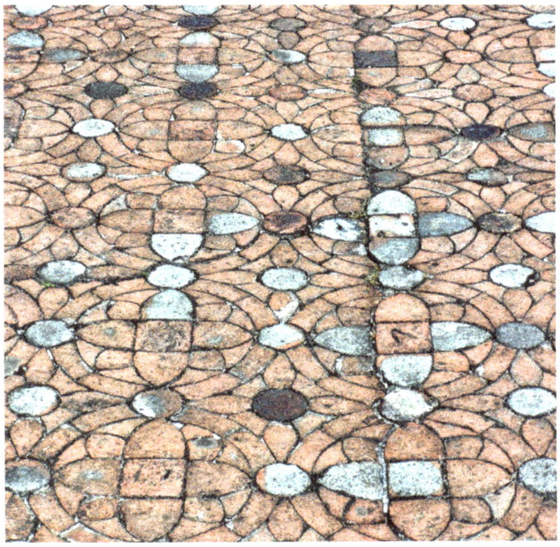

Gisborough Priory

St Mary • Augustinian 1119–1539

Virtually every monastic building at this early Augustinian priory of St Mary was flattened to create a landscaped area, but the little that is left is all the more impressive, standing supremely alone as a magnificent guardian of this once holy site, dominating both the town and surrounding pastoral landscape. The majestic east end gable of the priory church stands to its full original height of 29.6m (97ft) and its stunning visual impact is enhanced by the massive central window, alas now without its tracery, supported by slender stone shafts terminating in decorated turrets. The window is crowned by a gable enclosing a smaller, but rather ornate window with its tracery still intact. Flanking the main window are two gabled and turreted buttresses, each containing a low-level, broad lancet window, with smaller lights above. The massive buttresses that support this amazing structure have no doubt contributed to its survival. The scant outline revealed by nineteenth century excavations indicates that the church was 107m (352ft) long, with the presbytery alone comprising nine bays. Each arcade in the eight-bay aisled nave was supported by a clustered column on a moulded base, the remains of which can be identified at the western end. The north transept lay outside the modern boundary wall, while fragments of the south transept can be recognised, together with traces of a bench next to the west door of the nave. In the east end there is a cover slab of a medieval grave and the base of a tomb.

Parts of the south range have been excavated and include the south wall of the refectory with three large recesses with raised sills, and a doorway into an interesting vaulted service passage. This passage led to the dining hall from the buttery and pantry, and the square hatch in the south wall opened to the kitchen. Excavations have also revealed the cellarer's range, which comprises a vaulted undercroft of nine bays and an outer parlour leading to the cloister. The missing upper floor of this range contained the prior's lodging, hall and chapel. The oldest surviving feature is the great gate, which was later used as a gatehouse to a nearby mansion. It originally comprised the outer porch, now ruined, and inner hall and a porter's lodge on the ground floor with chambers above. The south wall of the porch has two arches: the smaller, single-door arch was for pedestrians, and the larger with double doors for wagons. In the centre of the inner court is a late seventeenth century dovecote, part of the now demolished Old Gisborough Hall, but this is not accessible to visitors.

Gisborough Priory was founded in 1119 for Augustinian canons by Robert de Brus, Lord of Cleveland, who, along with other wealthy benefactors, endowed the new foundation with much land, including the whole of the township of Guisborough. His brother William became the first prior, and was an ancestor of one of Scotland's most famous Kings, Robert the Bruce. The founder was buried here in 1142, and another Robert, the future King's grandfather, was also laid to rest at Gisborough in 1295, on the eve of the Scottish wars. As the priory grew in importance, eventually becoming the fourth richest house in England, the first stone church, already of a good size, was replaced by an even grander building. Construction started at the end of the twelfth century and took most of the next hundred years, but a catastrophic fire in 1289 gutted the almost completed building. The blame lay with a plumber, who was repairing a sprung joint in the lead roof. He took a bucket of red-hot coal up on the roof to heat the soldering irons, but forgot to bring it down at the end of the day. Some oak beams caught fire and, fanned by strong May winds, the flames consumed virtually the whole structure.

The present remains date from the third rebuilding started after the fire. In the fourteenth century, the priory suffered severely from frequent raids by the Scots and its fortunes, if not its influence, declined. It was a centre of the Pilgrimage of Grace rebellion and was finally surrendered to the Crown on Christmas Eve in 1539. The Deed of Surrender was signed by the prior and twenty-three canons. Henry VIII granted the priory to Sir Thomas Leigh on a 21-year lease, but in 1550 was given by his successor, Edward VI, to Sir Thomas Chaloner. Much of the fabric was razed to the ground, and stone 'quarried' from the priory can still be recognised in many buildings in the town.

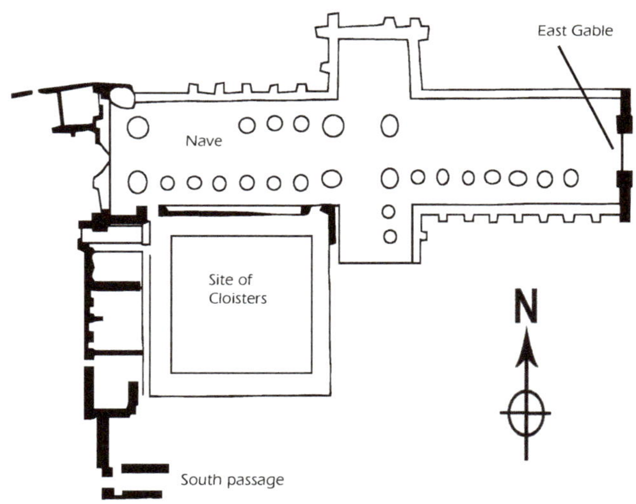

Photos - clockwise from top left

The majestic east gable still standing to its full height
Enough of the great gate has survived to show its entrance arches
Gothic window with parts of its tracery still in place
Vaulted service passage that led into the dining hall

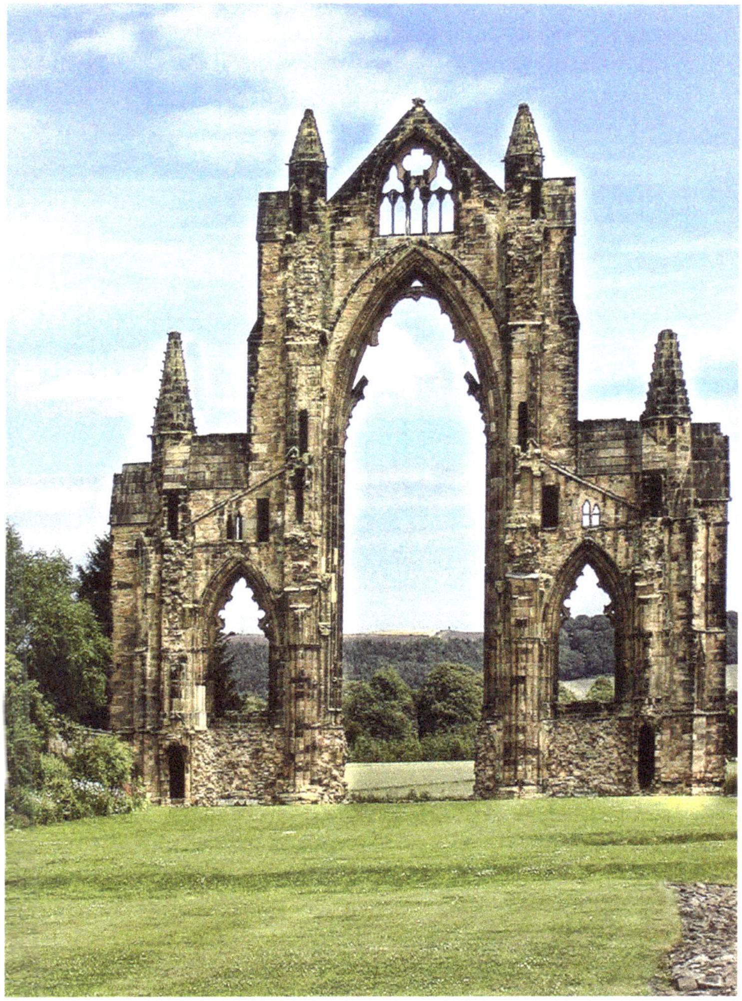

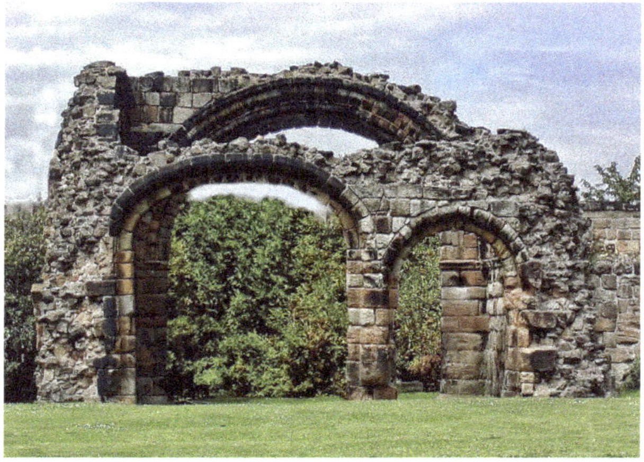

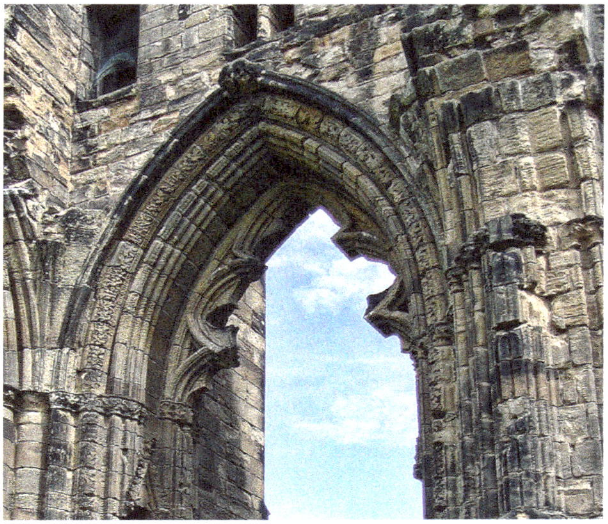

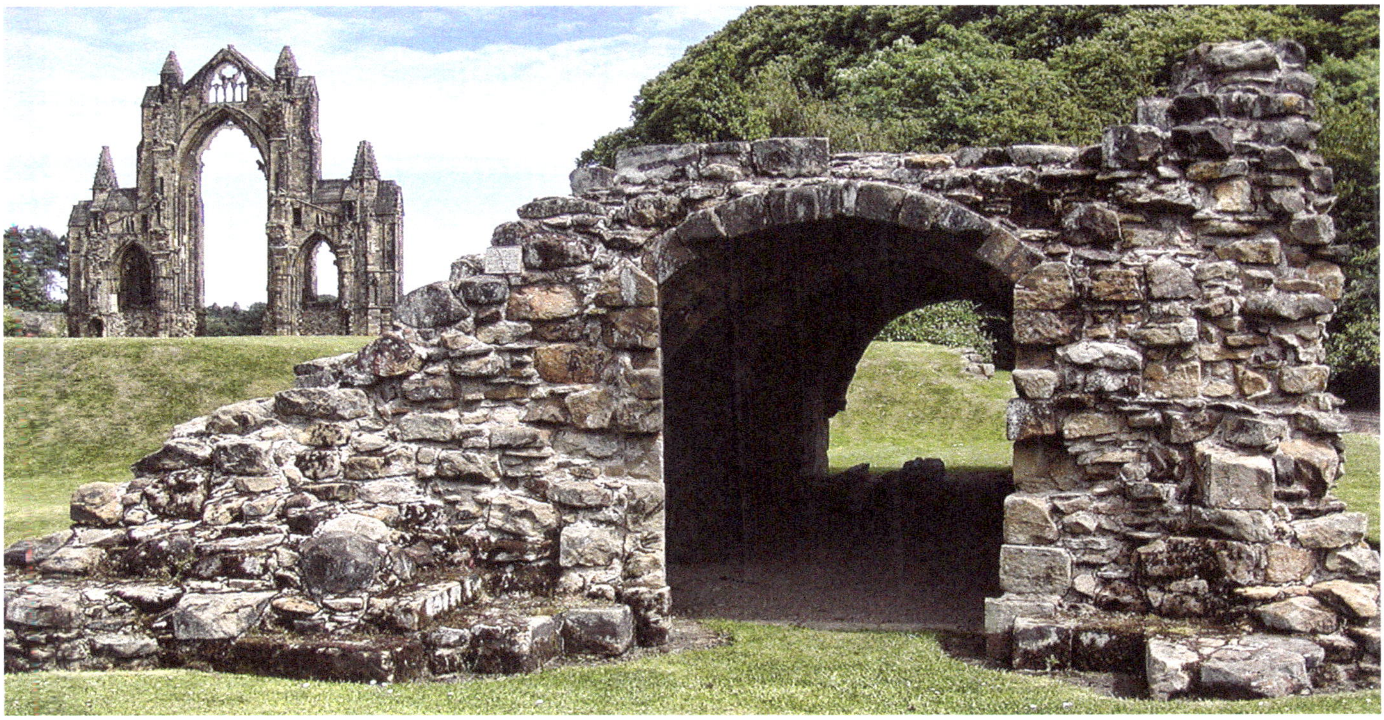

Goathland Hermitage

St Peter 1109–1114

A hermitage for Osmund, the priest, and two brothers was founded at Goathland in 1109, but ceased in 1114. In a charter addressed to Archbishop Thomas (1109-14), Nigel d'Albini and Osbert, Sheriff of Yorkshire, Henry I granted to Osmund and the brothers of 'Godelane' the hermitage for entertaining the poor. The brothers were to hold it free of all interference from the King's foresters and others, in perpetual alms. By a later charter, addressed to the same persons, the King gave licence to Osmund and the brothers to transfer themselves and their hermitage with all its appurtenances to the abbot and convent of Whitby, in perpetuity. The King enjoined the abbot and monks to receive the brethren to the rule of St Benedict, and confirmed the hermitage to Whitby when this was done. It has been conjectured that Goathland then formed a cell to Whitby, but this cannot be substantiated, and nothing is known of Goathland after it passed to Whitby. It would appear that at some time, the hermitage had been turned into a house for the abbot as, in December 1538, Henry Davell, Abbot of Whitby, leased to Robert Cokerell of 'Godland' one Abbot House, for eighty-one years at a yearly rent of 20s.

Grosmont Priory

St Mary • Grandmontine c1200–1539

Not a vestige is left of this alien priory of the Grandmontine Order. But strolling along the valley of the River Esk, with barren moorland rising sharply to a great height on each side, it is still possible to at least appreciate the isolation of the small number of monks who kept this poor house functioning for more than three hundred years. It was founded c1200 on the north bank of the river by Joan Fossard, wife of Robert de Torneham, who gave a mansion and arid land in the Forest of Egmont and the advowson of the church at Lockington to the abbey of Grandmont in Normandy. This charter was sanctioned by her husband, who added further land, and both charters were confirmed by King John in the fifteenth year of his reign (1213-14). The monks may initially have come from Grandmont but, by 1294, it was recorded that the brothers under the corrector, Roger de Cresswell, were Englishmen. This would suggest that the house was colonised from Craswall, Herefordshire, one of three houses of the Order in England.

Its history is as bare as the desolate moorland, and its internal life is only touched upon in 1387, when Pope Urban VI directed the abbot of Whitby to enquire into rumours that successive priors had alienated some of the properties and rights to the grave injury of the house. The outcome of these enquiries has not been recorded. During the wars with France, the abbot of Grandmont obtained licence from Richard II in 1394-95 to sell the Priory of Eskdale, as it was then known, to one John Hewitt and it thus became an English house. In the *Valor* of 1535, the clear annual value of the priory was returned as only £12 2s, but it survived the closure of the lesser monasteries until it was finally suppressed in 1539. Only Prior James Egton and four monks were then in residence. The priory and its lands were granted in 1544 to Edward Wright who sold it the following year to Sir Richard Cholmley. Nothing now remains of the buildings, but a description, with measurements, was given at the Dissolution. The church had an apsidal choir, nave, bell-tower and north chapel, with the typical claustral complex comprising a sacristy, chapter house, warming room, refectory, kitchen and prior's lodgings.

Hackness Priory

St Peter • Benedictine c1095–1539

The famous Hilda, Abbess of Whitby, founded a convent for Benedictine nuns at Hackness shortly before her death in AD 680. Ailing greatly during the last years of her life, she had intended to end her days at Hackness, but died at Whitby in the early hours of the morning. At that time, Begu, a nun at Hackness, was sleeping in the dormitory with the other nuns when she suddenly heard the bell that called them to prayer when a soul was passing away. She immediately had a vision that the roof of the house opened to a light-filled sky and Hilda was borne to heaven by angels. Begu, later St Begu, hurried to bring the news of Hilda's passing to Prioress Frigyth who ruled in the absence of Abbess Hilda. All the nuns arose and prayed for the soul of the abbess until, at dawn, monks arrived to confirm Hilda's death. Begu lived at Hackness for another ten years, dying there in AD 690. When, around 1125, the monks of Whitby were seeking holy relics to replace those of Hilda, which had been translated to Glastonbury after the Viking raids of the tenth century had left their monastery in ruins, a supposed revelation directed them to Hackness where a sarcophagus was uncovered bearing the inscription *Hoc est sepulchrum Begu.* Its contents were transferred to Whitby, where miracles were soon being reported.

Nothing is known of the subsequent history of the house until William de Percy gave to the re-founded Benedictine abbey at Whitby the church of St Peter at Hackness, as well as some land in the vicinity in c1095. It is said that Prior Serlo and some monks left Whitby for Hackness due to problems with robbers and sea-pirates who ravaged the abbey, and that some monks remained after Serlo died in 1100. There is no evidence that Hackness was a distinct cell of Whitby, but it has been recorded that four monks were in residence at the time of the Dissolution in 1539.

Handale (Grendale) Priory

St Mary • Cistercian nuns 1133–1534

This small and poor Cistercian nunnery to the Blessed Virgin Mary is largely a closed book, the only recorded event of note was an unsuccessful action brought in 1301 by Prioress Ivetta, who claimed that she was seized, imprisoned and suffered other indignities at Yarm. It was founded and endowed in 1133 by William de Percy of Dunsley, probably for Benedictine nuns, but was certainly a Cistercian house before 1504. The priory was surrendered in 1534 by Prioress Anne Lutton and ten nuns. Its clear annual value was just £13 19s. The priory mill was used for the manufacture of cotton garments after the Dissolution and in the eighteenth century, the priory ruins were incorporated into the existing farmhouse and walled garden. There are no visible remains of the buildings and the only reminders are dry fishponds to the south, and the pedestal of a stone cross and tomb slab located at the base of a medieval wall.

There was no village of Handale and the area was formerly a mixture of open farmland and dense woods. The name only survives in the legend of the Handale Serpent, which has been described as a 'loathly worm'. It is said that the hypnotic power lured the local maidens into its lair, many of whom were never seen again. However, one day a handsome knight named Scaw arrived and enquired about the shortage of comely maidens. When told of the serpent, he engaged him in a fearsome battle, but found the serpent too strong. Weary from his exertions, Scaw tripped over a fallen tree and, as he lay there, he plunged the sword into the only weak part of the serpent's body, his throat, and killed him. When he searched the lair, he found a maiden, Emma Beckwith, whom he lived with happily ever after. Long after Scaw died, a tomb was found at Handley Priory in 1830, with a sword and the words 'snake slayer' carved into the lid. Inside the tomb, the skeleton, believed to be of Scaw, held a 1.2m (4ft) long sword.

Hood Abbey

St Mary • Savignac/Augustinian 1139–1145

When the Savignac monks, who came from Furness Abbey and had set up Calder Abbey in 1135, were forced out by Scottish raiders, Abbot Gernon and his twelve companions travelled across the Pennines and were eventually granted land by Roger de Mowbray at Hood near Thirsk in 1139. The community lived in a hermitage of Robert de Alneto, but soon found their facilities too small, as a result of which the founder gave them a more suitable site at Old Byland, to which they moved in 1143. The buildings at Hood were taken over for a period of two years by Augustinian canons who were sent from Bridlington to establish Newburgh Priory near Coxwold, on land also given by Roger de Mowbray. When the new monastic buildings at Newburgh were ready in 1145, the canons vacated Hood, although one appears to have continued serving the church of St Mary. Hood may have remained as a cell to Newburgh, but was more likely little more than a grange. A medieval barn behind the later house built on the site may have been part of this grange. This incorporates a stone coffin and two trefoil window heads built into a wall, and a plain medieval doorway.

Hutton Lowcross Priory

St Mary • Cistercian nuns c1162–c1166

A priory for Cistercian nuns was founded c1162 by Ralph de Neville, but the community was transferred to a new site at Thorp, later to become known as Nunthorpe, in c1166. Nothing is known of the short period at Hutton Lowcross, nor of the reasons for the removal of the nuns.

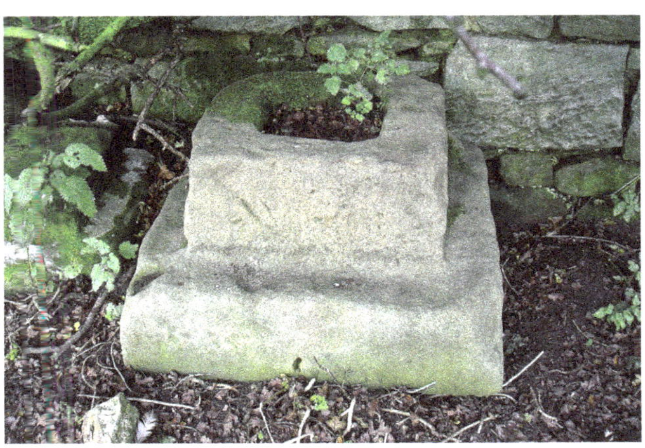

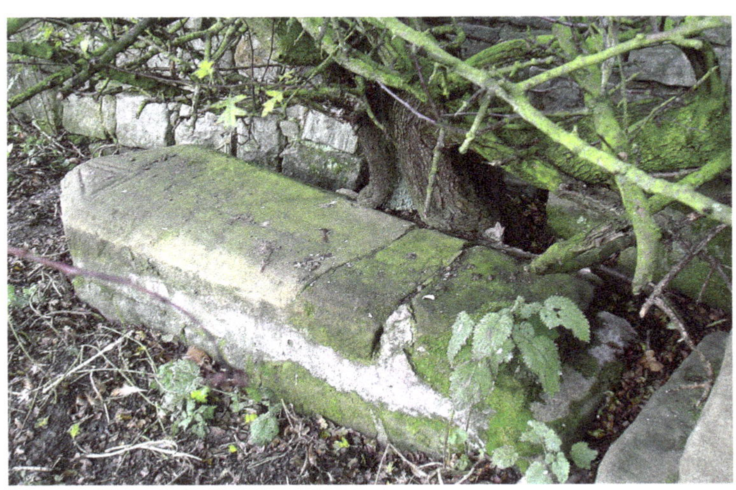

Photos from Handale Priory courtesy of John Lawson

Jervaulx Abbey

St Mary • Cistercian 1156–1537

Hidden behind the boundary wall of the Marquis of Ailesbury's estate and screened by mature trees, Jervaulx Abbey reposes in a green valley where sheep graze freely and nature has been left to encroach on what was a surprisingly large monastic settlement. Once known as Yorevale Abbey, derived from Yore (the valley of Ure), it was given a French spelling by a former Marchioness of Ailesbury. Although established in its present location in 1156, the foundations of a Cistercian abbey had been laid in 1145 in the time of King Stephen, when Akarius fitzBardolph bequeathed land at Fors in Upper Wensleydale near Askrigg to Peter Quinciano, a monk of Savigny. Disapproved of by Serlo, the then abbot of Savigny, Fors came under the authority of Byland Abbey, which provided assistance to the fledgling brotherhood and supplied John de Kinstan as abbot and twelve monks to Fors. The confines and sterility of the land made it untenable, however, forcing the community to give up the unequal struggle.

This all changed when Conan, the son of the Earl of Richmond, increased his endowment and removed the abbey to a much more pleasing and fertile location in the parish of East Witton. Ancient manuscripts tell a romantic story of the travails of the monks to the present site. On travelling from Byland to Fors, John de Kinstan and his twelve monks were said to have lost their way in dense woods, but were guided to safety by a vision of the Virgin Mary and Child, who said; "Ye are late of Byland but now of Yorevale." A large church was built and dedicated, like most Cistercian abbeys, to the Virgin Mary. Under the patronage of Harveus, son of Akarius, and other later benefactors including Henry fitzHugh, who lies buried in the church, Jervaulx Abbey gained in wealth and influence. At the height of its power it owned half of the valley of the Ure.

The last abbot of Jervaulx, Adam Sedbar, who was elected in 1533, found himself implicated in the Pilgrimage of Grace opposition movement against the dissolution of the monasteries ordered by Henry VIII. He was taken to the Tower of London and interrogated, and although the charges proved unsubstantiated, Sedbar was hanged at Tyburn for his 'insubordination' in June 1537. As a result, the abbey was forfeited to the Crown and suffered more complete destruction than other religious houses, to ensure that any recolonisation by other defiant monks was made impossible. At the Dissolution, Jervaulx Abbey was valued at up to £455. The site was then given by the King to Maltham, Earl of Lenox. Much of the stone was later removed and used as local building material.

Yet, there is still much to explore at Jervaulx. Although only foundations now trace the outline of the church, it is approached through the south-west door with its beautiful Norman dog-tooth decoration. There are also several altars and interesting tombs, including the weathered cross-legged effigy of Lord Henry fitzHugh, the abbey's great benefactor, between the two transepts. Parts of other important buildings still stand almost to their full height. One of the most notable examples is the virtually complete west wall of the 53m (173ft) long monk's dorter, with its well-preserved lancet windows in the upper storey.

On the east side of the cloister, six steps lead down to the chapter house. Most of the columns used to support the vaulted roof remain perfect to the height of the springing, with their finely decorated capitals still intact, as are the stone seats for the monks and abbot. The abbot's seat is in the middle of the east side. There is much more, including the monk's infirmary, chapel and kitchen, abbot's lodging, and meat kitchen with wide fireplaces, ovens and a trough for washing up. Also still in evidence are the lay-brothers infirmary and reredorter. Several tombs can be found in the church and chapter house. With a systematic approach and a little imagination, this relatively unknown jewel in North Yorkshire will yield up far more than first expected.

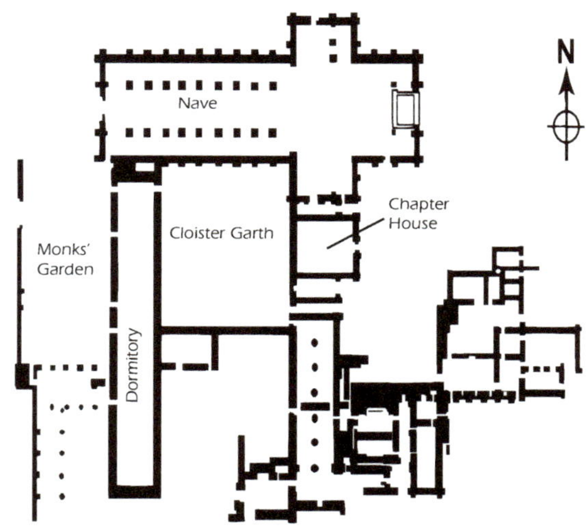

Photos – clockwise from top

The monks' dormitory, the most prominent survival
Monks' infirmary and chapel
Beautiful Norman archway into the church and stairs to the dormitory
Finely decorated column capital in the chapter house
Archway into the parlour
Chapter house with five of six columns and stone seats

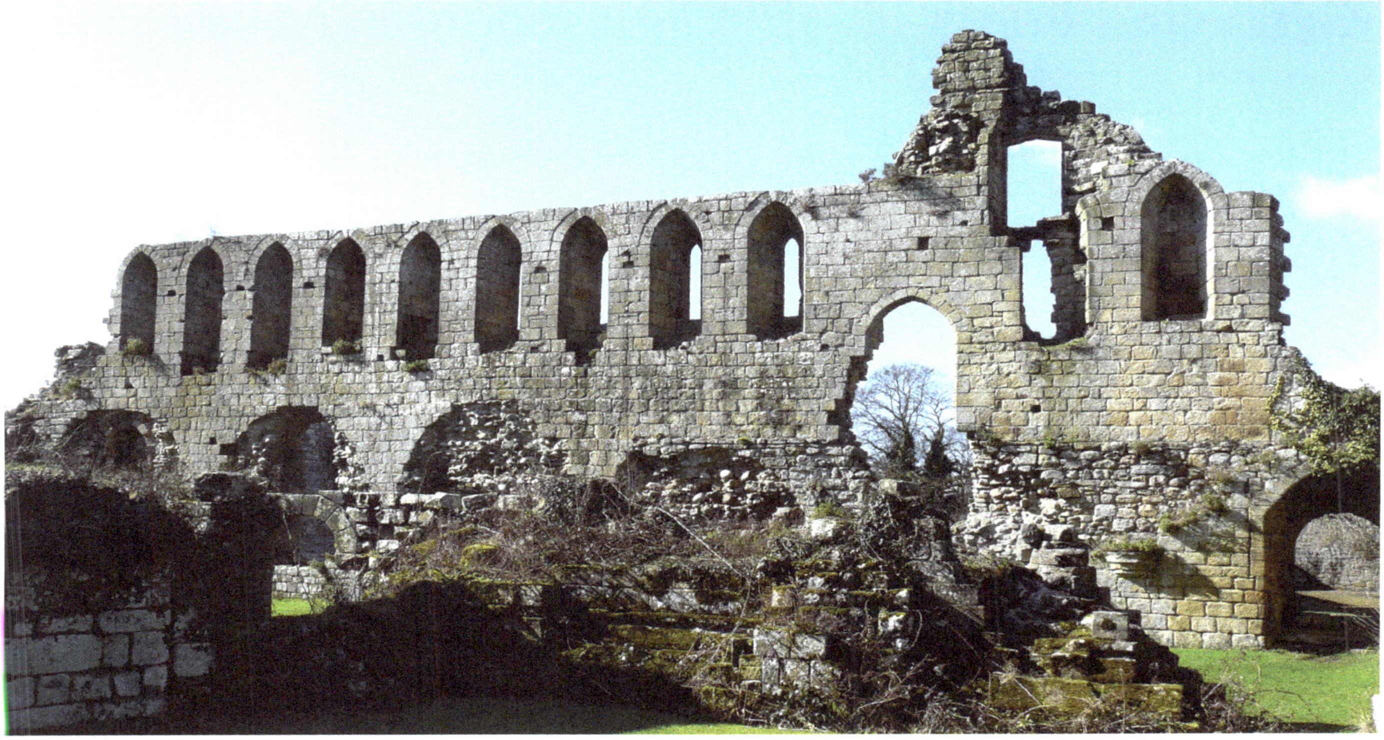

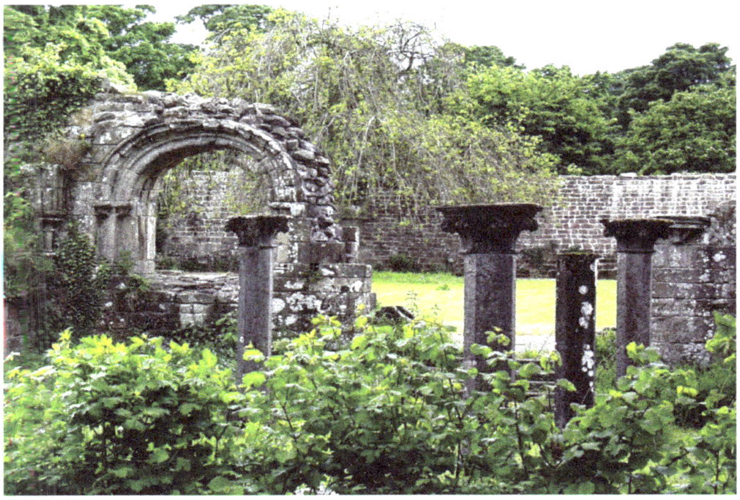

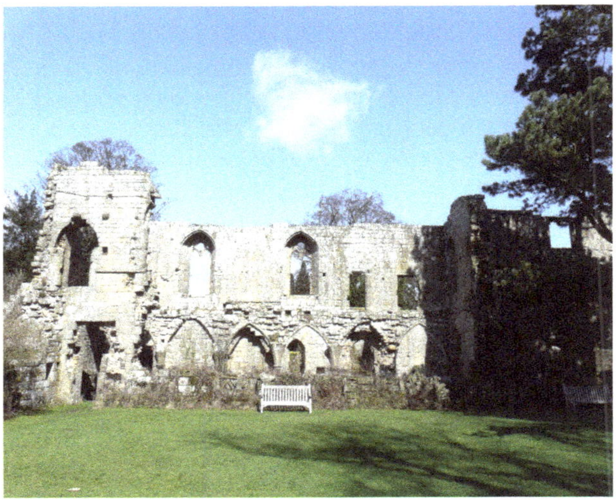

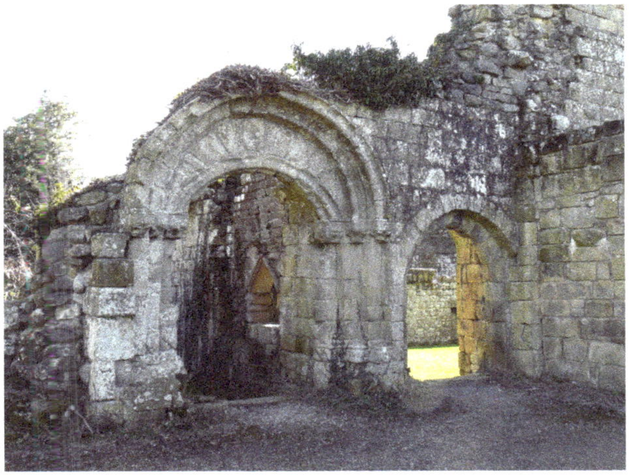

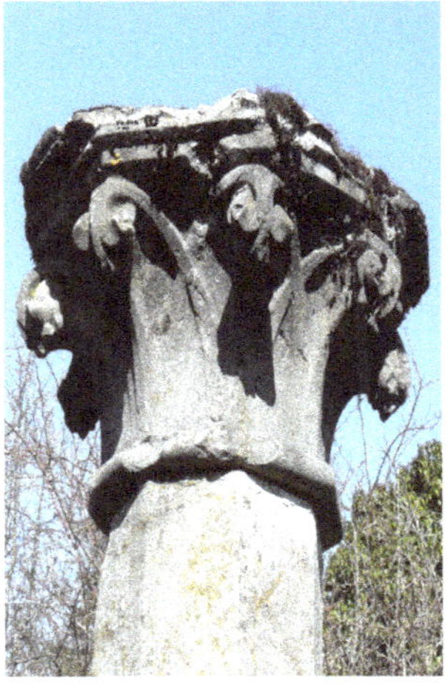

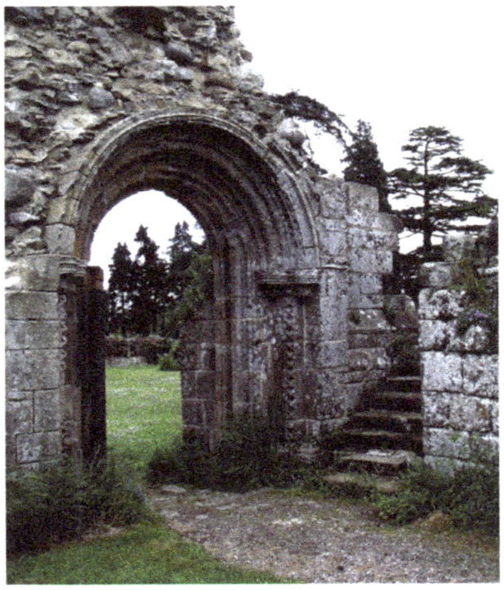

Keldholme Priory

St Mary • Cistercian nuns +1100–1536

Two stone coffins incised with foliated crosses built vertically into the garden wall of a modern house, and now almost obliterated by rampant vegetation, and fragments of pillars are all that has survived of this small Cistercian nunnery dedicated to St Mary. The coffins are thought to be of a Keldholme nun and a monk from a neighbouring monastery who conceived a child together. According to the tale, compassion prevailed and they were allowed to jointly raise the child until such time it could be admitted into fellowship. Upon death, however, they were buried upright, which was believed to complicate heavenly salvation. This story, whether true or not, forms part of a chequered history. Founded in the reign of Henry I by Robert de Stuteville in a curve of the River Dove below Spaunton Moor, the small priory never obtained the grant of any church and always remained poor, in spite of the patronage passing by marriage to the lords of Liddell early in the thirteenth century. It suffered an almost permanent series of violent disputes and internal wrangling and disobedience, which in the fourteenth century called for the intervention of the archbishop, although his injunctions did not reveal any particular misdemeanours. This sorry state of affairs did little to ensure a comfortable living and the 'nuns of Dove' had to board young girls and widows to supplement their income. It was reported that the priory possessed a piece of the true cross and a finger of St Stephen, which would have encouraged pilgrims to Keldholme, but this did not seem to have improved its fortunes by much. Income was largely derived from a thriving wool trade with Italian merchants, which amounted to twelve sacks per annum. Before its suppression in August 1536, signed by Prioress Elizabeth Lyon, five nuns, chaplain Sir John Porter, and twelve servants and boys, it had been valued at a lowly £29 6s.

Kildale Crutched Friars

1310– +1313

Arnold de Percy granted a chapel and ten acres of land in his park at Kildale to the Crutched Friars, also known as the Friars of the Cross. The grant was made without royal licence, but Edward II pardoned the friars in 1310. However, William Greenfield, Archbishop of York and sometime Chancellor of England, put the house under interdict, because the friars celebrated divine service without his permission and the Order was not approved by the pope. The use of the chapel was forbidden in 1314-1315. The friars may have moved away, as nothing further has been recorded.

Lastingham Abbey

St Mary • Benedictine 1078–1086

The thirteenth century church of St Mary in the small village of Lastingham in a green hollow on the edge of the vast North Yorkshire Moors hides what was left of an unfinished abbey, when the monks deserted the site in 1088 and set up St Mary's Abbey in York. The reason for this abrupt departure is not known. Narrow stone steps take the visitor down to an amazing crypt, which is not only of unusual and probably unique design, but has survived virtually unaltered over the centuries. The crypt has a chancel, aisles, eastern apse and stumpy columns with heavy carved capitals and bases and is in effect a church within a church. Historians believe that this grand structure was intended to receive relics of St Cedd, who had established a Saxon monastery on the same site in AD 658 at the request of King Aethelwald. St Cedd died of the plague in AD 664 and, according to the Venerable Bede, was buried to the right of the altar. He entrusted the abbey to his even more famous brother, St Chad, who is said to have ruled with wisdom and kindness.

Lastingham was probably destroyed by the Danes in the ninth century, but in 1078, Abbot Stephen, who had left Whitby Abbey after a quarrel, refounded the abbey as a Benedictine house with nine monks. A substantial church was planned, and the two massive eastern piers would have supported the tower. Abbot Stephen first built the crypt over the place where St Cedd is thought to have been buried, but ten years later the monks abruptly left, with only the crypt and apse of the church completed. The apse was incorporated in the present parish church, which was built in the thirteenth century. The tower is of later date. Of note within the crypt is a collection of twelve Anglo-Saxon stone fragments, including crosses of late eighth-tenth century date, a hogback of the mid-tenth century, and several other, even older parts. Close to a nearby bridge are the old wells of St Cedd and St Chad, erected in the nineteenth century. St Cedd's Well was built using twelfth century stone from Rosedale Abbey.

Photos - clockwise from top left

Stone coffin from Keldholme Priory incised with foliated cross
Thirteenth century church of St Mary at Lastingham
Pier supporting vault
Rare crypt with chancel, aisles and estern apse
Old well of St Cedd
Doorway into the crypt

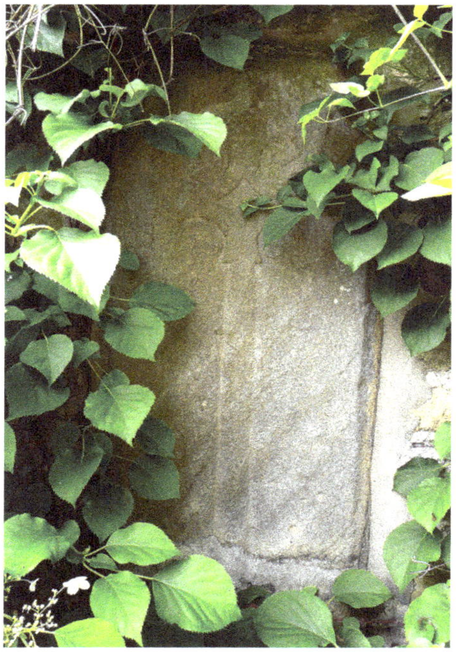

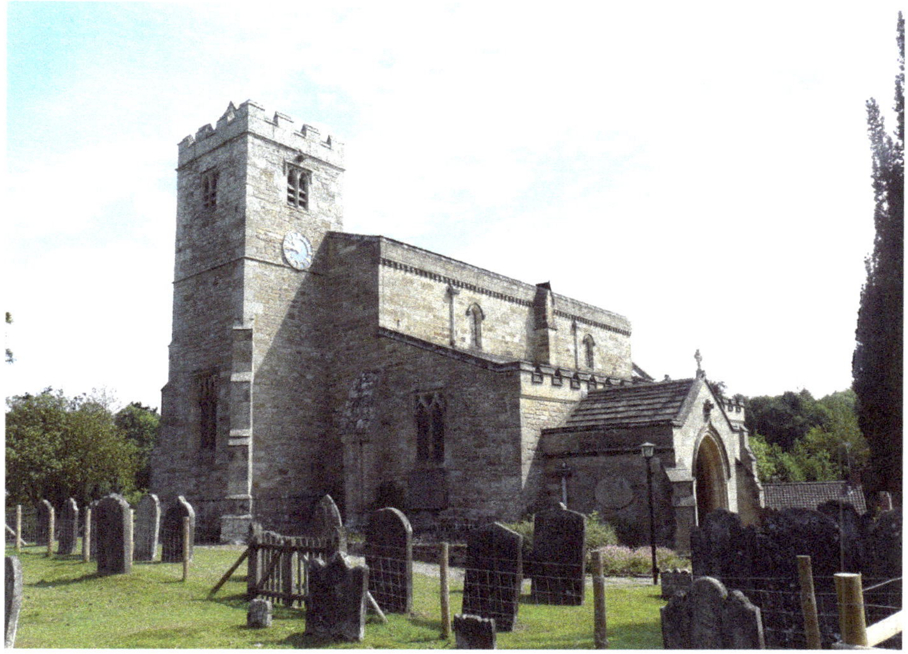

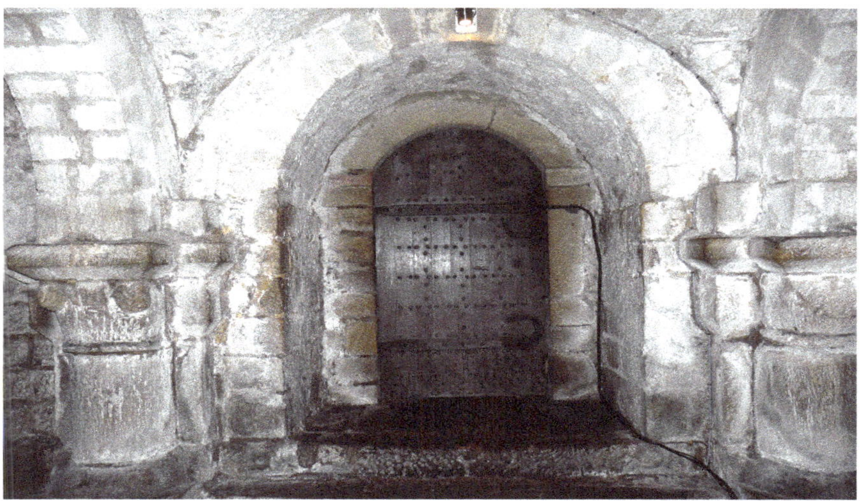

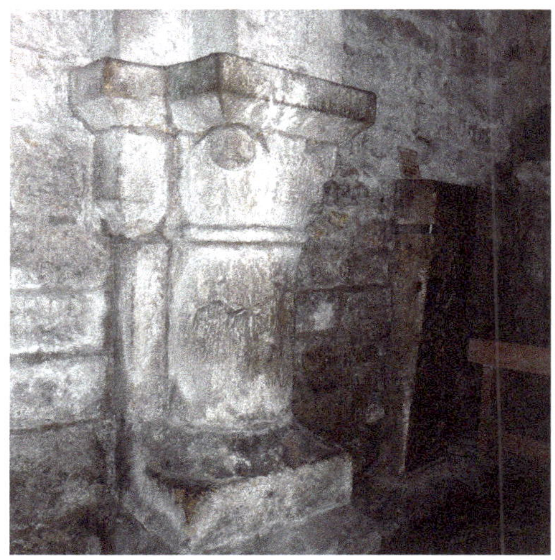

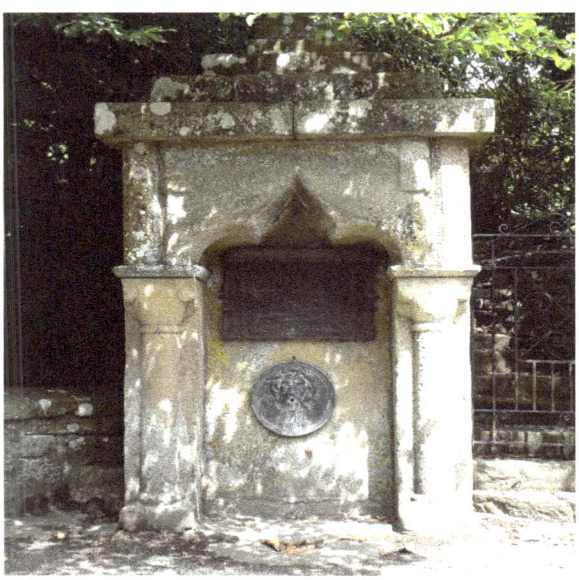

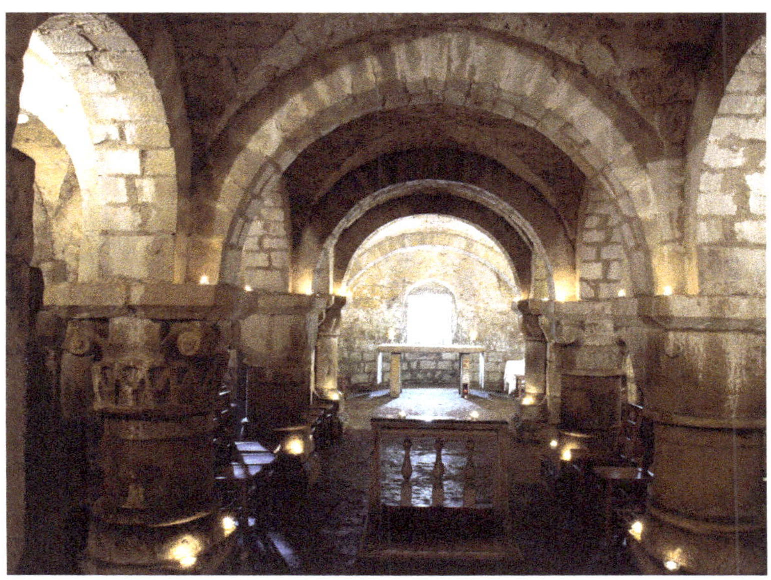

Malton Priory

St Mary • Gilbertine 1150–1539

The Priory of St Mary at Old Malton was one of the few monastic houses of the Gilbertines, the only full British monastic Order, and the church is the sole surviving example where worship continues to this day. Of the original aisled church, which was more elaborate than those of most other Gilbertine houses with transepts, crossing tower and twin west end towers, only the nave and the west façade remain standing. The church exhibits a mix of architectural styles progressing from massive round columns and arches to the fine Early English of the west front dating from around 1200, and the transitional Romanesque of the west doorway itself. The five orders of moulding are distinguished by Norman and Early English motifs and colonettes with stiff-leaf capitals. The surviving tower has elegant shafted windows, one with 'Beverley rose' decoration characteristic of East Yorkshire, and quatrefoil openings above the twin-bell openings. One of the octagonal eastern piers is known as 'The Prior's Column', which is elaborately panelled with a carved inscription on the capital referring to Prior Robert Shotton (1498-1518), under whose mastership major repairs and rebuilding were undertaken. The description, which includes a rebus of an arrow through a barrel, is partly inverted, suggesting that it may have been the work of an illiterate carver who copied it wrongly from a sketch. Of great interest are the medieval misericords, of which seven have survived. These include a kneeling Bactrian camel, an owl with upraised wings, eagle, hare or rabbit in crouching position, a heraldic lion, griffin, and an elaborate design of a pineapple. The other misericords date from the nineteenth century.

At the back of the church are a number of carved stones found in and around the churchyard, including Saxon and Anglo-Scandinavian cross-heads, a small Roman altar and fragments from the monastic buildings. There is also a thirteenth century tomb slab with an incised cross, probably that of a prior. A few ruinous elements at the east end outside include two massive pillars from the central tower, and an interesting processional doorway that led from the now missing cloister into the south aisle of the church. Its waterleaf capitals date it to about 1180. In the wall close to the doorway are the remains of a holy water stoup. Also among the earliest work is a re-erected doorway in the churchyard, which may have been the entrance to the chapter house but for many years was used as a cattle trough. Its elaborate Norman beakhead decoration and scalloped capitals are worth noting. St Gilbert is said to lie buried in the priory church. Of the associated monastic buildings virtually nothing has survived, except for a vaulted undercroft below an outbuilding at Abbey House. The Doodles, a small nearby area of wooded wetland and earthworks, is thought to have been the priory's fishponds.

Fragments of Saxon carved stone crosses suggest that there was a church on this site, although nothing has survived from this early structure. This was probably due to the burning of the village by an army led by Archbishop Thurstan of York in 1138, when the local lord, Eustace fitzJohn, sided with Scottish King David, who had invaded England, but was later repelled in the famous Battle of the Standard on Cowton Moor near Northallerton. It was Eustace fitzJohn who founded the priory in 1150, probably in expiation. Eustace endowed his foundation with farmland and a number of churches, and several more grants from other benefactors increased the priory's possessions and brought in a fair income, mostly from wool production, rent and mills. This contributed towards major building works, which, according to an account by William of Newburgh on the deaths of three monks from poisoning during the process of burning lime, was still in progress in 1197.

But heavy borrowing from the Jews, the paying off of debts of benefactors, poaching of cattle and stealing of corn by the townsfolk for the war against the Scots, plunged the priory at times into debt. Sometime in the late fifteenth century, the north-west tower collapsed in a fire, causing major damage to the north aisle, whose piers were remodelled as a result in the Perpendicular style. With income under £200, Malton priory was scheduled to be closed in 1536, but the influence of Prior Robert Holgate ensured its survival for four more years. However, the prior was accused of participation in the Pilgrimage of Grace and arrested, but his fate is unknown. In December 1539 the then prior and nine canons finally surrendered this, the last house of the Gilbertines.

The monastic complex was used as a ready-made quarry. The central tower was taken down in 1636, and the church sustained minor damage from cannonballs during the Civil War. The process of quarrying continued and by 1728 most of the monastic buildings were in ruins, although the cloister walls were then still standing. By 1733, the south aisle, chancel and the transepts had all either fallen or had been demolished, as was the north-west tower. The rest of the church was semi-ruinous and the parish was granted permission to take down the north aisle, to reduce the height of the roof by 2.4m (8ft), and to shorten the east end of the aisle by 11m (36ft). A stone rood screen may also have been demolished at that time. Major reconstruction work was started in 1877, when the parish was faced with the imminent collapse of the remaining tower.

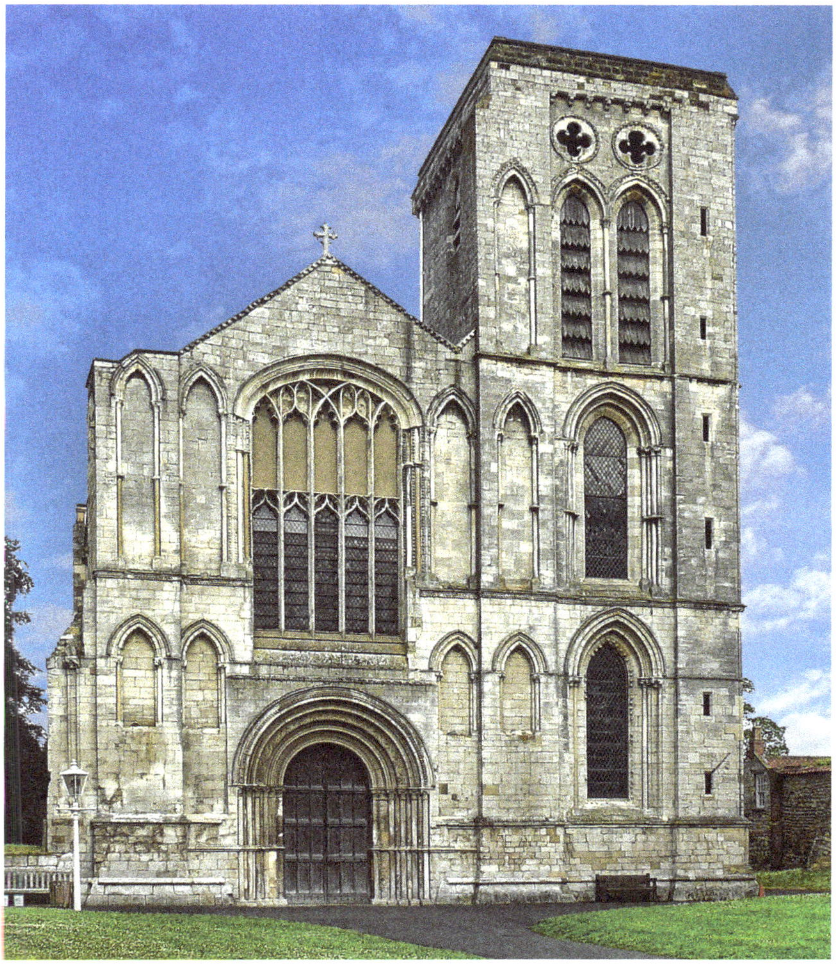

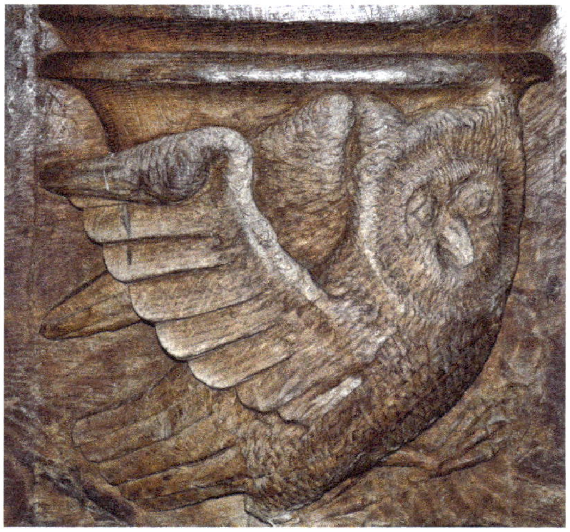

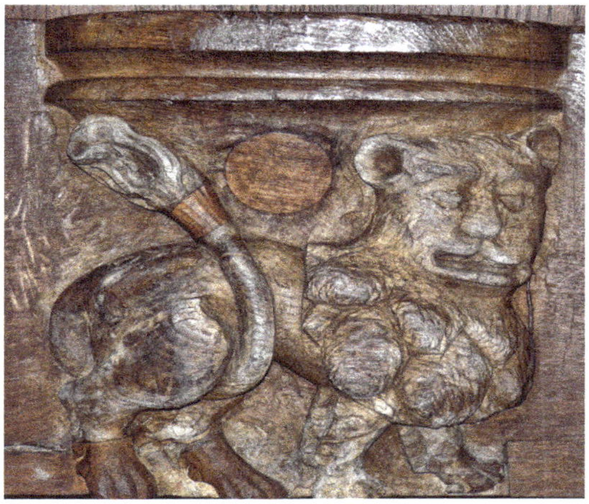

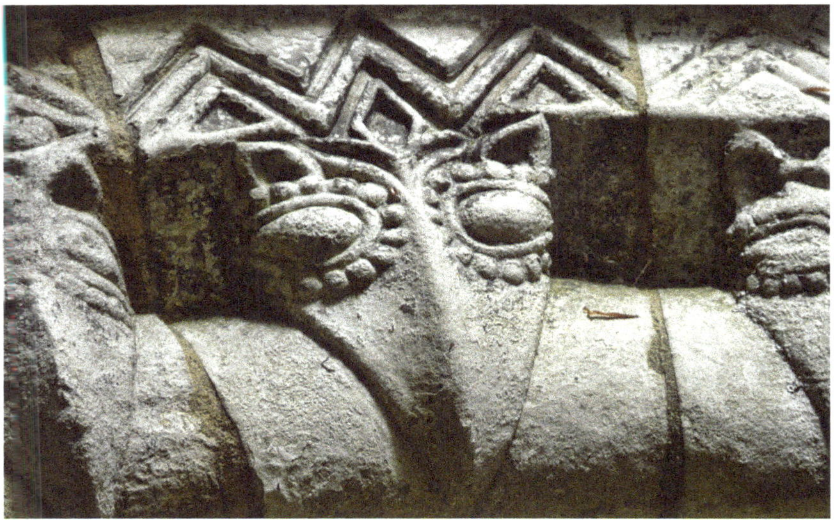

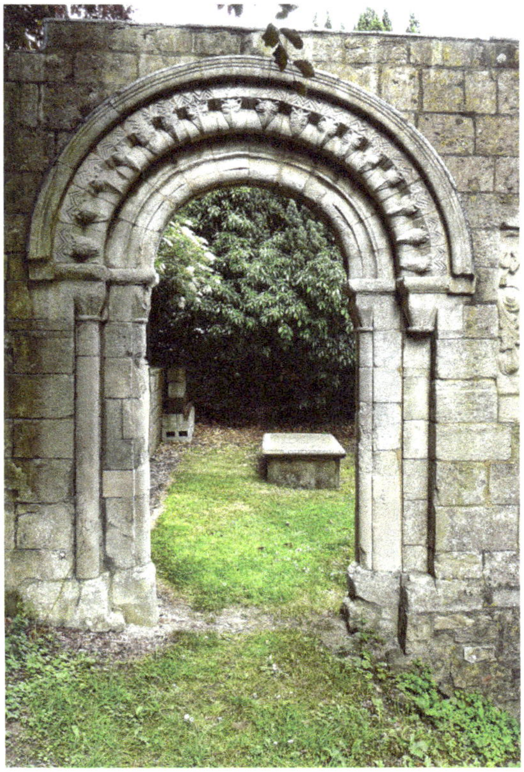

Photos - clockwise from top left

Nave and west front of former priory church
Medieval misericord of owl with upraised wings
Medieval misericord of heraldic lion
Re-erected Norman doorway, probably from chapter house
A fine example of Norman beakhead decoration on doorway

Marrick Priory

St Mary and St Andrew • Benedictine nuns 1156–1539

Almost within hailing distance of Ellerton Priory, but on the north side of the Swale, lies Marrick Priory, founded around 1156 by Roger de Aske as a Benedictine nunnery dedicated to St Mary and St Andrew. Its setting in the middle reaches of Swaledale is equally as beautiful as Ellerton, its slightly raised position providing shelter on the hillside while being high enough above the flood level to be safe from sudden surges of one of the swiftest rivers in England. The founder granted the church of St Andrew at Marrick, together with a carucate of land, and Conan, Earl of Richmond, confirmed his gift and those of other benefactors. Several of Roger's daughters became nuns. The community received many other donations, including the hospital known as Spital on Stainmoor, but income from this and the wool trade was insufficient to maintain the nuns much above subsistence level.

Almost nothing is known of its history, but what little has been written down suggests an unexceptional existence. Details of only one visitation are known. This occurred in 1252 under the archepiscopate of Walter Gray, when several notices were issues, although these were of a general nature, such as nuns were not to be left alone with guests, were not to sit with visitors outside the cloister after curfew, and no man or woman were to be admitted without the bishop's licence. When Scottish raiders despoiled Ellerton Priory in the fourteenth century, Marrick is also thought to have suffered damage, as a sudden drop in papal taxation from £66 12s in 1291 to a nil valuation in 1318 would indicate. While, for some unexplained reason, the priory escaped the closure of the lesser monasteries in spite of its annual value having been assessed at only £48 13s, it was finally surrendered in September 1539. The prioress, Christabella Cowper, and the sixteen nuns then in residence were pensioned off. The site and demesne lands were at first leased and then purchased in 1545 by Sir John Uvedale, secretary of the Council of the North, who had coveted Marrick and was present at the eviction of the nuns. The priory church was later used by the parishioners, but was left to gradually become derelict and a home for stray chickens.

The present remains include an almost complete church, but only the thirteenth century tower stands as first built, with the rest re-erected in 1811. Ruins of the medieval chancel survive to the east, including window tracery and a sedilia. Farm buildings are attached to the north side of the tower and include the Prioress' House. The Marrick Priory complex is now a Diocesan Youth Centre and is not open to the public, although it can be viewed from an adjoining footpath.

Marton Priory

St Mary • Augustinian canons/nuns 1158–1536

One the road from Stillington to Helmsley, a farmhouse called Marton Abbey built out of the ruins, together with undulating earthworks and a moat that surrounded it, are the only reminders of this unique double house of Augustinian canons and nuns, founded in 1158 by Bertram de Bulmer. The priory was granted lands at Burnsall and Thorpe, and prospered with further endowments of lands and churches confirmed by Henry II. By 1167, the nuns had moved three kilometres south to Moxby, thus changing the foundation to a quasi-double house with the two sexes accommodated in separate establishments, albeit in close proximity to each other. Its annual income of £183 2s brought Marton Priory only just within the limit for the lesser monasteries, forcing Prior Thomas Godson and fifteen canons to surrender to Henry VIII's commissioners in 1536. The priory was granted to the archbishop of York.

Middlesbrough Priory

St Hilda • Benedictine 1119–1536?

A few stones built into a brewery are all that remains from the priory of St Hilda, a cell of Whitby Abbey. The ground on which it stood was consecrated as early as AD 686, when St Cuthbert established a monastic community at the request of St Hilda, Abbess of Whitby. The history and fate of this foundation has been lost, but religious life was revived in 1119, when Robert de Brus, Lord of Cleveland and founder of Gisborough Priory, granted the church of St Hilda in Middlesbrough to the abbey of Whitby, together with land at Newham. The gift was confirmed by Henry I, and in 1130 by Archbishop Thurston. The twelve Benedictine monks installed to maintain this cell later received further gifts of land in the neighbourhood, but for reasons unknown, the priory became impoverished and by the middle of the fifteenth century, only the prior and one monk remained. In a return made in 1527, the clear annual value of the priory was just £12. After its dissolution, probably in 1536, the priory fell into ruin and its possessions were granted by Queen Elizabeth I to Thomas Reeve.

Photos of Marrick Priory – clockwise from top

Marrick Priory from the south bank of the River Swale
Ruins of medieval chancel
Former room of prioress
Unusual font in chapel
Thirteenth century tower of priory church

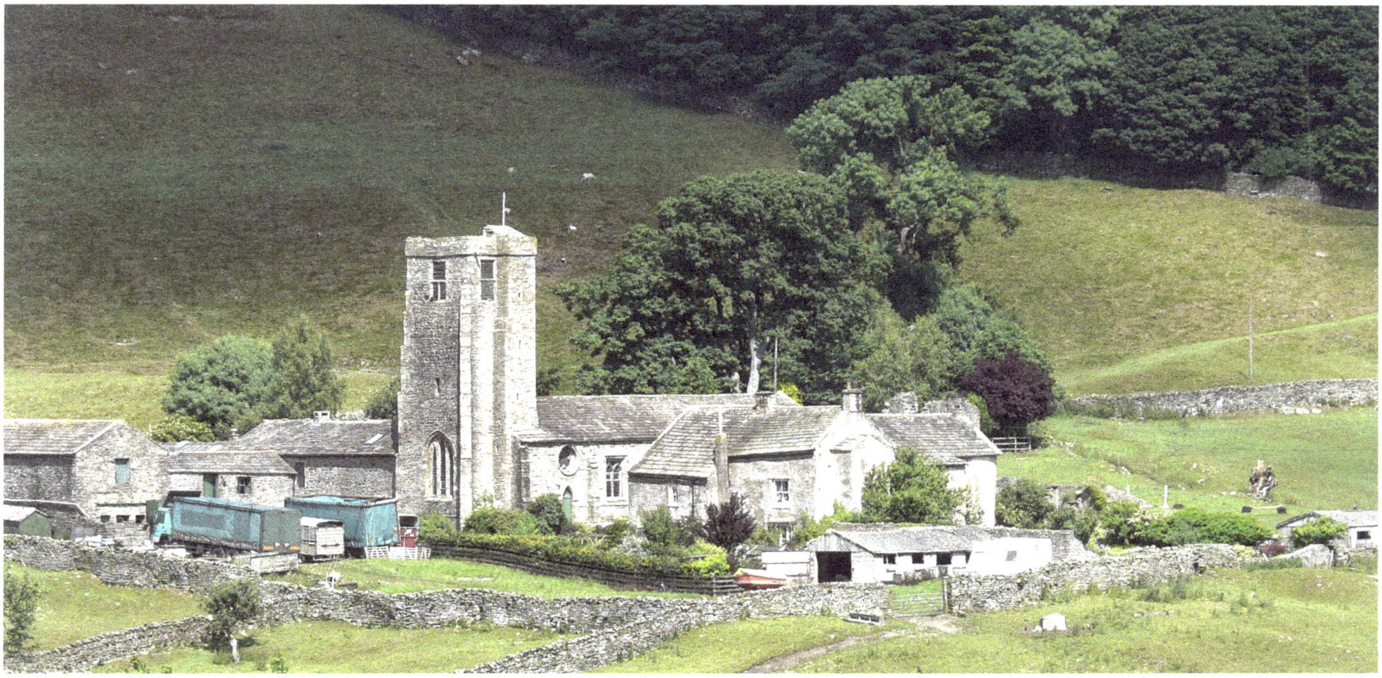

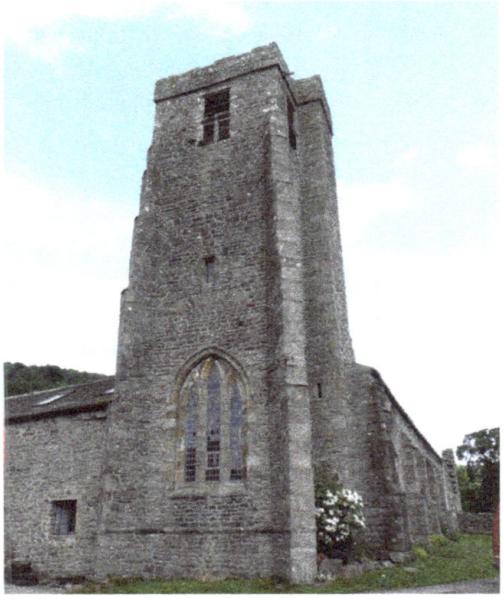

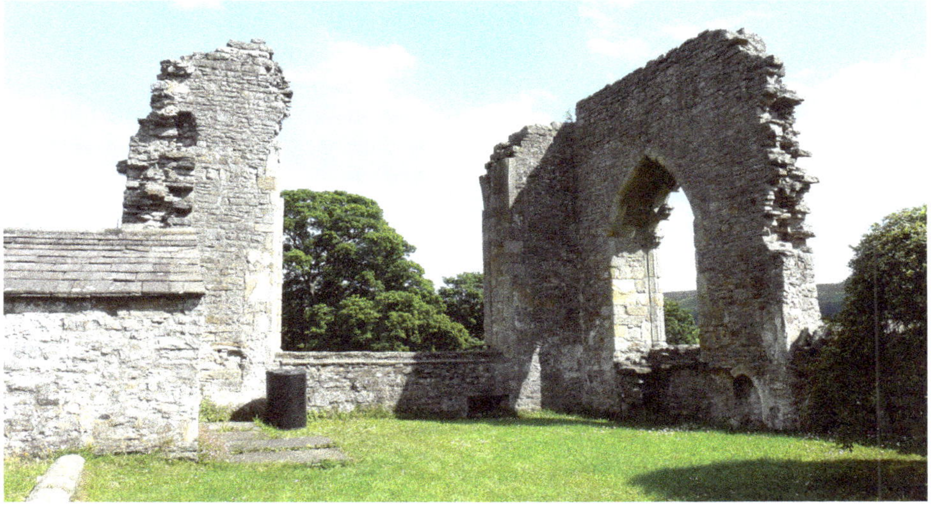

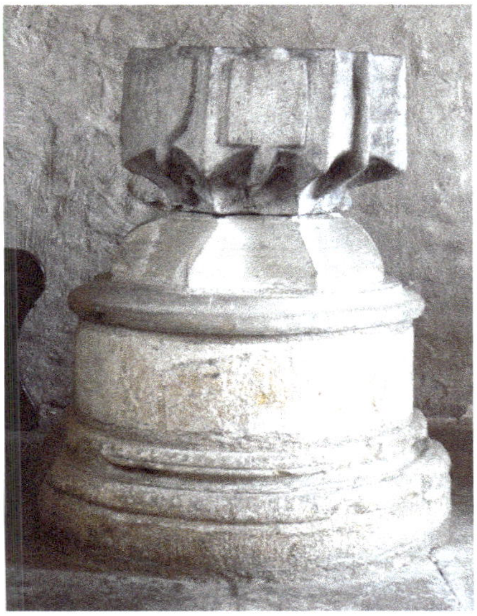

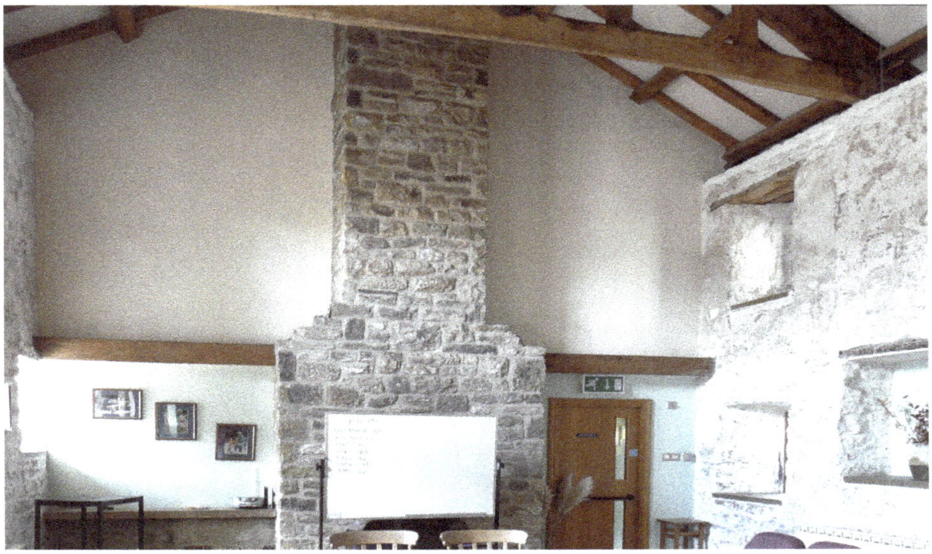

Mount Grace Priory

Assumption of the Virgin & St Nicholas • Carthusian 1398–1539

A visit to Mount Grace provides a unique experience, the priory being one of only nine medieval Carthusian monasteries, or Charterhouses, to be founded in Britain, and the only one accessible to the public. Situated on a raised terrace below the wooded escarpment of the Hambleton Hills in the North Yorkshire Moors, this isolated and peaceful location ideally suited the Carthusian monks, who lived virtually as hermits in individual cells, but within the community. Once through the doorway of the seventeenth century mansion, which was converted from the priory guesthouse and now forms the entrance to the ruins, one becomes immediately aware that Mount Grace is different from other monastic sites. There are no grand church and elaborate monastic buildings around the cloister, and the general impression is of a humble and harsh existence. The church, which stands to a good height and still has some fine Gothic arches and remains of intricate window tracery, is rather small and solid, because the Carthusian mass was a simple affair without elaborate rituals, and visitors were discouraged.

Yet in complete contrast, the great open cloister is a huge area, which dominates the site. Grouped around the edge are the remains of monastic cells, where twenty-five monks spent the day in prayer, work and meditation, leaving only for the three daily collective attendances in church. At midnight, they rose from their beds to give thanks. Additional cells had to be squeezed into the site to the north of the church because of the demand for places, but this still left a waiting list. Although the monks clearly lived a life of deprivation, their cells, probably better described as cottages, were rather well appointed. Each had two storeys, with a living room, study and bedroom on the ground floor, and a workroom on top. Each cell was also surrounded by its own cloister and garden. Lay-brothers, who were responsible for all the manual work, left food for the monks in little recesses beside each door. Only on Sundays and feast days were the monks allowed to dine together and meet to discuss business and discipline. If ill, monks were tended in their cells, which explains the absence of an infirmary in Carthusian monasteries. One cell has been reconstructed in the cloister to provide an insight into the life of "Christ's Poor Men", as they were called.

A fascinating feature was the water supply to the priory. Water for drinking was brought from spring-houses on the hillside above, one of which is still in place. At the centre of the cloister stood an octagonal 'water house', from which water was pumped by hand to a storage tank and distributed to every part of the priory by lead pipes. The monks' cells incorporated a latrine over a stone channel, which was flushed by running water. Each had a wooden seat and a candle niche to provide light.

The solitary lifestyle, which never wavered, attracted much royal patronage, with Richard II, Edward IV and Henry V particularly generous, granting lands stretching from Teesside in the north to as far as Ware down south. Mount Grace Priory was founded in 1398 by Richard II's nephew, Thomas de Holand, Earl of Kent and Duke of Surrey, who unfortunately lost his head for treason against his uncle's successor, Henry IV, just two years later. Work on the stone gatehouse and church was begun in 1400, while the monks were given wooden cells around the cloister. As the priory's fortunes improved, the church was enlarged in 1415 and the wooden cells replaced by stone buildings. Further expansion followed with the addition of chapels around the nave and presbytery to say mass for those who had chosen the church as their final resting place. Much of this building programme, which continued until the suppression, was funded by Henry's half-brother Thomas Beaufort, who was buried there in 1427. Prior John Wilson and sixteen monks surrendered Mount Grace to Henry VIII's commissioners at the end of 1539. The priory was immediately stripped of its roofing lead and partially demolished.

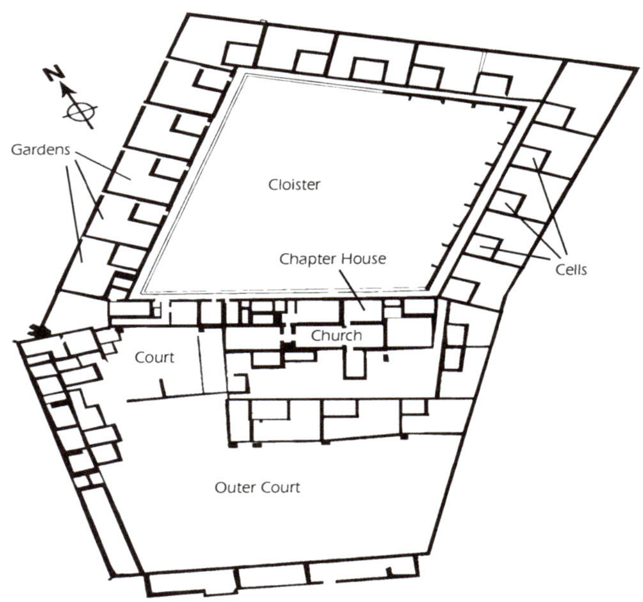

Photos - clockwise from top

The modest Carthusian church
Recesses beside door for the monks' food
The monks' cells with their own cottage garden
Water pumped from spring-houses on the hillside
The cells grouped around a large cloister garth

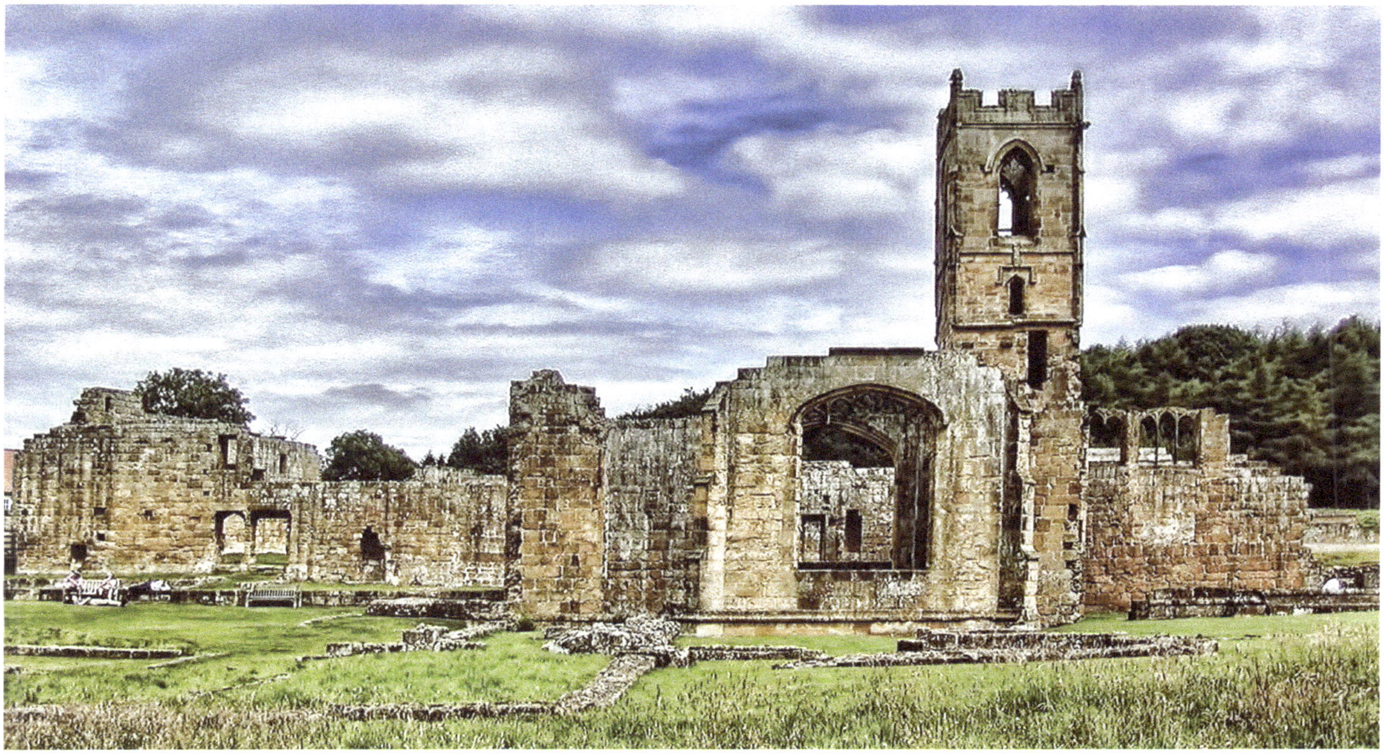

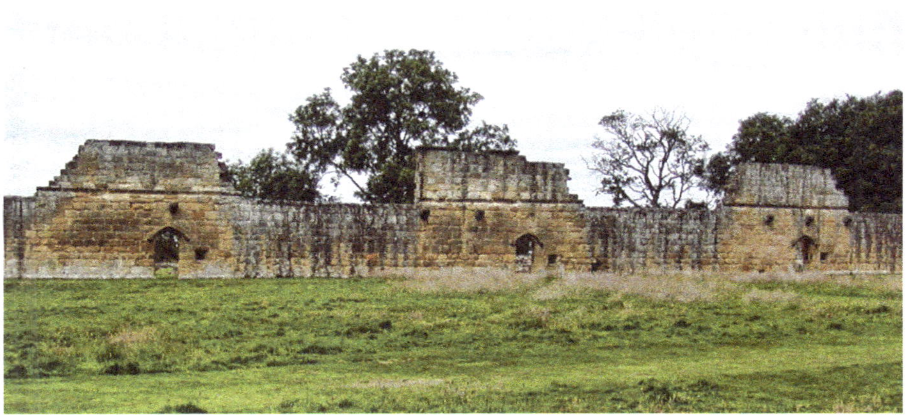

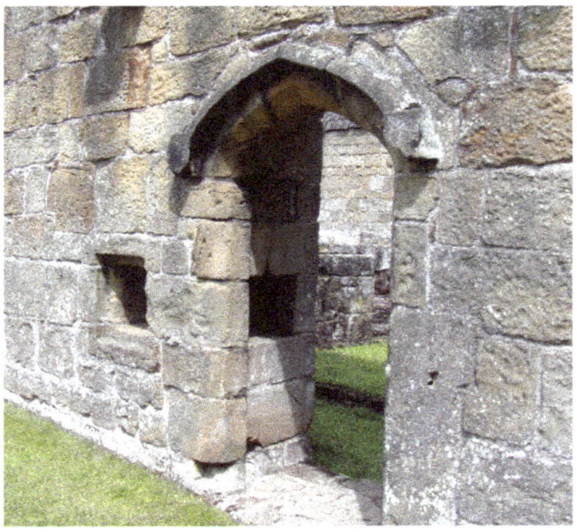

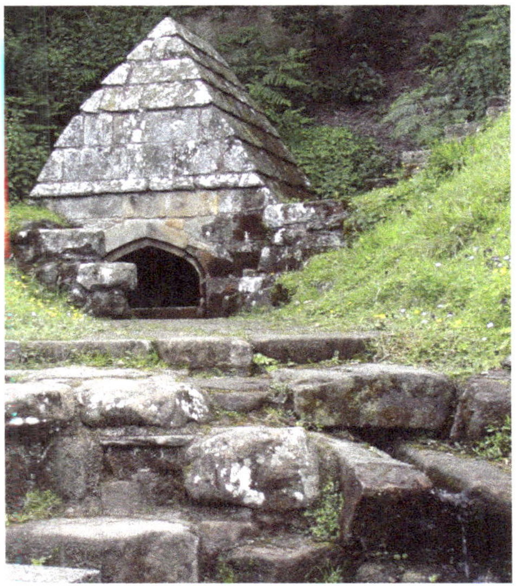

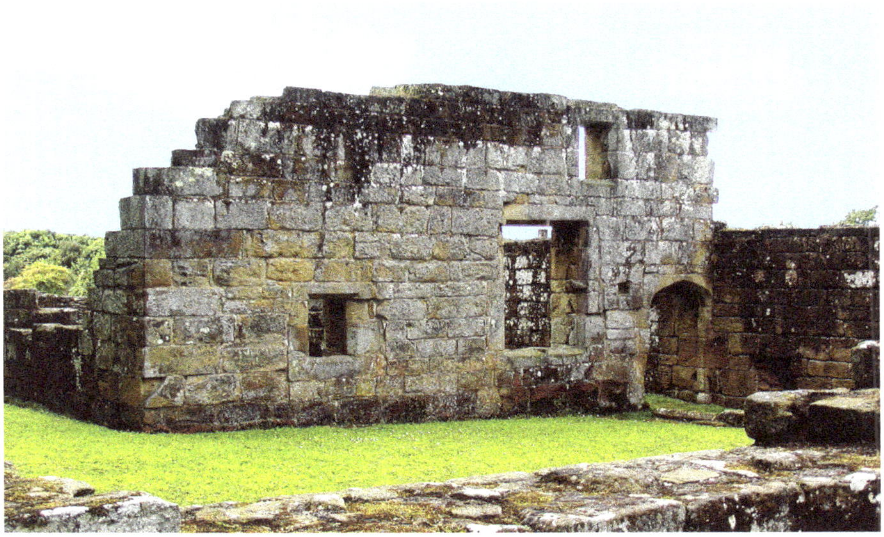

Moxby Priory

St John the Evangelist • Augustinian canonesses 1158–1536

Only earthworks of the ancillary structures on the west bank of the River Foss remain of this Augustinian house of nuns, comprising principally a moated enclosure thought to have been a medieval garden, part of a mill dam and the site of the monastic mill that was driven by the river. The main claustral buildings are overlain by Moxby Hall, but the exact location of the church has not been established. The priory was founded by Bertram de Bulmer in 1158, initially at Marton, some three kilometres to the north, as a double house of canons and nuns. However, for reasons unknown, the nuns had moved to Moxby by 1167 on land granted by Henry II.

Moxby Priory was a rare example of a quasi-double house accommodated in entirely separate establishments, and is unique in that it is the only known example of a double house of the Augustinian Order. Various injunctions issued following visitations ordered healthy nuns to keep out of the infirmary, not to take in girls over twelve without licence, not to leave the precincts of the house and wander in the woods, and not to gossip with seculars, but none of these indiscretions were serious. In 1317, the nunnery was burdened with having to supply fourteen loaves each week to the Friars Minor of York. Following devastation by the Scots in 1322, the nuns were dispersed, but returned three years later. More Scottish raids followed, pushing the priory heavily into debt and leaving all of its buildings in ruins. With an annual income valued at only £32 6s, the priory was closed in the first wave of the Dissolution of the lesser monasteries in August 1536 when Prioress Philippa Jennyson and nine nuns surrendered. The nunnery was then converted into a family mansion, which was itself demolished in the 1850s.

Newburgh Priory

St Mary • Augustinian c1150-1538

Apart from the name, there is little to remind of the medieval priory that once stood on this site, as the monastic buildings were converted into an imposing country mansion by Sir William Bellasis, nephew of one of Henry VIII's chaplain, Anthony de Bellasis, who, with his brother Richard, was responsible for the Dissolution of Newburgh and eight other monastic houses in the north. The area is still unspoilt, however, with breathtaking views of the Howardian Hills near Coxwold and the Kilburn White Horse in the distance, making it easy to imagine the wonderful environment enjoyed by the Augustinian canons. Founded in 1145 by Roger de Mowbray on lands granted by William the Conqueror to his father Robert de Mowbray, the priory was well endowed with the church of St Mary *'de Novo-Burgo'*, many other churches in North Yorkshire, and land and woods under the adjoining hills. The priory was colonised from Bridlington, but the canons first settled at Hood, which had been vacated by the monks of Byland.

Its history appears to have proceeded with little excitement, its isolated location probably being responsible for the dearth of surviving records. What little is known did not indicate a well-ordered house. The prior was disgraced in 1252 for treating brethrens inequitably and imputing crimes to them, for wasting the goods of the church and keeping an extravagant household. Archbishop Giffard held a visitation in 1275 during which he found the priory heavily in debt and ordered the prior to cease any unnecessary building work. The archbishop and several of his successors over the next two hundred years issued a series of injunctions in respect to indiscipline, poor behaviour of the canons, failure to distribute alms to the poor, trading in horses, having a superfluity of dogs, allowing strangers in the refectory, keeping of useless and wasteful servants, and wearing 'novelties in dress'. One compassionate moment occurred in 1404, when a canon with an impediment of his tongue was freed from the obligation to sing mass in a loud voice. In 1503, Margaret Tudor stayed a night at the priory during her progress to meet her husband, James IV of Scotland.

In the *Valor Ecclesiasticus* of 1535, the clear annual value was assessed at a respectable £367 8s, its income being derived from advowsons and properties in Yorkshire, Durham, Leicestershire and Lincolnshire. It was surrendered in 1538 to the King's commissioners, Drs Legh and Layton, by the prior, William Lenewood, and seventeen canons. The commissioners recorded that the canons had the girdle *'Sancti Salvatoris'*, which, as it was said, was good for those in childbirth, and also venerated an arm of St Jerome. The priory church was completely demolished, but the remaining buildings were converted into a country mansion in 1546, which, apart from some alterations and building work carried out between 1760 and 1780, remains much as it was when first built and will no doubt incorporate some medieval stone within its walls.

The house apparently hides a secret that has yet to be revealed. A brick-built tomb high in the roof is said to hold the mortal remains, minus head, of Oliver Cromwell. His daughter Mary, who was married to Lord Fauconberg, who then lived at Newburgh Priory, recovered her father's headless remains from his burial site near the Tyburn gibbet and brought them to the house for re-interment. The tomb has never been opened to prove the story.

Northallerton Austin Friars

In 1340, William de Alverton gave eight acres of land to the Austin Friars, to enable them to build a church and place to live, but nothing at all is known of its subsequent history. It has been suggested that the foundation never took place. The site of the priory is now occupied by the Fleece Inn and the two buildings to the south.

Northallerton White Friars

St Mary c1356–1538

About the year 1354, Thomas Hatfield, Bishop of Durham, granted the Carmelite friars a croft and pasture for the foundation of a religious house, which was established in 1356 and dedicated to St Mary. Other sources suggest, however, that the founder was King Edward III, or John Yole and his wife Helena, by licence from the King. Walter Kellaw, who was Prior Provincial of the Carmelites in England, is said to have been buried in Northallerton in 1367. Kellaw was also confessor to the Neville family, noted benefactors to the Carmelites, who also obtained many bequests from local people. In 1456, it came to prominence when a Provincial Chapter was held in Northallerton, with a second chapter following in 1514. Prior William Umefray, five friars, and five novices signed the Deed of Surrender in December 1538. The site of the priory was granted to Richard and Henry Vavasour in 1553. The priory was located in the east of the town in an area now known as Friarage Fields, but nothing can now be seen. Some fifty years ago, the gateway of the priory was visible, built into the wall of a now demolished lemonade factory. Recent excavations during building works discovered the remains of eight friars.

Nunthorpe Priory

St Mary • Cistercian nuns 1162–1189

The Cistercian nuns had first established themselves at Hutton Lowcross near Guisborough in 1162, but moved in c1166, when they were given two pieces of land and a mill at Thorp, later to become known as Nunthorpe, probably in the grounds of the present Nunthorpe Hall. The nuns acquired a reputation for dissolute behaviour and mismanagement, which clearly continued after the move to Baysdale in 1189, facilitated with a grant from Guy de Bovingcourt. The nuns retained their possessions at Nunthorpe until the Dissolution.

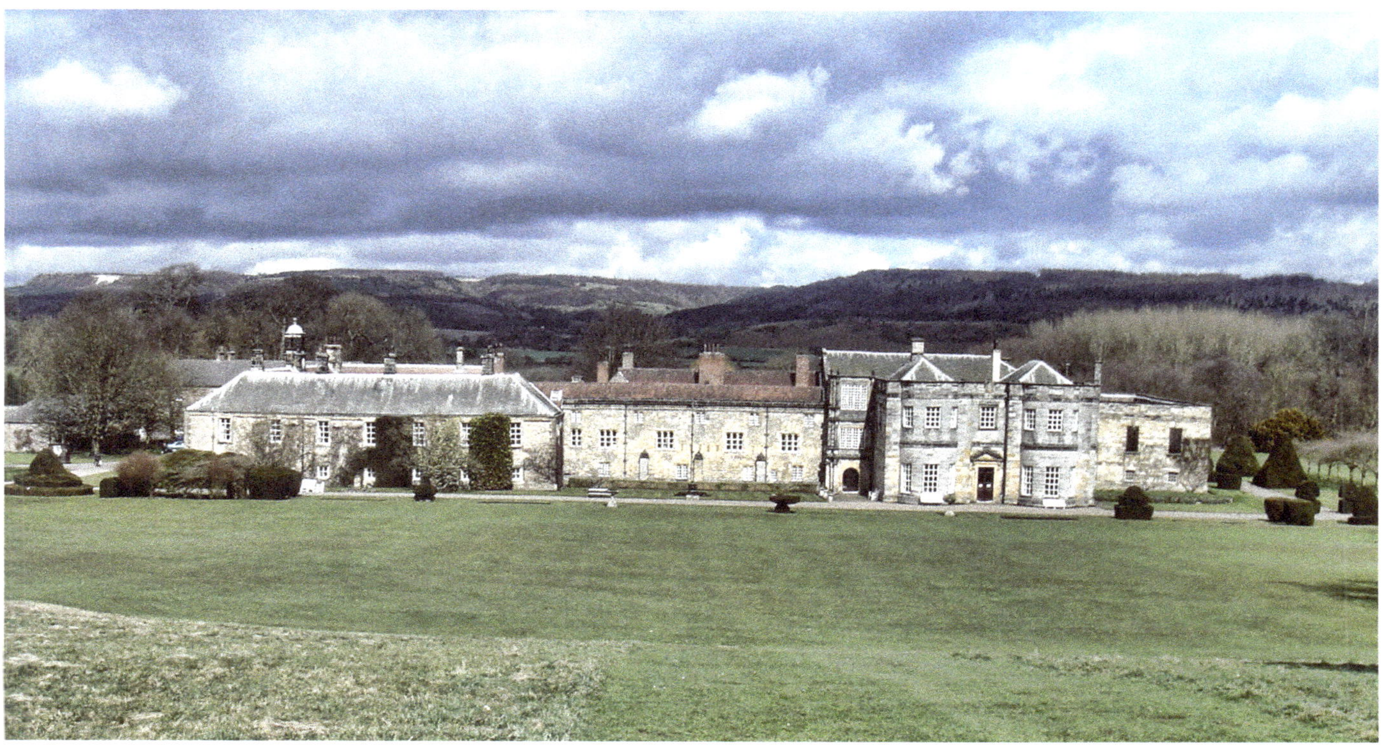

The imposing mansion of Newburgh Priory now exhibits little of its medieval past, but remains in an unspoilt location framed by the Howardian Hills

Richmond Priory

St Martin • Benedictine c1100–1539

The picturesque ruins of the Benedictine Priory of St Martin are on private land on the edge of town and can only be viewed from the nearby road, unless permission is granted by the owner of the land. When wandering through the sparse and neglected remains, now shared with grazing sheep and farm machinery and implements, it is difficult to imagine that this richly endowed house once had a profound influence on the people of Richmond. The ruins are situated on a terrace south of the River Swale and include a small, predominantly Norman church, several of whose walls stand to first floor level, with the west gable notable for its twelfth century segmental-arched doorway and later fifteenth century window above. Several building periods up to recent times are noticeable in the small fifteenth century embattled gatehouse tower, which, nevertheless, retains some of its medieval fabric. The standing remains are linked by various medieval walls, which reflect the extent of the claustral layout.

The Priory of St Martin was established c1100 as a cell of St Mary's Abbey at York by Wymar, steward to Stephen, Earl of Richmond. It initially housed nine or ten monks under Prior John de Poppleton and retained a considerable degree of independence from the mother house. The priory was given several manors, as well as the hermitage of St Thomas of Bordelho for the reception of leprous brethren. All trace of the site of this hermitage has long since disappeared, but in all probability it stood at the foot of the precipitous slope now known as Sleegill. In 1147, the remote priory hosted an ecclesiastic assembly of some importance. After the death of Henry Murdac, Archbishop of York, Pope Eugenius III issued a mandate to the local clergy to elect his successor. The assembly should have been in York, but William de St Barbara, Bishop of Durham, who had made an implacable enemy of William, Earl of York, feared for his life if he set foot in York and refused to attend there. The recorded history thereafter is sparse, but the priory appears to have gradually declined in wealth and numbers, leading to a shortening of the church. By 1381, only the prior and one monk were resident. Daily life would seem to have proceeded without upheaval until 1478, when a bitter dispute arose between the prior and the abbot of Easby over ownership of certain possessions. In the *Valor* of 1535, the net income of the house was assessed at just £47 16s. It was dissolved in 1539 and passed through several hands. Extensive quarrying left it ruined.

Richmond Grey Friars

1258–1539

The lone Gothic tower that forms the centrepiece of the town's well-tended Friary Gardens may be thought of as an attractive folly, but it is all that remains above ground of the medieval Franciscan priory, which was founded by Radulph fitzRadulph, Lord of Middleham, in 1258. It can be reached from the marketplace by the present-day Friar Wynd, over the same route the friars took in medieval times. The pinnacled bell tower itself was constructed in the fifteenth century and now stands guard over a few fragments of the chancel and south aisle nearby, and the buried remains of other buildings. It dates to a period of expansion of the priory, much of which is known from a survey of 1386. This listed, apart from the church, a guest house, a washroom 'where the friars commonly wash themselves when they come to the house tired and weary', a study next to the dormitory, refectory and parlour. An early small cloister lay immediately to the north of the nave of the first church, but when the church was enlarged early in the fourteenth century by the addition of a south aisle, a 'great cloister' was created by extending the priory to the north.

The friars played an important and active role in the life of the town and their sermons were always well attended. In 1314, the archbishop of York sent instructions to the warden to preach against the Scots and rouse resistance, and in 1492, the friars became involved in a dispute with the abbot of nearby Easby over the possessions of an anchoress. A curious fifteenth century ballad 'The Felon Sow of Rokeby and the Freres of Richmond' recalls an attempt by Friar Middleton and two men to catch a savage sow given to them by Ralph Rokeby of Morton 'to mend their fare', when Friar Theobald was warden. To calm the terrible beast, the friar began to read 'in St John his Gospell', but 'The sow she would not Latin heare, but rudely rushed at the frear'. The three men fled from the 'feind of hell'.

At the height of its influence, the house probably numbered some thirty friars, but this had shrunk to just thirteen plus the warden, Dr Robert Sanderson, when it was surrendered to the King's commissioners in January 1539. After a short period under lease from the Crown, the property passed into private ownership. The warden's house, which survived the demolition, eventually became the headmaster's house of Richmond Grammar School and still survives as part of the now hospital's southwest corner.

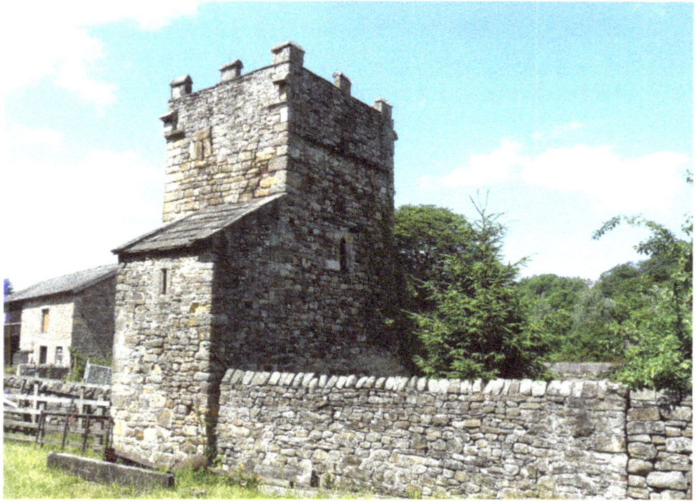

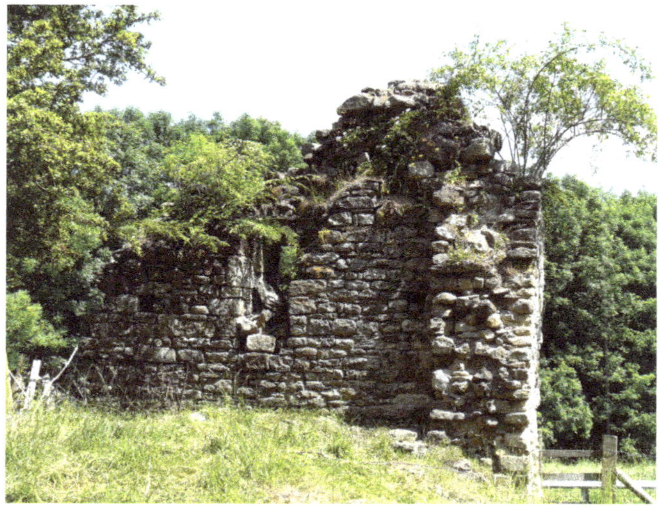

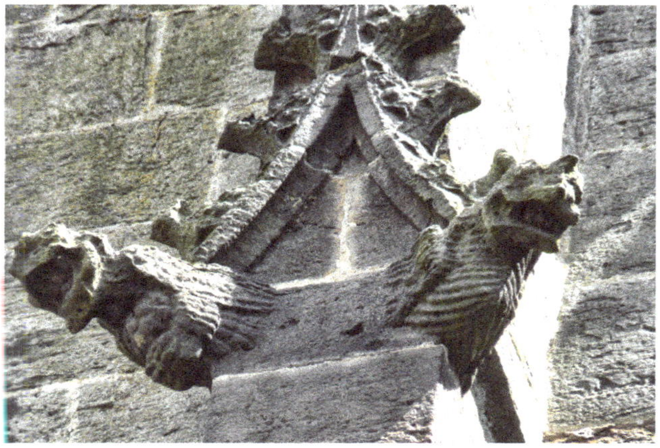

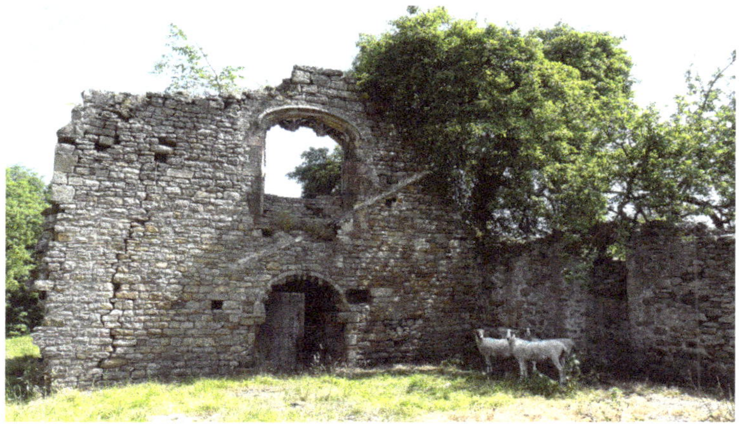

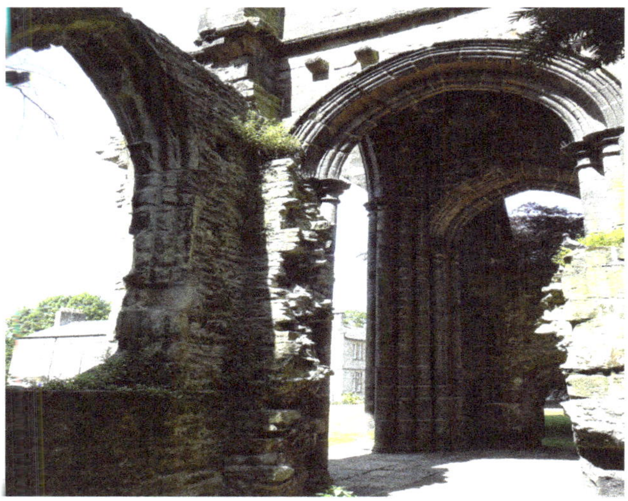

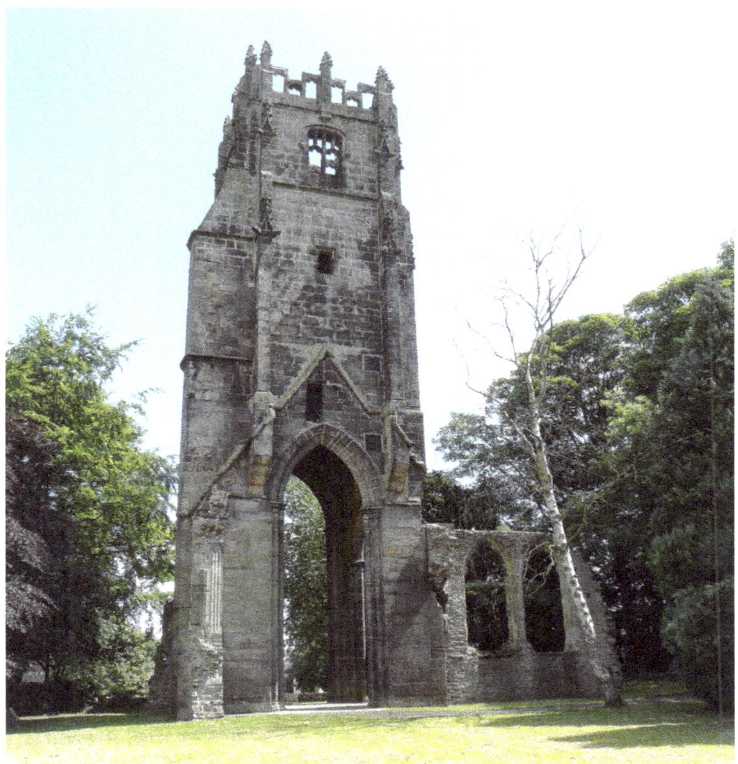

Photos – clockwise from top left

Gatehouse tower at Richmond Priory
Ruined nave wall of priory church
West front with doorway and window
Pinnacled bell tower of Grey Friars
Fragment of chancel
Carvings of mythical beasts

Rievaulx Abbey

St Mary • Cistercian 1132–1539

There can be few more spectacular views of an English monastic site than that of Rievaulx Abbey from the terrace high above. Tucked away in a hollow under the steeply wooded hillside, the tall, skeletal walls of the church soar above the little River Rye in Ryedale in perpetual defiance of the destructive power visited upon its hallowed halls by man and the elements. In the earliest accounts of Rievaulx, the site was described as the "awe-inspiring and solitary place," a description that has stood the test of time well. No matter how long and tiring the journey, a visit to Rievaulx should be of the highest priority and the massive church the first place to pause at in humble admiration. Although the aisle walls have long gone, leaving only the 50m (165ft) long nave arcading, the upper clerestory windows atop the tall, yet elegant columns reach for the sky in a bold gesture of worship. The transepts, partly Norman and partly Early English, are almost complete and the crossing is dominated by its 21m (70 ft) high arch between the nave and the choir. The nine-bay nave is marked only by low walls. The church was 104.5m (343ft) long, but because of the confines of the site and orientation of the steep hill and the river, it faces north to south, rather than the conventional east to west. There are remains of a galilee porch and entrance to church.

Of the other claustral and domestic buildings, some still stand to full height, while there are mere vestiges of others. Among the most impressive is the vast monks' refectory, which was built over the cellarium and is entered from the cloister via an arched doorway flanked by lavers. The remains of the reading pulpit are recognisable. A corner of the cloister arcade has been reconstructed. The rectangular chapter house is notable for the apse at one end and the shrine to St William of Rievaulx, the first abbot, which can be seen in one of the windows. The large dormitory once housed 140 monks, and alongside is the infirmary cloister, which provided a garden of recuperation for sick and infirm monks.

Rievaulx Abbey's history goes back to 1132, when it was founded on land given by Walter l'Espec, Lord of Helmsley, at a place called Blackmore, in the woods near Helmsley. There, the monks from Clairvaux set up the first Cistercian abbey in England's north, calling the new foundation "Our Lady of Rievaulx." The first abbot, William, one of St Bernard's own disciples, immediately set about constructing the church and other monastic buildings, which proceeded at great speed, while also training his monks in the Cistercian way. Even more celebrated was the third abbot St Aelred, under whose abbacy Rievaulx achieved great repute and grew in size to 140 monks and probably up to 500 lay-brothers and servants. St Aelred was a renowned scholar and the most prominent religious figure in the twelve century, who, among others, was responsible for the *Genealogia Regum Anglorum,* written to instruct Prince Henry, later King Henry II, in the history of Saxon Kings. His shrine behind the high altar in the rebuilt presbytery became a popular place of pilgrimage.

The daily life at the abbey appears to have been unremarkable, with only the occasional differences over tithes and taxes disturbing the even temper of its existence. By the mid-fourteenth century, the Black Death and mounting debts incurred from an ambitious building programme had reduced the community to barely a dozen monks and a similar number of lay people. Although the situation improved towards the end of the century, the abbey never fully recovered. Soon, other storm clouds were gathering that would lead to the end of monasticism in the British Isles. Abbot Thomas Helmesly tried to resist Henry VIII's plan for the dissolution of the abbey and was deposed, but Richard Blyton, who was put in his place, signed the Deed of Surrender in 1539. At the time, there were twenty-two monks in residence and slightly more than 100 paid servants. The abbey

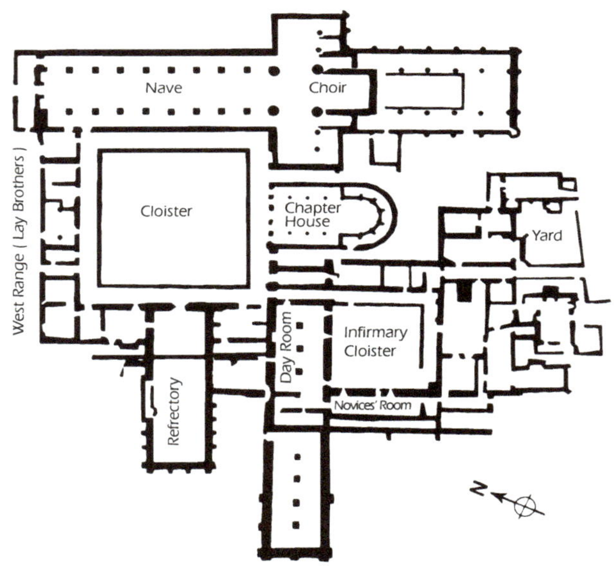

Photos – clockwise from top

Soaring nave and transepts of the magnificent abbey church
Slender flying buttresses supporting the lofty nave arcade
Foundations of the apsidal chapter house
The spectacular refectory entered via an arched doorway flanked by lavers

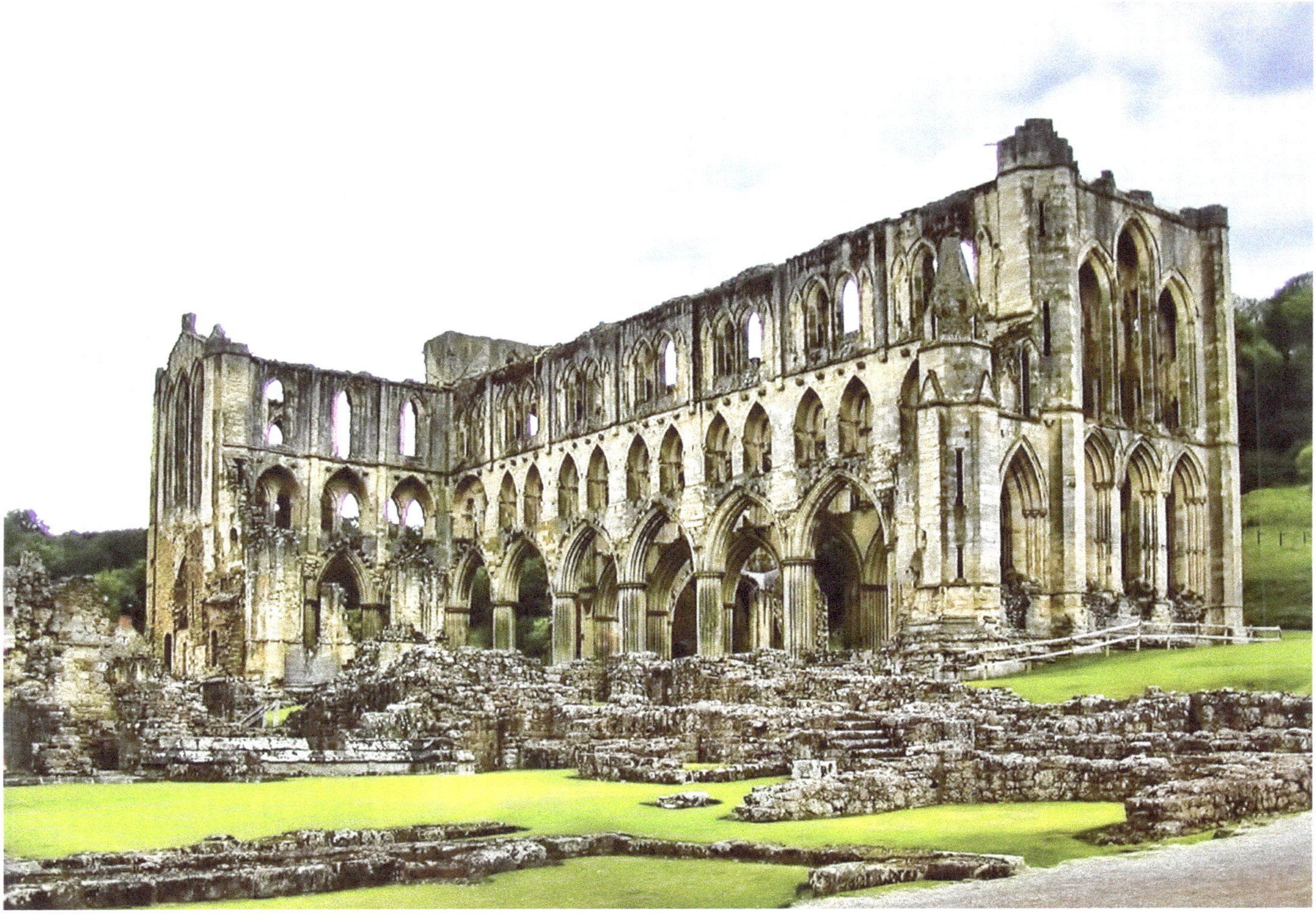

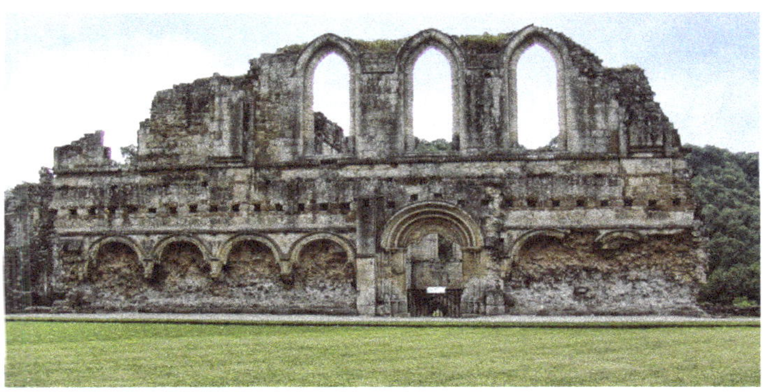

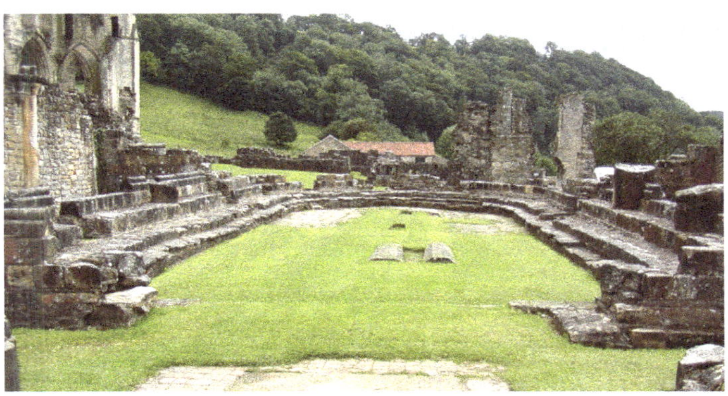

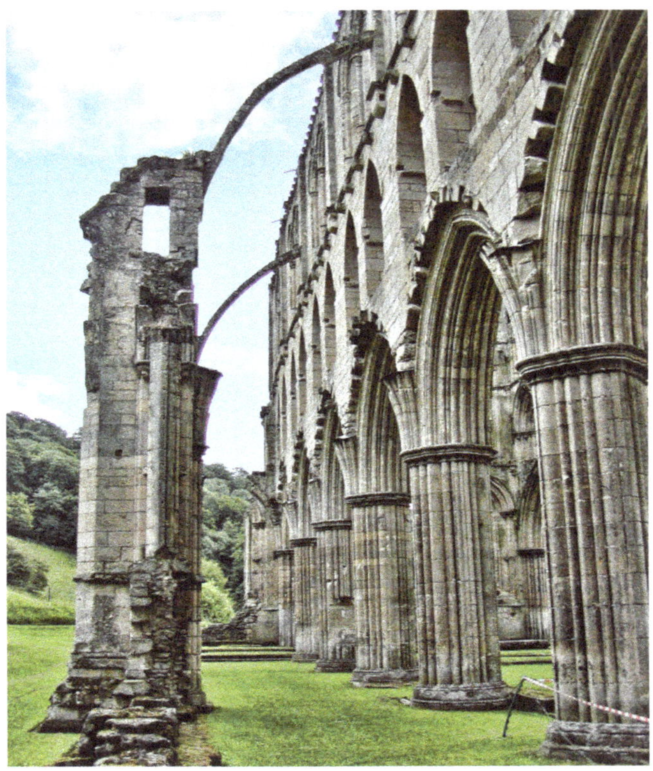

Rosedale Priory

St Mary and St Laurence • Benedictine nuns 1154/58–1536

Barely an hour's walk from Lastingham along picturesque Rosedale is the village of Rosedale Abbey. Any search for an abbey, however, will prove fruitless, as there was only a small Benedictine Priory for nuns. The present parish church of St Mary and St Laurence was built over the foundations of the priory chapel, and a few signs of the old building can be found inside the parish church, including a memorial tablet to one of the nuns and an old stone seat. In the garden outside the west door is a small turret, which is believed to have given access from the nave of the church to the dormitory above. The present school and its playground occupy part of the space of the cloister. The priory was founded by William of Rosedale in 1154 or 1158, probably for unmarried ladies of the local gentry, although it has also been suggested that the foundation date was in the reign of Richard I, after 1189, and the founder was Robert fitzStuteville. The house has been referred to as Augustinian, Benedictine and Cistercian, but is most likely to have been a Benedictine foundation. It never had more than nine nuns in the charge of a prioress, but these are credited with having been the first people to commercially farm sheep in the region, which proved very successful.

A series of visitations by Archbishop Greenfield in 1306, 1310 and 1315 resulted in several injunctions, the principal digressions being maladministration, which pushed the priory into poverty and the buildings into disrepair. The nuns were also ordered to stop taking puppies into the church and to stop wearing coloured clothing. They were also to cultivate charity. Archbishop William Melton, in 1321, sent a nun who had abandoned her religious faith to Handale Priory, where she was to undergo her penance. She was to be last in the convent, talk to no one, and was forbidden to leave the precincts of the priory. Every Friday she was to fast on bread and water, was to abstain from eating fish on Wednesdays, and was to be disciplined in chapter. In 1322, Scottish raids severely ravaged the area and the nuns were, for a time, dispersed to other houses. Its net worth by the time of the *Valor* in 1535 had shrunk to just £37 and, as a lesser house, was duly dissolved in 1536. Many of its buildings survived for two hundred years, but were then dismantled to provide stone for new homes needed to house workers in the expanding mining industry.

Scarborough Black Friars

-1252–1538

This large house of the Dominicans was established before 1252, but its establishment and early history was marked by disputes with the Cistercians, who complained frequently to the King that their presence, and that of the Franciscans in the town, diminished their revenues. Nevertheless, the friars prospered, largely through the benefice of Isabel de Beaumont, second wife of John de Vescy, sometime Governor of Scarborough Castle. Isabel built the nave of the church, cloister and dormitory c1291 at her own cost, and bestowed many other gifts. The castle featured again in the life of the friars in 1312, when a besieged Piers Gaveston was persuaded to confer with the earls of Pembroke and Warenne, and Henry Percy, in the friary church. There, in the presence of the Body of Christ, with their hands upon the Gospels, they swore that if the Lord Peter would go home with them they would either make peace between him and the magnates, or bring him back safe and sound to the castle. Gaveston agreed and was promptly seized and executed by the Earl of Warwick. Over the years, the house acquired more land and bequests, but later appears to have slid into poverty. There were fifteen friars in residence at the end of the fifteenth century. The last prior, John Newton, surrendered the house to Richard Ingworth, Bishop of Dover, in March 1539. Friar's Way marks the site of the Dominican house, but nothing is now left. A map dated c1538 shows a single-aisled church with a squat tower.

Scarborough Grey Friars

1272–c1538

The Franciscans settled in Scarborough in 1239, but the establishment of their house was strongly resisted by the Cistercian monks, who appealed to the pope for support. However, a compromise was reached, which in 1245 resulted in the friars moving to a new site in the parish of Scalby. The bailiffs were ordered by Henry III to assist the friars in removing their church and buildings to the new site. In yet another twist in the saga, the friars returned to Scarborough in 1272 to a site that abutted the cemetery of St Sepulchre and, while it is not known if the Cistercians objected to this new settlement, a dispute broke out again in 1281, probably as a result of the enlargement of the church. The friars survived an order by the Abbot of St Albans, as 'conservator of the rights of the Cistercians', to leave town, and peace returned. Although the friars received money and other bequests, the house remained poor, a fact that was referred to by the bishop of Dover, who received the surrender from the warden, Richard Chapman, in March 1539. On a map dated c1538, the priory church is depicted as having an impressive nave and tall tower with pyramidal pinnacles, but nothing at all is now left.

Scarborough White Friars

1319–1539

The opposition of the Cistercians to the Dominicans did not apply to the Carmelites, which received their consent for the founding of a house within the parish of St Mary, on land granted by Edward II in 1319. A licence to build a chapel and bell-tower was granted in 1320-1. The friars received a number of bequests, but little is otherwise known until the final years of its existence. Before the 1536 northern rebellion, which became known as the Pilgrimage of Grace, Prior John Boroby sowed discontent by collecting and distributing seditious prophesies. Although he was examined at York, he survived to surrender the now impoverished house to the bishop of Dover in March 1539. According to Egan, there were eight friars c1500. The priory lay behind the Queen Street Chapel, but nothing has survived above ground.

Skewkirk Priory

All Saints • Augustinian 1114–1540

Skewkirk Hall stands on the site of a small priory cell dependent on Nostell Priory. The hall was first built in the sixteenth century using stone from the priory, but has since been rebuilt entirely in brick. The only visible evidence of re-used material from the priory is a small, single-light, arched window inserted into the south wall of adjacent buildings. The priory cell was founded in 1114, when Geoffrey fitzPain, who was a man of great distinction in the time of Henry I, donated the chapel of All Saints at Skewkirk, near Kirk Hammerton, to the Augustinian canons of Nostell Priory.

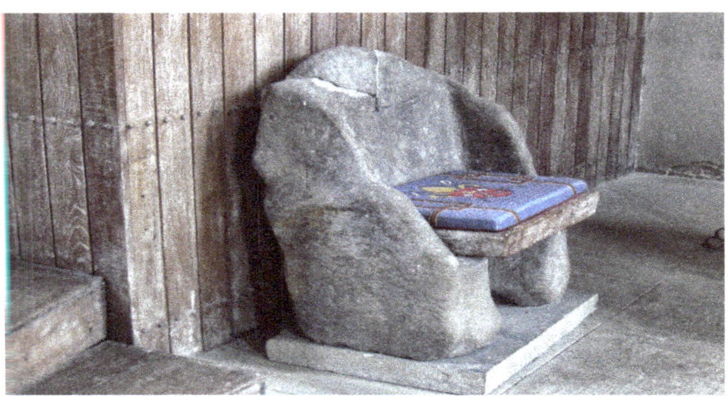

Photos of Rosedale Priory - from left

Old stone seat

Small turret thought to have provided access to church from dormitory

Stocking Abbey

St Mary • Cistercian 1147–1177

In 1147, Roger de Mowbray, who had given land to the Savignac monks at Hood, near Thirsk in 1139, and then a new site at Old Byland in 1143, granted the monks 'two carucates of wasteland in the territory of Cukwald (Coxwold) below the hill of Blakhou', which elsewhere was called Stocking. By then, the Savignac Order had been integrated into the Cistercians. It would appear that the monks built a small stone church, a cloister and other buildings and offices, probably to have a base while they cleared and drained swampy and overgrown land at their intended home at Byland, to which they finally moved in 1177.

Swainby Abbey

St Mary • Premonstratensian -1190–c1212

A monastery of Premonstratensian canons was founded at Swainby in the Vale of Mowbray sometime before 1190 by Helewise, daughter of Ranulph de Glanville, Lord Chief Justice of England under Henry II, but moved to Coverham in c1212, so, it is said, that Ranulph fitzRobert could hear the sound of the abbey bells in his castle at Middleham. Helewise died in 1195 and was buried at Swainby, but her remains were later re-interred in the chapter house at Coverham.

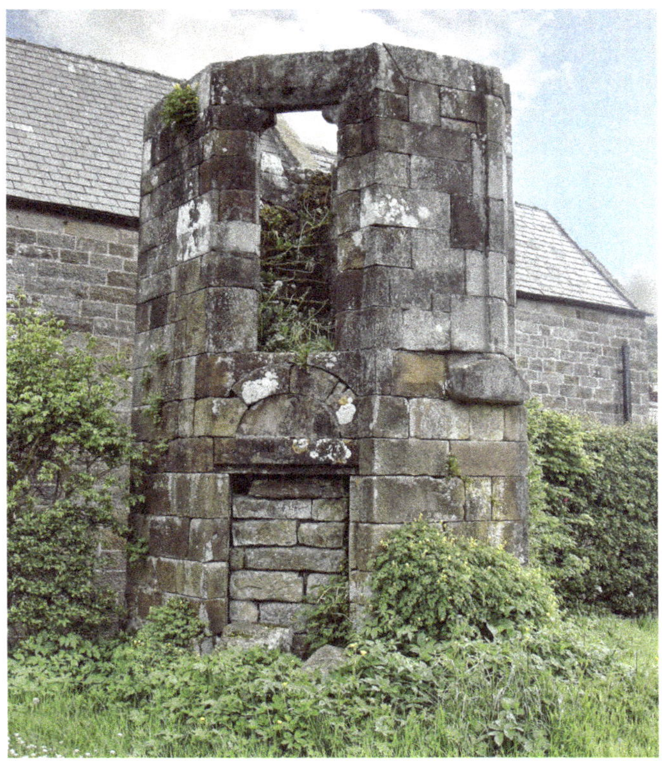

Whitby Abbey

St Peter & St Hilda • Benedictine -1077–1539

For centuries, seafarers looked upon the soaring church of Whitby Abbey as a shining beacon to guide them along the treacherous coast. But, while prior to the wilful destruction of this sacred place, its pale lights reached far out to sea and the distant chime of its great bells brought certainty to sailors blindly feeling their way through heavy mists, its shattered walls are now dark and lifeless and the bells ring no more. Today's fleet, of course, no longer needs to rely on the towering church for safe passage, but those onboard, as well as the visitor strolling along the seafront of the small fishing town 80m (250ft) below, can still appreciate its magnificent presence. Windswept, desolate and precarious, even foreboding as darkness falls, Whitby Abbey matches every mood. Its very exposed position will, unfortunately, continue to accelerate its decay, so hurry before it is too late.

It is, perhaps, appropriate that parts of the church alone survive, all other monastic dwellings having long since vanished, their walls dismantled and the masonry incorporated into a nearby building. A few excavated foundations, nevertheless, provide some indication of the extent of what was a large foundation. The presbytery of the church, with its great eastern front dominating the skyline, remains, along with seven bays of the choir and sanctuary, and the three-bay buttressed transept, the entire western side having been blown down in 1763. Portions of the decorated nave still stand defiantly, with two tiers of graceful lancet windows continuing to throw light into the interior of the high church, whose vaulting rose 18m (60ft) above the floor. The 45m (150ft) high crossing tower, alas, collapsed in 1830. With a length of 110m (360ft) and width of 21m (69ft), each transept stretching 45m (150 ft) across, it was one of the largest and most impressive monastic churches in the land.

Almost all of the present ruins date from the 1220s, but there has been a religious foundation on the site since the early days of Saxon Christianity. The story goes that when Oswald, King of Northumbria, faced a battle against formidable adversaries in AD 655, he vowed to found twelve monasteries if victorious. That he was, and true to his word, he began making good his promise by sending his infant daughter Aelfleda to the monastery at Heretu (now Hartlepool), over which the saintly Hilda presided. Two years later, in AD 657, Hilda and Aelfleda made their way across the Vale of Pickering to the coast and established the monastery of Streonshalh, in its much later reincarnation to become known as Whitby Abbey. Hilda proved a highly respected abbess, ruling a double community of men and women and considerably increasing the abbey lands. People came from far and wide to seek her counsel. Here the great Synod of Whitby was held in AD 664, to determine the controversy over the observance of Easter. Little is known of the buildings raised by St Hilda, although the remnants of the small cells in her double monastery were excavated in the last century, but have since been covered over.

The monastery prospered even after St Hilda's death in AD 680, when Aelfleda became abbess, but was left in smoking ruins by Danish raiders in AD 867, a fate that befell many religious and secular establishments in the northeast. It is said that the then abbot, Titus, fled to Glastonbury with St Hilda's relics. For 200 years, the site appears to have been unoccupied, but in 1073, three monks were despatched from Evesham to revive the destroyed religious establishment, one of whom, Reinfrid, refounded Whitby as a Benedictine house. After many years of service, Reinfrid was accidentally killed at Ormesbridge, when a piece of timber fell on him. With gifts from Hugh Lupus, first Earl of Chester, and William de Percy, and privileges granted by William the Conqueror, later confirmed by Henry I, Whitby grew in importance and was elevated to abbey status probably before or in 1109, when William de Percy II was named as abbot. Among its many possessions were the town and port of Whitby, the town of Hackness, many churches and chapels, seven mills and considerable swathes of land. Its coastal position, however, left the abbey open to occasional forays by Norwegian pirates, who partially destroyed it in the middle of the twelfth century. The monks were also persecuted by the founder, William de Percy, who repented of his foundation gift, forcing Prior Stephen and some of the monks to leave for Lastingham and thence to York to found St Mary's Abbey. Whitby Abbey was rebuilt, but its subsequent history was relatively uneventful. The only recorded visitation was in 1320 by Archbishop Melton, who found the abbey heavily in debt and issued several injunctions, although none reflected too badly on the community. Whitby was surrendered to the Crown by Abbot Henry Davell and twenty-one monks in December 1539. In the *Valor* of 1535, Whitby Abbey had a clear annual value of £437 2s. It was granted to John, Earl of Warwick.

Photos - clockwise from top left

The great eastern front reflected in Abbey Pond
Thirteenth century choir
Door into the nave
Carved stone figures
View of abbey ruins from the west

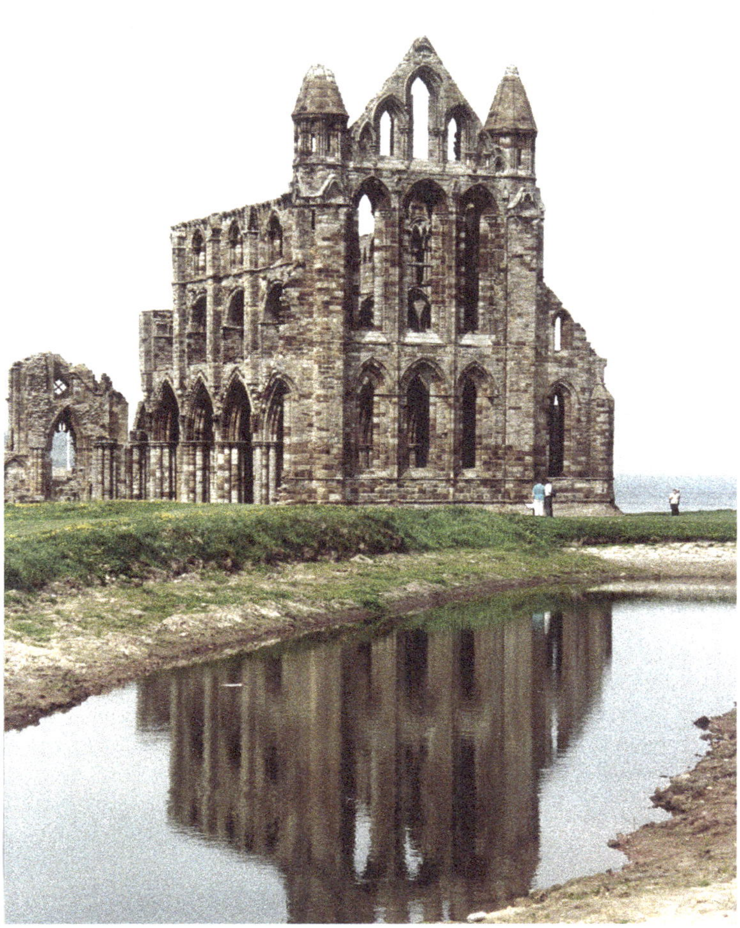

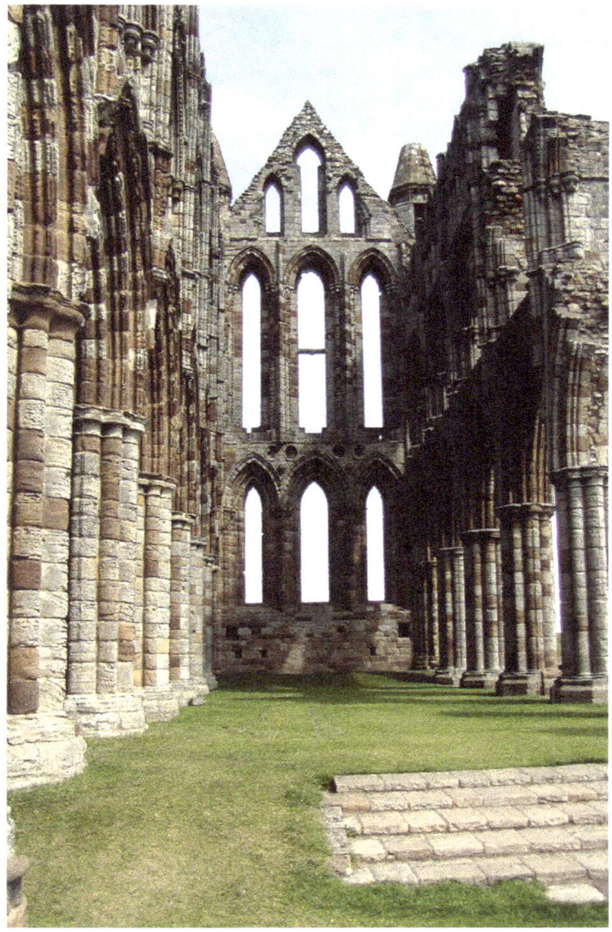

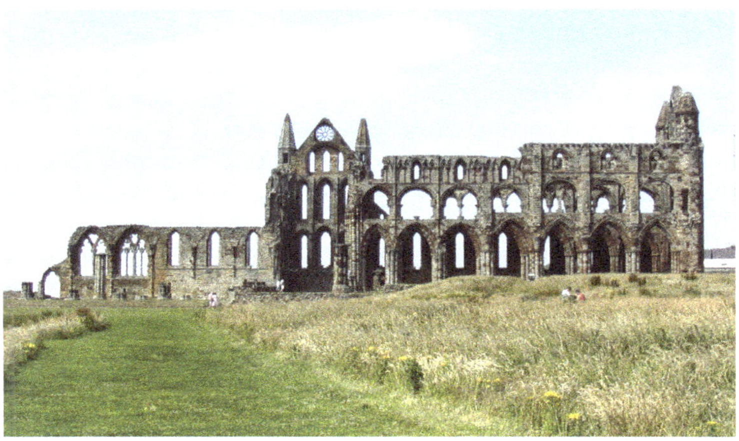

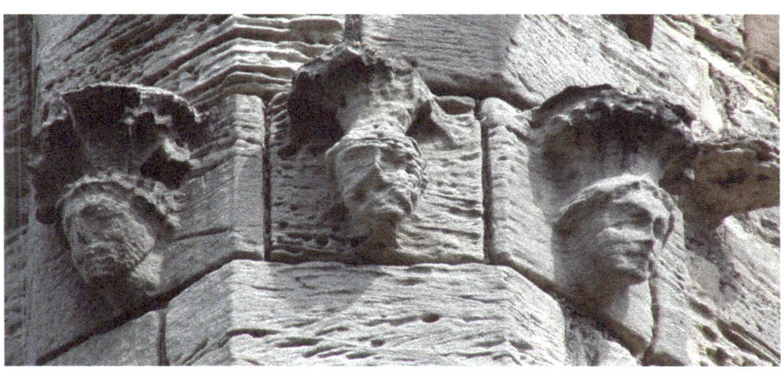

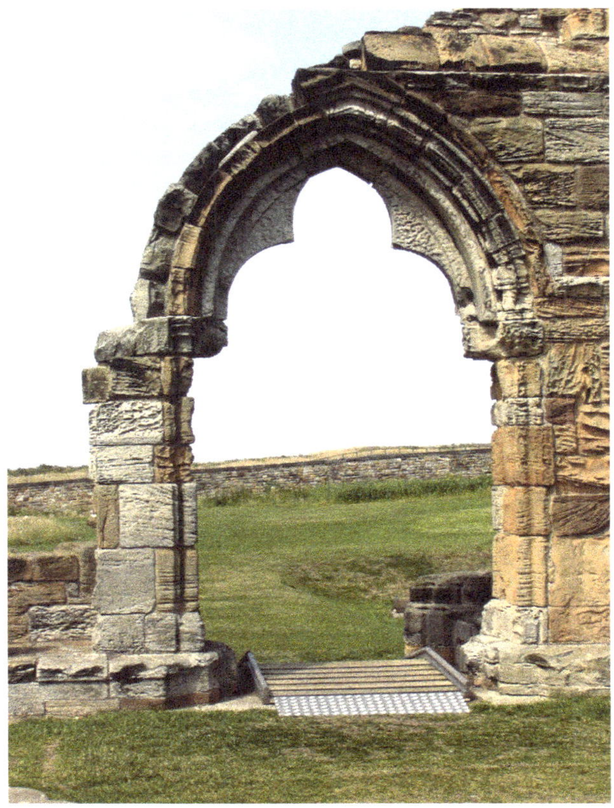

Wykeham Priory

St Mary and St Michael • Cistercian nuns c1153–1539

Little remains from this priory of Cistercian nuns except a 40m (130ft) long by some 6m (20ft) high section of the north wall of the priory church, now serving as a garden wall. The wall incorporates a fourteenth century three-light window, a door with a semi-circular arch in-filled with fragments of decorative stonework, and two blocked arches, which led into the north transept. This last reminder is situated in private grounds of a large country house and not accessible to the public. In a survey of 1540, the church was described as having been 28m (90ft) long and 6.5m (22ft) wide, with an 18m (60ft) square cloister to the south.

The lack of physical presence obscures a less than ideal monastic existence. While not much of note happened in the early period, an accidental fire at the beginning of the fourteenth century destroyed the church, cloister and twenty-four other houses and deprived the nuns of all their books, vestments and other belongings. A twenty-year waiver by Edward III of an annual payment for lands held by the priory in the Honour of Pickering relieved the hardship somewhat, but did not halt the moral decline that had set in. Several visitations discovered a spiritual vacuum among the community, which led to Prioress Isabelle Westirdale being relieved of her post in 1444 for carnal knowledge of several men, both inside and outside the priory. A number of nuns also at varying times had succumbed to the pleasures of the flesh. Founded c 1153 by Pain fitzOsbert, the priory was dissolved in 1539, when Prioress Katherine Nendyk and twelve nuns signed the Deed of Surrender. Its value at the time was a modest £25 17s. The site was granted to Francis Poole.

Yarm Black Friars

The Annunciation • -1266–1538

The Friars Preachers settled at Yarm in or before 1266, in which year Henry III gave them ten oaks in Galtres Forest. The friars also received several grants of land and subsequent bequests were numerous including, in 1291, a gift of money from the executors of Queen Eleanor. In 1302, some locals entered the close of the prior, threw down some walls, broke his gates and carried away the timber, and beat his servants. Two years later the prior obtained a writ against another group who drove its cattle onto the grass within the close. Edward I, II and III gave food to the friars, on which occasions the community varied from twenty-eight to thirty-three in number. Edward III also contributed to the repair of the cloister in 1335. The church appears to have been rebuilt at the beginning of the fourteenth century, but nothing is now left. The priory was surrendered in December 1538 to William Blytheman by Miles Wilcock the prior, eleven friars, and six novices. A modern mansion known as the Fryarage now stands on the site.

Yedingham Priory

St Mary • Benedictine nuns -1163–1539

Little remains of this twelfth century house of Benedictine nuns dedicated to the Blessed Virgin, and what there is makes it difficult to piece together the probable layout of the priory complex. Nevertheless, the beautiful countryside between the Yorkshire Wolds and North Yorkshire Moors makes the discovery of parts of the south wall of the aiseless church now incorporated into a cowshed, standing on the north side of the River Derwent, an exciting experience. Of particular interest are an intact blocked east doorway with two-centred arch and two orders with stiff-leaf decoration, an intact west processional doorway with a single chamfered segmental arch, and to the north, a piscina with stiff-leaf and trefoiled canopy. All date from the late twelfth century.

Yedingham Priory, also known as *Parvo Marisco* or Little Marais, which in modern English means Little Marsh, was founded in or before the year 1163 by Helewise de Clere, whose husband Roger de Clere granted it all his lands. Its foundation charter provided for the accommodation of nine nuns. Other benefactors soon added to the endowments and it is thougt that the community probably increased to the usual twelve nuns under a prioress. The priory church was not consecrated until 1241. Poverty soon afflicted the community, prompting Archbishop Wickwane in 1280 to entrust the financial affairs of the priory to Robert de Brus. Archbishop Greenfield issued several injunctions following a visitation in 1314, but none were too serious. By 1456, the priory buildings had become so ruinous that a forty-day indulgence was granted to all penitents who assisted in the repair. In the *Valor* of 1535, the house was valued at only £26 6s but survived until finally dissolved, most likely in 1539, when the prioress, Agnes Bradrigge, and nine nuns signed the Deed of Surrender. The site was granted to Robert Holgate, Bishop of Llandaff, and afterwards Archbishop of York, in exchange for the handover to the King of several manors belonging to the See.

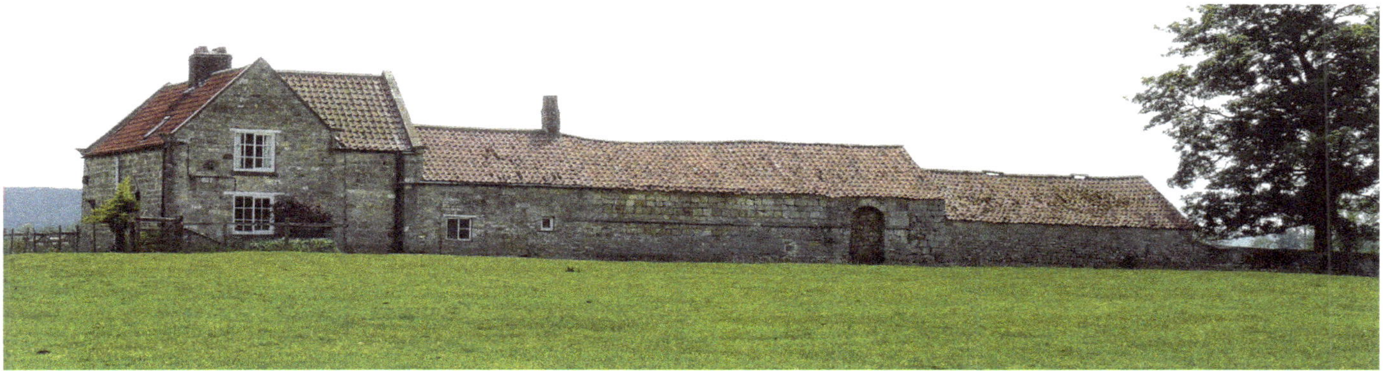

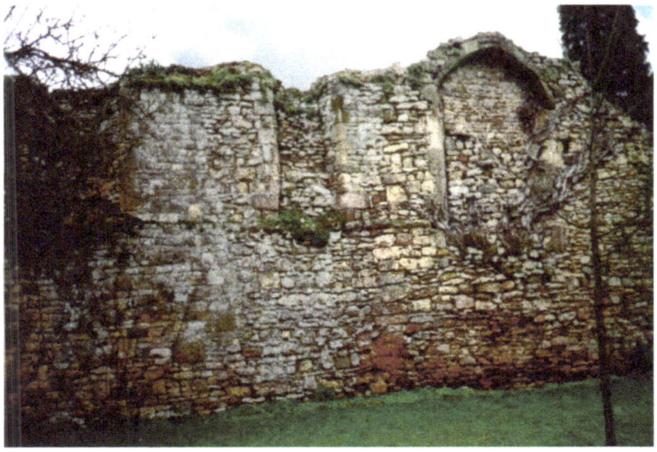

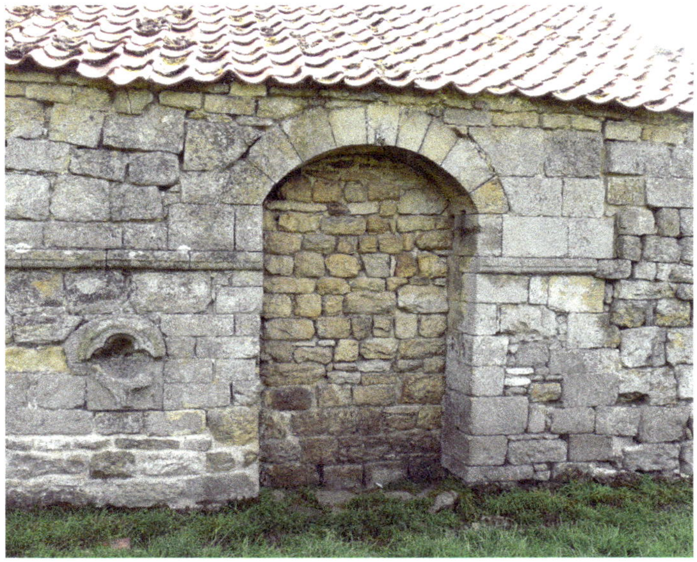

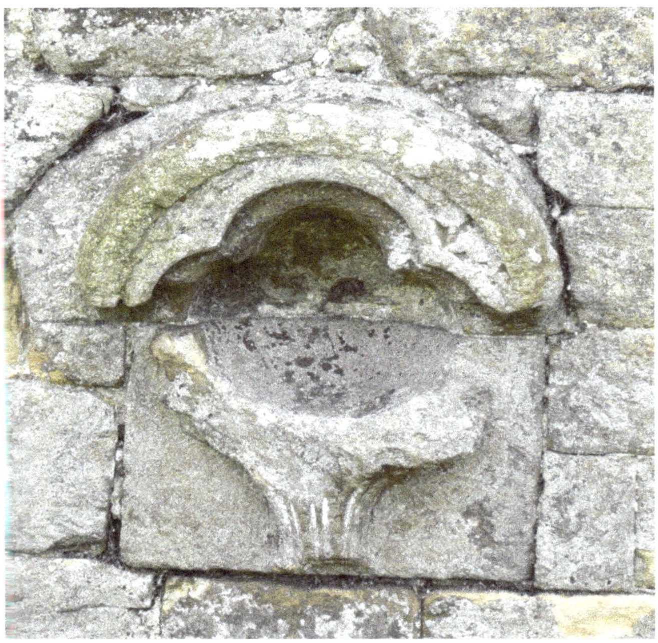

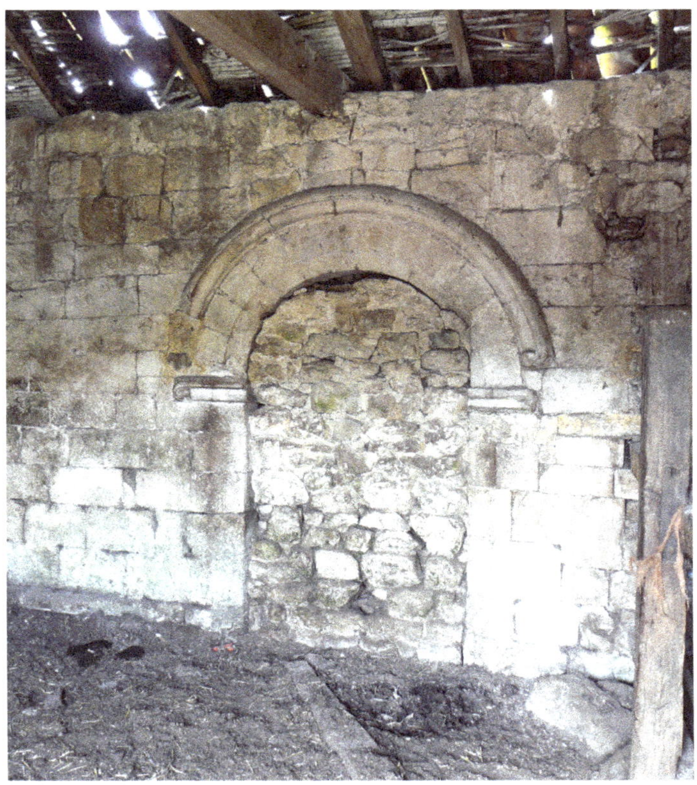

Photos – clockwise from top

Remains of Yedingham Priory
Processional doorway
Blocked doorway with two-centred arch
Piscina with trefoiled canopy
North wall of Wykeham priory church

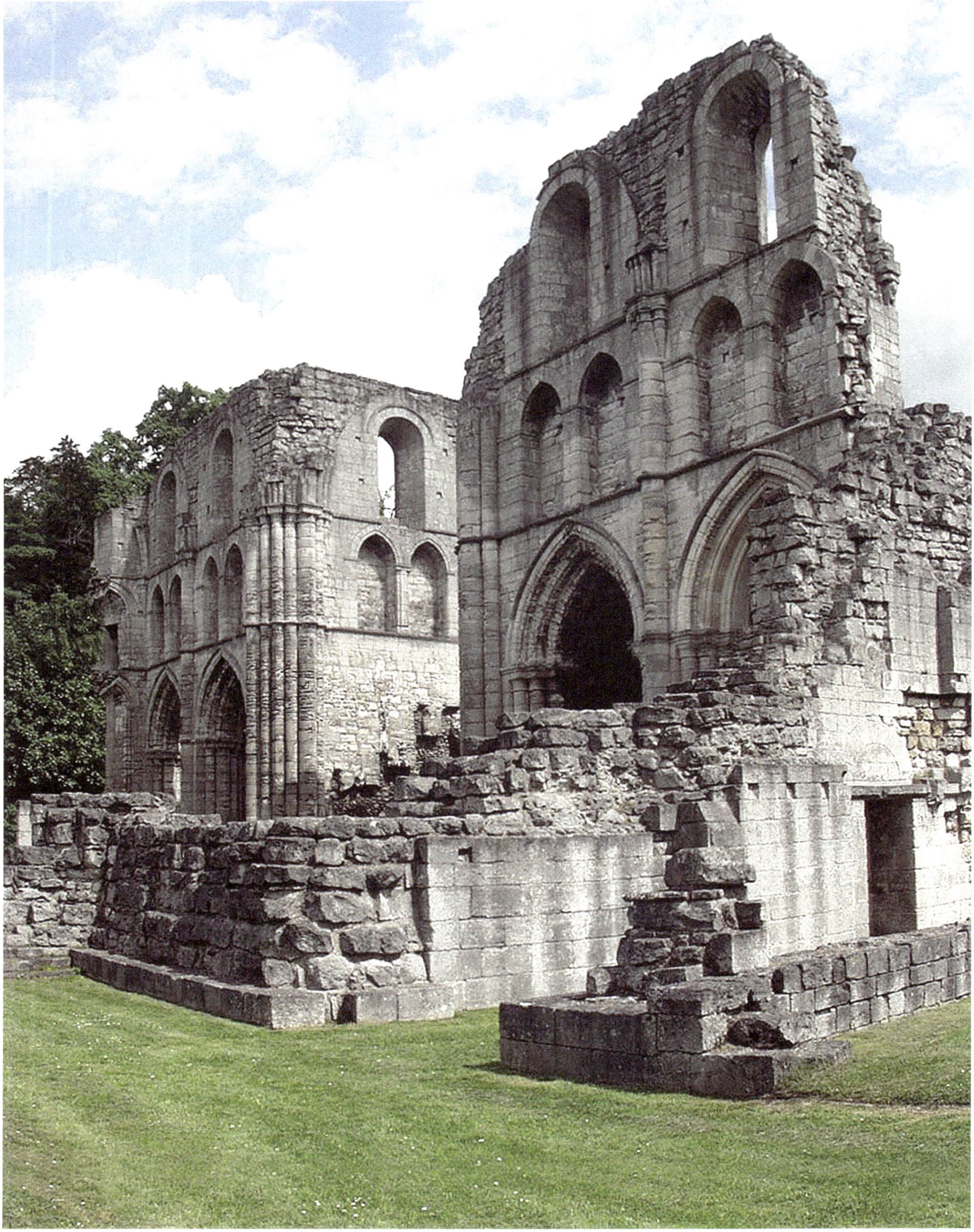

Roche Abbey

Allerton Mauleverer Priory

St Martin • Benedictine +1100–1414

This Benedictine priory came into being in the reign of Henry I, when Yorkshire landowner Richard Maleverer gave a chapel and one carucate of land to the Holy Trinity at York, which was a dependency of the abbey of St Martin at Marmoutier near Tours. By 1110, the priory had come under the direct control of Marmoutier, and Archbishop Thomas of York (1109-1114) turned the chapel into the parish church. There is, alas, nothing on record of its internal history, but as an alien priory it must have suffered from the frequent seizures by the Crown. Along with all other remaining alien houses, it was suppressed in 1414, and its revenues were later settled on Henry VI's new King's College, Cambridge.

Arthington Priory

St Mary • Cluniac nuns c1155–1540

Nothing at all remains of this small and poor house, one of only two Cluniac nunneries in England. It was founded c1155 by Peter de Arthington and endowed with gifts of land and Maltby Church. Few records exist of the internal history of the priory but, following visits in 1307 and 1315, Archbishop William Greenfield had to enforce discipline on a number of nuns and, on one occasion, on the prioress herself. Arthington Priory was valued at only a little over £11 and was formally surrendered by Prioress Elizabeth Hall and eight nuns in November 1540. The priory and lands were given to Archbishop Cranmer in 1543 and, in 1585, a house was built on the site, using stone from the priory.

Barnoldswick Abbey

Mont St Mary • Cistercian 1147–1152

The Cistercian Abbey of Mont St Mary, founded by Norman nobleman Henry de Lacy in 1147, was a short-lived daughter house of Fountains Abbey, which sent twelve monks and ten lay-brothers. The community suffered frequently from robbers and also from resentment by the local population. This came to a head when the monks tore down the existing church, either out of anger or to make way for the new abbey. In 1152, Abbot Alexander and his monks abandoned Barnoldswick and built a new abbey at Kirkstall near Leeds. Having left Barnoldswick without a church must have pricked their conscience for the monks returned in 1160 to build the church of St Mary-le-Gill, some distance away from the settlement on the banks of Gill Syke in an idyllic steep-sided valley. Legend has it that the monks built it in isolation to put as much distance as possible between themselves and the inhabitants. Apart from minor earthworks and the faint outline of buildings, nothing can be seen of the original foundation, but the medieval church is worth a visit. Although not much remains of the original structure of the church, the font may date from an early period, and also of note inside are the arms of Kirkstall, three daggers, faintly etched on an inside wall.

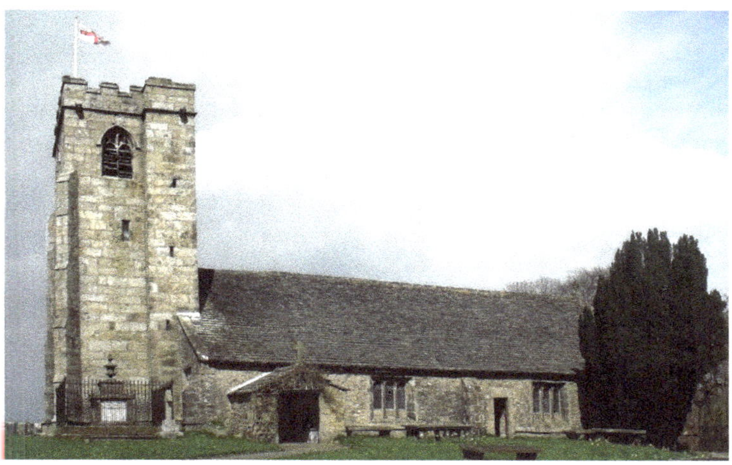

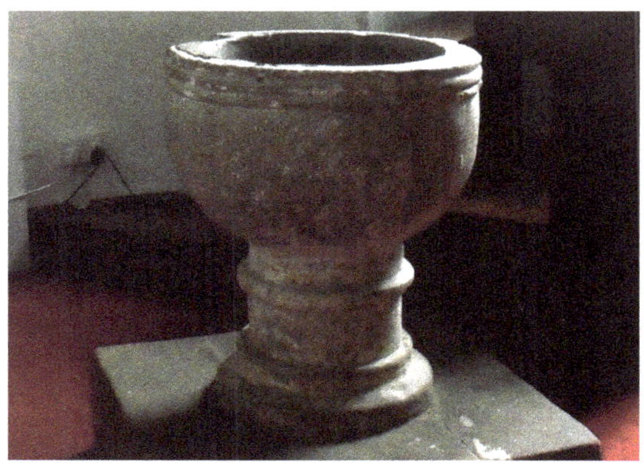

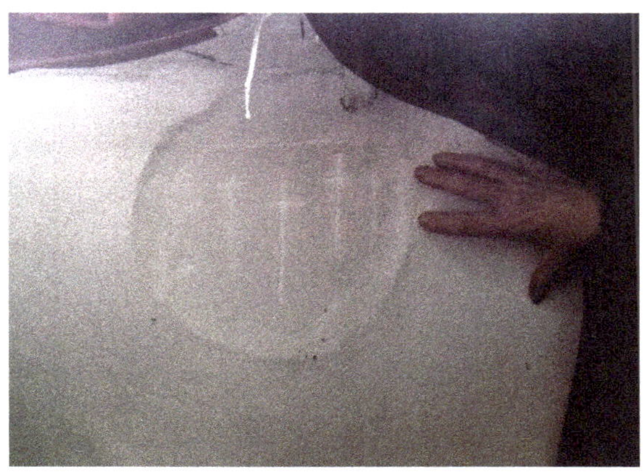

Photos of Barnoldswick Abbey – clockwise from above

St Mary-le-Gill at Barnoldswick
Early medieval font
Arms of Kirkstall Abbey

Bolton Priory

St Mary & St Cuthbert • Augustinian 1154–1539

Overlooking the River Wharfe and surrounded by verdant parkland and wooded hills, Bolton Priory, now known as Bolton Abbey, never fails to delight the visitor or casual wanderer who stops to admire this hallowed place. The priory was founded when Lady Alice de Romille, the owner of nearby Skipton Castle, donated land next to the village of Bolton-in-Wharfedale, for "the wellbeing of my soul and those of my forebears and descendants". After spending some years enduring harsh conditions on higher ground near Embsay, a group of black-robed Augustinian canons and their prior arrived at Bolton in 1154 to make a new start. The site was a huge improvement on their previous abode, with the surrounding hills protecting it from the harshest winter weather, and the closeness of the river providing a useful artery for supplies. A rough stone shelter was built, signs of which can still be seen today in the base stones of the ruined high altar. The canons quickly became popular, as unlike some other religious Orders, the Augustinians went out into the community to teach, run hospitals, and serve as local priests.

The priory began to thrive, with income derived mainly from agricultural produce, tithes and rents from farms, mills and lead mines in the area. The canons also brewed fine ale, for which the cold and clear waters of the Wharfe must have been perfect. Moneys thus received paid for the canons' community work and met the heavy expenses of expanding the monastic buildings and erecting a magnificent church of great architectural beauty, which had few equals in the country. The number of canons remained relatively small, although it is thought that at times some 200 workers, labourers and servants were dependent on the priory. But, life was not always idyllic. Severe winters and failing crops led to occasional poverty, and illness deprived the priory of canons and workers. Intermittent raids by marauding Scots also interrupted the religious and secular work at the priory.

Worse was to come under Henry VIII with the Dissolution of England's monastic houses. Bolton could not escape and was suppressed in January 1539. Most of the estate was sold to the Clifford family, and later passed to the Cavendishes, Dukes of Devonshire, who still own the land. Slowly, the domestic buildings were dismantled, and the church crumbled, except for the nave, which was saved by Prior Moone to serve as the parish church. A new east wall was built to block off the ruined choir, and restoration work and new decorations over the following centuries have provided a wonderful place of worship, keeping alive the legacy of the Augustinian canons who had tirelessly prayed and worked there for 400 years.

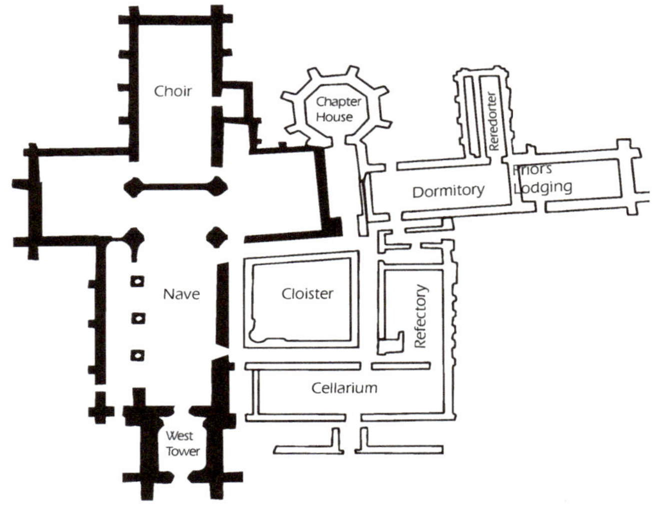

The exquisite west doorway with its rich thirteenth century carvings leads into the church, where the eyes have difficulty in taking in all the splendour, including the painted east wall, the six soaring lancet windows in the south wall, which tell the gospel in stained glass by Pugin, and the base of the night stairs in the south transept that once led to the dormitory. Two doors lead out into the cloister, octagonal chapter house and domestic buildings, of which only foundations now remain. But the ruined choir, the crossing pillars that once carried a central tower and north and south transepts are still standing to a good height. The graceful arcading above the choir stalls, the one window retaining its delicate tracery, but most of all, the lofty east window, give the priory its romantic appeal. Cross the bridge over the Wharfe and climb a little way up the hill. The view over the ruins reflected in the clear water is unforgettable.

Photos of Bolton Priory - clockwise from top

The romantic ruins overlooking the verdant Wharfe Valley
Blind arcading and traceried window in ruined choir
Remains of the octagonal chapter house
Piscina under Gothic arcading

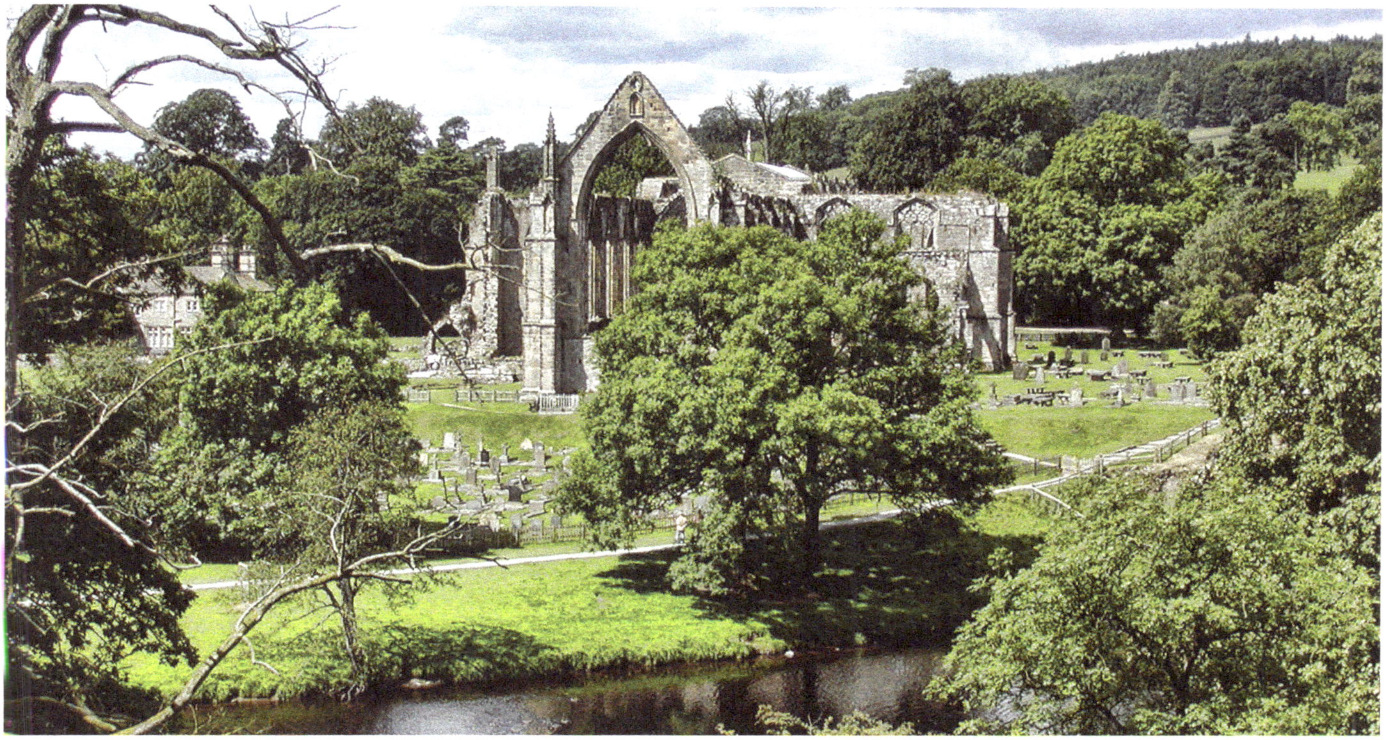

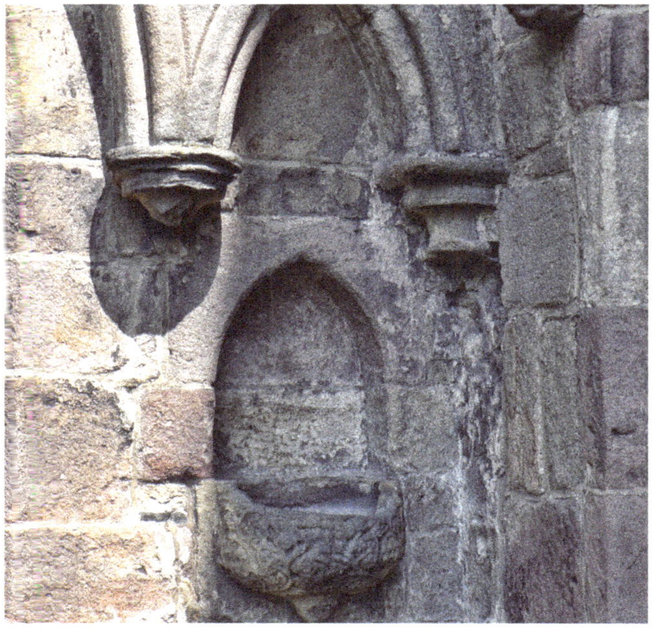

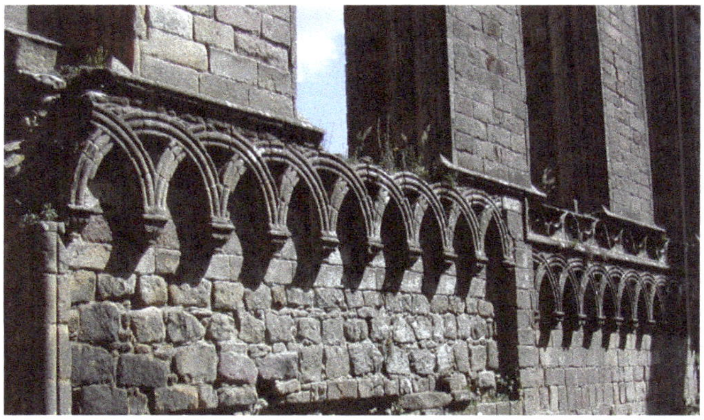

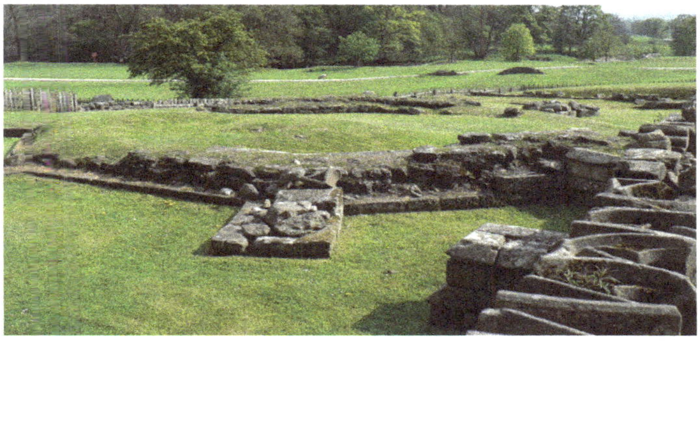

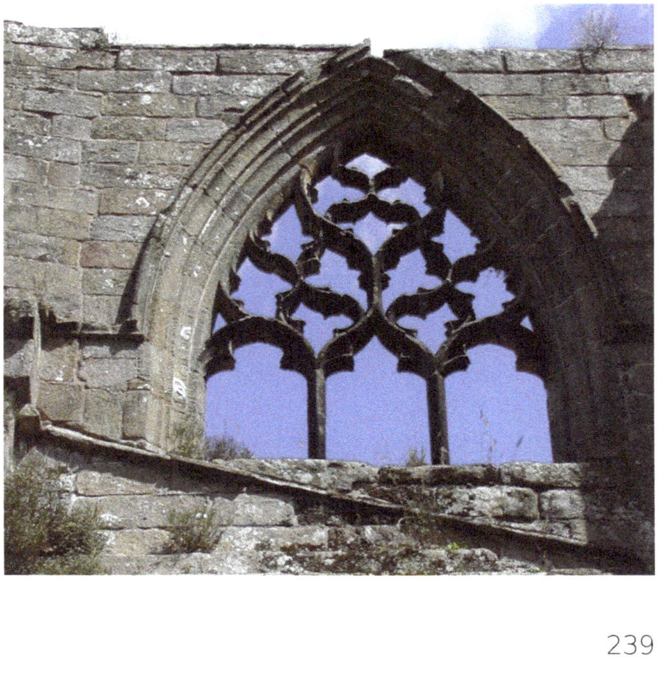

Doncaster Grey Friars

-1290–1536

Information about the Grey Friars site is scarce, but it had completely vanished by 1842, when the River Don navigation canal was cut. Excavations then revealed foundations of Warmworth stone, some dressed stone, and pinnacles and foliated crockets. The turreted gate and chapel on the great Friars' Bridge are also no more. As was the rule of the Order, the Friars Minor established themselves on a seven-acre site in the poorest quarter of the town, in Marsh Gate, at the south-eastern extremity of an island formed by the Rivers Cheswold and Don. The founder has not been identified, nor has the exact date of its foundation, although it is known that it was in existence in 1290. There were thirty friars in the house in 1299-1300, when Edward I gave them money for food, but numbers appear to have declined thereafter. In 1332, Warden Thomas de Saundeby and four friars were sued by John de Malghum for having seized and imprisoned him, and the friars had to face further suits in later years. In spite of these blots on their character, the friars were well thought of by the local populace and obtained a continuous flow of benefactions, which helped to sustain their house until its dissolution in November 1538, when Warden Thomas Kirkham, six friars and three novices surrendered the house to Sir George Lawson. In 1536, Robert Aske, the leader of the northern Pilgrimage of Grace, resided in the Grey Friars house.

Doncaster White Friars

-1350–1538

Unlike the Franciscans, the Carmelites established themselves in the higher and drier part of the town, having at their disposal a site of 100 acres, granted to them by John de Nicbrothere of Eyam. Unfortunately, nothing at all has survived above ground and the site today is marked only by roads. The church was not required for the parish and was thus demolished, but the abbey gateway survived into the eighteenth century. According to Speed, the house was founded by John of Gaunt, Duke of Lancaster, before 1350 in the reign of Edward III. The earliest record of the house was in 1346, when it was described as being a right goodly and flourishing house. In 1399, Henry Bolingbroke, soon to become Henry IV, lodged at the priory, as did Edward IV in 1470. King Henry VII, on his first progress to the north, heard mass in the Carmelite church in 1485, and in 1503, his daughter, Princess Margaret, stopped in the priory on her way north to marry King James of Scotland. A figure of the Blessed Virgin, known as 'Our Lady of Doncaster', is said to have been in the priory church. In November 1538, the last prior, Lawrence Cooke, and six friars surrendered the house to the King's commissioners, Bellasis and Blithman. Cooke, in retaliation for allowing the leaders of the Pilgrimage of Grace rebellion in the north to use the Carmelite priory as their headquarters in 1536, was immediately confined in the Tower of London. He was hanged at Tyburn in August 1540. The Carmelite site, together with the title Lord Carlingford, was acquired by the Swift family.

Drax Priory

St Nicholas • Augustinian c1130–1536

Only earthworks, scattered stones and buried remains remind of this house of Augustinian canons founded in the early1130s in the reign of Henry I on the south side of the River Ouse by William Paynel, who endowed the Priory of St Nicholas with lands and property spread over a wide area in Yorkshire, Leicestershire and Lincolnshire. It is a sad sight, but with the monstrous cooling towers and chimneys of Drax Power Station now looming large on the horizon, it is probably just as well that the soil has drawn a veil over this once holy place. Some relics of the priory, including fine sculptures of saints, apostles, abbots, bishops and Kings, can be found in Drax Church under the splendid fifteenth century clerestory, adorned outside with a fine show of gargoyles and battlements. Fine medieval carvings, also believed rescued from the priory, adorn the ends of the pews, including one with a man falling on his head, thought to represent Balaam and his ass.

Drax Priory did not have an easy history, suffering as it did from frequent inundations of the Rivers Ouse and Aire, in spite of the surrounding moat, and the loss of cattle, which so impoverished the house that it was, according to Archbishop Melton in 1324, hindered from its work of piety and hospitality. Furthermore, frequent invasions of the Scots and other enemies caused the canons to seek a licence to crenellate the church and belfry in 1362. With its suppression in August 1536, Prior William Emson, nine canons and twenty-nine servants lost their livelihood. Drax Priory was granted by Henry VIII to Sir Marmaduke Constable for services rendered and completely demolished.

Ecclesfield Priory

Benedictine -1100–1539

The Benedictine abbey of St Wandrille in Normandy established a small satellite in Hallamshire on estates granted by Countess Judith. The exact date of foundation has not been ascertained, but is thought to have taken place in the last years of the eleventh century. The first record, dated 1141, lists the priory possessions as a church with chapels, tithes and one mill. As an alien house, it was subject to several repossessions by the Crown, the final time in 1386, when it was given to the Carthusian monastery of St Anne in Coventry. Now in English hands, it survived until the Dissolution. The entire estate passed to the earls of Shrewsbury in 1539. Ecclesfield Priory was located just north of the present parish church on a site now occupied by a private house, which incorporates parts of the monastic chapel, including a three-light trefoil-headed window, stone piscina, aumbry with its original wooden doors, narrow windows, and doorways with stone surrounds.

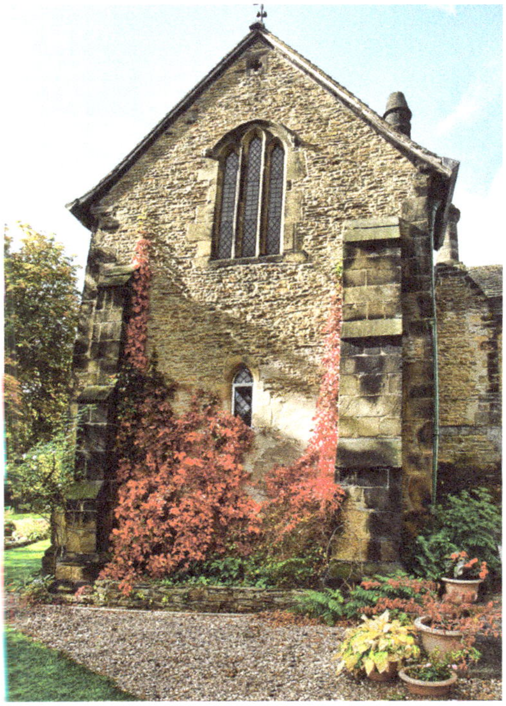

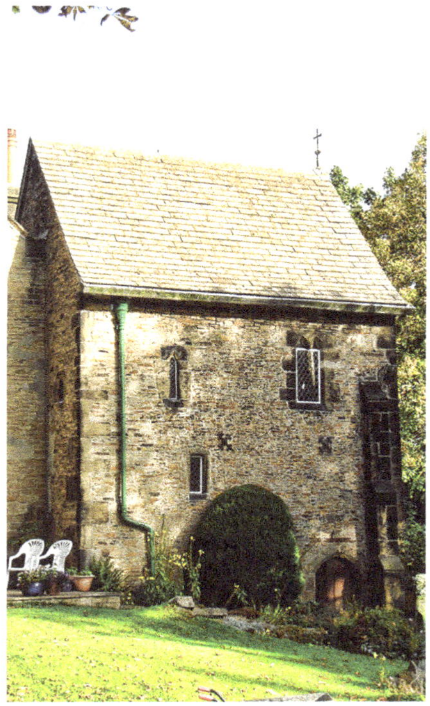

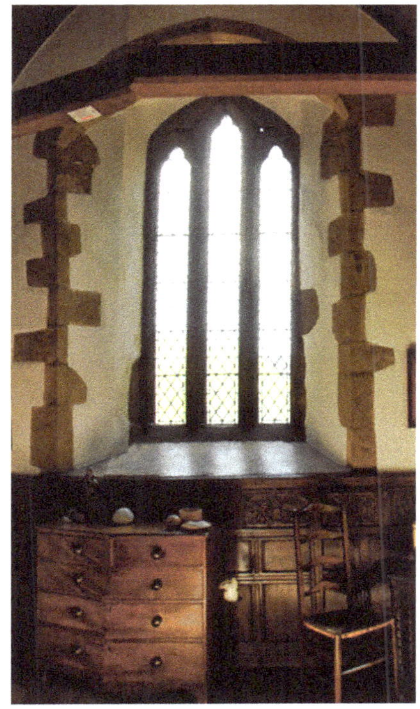

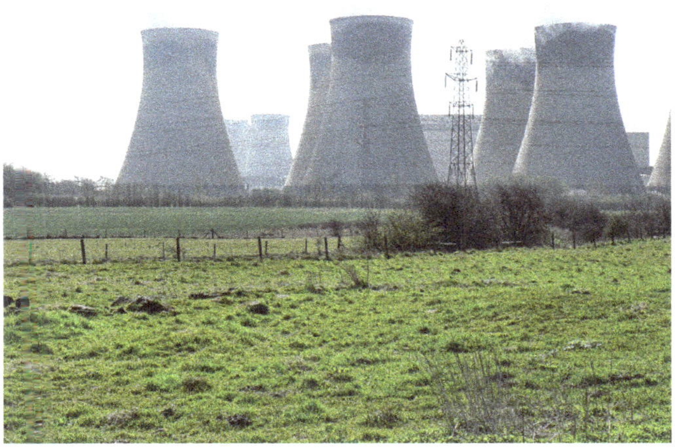

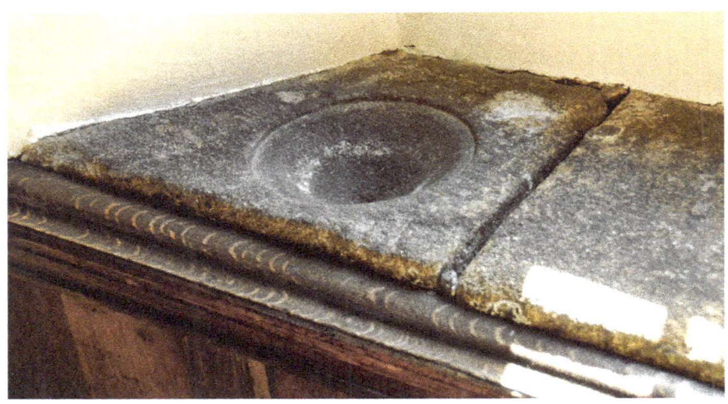

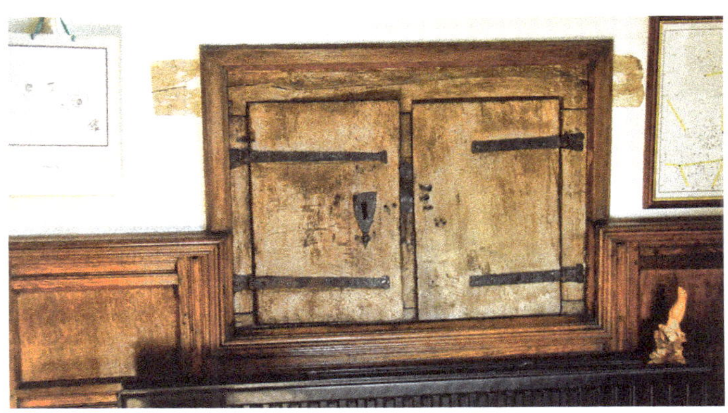

Photos - clockwise from top left

Chapel at Ecclesfield, now a private home, with three-light trefoil window
Stone piscina in former chapel
Aumbry with original wooden doors
Scattered stones of Drax Priory

Embsay Priory

St Mary and St Cuthbert • Augustinian 1120–1536

Apart from the uncovering of the cloister foundations during the building of the present church of St Mary, almost nothing is known of the priory's layout, and nothing has survived. It was founded in 1120 for Augustinian canons under Prior Reynald by William de Meschines and his wife Cecile de Romille, Lady of Skipton Castle. Dedicated to St Mary and St Cuthbert, it was endowed with land and several churches, to which were later added the mills at Silsden and Harewood. A Celtic double monastery in charge of a prioress may have stood on the site some centuries before, but was probably destroyed by the Danes in AD 867. In spite of the stunning landscape around Embsay, the harsh conditions on the high moors soon drove the canons down to the milder and more pleasant surroundings along the banks of the nearby Wharfe, where they established Bolton Priory. However, medieval records show that a small group of canons maintained Embsay Priory until its Dissolution in 1536 after which it fell into a state of total disrepair. It is thought that stone from the priory was used to build Embsay Kirk in 1780.

Esholt Priory

St Mary and St Leonard • Cistercian nuns c1172–1539

The grand Queen Anne style of Esholt Hall, built by Sir Walter Calverley between 1706 and 1709, now standing in the shadows of the Bradford Water Treatment Works, incorporates a number of fragments of this Cistercian nunnery dedicated to St Mary and St Leonard. Looking out across Airedale towards the fast-flowing River Aire, and the sprawling suburban expanse of Leeds, it takes imagination to picture this area, which, when the priory was founded in 1172 or earlier, was the most heavily wooded area in the West Riding of Yorkshire. Indeed, the very name Esholt is derived from the Saxon words Esche, meaning ash, and Holt translating as wood. In keeping with the Cistercian ideal, the nuns sought out sparsely populated areas with running water, and it is rather disappointing that its one time existence has escaped the consciousness of even most local people. Its sparse remains are still hidden away on private land, and the present owners have done little to enable the public to enjoy the few ancient vestiges that tell a fascinating story.

Set high into the external wall of what was once a washhouse at the rear of the main hall, is a stone tablet, probably the tomb slab, of Elizabeth Pudsey, who is generally regarded to have been the last prioress, although this distinction has also been conferred on Joan Jenkynson. The name of Elizabeth Pudsey is still clearly legible above three shields. The first and third shields contain the letters L.H.S. and M.R., while the central shield shows the armorial bearing of the le Wards, founders of the house. The initial 'R' denotes, in all probability, the particular member of the family when the tablet was erected, although his identity is not known. The cellars contain some small twelfth century windows, and there is also an early fireplace within the hall. Two drains date from the twelfth and fourteenth centuries. On the edge of the Aire and alongside a free-flowing beck stand the remains of the priory's fulling mill, now overgrown and neglected, but still in excellent condition. Unfortunately, the original stonework is hidden by a post-Dissolution facing in the same stone and construction. The fulling mill was operated by two water wheels, one powered by water from the Aire in winter, and the other by the beck that runs alongside, when the Aire was at low level during the summer. Stories of a passage running from the priory to the mill have not been verified but a small doorway in the wall of the mill could have been the exit from the passageway.

Built by the side of a stream, the priory was founded by either Geoffrey de Haget or Simon le Ward, his wife Maud, and their son William, who gave large tracts of land, confined mostly to Yeadon. It was confirmed as a priory of the Cistercian Order by Pope Lucius III in 1184. The fact that no reference has been found of any name of prioress before 1300, lends credence to Dugdale's assertion that St Mary and St Leonard was a cell to Sinningthwaite. It is known that in 1172 a place called Escheholt in Airedale was confirmed by a Bull of Pope Alexander III to the nuns at Sinningthwaite. The first known prioress was Juliana de Wodehall, who had been a nun at Sinningthwaite. The priory suffered from flooding of the nearby River Aire, which, in spite of regular grants and gifts, partly contributed to the poor financial state it found itself in by1318, when Archbishop Melton urged moderation. The nuns were very adept at brewing large quantities of ale, much more than allowed, enabling them to sell the surplus to improve their finances, thereby incurring the displeasure of the archbishop of York. The archbishop also threatened to close the priory down if the nuns didn't stop selling their favours to travellers coming up and down the valley. In spite of these less than spiritual, if entrepreneurial activities to boost income, the house remained poor. In 1445, Archbishop Kemp granted an indulgence of 100 days to all who were prepared to help towards the restoration of the bell tower, which had fallen into ruin.

The end came in 1539 when the deed of surrender was signed by Prioress Joan Jenkynson and ten nuns, including Elizabeth Pudsey, which was also described as prioress, but with the added note that she was "too decrepit and not able to ride or walk". Its annual value was only £13 5s. For some unknown reasons, the priory had escaped the 1536 closure of the lesser houses. Priory and estates passed through several hands until coming by marriage to Walter Calverley, whose son built Esholt Hall.

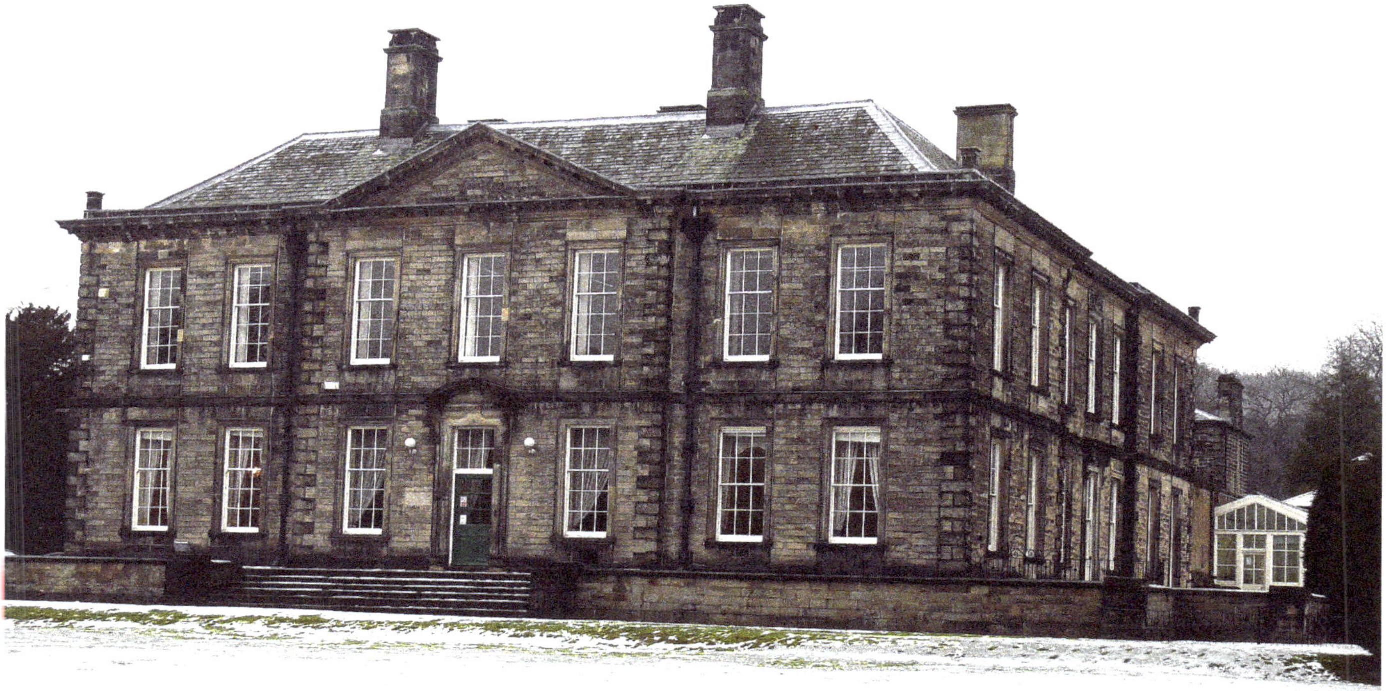

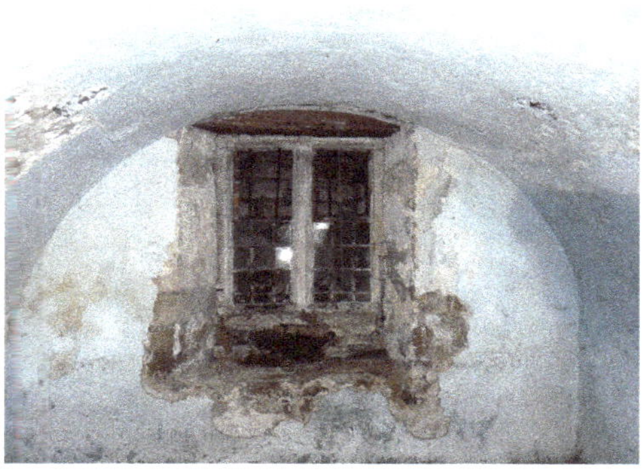

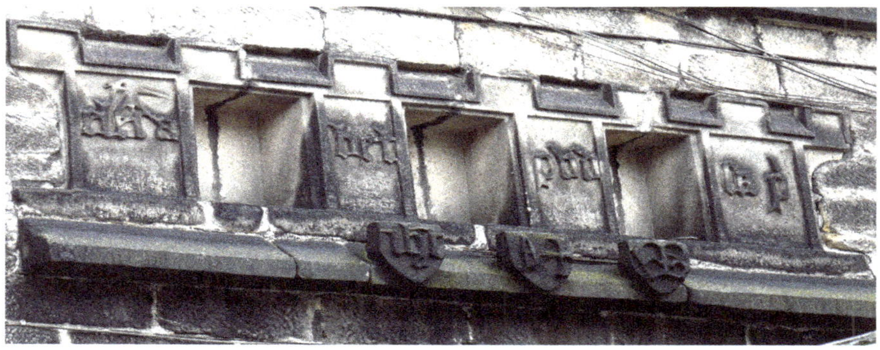

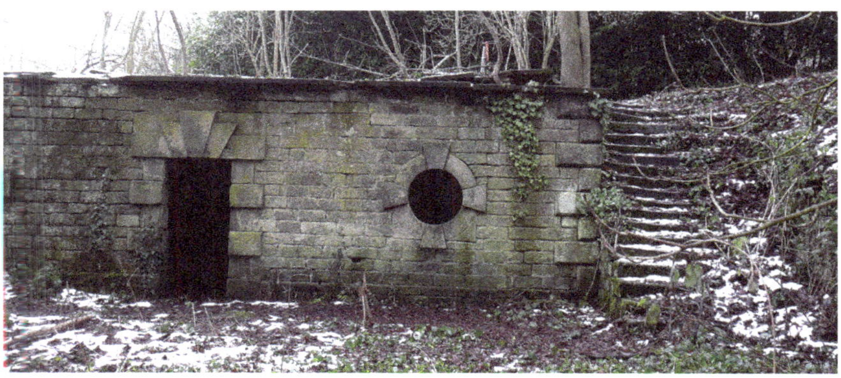

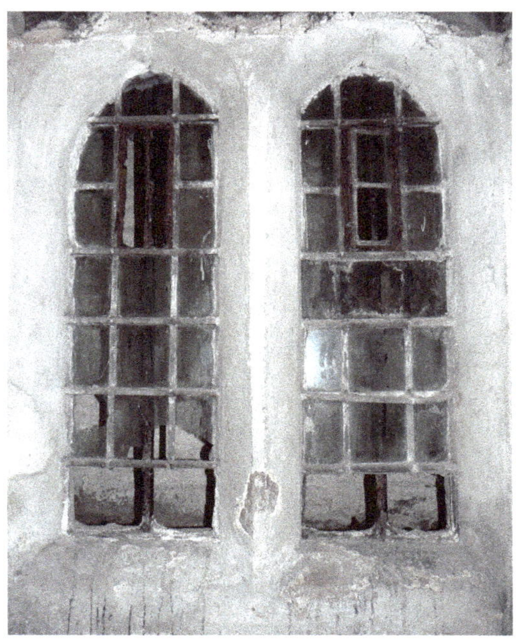

Photos of Esholt Priory – clockwise from top

Esholt Hall on site of Cistercian nunnery
Stone tablet of Prioress Elizabeth Pudsey
Narrow twelfth century windows in hall
Remains of priory fulling mill
Medieval window in cellars

Hampole Priory

St Mary • Cistercian c1150–1539

This Cistercian priory was situated in a pleasant vale on the high road between Wakefield and Doncaster, once surrounded by Barnsdale Forest. After its closure in November 1539, when it was handed to Henry VIII's commissioner, Thomas Leigh, a clerk of the Chancery, by Prioress Isabel Arthington and thirteen nuns, the stone was carted away to serve as free building material for local construction. As a result, remnants of the priory can be found in various farm buildings and gardens, although identification is now very difficult. Medieval arches support the ceiling of the cellars in Abbey House and at the gable end of the old school house is a niche and cross that may have come from the priory. The majority of the foundations of the priory buildings now lie beneath the village green and nothing remains *in situ* above ground.

Hampole Priory was founded c1150 by William de Clairfait, Lord of Hampole, and his wife, Avicia de Tanais, and endowed with lands in the near vicinity. Although a papal bull of 1156 by Pope Adain decreed that the nuns were to follow the Benedictine rule, by the twelfth century the nuns were claiming to be Cistercians. The reason for this change may be found in the fact that Cistercian male monasteries were exempt from paying tithes. However, Cistercian monks refused to recognise the claim of the nunneries until an instruction was given by Pope Alexander III that nuns must be accepted into the Order. Notwithstanding the pope's directive, contacts between male Cistercian houses and nunneries were discouraged and, in 1267, the guardianship of Hampole Priory was recorded as being under William de Bardney, a monk of the Benedictine Abbey of Whitby.

In spite of the advowsons of the churches of Adwick, Marr and High Melton, as well as revenues from three estates, the nuns' high living, preferring the latest fashions in clothing rather than their plain garments, brought the priory into debt. A visitation in 1315 exhorted the nuns to be more 'economical'. The situation improved after the great writer and hermit, Richard Rolle, gave counsel to the nuns. He is believed to have been buried in the priory church. At its suppression, it was valued at £63, which should have brought it within the first Act of 1536. However, while a report by Sir Brian Hastings after his visit in 1537 assured Cromwell that the nuns were "of good fame", and a promise of exemption from suppression, obtained in March 1538, it only delayed the inevitable.

Headley Priory

St Mary • Benedictine c1125–1414

There is some doubt as to the identity of the founder and the exact year of establishment. The reputed founder was Ypolitus de Bram, but it is more likely to have been Alexander Paynell and his wife Agnes, who had granted a site in Bramham Wood to the Benedictine monks of Holy Trinity in York, c1125, in the reign of Henry I. It is said that when St Robert (c1160-1218) escaped persecution at Knaresborough by fleeing to Headley, he was so dismayed by the laxity of the house that he soon departed in search of a more disciplined monastery. As Holy Trinity was dependent on Marmoutier Abbey, which was located outside Tours in Indre-et-Loire, France, Headley itself was also an alien house and as such, was suppressed by Henry V in 1414. Little is known of its near 300 years of history and there are no visible remains.

Healaugh Park Priory

St Mary • Augustinian +1161–1535

Set among trees in the fertile agricultural expanse to the southwest of York, well back from the road, what remained of this priory of Austin canons has been incorporated into farm buildings, and includes fragments of Perpendicular windows and two large fireplaces in a barn. Nothing is left of the priory church, but the nearby parish church of St John the Baptist is well worth a visit. It is notable for the ornately carved late Norman doorway, as well as Saxon remnants.

The origins of the priory date back to some years after 1161, when Bertram Haget granted land in Healaugh Wood for a hermitage to Gilbert, a monk from Marmoutier. In about 1203, a church was built in honour of St John the Evangelist and a community of canons from France under Prior William was established in 1218 by Jordan de St Maria, who had married Alice, one of Bertram Haget's daughters. The priory gained extensive possessions, although of little value, including nearby land and churches and the hospital of St Nicholas juxta Yarm, but soon became burdened by debt, which prevented the community from keeping the buildings in good repair. It also became afflicted by immorality and indiscipline, resulting in the forced resignation of several priors. Healaugh was suppressed in August 1535, when only Prior Richard Roundale, five canons and eight servants, boys and other workmen were left. Its clear annual value was £67 3s. It was granted to James Gage in 1540.

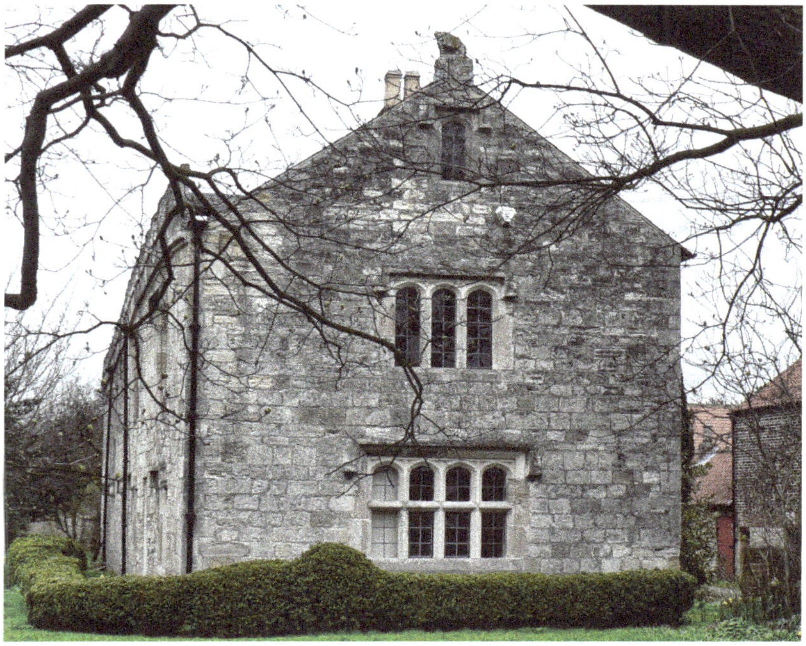

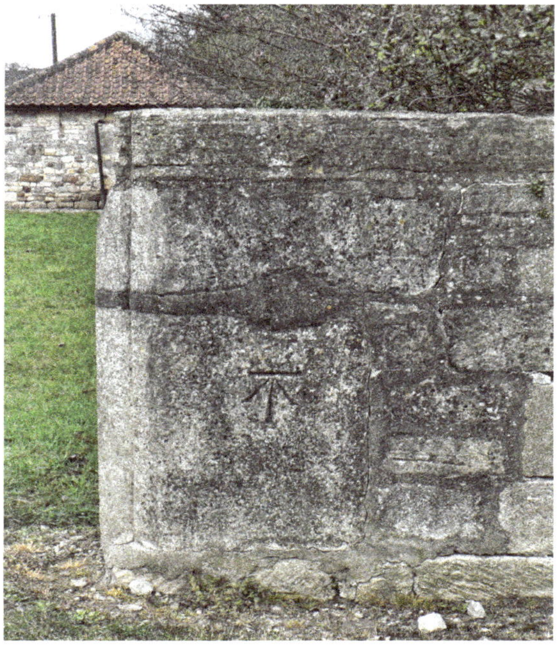

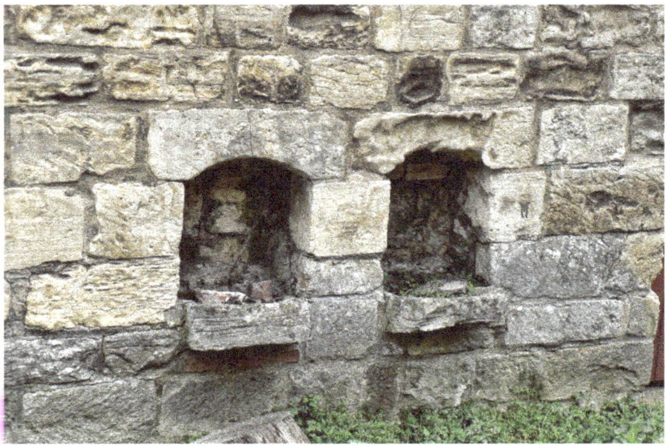

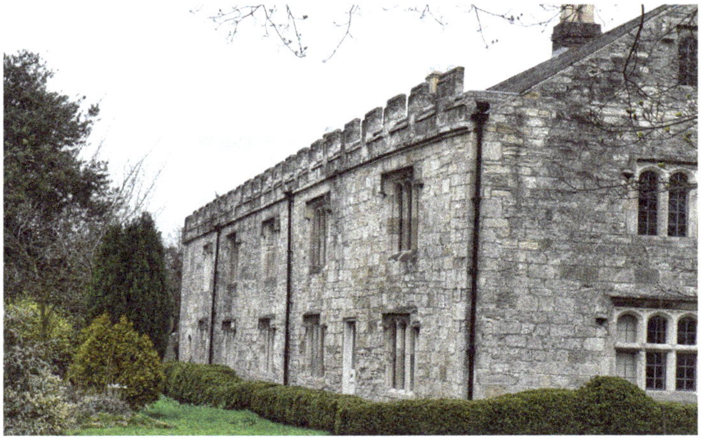

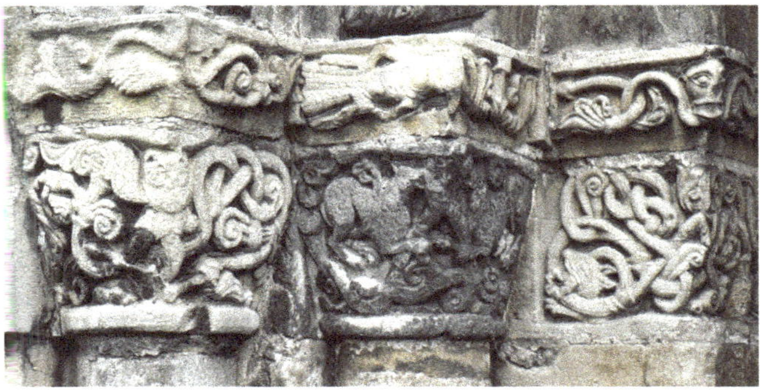

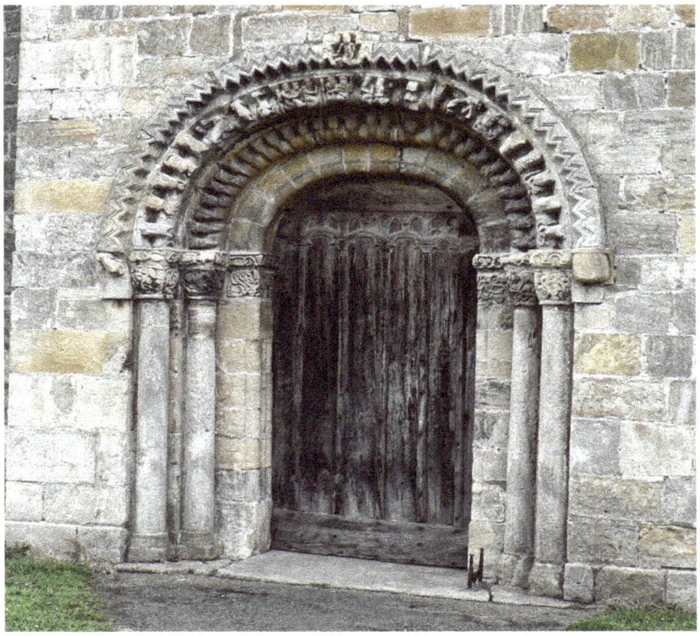

Photos of Healaugh Park Priory - from top left

Farmhouse incorporating priory remains
Mason mark on precinct wall
Another view of farmhouse
Late Norman doorway at Healaugh parish church
Decorated column capitals
Possible remains of piscinae

Kirklees Priory

St Mary & St James • Cistercian nuns -1138–1539

In the grounds of the vast Kirklees Park, in the midst of fields and ancient woodland still wonderfully isolated from the encroachment of urbanisation, stands the ruined gatehouse of this fascinating house of Cistercian nuns. It is the only building to have survived *in situ* to this day but provides a physical link to a tale of treachery and mystery involving none other than the swashbuckling Robin Hood. When Robin was struck down by illness, he is said to have travelled to the priory because the prioress, most probably Elizabeth de Stainton, who was a relative, was well-known for her medical skills. He was put up in an upper room of the gatehouse, where the prioress began the process of blood-letting to purge the body. When the bowl had filled with blood, the wound was to be sealed. However, so the story goes, the prioress had made a hole in the bowl so that Robin lost much more blood then was necessary, putting him into a seriously weakened state. Red Roger of Doncaster, a convent priest and lover of the prioress, was then sent to put Robin to the sword. Why the prioress wanted Robin dead remains a mystery. However, Robin managed to kill Red Roger and, after calling Little John on his horn and asking him to fetch his longbow, uttered the words: "Bury me where my arrow falls." Robin probably died in 1246 or 1247. In the latter year, Elizabeth de Stainton is said to have committed suicide. The discovery of her tomb in the nun's cemetery added a frisson of credibility to this intriguing tale.

The present monument deep in the heart of ancient woodland to the south-east near the River Calder, marked Robin Hood's Grave, is too far away to have been reached by a medieval archer, but human bones removed in the mid-eighteenth century from an unmarked grave half the distance from the gatehouse, could have been those of Robin Hood. The grave, like the gatehouse on private land and only accessible with special permission, is enclosed by a low stone wall and iron railings. The stone tomb slab has been chiselled away over the years, but set into the rear wall is a tablet with an apparently medieval inscription, which translated reads:

Here underneath this little stone
Lies Robert, earl of Huntington
Never was there archer as he so good
And people called him Robin Hood
Such outlaws as he and his men
Will England never see again
Died 24th kalendris December 1247

A legend it all may be, but it will keep the name of Kirklees Priory alive long after the gatehouse is no more.

Kirklees Priory was founded before 1138, during the reign of Henry I, by Reiner de Fleming, Lord of the manor of Wath-upon-Dearne, whose grant was confirmed by Henry III in 1236, and by William de Warenne sometime before 1240. The adherence of the nuns to their religious vows appear to have vanished very quickly, as they were often admonished by visiting bishops for indulging in worldly ways, including keeping dogs and going out dancing. But worse was to come. There were scandalous reports in 1315 about the nuns of Kirklees, particularly about one "Alice de Raggid, deceived by the allurements of frail flesh in great levity of mind, hath gone forth from her house and had wandered, in great peril, having long ago put off her religious habit". Two more nuns, Elizabeth de Hopton and Joan de Heton, were accused of admitting clergy and laymen to the "secret places of the monastery... from which suspicion of sin and great scandal arises". No further misdemeanours of a serious nature were reported subsequently and the nuns benefited from various bequests and the appropriation of Mirfield Church, granted by Pope Boniface IX c1400. With an annual value of only £19 8s, the poor nunnery was given a grant that avoided its closure as one of the lesser monasteries, but it finally fell in November 1539, when Prioress Joan Kyppes and seven nuns surrendered the priory.

Its buildings, with the exception of the gatehouse, were demolished and the stone used to build Kirklees Hall on the nearby hill. The depredations of weather, time and neglect have contributed to the poor state of the gatehouse. It is believed to date largely from the early sixteenth century and is of timber frame construction, partially encased in large dressed stone. The east gable is timbered only from the first floor up and the wall plates have decorative rosettes, and a flowing vine scroll interspersed with hunting dogs to the upper, and vertically carved stags to the lower part of the scroll. Below the tie beam is a four-light oriel window with wooden ovolo moulded mullions. A stone stair leads to the first floor, divided into two rooms, from one of which Robin Hood is said to have loosened his arrow. Of note in the south-facing room are decorative plasterwork bosses of alternate fleur-de-lys and flowers in vases.

Excavations have revealed that the church was only c25m (80ft) long with a 6m (20ft) wide nave and chancel, but no aisles and transepts. The cloister was some12m (40ft) square and still has the weathered base of its lavabo in the centre. Inscribed stone blocks mark the extremities of the church and cloisters. The medieval wall surrounding the nun's orchard still exists, but has a Tudor coping. The modern Three Nuns Inn stands on the site of the priory guesthouse, which was run as a hostelry following the Dissolution by three nuns, Cecilia Topcliffe, Joan Leverthorpe and Katherine Grace.

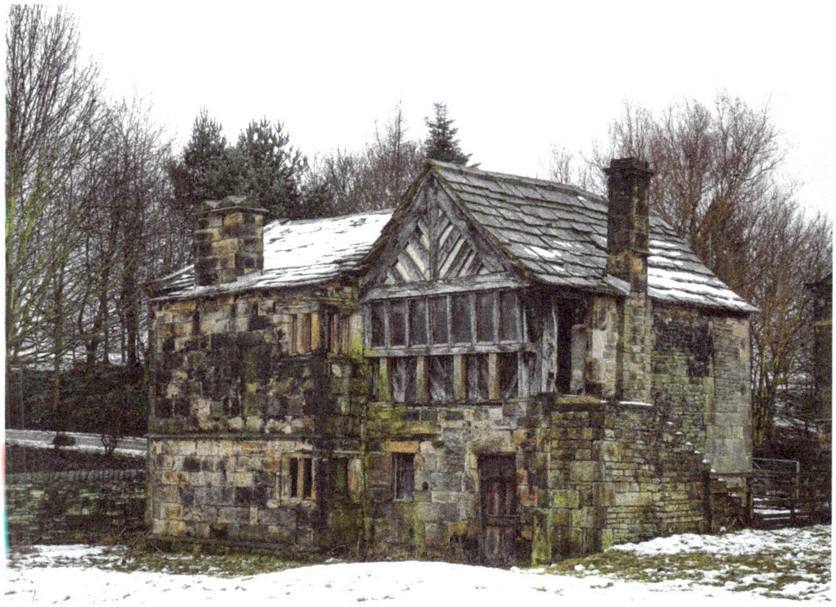

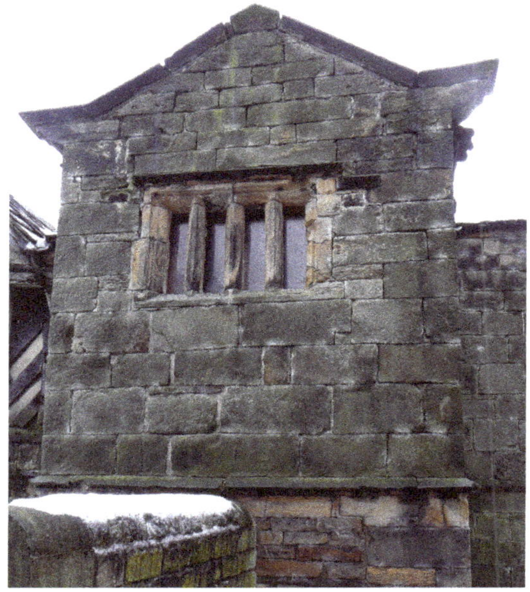

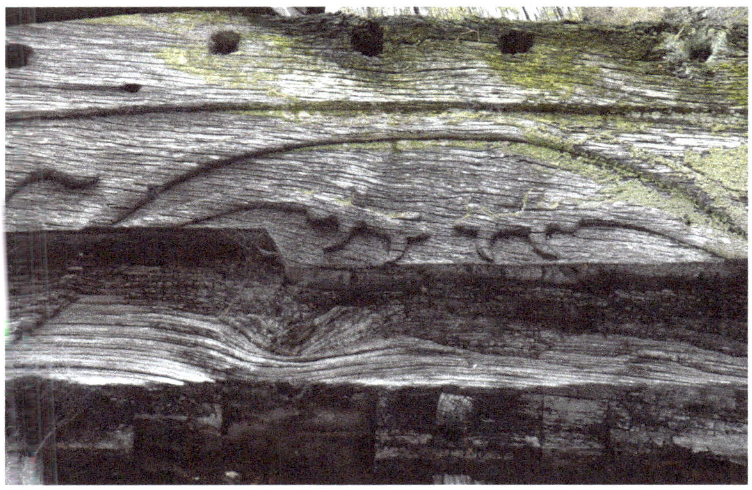

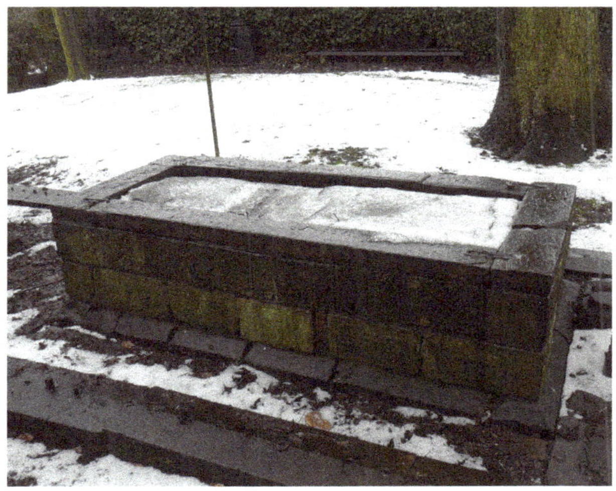

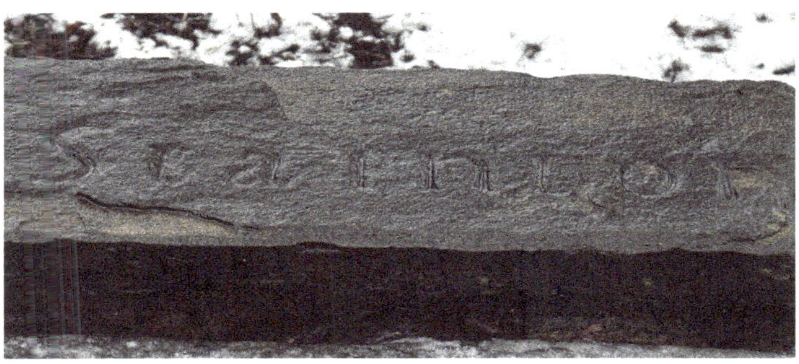

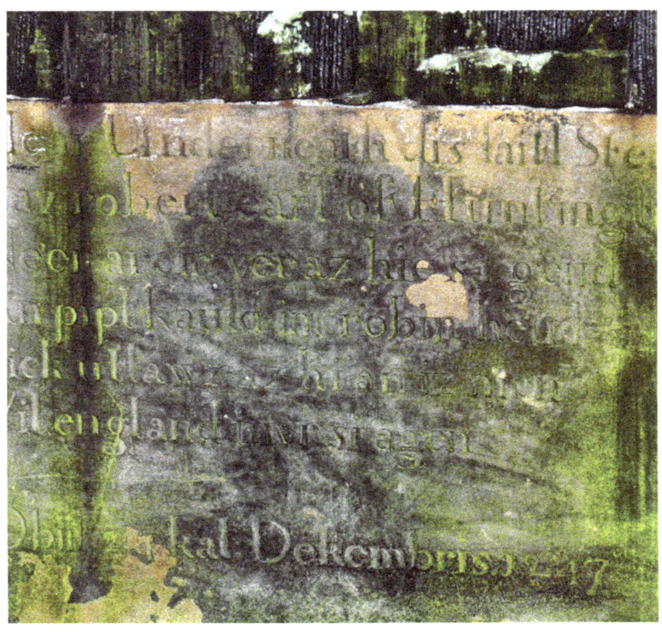

Photos – clockwise from top left

The gatehouse, the only substantial building left from this house of Cistercian nuns
Gable end with four-light stone window
Tomb of Prioress Elizabeth Stainton in the nuns' cemetery
Purported grave of Robin Hood
Inscription on edge of tomb slab
Wall plate with flowing vine scrolls and hunting dogs

Kirkstall Abbey

St Mary • Cistercian 1152–1540

Surrounded by landscaped parkland on the north bank of the River Aire, Kirkstall Abbey still retains its feel of seclusion, although the busy main road cutting through its precincts and the encroachment of the City of Leeds makes its present day location a far cry from the Cistercian ideal. When Kirkstall was founded in 1152, the beautiful Airedale Valley was still unspoilt and no doubt remained so until the abbey's closure in 1539. What impresses about this abbey and sets it apart from others is the completeness of most of its buildings, which still stand to their full height, notwithstanding the fact that much of the stonework was removed and used for local building projects. In the eighteenth century, the picturesque and romantic ruins, then overgrown with ivy, inspired many famous artists, such as JMW Turner, who came to Kirkstall to paint, and writers such as Horace Walpole.

In 1147, Alexander, the abbot of Fountains Abbey, left to found a monastery at Barnoldswick on lands of Henry de Lacy. The inhospitable climate and the opposition of local villagers towards the new religious community forced Alexander to seek out a more favourable location. This he found in Airedale on land owned by William Poitou, a vassal of Henry de Lacy. Thus in 1152, Alexander and twelve monks transferred from Barnoldswick to found an abbey at Kirkstall. The first buildings were of wood, but these were soon replaced by massive stone structures in the local Bramley Fall gritstone. Alexander was a man in a hurry, and the 68 m (224 ft) long by 19m (62ft) wide church, cloister and all surrounding buildings were completed before his death in 1182.

As no major rebuilding projects were undertaken subsequently, these twelve century buildings reflect the Cistercian credo of simplicity and are devoid of excessive adornment. In the early sixteenth century, Abbot William Marshall re-roofed the church and built a battlemented tower, the northwest side of which collapsed into the nave in 1779. Monastic life came to an abrupt end in 1539, when Abbot John Ripley surrendered to the commissioners of Henry VIII. Three years later, the estate was granted to Thomas Cranmer, Archbishop of Canterbury, but reverted to the Crown in 1556, when he was burnt to death.

Many of the abbey buildings were used for agricultural purposes, which probably saved them from total destruction. The highest remains are those of the crossing tower built between 1509 and 1527, but with the transepts and the nave still at eaves level, the abbey church dominates the site. There is an unbroken internal view along the length of the nave, with the eight towering columned arches particularly impressive. Each transept had three chapels, and in the south transept, the night stairs used by monks from the dormitory have survived, as has the dormitory block itself, which has a beautiful arched doorway. Two similar arches lead from the arcaded cloister into the chapter house, where the vaulted ceiling is supported by stout yet attractive clustered columns. The refectory exhibits fifteenth century alterations, which indicate a division to create an area where monks could eat meat, a clear reflection of the later relaxation of the Cistercian principles, which allowed only those who were ill to supplement their fish and vegetable diet with meat.

Parts of the lay-brothers' dormitory and refectory can be explored in the west range, where an interesting walled lane once gave access to the church. Elsewhere in the grounds are fragmentary remains of the Abbot's Lodge, a guesthouse and various domestic buildings including the meat kitchen, although only a few walls stand much above ground level. The Abbot's Lodge, built c1250, had three floors, with the basement reserved for servants, the main hall occupying the first floor, and the private living quarters taking up the top level. The separate lodging house for visiting abbots stood alongside. The extensive guesthouse, although comprising low walls only, shows signs of a kitchen, bakehouse and fireplaces.

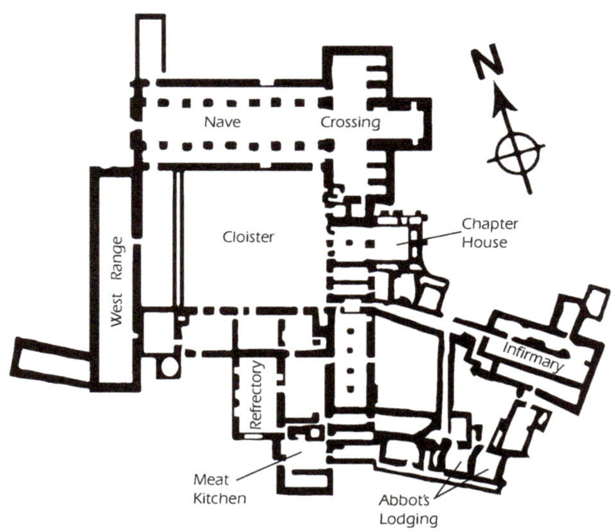

Photos - clockwise from top left

East end of cruciform abbey church
Processional doorway into church
Chapter house vestibule
Double trefoiled lavatorium
Abbot's Lodging
Narrow and lofty aisle of church

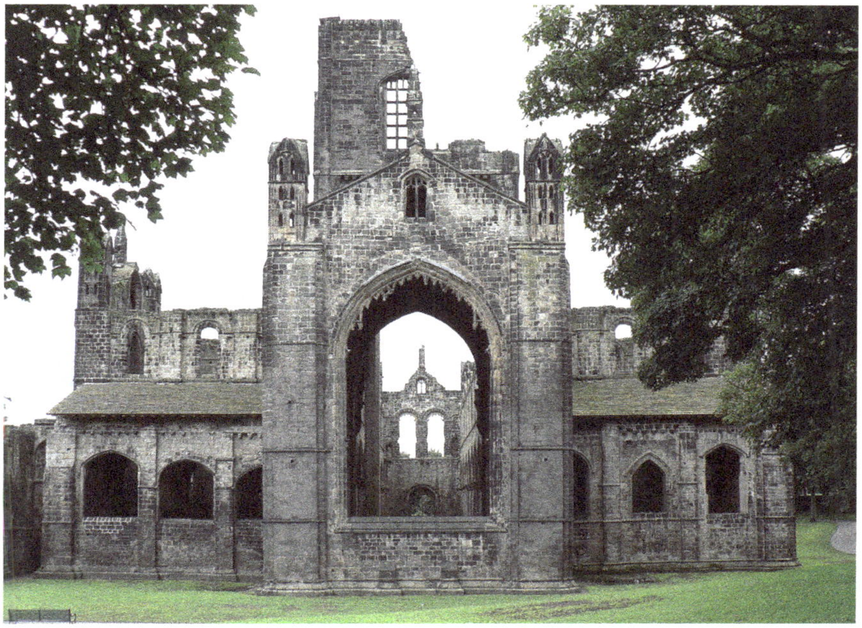

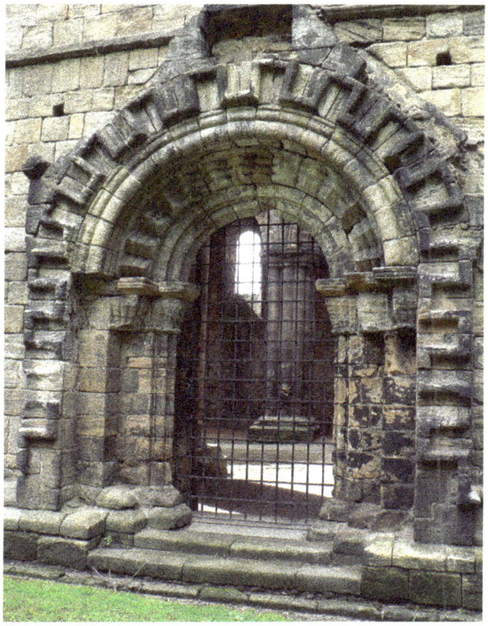

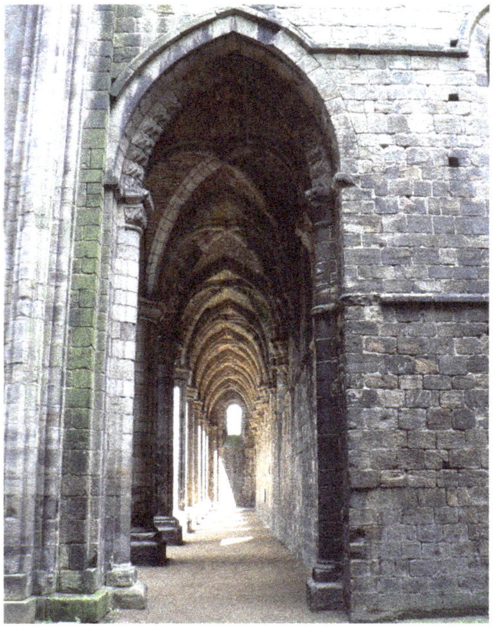

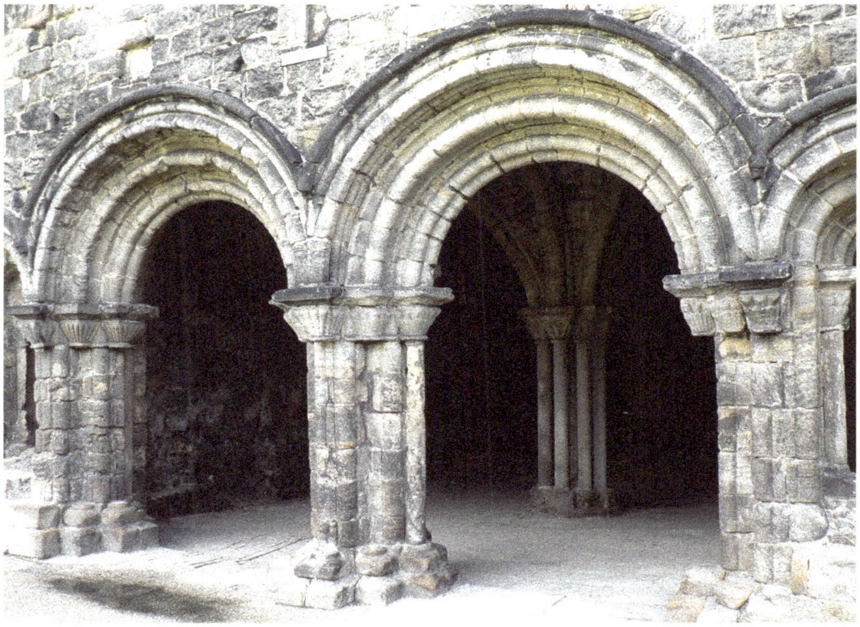

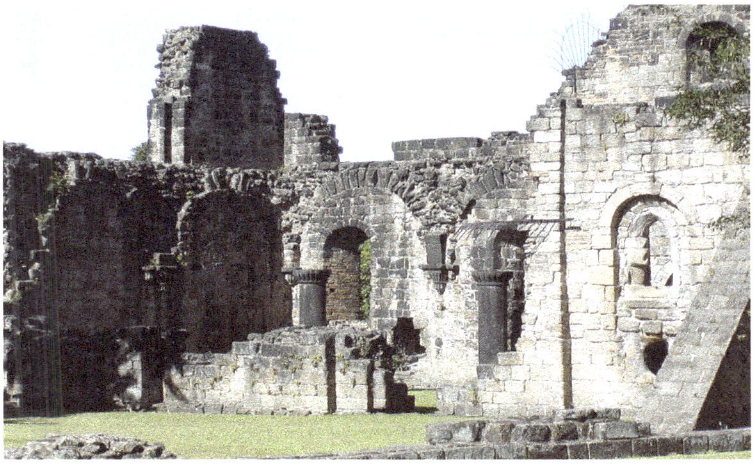

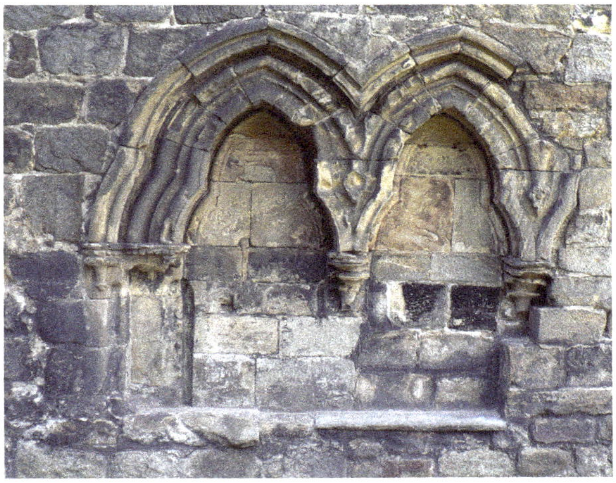

Knaresborough Priory

St Robert • Trinitarian c1252–1538

Inside a loop of the river Nidd there once stood a small priory dedicated to St Robert, whose vicissitudes took him from his hermit's cave, known as St Giles Chapel, to Spofforth, Headley and back again to Knaresborough. St Robert's cave can be reached via a pleasant stroll along the river, but, apart from some intriguing decorated masonry built into nearby walls, nothing remains of the priory buildings. The tentative beginnings of a priory can be found in the building of the Chapel of the Holy Cross by Robert's brother, Walter, Mayor of York, and subsequent granting of land in 1216 by King John, who was impressed by his piety when visiting Robert in his cave. Robert died in 1218 and his tomb in the chapel became a place of pilgrimage. Matthew Paris noted that "a medicinal oil is said to have flowed abundantly from his tomb". Friars of the Trinitarian Order for the Redemption of Captives in the Holy Land then settled on the land under the patronage of Richard, Earl of Cornwall, who became lord of the Honour of Knaresborough in 1235. The friars built a new church over the chapel in 1282 and acquired lands and the patronage of several churches in the area. The priory and its lands were laid waste by the Scots in 1318, but a writ of protection from Edward II and exemption from taxes helped the recovery. The community of friars was reduced from around a dozen to just six by 1360, probably the result of the Black Death. Minister Thomas Kent and ten friars surrendered the house in December 1538.

Monk Bretton Priory

St Mary Magdalene • Cluniac/Benedictine c1154–1538

The sandstone ruins of this priory are tucked away in a housing estate within a stone's throw of the industrial city of Barnsley, rather far removed now from the Cluniac ideal of seeking a place of worship in beautifully remote countryside. However, with a little inventiveness and peeling back of the centuries, the priory can be pictured wholly surrounded by green pasture and spreading woodland. Indeed, there are still views across wooded countryside from the priory grounds and when founded, it was called the priory of St Mary Magdalene on the Lund, from the Norse 'lundr' meaning a sacred woodland grove. What is a little more difficult to imagine is its layout, as no help is provided on the site. Accepting that it followed the usual monastic arrangement, a good starting point after entering the site through the late fourteenth century three-storey gatehouse is the cruciform church, which is still outlined by some remaining low transept and chancel walls, columns, carved doorways and windows. Although originally only 52 m (170 ft) long with a four-bay aisled nave, it had been much extended by the end of the fifteenth century. There are also some excavated stone coffins within the church precincts where the high altar would have been. These are thought to be those of the founder and his wife Matilda, or of some later benefactors.

Among other surviving remains is a two-storey building to the north of the church, which may have been a guesthouse or, more likely, an administrative centre doubling as a manorial courthouse. It is noteworthy for its rare medieval double pitched roof. As a result of the residential conversion incorporating much of the original monastic structures, the south wall of the refectory stands to a good height and still incorporates two beautiful windows. Parts of the west range also remain remarkably intact and a few fragments recall the cloister and chapter house. Of much interest is the sophisticated drainage system of the site, which included a series of sluice gates. There is much to see and admire and the visitor should not be put off by the rather grim industrial surroundings, for within its crumbling walls, the priory still offers time and space for quiet reflection.

The priory's early history was clouded by bitter conflict. Founded by Adam fitzSwain around 1154 for Cluniac monks, the close proximity of the Priory of St John, another Cluniac house at Pontefract established by the de Laceys, caused considerable rivalry and battle for control. The argument had an economic basis and involved the tithes payable to the two priories, and to another, St Oswald's at Nostell, by the various villages. The generous foundation grant had included large areas of land and income from churches and mills, and the priory's value was further increased in 1249, when Henry III granted a weekly market and annual fair. Another area of dispute arose about the election of its own priors. This was strongly opposed by Pontefract, which sent armed forces to take over. The Sheriff, Pope and King eventually became involved resulting in 1276 in a battle in which three monks were killed. Altogether, the quarrel went on for more than a hundred and fifty years, until finally settled in 1317. In the meantime, Monk Bretton had changed its allegiance in 1281 to the Benedictines, which removed one of the contentious issues.

After that time, apart from a severe fire towards the end of the fourteenth century, the history of Monk Bretton appears to have proceeded quietly and without great incidents. It remained a relatively small house of between eleven and thirteen monks, and was finally surrendered, in 1538. The contents were put up for sale, and most of the other buildings were dismantled to provide local landowners with building material. In 1589, the Earl of Shrewsbury bought the priory and some buildings were restored and converted into a private home by his fourth son, Henry Talbot.

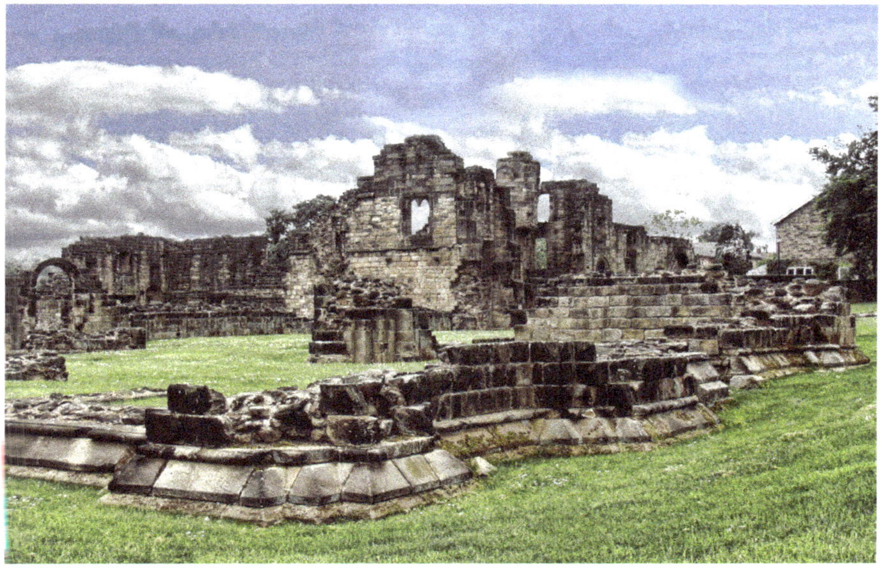

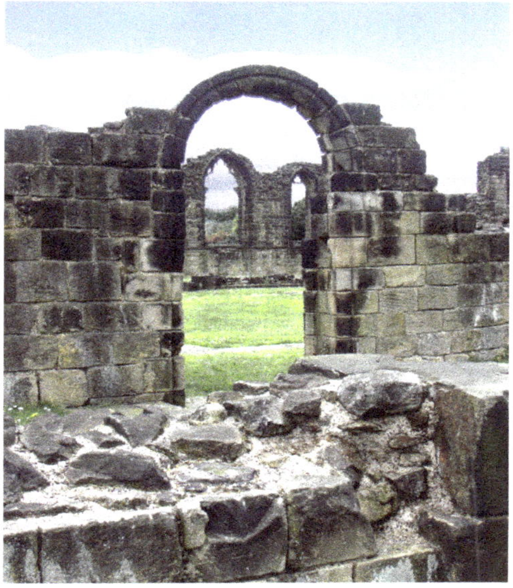

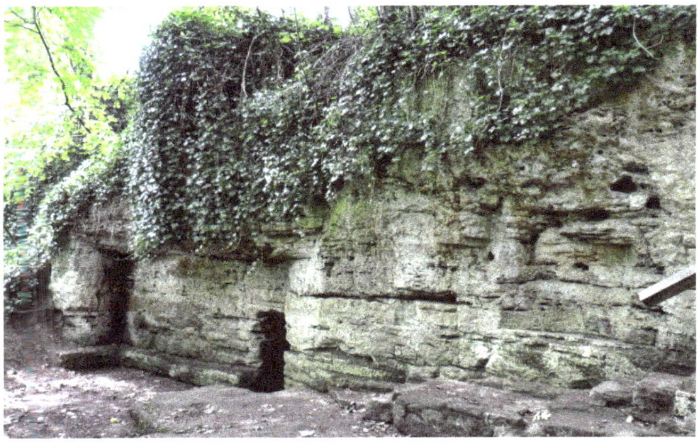

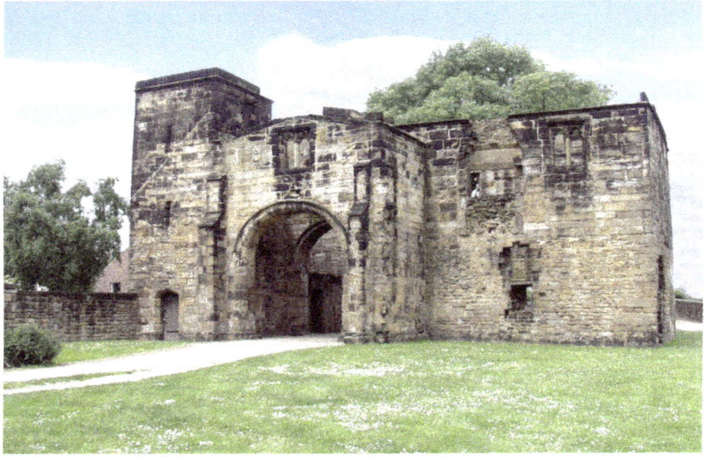

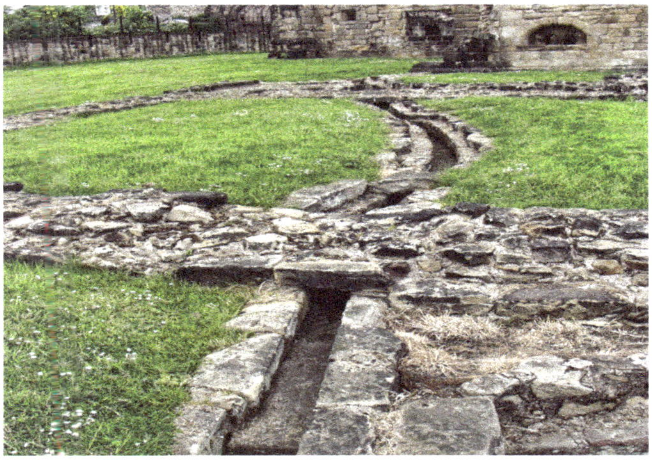

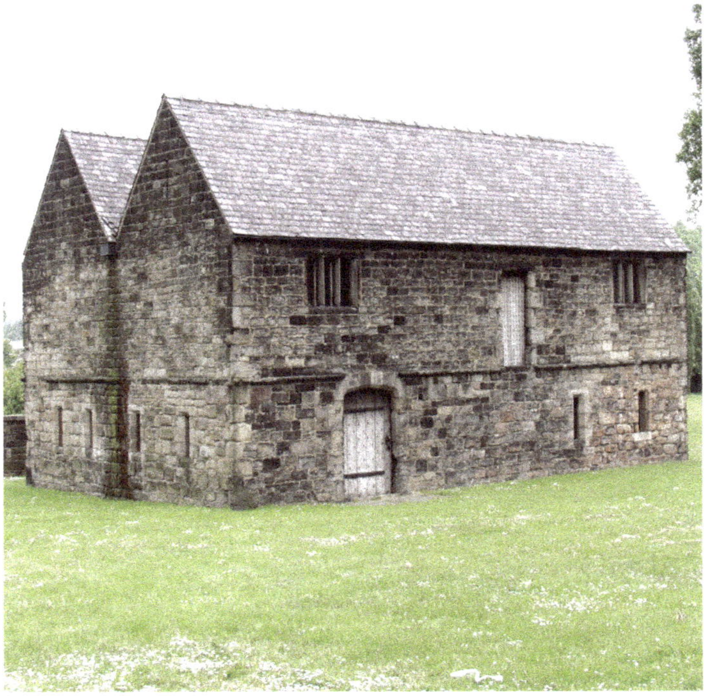

Photos - clockwise from top left

Monk Bretton priory ruins
Remains of priory church
Gatehouse and gate passage
Admin building with rare double-pitch roof
Drainage channels to River Dearne
St Robert's cave at Knaresborough

Nostell Priory

St Oswald • Augustinian c1114–1540

A clutch of mature trees now stands above the buried foundations of the former Augustinian priory dedicated to St Oswald, the martyred northern Saxon King who brought Christianity to the area. So thorough was the destruction that not a solitary stone can be seen above ground, nor has a single architectural carving been preserved for display inside the grand Palladian mansion that now stands on what was once holy ground. According to a royal charter of 1121-22, Ralph Adlave, chaplain and confessor to Henry I, discovered a group of hermits living in the woods around Nostell and, being impressed by their faith, asked the King's permission to regularise the community under the Augustinian rule. Henry I made a grant and other major benefactors, including Robert de Lacy, ensured that the abbey was richly endowed. Apart from five cells – Bamburgh in Northamptonshire, Breedon in Leicestershire, Hirst in Lincolnshire, and Erdislaw and Tockwith in Yorkshire – the canons possessed over thirty churches. While the priory suffered periods of impoverishment, disputes with the prior of Pontefract and archbishops of York, lawsuits and indispline, one highlight of an otherwise unremarkable history was the visit of Cardinal Wolsey, who stopped at Nostell on his way to York in 1530. Ten years later, in November 1540, Prior Robert Ferrer (later Bishop of St David's) and twenty-eight canons surrendered to Henry VIII's notorious commissioners, one of whom, Dr Legh, took possession of the priory. It then passed through several hands until acquired by the Winn family in 1650. The church and monastic buildings, which served as domestic dwellings, were razed to the ground to make way for the new Paladian mansion. Now a National Trust property, the mansion is well worth a visit for its Robert Adams interiors, the best accumulation of Chippendale furniture in the country, and an outstanding art collection.

Nun Appleton Priory

St Mary and St John the Evangelist • Cistercian nuns c1150–1539

The priory was founded c1150 by Eustace de Merch and his wife, Adeliz de St Quintin, on land near the River Wharfe. This grant and many other gifts were later confirmed by Thomas Becket, Archbishop of Canterbury, and, in 1205, by King John. While no great transgressions by nuns have been recorded, visitations in the thirteenth and fourteenth centuries uncovered a relaxed attitude towards hospitality to men and women, which not only had a negative effect on the religious life within the fairly large community, but also proved unacceptably expensive and plunged the priory into heavy debts. Although there is no record of the value of the house in the *Valor Ecclesiasticus*, according to the *Monasticon*, its clear annual value was £73 9s. Nun Appleton Priory was suppressed in December 1539. The office of prioress appeared to be vacant at the time, as only the sub-prioress and eighteen nuns were listed as having received pensions. A few fragments are all that can still be seen of this priory for Cistercian nuns dedicated to God, St Mary and St John the Evangelist. In Bolton Percy Church is the tomb slab of Prioress Agnes de Ryther.

Nun Monkton Priory

St Mary • Benedictine nuns 1172–1536

The picturesque setting near the confluence of the Rivers Nidd and Ouse, together with some glorious detail in the doorway and internal arcading make St Mary's Church one of Yorkshire's hidden gems. The fact that these features, part of the west wall and nave, have survived from the time when the church formed the heart of the small Benedictine priory of nuns, gives a visit added incentive. Hidden is the operative word as there is only one road in and out of the village and only a ghostly outline of the church can be glimpsed behind an ancient willow at the end of a tree-lined avenue of elms. The doorway is a lovely example of Transitional work with five orders of colonettes, chevron decoration and a trefoiled niche in the triangular pediment above. Of the four round-headed niches, two on each side of the doorway, only one still contains a statue. Three Early English lancets with dog-tooth ornaments lead the eye towards the top of the bell tower. Inside, the church is lit by six lancets with nail-head decorations, divided by recessed arcades of small twin arches with trefoiled niches above. The eastern end of the church is Victorian.

The small priory was founded in 1172 by William de Arches and his wife, Ivetta, and endowed with local lands and churches. Their daughter, Maud, became the first prioress, and it was to her and St Mary that the priory was dedicated. By the late thirteenth century it flourished, controlling property as far away as Durham. However, from accounts of the visitation in 1397 by Thomas de Dalby, Archdeacon of Richmond, the spiritual acuity of the community had by then given way to sinful pursuits, with the prioress and nuns reputed to have worn jewellery and furs, enjoyed fine food and wine, and succumbed frequently to the pleasures of the flesh. The tenth prioress Margaret Fayrfax was reprimanded for engaging in candle-lit suppers and more intimate pursuits with local cleric John Monkton. Nun Monkton Priory did not survive the suppression of the smaller monasteries and was closed in 1536, in spite of pleas by Henry VIII's second wife, Anne Boleyn, that it be spared. It was granted to Sir John Nevill in 1538. Much of the church and all other conventual buildings were then demolished.

Pontefract Priory

St Mary and St John • Cluniac c1090–1539

A search for any vestiges of Pontefract Priory will unfortunately be in vain. Only the name of Monk Hill recalls that there once stood an important religious establishment in the area, founded by Robert de Lacy as early as 1090 as a dependency of the Cluniac abbey of la Charité-sur-Loire, which supplied the first community of monks. Dedicated to St Mary and St John, the priory was destroyed during the Anarchy of King Stephen, but rebuilt soon after, being home to an average of twenty monks. The priory's history was marked by a lengthy dispute with the subordinate house of Monk Bretton, which was finally settled in 1280 when the latter renounced Cluny and became a Benedictine priory. In 1322, Thomas, Earl of Lancaster, one of the leaders of the baronial opposition to Edward II, was beheaded for treason at Pontefract Castle and buried in the priory church near the high altar. Many miracles are said to have been wrought at his tomb and the attempt to present the earl as a martyr aroused the anger of the King, who impounded the offerings. However, a chantry chapel was later dedicated to Thomas. The priory was relatively wealthy, being valued at £472 16s in the *Valor Ecclesiasticus*, and was able to stave off Dissolution until November 1539 when Prior James Thwytes, seven brethren and one novice surrendered it to the King's commissioners. The church and conventual buildings were completely destroyed

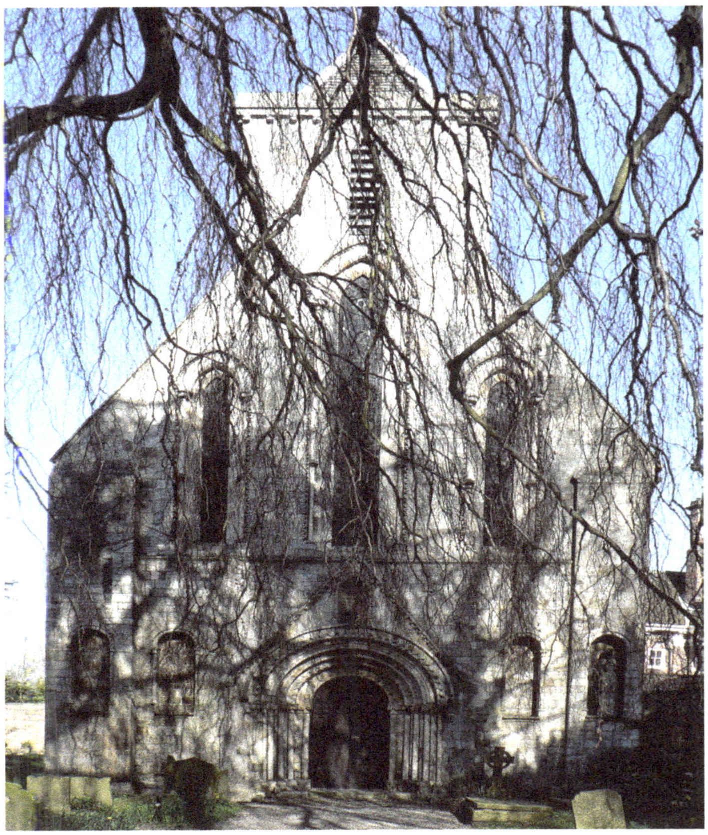

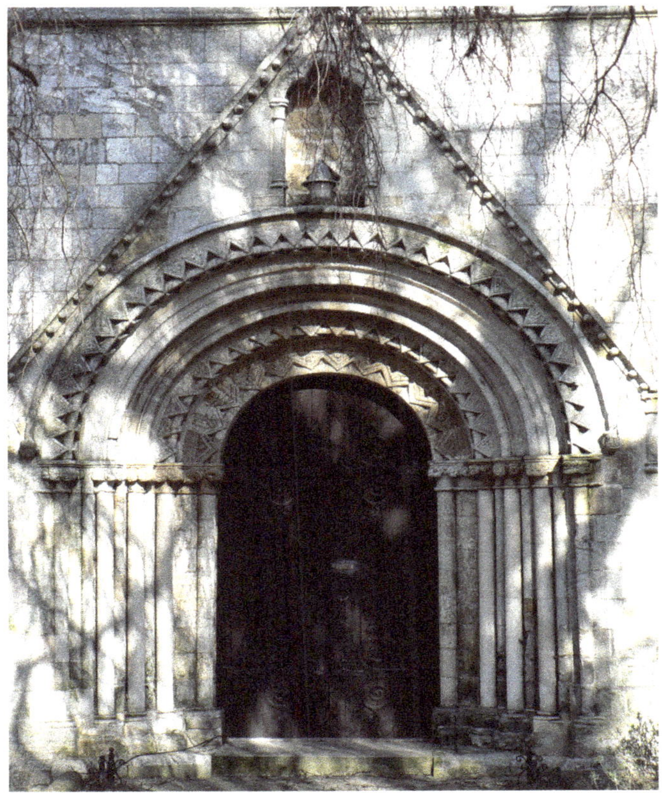

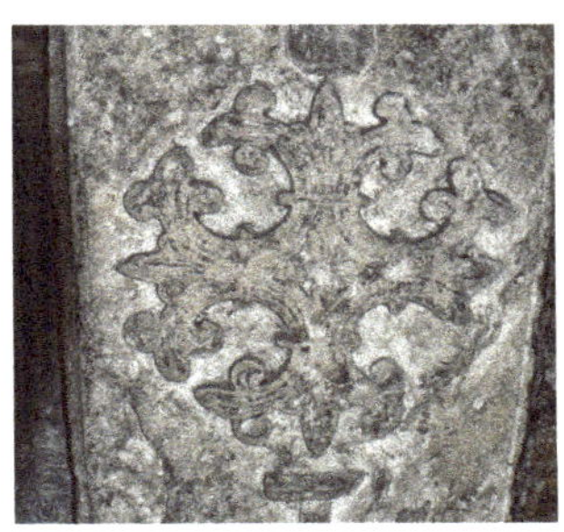

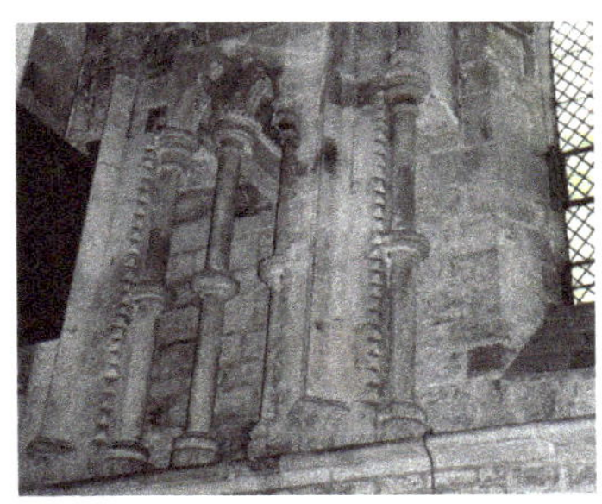

Photos of Nun Monkton Priory – clockwise from left

The well-hidden priory church of St Mary at Nun Monkton
Doorway with five orders of colonettes, chevron decorations and trefoiled niche above
The clerestory lancets divided by recessed arcades
Foliated cross incised on tomb slab

Roche Abbey

St Mary • Cistercian 1147–1538

Secluded in a deep valley overlooked by steep magnesian limestone cliffs to the north and straddling Maltby Beck, the ruins of Roche Abbey provide a charming tableau in the green pastoral landscape of South Yorkshire. Alas, only the transepts of the church remain to any great height, although these are among the most important examples of early Gothic architecture and alone are worth the long journey north. The remaining buildings survive only as low standing walls, and without the excavation programme of the Office of Works under Sir Charles Peers in the early twentieth century, even these would have been lost forever. The destruction of most of the abbey can be laid firmly at the door of the fourth earl of Scarborough, who, in 1775, commissioned Lancelot 'Capability' Brown to landscape the area to enhance his adjoining family seat at Sandbeck Park. Capability Brown was directed to create a picturesque setting for the ruins to reflect a "Poet's feelings and Painter's eye," but he completely disregarded the archeological importance of Roche Abbey and razed most of the monastic buildings to the ground, burying the foundations underneath huge grass parterres. Only the transepts were retained as 'romantic' features.

The east walls of both transepts, each pierced by two arches, which led into the chapels, stand almost to full height and remain the dominant features of the site. The early application of the Gothic style of architecture, characterised by lancet arches, ribbed vaulting and flying buttresses originated in the Paris area of France. It is believed that the master who designed the church, building of which started around 1180, came from the Aisne valley in the Laonois, a prolific area of Cistercian settlement. Also of note is the first application of a three-level design, with the middle storey composed of a pair of blind arches. There are slight variations in the construction of the lower arches, suggesting different building periods. The church was some 67m (220ft) long and 33.5m (110ft) at its widest, and comprised an aisled nave and monks' choir, with three entrances in the west front leading from a ceremonial galilee porch. The sedilia can be recognised in the south wall of the presbytery, although the rich canopy work has crumbled. Three heavy foundation blocks along the north wall once supported flying buttresses added in the fourteenth century to stabilise the structure.

Excavations have revealed the complete layout of the abbey, which can best be viewed from the cliff path running along the site boundary. From the south aisle of the church, six steps lead to the adjacent cloister, of which traces of the foundations to the arcades survive. A section of the arcade itself has been rebuilt from fallen fragments and is displayed in the on-site museum. Grouped around the cloister were the lay-brothers' refectory and dormitory, kitchens, and warming house between the monks' refectory and dormitory. The last two were later extended to accommodate an influx of new monks, which required spanning the stream. The arches carrying the southern ends of the buildings over the stream still exist. Later still, more buildings were constructed on the other side, including the abbot's lodging, kitchens, bakehouse and the infirmaries. Also of interest is the medieval roadway to the great arched gatehouse, and the huge fireplace in the meat kitchen.

Roche Abbey was founded in 1147 by Richard de Buili and Richard fitzTurgis, who owned land on both sides of what is now known as Maltby Beck, and was colonised by monks from Newminster in Northumberland. As other Cistercian abbeys, it was dedicated to the Virgin Mary, but took the name of *Sancta Maria de Rupe* from the rocky cliff to the north of the church. An over ambitious expansion programme brought the abbey into debt, but life appears to have been uneventful throughout its history until the Dissolution in June 1538, when the colony had been reduced from around 175 in the early years to just fourteen monks and four novices. In the *Valor Ecclesiasticus* of 1535, its net annual value had been assessed at £226 19s. Local people robbed the abbey of goods and building materials, leaving it in a ruinous state, only for the final vandalism to destroy the rest.

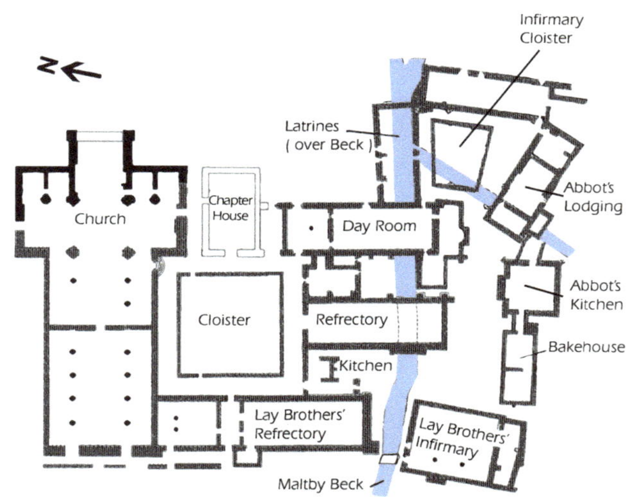

Photos - clockwise from top

Most of the abbey site reduced to low walls
The surviving transept walls, a fine example of early Gothic work
Remains of the Great Gatehouse
Huge brick fireplace in the meat kitchen
Massive clustered columns supporting the nave arcade

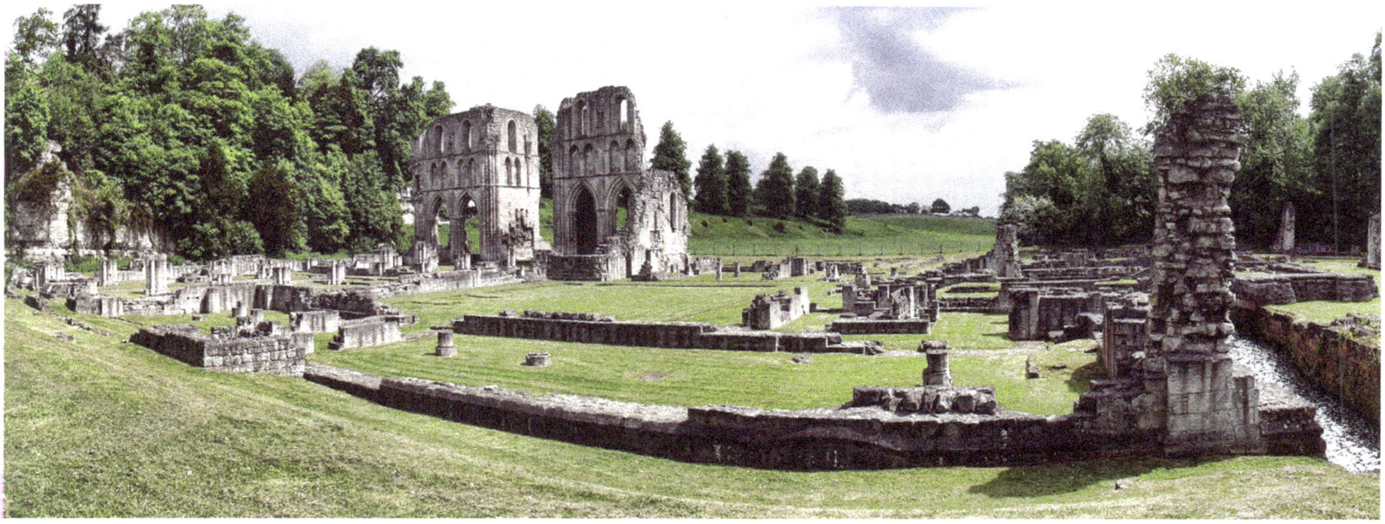

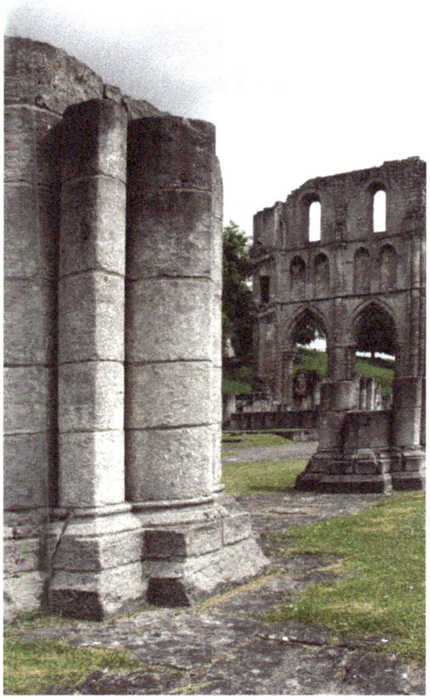

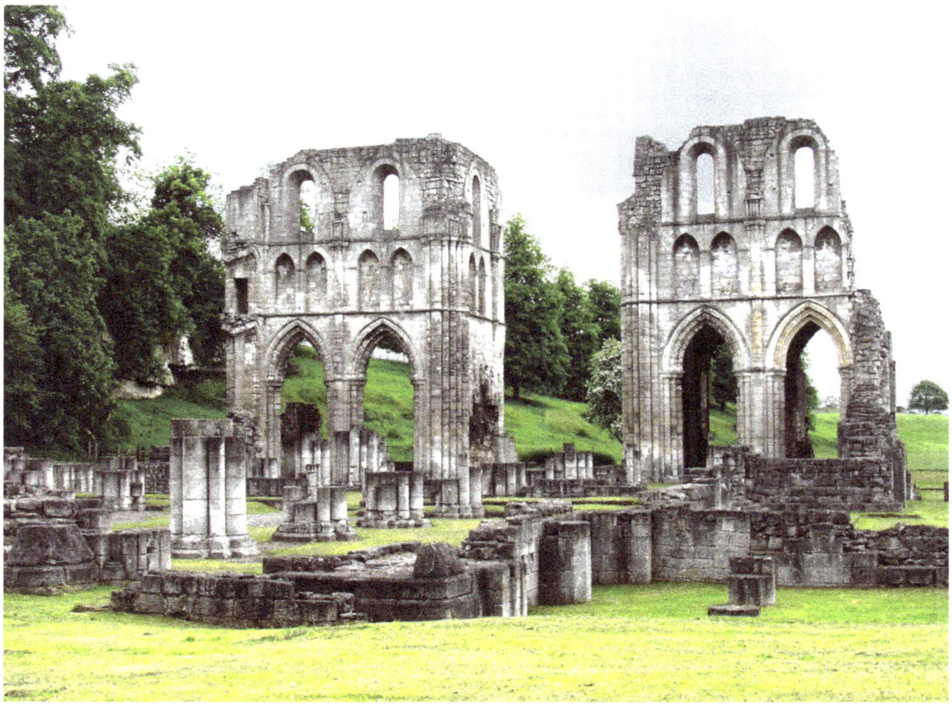

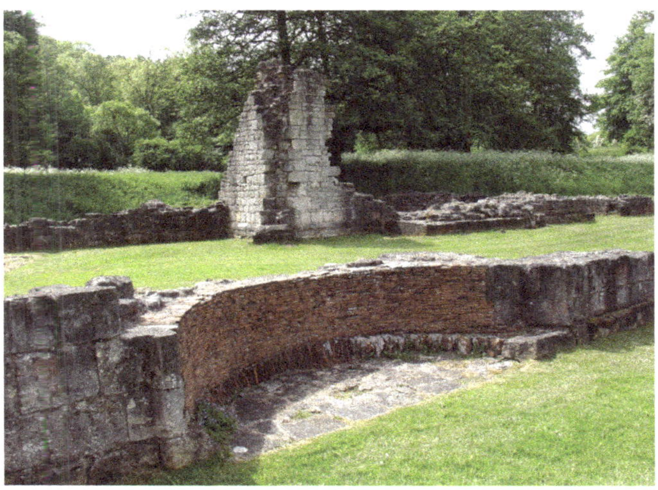

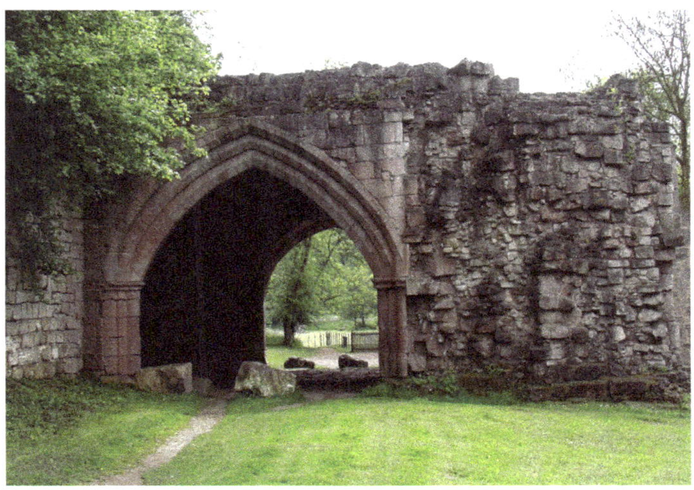

Sawley (Salley) Abbey

St Mary and St Andrew • Cistercian 1147–1536

Against the dramatic backdrop of Pendle Hill, the ruins of this Cistercian abbey on the banks of the River Ribble appear rather insignificant. This feeling is heightened by the fact that only some of the church walls, mainly the rubble core, stand to any substantial height. The stonework of the remaining monastic buildings barely extends above ground, although excavations have made it possible to gain an insight into the layout of the abbey. The shortened nave of the church is evidence of the early poverty of the abbey, and the arrangement of some of the other buildings indicates that there has been some remodelling during the abbey's existence, and possibly after its suppression.

Of particular interest are the remains of the monks' night stairs to the dormitory, leading from a corner of the south transept, and patches of medieval tiles that have survived in several areas throughout the church. The church had a crossing tower, and there were three chapels in each transept. The cloister lay in the angle between the nave and the south transept in the traditional Cistercian arrangement, with the chapter house to the east, refectory to the south, and the lay-brothers' range on the western side. Fragments of service buildings can be seen in the village and surrounding fields. A reminder of architectural embellishments is provided in the display of carved corbels and decorative stonework rescued from the rubble. Outlying earthworks of the monastic fields can also be recognised. True, Sawley Abbey was never a large abbey, but its stunning setting on the banks of the River Ribble, and an interesting history, make it beneficial for the traveller to break the journey, pause a while, and reflect on times long past.

Originally known as Salley Abbey, Sawley was founded by William de Percy II, son of Alan Percy 'The Great', in 1147. The first abbot, Benedict, with twelve monks and ten conversi came from Newminster in Northumberland, a daughter house of Fountains Abbey, but the new community soon found the going tough. Described as *"terra nebulosa et pluviosa"* (foggy and rainy), and later in the reign of Edward II as "for the most part barren and unfruitful," crops continually failed and serious consideration was given in the 1180s to abandon the site and move elsewhere. However, an endowment of a church, chapel and pension by Maud de Percy, Countess of Warwick, saved the abbey, which was then still under construction. Being located alongside an important north-south route, the monks were required to provide frequent hospitality to travellers, thus incurring greater expense. The community also suffered from frequent incursions by the Scots, who were responsible for "the cruel and inhuman spoliation of all their moveables and the horrible burning of some of their places".

The abbey became involved in two bitter feuds. Disputes over the patronage of nearby Gisburn church, settled by the archbishop of York in 1226, continued to fester and in 1285, the then abbot of Sawley took the vicar to court for "entering the Abbot's warren and carrying off game'. The move of Stanlaw Abbey to Whalley in 1296 was seen as a threat to the survival of Sawley, with the monks claiming that the close proximity of Whalley was pushing up the price of building materials, timber, salt, iron, and bark for the tannery, and imperilled its trade. The wrangle continued until settled by a commission of Cistercian abbots in 1305, when co-operation replaced confrontation. In 1306, the abbot and several monks were excommunicated, but the reason for this has not been recorded. The abbots of Sawley were summoned to Parliament on no less than nine occasions from 1294 to 1307.

The abbey was suppressed in May 1536. Apart from Abbot Thomas Bolton, there were twenty monks and twenty-one servants in residence. Its annual net worth had been assessed in the *Valor Ecclesiasticus* at £147 3s. During the uprising in the North, the so-called Pilgrimage of Grace, the monks returned under a new abbot, William Trafford. In October, hundreds of rebels descended on Whalley to force Abbot Paisley to join the revolt, but were dispersed upon the arrival of Thomas Stanley, Earl of Derby. Although Stanley promised immunity, both abbots, two monks from Sawley, and two local men were arrested and hanged for high treason at Lancaster Castle in March 1537. The abbey site and other property were granted to Sir Arthur Darcy de Gray, who also took possession of Fountains Abbey. Sawley Abbey was stripped of all its valuables and its buildings largely left to decay and the stone sold. A large house was built close to the claustral range, but this had been demolished by 1884. Fragments of it can still be seen.

Photos – clockwise from top

Chapels in transept of abbey church
Remains of abbey church
Fragments of tiled floor
Ornate stonework with carved face
Monks' reredorter
Foundations of chapter house

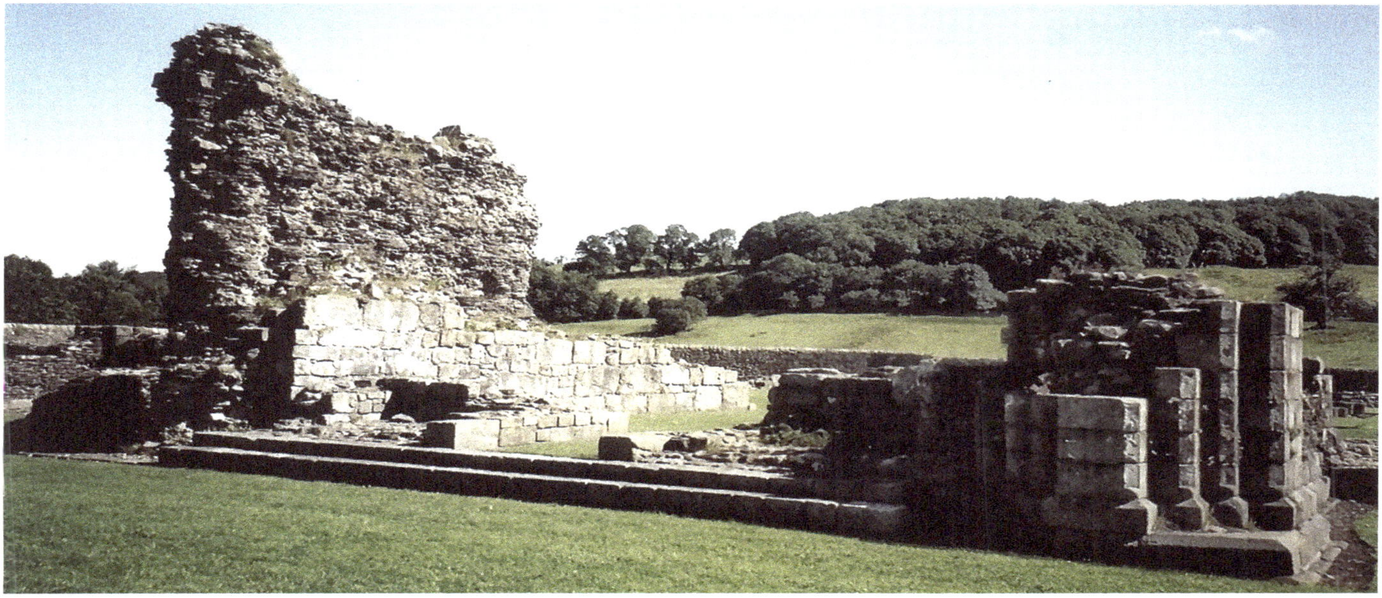

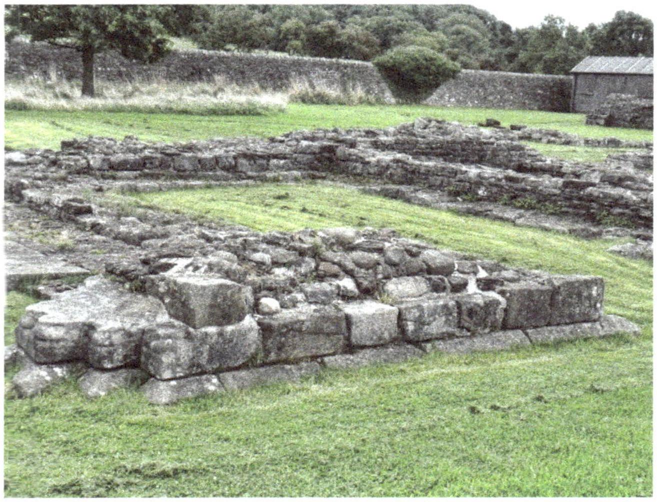

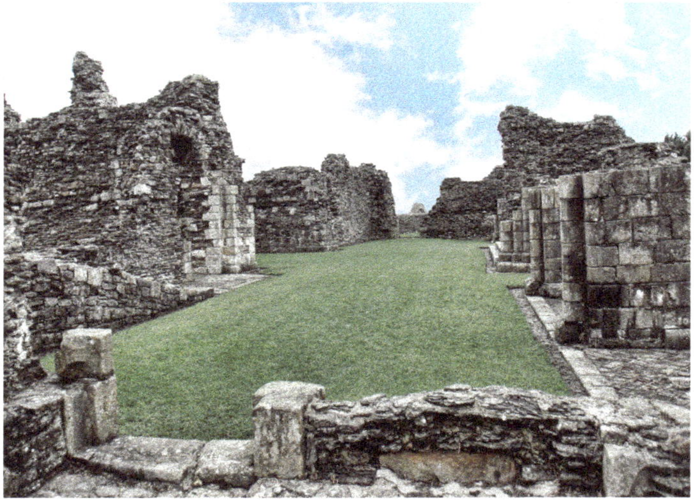

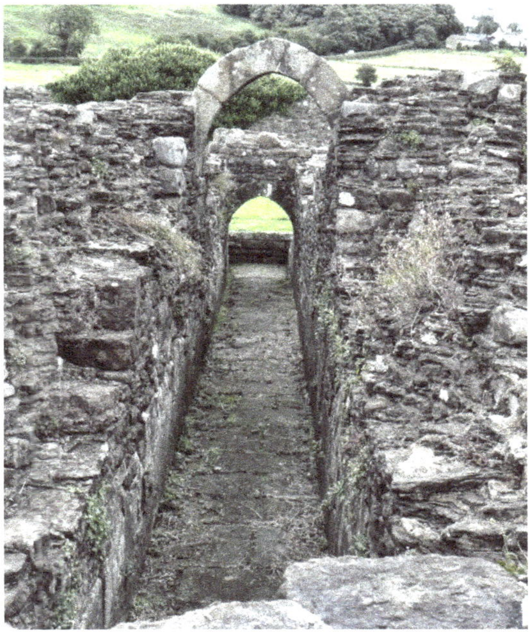

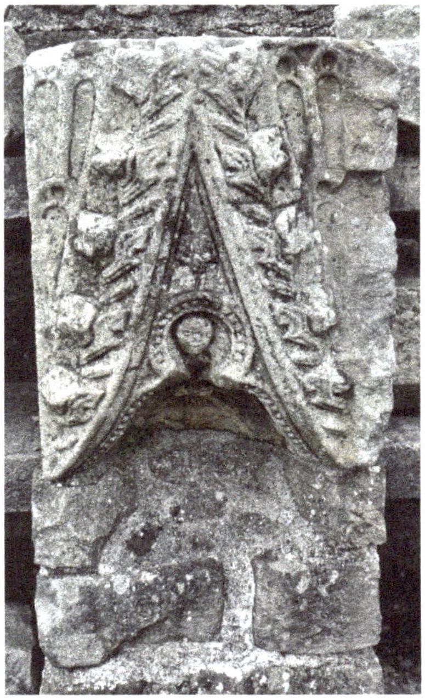

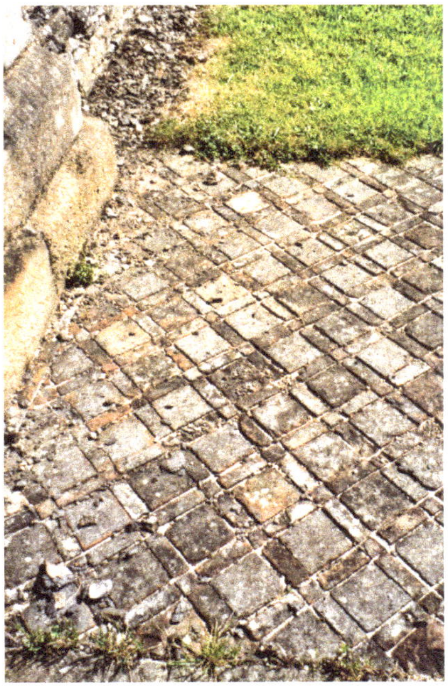

Selby Abbey

St Mary and St Germain • Benedictine 1069–1539

The magnificent abbey church, dedicated to St Mary the Virgin and St Germain, is all that is left of a huge abbey complex, once one of the most important in Yorkshire. It stands on high ground surrounded by the decaying industrial landscape of a town that has seen better days, yet serves as a beacon of hope for a population that has suffered heavily from the disappearance of vital trade. While the abbot's house and other monastic buildings were pulled down or fell into ruin after the Dissolution, the church survived as the parish church, at first unofficially, but legalised in 1618. The impressive gatehouse was dismantled in 1806. The appearance of the abbey church today is much as it was in medieval times, although floods and fire in more recent times have necessitated some repairs and rebuilding, especially after considerable damage caused by a fire in 1906.

The external appearance of the abbey church is low and powerful, with a mixture of Norman and Early Gothic, culminating at the chancel end in an abundance of fourteenth century buttresses, pinnacles and the tracery of the east window. Once through the west door, the visitor is faced by a mighty eight-bay nave with triforium and clerestory, the earliest parts dating to Norman times. The two eastern piers have trellis decoration, and the capitals throughout are rich and varied, ranging from scalloped, figurative and foliate to water-leaf designs. The post-fire roof incorporates a number of original bosses saved from the wreckage. The arcade spandrels support figures of saints. The four sedilia in the chancel are notable for the soaring filigree stonework, attributed to the celebrated architect, Henry Yevele. This attack on the visual senses is but a prelude to the *pièce de rèsistance*, the magnificent Jesse Window, one of the finest in England, which was constructed in 1340 and still retains its medieval glass, having been saved during a disastrous fire in 1340 when the wind changed direction. The chapter house, dormitory, treasury and other buildings suffered greatly and the church became in part ruinous. The window consists of seven lights, with beautiful flamboyant tracery above, which incorporates the Doom, representing men and women rising from their graves to go to judgment. St Michael is in the centre, with balance in hand, weighing souls. From Jesse reposing at the base of the window, the family tree branches spread upwards to the Lord in his Mother's arms in the top centre pane.

The abbey's history began in 1069 when Benedict, a monk from Auxerre, arrived in Selby with the dried finger of St Germain. Legend has it that a vision led him to that part of Yorkshire to found an abbey. He duly received a charter from William the Conqueror the following year, together with lands at Flaxley, Brayton and Rawcliffe. Benedict became the first abbot, but his tenure was cut short when he was forced to resign on the grounds of cruelty. When two monks tried to abscond with valuables from the abbey's treasury, he had them castrated. Morale among the community then reached such a low ebb that the monks talked about leaving Selby, and it was only the intervention of Henry I, the Conqueror's youngest son, who according to tradition was born in Selby, that monastic life continued and flourished under Abbot Hugh. Benedict's successor removed the abbey a short distance from Church Hill and began an extensive rebuilding in stone, including the wonderful cruciform church. Abbot Hugh himself toiled alongside the workmen for the same wage, which he donated to the poor.

Although on a slight eminence, the site chosen was only three feet above the water-table, with thin layers of sand above and clay below, presenting considerable engineering challenges. The thin layer of impervious clay essentially carried the enormous weight of the church, but also caused frequent flooding of the surrounding area. When the heavy central tower was added, it began to sink, cracking and distorting the adjacent arches, the effect on which can still be seen today. It took 130 years to realise Abbot Hugh's vision, but the end result was one of the most beautiful and influential abbeys in the north. The solid Norman pillars and arches later gave way to more elegant Early English designs, and, following the appointment of William Aslakeby as abbot in 1280, a new larger choir and the Jesse window at the east end completed the church much as it is today. In 1256, the abbey was granted the mitre, an honour it shared with St Mary's Abbey in York.

The abbey benefited financially from the wool trade, operation of a ferry across the Ouse, and markets and fairs, which attracted many visitors. Its coffers were further boosted by a succession of wealthy benefactors. However, soon after the appointment of Thomas de Whalley in the second half of the thirteenth century, he and several monks were accused of mismanaging abbey funds, and of loose living and immorality. Although the situation improved under William Aslakeby, later visitations again found the abbey heavily in debt and burdened by pensions, a situation that persisted through its remaining existence. Immorality and indiscipline also still bedevilled the community. Selby Abbey was dissolved in December 1539. The last abbot Robert Selby, Prior Robert Midgley and James Laye, the prior of the cell at Snaith, were pensioned off, together with twenty-three monks and two novices.

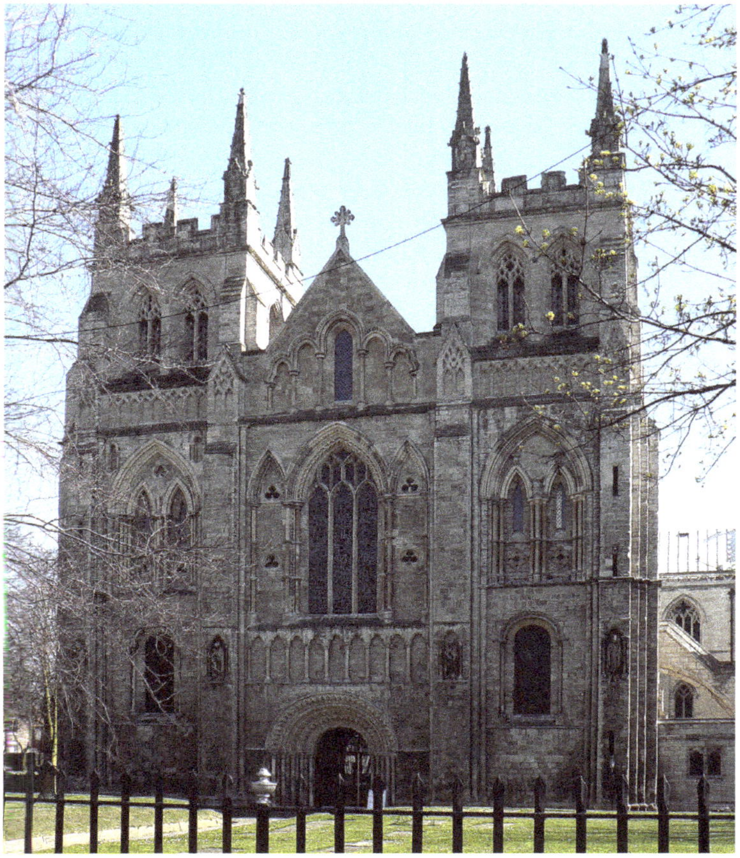

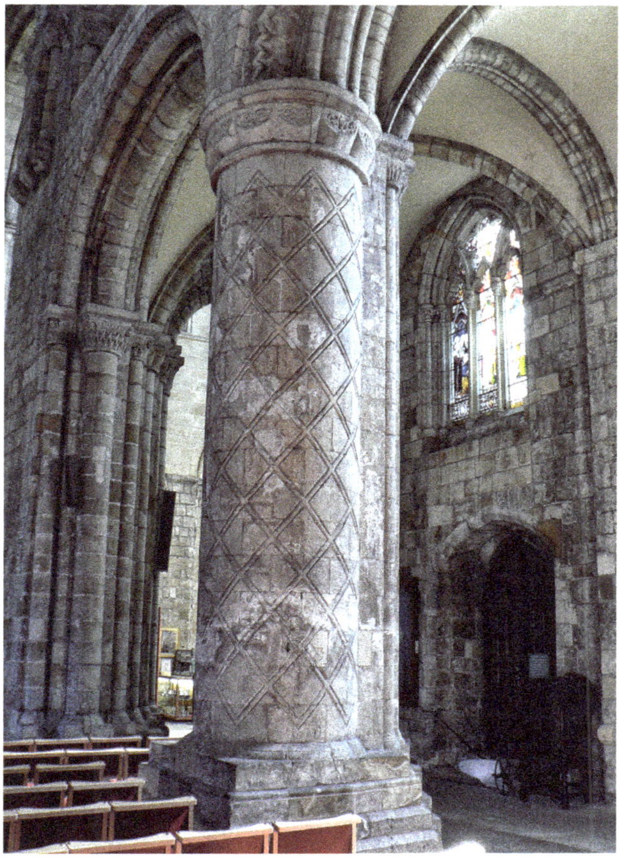

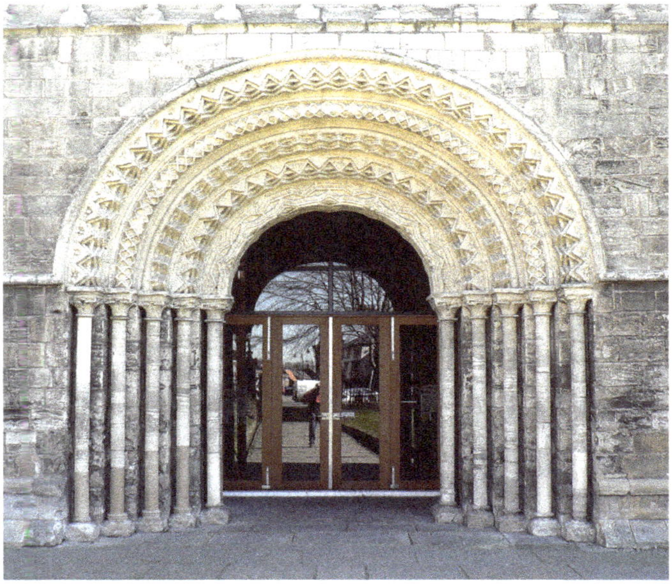

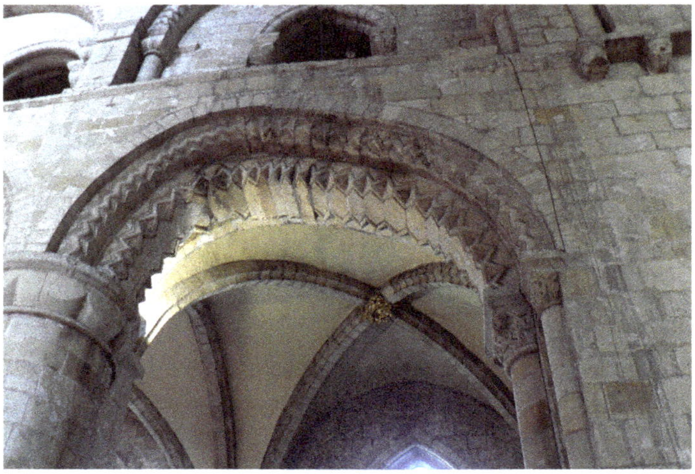

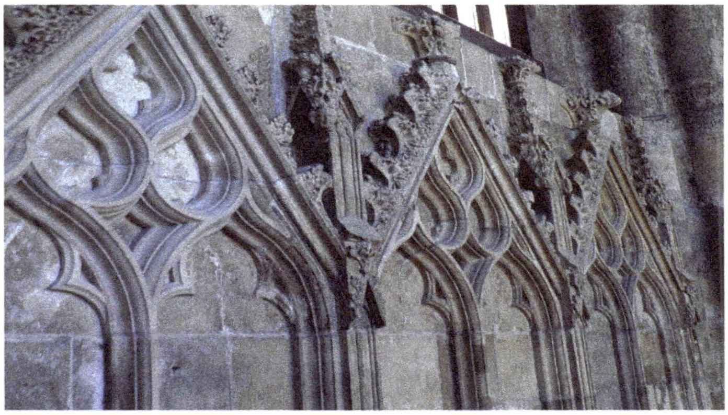

Photos – clockwise from top left

West front of abbey church with twin pinnacle towers
Pier in the nave arcade with trellis decoration
Distorted arches from the time when the central tower began to sink
Delicate filigree work on sedilia
Decorated west door arch supported on two sets of five colonettes

Sinningthwaite Priory

St Mary • Cistercian nuns c1160–1536

In the midst of a modern holiday complex stands a two-storey building that once was part of the south range of this Cistercian nunnery dedicated to St Mary the Virgin. The most noteworthy remains are a late Norman doorway on the northern side, with leaf capitals on plain freestanding columns, an arch with zigzag decoration intersecting across a roll-moulding, and two smaller blank arches alongside, which may have been part of arcading in the cloister. Stone carvings exist in the wall opposite, but nothing else is left. The moat surrounding the farm buildings, associated with the priory, is visible on aerial photos as earthworks.

The priory was founded c1160 by Bertram de Haget and his son and daughter, with the consent of his overlord, Roger de Mowbray. The nuns were gifted the site and the advowson of the church at Bilton, and later received land at Esholt in Guiseley near Leeds, on which was founded a house with nuns from Sinningthwaite.

No major incidents have been recorded of the life within the priory, but a visiting archbishop issued an injunction that "the door of the dorter was to be firmly locked, so that nuns cannot get out, and other persons cannot get in". The nuns were also ordered not to allow any man, to sleep in the wool-house under the dormitory, or within the inner cloister, where it would be possible to have access to the nuns, or the nuns to have access to that building. Clearly, some nuns had found temptation too great to resist. The nuns were also ordered to take greater care of the sick, not to leave the precinct without licence, and to limit visits by the Friars Minor to hear confessions. There were also allusions to the inadequacy of the clothing of the poorer nuns who were 'afflicted by the cold contrary to the honesty of religion'. In August 1536, Prioress Katherine Foster, the sub-prioress and nine nuns, together with eight servants, signed the Deed of Surrender. The priory had been valued at £60 15s.

Snaith Priory

St Lawrence • Benedictine c1310–1539

In the episcopate of Gerard, Archbishop of York (1101-08), the church of St Lawrence in Snaith was granted to the abbot of the Benedictine abbey of Selby, which derived considerable income from this valuable gift. At the time, Snaith, which is thought to mean 'enclosed by water', was a busy port with a harbour and ferry across the river to Selby, one of the few crossings of the Aire in the area. In 1310, the church and manor became a cell to Selby when Archbishop William Greenfeld directed that the abbot could place two monks and a secular priest permanently at Snaith. Several quarrels arose later over church and manor, but the abbot was always able to maintain complete jurisdiction over the priory. Snaith was a Peculiar, which enabled it to have its own ecclesiastical court and was largely exempt from the jurisdiction of the bishop. This would explain that whenever the bishop's visitors came to the priory to investigate reported 'indiscretions' the monks summoned the ferry to the Snaith bank, so that they could not cross the river! Snaith Priory was a staging post for pilgrims travelling from Lincoln to York, which brought some income to the monks, in exchange for their hospitality. When Selby was surrendered to the King's commissioners in December 1539, Snaith Priory also ceased to exist. The last prior, Jacob Laye, was pensioned off. The priory's value was assessed at only £12 2s.

The priory church has survived as the parish church. It stands in a peaceful, tree-lined churchyard adjacent to what was once the old Buttermarket and started life as a Saxon foundation, although very little of the original Saxon church remains. The present clerestoried building, 52m (170ft) long, dates from 1086. Of note within is a roodloft stair enclosed in a pillar, but the rood screen is no more. The east window of the Dawnay Chapel retains the only remaining fragments of fourteenth century glass, and also of note in the chapel is the tomb of Sir John Dawnay of 1493, which is adorned with painted shields. A stone in the chancel floor once held one of the biggest brass portraits in England. It was a mitred figure with a staff, perhaps an abbot of Selby. Near the chancel arch is a niche dedicated to St Sitha, whose only claim to fame is that she was martyred. According to local tradition, her head was cut off and she picked it up and ran three miles to the nearest church to warn other Christians. The only other shrine to that little known saint is in Bradford Cathedral. The unconsecrated building at the back of the church was the Consistory Court, which was used to try ecclesiastical matters and to deal with disputed wills and land settlements.

Photos – clockwise from top left

Parts of south range of Sinningthwiate Priory
Late Norman doorway with zigzag decoration
Carved stonework set into garden wall
Snaith Priory Church of St Lawrence
Roodloft stair within pillar
Tomb of Sir John Dawnay with painted shields
Niche of the little-known martyred St Sitha

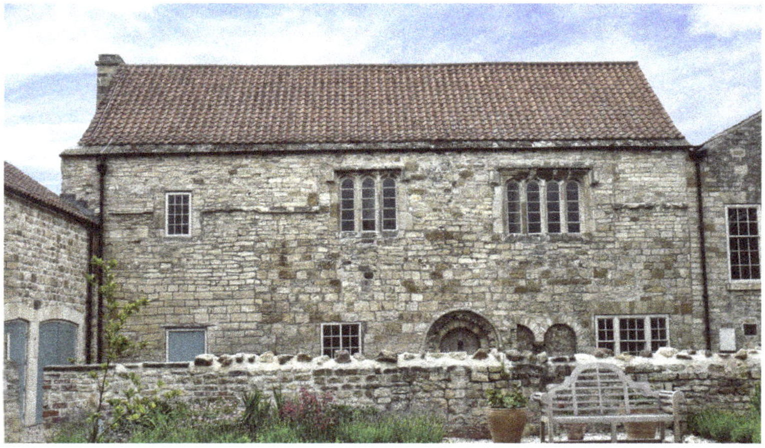

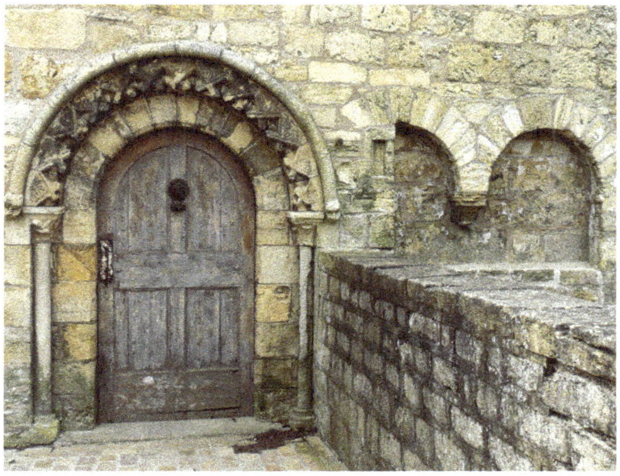

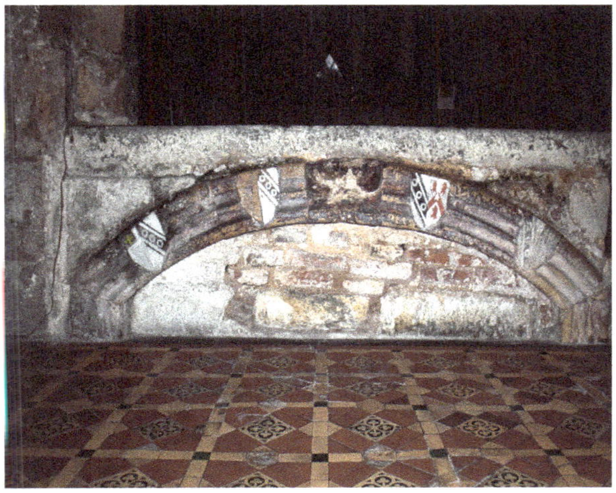

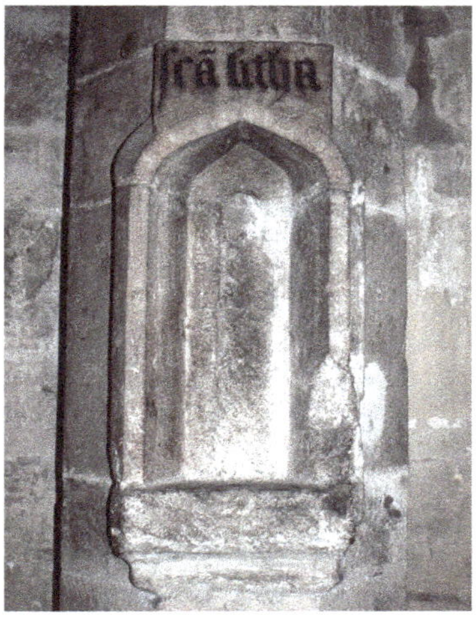

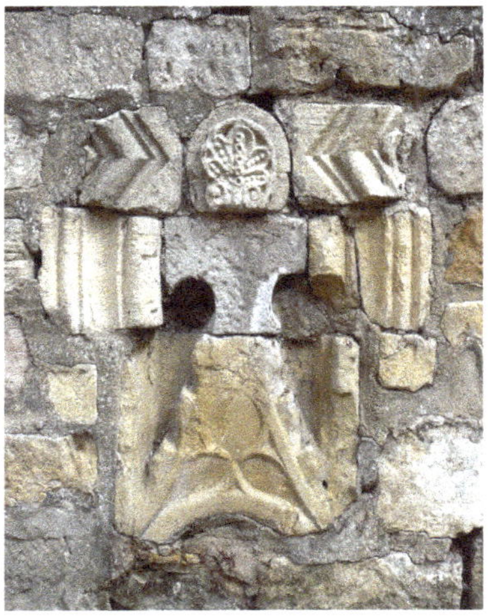

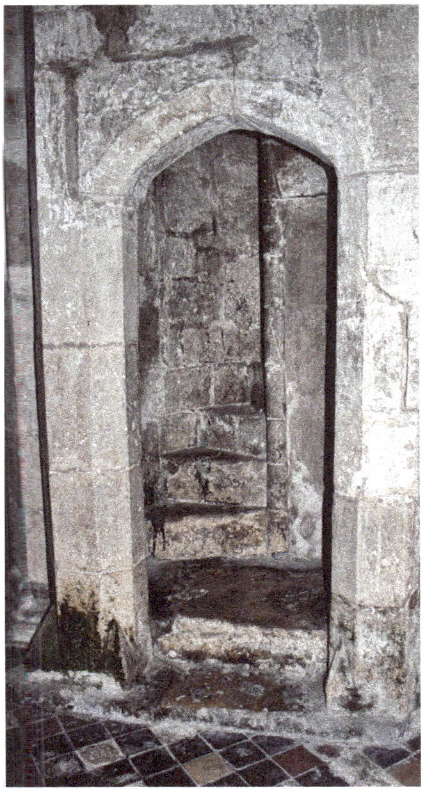

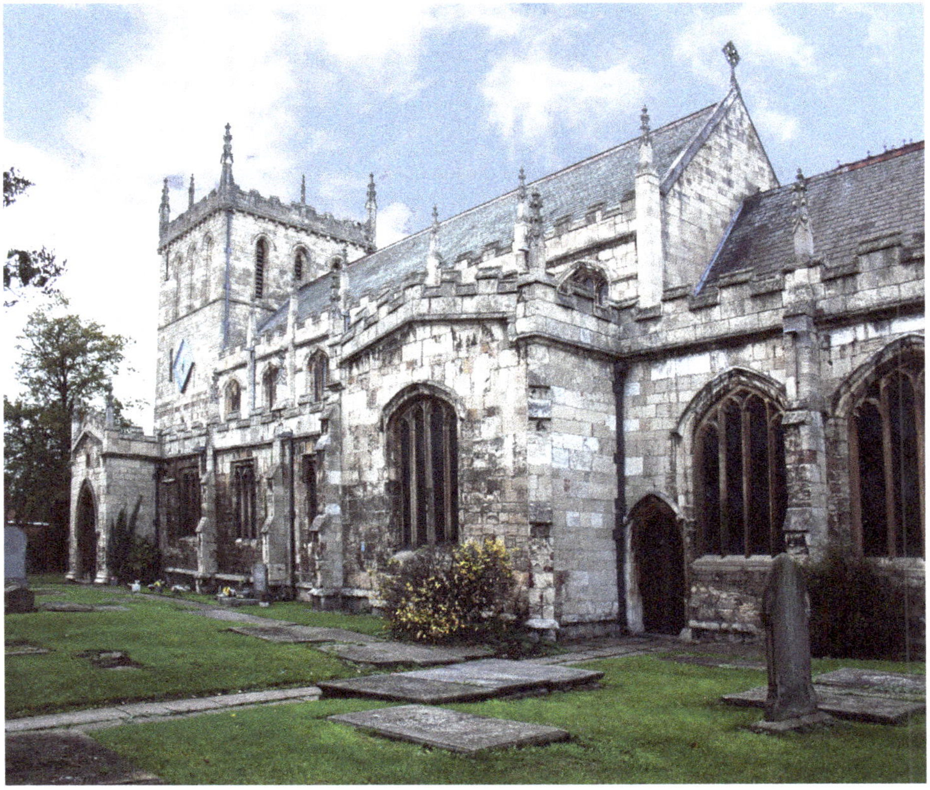

Tickhill Austin Friars

c1256–1538

Although only fragments have survived from Tickhill, these present a valuable snapshot of this house for Augustinian friars. Of particular interest is the near perfect former chapel door, which has a pointed arch and a double row of quatrefoils. It is now incorporated into a wall surrounding a kitchen garden. A few shields of arms can be seen in the desecrated walls of a building overlooking the flower garden. The house, known as The Friary, dates largely from the thirteenth and fourteenth centuries, with twentieth century alterations, although which dwellings of the original priory this formed part of is not at all certain. The more ornate west wing may have been the refectory, with the east wing thought to have been used for domestic purposes, as indicated by a fireplace and possible garderobe. It has also been suggested that the original entrance hall of the house was part of the priory chapel. Nevertheless, uncertainty apart, the presence of arches, stepped buttresses and a leper squint leaves no doubt over its ecclesiastical provenance. A visit to the parish church will reveal a richly painted alabaster monument, which was removed from the priory after the Dissolution. It bears the effigies of Sir Richard fitzWilliam, Knight, and Lady Lucy Nevill, and is adorned with the arms of the fitzWilliam, Clarel and Nevill families.

The priory was founded c1256 towards the end of the reign of Henry III by John Clarel, warden of Queen Eleanor's chapel in Tickhill Castle and canon of Southwell, who resided at nearby Clarel Hall. Over the years, the friars received gifts of arable land, orchards, meadows and pastures, as well as property in Tickhill and Newton on Derwent. The Clarel family remained great benefactors, which also included Thomas, Earl of Lancaster, Sir Hugh Hastings and, most importantly, the royal family. In 1276, Edward I granted a licence to inclose a lane between their dwelling and the land of William Clarel, and in 1279, the King gave four oaks for the building of the church. On the death of his mother, Eleanor of Provence, in 1291, the community received 40s from the executors of her will. His son, Edward II, and grandson, Edward III, were equally generous. Edward II gave six shillings for one day's food to the eighteen friars in 1300, and Edward III gave 4d to each of the twenty-four friars then in residence. In the fifteenth century, local landowner, Sir Richard fitzWilliam, inherited the patronage of the priory upon his marriage to Elizabeth, heiress of the Clarels of Aldwarke. Many of the founder's descendants were buried in the church. The priory was dissolved in November 1538 when Prior Richard Robinson and eight brethren signed the Deed of Surrender in the presence of the King's commissioner, Sir George Lawson. It was leased out, but following its sale by the Crown in 1589, the priory had numerous owners and tenants.

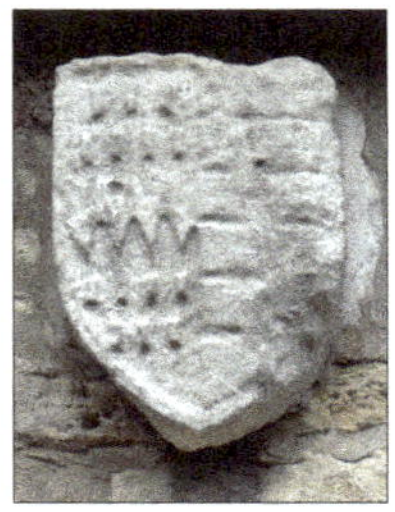
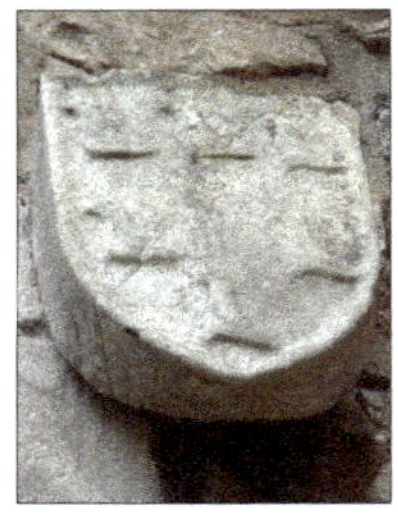
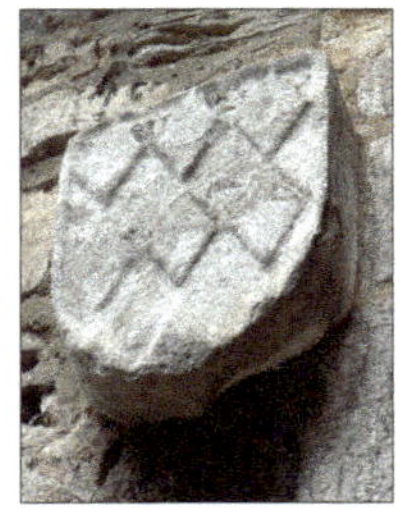

Woodkirk Priory

St Mary • Augustinian 1121/27–1540

Between 1121 and 1127, a small monastic cell of three or four Austin canons was established when the lord of the manor, William de Warenne, together with Ralph Lisle and his son, William, gave the parish church of St Mary to Nostell Priory. Just before his death in 1135, Henry I granted a royal charter for two three-day fairs, one to be held before the Feast of the Assumption of Mary, the other before the feast of the Nativity. These fairs were confirmed by King Stephen in 1136. Originally known as Woodkirk Fair, the tradition has survived to this day, although it is now known as Lee Fair, after Thomas Lee, a commissioner for Henry VIII, who acquired the priory's property after its dissolution in 1540 It was then valued at £47 0s. Almost nothing else is known of this small cell. The parish church was built on the site of the monastic church, and excavations in the 1960s uncovered part of the cloister to the north of the church, and foundations of buildings of the north and east claustral ranges. Finds are lodged in the Bagshaw museum in Batley.

Photos of Tickhill Austin Friars- clockwise from top

Thirteenth and fourteenth century priory building
Double arch starting outside and continued on the inside
Former chapel door with double quatrefoils
Painted alabaster fitzWilliam monument in parish church
Heraldic shields on desecrated walls (above)

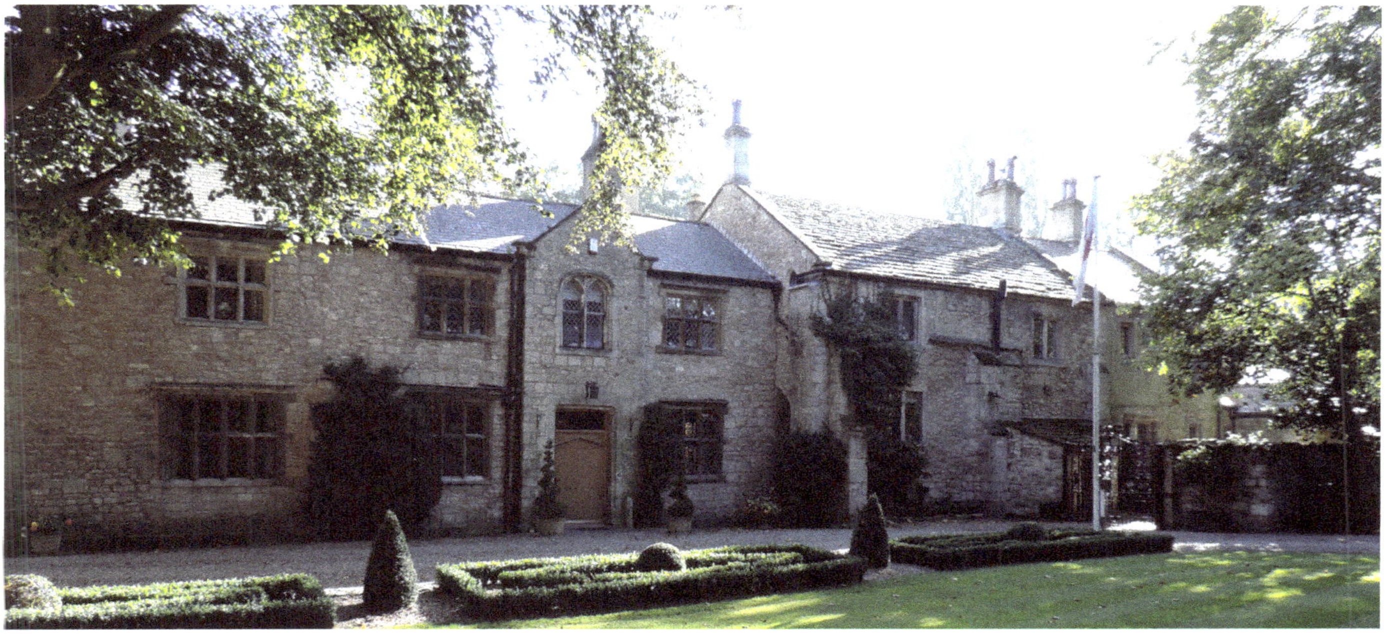

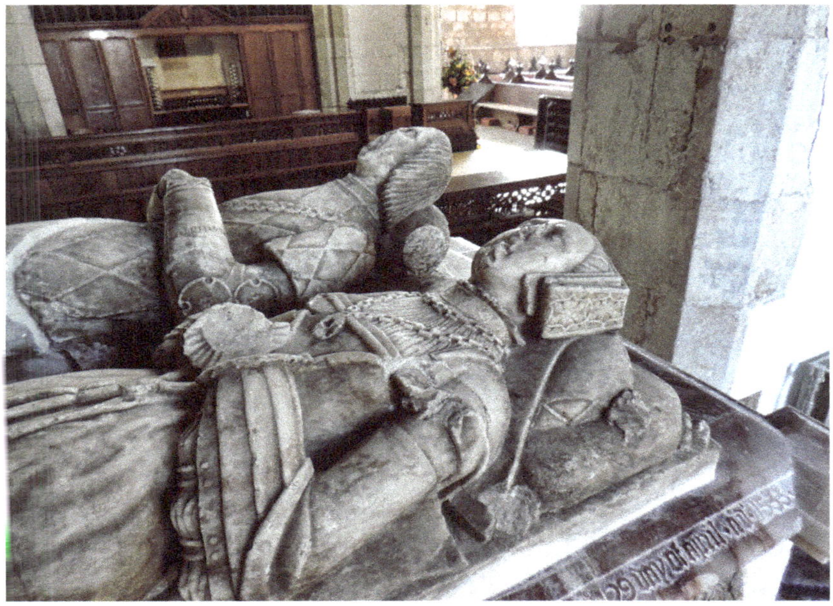

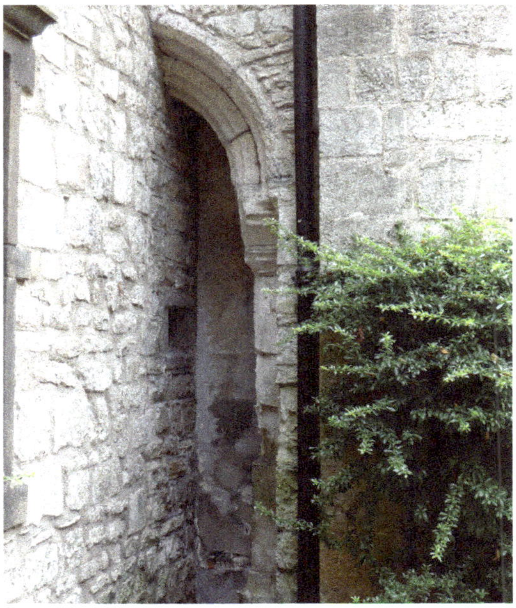

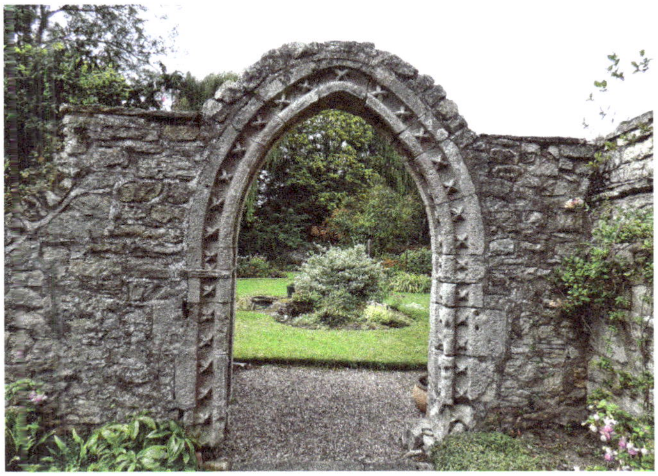

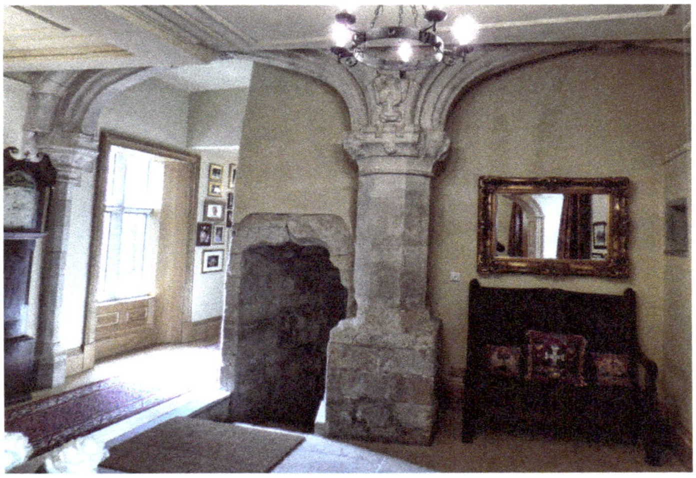

York St Mary`s Abbey

▪ Benedictine 1089–1539

The beautiful ruins of St Mary's Abbey, once the most influential and wealthiest Benedictine foundation in the north, stand to the west of York Minster, in the well-tended gardens of the Yorkshire Museum. Although the remains of the abbey are scant, its setting among flowers and manicured lawns make it a delightful place to visit. In the sun, the pale stone looks almost white, adding another dimension to the experience. What is particularly notable among the fine remains of the Gothic church, designed and built by architect Simon de Pabenham during the abbacy of Simon de Warwick between 1270 and 1294, is the richness of the surviving architectural detail, which indicates that the Benedictine monks soon deserted their principles of a simple monastic life. Indeed, it was dissatisfaction with this trend, which caused thirteen monks from the abbey to venture north and establish Fountains Abbey near Ripon in 1132.

Above ground, the most prominent feature is the north aisle of the nave with its fine decorated arches and blind arcading, which every four years forms the backdrop to the York mystery plays. Elaborate carvings also survive in parts of the transept, the west front and the outer wall of the chancel. Enough of the window tracery remains to reveal an alternating pattern between a single large circle over two lights and three small circles over three lights. Most surviving column capitals are decorated with stiff-leaf foliage, although more natural leaf applications can be seen in later parts of the wall. Apart from the picturesque abbey church, fragments of several monastic buildings are scattered throughout the park. These include the abbot's house, incorporated in the King's Manor, the timber-framed hospitium or guesthouse with adjacent remains of the watergate, the largely fifteenth century gatehouse in Marygate alongside St Olave's church, and the chapel of St Mary on the Walls. The vestibule of the chapter house, parlour and the south cloister walk have been reconstructed *in situ* within the museum, which also displays fragments of domestic buildings, and many statues, carvings and roof bosses salvaged from the abbey. It is also worth taking a look at the ruined St Leonard's Hospital, the largest medieval hospital in the north of England.

The abbey was founded for Benedictine monks by King William II, in atonement for the terrible deeds his father and he had committed in York. It replaced an earlier foundation, established by Count Alan of Brittany, Earl of Richmond, on a smaller site at nearby Marygate, dedicated to St Olave. The monks came from Whitby via Lastingham, and Stephen became the first abbot of the new foundation. When the King visited York in 1088, he decided that St Olave's was too constricted for a monastery and he himself, in the presence of an impressive gathering of Norman nobles and churchmen, laid the foundation stone in 1089 for a much bigger church sited on additional land next to St Olave's and dedicated to St Mary. This church was partially taken down in the late thirteenth century to make way for the Gothic church whose spectacular ruins still grace the Museum Gardens. The widespread acquisition of land, fairs, churches and tithes, both inside and outside Yorkshire, together with many royal privileges, made St Mary's Abbey the wealthiest and most powerful monastery in the North. The abbots became mitred in 1245 and regularly attended Parliament, collected taxes for King and Pope, and for many years housed the royal treasury for the defence of the northern lands.

The location of the abbey just outside the city walls, which provided its eastern boundary, caused considerable friction between the abbot and city officials over territorial and jurisdictional rights, as well as personal disputes between the abbey tenants and the citizens of York. The walls surrounding the abbey were constructed in 1266, following an attack by the citizens, who threatened to crucify the abbot, castrate the novices and murder the monks, over a dispute about the market at Bootham. Battlements were added to the walls in 1318 in response to the threat of a Scottish invasion. The uneasy relationship with the citizens took a turn for the worse in 1343 and 1350, when the monks were again threatened with violence and their food supplies were cut off. The abbey was besieged and the abbot and some monks fled. Conflict once more flared up in the mid-fifteenth century, when the city lost a court case over the abbey fish garths in the Ouse, which it claimed obstructed river navigation and therefore restricted commerce. These disputes should not, however, overshadow the fact that great benefits also accrued to the city from employment of labourers on the abbey's lands, specialist craftsmen such as masons, and charitable works undertaken by the monks. St Mary's Abbey was dissolved in November 1539, when Abbot William Thornton, who had been accused of having a sinful relationship with his housekeeper at Overton, the prior and forty-seven monks surrendered it to Henry VIII's commissioners. It was gradually dismantled and its stone used for many buildings in the city, including the eighteenth century reconstruction of St Olave's Church.

Photos - clockwise from top

North aisle of nave with fine decorations
Impressively ornate chancel arch
Timber-framed hospitium with watergate
Remains of gatehouse in Marygate
The ruined St Leonard's Hospital

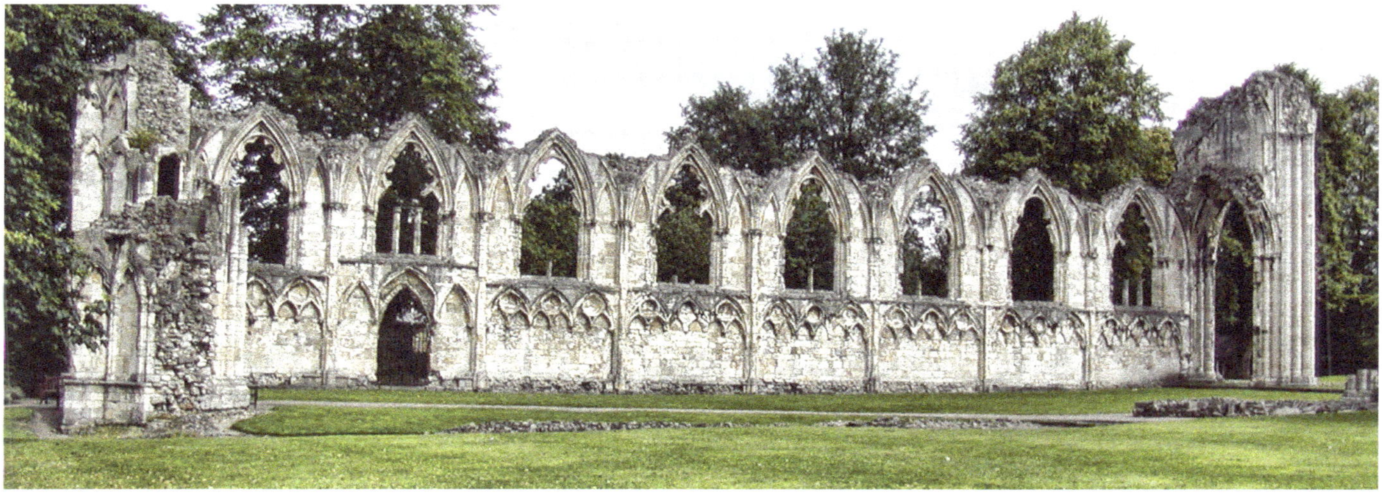

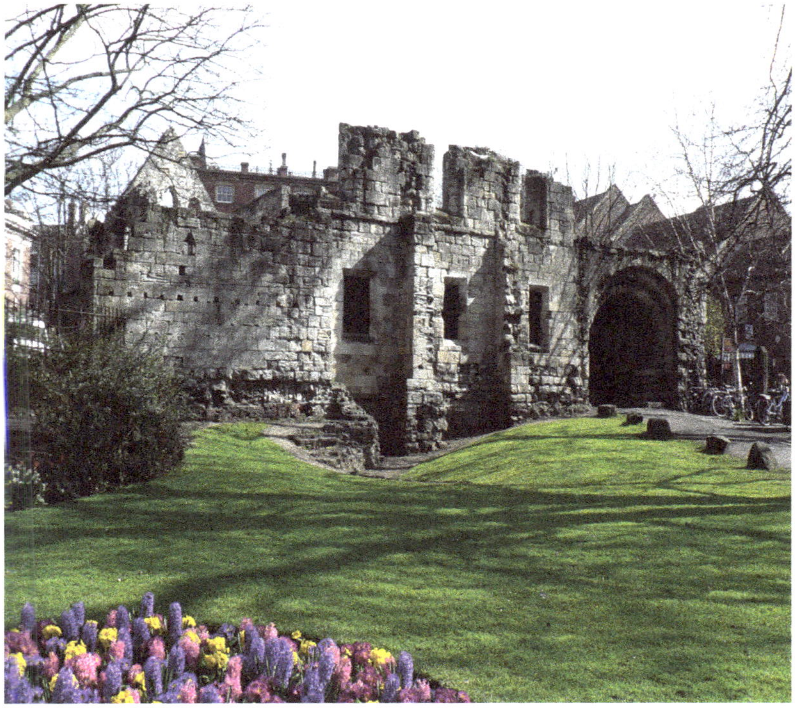

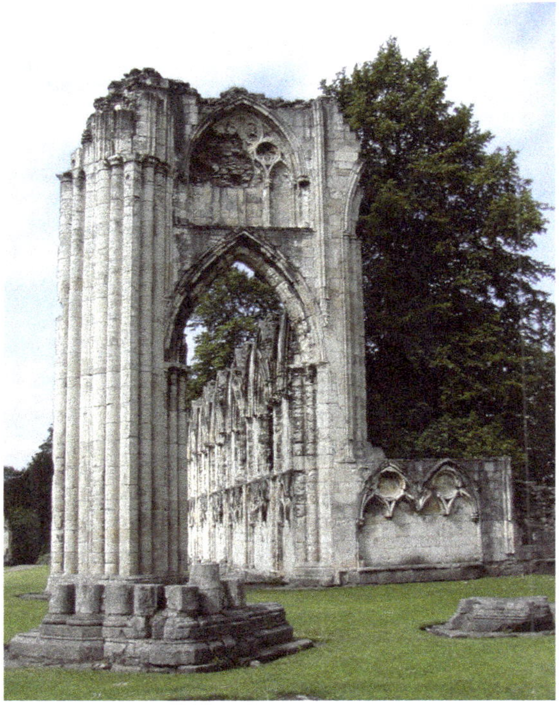

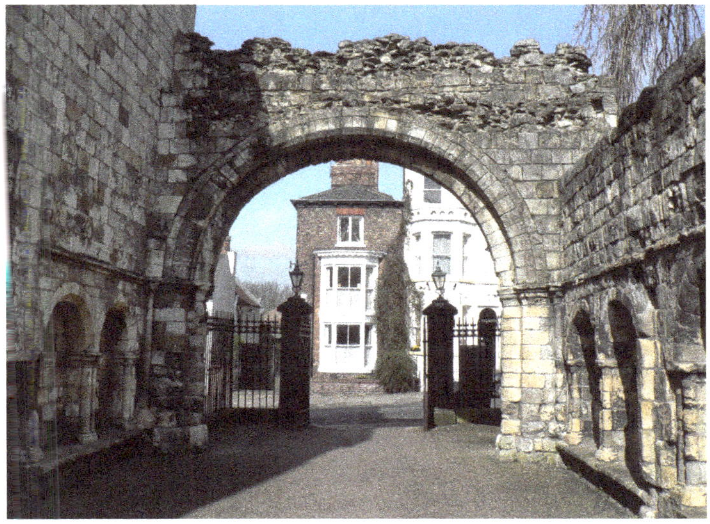

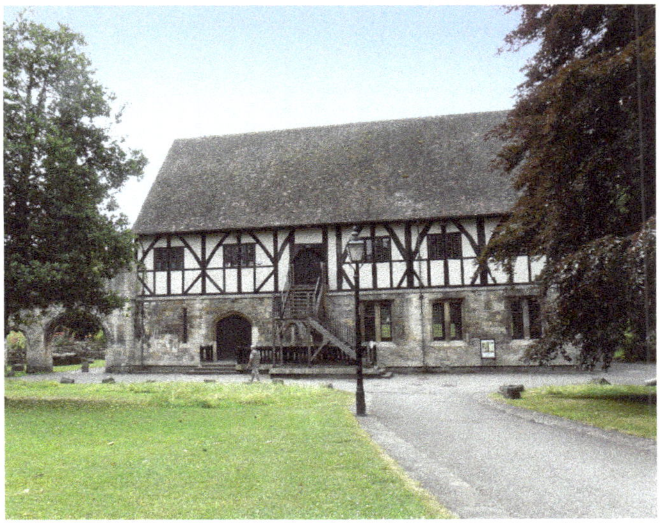

York Clementhorpe Priory

St Clement • Benedictine nuns c1130–1536

This priory for Benedictine nuns was founded without the walls of York about 1130 by Archbishop Thurstan, whose grants were confirmed by the dean and chapter. In 1192, Archbishop Geoffrey Plantagenet granted the priory to the abbey of Godstow in Oxfordshire. The prioress is said to have gone to Rome to appeal to the pope, who found in the nuns' favour, in spite of them being excommunicated by the archbishop. The nuns thus regained their independence. The history of the house was largely unremarkable, but it was often plagued by minor misdemeanours, internal dissent, and a non-observance of the rules. It was also in debt, which prompted Archbishop Melton after a visitation in 1317 to order the nuns to cease supplying loaves to the Friars Minor and Friars Preachers of York. He also forbade to allow little girls, or males of any age, or secular women, to sleep in the dormitory with the nuns. The *Valor Ecclesiasticus* of 1535 showed an annual value of the nunnery of only £55 11s, and in August 1536, eight nuns and nine servants surrendered the house to the King's commissioners, Dr Thomas Legh and Dr Richard Layton, who reported that pilgrimages were made to the priory because of the presence of some milk of the Blessed Virgin!

York Fishergate Priory

All Saints • Benedictine +1097-1536?

Every trace of this small priory cell to Whitby Abbey vanished amid the many changes the area in the vicinity of Fishergate Bar has undergone, and its exact location is no longer known. The church of All Saints was granted by William II (1087-1100) to the prior of Whitby, on the condition that some of the monks should be present there at all times. A charter of confirmation by Archbishop Murdac (1145-53) ratified All Saints as "a proper cell for monks of Wyteby free and clear from every Episcopal usage". Its modest revenues were derived from lands in Bustardthorpe and other properties in the neighbourhood, but these were insufficient to sustain the three or four monks in residence and any shortfall is likely to have been made up by the mother house. It has been suggested that the monks were recalled to Whitby before 1536. By that time, the church had already fallen into disuse and had disappeared altogether by 1539.

York Holy Trinity Priory

• Benedictine 1089–1538

Behind Micklegate Bar, through which Kings usually entered the city, and in the shadow of the town wall stood the Benedictine priory of the Holy Trinity. It was the oldest monastic site in York, as there was a Minster here before the Norman Conquest. It suffered almost complete destruction by fire in 1069 during the Harrying of the North, and was described in the Domesday Book of 1086 as "a ruined and poverty stricken church". It was refounded by Ralph Paynell in 1089 and granted to the French abbey of St Martin of Tours (Marmoutier), which was located outside Tours in Indre-et-Loire. The French abbot sent Benedictine monks to York to take over and revive the priory, which was given fourteen churches, extensive lands and several fisheries bynumerous benefactors.

It is now completely submerged in modern development and the only reminder is the five-bay, aisled nave and west front of the present church of the Holy Trinity, and the fifteenth century north-west tower. The church was largely rebuilt after the great fire in York in 1137 and dates from the late twelfth century. It continued as the parish church after the Dissolution, but suffered severe damage in 1551, when the central Norman tower fell in a freak storm and destroyed the choir and transepts. Its stone was used to repair the city walls and Ouse Bridge. The church was restored, but is now only half the size it once was. Nevertheless, it is the only monastic church in York still in use. The life of the monks of Micklegate is explored in an interactive exhibition in the church. Sections of the choir walls are preserved in the rectory gardens. The thirteenth century gateway to the priory was demolished in 1850 to make way for the building of Priory Street. The gateway was the starting point for the York Mystery Plays in medieval times.

As an alien priory, its monks often suffered persecution, which became particularly prevalent during the Hundred Years' War with France, when the priory was charged with harbouring spies and sending supplies to the enemy. In spite of such harassment, it survived the closure of all alien houses by Henry V in 1414, and in 1426 successfully petitioned the new King Henry VI for naturalisation and was given responsibility of the hospital of St Nicholas. However, the wars with France had pushed the community into poverty, which was eased somewhat by the granting of exemption from taxes in 1446. Further help came from Richard, Duke of Gloucester (later Richard III), in 1478. The priory was dissolved in 1538 and, together with its estates, was granted to Leonard Beckwith of Stillington, near York. Although the prior was implicated in the Pilgrimage of Grace, he avoided being tried and was pensioned off.

York St Andrew's Priory

Gilbertine 1195/1202–1538

From its origins in c1050 through its early history, the church of St Andrew underwent several complex and confusing ownership changes until it was given by Hugh Murdac, prebendary of Driffield, rector of Bamburgh and later 'disputed' archdeacon of Cleveland, between 1195 and 1202 to the Gilbertine order. The priory, located between the Foss and Fishergate, was founded for twelve canons. The canons appear to have been substantial landowners within the city of York and further afield, but by 1335, the priory was impoverished, as a grant was made for the repair of the priory buildings. Little has come to light about life of the community, but it is known that the canons had access to the Ouse, which they used for transportation and fishing. Excavations of the church some twenty-five years ago discovered a considerable number of male skeletons with injuries inflicted by blade and arrow, suggesting that a battle may have taken place on the site in the eleventh century, but burials continued well into the thirteenth century, including also of women and children. It has been suggested that the Gilbertine priory had a specialist infirmary, in which people with weapon injuries were treated. There was no assessment of the value of the priory in the *Valor* Ecclesiasticus of 1535, but other evidence suggests an annual value of £59 5s. This would have brought it within the scope of the closure of the lesser monasteries, but it was saved following an appeal to the King by Robert Holgate, Master of the Order of Sempringham. The reprieve was short-lived, and St Andrew's Priory was surrendered to the King's commissioners by Prior John Lepington and three canons in 1538. The buildings were demolished and subjected to wholesale robbing of its stone for building material. A limekiln was built in the cloister garth, and the north range may have remained in use for a time as a stable block or store.

York St Olave's Priory

Benedictine -1086-1089

A community of Benedictine monks arrived at the church of St Olave before 1086, having travelled from Whitby via Lastingham. When the canons of York Minster disputed the foundation, King William II granted more adjacent land and laid the foundation stone himself of St Mary's Abbey in 1089. The site of St Olave's had in any case become too small, so the monks readily moved next door. Nothing is left from the monastic church, with the oldest part, the tower, dating from the fifteenth century. The remainder is later still.

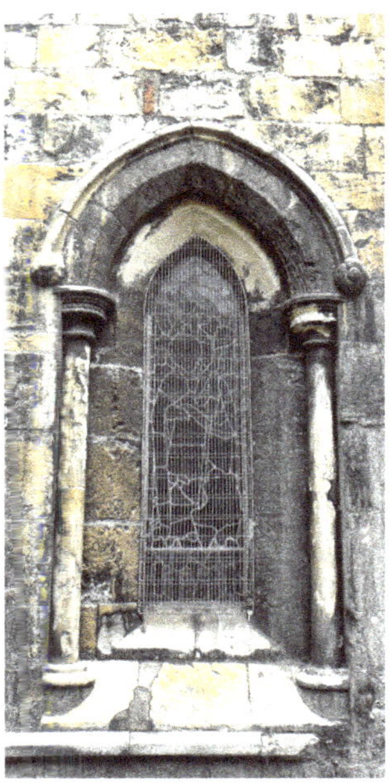

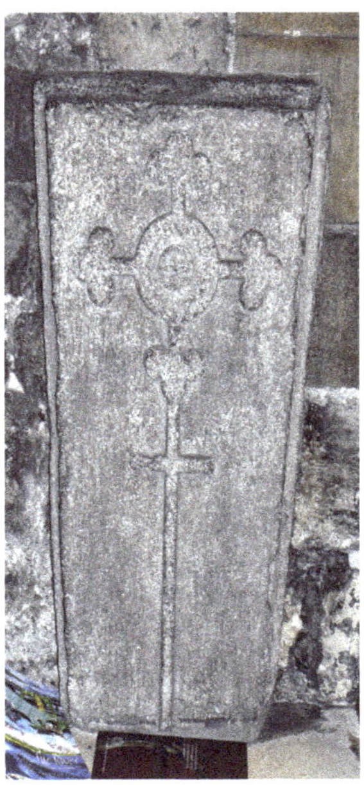

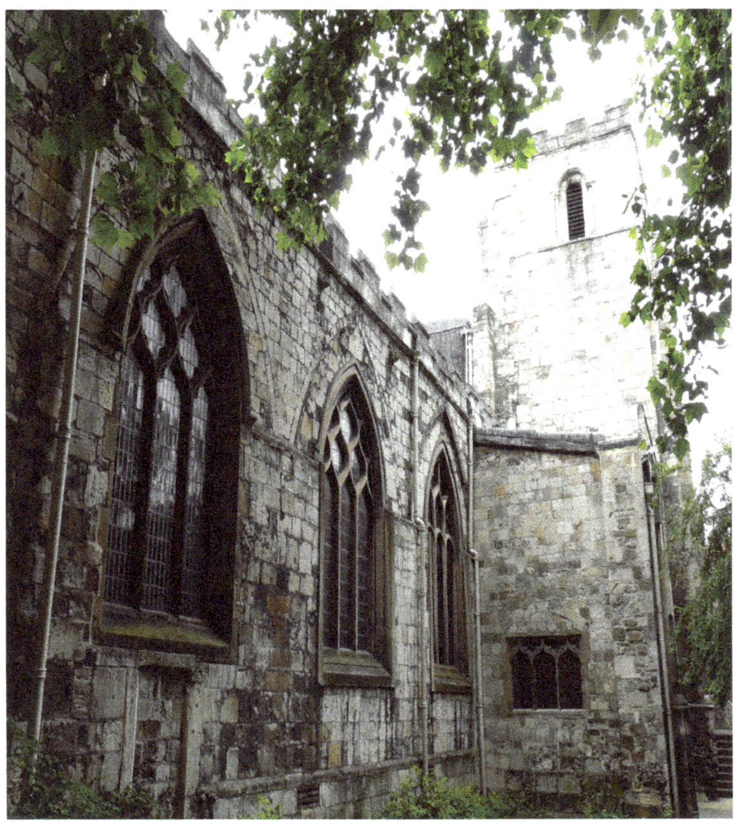

Photos of Holy Trinity Priory - from the left

Gothic window with arch supported by slender columns
Tomb slab with incised cross
The much reduced and restored former priory church of the Holy Trinity

York Austin Friars

1272–1538

The Augustinian friars established themselves in 1272 on a constricted site between present-day Lendal Street and the north bank of the Ouse, within a stone's throw of the Dominican priory across the river. The friars bought seven houses to form the heart of the priory, which they enclosed with a wall. The main gate opened onto Lendal Street. Nothing at all is left and little is known of its history, other than it housed thirty-five friars in 1300, and maintained an extensive library. Along with the other friaries in the city it was dissolved in 1538.

York Black Friars

St Mary Magdalene • 1227–1538

The Dominican friars first moved into a building in Goodramgate, which they handed over to the archbishop. But in 1227, under instruction from Henry III in consultation with the city authorities, the friars were given the chapel of St Mary Magdalene and adjacent land on the south bank of the Ouse, just within the city dyke. Free access to the river was granted through the dyke. Henry III made over several gifts of timber for the construction of the priory buildings and a surrounding wall, which continued for several decades. The expansion of the precinct was blocked on the south-eastern flank at Toft Green, which was used by the city authorities for storing arms and other defensive purposes and was also the site of horse and cattle fairs. The priory was an important house for the Dominicans, who often held Provincial Chapters there during the later thirteenth and fourteenth centuries. It received gifts from succeeding monarchs and numerous bequests from all sections of the populace. At its peak, it supported a community of up to 60 black friars. In 1385 it received an important relic, the right hand of St Mary Magdalene, which was brought over from France by Sir Robert Stapleton, who is said to have been buried in the church, along with many other important personages. A fire destroyed the priory buildings, books and vestments in about 1455, but an indulgence proclaimed by Archbishop Gray helped the rebuilding effort. Prior John Pickering was one of the organisers of the Pilgrimage of Grace in 1536 and was hanged at Tyburn in May 1537. He was a great writer of letters and had composed a song that became popular with the insurgents. Modern buildings have obliterated what was left of the priory after the Dissolution in November 1538, when Prior Brian Godson, six friars and four novices signed the deed of surrender.

York Crutched Friars

c1307–c1310

The Crutched Friars, or Friars of the Cross, had come to England from Italy in the mid-thirteenth century and settled in York c1307, in the early reign of Edward II. However, William Greenfield, Archbishop of York and sometime Chancellor of England, put the house under interdict, because the friars celebrated divine service without permission and the Order was not approved by the pope. The friars had moved by 1310, possibly to Kildale, where they also failed to escape the long arm of the archbishop. The friars were so named for carrying a staff surmounted by a wooden cross.

York Grey Friars

St Francis • c1230–1538

The Franciscans, or Friars Minor and often referred to as the Grey Friars, came to York around 1230. They established themselves on a site that soon proved too small, occasioning a move to a location in the parish of St Mary Castlegate, between the River Ouse and the moat of York Castle. The King himself helped to finance the original construction with grants of timber and the house became the head of one of the seven administrative custodies of the Order. The first custodian, Martin of Barton, was personally associated with Francis of Assisi. The priory became a noted centre of learning, with several of its friars sent elsewhere to lecture on theology, among them Adam of York and Thomas of York. The church was rebuilt at the end of the thirteenth century, when the community of friars numbered fifty-two. The sheer size and sumptuous accommodation of the priory is illustrated by the visit of Edward III and his mother, Isabella of Valois, who, together with more than 600 knights and ladies, stayed at the priory in 1327. Edward II had made it his court and headquarters in 1319, following his abortive siege on Berwick. Richard II also stayed at the priory while visiting York.

The large precinct of the priory was walled, which, on the south-eastern boundary incorporated the city wall, and extended southwards to the edge of the Ouse. A small postern gate for the friars existed in the city wall. As the friars drew water from the Ouse for baking and brewing, the King, in 1380, ordered the local butchers not to clean animal skins in, and dump offal into the river or in lanes near the priory. The priory had sanctuary privileges and close royal connections. Dissolution came in November 1538, when the priory was surrendered by a warden and twenty friars, with 'no murmur of grudge', and its buildings left to decay. The area has since been built over.

York Sack Friars

c1260–1312

The Friars of the Sack, or Friars of the Penance of Jesus Christ, established themselves in the city c1260 but the priory was not disbanded until 1312, even though the Order was suppressed by the Council of Lyons in 1274, which forbade the Order to admit new members. There appear to have been two friars in 1300, when Edward I gave them alms, but on the death of the friars, their land was sequestered by the Crown and rented by Edward II in 1312 to Robert de Roston. It was located in the parish of St Nicholas, Micklegate, but not a vestige has survived.

York White Friars

St Mary • -1253–1538

A Carmelite priory was first mentioned in York in 1253 when the friars received a grant from the King, with further benefactions received in the following years. It was then located outside the city walls in Bootham, before moving in 1295 on to land given by William de Vescy in the parish of St Saviour.

Although the extent of the priory is uncertain, it was probably bounded in part by Hungate and Fossgate, with a gateway into the latter. The site was completely built over only fifty years ago, at which time only a single fragment of the precinct wall had survived alongside Black Horse Passage. In 1253, Henry III gave six oaks in Galtres Forest for the building of their church and, in 1300, King Edward I gave eight oaks for the construction of a new church, which was later extended when additional land became available. In 1301, the Carmelites reached an accommodation with the parish and St Mary's Abbey over tithes, burial rights and other concerns of mutual interest. At that time about two dozen friars were in residence, but in 1337, Royal alms indicated that the community had grown to forty-two. In 1314, the friars had obtained permission to build a quay on the King's fishponds in the Foss, to enable them to transport necessary supplies by water. The priory became the senior house of the York Distinction, one of four regional groups in the country established by the Carmelites in the early 1300s. It had a reputation for being a regional study centre, offering theology courses. Prior Simon Clarkson, ten friars and three novices signed the surrender document in November 1538.

Key to medieval map of York

A Clifford's Tower
B York Castle
C Old Baile
D St Leonard's Hospital

E Bootham Bar
F Monk Bar
G Fishergate Bar
H Micklegate Bar

J Ouse Bridge
K Foss Bridge

L White Friars
M Grey Friars
N Black Friars
O Austin Friars
P St Andrew's Priory
Q Clementhorpe Priory
R Fishergate Priory
S St Olave's Priory
T St Mary's Abbey
U Holy Trinity Priory

Crutched Friars - exact location unknown
Sack Friars - exact location unknown

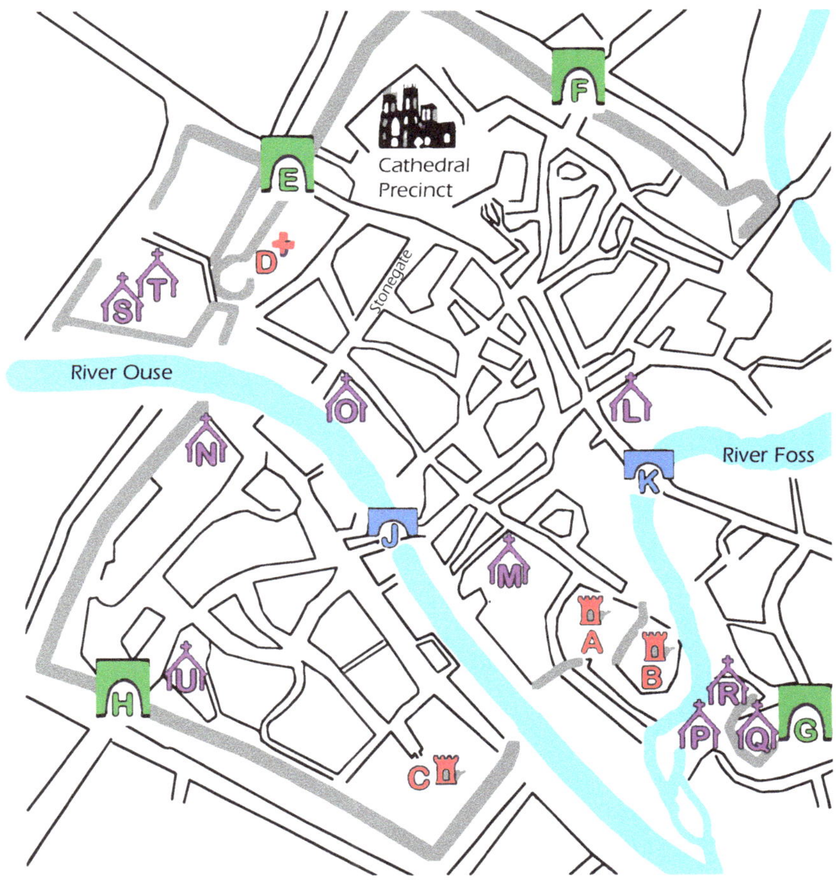

Timeline

400	St Augustine of Hippo writes rules for Augustinians; organised Order not founded until the eleventh century
529	St Benedict founds Benedictine Order
597	St Augustine establishes first Benedictine monastery in England at Canterbury
601	Monastery is established at Glastonbury
635	St Aidan founds religious community at Lindisfarne (Holy Island)
657	St Hilda becomes Abbess of Streonshalh, later known as Whitby
664	Great Synod of Whitby
685	St Cuthbert becomes bishop of Lindisfarne
910	Cluniac Order founded at Cluny by monk Berno and Count William of Aquitaine
970	St Dunstan becomes Archbishop of Canterbury
1065	Dedication of Westminster Abbey
1066	William of Normandy defeats King Harold at Battle of Hastings and becomes William I (William the Conqueror)
1070	Lanfranc becomes Archbishop of Canterbury
1078	First Cluniac house founded in Lewes, Sussex
1084	Carthusian Order founded by St Bruno at La Grand Chartreuse near Grenoble
1087	William dies and is succeeded by his third son, William II (Rufus)
1088	Rebellion of the barons; Bishop Odo banished
1098	Abbot Robert establishes the Cistercian Order at Citeaux in Burgundy
1100	Rufus is killed in New Forest; Henry I, youngest son of Conqueror, becomes King
1106	First Augustinian house established in England
1109	Bernard of Abbeville founds reformed Benedictine Order of Tiron at Thiron in northern France
1112	Vitalis of Savignac founds Savignac Order near Mortain in Normandy
1114	Canons Regular of the Holy Sepulchre founded in Holy Land
1121	Premonstratensian Order founded by St Norbert at Premontré near Laon
1127	First Savignac house established at Furness
1128	First Cistercian abbey in England established at Waverley in Surrey
1131	Gilbert, Rector of Sempringham in Lincolnshire founds Gilbertine Order reviving double monasteries of Saxon times
1135	Henry I dies of lamphreys and his nephew Stephen seizes the throne claimed by Henry's daughter, the Empress Matilda, leading to Civil War (Anarchy)
1141	Matilda briefly reigns after capturing the King at the Battle of Lincoln
1143	First Premonstratensian house founded at Newhouse in Lincolnshire
1147	Savignac Order absorbed into Cistercians
1153	End of Civil War (Anarchy)
1154	Henry II, son of Matilda, becomes King on death of Stephen; first Angevin King
C1155	Foundation of Carmelites (Order of Our Lady of Mount Carmel)
1162	Thomas Becket is installed as Archbishop of Canterbury
1170	Becket is murdered at Canterbury
1182	First Carthusian monastery founded at Witham in Somerset
1189	Richard I (Cœur de Lion) succeeds his father after Henry's death
1198	St John de Matha and St Felix of Valois found the Order of the Most Holy Trinity, known as Trinitarians, near Cerfroid, France
1199	Richard dies at siege of Chalus; his brother John (Lackland) is made King
1206	Stephen Langton elected Archbishop of Canterbury
1209	Order of Friars Minor (Franciscans) founded by Francis of Assisi
1215	Magna Carta signed at Runnymede; civil war ensues
1216	John dies and is succeeded by nine-year old Henry III (Plantagenet); Peter des Roches, Bishop of Winchester, becomes the King's guardian; St Dominic founds Order of Preachers, more commonly known as Dominicans
1221	Dominican Order settles at Oxford
1224	Franciscan Friars arrive in Canterbury
1230	Austin Friars establish themselves in Suffolk
1242	Carmelites establish base at Hulne in Northumberland
1244	Foundation of the Austin Friars
1245	Rebuilding starts of Westminster Abbey
1263	Rebellion of Simon de Montfort; Civil War
1267	Treaty of Montgomery acknowledges Llywelyn ap Gruffydd as Prince of Wales by Henry III

1272 Henry dies and is succeeded by his son who becomes Edward I (Longshanks)
1274 Second Council of Lyons; suppression of minor mendicant Orders
1283 Edward I completes conquest of Wales after death of Llywelyn
1284 Statute of Rhuddlan provides constitutional basis for governance of North Wales
1291 *Taxatio Ecclesiastica*; detailed valuation for taxation of all ecclesiastical property in England and Wales, compiled under the order of Pope Nicholas IV
1307 Death of Edward while marching on Scotland; his son becomes Edward II
1326 Edward forced to abdicate by his wife Isabella and her lover, Roger Mortimer
1327 Edward horribly murdered at Berkeley Castle; his son acceeds as Edward III
1337 Beginning of Hundred Years' War with France
1344 Bridgettine Order of nuns founded in Sweden by Saint Birgitta
1348/9 Black Death robs monasteries of monks and lay-brothers leading to slow decline
1377 Richard II, son of the Black Prince, becomes King upon the death of his grandfather
1399 Death of John of Gaunt, Duke of Lancaster, third son of Edward III; Henry Bolingbroke, his son, becomes Henry IV after forcing Richard to abdicate
1400 Richard dies in prison in Pontefract, probably murdered
1400 Start of Owain Glyndŵr's revolt against the English rule of Wales
1413 Henry V, son of Henry IV, becomes King
1414 Closure of alien priories by Henry V under act of Parliament of Leicester
1415 Battle of Agincourt; foundation of Syon Abbey, the only Bridgettine monastery in the British Isles
1422 Nine-months old son of Henry V becomes Henry VI after death of his father; England and France ruled by the dukes of Bedford and Gloucester
1453 End of the Hundred Years' War
1455 Wars of the Roses between houses of York and Lancaster
1460 Richard Neville, Earl of Warwick, known as the 'Kingmaker', crushes opposition to Edward; Henry VI captured and imprisoned
1461 Edward IV, eldest son of Richard, Duke of York, is proclaimed King after defeating Lancastrians at Battle of Mortimer's Cross
1470 Henry VI regains throne with the help of Warwick
1471 Henry deposed and murdered; his son, Prince Edward, killed at Battle of Tewkesbury
1483 Edward V becomes King after the death of his father, but together with his brother Richard is taken to the Tower of London by his uncle Richard, Duke of Gloucester, and probably murdered; the duke assumes Crown as Richard III
1485 Richard killed at Battle of Bosworth, which marks the end of the Wars of the Roses; Henry Tudor, son of Edmund Tudor is crowned Henry VII; first of the Tudor kings
1509 Henry dies and his second son becomes King as Henry VIII
1525 Cardinal Wolsey closes 30 small monasteries to fund his new colleges at Ipswich and Oxford
1534 Act of Supremacy, which recognised Henry VIII as the 'Supreme Head of the Church of England
1535 *Valor Ecclesiasticus*, survey of revenue and income of all ecclesiastical property in England, Wales and parts of Ireland, ordered by Henry VIII
1536 Henry confirms break with Rome after Pope's refusal to grant him a divorce; Act of Suppression closes small monasteries with income of less than £200
1536/7 Pilgrimage of Grace rebellion against closure of religious houses in the North
1537/40 King's Commissioners compel abbots to surrender remaining abbeys and priories
1540 Closure of last monastery completes the Dissolution
1547 Edward VII, son of Henry VIII and Jane Seymour, becomes King after the death of his father
1553 On Edward's death, Lady Jane Grey, great-granddaughter of Henry VII, is proclaimed Queen to prevent the succession of Mary and Elizabeth. Her reign lasts just nine days
1553 Mary, daughter of Henry VIII and Katherine of Aragon, takes the throne as Mary I. She restores Roman Catholicism, in the process burning many religious dissenters at the stake, which earns her the sobriquet of Bloody Mary
1558 Elizabeth, daughter of Henry VIII and Anne Boleyn, assumes the throne as Elizabeth I after the death of Mary through illness, becoming the last Tudor monarch. The Act of Supremacy re-establishes the Church of Engand's independence from Rome.

Medieval Catholic Popes 1066-1558

The chronological list of popes corresponds to the latest Annuario Pontificio, published every year by the Roman Curia. Shown under the heading of I Sommi Pontifici Romani (The Supreme Pontiffs of Rome), it lists those considered the legitimate succession and explicitly excludes the so-called antipopes, who opposed many of the chosen popes, especially in the eleventh, twelfth, fourteenth and fifteenth centuries.

1061-1073	Alexander II
1073-1085	Saint Gregory VII
1086-1087	Blessed Victor III
1088-1099	Blessed Urban II
1099-1118	Paschal II
1118-1119	Gelasius II
1119-1124	Callistus II
1124-1130	Honorius II
1130-1143	Innocent II
1143-1144	Celestine II
1144-1145	Lucius II
1145-1153	Blessed Eugene III
1153-1154	Anastasius IV
1154-1159	Adrian IV
1159-1181	Alexander III
1181-1185	Lucius III
1185-1187	Urban III
1187	Gregory VIII
1187-1191	Clement III
1191-1198	Celestine III
1198-1216	Innocent III
1216-1227	Honorius III
1227-1241	Gregory IX
1241	Celestine IV
1243-1253	Innocent IV
1254-1261	Alexander IV
1261-1264	Urban IV
1265-1268	Clement IV
1271-1276	Blessed Gregory X
1276	Blessed Innocent V
1276	Adrian V
1276-1277	John XXI
1277-1280	Nicholas III
1281-1285	Martin IV
1285-1287	Honorius IV
1288-1292	Nicholas IV
1294	Saint Celestine V
1294-1303	Boniface VIII
1303-1304	Blessed Benedict XI
1305-1314	Clement V
1316-1334	John XXII
1334-1342	Benedict XII
1342-1352	Clement VI
1352-1362	Innocent VI
1362-1370	Blessed Urban V
1370-1378	Gregory XI
1378-1389	Urban VI
1389-1404	Boniface IX
1404-1406	Innocent VII
1406-1415	Gregory XII
1417-1431	Martin V
1431-1447	Eugene IV
1447-1455	Nicholas V
1455-1458	Callistus III
1458-1464	Pius II
1464-1471	Paul II
1471-1484	Sixtus IV
1484-1492	Innocent VIII
1492-1503	Alexander VI
1503	Pius III
1503-1513	Julius II
1513-1521	Leo X
1522-1523	Adrian VI
1523-1534	Clement VII
1534-1549	Paul III
1550-1555	Julius III
1555	Marcello II
1555-1559	Paul IV

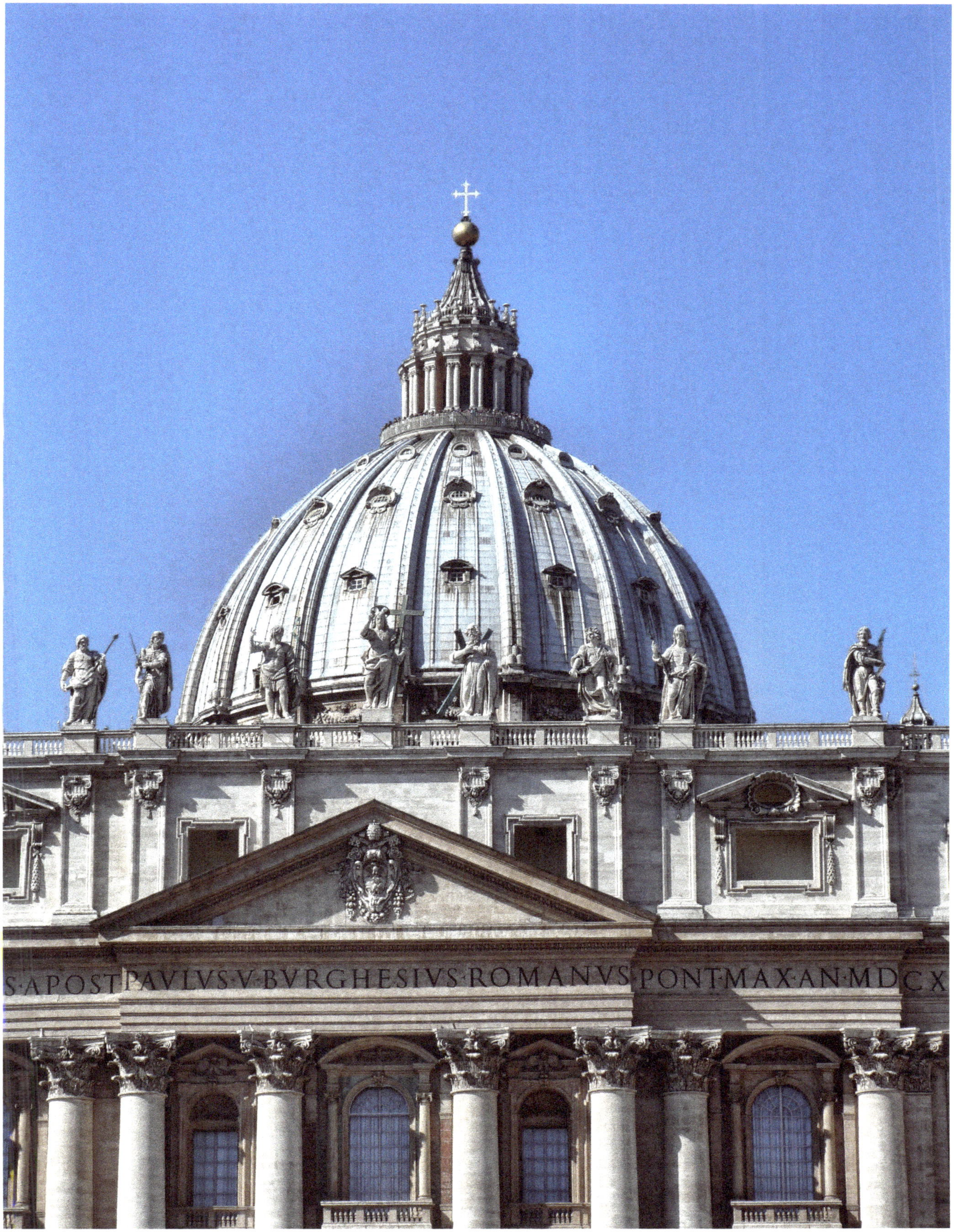

St Peter's Basilica, Rome

Medieval Archbishops of Canterbury 1066-1558

The first archbishop of Canterbury was Augustine who was sent by Pope Gregory I to England to convert the natives to Roman Christianity. Landing in Kent in AD 597, he quickly converted Ethelbert, King of Kent, along with many of his subjects. After establishing a Benedictine monastery, he was appointed archbishop in AD 601. One of the most notable archbishops before the Norman Conquest was Dunstan, Abbot of Glastonbury, who revived monasticism in England following the devastation by the Danes and reformed the English Church, a process that was carried on by Lanfranc, a close ally of William the Conqueror.

1052 - 1079	Stigand	Concurrently Bishop of Winchester; deprived of both Sees
1070 – 1089	Lanfranc	Abbot of St Étienne, Caen
1093 – 1109	Anselm	Abbot of Bec; canonised: St. Anselm
1109 – 1114	See vacant	
1114 – 1122	Ralph d'Escures	Translated from Rochester
1123 – 1136	William de Corbeil	Prior of St. Osyth
1136 – 1139	See vacant	
1139 – 1161	Theobald of Bec	Abbot of Bec
1161 – 1162	See vacant	
1162 – 1170	Thomas Becket	Previously Archdeacon of Canterbury and Lord Chancellor; murdered in Canterbury Cathedral; canonised: St Thomas of Canterbury
1170 – 1173	See vacant	
1173	(Roger de Bailleul)	Abbot of Bec; elected but declined the See
1174 – 1184	Richard of Dover	Prior of Dover
1184 – 1190	Baldwin of Forde	Translated from Worcester
1191	(Reginald fitzJocelin)	Translated from Wells; elected, however, appeals were sent to Pope Celestine III, but Reginald died before they were heard
1191 – 1193	See vacant	
1193 – 1205	Hubert Walter	Translated from Salisbury; Lord Chancellor; Chief Justiciar
1205 – 1206	(Reginald)	Sub-prior, elected but set aside by King John
1205 – 1206	(John de Gray)	Bishop of Norwich; chosen by the monks but set aside by Pope Innocent III
1207 – 1228	Cardinal Stephen Langton	Created a cardinal in 1206
1228 – 1229	(Walter d'Eynsham)	Elected but set aside by King Henry III of England and Pope Gregory IX
1229 – 1231	Richard le Grant	Formerly Chancellor of the See of Lincoln
1231	(Ralph Neville)	Bishop of Chichester, election quashed by Pope Gregory IX
1232	(John of Sittingbourne)	Election quashed by Pope Gregory IX
1232 – 1233	(John Blund)	Election quashed by Pope Gregory IX
1234 – 1240	Edmund Rich	Prebendary of Salisbury; canonised: St. Edmund of Abingdon
1241 – 1270	Boniface of Savoy	Translated from Belley in France
1270 – 1272	(William Chillenden)	Prior of Christ Church, Canterbury; elected but set aside by Pope Gregory X
1273 – 1278	Cardinal Robert Kilwardby	Created a cardinal in 1278 and resigned
1278 – 1279	(Robert Burnell)	Bishop of Bath & Wells; elected but set aside by Pope Nicholas III
1279 – 1292	John Peckham	English Provincial of the Franciscan Order
1294 – 1313	Robert Winchelsea	Formerly Archdeacon of Essex; Chancellor of Oxford
1313	(Thomas Cobham)	Election quashed
1313 – 1327	Walter Reynolds	Translated from Worcester; Lord Chancellor, Lord Treasurer
1328 – 1333	Simon Meopham	Prebendary of Chichester Cathedral, excommunicated
1333 – 1348	John de Stratford	Translated from Winchester; Lord Chancellor
1348 – 1349	(John de Ufford)	Dean of Lincoln, Lord Chancellor; died of plague before consecration

1349	Thomas Bradwardine	Died of plague
1349 – 1366	Simon Islip	Prebendary of St. Paul's; secretary to the King and Keeper of the Privy Seal
1366	(William Edington)	Bishop of Winchester; elected but refused the See
1366 – 1368	Cardinal Simon Langham	Translated from Ely; created a cardinal in 1368 and resigned the See
1368 – 1374	William Whittlesey	Translated from Worcester
1374	Cardinal Simon Langham	Elected a second time, but Pope Gregory XI refused to confirm the election
1375 – 1381	Simon de Sudbury	Translated from London; Lord Chancellor; beheaded during the Peasants' Revolt
1381 – 1396	William Courtenay	Translated from London; Lord Chancellor
1396 – 1397	Thomas Arundel	Translated from York; Lord Chancellor; charged with high treason under Richard II, fled but restored later
1397 – 1399	Roger Walden	Deprived
1399 – 1414	Thomas Arundel	Restored by Henry IV
1414 – 1443	Henry Chichele	Translated from St.David's
1443 – 1452	John Stafford	Translated from Bath & Wells; Lord Chancellor; Lord Treasurer
1452 – 1454	Cardinal John Kemp	Created a cardinal in 1439; translated from York; Lord Chancellor
1454 – 1486	Cardinal Thomas Bourchier	Translated from Ely; Lord Chancellor; created a cardinal in 1467
1486 – 1500	Cardinal John Morton	Translated from Ely; Lord Chancellor; created a cardinal in 1493
1501	(Thomas Langton)	Bishop of Winchester; died five days after being chosen
1501 – 1503	Henry Deane	Translated from Salisbury
1503 – 1532	William Warham	Translated from London; Lord Chancellor until 1515
1533 – 1555	Thomas Cranmer	Archdeacon of Taunton; excommunicated by Rome and deprived for heresy 1553; put to death by burning, 21 March 1556
1556 – 1558	Cardinal Reginald Pole	Dean of Exeter; created a cardinal in 1536

The Pope's refusal to sanction the annulment of Henry VIII's marriage to Katherine of Aragon led to the break with Rome, which culminated in the 1534 Act of Supremacy, which declared that the King was the "Supreme Head on earth of the Church of England". There followed the Dissolution and destruction of the monasteries, which was carried out between 1536 and 1540. Papal jurisdiction was reinstated by Mary I in 1553, but after Elizabeth succeeded to the throne, the Act of Supremacy of 1558 re-established the Church of England's independence from Rome.

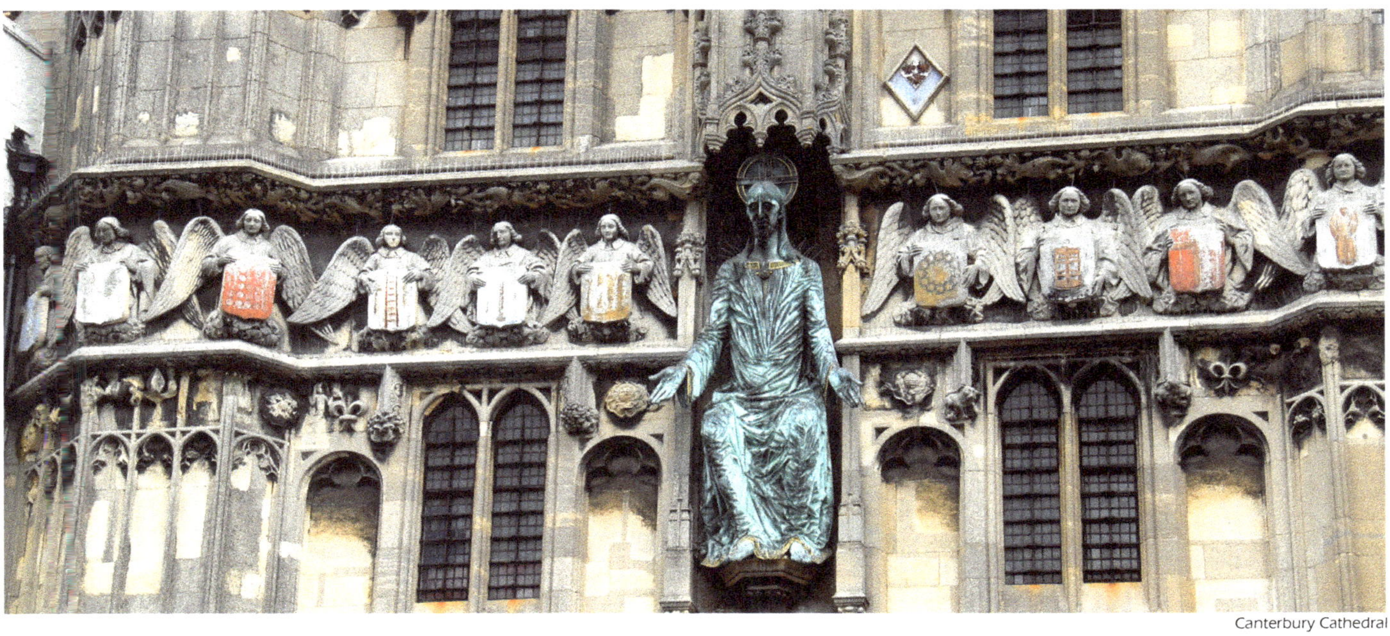

Canterbury Cathedral

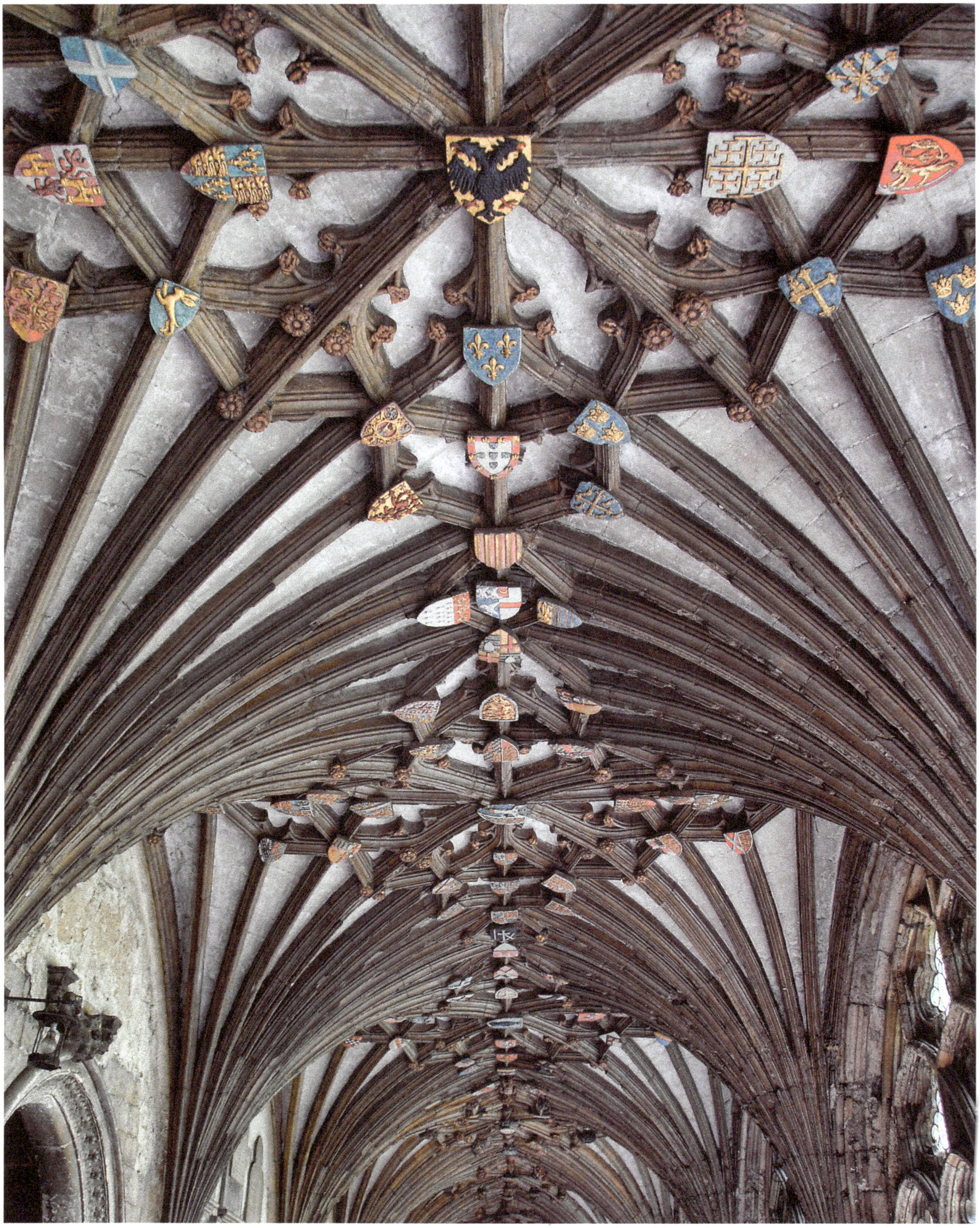
Canterbury Cathedral

Glossary

Abbacy Office of an abbot or abbess
Abbess Female Head of Abbey; abbot
Abbot Head of Abbey; abbess
Advowson Patronage of a parish church
Aisle Lateral division of church flanking the nave or chancel
Alien Priory A small religious foundation dependent on a foreign mother house
Almoner Monastic official charged with managing charitable donations to the poor
Altar Flat-topped wooden or stone table containing the cross
Ambulatory Processional aisle running around east end of church
Apostasy Act of a religious leaving the monastery without licence
Appropriation Transfer of a parish church, with all tithes and income, to a religious house
Apse Semi-circular projection, usually at east end of church; apsidal
Arcade Row of arches supported by columns; blind arcades
Arch Curved structure across an opening
Archbishop Ecclesiastical official who rules an archdiocese
Archdeacon Ecclesiastical official who oversees an archdeaconry
Archdeaconry Ecclesiastical administrative unit
Archdiocese An area of ecclesiastical jurisdiction ruled by an archbishop
Archiepiscopate Office or archdiocese of an archbishop
Ashlar Worked stone with flat surface, usually of regular shape and square edges
Aumbry Cupboard or recess to hold sacred vessels; ambry; almery

Ball flower Ball ornament surrounded by flowers
Barrel-vault Arched semi-cylindrical vault
Belfry Bell-tower or campanile
Benefactor Donor supporting community with financial or other aid
Bishop Ecclesiastical official who oversees a diocese
Bishopric Another term for diocese
Black Death Bubonic plague that took many lives throughout Britain and Europe
Blind arcading Line of arches on a solid wall for decoration
Boss Ornamental projection in ribbed vaults used to hide joints
Bovate Land area measurement equivalent to about 15 acres
Bull Authoritative papal letter
Burgess Political official or representative
Burgh Settlements typically under the protection of a castle
Buttress Projecting masonry on wall for additional strength

Calefactory Warming house; the only room beside the kitchen in which a fire was allowed
Canon Chapter member
Canonical Hours Seven daytime Offices of Lauds, Prime, Terce, Sext, None, Vespers and Compline, and nighttime Office of Vigils
Capella ante portas Chapel by the gate used by laypeople and pilgrims
Capital Uppermost part of column or shaft, often decorated
Cartulary Book of monastic records
Carucate Land area measurement equivalent to around 120 acres, thought to be the amount of land that a team of eight oxen may plow annually
Cathedral Priory A monastic community attached to a cathedral
Cellarer Official in charge of monastery provisions in the cellarium
Cellarium Store room for provisions and office of cellarer
Chamfer Surface formed by cutting squared edge, usually at an angle of 45o
Chancel East end of church containing the altar, separated from the nave by the rood screen
Chantry Chapel Permanent endowment where mass was said
Chapter House Meeting place of chapter
Chevet semi-circular projection at east end of church, especially in Gothic design; apse

Chevron Zigzag design
Choir Part of a church between presbytery and pulpitum; also known as quire
Clas Ancient mother churches in Wales
Claustral Pertaining to a cloister; claustral buildings
Clerestory Upper storey of nave with windows to admit light to central part of church
Cloister Four-sided covered walk around the garth and between the monastic buildings
College A community made up of secular canons
Collegiate Church Church staffed by a college of secular canons
Colonettes slender columns used as a decorative rather than supporting element
Column Circular supporting stone shaft with base and capital; pillar
Corbel Timber or stone projection to provide support
Conversi Adult converts to religious life; lay-brothers
Cornice Moulded horizontal projection along top of wall
Corrodian A pensioner living in a monastic community who paid for accommodation and food for the rest of his/her life
Credence table Small table in sanctuary where bread, wine and water are placed before Mass
Crossing Central space where east-west axis of church is crossed by north-south transept
Crossing tower Tower surmounting central space
Crusades Military expeditions to fight Muslims for control of Holy Land
Crypt Sub-chamber of church, usually underground

Daughter house Monastic community founded by members of another house
Daystairs Stairway giving access to the dormitory via a claustral walkway
Decorated Rich detail style of Gothic architecture
Demesne Land held by a tenant for his or her own use
Dissolution The suppression of English and Welsh monasteries by Henry VIII, 1536-1540
Dogtooth Diagonal indented decoration
Dormitory Monastic sleeping quarters; dorter
Divine Office Set of prayers, canonical hours, recited at certain times of the day and night
Double monastery Monastic community housing both male and female religious in segregated accommodation

Early English Style of earliest Gothic architecture, mainly thirteenth century
Effigy Carved likeness of a person
Episcopal Governed by a bishop
Eremite A hermit, anchorite or anchoress
Excommunication Exclusion from Church membership

Fan-vault Concoidal vault in which length and curvature of ribs are equal
Flying buttress Free-standing buttress linked to the building by part of an arch
Frater Monastic refectory or dining hall

Galilee Porch attached to west end of church
Gargoyle Carved ornament, usually grotesque, to take rainwater away from roofs
Garth Area enclosed by the cloister
Gatehouse Main entrance to monastery, usually highly decorated
General Chapter Annual meeting of the heads of all abbeys
Gothic Style of architecture, twelfth-sixteenth century, characterised chiefly by pointed arches
Grange Farm worked by hired workers and supervised by lay-brothers
Groin Edge of intersecting vaults
Grotesque Carving or sculpture of of a figure, animal or hybrid

Indulgence Pardon issued by an ecclesiastical authority for a sin previously committed
Infirmarian Monastic official in charge of the infirmary
Infirmary Hospital, sick quarters for monks, often with its own cloister

Kitchener Monastic official in charge of the kitchen

Lady Chapel	Chapel at east end of church dedicated to the Virgin Mary
Lancet	Slender and tall window with pointed head
Lavabo	Basin for washing; water jug
Lavatorium	Trough with running water where monks washed their hands before meals
Lay-Brother	Man belonging to religious order but not ordained
Legate	Representative of the papacy
Manor	Group of lands managed as an economic and administrative unit
Mass	Chief Christian religious ritual
Mendicant	Reliance on charity or begging for subsistence
Minster	Large church originally linked to a monastery
Misericord	Place where comforts such as warmth could be obtained
Mitre	Ecclesiastical pointed cap worn by bishops and some privileged abbots
Monk	Man who has taken vows and joined religious community
Mother house	Principal monastic community
Mullion	Vertical division between lights of a window
Narthax	Small porch at west end of church
Nave	Main body of a church, extending westwards from the screen or crossing
Nightstairs	Stairway giving access to the church from the dormitory
Novice	Member of a monastic community who has not yet been professed
Obedientiary	Head of a department managing the community's holdings
Ogee	Double-curved arch, pointed and convex above, concave below
Oratory	Small cell attached to a chapel
Oriel	Projecting window in wall
Parlour	Only place were talking was allowed in Cistercian Order
Perpendicular	English architectural style, c 1330-1540
Pilaster	Shallow pier used to buttress wall
Pilgrimage of Grace	Popular uprising in the north against the dissolution of the monasteries, 1536-7
Piscina	Carved shallow basin in south wall niche near altar for washing sacred vessels
Plinth	Projecting base of a wall or column
Prebend	Stipend assigned to a canon or member of the chapter
Presbytery	East end of church containing the high altar
Prior	Second in command after abbot; head of Priory
Pulpitum	Screen between the nave and quire of church, often supporting a gallery
Quatre-foil	Four-lobed
Quire	Part of church between presbytery and pulpitum with stalls for the monks; choir
Recusant	A religious dissenter
Refectory	Communal dining hall; frater
Reredorter	Building containing latrines, usually flushed by a channel of running water
Reredos	Wall covering or screen behind altar decorated with the twelve apostles
Respond	Half-column with capital and base where arch joins a wall
Retroquire	Area behind the high altar between pulpitum and rood screen
Rib-vault	Vault or arch supported by projecting bands of stone
Romanesque	Architectural style from eighth to twelfth century with rounded arches
Rood screen	Stone or wooden division between nave and quire
Sacristy	Room for keeping sacred vessels and vestments
Sanctuary	Part of church to the east of the altar
Scriptorium	Room used for writing and the copying of books
Sedilia	Stone seat for officiating clergy recessed in the wall on south side near altar
See	Ecclesiastical area under the control of a bishop
Sepulchre	Tomb

Slype	Covered way or passage
Springing	Level at which an arch or vault rises from its supports
Squint	Small opening in wall of church giving view of altar from outside
Stiff-Leaf	Formalised three-lobed carved foliage
Stringcourse	Continuous horizontal mouldings on façade of a building or around its walls
Suffragan bishop	Assistant to a diocesan bishop
Tracery	Decorative intersecting rib-work in upper part of a window
Transept	Transverse part of a cruciform-shaped church, set at right angle to the main axis
Transitional	Period in which Norman architecture was giving way to Gothic
Transom	Cross-beam or horizontal division of window
Trefoil	Three-lobed
Triforium	Arcaded gallery between main arcade and clerestory
Undercroft	Vaulted underground room or basement supporting a principal chamber above
Vault	Arched stone roof or ceiling, sometimes relieved by stone ribs
Vesica	Shape formed by the intersection of two circles of equal radius
Visitation	Inspection of a monastic community by an ecclesiastical authority
Visitor	Ecclesiastical official with the right of visitation
Voissor	Wedge-shaped element used in building an arch or vault
Waterleaf	Leaf-shaped ornamental motif at top of columns; introduced by Cistercians
Warming house	Room where communal fire was kept burning during the winter

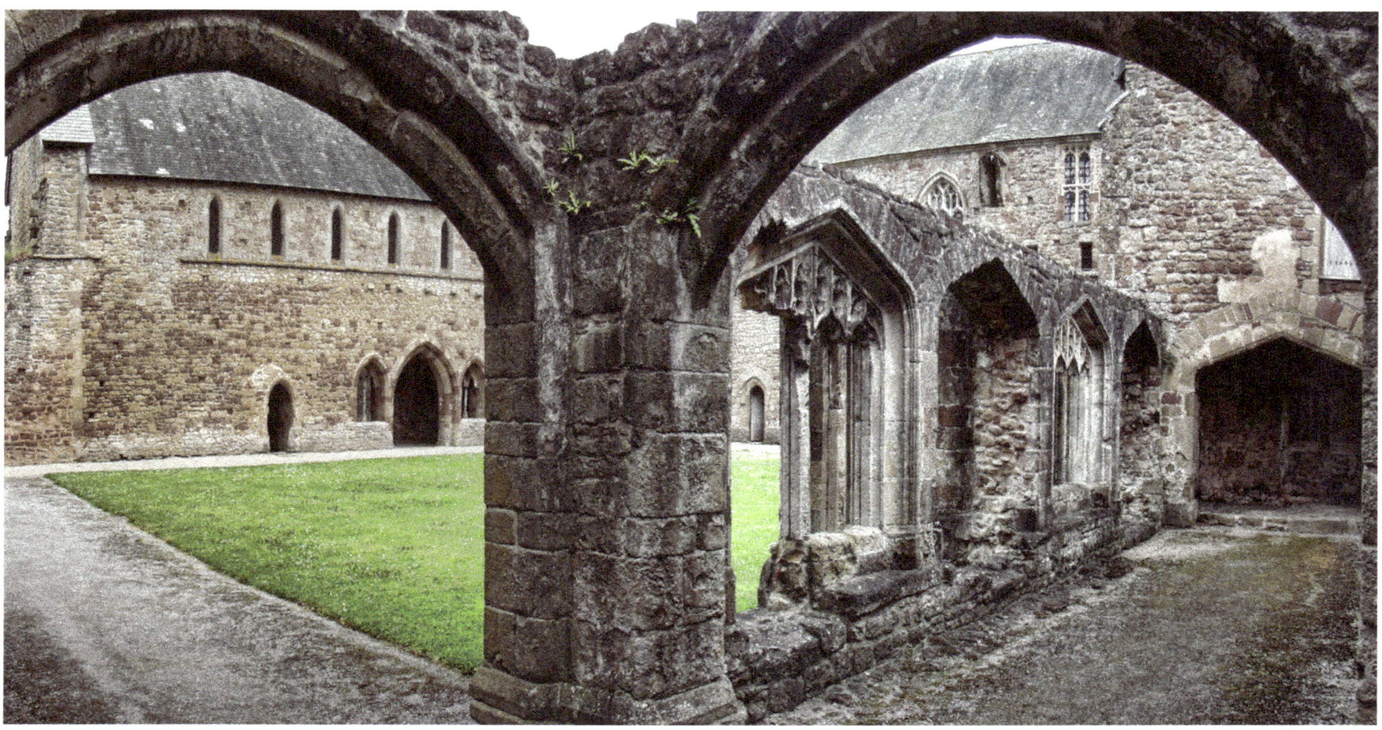

Cleeve Abbey

Index By Counties - Volume 1 - Northern England

Index - Alphabetical Volume 1 Northern England

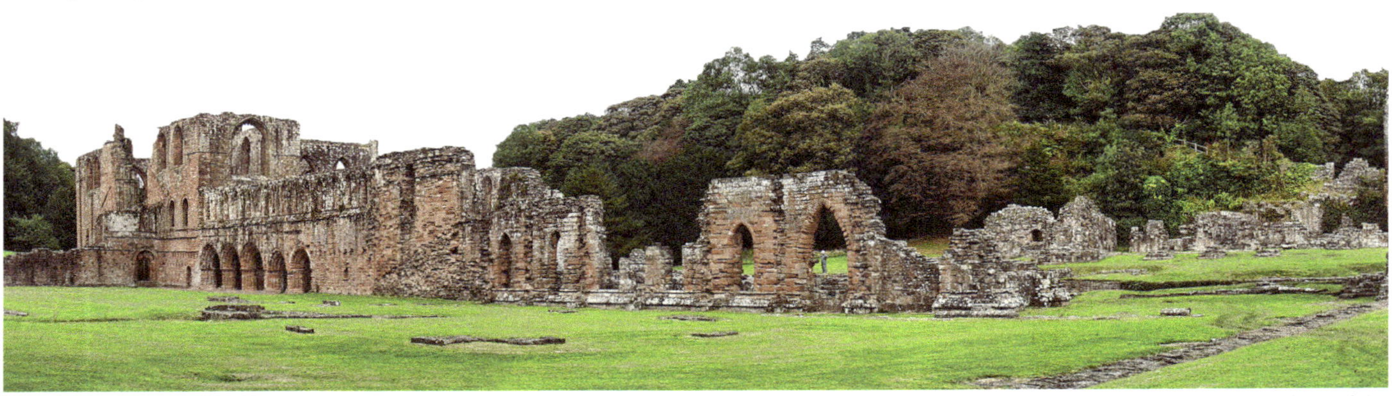

Furness Abbey

Lightning Source UK Ltd.
Milton Keynes UK
UKHW051334190719
346398UK00005B/36/P

9 780995 847606